March 1998.

The GUINNESS Book of

Rail

Facts and Feats

The GUINNESS Book of

Rail

Facts and Feats

Third Edition

by

John Marshall

GUINNESS SUPERLATIVES LIMITED
2 CECIL COURT, LONDON ROAD, ENFIELD, MIDDLESEX

Acknowledgements

In addition to those persons and organisations mentioned in the first and second editions I should like to record my gratitude to the following: Argentine Railways; Association of American Railroads; Philip Atkins, Librarian, National Railway Museum, York; Austrian Federal Railways; Maurice Barbey; Canadian National Railways; Climax Molybdenum Co, Colorado; J R Colombo, Toronto; Ray Corley, Toronto; W J K Davies; Denver & Rio Grande Western RR; A. Eaton; John Edgington of the NRM Library; Angel Ferrer, Argentina; Japanese National Railways; P M Kalla-Bishop; John Knowles; Omer Lavallee, Montreal; R M Robbins; J. Schmid, Swiss National Tourist Office, London; K F Schulze, Toronto; P W B Semmens of the NRM; J N Slater, Editor, *The Railway Magazine*; Southern Pacific Transportation Co; Alf Trumper, Brisbane; Dave Wilkie, Victoria, BC; J P Wilson; Ean Wood.

Once again I must thank my sons Andrew and Simon and my wife Ann for their co-operation and helpful criticism; my colleague K B Smith for further assistance with the stamp section; and finally, the staffs of Bolton and Manchester Public Libraries.

J M, Bolton, Lancashire, 1978

Editor: Beatrice Frei
Illustrations: Photos taken by the author, except where credited otherwise.
Maps and diagrams drawn by the author

First published in 1971
Second edition 1975
Third edition 1979
Second imprint 1981

Published in Great Britain by
Guinness Superlatives Ltd, 2 Cecil Court,
London Road, Enfield, Middlesex

ISBN 900424 56 7

Set in Times New Roman Series 327
Printed and bound in Great Britain by
Butler & Tanner Ltd, Frome and London

Contents

Introduction

The construction and operation of railways confronted man with a challenge which resulted in many outstanding achievements. Over the years the facts concerning these achievements have formed the foundations of railway history. The feats have become incidentals of the history. This is a book concerned largely with the facts and feats of railways and, as is appropriate, the material is presented in a direct and factual manner, without emotion, nostalgia or partisanship.

As a railway historian I realise that history is not simply a collection of facts arranged in chronological order. History relates the facts to each other and to society, and their reasons for happening. In the course of his researches the railway historian will come upon numerous facts, and feats of technology which, in their day, were as remarkable as landing on the Moon in 1969. It was the skill and courage of the 19th-century engineers which made possible modern engineering technology.

In this third edition these facts of railway history and the achievements of the engineers are brought together, and because today's events are tomorrow's history, the most recent railway achievements are included. The material, which has been updated throughout is illustrated by about 200 photographs in black and white and 35 in colour. Since railway history is essentially a human story a section of the book is devoted to railways in human affairs and the arts. To give space for new material, the biography section, 'The Pioneers', has been omitted from this edition; all the information can be found in the author's *Biographical Dictionary of Railway Engineers* (David & Charles, 1978). For historical interest, years of birth and death are given in the index.

Although this is not a book designed to stir the emotions it is realised that, of all man's inventions, the railway perhaps most directly affects his emotions. At any time or season a busy station like Glasgow Central or King's Cross, London, can be a fascinating place; even a long wait on the platforms of Crewe in the small hours, wearying or exasperating, and chilling, as it may be at the time, comes to be looked back upon as an experience one would not have missed. The steam locomotive alone has thrilled people ever since the first decade of the 19th century and has aroused a following which in some instances can only be described as fanatical. One has only to visit a railway preservation centre to find enthusiasts from all walks of life lovingly restoring old engines and developing practical skills which once they never knew they had.

The modern railway began in Britain and North America, almost simultaneously, in 1830 and these countries became the world's biggest producers of locomotives and railway equipment. So it is natural that one finds the greatest interest in railways among English-speaking peoples; in Australia, Britain, Canada, New Zealand and the USA one can number railway enthusiasts in thousands. Elsewhere one can find them, but more as individuals or in small groups. Where there is a fairly large following, as in France, Germany or Japan, it is of comparatively recent origin. For a publication like *The Railway Magazine* to succeed from its start in 1897 there must have been a large number of British enthusiasts at the time. And, going back to the beginning, where could one find two greater railway enthusiasts than George and Robert Stephenson?

Section 1
THE BEGINNINGS

The principle of a railway, a track which guides vehicles travelling along it, dates back to Babylonian times, about 2245 BC. Parallel lines of stone blocks with grooves in the centres, with a gauge of about 1·5 m (5 ft), can still be found.

The ancient Greeks used grooved stone wagonways with a gauge of 1·626 m (5 ft 4 in). Remains of these can be found all over Greece, principally between Athens and Piraeus.

The oldest known illustration of anything resembling a railway is a window high up in the Minster of Freiburg-im-Breisgau, Germany, dating from about 1350. It was presented by Johann Snewlin der Gresser who owned the Schauinsland Mines, and shows a miner pushing a box-like vehicle.

One of the earliest illustrations of a mine railway is found in a book published by Johan Haselberger of Reichenau in Lower Austria about 1519 with a title beginning *Der Ursprung gemeynner Berckrecht wie die lange Zeit von den Alten erhalten worde*. . . . It shows a man pushing a small truck along a wooden railway.

A Flemish painting, dated 1544, entitled *Les Travaux de la Mine*, on a wood panel 106·7 × 55·9 cm (42 × 22 in) was discovered about 1940. It shows a miner pushing a four-wheeled truck along a railway out of a mine. The painter probably obtained his information from the above book.

The earliest record of a railway in the generally accepted sense is an illustration of a narrow-gauge mine railway at Leberthal in Alsace in *Cosmographiae Universalis* by Sebastian Münster (1489–1552), dated 1550.

Rail wagons were described and illustrated by Georg Bauer (1494?–1555), (in English 'George Farmer') who called himself Georgius Agricola, in *De Re Metallica*, first published in 1556.

Mine truck as illustrated by Georg Bauer, 1516. Note the guide pin (*Leitnagel*) which ran between the wooden rails and kept the wagon on the track (The Science Museum, London)

A mine wagon with flanged wooden wheels, some wooden track with a gauge of 480 mm (1 ft 6⅞ in), and a switch or point with one blade, as used in gold-mines in the Siebenbürgen in Transylvania, is stored in the Verkehrs und Baumuseum, Berlin. They are said to date from the late 16th century which, if correct (and this is doubtful) would establish that railways were in general use in central Europe in the late Middle Ages. Transylvania is now part of Romania.

The first recorded 'railway' in Britain was a line about 3 km (2 miles) long, made of baulks of timber, from coal-pits at Strelley to Wollaton near Nottingham. It was built by Huntingdon Beaumont between October 1603 and October 1604. Beaumont then established the wagonways on Tyneside, between 1605 and 1608.

Flanged wooden wheels were used on English wagonways from about 1660 or earlier. They were generally turned with the grain lengthways, that is parallel to the axle. Elm was preferred, but beech, oak and ash and even softwood were used. One example discovered at Broseley, near Ironbridge in Shropshire, probably dates from this period. It measures 241 mm ($9\frac{1}{2}$ in) diameter over the flange and 203 mm (8 in) over the tread which is 95 mm ($3\frac{3}{4}$ in) 'wide' (along the grain).

The idea for the flanged wheel was a direct outcome of the guide-pin (*Leitnagel*), allowing a much wider gauge to be used with corresponding greater stability and carrying capacity. For the guide-pin (see Georg Bauer's illustration) the rails had to be close together and on this narrow-gauge wagons were small and easily upset.

The first recorded use of the word 'railway' was in 1681 at Pensnett about 4 km ($2\frac{1}{2}$ miles) north-east of Stourbridge, in Staffordshire, England (now West Midlands).

'Railroad' was first used at Rowton on the Tarbatch Dingle line near Coalport on the River Severn in Shropshire in 1702. The two words were then used indiscriminately in Britain until about 1850 after which 'railway' became standard. In North America this was reversed and 'railroad' became the more widely used term.

The word 'waggonway' was first recorded at Broseley in Shropshire in 1631. It became widely used on Tyneside where it lasted until about 1800.

The earliest discovered record of the word 'tramroad' was in the Minutes of the Brecon & Abergavenny Canal Company, in South Wales, on 17 October 1798. This referred to the L-shaped iron rails or plates and was generally used in this connection. 'Tramway' generally denoted a light railway or mineral railway.

The word 'tram' is believed to derive from a Swedish dialect word *tromm* meaning a log, and probably originated with the old wooden railways or with the frame on which baskets of coal were carried.

Strips of wrought iron on the tops of wooden rails to protect them from wear were introduced in Britain by or before 1716.

The most famous of the early British wagonways was the Tanfield Wagonway in County Durham. The first section was built in 1725 and it was extended in 1726. It was a double-track wooden railway with a gauge of 1·219 m (4 ft), and was converted to iron rails in 1839. The Tanfield, or Causey, Arch built in 1727 by master-mason Ralph Wood, has a span of 32 m (105 ft) and is probably **the world's oldest major railway bridge.** It carried the wagonway over the Beckley Burn near Causey at a height of 24·38 m (80 ft) with a semi-elliptical arch 6·9 m (22 ft $7\frac{1}{2}$ in) wide with a rise of 10·5 m (35 ft) and remained in use until the late 1760s. It remained the largest arch in Great Britain until surpassed by the 42·67 m (140 ft) span over the Taff at Pontypridd, Wales, built by William Edwards in 1755.

Part of the Tanfield line remained in use for coal traffic until 18 May 1964.

The use of 'check rails' on curves is known to date from 1729, and may be earlier, when they were recorded on a wagonway at Ravensworth in County Durham. The back of the wheel flange on the inside of the curve bears against the check rail and so prevents the outer flange from mounting the running rail. Check rails are also used on bridges and viaducts to prevent derailments.

Cast-iron flanged wheels were made at Coalbrookdale in Shropshire, England, from 1729.

The first railway in Scotland was the Tranent–Cockenzie Wagonway, about 16 km (10 miles) east of Edinburgh, laid down with wooden rails in 1722. Part of the line was used on 21 September 1745 in the course of a battle with the Young Pretender, Prince Charles Edward. Iron rails were used from 1815. It continued as a horse tramway until after 1880 when part of it was converted into a steam colliery railway.

A wooden wagonway was constructed by Ralph Allen (1694–1764), the Post Office reformer, at Prior Park, Bath, England, in 1731 to convey stone from quarries to the town. The well-known engraving by Anthony Walker, published in 1752, was the first illustration of an English railway. This was the first railway in Britain on which the use of flanged wheels is positively recorded.

The first railway authorised by Parliament in Britain was the line from a colliery at Middleton into Leeds, Yorkshire, constructed under an Act granted to Charles Brandling, Lord of the Manor of Middleton, on 9 June 1758. It was described in the Act as a

A section of oak track, dating from the mid-18th century, from Groverake Mine near Blanchland, County Durham. The rails are 1·79 m (5 ft 10½ in) long, about 89 mm (3½ in) square, and are laid to a gauge of about 457 mm (1 ft 6 in) on sleepers 825 mm (2 ft 8½ in) long. The photograph, taken in the National Railway Museum, York, in October 1978, also shows an 'L' section plateway rail, a cast-iron 'fish-bellied' rail, and some early wrought-iron rail on stone block sleepers

Set of wheels from a Blenkinsop/Murray locomotive of 1812, preserved at the National Railway Museum, York, on some of the original rails. The actual track is supposed to have had teeth on one side only to facilitate travelling round curves, but this example, to a gauge of 1·53 m (5 ft ¾ in), has teeth on both rails. The wheels are 768 mm (2 ft 6¾ in) diameter and the 20-toothed gear wheels have a mean pitch diameter of 952 mm (3 ft 1½ in)

'wagonway' and was **the first on which steam locomotives were commercially used.** It had a gauge of 1·53 m (5 ft ¾ in). The first two engines, built by Matthew Murray of Leeds to an order by John Blenkinsop, first ran on 12 August 1812. Because Blenkinsop believed that smooth wheels would not grip the rails, it was propelled by a toothed wheel engaging on a rack on one of the rails. Two more similar engines were built in 1813. The rack engines continued in service until 1835. The wheels of one are preserved on a section of original track in the National Railway Museum, York.

A portion of the Middleton Railway is still active, preserved by the Middleton Railway Trust, founded in 1959 with the co-operation of the National Trust. Steam locomotives are still at work after 163 years—a world record.

The 'standard gauge' of 1·435 m (4 ft 8½ in) was first established on the Willington Colliery wagonway system near Newcastle upon Tyne, England. Killingworth Colliery, where George Stephenson began his railway work, was part of this system. The first section of 4·828 km (3 miles), from Killingworth Moor to Willington Quay on the Tyne, was built in 1764–5. It had wooden rails.

Cast-iron bars on the tops of wooden rails were first recorded in use at Coalbrookdale, Shropshire, in 1767. They served a double function: to protect the rails from wear; and to act as a store for stocks of pig-iron during a period of low prices and at the same time to enable the furnaces to remain in operation. They were 1·524 m (5 ft) long, 10·2 cm (4 in) wide and 32 mm (1¼ in) thick. The men who fixed these were known as 'plate-layers', a term still in use today for permanent-way men.

The first use of a railway as a canal feeder was from Caldon Low Quarries in Staffordshire to Froghall Wharf for which the Trent & Mersey Canal Company obtained an Act on 13 May 1776, the second British Railway Act. The canal was authorised in 1766 and completed at the same time as the railway in 1777. The course of the railway can still be traced.

Iron flanged rails or 'plates' were introduced in England by John Curr of Durham, while he was viewer of the Duke of Norfolk's collieries at Sheffield in 1787. They were first used only underground in Sheffield Park Colliery. The 'L'-shaped rails, laid on wooden sleepers to a gauge of 610 mm (2 ft), were 1·829 m (6 ft) long and weighed 21–22 kg (47–50 lb) each. Their first use on surface lines was in 1788 on the Ketley inclined plane in Shropshire. They were cast at Ketley Ironworks and were laid on longitudinal timber bearers, 356 mm (14 in) square. The rails were 1·829 m (6 ft) long, 203 mm (8 in) wide, 50 mm (2 in) thick and the flange was 76 mm (3 in) high.

The flanged iron plates cast at Coalbrookdale rapidly replaced the cast-iron bars on wooden rails for flanged wheels used around Coalbrookdale since 1767.

Flanged rails were inefficient compared with edge rails and their use was restricted to mineral lines on which wagons were pulled by horses. Their most concentrated use was probably in South Wales, in the Forest of Dean in Gloucestershire and around Coalbrookdale. **The world's first steam locomotive**, Richard Trevithick's of 1803 (see pp. 107 and 108) was designed to run on flanged rails but proved too heavy for them. On the Peak Forest Tramroad in Derbyshire they continued in use until the 1920s and in the Forest of Dean until 1952.

The principal advantage of a 'plateway' was that flat-wheeled wagons could make part of their journey by road and part by rail. It was the first 'road-rail' device. Flanged rails formed a side track in the evolution of railways and were not in the direct line of development.

The oldest surviving railway wagon in Britain is a quarry truck of 1797 from the Peak Forest Canal Company, Derbyshire. It can be seen at the National Railway Museum, York. It ran on flanged rails.

Cast-iron edge rails for flanged wheels were first used in South Wales about 1790. They were 1·829 m (6 ft) long, 76 mm (3 in) wide at the bottom, 64 mm (2½ in) at the top and about 50 mm (2 in) thick.

'Fish-bellied' cast-iron rails were designed by William Jessop in 1792 and were laid in 1793–4 on the railway from Nanpantan to Loughborough in Leicestershire. They had a broad head on a thin web, deepest in the centre (see illustration). One end had a flat foot which was nailed into a peg in a stone block. The other end had a round lug which fitted into a slot in the foot of the next rail. These were the true ancestors of the modern rail.

The first malleable iron edge rails were used at Walbottle Colliery near Newcastle upon Tyne in England in 1805. They were faulty, however, and were replaced by cast-iron 'fish-bellied' rails.

Wrought-iron rails were first used on Lord Carlisle's Railway in Cumberland, between 1808 and 1812 when about 5·632 km (3½ miles) were relaid with wrought-iron bars on stone block sleepers.

Lord Carlisle's Railway was built as a wooden railway, begun in 1775 and completed in 1799, but was soon relaid with cast-iron rails. In 1836 the company bought the Stephensons' *Rocket* from the Liverpool &

A wagon from the Peak Forest Tramroad, Derbyshire, preserved on some of the original flanged rails at the National Railway Museum, York. The 'gauge' over the rail flanges is 1·27 m (4 ft 2 in). The wheels are 457 mm (18 in) diameter, wheelbase 768 mm (2 ft 6¼ in) and the wagon body 2·08 m (6 ft 10 in) long and 1·27 m (4 ft 2 in) wide

The frame and wheels of a wagon from the Belvoir Castle Railway, Leicestershire, on some of the original fish-bellied cast-iron rails of 1815 at the National Railway Museum, York. The rails, 914 mm (3 ft) long and weighing 18 kg (40 lb) each, were laid to a gauge of 1·333 m (4 ft 4½ in). The wagon wheels are 610 mm (2 ft) diameter, with a wheelbase of 914 mm (3 ft)

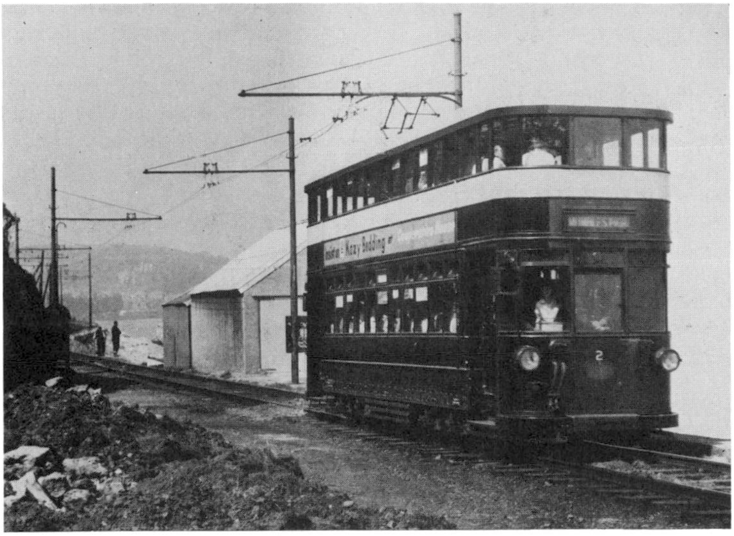

One of the electric cars on the Swansea & Mumbles Railway approaching Mumbles in July 1959

Manchester Railway and used it until 1840.

An improved method of rolling wrought-iron rails was patented by John Birkinshaw at the Bedlington Ironworks, Northumberland, on 23 October 1820. They had a swelled upper edge and were in 5·486 m (18 ft) lengths. The patent even included welding the rail ends.

The first recorded use of flanged wheels in eastern Europe was in 1794 at the Oraviga Mines in the Banat, Hungary. They were wooden rollers 200–230 mm (8 or 9 in) diameter with flanges about 355 (14 in) diameter between the rails. The rollers were turned with the grain across them and frequently split. They lasted, at best, about a year. The use of flanged wooden wheels in the Banat and Transylvania dates from about 1774, possibly even earlier.

The oldest wagon with flanged wheels in Britain, also at the National Railway

The opening of the Stockton & Darlington Railway on 27 September 1825, showing *Locomotion* and train passing over Skerne Bridge at Darlington as shown in a painting by John Dobbin (1815–88). The original watercolour, dating from 1871, is in the Borough of Darlington Museum

Museum, is from the Belvoir Castle Railway in Leicestershire. This was a 1·333 m (4 ft 4½ in) gauge railway with 'fish-bellied' cast-iron rails 914 mm (3 ft) long, laid in 1815 by the Butterley Company of Derbyshire, to carry supplies from the Grantham Canal up to Belvoir Castle. Wagons were pulled by horses, until the line closed in 1918. It was dismantled in 1940, but parts near Belvoir Castle remain *in situ*.

The first public goods railway in the world to be sanctioned by Parliament was the Surrey Iron Railway, on 21 May 1801. It was 1·219 m (4 ft) gauge and opened from Wandsworth to Croydon on 26 July 1803 and was extended by the Croydon, Merstham & Godstone Railway, incorporated by Act of Parliament on 17 May 1803, and opened from Croydon to Merstham on 24 July 1805.

The first railway to carry fare-paying passengers was the Oystermouth Railway, also known as the 'Swansea and Mumbles Railway', incorporated by Act of Parliament on 29 June 1804. It was opened about April 1806 and carried passengers from 25 March 1807. Horse-traction was used at first, and even sail-power was tried.

From about 1826 horse-buses began plying along a turnpike road beside the railway and completely stole the passenger traffic; probably the first instance in the world of a railway succumbing to road competition!

Passenger traffic was resumed in 1860 after the track was relaid. Steam-power was introduced on 16 August 1877 and lasted for 52 years until, on 2 March 1929, electric double-decked cars were put in service. They were the largest electric tramway cars in Britain, seating 106 passengers.

For goods traffic a petrol locomotive was obtained in 1929 and a diesel in 1936, making in all seven forms of motive power on one short railway.

For the second time, on 5 January 1960, the railway succumbed to a bus service. This time, however, it was dismantled.

It was the first railway in the world to celebrate 150 years of passenger services.

The first 'proper' railway in Scotland was the Kilmarnock & Troon Railway, incorporated on 27 May 1808 and opened for horse-drawn traffic on 6 July 1812. Steam-traction was introduced in 1817.

The oldest portion of the former Midland Railway, England, and one which still survives, was the Mansfield & Pinxton Railway in Nottinghamshire, incorporated on 16 June 1817 and opened on 13 April 1819. It was taken over by the MR in 1848, completely rebuilt, and reopened for steam-traction on 9 October 1849.

The first public railway to use steam from the beginning was the Stockton & Darlington Railway, opened on 27 September 1825. Steam locomotives were used at first only for goods trains, and for passenger trains from 1833.

The steam locomotive first established itself as a reliable form of motive power at the Rainhill Trials on the Liverpool & Manchester Railway from 6 to 14 October 1829. The locomotives entered included *Rocket* (George and Robert Stephenson), *Sans Pareil* (Timothy Hackworth) and *Novelty* (Braithwaite and Ericsson). The £500 prize was awarded to the *Rocket* on the last day.

The Canterbury & Whitstable Railway was opened on 3 May 1830. Stephensons' locomotive *Invicta* was driven by Edward Fletcher, later to be locomotive superintendent of the North Eastern Railway. It inaugurated the first regular steam passenger service over a mile of the line between Bogshole Farm and South Street, Whitstable.

After years of display in the open at Canterbury, *Invicta* is being restored at the National Railway Museum, York, for display under cover in a museum at Canterbury.

The world's first 'modern' railway was the Liverpool & Manchester. The first of its several Acts received the Royal Assent on 5 May 1826 and the entire railway was opened on 15 September 1830.

It was the first public railway to be operated entirely by locomotives, except for winding engines at Edge Hill, Liverpool, for working traffic to and from the docks, Crown Street, and later Lime Street Station. It was the first to have double track throughout and the first to operate passenger trains to a timetable with freight trains fitted into 'paths' in between. It was also the first to operate all the traffic itself with its own vehicles and locomotives.

It is still a busy main line today, with 15 to

The opening of the Liverpool & Manchester Railway at Edge Hill, Liverpool, on 15 September 1830, from a drawing by Isaac Shaw made from the mouth of the Wapping Tunnel. The 'Moorish Arch' housed the boiler and winding engine for winding trains up and down the incline to the goods station at Wapping.

The same view at Edge Hill after the closure of the Wapping line on 1 November 1965. The winding engine went out of use on 11 May 1896 and the Moorish Arch was removed

20 passenger trains each way between Liverpool and Manchester daily.

The first railway amalgamation to be authorised by Act of Parliament was the formation of the North Union Railway on 22 May 1834, uniting the Wigan Branch Railway with the Wigan & Preston Railway

EARLY RAILROADS IN THE USA

While in Britain and northern Europe the railway had to be fitted into an already highly developed agricultural or industrial environment, and brought into well-established towns, in North America, except in the older eastern States, the railroad opened up the country. The early railroad-builders were pioneers, often even explorers. In many towns the railroad station was the first building. One can note this pattern, for example, in Denver, Colorado, where the older streets are laid out parallel to or at right angles to the railroad, and only the later portion of the city is planned on a north–south axis. Thus railroad history in the USA and Canada is much more bound up with the growth of the country than it is in Europe.

The first railroad in North America was a short length of wooden track laid on Beacon Hill, Boston, Massachusetts, in 1795 to carry building material for the State House. A railway was laid on the same hill in 1807 to carry bricks. It was operated by Silas Whitney.

In 1811 a railway was built at Falling Creek near Richmond, Virginia, to serve a powder-mill. Another was built at Bear Creek Furnace, near Pittsburgh, Pennsylvania in 1818.

The first American railroad charter was obtained on 6 February 1815 by Colonel John Stevens of Hoboken, New Jersey, to build and operate a railroad between the Delaware and Raritan rivers near Trenton and New Brunswick. Lack of financial backing prevented construction.

The first steam locomotive in North America was built by John Stevens in February 1825 and was tested on a circular track at his home at Hoboken. It had four flat-tyred wheels guided by four vertical rollers running against the insides of the rails, and it was propelled by a central toothed rack.

John Stevens was granted another railroad charter on 21 March 1823 for a steam-powered railroad from Philadelphia to Columbia, Pennsylvania. The company was incorporated under the title of the 'Pennsylvania Railroad' which established that name as the oldest among the numerous railroad companies of the USA. It was 1829, however, before any part of the railroad was opened, and the whole line was not opened until 16 April 1834.

The Delaware & Hudson Canal Company obtained one of the first USA railroad charters on 23 April 1823, for a line from Carbondale to the canal at Honesdale in the Lackawanna Valley. The railroad was built by

Tom Thumb, the first steam locomotive on the Baltimore & Ohio Railroad, built by Peter Cooper in 1829 (Smithsonian Institution, Washington)

John Bloomfield Jervis (1795–1885) and was opened on 9 October 1829, with a gauge of 1·295 m (4 ft 3 in).

For this railroad a steam locomotive named *Stourbridge Lion* was obtained from Foster, Rastrick & Company, Stourbridge, England, and it was tried on the line on 8 August 1829, driven by Horatio Allen. However, it was too heavy for the wooden rails covered with iron strips, and for many years afterwards the line was worked as a gravity railroad. It later became part of the present Delaware & Hudson system.

Steam operation was resumed in 1860. The *Stourbridge Lion* was unquestionably **the first sub-standard-gauge locomotive in the Western Hemisphere.**

The *Stourbridge Lion* weighed 8 tons and measured 4·572 m (15 ft) high and 2·311 m (7 ft 7 in) wide. It ran only a few trial trips. About 1845 the boiler and one cylinder were sold to a foundry for use as a stationary engine and the boiler worked until 1871. This and a few other parts are preserved in the Smithsonian Institution, Washington DC. A full-size operating replica built by the Delaware & Hudson Railroad in 1932 is exhibited at Honesdale, Pennsylvania.

The first railway corporation in the USA to build and operate a railroad was the Granite City Railway Company, incorporated in Massachusetts on 4 March 1826.

The first railroad in the USA to offer a regular service as a public carrier was the Baltimore & Ohio Railroad. This was chartered on 28 February 1827. The first stone was laid on 4 July (Independence Day) 1828, and the first 21 km (13 miles) between Baltimore and Ellicott's Mills, Maryland, were opened for passenger and freight traffic on 24 May 1830. It was the first double-track railroad in America. The first fare-paying passengers were carried on 7 January 1830 from Pratt Street, Baltimore, to the Carrollton Viaduct. Horse-traction was used until July 1834. This line was closed to passengers on 31 December 1949.

The first steam locomotive on the Baltimore & Ohio Railroad, *Tom Thumb*, was built in 1829 by Peter Cooper (1791–1883) and was first run on 25 August 1830 from Baltimore to Ellicott's Mills and back. It developed only 1·43 hp which, however, was more than three times that of the Stephensons' *Rocket*. It had a vertical boiler.

The first Baltimore & Ohio rails were 150 mm (6 in) square wood baulks topped by iron strips. Mount Clare Station, Baltimore, was completed on 24 May 1830 and is the oldest surviving railroad station in the USA (see photograph p. 201).

The first train into Washington was run by the Baltimore & Ohio on 24 August 1835. In 1842, shortly after Charles Dickens had travelled on it, the railroad was extended to Cumberland, Maryland.

The Baltimore & Ohio could claim more 'firsts' than probably any other railroad. Besides the above, and matters mentioned elsewhere, it was the first railroad:

- to print a timetable advertisement, in the *Baltimore American* on 23 May 1830;
- to declare a dividend, in January 1831;
- to carry troops in the USA, on 30 June 1831;
- to operate a train at 48 km/h (30 mph), on 30 August 1831;
- to use iron wheels on passenger cars, in 1832;
- to operate a railroad workshop in America, at Mount Clare, in 1833;
- to carry a US President, on 6 June 1833 when Andrew Jackson travelled from Ellicott's Mills to Baltimore;
- to install a turntable, at Mount Clare Shops, in 1834;
- to secure a Government contract for carrying US mail, on 1 January 1838. (Mail was carried on the B. & O. from January 1832);
- to install a telegraph line in America, from Baltimore to Washington, in 1844; the first message was transmitted through Mount Clare Station on 24 May 1844;
- to use iron box cars, forerunners of all-steel cars, in 1844;
- to test an electrically operated locomotive (Page's), on 29 April 1851;
- to run a through service from the Atlantic coast to the Mississippi River, on 21 June 1857;
- to construct a grain-elevator for the export trade, at Locust Point, in 1872;
- to operate a railway express company, on 1 August 1877;
- to operate a streamlined passenger train,

Baltimore–Washington, from May to August 1900;

- to retain its charter name in the USA for a century, on 28 February 1927;
- to operate an air-conditioned car, the diner *Martha Washington*, in April 1930;
- to operate a streamlined diesel-electric locomotive on long-distance passenger services, the *Royal Blue*, on 25 May 1935;
- to offer a scheduled car-load freight service, inaugurated in 1947;
- to place strata-dome cars in regular service in the eastern USA, in 1949.

Washington became linked with New York in January 1838 by a chain of railways with ferries across major rivers and stage-coaches between stations in cities.

The first regular steam railroad in the USA was the South Carolina Railroad, opened on 15 January 1831. It now forms part of the Southern Railway system.

The first successful steam locomotive to be built in the USA, *Best Friend of Charleston*, was built by West Point Foundry, New York, for the South Carolina Railroad in 1830 and was first tested with passengers on 14 December. It entered service on Christmas Day. It had a vertical boiler, weighed under 4 tons and developed about 6 hp.

The 'Best Friend of Charleston' had the distinction of **the first locomotive boiler explosion** in the USA. On 17 June 1831, while it was being turned on the 'revolving platform' the Negro fireman held down the safety-valve to stop the steam escaping. In a few minutes the boiler blew up, injuring the fireman and several others including Mr Darrell, the engineer.

The first steam train in New York State was pulled by the *De Witt Clinton* on the Mohawk & Hudson Railroad from Albany to Schenectady on 9 August 1831. This engine was also built at the West Point Foundry. It was a 0–4–0 with cylinders 140 × 460 mm ($5\frac{1}{2}$ × 16 in), and 1·371 m (54 in) wheels, and weighed 4 tons.

One of the earliest constituents of the Pennsylvania Railroad, the Newcastle & Frenchtown Turnpike & Railway Company, was opened in July 1831; it was 27·842 km (16·19 miles) long. Steam-power was used from October 1832.

US mail was first carried by rail on the South Carolina Railroad (now part of the Southern Railway) in November 1831, and on the Baltimore & Ohio in January 1832.

The first American railroad tunnel was Staple Bend Tunnel, 275 m (901 ft) long, 6·437 km (4 miles) east of Johnstown, Pennsylvania, on the Allegheny Portage Railroad opened on 7 October 1834. Work on the tunnel began in 1829 and it was built by J. & E. Appleton at a cost of $37,498.84. It is 6·096 m (20 ft) wide, 5·791 m (19 ft) high, and it is lined with cut stone for 45·72 m (150 ft) at each end.

This section of the Pennsylvania Railroad, linking canals between Johnstown and Hollidaysburg, formed part of the route between Philadelphia and Pittsburgh. It was abandoned when the Pennsylvania Railroad opened its new route across the mountains, including the famous Horseshoe Bend, on 15 February 1854.

Charles Dickens travelled over the Portage Railroad in 1842 and described the journey in his *American Notes*.

By 1835 over 200 railway charters had been granted in eleven States and over 1600 km (1000 miles) of railway were open. For the development of railway mileage in the USA see p. 96.

The first iron railway bridge in the USA was probably one on the Reading Railroad near Manayunk, Pennsylvania, first used on 4 May 1845.

The Great Lakes were first joined by rail to the Atlantic seaboard in December 1842 when, except for the crossing of the Hudson River at Albany, New York, there were continuous rails from Boston to Buffalo on Lake Erie.

The first unbroken line of rails between the Atlantic and the Great Lakes was the New York & Erie (now Erie Lackawanna), completed from Piermont, New York, on the Hudson River to Dunkirk, NY, on Lake Erie and formally opened to through traffic in May 1851.

The first locomotive in Chicago was the *Pioneer*, weighing 10 tons, built by Matthias Baldwin of Philadelphia. It arrived by sailing-ship on 10 October 1848 and made its first run

Staple Bend Tunnel, Pennsylvania, built in 1829–30 as part of the Allegheny Portage Railroad, and the first railroad tunnel in North America (United States Department of the Interior, National Park Service, Western Pennsylvania Group)

out of Chicago, pulling two cars, on 25 October.

Chicago became linked by rail to the eastern cities on 24 January 1854, but several changes of trains were necessary.

The first locomotive west of the Mississippi, *The Pacific*, ran the 8 km (5 miles) from St Louis to Cheltenham on 9 December 1852.

The first railroad to reach the Mississippi was the Chicago & Rock Island (now Chicago, Rock Island & Pacific), completed to Rock Island, Illinois, on 22 February 1854, opening up through rail communication to the eastern seaboard.

The first railroad bridge across the Mississippi, at Davenport, Iowa, was opened on 21 April 1856. It was partly burned down on 6 May after a collision by the steamer *Effie Afton*, but was rebuilt and reopened on 8 September 1856.

The first railroad in the Pacific coast region was opened on 22 February 1856, when the locomotives *Sacramento* and *Nevada*, which had arrived by sailing-ship round Cape Horn, ran from Sacramento to Folsom, California, 35·406 km (22 miles).

The first southern rail route between the Atlantic seaboard and the Mississippi, from Charleston to Memphis, was completed on 1 April 1857.

Rail traffic first reached the Missouri River at St Joseph on 14 February 1859. The first bridge across the Missouri, at Kansas City, was opened on 4 July (Independence Day) 1869, establishing a through route from Chicago.

The first locomotive in the Pacific North-west, the *Oregon Pony*, arrived at Portland, Oregon, on 31 March 1862.

The first American transcontinental railroad, from the Missouri River to the Pacific, was authorised by an Act signed by President Lincoln on 1 July 1862 and was completed in 1869.

The first railroad bridge in the USA with an all-steel superstructure was completed in 1879 at Glasgow, Missouri, on the Chicago & Alton Railroad, now part of the Illinois Central Gulf RR.

EARLY RAILWAYS IN CANADA

The first railway in Canada about which there is any positive information was a double-track balanced incline 152 m (500 ft) long built at a cost of £695 by the Royal Engineers in 1823 to carry stone from a wharf on the St Lawrence to the top of the escarpment at Quebec during construction of the Citadel. It was worked by a horse gin, but later references to boiler repairs suggest that the gin may have been replaced by a steam-engine, and that it lasted into the 1830s.

Coal-carrying railways were built in Nova Scotia at Pictou in 1827 and North Sydney in 1828. Both used horses. They were standard, 1·435 m (4 ft 8½ in) gauge and were probably the first in North America to use iron rails, which were cast in 1·524 m (5 ft) lengths.

Canada's first steam railway was a line 26·5 km (16½ miles) long operated by 'The Company of Proprietors of the Champlain & Saint

Samson, built by Timothy Hackworth in 1839 for Nova Scotia; one of the three first coal-burning locomotives in Canada (The Science Museum, London)

Lawrence Rail Road'. It was chartered in 1832 and opened from Laprairie on the St Lawrence to St John on the Richelieu on 21 July 1836 with a gauge of 1·676 m (5 ft 6 in). (See 'The Provincial Gauge', below.)

The first locomotive was ordered from Robert Stephenson & Company, Newcastle upon Tyne, on 26 October 1825. During trials before the railway was opened the water in the boiler was allowed to get so low that several tubes were burnt out and had to be temporarily plugged so that the engine was unable to produce its maximum power on the opening day. It was named *Dorchester* after the delivery of a second locomotive in 1837. Compartment-type cars were used, built at Troy, NY, in 1836.

The oldest charter of a constituent of Canadian Pacific was that incorporating the St Andrews & Quebec Railroad Company in March 1836, for a railway from St Andrews, New Brunswick, to Lower Canada.

The first coal-burning locomotives in Canada, *Samson* (illustrated above), *Hercules* and *John Buddle* worked on a 9·656 km (6 mile) railway built in 1839 to carry coal from the Albion Mines to Pictou Harbour, Nova Scotia. *Samson* is preserved at New Glasgow, NS.

The Erie & Ontario Railway, built in 1839, was the first railway in Upper Canada. It ran round Niagara Falls from Queenston to Chippawa. The original gradients were too steep for locomotives, and horses were used. It was later rebuilt with easier grades and in 1854 was reopened with locomotive operation. It was thus the third railway in Upper Canada to use locomotives. The Great Western and the Ontario, Simcoe & Huron Union Railway, both opened in 1853, used steam locomotives from the start.

The Montreal & Lachine Railway was opened in 1847, using an 18 ton American locomotive which took 21 min to cover the 13 km (8 mile) journey. The gauge was officially 1·448 m (4 ft 9 in).

The first locomotive from Great Britain to be imported into Lower Canada was the *James Ferrier*, built at Dundee, Scotland. It made its first trip on the Montreal & Lachine Railway on 24 July 1848.

The oldest operating constituent of the Canadian Pacific Railway was La Compagnie du Chemin à Rails du Saint Laurent et du Village d'Industrie, 19 km (12 miles) long from Village d'Industrie (now Joliette, Quebec) to Lanoraie on the St Lawrence about 56 km (35 miles) north-east of Montreal. Regular services began on 6 May 1850. It came into the possession of what is now CP Rail with the purchase of the Eastern Division of the Quebec, Montreal, Ottawa & Occidental Railway in September 1885, and part of it is still in use.

The first international railway link in North America was opened from Laprairie, Quebec, to Rouses Point, New York, on 16 August 1851. By international agreement, **the first of its kind in the world**, rolling stock of a foreign railway was given free entry into Canada or the USA. This arrangement still operates.

The first steam train in Upper Canada ran from Toronto to Aurora, 48 km (30 miles), on 16 May 1853. This was the first section of the Northern Railway from Toronto to Collingwood on Georgian Bay, Lake Huron, completed in 1855. It is now part of the Canadian National system.

The railways of Canada grew from 35 km (22 miles) in 1846 to 106 km (66 miles) in 1850 and to 3325 km (2065 miles) by 1860.

The Provincial Gauge, 1·676 m (5 ft 6 in), began on the St Lawrence & Atlantic Rail Road which, with the Atlantic & Saint Lawrence Rail Road in the USA, linked Montreal with Portland, Maine, to provide an ice-free port for Montreal in winter.

The first section, between Longueuil and St Hyacinthe, was opened in December 1848. The non-standard gauge was chosen in an attempt to force Canadian winter traffic on to the line. The actual gauge may have been influenced by the purchase of the first two locomotives from the Arbroath & Forfar Railway in Scotland which was changed from 5 ft 6 in to standard gauge in 1847 and whose broad-gauge stock was sold in December 1848. The explanation given for the broad gauge was that it would hamper invasion and that changing trains at the breaks of gauge would give passengers 'healthful exercise'. The 'Provincial Gauge' was officially adopted by legislation on 31 July 1851; it was repealed by the Dominion Government in 1870.

The Great Western Railway of Canada, begun at London, Ontario, in 1847, was forced to adopt a third rail. It was opened from Niagara to London in 1853. The Grand Trunk Railway, chartered in 1852, was also built to the 1·676 m (5 ft 6 in) gauge.

The first railway tunnel in Canada, at Brockville, Ontario, opened in 1860 and used by Canadian Pacific trains until 1974. The photograph, taken on 14 September 1957, shows the south portal (R F Corley)

The broad gauge held out until 1871, by which time most Canadian and USA railways had adopted standard gauge. Conversion of the Grand Trunk system took until September 1874. The Intercolonial Railway between Halifax and St John, New Brunswick, was converted to standard gauge by 1875, and the connection from Halifax to Rivière du Loup was opened on 1 July 1876, bringing the mileage of the Intercolonial to 1127 km (700 miles).

Canada's first sub-standard-gauge steam-operated railway was the 1·067 m (3 ft 6 in) gauge Lingan Colliery Tramway on the island of Cape Breton, built in 1861. The first locomotive was a Black Hawthorn 0–4–0 saddle tank built in Gateshead, County Durham, in 1866.

The Glasgow & Cape Breton Coal & Railway Company operated the first steam-worked narrow-gauge railway in Canada. The 914 mm (3 ft) gauge line was opened in May 1871, using a Fox, Walker 0–4–0 tank engine, built in Bristol.

The first locomotive to be built in Canada was named *Toronto*. It was built at the foundry of James Good, Toronto, and made its first run on 16 May 1853 on the Ontario, Simcoe & Huron Union Railway, later renamed the Northern Railway.

Through trains were inaugurated between Montreal and Toronto on 27 October 1856 by the Grand Trunk Railway, later part of the Canadian National Railways.

Canada's first railway tunnel was opened by the Brockville & Ottawa Railway on 31 December 1860. It was about 540 m (a third of a mile) long, passing beneath the town of Brockville, and was used by Canadian Pacific Rail until abandoned in 1974.

The first railway in British Columbia was built in 1861 at Seton Portage, 225 km (140 miles) north of Vancouver. It had wooden rails, and cars were drawn by mules.

FURTHER RAILWAY DEVELOPMENTS

The railway was introduced to France by an Englishman, William Wilkinson (*c* 1744–1808), who built a line in 1778–9 at Indret at the mouth of the Loire to serve a new ordnance factory. It was used until about 1800.

The first recorded use of the French term 'chemin de fer' was in 1784 by a Frenchman named de Givry, reporting on a visit to Coalbrookdale in Shropshire, England.

The first public railway in France, from Saint-Etienne to Andrézieux, was begun in 1824 and formally opened on 1 October 1828. The Concession had been granted on 26 February 1823. The railway was used unofficially from May 1827. Passenger traffic began on 1 March 1832, but horse-traction was used until 1 August 1844. Cast-iron 'fish-bellied' rails were used. It was extended from Saint-Etienne to the Loire in 1828 using wrought-iron rails.

On 7 June 1826 a Concession was granted for the Saint-Etienne–Lyon Railway and the section from Givors to Rive-de-Gier was opened on 25 June 1830.

It was on this line that Marc Séguin tried out his locomotive on 7 November 1829.

The remainder of the railway was opened from Lyon to Givors on 3 April 1832, and from the Rive-de-Gier to Saint-Etienne for goods on 18 October 1832 and passengers on 25 February 1833.

In Austria-Hungary the first railway opened on 7 September 1827, from Budweis (now Budejovice, Czechoslovakia) to Trojanov, with horse-traction. It was the first section of the Linz–Budweis Railway. Locomotives were not used until 1872.

The great Doric Arch which fronted on to Euston Road, London, at the terminus of the London & Birmingham Railway. It was demolished in 1962 when the present Euston Station was built (British Rail)

The first railway wholly in modern Austria was the Kaiser Ferdinand Nordbahn from Vienna to Floridsdorf and Deutsch Wagram, 17·7 km (11 miles) long, opened on 23 November 1837. It was the first railway in Austria to use steam locomotives.

The first railway in Ireland was the Dublin & Kingstown (now Dun Laoghaire) Railway, opened on 17 December 1834. It was standard gauge but was converted to the Irish standard of 1·600 m (5 ft 3 in) in 1857. The first locomotive, the 2–2–0 *Hibernia*, was built by Sharp Roberts & Company, Manchester.

The first section of the Ulster Railway, from Belfast to Lisburn, was opened on 12 August 1839. The gauge was originally 1·880 m (6 ft 2 in).

A story, possibly apocryphal, relates how an army officer was asked to settle the Irish gauge question. He simply rounded off the gauges to 6 ft and 4 ft 6 in, added them together and divided by 2. The result, 5 ft 3 in (1·600 m), became the Irish standard gauge which also found its devious way into Brazil and Australia, by the employment of Irish engineers.

The Ulster Railway was converted to 1·600 m (5 ft 3 in) gauge in 1847.

The first railway in Belgium, from Brussels to Malines, 23·35 km (14·5 miles), was opened on 5 May 1835. It was built and worked, as part of a planned national system, by the Belgian Government and was thus **the first nationalised railway**. The first two locomotives, inside-cylinder 2–2–2s, *La Flèche* and *Stephenson*, were built by Robert Stephenson & Company at Newcastle upon Tyne.

The first railway in Germany, the Ludwigsbahn from Nuremberg to Fürth, was opened on 7 December 1835. Robert Stephenson & Company again built the first locomotive *Der Adler*, similar to the Belgian locomotives.

The first railway in Russia was the St Petersburg & Pavlovsk Railway, built to a gauge of 1·829 m (6 ft). The first portion, Pavlovsk to Tsarskoe Selo, was opened to horse-traction on 9 October 1836. The entire railway was opened on 30 October 1837.

The first railway in London was the London & Greenwich Railway incorporated on 17 May 1833, and opened on 8 February 1836 from Spa Road to Deptford, extended to London Bridge on 14 December 1836 and to Greenwich on 24 December 1838. The railway, 6 km (3¾ miles) long, was almost entirely on a brick viaduct of 878 arches. **It was the first 'overhead railway'.**

The first British trunk railway was the Grand Junction Railway from Birmingham to Warrington, engineered by Joseph Locke and opened on 4 July 1837. It became part of the London & North Western Railway on the formation of that company on 16 July 1846. It had already absorbed the Liverpool & Manchester Railway. With the opening, on 17 December 1846, of the Lancaster & Carlisle Railway, of which Locke was again engineer, it formed a section of the main line from London (Euston) to Carlisle.

The opening of the Caledonian Railway from Carlisle to Glasgow and Edinburgh, again engineered by Locke, on 15 February 1848 completed the West Coast route from London to Scotland.

The first railway across England was the Newcastle & Carlisle Railway, opened on 18 June 1838. It became part of the North Eastern Railway on 17 July 1862.

The oldest main line into London, the London & Birmingham Railway, was opened from London (Euston) to Birmingham on 17 September 1838. With the Grand Junction and the Manchester & Birmingham railways it became a part of the London & North Western Railway on 16 July 1846.

Birmingham was bypassed by the opening of the 64 km (39¾ mile) Trent Valley line from Rugby to Stafford on 15 September 1847, now part of the West Coast main line.

The first section of the Great Western Railway, engineered by I K Brunel, was opened from London (Paddington) to Maidenhead on 4 June 1838. It had a nominal gauge of 2·134 m (7 ft). It was extended to Twyford on 1 June 1839, to Reading on 30 March 1840, and was completed to Bristol on 30 June 1841. Brunel was then only 35 years old. The present Paddington Station was designed by Brunel and opened on 16 January 1854. (See Frith's *The Railway Station.*)

The first railway in the Netherlands was

Full-size replica, built in 1939, of *De Arend* (The Eagle), the first locomotive in the Netherlands. The original was built in 1839 by Longridge of Bedlington, Northumberland. The photograph was taken at the Netherlands Railway Museum, Utrecht, and shows the engine with replicas of 1st, 2nd and 3rd class coaches.

opened from Amsterdam to Haarlem on 24 September 1839. The first locomotive, *Arend* (Eagle), was built by R B Longridge & Company at Bedlington, Northumberland (Works No 119), and was scrapped in 1857. A full-size replica stands in the Netherlands Railway Museum, Utrecht.

The first Netherlands railway timetable was published on 14 April 1850.

The first railway in Italy, from Naples to Portici, opened on 4 October 1839.

The oldest principal section of the East Coast route, the Great North of England Railway from York to Darlington, was opened on 4 January 1841 for goods trains and on 30 March for passengers.

The first trans-Pennine railway, the Manchester & Leeds, was opened throughout on 1 March 1841. On 9 July 1847 it became the Lancashire & Yorkshire Railway. It passed beneath the Pennine watershed between Littleborough and Todmorden in the Summit Tunnel, 2638 m (2885 yd) long.

The first conference of railway managers was held in Birmingham, England, on 19 January 1841, to draw up a code of rules, signalling, etc.

The Railway Clearing House to settle rates for through traffic over different British railway companies' systems began operating on 2 January 1842. The Irish Railway Clearing House was established on 1 July 1848.

Switzerland's first railway, from Basel to St Ludwig (now Saint-Louis, France), opened on 15 June 1844. The Zürich–Baden Railway (opened on 9 August 1847) was the first railway entirely in Switzerland.

The year when the greatest number of railway Acts was passed was 1846, during the 'Railway Mania', when 272 Bills received the Royal Assent in Britain.

The first steam railway in Hungary from Pest to Vacz, 33 km (20½ miles), was opened on 15 July 1846. An early line from Pest to Köbanya was opened in August 1827.

The oldest railway in modern Denmark is the Copenhagen–Roskilde Railway, opened on 26 June 1847. (The Altona–Kiel Railway, opened in 1844, was afterwards annexed with its territory by Prussia.)

The first railway in Spain, 27 km (17 miles), from Barcelona to Mataró, was opened on 28 October 1848. The first locomotive was also named *Mataró*.

Robert Stephenson's Britannia tubular bridge over the Menai Strait from the Anglesey shore on 26 July 1972, in course of rebuilding into a steel arch bridge following severe fire damage in 1970. The arches are complete and the Stephenson tube is being cut up from the far (Bangor) end. A road deck is to be added above the railway

A through railway between London and Aberdeen was completed with the opening of the Scottish North Eastern (later Caledonian) Railway between Perth and Aberdeen on 1 April 1850.

The first section of the Great Northern Railway (England), from Louth to Grimsby, 22·5 km (14 miles), was opened on 1 March 1848.

The 'East Coast route' from London (Euston) to Edinburgh via the Midlands was completed in 1848 with the opening, on 29 August, of a temporary bridge over the Tyne between Gateshead and Newcastle and, on 10 October, a temporary viaduct over the Tweed at Tweedmouth.

The Tyne bridge was replaced by Robert Stephenson's High Level Bridge, opened for rail traffic on the upper deck on 15 August 1849, and for road traffic below on 4 February 1850.

The Royal Border Bridge across the Tweed, also by Robert Stephenson, was opened on 29 August 1850.

The Great Northern Railway trains reached Doncaster from London via the 'Loop' from Peterborough through Boston and Lincoln on 7 August 1850. From Lincoln to Retford trains ran over the Manchester, Sheffield & Lincolnshire Railway.

King's Cross became the terminus of the East Coast route when the GNR was extended from Maiden Lane on 14 October 1852. The 'Towns Line', Peterborough (Werrington Junction)–Grantham–Newark–Retford, was opened on 1 August 1852.

North of Doncaster the route to York lay over the Lancashire & Yorkshire Railway and the York & North Midland (later North Eastern) Railway. The NER direct line Doncaster–Selby–York was opened on 2 January 1871.

North of Darlington trains ran via Leamside to Newcastle until 1872 when they were routed over a new line via Durham.

The Chester & Holyhead Railway was completed with the opening of Robert Stephenson's tubular bridge over the Menai Strait on 18 March 1850. It formed the northern part of the main line between London and Dublin.

The first railway in India, part of the Great Indian Peninsula Railway, was opened on 18 April 1853 from Bombay to Thana. The gauge of 1·676 m (5 ft 6 in) became the Indian standard.

The first railway in South America was opened on 3 November 1848. It ran from Georgetown to Plaisance, 8 km (5 miles), in British Guyana. It formed part of the standard gauge

East Coast line, 98 km (61 miles), and was closed on 30 June 1972.

The oldest steam locomotive in South America, Caldera & Copiapo Railway No. 1, built in 1850 and now preserved at Copiapo, about 1000 km (621 miles) north of Santiago, Chile (Ricardo Kelly)

The first railway in Chile ran from the port of Caldera to Copiapo 396 m (1300 ft) above sea-level, a distance of 80·5 km (50$\frac{1}{4}$ miles). The company was formed locally in October 1849; the line was laid out by William Wheelwright and built by Allan and Alexander Campbell of Albany, New York, and was opened on 25 December 1851. Locomotive No. 1 *Copiapo*, illustrated, built by Norris Brothers of Philadelphia, USA, in 1850 is **the oldest steam locomotive in South America**. It was standard gauge and worked until 1891. The railway was taken over by the Chilean Government in 1911 and later converted to metre gauge.

Copiapo is unique in being the only surviving American 4–4–0 of the 1850 period and, unlike other preserved early American locomotives, all of which have been extensively rebuilt, it is almost in its original form. The engine had about 60 m^2 (645 ft^2) heating surface, cylinders 330 × 660 mm (13 × 26 in), coupled wheels 1·524 m (5 ft), and weighed 19 tons in working order.

The first railway in Brazil was the 1·676 m (5 ft 6 in) gauge line, 16 km (10 miles) from Maua at the end of the Bay of Rio to the foot of the Petropolis Serra. It was opened on 30 April 1854 and was later converted to metre gauge. On its extension to Petropolis it climbed the Sierra de Estrella for 6·437 km (4 miles) with a Riggenbach rack. In 1897 it became part of the Leopoldina Railway.

From 1862 the Dom Pedro II Railway (later Central of Brazil) established 1·600 m (5 ft 3 in) as the Brazilian broad gauge.

The first sub-standard-gauge railway in South America and probably the first steam-operated sub-standard-gauge public railway in the Western Hemisphere was the 1·067 m (3 ft 6 in) gauge União Valenciana Railway in Brazil. Baldwin Locomotive Works of Philadelphia built three locomotives for this line in 1869.

The first railway in Argentina from Plaza del Parque in Buenos Aires to the suburb of Floresta, 9·9 km (6·2 miles), was opened on 30 August 1857. It was built to 1·676 m (5 ft 6 in) gauge because its first locomotive, named *La Portena*, and built in 1856 by E B Wilson & Company, Leeds, was originally intended for India, and this established the 5 ft 6 in gauge in Argentina.

The first railway on the African continent was opened in January 1856 between Alexandria and Cairo, 208 km (129 miles), standard gauge.

The first railway in Norway, from Christiania (later Oslo) to Eidsvoll, 67·6 km (42 miles), was opened on 1 September 1854.

The first railway in Portugal, from Lisbon to Carregado, 37 km (23 miles), was opened on 28 October 1856.

The oldest portions of the Swedish State Railways, from Gothenburg to Jonsered and Malmö to Lund, were opened on 1 December 1856.

EARLY AUSTRALIAN RAILWAYS

The Australian Agricultural Company constructed an inclined tramway of iron rails to carry coal from its mines at Newcastle to Port Hunter in 1827, and another there in 1830.

The first locomotive in New South Wales, Australia, 'Class 1' 0–4–2 No. 1 built by Robert Stephenson & Company in 1854 for the Sydney & Goulburn Railway. It is shown on display in the forecourt of Sydney Station at the Centenary celebrations on 19 August 1955 (J L N Southern)

In Tasmania in 1836 a wooden railway 8 km (5 miles) long was laid across a peninsula. Passengers paid a shilling to ride in trucks pushed by convicts to avoid a stormy sea journey.

Australia's first steam-operated railway was the 4 km (2½ miles) long 1·600 m (5 ft 3 in) gauge Melbourne & Hobson's Bay Railway, opened from Flinders Street, Melbourne, to Sandridge, Victoria, on 12 September 1854.

The first passenger railway, however, was the 11·265 km (7 mile) Port Elliot & Goolwa Railway in South Australia, also 1·600 m (5 ft 3 in) gauge, opened with horse-traction on 18 May 1854.

The first railway in New South Wales was opened from Sydney to Panamatta Junction, now Granville, on 26 September 1855. It was built by the Sydney Railway Company, but was taken over by the New South Wales Government before opening.

The first locomotive in New South Wales was 'Class 1' 0–4–2 No. 1, built by Robert Stephenson & Company at Newcastle upon Tyne, England, for the Sydney & Goulburn Railway in 1854, to a design by J E McConnell. It weighed 45 tons 5 cwt, and worked the first train from Sydney, where it is now preserved.

In South Australia the 1·600 m (5 ft 3 in) gauge railway from Adelaide to Port Adelaide, 12 km (7½ miles), was opened on 21 April 1856. It was built and worked by the Government.

In Queensland the first railway, to a gauge of 1·067 m (3 ft 6 in), was opened in July 1865, between Ipswich and Grandchester, 33·297 km (20·69 miles), in the Southern Division. **Queensland was the first railway system in the world to adopt a sub-standard gauge for main lines.**

On 14 June 1883 the railways of New South Wales and Victoria met at Albury, after the completion of the bridge over the Murray River.

The first 'proper' railway in Tasmania, to a gauge of 1·600 m (5 ft 3 in) as in South Australia, was opened in 1871 between Launceston and Deloraine, 72·4 km (45 miles). It was taken over by the Government in 1872 as was the later Launceston–Hobart line, opened in 1876. The lines were converted to 1·067 m (3 ft 6 in) gauge, standard in Tasmania, in 1888. The first 1·067 m (3 ft 6 in) gauge line was opened in 1885.

In Western Australia the first railway was a 1·067 m (3 ft 6 in) gauge private timber-carrying line from Yoganup to Lockville, 19 km (12 miles) opened on 6 June 1871. It was worked by horses until August when the locomotive *Ballarat* arrived from Ballarat, Victoria, where it was built.

The first railway in South Africa, from Durban to The Point, was opened by the Natal Railway on 26 June 1860. It was acquired by the Natal Government on 1 January 1877.

Cape Province's first railway was opened to Eerste River on 13 February 1862 and extended to Wellington in 1863.

The first railway in Pakistan was the 169 km (105 mile) line from Karachi to Kochi, opened on 13 May 1861.

New Zealand opened its first steam railway from Christchurch to Ferrymead with 1·600 m (5 ft 3 in) gauge on 1 December 1863.

The first railway in Sri Lanka (Ceylon), from Colombo to Ambepussa, was opened on 2 October 1865.

The first railway in Greece, from the harbour at Piraeus to Athens, was opened in 1869.

The first railway in Japan, from Yokohama to Sinagawa, was opened on 12 June 1872. It was completed to Tokyo on 14 October.

Japanese railways in the ten years from 1880 to 1890, grew from 158 km (98 miles) to 2348 km (1459 miles). By 1974 the total was 27 283 km (16 953 miles), and it is still increasing.

China had no railway until 1876 when a 762 mm (2 ft 6 in) gauge line was opened from Shanghai to Woosung, about 32 km (20 miles). It was operated by two tiny 0–4–0 saddle tanks, built by Ransome & Rapier, England. The engineer was John Dixon (1835–91), nephew of John Dixon of the Stockton & Darlington Railway.

The Chinese were hostile and suspicious and, following a fatal accident, as soon as the redemption money was paid, in October 1877, the railway was bought by the Government and the entire outfit was torn up and dumped on Formosa.

The first permanent railway in China was the standard-gauge Tongshan–Hsukuchuang line, opened in 1880, extended to Lutai in 1886 and Tientsin in 1888. It now forms part of the Peking–Mukden section of the Chinese People's Republic Railways. Steam-traction was introduced in 1883.

After this, Chinese railway mileage grew rapidly. By 1900 it was 2346 km (1458 miles); in 1977 it was about 35 000 km (21 750 miles).

The first railway in Burma was the metre-gauge line between Rangoon and Prome, 257 km (160 miles) opened on 1 May 1877.

The first railway in Tibet, from Sining to Lhasa, was begun by China in 1975. One of the tunnels will be 5·8 km (3·6 miles) long.

Section 2
THE LINES

RAILWAY GAUGES
or measurement between the inner edges of the rails

Standard gauge, 1·435 m or 4 ft 8½ in, is used in Great Britain, Canada, the USA, Mexico, Europe (except Ireland, Spain, Portugal, Finland and the USSR), North Africa, the Near Eastern countries, the Australian Commonwealth Railways and New South Wales, China and South Korea; also some lines in Japan, Western Australia and Victoria. In South America it is found in Paraguay, Uruguay, the North Eastern Region in Argentina, the Central and Southern Railways of Peru, Venezuela and short lines in Brazil.

Other principal gauges:

Wide gauges
1·676 m (5 ft 6 in) India, Pakistan, Sri Lanka (Ceylon), Spain, Portugal, Argentina, Chile.
1·600 m (5 ft 3 in) Ireland, South Australia, Victoria, Brazil.
1·520 m (4 ft 11⅞ in) USSR, Finland (the gauge was 1·524 m or 5 ft until 1 January 1972).

Sub-standard gauges
1·067 m (3 ft 6 in) Queensland, South and West Australia, Tasmania, New Zealand, South Africa, Rhodesia, Malawi, Ghana, Nigeria, Sudan, Japan, Indonesia, Newfoundland, some lines in Norway and Sweden, and in Ecuador and Chile. South African Railways are now 1·065 m.
1·05 m (3 ft 5¼ in) Algeria, Syria, the Lebanon and Jordan.
1 metre (3 ft 3·375 in) principal lines in Burma, Thailand (Siam), Vietnam, Malaysia, East Africa and Cambodia, Brazil, Argentina, Chile, Bolivia; secondary lines in Switzerland, Portugal, Greece, India, Pakistan, Iraq.

For narrow gauges, less than 1 metre, see 'Narrow-gauge railways' in the section Miscellany.

The world's mean track gauge works out to exactly 1·400 m or 4 ft 7⅛ in, close to the standard gauge of 1·435 m or 4 ft 8½ in.

The first metre-gauge railway was probably that built by George Stephenson to connect his limestone quarry at Crich in Derbyshire with the limeworks beside the North Midland Railway at Ambergate. The first section was opened in March 1841 and the line was completed to Cliff Quarry in 1846. The railway worked until 24 May 1957 and the limeworks closed on 2 October 1965. Today the Cliff Quarry is the site of the Crich Tramway Museum (qv).

Metre-gauge mineral railways were built in Algeria in 1865–6 and in Greece in 1869.

The earliest known passenger train service on a metre-gauge railway was operated by the Bombay, Baroda & Central India Railway between Delhi and Rewari, 84 km (52½ miles), opened to passengers on 14 February 1873.

The establishment of the metre gauge for secondary lines in India was somewhat devious. The choice of gauge was left to Lord Mayo (b 1822 and Viceroy of India from 1869 until his assassination in 1872). He decided that the minimum width of a carriage to seat four aside should be 6 ft 6 in (1·981 m) and that the gauge should be not less than half that width. So the British Government agreed on a gauge of 3 ft 3 in (990 mm), but as a commission was then considering the introduction of the metric system in India the gauge was fixed at 1 metre, although another 90 years were to pass before the metric system was adopted.

The metre gauge holds second place in the world's route mileage. Out of about 1 126 500 km or 700 000 route miles in 1930 about 112 650 km or 70 000 miles were metre gauge. Third place is held by the 1·067 m (3 ft 6 in) gauge with a route length of 75 640 km (47 000 miles).

Triple-gauge track at the south end of Gladstone Yard, South Australia, on wheat silo discharge tracks, in 1973; 1·067 m (3 ft 6 in), 1·435 m (4 ft $8\frac{1}{2}$ in) and 1·6 m (5 ft 3 in) (A. Grunbach)

Australia has three different gauges. Out of over 40 240 km (25 000 miles) nearly half is 1·067 m (3 ft 6 in) gauge and the remainder is almost equally divided between 1·435 m (4 ft $8\frac{1}{2}$ in) and 1·600 m (5 ft 3 in).

The 1·600 m (5 ft 3 in) was the result of employing an Irish engineer, F W Shields; the 1·067 m (3 ft 6 in) was adopted as an economy measure. Plans to unify the system have been discussed since 1897.

Perth to Kalgoorlie is now partly dual-gauged from Perth to Northern, with standard and 1·067 m (3 ft 6 in). Port Pirie to Broken Hill is now standard gauge.

South Australia has all three gauges. At Peterborough on the Port Pirie–Broken Hill section and at Gladstone there is triple-gauge track, thus:

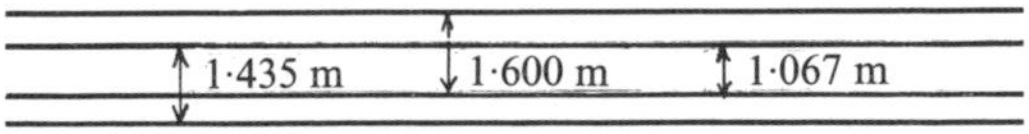

A gauge of 5 ft (1·524 m) was used at first on the Eastern Counties, Northern & Eastern and London & Blackwall Railways, England.

For the Great Western Railway, England, I K Brunel (see p. 23) adopted a gauge of 7 ft (2·134 m). After a while a $\frac{1}{4}$ in (6 mm) was added to give greater clearance.

A Royal Commission on railway gauges was appointed by the British Government on 25 June 1845. Its report, published in 1846, recommended that future railways should be built to standard gauge, except on the Great Western (where the standard gauge was always referred to as the 'narrow gauge').

The last railway to be built to the 7 ft gauge was the 6·8 km ($4\frac{1}{4}$ mile) branch of the West Cornwall Railway from St Erth to St Ives opened on 1 June 1877.

The last broad-gauge trains of the Great Western Railway ran on 20 May 1892. Gauge conversion was completed by 23 May.

A gauge of 2·4 m (8 ft) was used on a lumber railway in Oregon, USA, in 1885.

TRACK
(For early developments see 'The Beginnings')

The first steel rails were made by Robert Forester Mushet and were laid experimentally at Derby Station on the Midland Railway, England, early in 1857, on a heavily used line. They remained in use until June 1873.

The first steel rails on the London & North Western Railway were laid at Chalk Farm, London, in 1862.

The first steel rails in the USA were laid by the Pennsylvania Railroad in 1863 at Altoona and Pittsburgh under the supervision of John Edgar Thomson (1808–74), the third president of the PRR and himself an engineer.

The word 'sleeper' originated from the 'dormant timbers' placed beneath the rails and was certainly in use in England in the early 18th century. North Americans adopted the word 'tie', the French 'la traverse'. In German it is 'die Schwelle', simply 'joist'.

British Rail consumes about 2 500 000 sleepers annually. Each timber sleeper measures 2·591 m (8 ft 6 in) × 254 mm (10 in) × 127 mm (5 in) in softwood or 120 mm ($4\frac{3}{4}$ in) in hardwood.

The number of sleepers per kilometre in Britain is from 1320 to 1540 (2112 to 2404 per mile) according to loadings, foundations, curves, etc. In exceptional situations as many as 1650 (2040 per mile) may be used.

The maximum British axle load is 25 tons,

but in the USA where loads can be up to 34 tons per axle, 1875 to 2188 ties per km (3000 to 3500 per mile) are used.

In Britain there are about 9 000 000 pre-stressed concrete sleepers in use. They measure 2·515 m (8 ft 3 in) long and weigh 267 kg (588 lb) with fastenings, compared with 107·5 kg (237 lb) for a chaired and creosoted wooden sleeper. They have an estimated life of from 44 to 50 years, more than double that of a wooden sleeper. They became popular during the wartime timber shortage and are now standard for plain line. Mechanical handling has largely overcome the weight problem. Experiments are being made with concrete beams for points and crossings.

Steel sleepers are extensively used on the continent of Europe and in other parts of the world. They can still last from 40 to 50 or even 80 years and then still have scrap value. In Switzerland 70 per cent of the Federal system and the whole of the Rhaetian and other metre-gauge systems are laid with steel sleepers. Greece, Congo Republics, systems in West, East and South Africa use steel sleepers for 90–100 per cent of the track.

In India steel sleepers are used on 12 381 km (7694 miles) of 1·676 m (5 ft 6 in) gauge track and on 2306 km (1433 miles) of metre-gauge track.

In Britain steel sleepers are little used, largely because of the difficulty of packing ballast beneath. Corrosion can be minimised by resilient tar coatings or by the addition of a small percentage of copper to the steel.

The latest type of track construction in Britain, known as PACT (Paved Concrete Track) is being experimented with at Radcliffe on Trent near Nottingham (1970), and at Duffield north of Derby (1972). It consists of a continuous concrete slab on which the rails are fixed. This eliminates sleepers and ballast, significantly reduces maintenance, and provides a better line for high-speed trains, giving a smoother ride. The new track is expected to be highly suitable for use in tunnels, particularly the Channel Tunnel, and for rapid transit lines. It is already in use on part of the new electric main line in Glasgow.

On French Railways (SNCF) it has been used in the new Sainte-Devote Tunnel under Monte Carlo and in an experimental cutting near Limoges.

It has been used on 270 km (167 miles) out of 400 km (248 miles) of the 1975 extension of the Shinkansen from Okayama to Hokata in Japan.

Freight train with a Class 37 diesel locomotive passing over the 1·8 km (1·1 mile) length of Paved Concrete Track (PACT) at Duffield, north of Derby, brought into use on 13 August 1972. The line carries about 40 passenger and 30 freight trains daily with minimal maintenance (British Rail)

Pandrol rail clips in use with wooden sleepers on the main line at Durham

In New Zealand it is being used inside the new Kaimai Tunnel in the North Island (qv).

Before it can be used extensively on main passenger lines train toilet facilities will have to be altered so that they no longer deposit waste on to the track. At present the ballast acts as an efficient filter-bed.

The simplest, most ingenious and most effective rail fastening is probably the 'Pandrol'. The principal component is a spring-steel clip quickly driven into place with a hammer, and as easily removed. Its resilience makes it unaffected by vibration, it will not work loose, and it prevents 'rail creep' (the tendency for rails to move in the direction of the traffic when a train is braking). It is suitable for wood, concrete or steel sleepers, and on the last can be insulated for track-circuiting. Rail changing is simplified and the clips can be reused. It is eminently suitable for use with the new PACT construction. One of its greatest advantages is its low cost.

'Pandrol' rail fastenings were first used on British Railways in 1959 just south of Peterborough on the former Great Northern main line. Since then it has become standard on British Rail and the 50 millionth clip was delivered during 1972. It has also been adopted in many other countries throughout the world.

Insertion and extraction have now been mechanised to reduce line-occupation periods. The 'Pandriver' travels along the track at about 0·75 km/h (0·5 mph), enabling a man to place clips in position ahead of the machine ready for driving. The 'Pandrex' knocks out clips at a track speed of 3 km/h (2 mph).

The standard British flat-bottomed rails measure 159 mm (6$\frac{1}{4}$ in) high, 140 mm (5$\frac{1}{2}$ in) wide across the foot, 70 mm (2$\frac{3}{4}$ in) across the head and have a nominal weight of 55·79 kg/m (113 lb/yd). They are rolled in 18·288 m (60 ft) lengths. In Germany 30 m (98 ft 5 in) is common. They are then welded into continuous lengths first at the depot into 182·88 m, 219·46 m, 274·32 m or 402·3 m (600 ft, 720 ft, 900 ft or 1320 ft), and into greater lengths at the site.

London Transport use a 47·6 kg/m (95 lb/yd) 'bull-head' rail in chairs, mounted on sleepers of jarrah on underground lines.

USA railroads use rails of a standard length of 11·887 m (39 ft). Some, however, use lengths of 13·716 m and 18·288 m (45 ft and 60 ft). Rail weights on Class 1 railroads vary from 22·3 to 86·3 kg/m (45 to 174 lb/yd). On trunk lines the weights range upwards from 42 kg/m (85 lb/yd). Rail joints are generally staggered.

'Fish-plates' for joining rail ends were introduced in 1847 by William Bridges Adams and Robert Richardson, and their use became general in Britain during the late 1840s and early 1850s. Previously the ends of rails rested in wide 'joint chairs' in which the rails could become loose. Standard fish-plates are 507 mm (1 ft 8 in) long with four holes at 127 mm (5 in) centres. Even with secure fish-plates the fracture of rail ends has always been a problem, and during the 1930s the London, Midland & Scottish Railway experimented with short two-hole fish-plates which allowed the sleepers and chairs to be brought close to the rail ends to give better support. Modern track with heavy-section long-welded rails has practically eliminated this danger.

The longest stretch of unbroken four-track line in the world was 551 km (342·5 miles) between Castleton and Dunkirk, New York, USA. Except for a 3·2 km (2 mile) break at Dunkirk the four-track line extended from Castleton to Collinwood, Cleveland, 762·5 km (473·75 miles). Today most of this length has been converted to two tracks using Centralised Traffic Control (CTC).

The latest weed-killing train on British Rail went into operation in the summer of 1975. It is able to operate at 72 km/h (45 mph) in both directions. It is the sixth type produced in association with Fisons Ltd in the past 20 years.

LONGEST STRAIGHTS

The world's longest straight stretch is on the standard-gauge Transcontinental Railway of the Commonwealth Railways of Australia, across the Nullarbor Plain, 478 km (297 miles), from km 798 (mile 496) between Nurina and Loongana, Western Australia, to km 1276 (mile 793) between Ooldea and Watson, South Australia. It was completed in 1917. In one year 712 km (442 miles 44 chains) of track was laid, with a maximum for one day of 4 km (2 miles 40 chains), unballasted at the time. This is a record in Australia. (For the world record see 'Some USA Facts and Feats'.)

The Buenos Aires & Pacific Railway, Argentina (Central Region), is dead straight and almost level for 330 km (205 miles) between Junin and MacKenna, on the 1·676 m (5 ft 6 in) gauge line from Buenos Aires to Mendoza where it connects with the metre-gauge South Transandine line.

In the USA the longest straight is the 126·914 km (78·86 miles) on the former Seaboard Air Line Railway between Wilmington and Hamlet, North Carolina. ('Air Line' is an American term meaning 'direct'.) It is now part of the Seaboard Coast line which also has a 92·376 km (57·4 miles) straight between Okeechobee and West Palm Beach, Florida. Other long straights in the USA are:

Rock Island Railroad between Guymon, Oklahoma, and Dalhart, Texas, 114·163 km (71·94 miles)
Conrail (formerly New York Central, later Penn Central) between Air Line Junction (West of Toledo) and Butler, Indiana, 110·229 km (68·49 miles)
Monon Railroad between Brookston and Westville, Indiana, 103·836 km (64·52 miles)
Illinois Central Gulf between Edgewood and Akin Junction, Illinois, 101·324 km (62·96 miles)
Atlantic Coast line between Waycross and Kinderlou, Georgia, 96·721 km (60·1 miles)

There are, or were, five more lengths over 80 km (50 miles).

In Rhodesia is a 112·65 km (70 mile) straight between Sawmills and Dett on the Bulawayo–Waukie main line.

In Russia the Moscow & St Petersburg (Leningrad) Railway is almost straight and level for 643·74 km (400 miles). It was begun in 1843 and opened on 13 November 1851. It adopted the 1·524 m (5 ft) gauge, then standard in the Southern States of the USA, and so established the Russian standard gauge of 5 ft.

The longest straight in England is 29 km (18 miles) between Barlby and Staddlethorpe Junctions on the former North Eastern Railway Selby–Hull line (opened by the Hull & Selby Railway on 1 July 1840). Next is the 25·75 km (16 miles) on the former Great Northern Railway Boston–Grimsby line between Boston and Burgh-le-Marsh, Lincolnshire, opened throughout on 1 October 1848.

The former South Eastern Railway between Tonbridge and Ashford, opened throughout on 1 December 1842, is nearly straight for 38·6 km (24 miles), but has a slight deviation between Staplehurst and Headcorn.

RAILWAY CURVES

In Great Britain curves are described by their radius in chains (1 chain = 66 ft = 20·12 m). European continental railways measure the radius in metres. In the USA railway curves are described by the number of degrees in the angle subtended at the centre of a circle of equal curvature by a chord 100 ft (30·48 m) long, so that the flatter the curve, the smaller is the angle. By the sine formula it can easily be worked out that a curve of 1° has a radius of 5734 ft or 86·9 chains or 1747·8 m. The radius of a curve is calculated by dividing 1747·8 or 86·9 by the number of degrees. Thus a curve of 10° has a radius of 174·78 m or 8·69 chains, suitable only for sidings or slow traffic. The number of degrees is obtained by dividing 5734 by the radius in feet, or 86·9 by the radius in chains, or 1747·8 by the radius in metres.

The radius of a curve, in feet, is obtained by measuring the versine, or offset, of the rail from the centre of a chord, usually of either 100 ft or 1 chain, and using the formula $R = 3L^2/2V$ where L = length of chord in feet, and V is the versine in inches. In metric units the formula becomes $R = 125L^2/V$ where R = radius in metres; L = length of chord in metres; V = versine in millimetres. On single lines the versine is measured on the outer, or 'high' rail and on double lines on the outer rail of the inner track.

Super elevation, or cant, obtained by tilting the track so that the outer rail is higher than the inner, is applied on curves to move the centre of gravity of vehicles towards the inside of the curve. Its extent depends on the radius of the curve and the speed of the traffic. The maximum cant is 152 mm (6 in).

Transition curves, with gradually increasing cant and reducing radius, are needed to ease a train smoothly from a straight track into a curve and in the reverse direction out again into a straight or a reverse curve.

Check rails are fitted to the inside of lower, or inner, rails on curves of less than 200 m (10 chains) radius in Britain. These guide the flanges of the inner wheels and reduce wear on the outer rail.

GRADIENTS

Railway gradients in Britain are described as a ratio, eg 1 in 100. In North America a 'per cent' description is used for the units rise per 100 horizontal units. In some European continental countries a 'pro mille' ($^0/_{00}$) or per 1000 description is used: eg $25^0/_{00} = 2{\cdot}5$ per cent = 1 in 40.

Bury 2–2–2, built by Bury, Curtis & Kennedy, Liverpool, in 1846, for the Great Southern & Western Railway, Ireland; photographed on Cork Station on 29 May 1978 (Simon Marshall)

Cars on the 838 mm (2 ft 9 in) gauge Volk's Electric Railway at Brighton on 4 August 1976 (see p. 153) (Simon Marshall)

The Pfaffenberg–Zwenberg Bridge, Austria. The Falkenstein Bridge is just hidden behind the hill beyond (see p. 55)

Trains at the summit of the Snowdon Mountain Railway, Wales, 1064 m (3493 ft), the highest railway in Britain

The steepest railway in the world is the Swiss funicular (cable-worked) incline between Piotta and Piora (Lake Ritom) in Canton Ticino, with a gradient of 1 in 1·125 (88 per cent). It is closely approached by the Châtelard-Barberine funicular south of Martigny, Switzerland, with a gradient of 1 in 1·15 (87 per cent). Both lines were built for transport of materials for hydro-electric schemes and were later adapted for passengers.

Looking up the steepest railway in the USA from the bottom of the Royal Gorge in Colorado

The summit of the Middleton Incline on the Cromford and High Peak Railway, in July 1940. The winding engine house on the left has been restored together with the condensing beam winding engine built by the Butterley Company in 1825

The steepest railway in the USA is the 472·440 m (1550 ft) long cable-worked incline down to the famous 'hanging bridge' at the bottom of the Royal Gorge, Colorado. It has a gradient of 64·6 per cent, or 1 in 1·55. It was opened on 14 June 1931. The engineer was George F. Cole. The journey takes five minutes.

The world's steepest rack railway is the Pilatus Railway in Switzerland with a gradient of 50 per cent (1 in 2). (See 'Mountain and Rack Railways'.)

The steepest incline worked by adhesion is the 9 per cent (1 in 11) between Chedde and Servoz, on the electric Chamonix line of the South-Eastern Region of the French National Railways.

The steepest standard-gauge incline on the French National Railways is 1 in 23 (4·3 per cent) between Urdos and Les Forges on the French side of the Somport Tunnel in the Pyrenees.

The steepest adhesion-worked incline in Great Britain was the 1 in 14 (7 per cent) Hopton Incline on the Cromford & High Peak Railway in Derbyshire, opened in 1831 and closed in 1967. It was originally cable worked.

The original C. & HPR included five other cable-worked inclines with gradients ranging from 1 in 7 (14·3 per cent) to 1 in 16 (6·25 per cent), and a short one at Whaley Bridge worked by a horse gin and endless chain, which continued in use until 9 April 1952.

The steepest main-line gradient in the USA is the Saluda Hill on the Southern Railway, 54·718 km (34 miles) south of Ashville, North Carolina. The grade is 4·7 per cent (1 in 21·4).

The steepest standard-gauge incline in the USA was on the north side of the Ohio River at Madison, Indiana, on the Madison & Lafayette Railroad, opened on 1 April 1839. It was 2·146 km (7040 ft) long and rose 131·369 m (431 ft) on a gradient of about 1 in 17 (5·89 per cent).

From 1866 it formed part of the Jeffersonville, Madison & Indianapolis Railroad, whose master mechanic Reuben Wells designed a massive 0–10–0 tank engine, built in 1868, to work the incline. The engine can still be seen today, in the Children's Museum, Indianapolis.

The world's greatest 'main-line' inclines are on the 1·600 m (5 ft 3 in) gauge São Paulo Railway in Brazil. The railway has to rise about 800 m (1700 ft) from the port of Santos to São Paulo in a distance of 79 km (49 miles). The British engineer James Brunlees (1816–92) built the first line in 1851–7. It included a single-track incline 8·5 km (5·28 miles) long on a gradient of 1 in 10 (10 per cent). It was worked by a cable on the 'tail-end' principle.

In 1900 a new double-track line was opened, 11 km (6·8 miles) long worked in four inclined sections with continuous cables. The old incline remained in use for freight.

By 1958 traffic on the inclines was nearing their limit of 9 000 000 tons per annum, so in 1968 it was decided to rebuild the original incline for rack operation, electrified at 3000 V dc. The new incline was opened in 1974. It includes a concrete viaduct 260 m (853 ft) long at Grota Funda and a span of 63 m (206 ft) over the River Mogi. It is operated by rack and adhesion locomotives of 2820 kW (3800 hp) and has a capacity of 21 000 000 tons per annum at only a third of the operating cost of the cable incline. The 1900 cable inclines are being retained for emergency use.

The steepest gradient over which standard-gauge passenger trains were worked by adhesion in Great Britain was probably the Lowca Light Railway in Cumbria which was 1 in 17 (5·9 per cent) between Rose Hill and Copperas Hill. Between 2 June 1913 and 31 May 1926 passenger trains were worked over it by the Furness Railway and its successor, from 1 January 1923, the London Midland & Scottish.

The Chequerbent Incline on the Kenyon–Leigh–Bolton branch of the London & North Western Railway in Lancashire, once 1 in 30 (3·33 per cent), was so affected by mining subsidence that a short stretch became 1 in 19·5 (5 per cent). At this place one end of a coach was nearly 1 metre higher than the other end. The line was originally part of the Bolton & Leigh Railway, the first public railway in Lancashire, opened on 1 August 1928. Passenger services ran from 13 June 1831 to 3 March 1952.

On the 1·219 m (4 ft) gauge Glasgow Subway there are gradients of 1 in 18 (5·5 per cent) and 1 in 20 (5 per cent) on the sections under the Clyde.

Several railways with rope-worked inclines carried passengers at one time. The best known was the Beck Hole Incline near Goathland on the Whitby & Pickering Railway, 1 in 10 (10 per cent), which carried passengers from 1836 to 1865. A runaway disaster led to the construction of the present deviation line through Goathland. (See 'North Yorkshire Moors Railway'.)

The steepest gradient in Britain over which standard-gauge passenger trains work today is the 1 in 27 (3·7 per cent) on the Mersey Railway from the bottom of the Mersey Tunnel up to James Street Station, Liverpool. (See Merseyrail.)

From Middleton Junction to Oldham the branch of the Lancashire & Yorkshire Railway opened in 1842 rose for 1·2 km ($\frac{3}{4}$ mile) at 1 in 27. Passenger services ended in 1958 and the line was closed completely on 7 January 1963.

The Pwllyrhebog Incline on the Pwllyrhebog branch of the Taff Vale Railway in South Wales, opened in 1863, climbed at 1 in 13 for 0·8 km ($\frac{1}{2}$ mile), then at 1 in 29 and 1 in 30. Trains were assisted by a rope and winding engine. It was closed on 1 July 1951. For working the incline the locomotive superintendent Tom Hurry Riches (1846–1911) designed the 'H' Class 0–6–0 tanks of which three were built by Kitson, Leeds, in 1884. They had a dome over a firebox specially designed to avoid its becoming uncovered by water on the steep incline.

In Scotland the Causewayend Incline near Manuel, about 3·219 km (2 miles) west of Linlithgow, Stirlingshire, included 804 m ($\frac{1}{2}$ mile) at 1 in 23 (4·4 per cent). The Commonhead Incline near Airdrie, Scotland, included a short stretch of 1 in 23. Passenger trains ran until 1 May 1930 on both these lines.

On the former Brecon & Merthyr Railway in Wales, in the 11·667 km (7·25 miles) from Talybont-on-Usk to Torpantau the line climbed 281·94 m (926 ft) on gradients of 1 in 38–40 (2·7–2·5 per cent).

The Canterbury & Whitstable Railway in

One of the numerous viaducts on the Plymouth–Penzance section of the former Great Western in Cornwall. Class 52 diesel hydraulic No. 1013 *Western Ranger* seen crossing Moorswater viaduct near Liskeard in July 1976. One of the piers of Brunel's earlier timber viaduct can be seen (see p. 70)

The Seikan Tunnel, Japan, showing the construction tunnel on the left (see p. 91) (Japanese National Railways)

The oldest steamable locomotive in Britain, the 0–4–0 well tank Shannon built in 1857 for the Sandy & Potton Railway photographed at the Great Western Society's Didcot depot in August 1977 (see p. 139) (Simon Marshall)

The first British Railways Standard locomotive, No. 70000 *Britannia* near Bewdley on the Severn Valley Railway, 9 September 1978 (see p. 140) (Andrew Marshall)

Deltic diesel-electric No. 55008 on a Newcastle–London train at York, 23 August 1978 (see p. 145) (Andrew Marshall)

Kent, opened on 3 May 1830, included 543 m (594 yd) at 1 in 28 (3·5 per cent).

The self-acting inclined plane on which descending loaded wagons pull empties up was patented by Michael Menzies, a Scottish advocate, in 1750.

The principle was first used on the Schulenberg Railway in the Harz Mountains in Germany in 1724.

The first use of a steam winding engine to draw wagons up an incline was about 1805.

The world's toughest and longest gradient is on the standard-gauge Central Railway of Peru. In 172 km (107 miles) the line rises 4775 m (15 665 ft). This gives an *average* gradient of 1 in 36 (2·8 per cent), but this includes stations and reversing switches. The normal gradient is 1 in 25 (4 per cent), with long stretches of 1 in 20 (5 per cent) or steeper. The line was begun by Henry Meiggs in 1870 and completed to Oroya in 1893, and it was opened to Huancayo, 332 km (206 miles), on 8 September 1908.

On the Burma State Railways the line between Mandalay and Lashio climbs for 19·312 km (12 miles) continuously at 1 in 25 (4 per cent). This section includes the Gokteik Viaduct (see p. 65).

The steepest main line in Australia is 1 in 33 (3 per cent) up the Blue Mountains between Sydney and Lithgow, New South Wales.

The steepest adhesion-worked railway in Australia was 1 in 19 (5·3 per cent) between

The Viso zigzag at km 112 on the Peru Central Railway. The upper level can be seen in the centre of the photograph and in the top right corner

Westbound goods train at Woodford on part of the 1 in 33 climb to Katoomba between Sydney and Lithgow, New South Wales, headed by 2–8–0 'Standard goods' No. 5187 and three-cylinder 4–8–2 No. 5701, about 1950 (G C Taylor)

Campbelltown and Camden, New South Wales. It was opened as a tramway in 1879 and became a branch of the railway system in 1901. It was closed on 31 December 1962, though an enthusiasts' special was run over it the following day. Normal trains consisted of a carriage and two wagons hauled by a '20' Class 2–6–4 tank engine. On Good Fridays up to three pilgrims' specials were run, eight or nine coaches with two '20' Class engines in front and one behind.

Australia's steepest railway was a section of the 1·067 m (3 ft 6 in) gauge Emu Bay Railway in Tasmania where the line rose at 1 in 16 (6·2 per cent) between Queenstown and Strahan. An Abt rack was used. It was closed in 1963.

ZIGZAG INCLINES, OR SWITCHBACKS*

The use of zigzag or switchback locations on railways for overcoming abrupt height differences dates back to the 1840s when they were used on a coal line at Honesdale in Pennsylvania, and on the Ithaca & Oswego Railroad, New York. Their first use on a main line was on the Great Indian Penninsula Railway at Bhore Ghat on the line from Bombay to Poona, begun in January 1856 and opened on 14 May 1863. With a ruling grade of 1 in 37 (2·7 per cent), 25·5 km (15·86 miles)

*The word 'switchback' can also mean alternating up and down gradients.

long, it overcame a height difference of 558 m (1831 ft) from Karjat at the foot up to Khandala. There were 25 tunnels totalling 5·653 km (2 miles 475 yd). On the Bombay–Calcutta main line the incline up the Thull Ghat was begun in 1857 and opened on 1 January 1865. It was originally 15 km (9·326 miles) long, rising 296 m (972 ft) with a ruling gradient of 1 in 37 (2·7 per cent) and 13 tunnels totalling 2·315 km (1 mile 772 yd) and including **the highest viaduct in India**, the Ehegaon Viaduct (qv). Realignment of the Thull Incline, begun in October 1913 and brought into use in September 1918, abolished the zigzags. The line to Poona was similarly realigned, and electrified, in 1929.

While these lines were under construction the Great Western Railway of New South Wales, Australia, was being laid out over the Blue Mountains west of Sydney, by John Whitton (1819–98). At Lapstone, 64·4 km (about 40 miles) from Sydney, it climbed the mountain face by the 'Little Zig Zag', opened on 13 July 1867, and 80 km (50 miles) farther descended again by the 'Great Zig Zag' at Lithgow, opened on 18 October 1869. The Lapstone zigzag was bypassed by the Lapstone deviation in 1892 and this in turn was avoided by the Glenbrook deviation in 1913.

The Lithgow zigzag was bypassed by the deviation line opened on 16 October 1910. Both zigzags are now accessible by road and on foot, and on 30 August 1975 trains began running on a 1·067 m (3 ft 6 in) gauge railway laid on the middle section of the Lithgow zigzag by the Lithgow Switchback Railway Co-operative Society, using preserved locomotives and rolling stock. The area is now administered by the Zig Zag Trust, Lithgow.

The next use of the principle for main-line work was on the Peru Central Railway (qv), 1870–93, and on the Darjeeling Himalayan Railway, (qv), opened in July 1881. They can also be found on the 1·067 m (3 ft 6 in) gauge Guayaquil–Quito Railway in Ecuador, completed in 1908, and on the 914 mm (3 ft) gauge Cuzco–Santa Ana Railway in Peru.

Besides their use for temporary lines, such as over the Cascade Mountains during the construction of the first Cascade Tunnel in 1892–1900 (qv), other examples of zigzag locations are too numerous to list fully.

In England the most notable zigzag railways were both freight-only lines, on the North Eastern Railway: down to the Loftus iron-mine near Skinningrove, Cleveland, opened on 21 April 1865, and from Tweedmouth down to the dock, opened on 16 October 1878. The Skinningrove branch was closed on 1 May 1958 and the Tweedmouth Dock branch in 1965.

The Central Railway of Peru is not simply the world's highest railway; it is also the most wonderfully engineered. It climbs from just above sea-level at Callao to 4783 m (15 694 ft) in Galera Tunnel in a distance of 173·5 km (107·8 miles) and drops again to Oroya, 3726 m (12 224 ft), in a further 49 km (30 miles), by means of six double zigzags and one single zigzag on the main line and three double zigzags on the Morococha Branch, with 67 tunnels and 59 bridges, some of these major engineering works in themselves.

It was laid out and constructed under the direction of Henry Meiggs, but he died in 1877 when construction had reached Cacray, and further work was delayed by the Peru-Chile War in 1879. In 1893 it was completed to Oroya along the route already laid out by Meiggs. The mountain above the summit is named Mount Meiggs after the great engineer and contractor. Heights, distances and dates are shown on the adjoining map.

In April 1955 a spur was opened from the

The author (right) at the world's highest railway summit, La Cima, on the Morococha Branch of the Peru Central Railway, 4818 m or 15 806 ft. Until recently a spur branched off just beyond the right of the picture to serve a mine, reaching an altitude of 4830 m (15 848 ft), but it is now removed. This section, from Ticlio to Morococha, appeared to be out of use at the date of the photograph, 5 October 1974 (John Knowles)

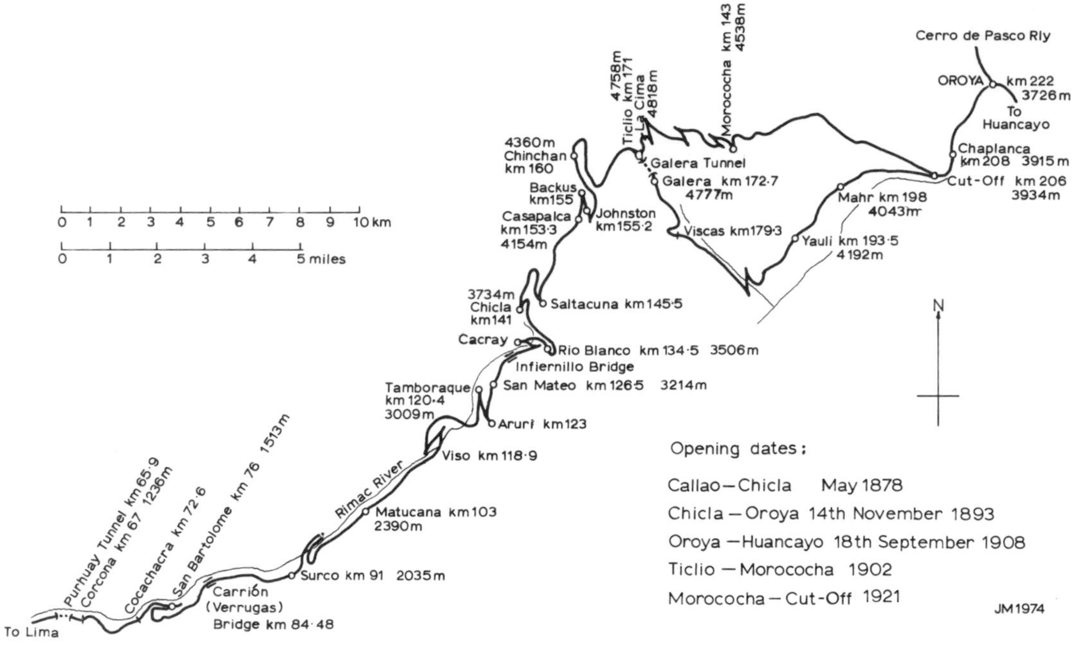

Map of the Peru Central Railway

Morococha Branch at La Cima to the Volcán Mine overlooking Ticlio, reaching a world record altitude of 4830 m (15 848 ft), but it has recently been abandoned and dismantled.

The world's highest railway junction, 4758 m (15 610 ft) at Ticlio on the Peru Central Railway, on 6 October 1974. The main line passes beneath Mount Meiggs in the background in the Galera Tunnel, the world's highest railway tunnel. The line curving round in the foreground descends to Casapalca. The Morococha Branch can be seen climbing to the left, and above it is the Volcan Mine, until recently served by a branch from La Cima which reached a record altitude of 4839 m (15 848 ft)

The world's highest railway junction is at Ticlio 4758 m (15 610 ft), on the Central Railway of Peru where the line divides, the main line passing beneath Mount Meiggs in the Galera Tunnel (qv) and the Morococha Branch climbing to the world's highest railway summit at La Cima, to rejoin the main line at Cut-Off above Oroya.

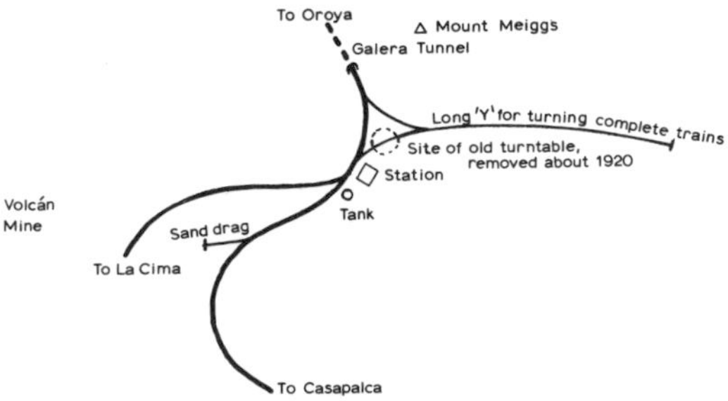

Ticlio, Peru Central Railway (not to scale), from information supplied by Brian Fawcett

The highest railway in Great Britain is the summit terminus of the 800 mm (2 ft $7\frac{1}{2}$ in) gauge Snowdon Mountain Railway, 1064 m (3493 ft). The 8 km (5 mile) Abt system rack railway was opened on 19 April 1897 and still uses Swiss-built steam locomotives.

PRINCIPAL RAILWAY SUMMITS OVER 1000 M (3250 FT) ABOVE SEA-LEVEL**

Summit	Railway	Gauge	Altitude m	ft
La Cima	Peru Central, Morococha Branch†	standard	4818	15806
Condor	Bolivian National (former Antofagasta & Bolivia), Potosi Branch‡	metre	4787	15705
Galera Tunnel	Peru Central†	standard	4781	15688
Caja Real	Yauricocha, Peru†	standard	4602	15100
Chaucha	Yauricocha, Peru†	standard	4564	14974
Km 41	Yauricocha, Peru†	standard	4538	14888
Chorrillos	Argentine Railways (North Transandine)	metre	4475	14682
Crucero Alto	Southern of Peru†	standard	4470	14666
Yuma	Bolivian National (former Antofagasta & Bolivia)‡	metre	4401	14440
Alcacocha	Cerro de Pasco, Peru	standard	4385	14385
La Raya	Southern of Peru	standard	4314	14153
Pike's Peak	Manitou & Pike's Peak, Colorado, USA	standard*	4302	14109
Jeneral Lagos	Bolivian National (former Arica–La Paz)	metre	4257	13963
La Cima	Cerro de Pasco, Peru	standard	4214	13822
Cuesta Colorado	Bolivian National	metre	4137	13573
El Alto	Guaqui–La Paz	metre	4106	13471
Escoriani	Bolivian National	metre	4057	13310
Between Potosí and Sucre	Bolivian National	metre	4033	13231
Comanche	Bolivian National (former Arica–La Paz)	metre	4031	13225
Kenko	Bolivian National (former Antofagasta & Bolivia)	metre	4004	13134
Muñano	Argentine Railways (North Transandine)	metre	4000	13120
Ascotan	Bolivian National (former Antofagasta & Bolivia)	metre	3959	12982
Socompa	Antofagasta–Salta (Argentina)§	metre	3908	12822
Tres Cruces	Argentine Railways	metre	3693	12116
Urbina	Guyaquil–Quito (Ecuador)	1·067 m (3 ft 6 in)	3609	11841
Pumahuasi	Argentine Railways	metre	3559	11674
Climax spur	Burlington Northern (former Colorado & Southern), USA	standard	3472	11390
Jungfraujoch	Jungfrau, Switzerland	metre	3454	11332
Fremont Pass	Burlington Northern (former Colorado & Southern), USA	standard	3450	11318
Villazon	Villazon–Atocha (Bolivian National)	metre	3447	11308
Iturbe	Argentine Railways	metre	3343	10965
La Cumbre	Chilean Transandine	metre*	3191	10466
Tennessee Pass Tunnel	Denver & Rio Grande Western, Colorado, USA	standard	3116	10239
Monarch	Denver & Rio Grande Western, Colorado, USA	standard	3093	10148
Gornergrat	Gornergrat, Switzerland	metre*	3088	10134
La Cima	National Railways of Mexico	standard	3054	10020
Cumbres Pass	Cumbres & Toltec Scenic Railroad (former Denver & Rio Grande Western), Colorado, USA	914 mm (3 ft)	3053	10015
El Oro	National Railways of Mexico	standard	3041	9977
Silverton	Denver & Rio Grande Western, Colorado, USA	914 mm (3 ft)	2831	9288
Veta Pass	Denver & Rio Grande Western, Colorado, USA	standard	2817	9242

PRINCIPAL RAILWAY SUMMITS OVER 1000 M (3250 FT) ABOVE SEA-LEVEL**

Summit	Railway	Gauge	Altitude m	Altitude ft
Moffat Tunnel	Denver & Rio Grande Western, Colorado, USA	standard	2817	9239
Timboroa	East African	metre	2783	9131
Schneefernerhaus	Bavarian Zugspitz, Germany	metre*	2650	8692
Nanacamilpa	National Railways of Mexico	standard	2561	8400
Acocotla	National Railways of Mexico	standard	2542	8337
Near Addis Ababa	Franco Ethiopian	metre	2470	8104
Sherman	Union Pacific, Wyoming, USA	standard	2443	8013
Cerro Summit	Denver & Rio Grande Western, Colorado, USA	standard	2429	7968
Las Vigas	National Railways of Mexico	standard	2415	7923
Near Asmara	Northern Ethiopian	950 mm (3 ft 1½ in)	2412	7911
Kikuyu	East African	metre	2395	7857
Asmara	Eritrean	metre	2394	7854
Rothornkulm	Brienzer Rothorn, Switzerland	800 mm (2 ft 7¼ in)*	2349	7707
Quezaltenango	Guatemalan State	standard	2332	7650
Raton Pass	Santa Fé, USA, Colorado/New Mexico	standard	2312	7586
Soldier Summit	Denver & Rio Grande Western, Utah	standard	2268	7440
Ghoom	North Eastern, India (former Darjeeling Himalayan)	610 mm (2 ft)	2258	7407
Bernina Hospice	Rhaetian, Switzerland	metre	2257	7403
Asit	Turkish State	standard	2256	7402
Kan Mehtarzai	Pakistan	762 mm (2 ft 6 in)	2222	7291
Nilgiri Hills	Nilgiri, India	metre*	2217	7275
Nurabad	Iran State (Trans Iranian, southern section)	standard	2217	7274
Furka Tunnel	Furka Oberalp, Switzerland	metre	2163	7098
Sierra Nevada	Southern Pacific, USA	standard	2147	7043
Gaduk	Iran State (Trans Iranian, northern section)	standard	2112	6929
Tip Top, near Colorado Springs	Chicago, Rock Island & Pacific, USA	standard	2097	6880
Nederhorst	South African	1·065 m (3 ft 6 in)	2095	6871
Pilatus	Pilatus, Switzerland	800 mm (2 ft 7½ in)*	2070	6791
Kleine Scheidegg	Wengernalp, Switzerland	800 mm (2 ft 7½ in)*	2061	6762
Oberalp Pass	Furka–Oberalp, Switzerland	metre	2045	6711
Rochers de Naye	Glion–Rochers de Naye, Switzerland	800 mm (2 ft 7½ in)*	1973	6473
Belfast	South African	1·065 m (3 ft 6 in)	1970	6463
Schynige Platte	Schynige Platte, Switzerland	800 mm (2 ft 7½ in)*	1967	6453
Nuria	Mountain Railways Co, Spain (Ribas–Caralps–Nuria)	metre*	1964	6443
Shelabagh	Pakistan	1·676 m (5 ft 6 in)	1950	6398
Near Butte, Montana	Burlington Northern (former Northern Pacific), USA	standard	1929	6329
Near Butte, Montana	Chicago, Milwaukee & Pacific, USA	standard	1925	6317
Mount Washington	Mount Washington, New Hampshire, USA	standard*	1918	6293

PRINCIPAL RAILWAY SUMMITS OVER 1000 M (3250 FT) ABOVE SEA-LEVEL**

Summit	Railway	Gauge	Altitude m	ft
Montenvers	Chamonix–Montenvers, France	metre*	1913	6276
Pattipola	Sri Lanka Government	1·676 m (5 ft 6 in)	1898	6226
Albula Tunnel	Rhaetian, Switzerland	metre	1823	5981
Shafter	Western Pacific, USA	standard	1799	5903
Hoch Schneeberg	Austrian Federal	metre*	1798	5898
Near Zebdāni	Syria	1·050 m (3 ft 5½ in)	1794	5885
Kolpore	Pakistan	1·676 m (5 ft 6 in)	1791	5874
Puerto de Navacerrada	Spanish National	1·676 m (5 ft 6 in)	1761	5777
Rigi–Kulm	Arth-Goldau–Rigi; and Rigi, Switzerland	standard*	1750	5741
Johannesburg	South African	1·065 m (3 ft 6 in)	1748	5735
Arosa	Rhaetian, Switzerland	metre	1742	5715
Wendelstein	Wendelsteinbahn, Austria	metre*	1723	5653
Near Marandellas	Rhodesia Railways	1·067 m (3 ft 6 in)	1688	5538
Between Tananarive and Antsirabe	Madagascar Railways	metre	1687	5534
Zermatt	Brig–Visp–Zermatt, Switzerland	metre*	1650	5415
Wolfgang	Rhaetian, Switzerland	metre	1633	5358
Great Divide	Canadian Pacific	standard	1625	5332
Monte Generoso	Monte Generoso, Lugano, Switzerland	800 mm (2 ft 7½ in)*	1620	5315
Between Peking and Suiyuan	Peking–Suiyuan, China	standard	1585	5200
Near El Alto	Costa Rica Northern	1·067 m (3 ft 6 in)	1547	5075
Paisano, Texas	Southern Pacific, USA	standard	1547	5074
Taurus	Turkish State	standard	1494	4900
Between Beirut and Zahle	Lebanon State	1·050 m (3 ft 5½ in)	1487	4879
Leysin	Aigle–Leysin, Switzerland	metre*	1453	4767
La Molina	Spanish National	1·676 m (5 ft 6 in)	1420	4659
Kalaw	Union of Burma Railways	metre	1405	4610
La Cañada	Spanish National	1·676 m (5 ft 6 in)	1380	4526
Near Ben Lomond	Public Transport Commission of New South Wales, Australia	standard	1377	4517
Brenner Pass	Austrian Federal	standard	1370	4496
Mekiri	Nigerian	1·067 m (3 ft 6 in)	1370	4494
Crow Nest Pass	Canadian Pacific	standard	1359	4459
Near Batna	Algerian National	standard	1313	4308
Arlberg Tunnel	Austrian Federal	standard	1311	4308
Mont Cenis Tunnel	Italian State	standard	1306	4284
Taugevatn, near Finse	Norwegian State (Bergen–Oslo line)	standard	1301	4265
Saanenmöser	Montreux–Bernese Oberland, Switzerland	metre	1275	4183
Rivisondoli	Italian State	standard	1267	4156
Lötschberg Tunnel	Bern–Lötschberg–Simplon	standard	1240	4068
Near Horse Lake	British Columbia Railway, Canada	standard	1208	3963
Tauern Tunnel	Austrian Federal	standard	1183	3381

PRINCIPAL RAILWAY SUMMITS OVER 1000 M (3250 FT) ABOVE SEA-LEVEL**

Summit	Railway	Gauge	Altitude m	Altitude ft
Connaught Tunnel	Canadian Pacific	standard	1154	3787
St Gotthard Tunnel	Swiss Federal	standard	1151	3780
Yellowhead Pass	Canadian National	standard	1133	3717
Maan	Hedjaz	1·101 m (3 ft 5¼ in)	1128	3700
Snowdon	Snowdon Mountain, Wales	800 mm (2 ft 7½ in)*	1064	3493
Kolasin	Jugoslav State	standard	1032	3385

*Whole or part rack.
**Abandoned railway summits in Colorado, USA, over 3050 m (10 000 ft) are listed under 'Some USA Facts and Feats', p. 96.
†The Central and Southern Railways of Peru and the Yauricocha Railway became part of the Peruvian National Railways on 1 December 1972.
‡In 1907 the Antofagasta & Bolivia Railway built a branch from Ollogue in Chile, close to the Bolivian border, to copper-mines at Collahuasi, reaching a height of 4826 m (15 835 ft) at Punto Alto. It is now disused beyond Yuma, 4401 m (14 440 ft). The Condor summit on the Potosí Branch is now **the highest over which passenger trains are worked**. The Bolivian lines of the A. & B. were nationalised on 1 November 1964.
§The Antofagasta–Salta Railway is divided between the Chilean National Railways and the Argentine Railways North Western Region.

The second highest is the summit of the 1·067 m (3 ft 6 in) gauge Snaefell Railway in the Isle of Man, at a height of 620 m (2034 ft). The Fell centre rail (see 'Mountain Railways') is used only for braking. The railway was opened on 21 August 1895. Electric traction is used; the cars have overhead bow-type collectors. On 1 June 1957 the undertaking was transferred to the Manx Government.

The highest summit on British Rail is at Druimuachdar, 452 m (1484 ft), between Dalnaspidal and Dalwhinnie on the former Highland Railway main line from Perth to Inverness, Scotland, opened in 1863.

In 1902 a 12·472 km (7¾ mile) branch was opened from the Caledonian Railway Glasgow–Carlisle main line, at Elvanfoot, to Wanlockhead, the highest village in Scotland. The station was at a height of 431 m (1413 ft), but the line climbed to 456 m (1498 ft). It closed on 2 January 1939.

At Waenavon in South Wales the London & North Western Railway reached a height of 427 m (1400 ft). It was closed to passengers on 5 May 1941 and closed entirely on 23 June 1954.

On the Great Western Railway, England, the terminus of the branch to Princetown on Dartmoor was at a height of 418 m (1373 ft). It was closed on 5 March 1956.

Stainmore Summit on the former Stockton & Darlington–Kirkby Stephen line was 417 m (1370 ft) above sea-level. It was opened in 1861 and closed on 22 January 1962.

At Weatherhill, County Durham, on the former Stanhope & Tyne Railway, later the North Eastern Railway, the rails stood at 420 m (1378 ft). From here a private mineral branch, opened in 1846, ascended to about 509 m (1670 ft) at the top of the incline down to Rookhope. **This was the highest point reached by standard-gauge rails in Britain.** A private passenger service operated over it until about 1921. It is now abandoned, but makes an interesting walk.

The lowest point on British Rail is the bottom of the Severn Tunnel, 43·889 m (144 ft) below Ordnance Datum.

The lowest point reached by any surface railway in the world was Jisr el Majame near Samakh (Zemach), 213·36 m (700 ft) below sea-level, where the 1·042 m (3 ft 5¼ in) gauge line from Haifa in Israel to Derraa crossed the River Jordan just south of the Sea of Galilee. At Derraa it joined the Hedjaz Railway from Damascus to Medina. It was begun in 1901 and opened through to Medina, on 31 August 1908. The Haifa–Derraa section is at present out of use for political reasons.

(See also 'Southern Pacific'.)

Mine railways are found at far greater depths.

TRANSCONTINENTAL RAILWAYS

The longest railway in the world is the Trans-Siberian, from Moscow to Vladivostok—9336 km (5801 miles). It was opened in sections. By ferry across Lake Baikal and via the Chinese Eastern Railway through Manchuria, through communication was established on 3 November 1901. In 1904, while Lake Baikal was frozen over, rails were laid across the ice, but the first locomotive plunged through a gap and was lost.

The Circum–Baikal line, round the south of the lake, was opened on 25 September 1904. The 1931 km (1200 mile) Amur line, opening up through travel entirely on Russian soil, was begun in 1908 and completed in 1916.

The Baikal–Amur Magistral northern line, begun with forced labour in 1938, is expected to be open in 1982, reducing the distance by about 500 km (310 miles). It involves moving 283 000 000 m^3 (10 000 million ft^3) of earth, and includes a tunnel 15 km (9·3 miles) long.

According to the Thomas Cooke International Timetable the Trans-Siberian Express covers the journey in 7 days 2 hours.

The first railway from the Atlantic to the Pacific was the 1·524 m (5 ft) gauge Panama Railroad, 77 km (48 miles) long, across the Isthmus of Panama, between Aspinwall and Panama. It was opened on 28 January 1855. Surveys were made as early as 1828.

The first big step towards an American transcontinental railroad was taken on 21 April 1856 when trains first crossed the Mississippi between Rock Island, Illinois, and Davenport, Iowa.

The first American transcontinental railroad was completed on 10 May 1869 when the last spike was driven at Promontory, north of the Great Salt Lake, Utah, uniting the Central Pacific and Union Pacific railroads. Because the point of joining had not been previously established, and because the companies were receiving up to $48 000 a mile in Federal loans for track-laying, rival grading gangs passed one another and the UP gangs went on constructing 362 km (225 miles) of parallel grading until they were officially stopped. The section from Promontory to Ogden was taken over by the Central Pacific.

The railway ran from Omaha, Nebraska, to Sacramento, California, 2776 km (1725 miles). The old Western Pacific Railroad (no relation to the present Western Pacific) was opened from Sacramento to Oakland opposite San Francisco, a further 148 km (92 miles), on 8 November 1869. It was consolidated with the Central Pacific on 23 June 1870. Passengers crossed by ferry to San Francisco.

Through communication between the Atlantic and Pacific coasts was finally established in 1877 when the first bridge was opened across the Missouri near Omaha. The present bridge, 533·44 m (1750 ft) long, was built in 1886.

The Central Pacific became a part of the Southern Pacific Railroad when that company was formed in 1884. It was fully absorbed in 1958.

The Lucin Cut-off across the Great Salt Lake, totalling 166 km (103 miles), was opened on 8 March 1904 and shortened the journey between Ogden and Lucin by 67·6 km (42 miles), making the original Promontory route redundant. (See 'The world's longest railway water crossing', p. 85.) The old line, however, with its curves equivalent to 11 complete circles, was not abandoned until 1942.

A short section at Promontory was relaid in 1969 for the enactment of the Centenary celebrations. For the benefit of crowds of visitors the 'last spike' suffered numerous drivings and extractions.

The first railway across Canada, the Canadian Pacific, was completed at a place named Craigellachie in Eagle Pass, British Columbia, when the Eastern and Western sections were joined on 7 November 1885. Its completion within ten years was a condition of British Columbia entering the Confederation, on 20 July 1871. The first sod was cut on 1 June 1875 at Fort William, on the left bank of the Kaministiquia River. The main contract was signed on 21 October 1880 by which year 1126 km (700 miles) were under construction. The Canadian Pacific Railway Company was incorporated on 15 February 1881; construction began on 2 May 1881, and throughout 1882 4 km (2·5 miles) of track were laid every day. The Prairie Section was finished as far as Calgary on 18 August 1883 and the Great Lakes Section on 16 May 1885, thanks to the devotion and energy of William Cornelius Van Horne. The section through the rock and muskeg north of Lake Superior

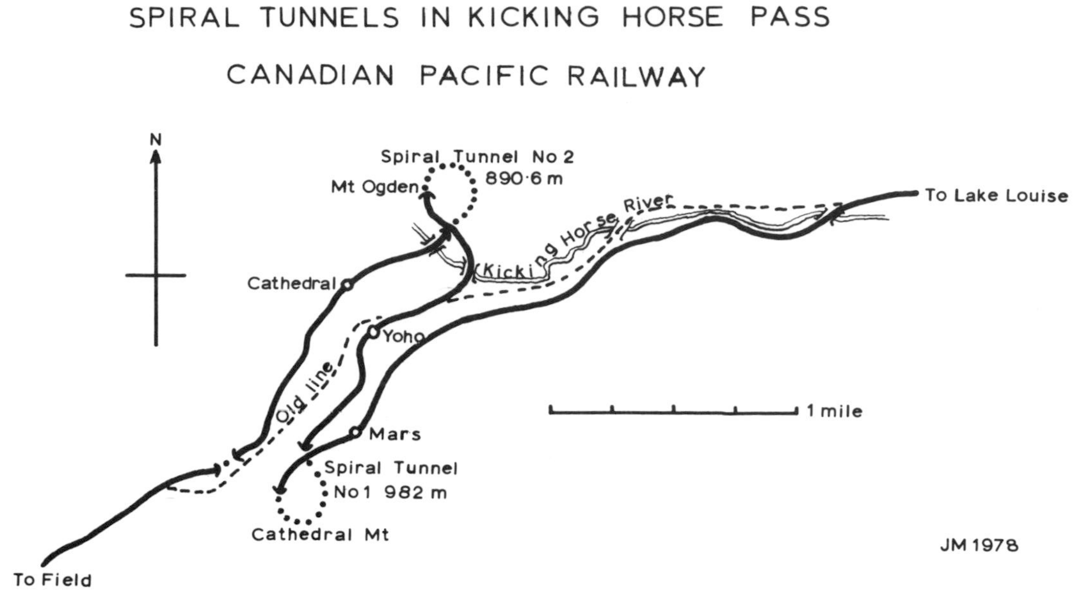

Map of the spiral tunnels in Kicking Horse Pass

was almost as difficult as the construction through the British Columbia mountains.

Transcontinental services began with the departure of the first train from Montreal on 28 June 1886. It arrived at Port Moody on 4 July. The 19·3 km (12 mile) extension to Vancouver was opened on 23 May 1887.

From Montreal to Vancouver, 4633 km (2879 miles) the journey takes three days on 'The Canadian' transcontinental train.

An alternative route through the Rockies at Crow's Nest Pass, through a rich coal region close to the USA border, was begun in 1897 and completed in 1930. It crosses the great Lethbridge Viaduct over the Oldman (formerly Belly) River (see p. 77), and another 45·8 m (147 ft) high over the same river at Fort Macleod.

Canada's second transcontinental railway began in eastern Canada as the Grand Trunk Railway which, by 1900, owned and operated a network of lines covering Ontario and Quebec, including the former Great Western Railway with which it amalgamated in 1882, and also the Grand Trunk Western to Chicago, and a line from Montreal to the Atlantic at Portland, Maine. After unsuccessful proposals to extend westwards through the USA, the GTR finally agreed that the Government should build the Eastern Division of the National Transcontinental Railway between Moncton and Winnipeg, and for the newly created Grand Trunk Pacific Railway, as a subsidiary of the GTR to build from there to the Pacific Coast at Prince Rupert, 885 km (550 miles) north of Vancouver. With Government aid the GTP was built to the same high standards as the Grand Trunk had been.

Both the National Transcontinental Eastern Division and the Grand Trunk Pacific were begun in 1905. The National Transcontinental was opened in stages from June to November 1915. It included the great Quebec Bridge (qv) over the St Lawrence, not opened until 1917. The GTP was completed at a point 671 km (417 miles) east of Prince Rupert on 7 April 1914 and complete services began in September.

From Winnipeg the GTP passed through Edmonton and through the Yellowhead Pass by which it made the lowest crossing of the Rockies, with the easiest grades, of any North American transcontinental railway.

The Canadian Northern Railway, Canada's third transcontinental line, was inspired by two men, William Mackenzie (1849–1923) and Donald Mann (1853–1934). It was made up of a number of separately incorporated railways and by 1903 had grown to 554 km

(344 miles) in the east, and to 2192 km (1362 miles) in the west. By 1905 the western lines had reached Edmonton and Prince Albert, and in the east Hawkesbury was linked to Ottawa. Surveys through the Yellowhead Pass began in 1908 and on 4 October 1915 the Canadian Northern was opened to Vancouver, through the Fraser River Canyon which it shared with the Canadian Pacific. The Canadian Northern had now grown to 15 067 km (9362 miles) and extended from Quebec to Vancouver, with additional lines in Nova Scotia and in the USA (the Duluth, Winnipeg & Pacific).

In 1917, to aid the war effort, over 161 km (100 miles) each of the Grand Trunk Pacific and Canadian Northern tracks were removed between Lobstick Junction, Alberta, through the Yellowhead Pass, to Red Pass Junction where the Prince Rupert and Vancouver lines diverged, to make a joint line of the two competing sections.

Soon after opening the transcontinental line the Canadian Northern was in financial difficulties and, following careful consideration by the Government, *Canadian National Railways* was formed to acquire the Canadian Northern Railway. In 1919 the Grand Trunk Pacific was allowed to go into receivership. On 21 May 1920 the Government took formal possession of the Grand Trunk Railway and in September 1920 met the debenture obligations as *de facto* proprietor of the Grand Trunk Pacific. The Grand Trunk Acquisition Act was passed on 5 November 1920. In 1923, under an Order in Council, the control of all Government railways including the Grand Trunk and the Intercolonial Railways passed to the Canadian National Railways under a president and board of directors appointed by the Government. In 1949 the Newfoundland Railway was absorbed.

In 1923 the Canadian National Railways had 33 109 km (20 573 miles) of route, and the

Eastbound 'Super Continental', the transcontinental train of the Canadian National Railways, crossing the Yellowhead Pass at the summit of the railway, at 1133 m (3717 ft) the lowest crossing of the Canadian Rockies (Canadian National)

Canadian Pacific Railway 21 828 km (13 563 miles), making them among the world's largest railway systems.

In the USA no single railroad company operates from the Atlantic to the Pacific, with the possible exception of the Southern Pacific (see below). Following the Union Pacific–Central Pacific, the other major transcontinental routes were completed as follows:

- **The Atchison, Topeka & Santa Fe** from Kansas City joined the Southern Pacific from California at Deming, New Mexico, on 8 March 1881. The Santa Fe completed its own through route from Chicago to California on 1 May 1888.
- **The Southern Pacific** from California to New Orleans on the Gulf of Mexico was formally opened on 12 January 1883. (See 'Pecos Bridge' and 'Southern Pacific'.)
- **The Northern Pacific, the first to the Pacific North-west**, was completed at Gold Creek, Montana, on 8 September 1883.
- **The Oregon Short Line and the Oregon Railway & Navigation Company**, forming the Union Pacific route to the Pacific North-west, were connected at Huntingdon, Oregon, on 25 November 1884.
- **The Great Northern Railway** between the Great Lakes and Puget Sound at Everett, Washington, was completed on 6 January 1893.

On the Pacific Coast Extension of the **Chicago, Milwaukee & St Paul** (now the Chicago, Milwaukee, St Paul & Pacific, or The Milwaukee Road) the last spike was driven at Garrison, Montana, on 19 May 1909.

- **The Western Pacific**, the western extension of the Denver & Rio Grande main line from Denver to Salt Lake City, was opened throughout to San Francisco on 22 August 1910, making its famous passage through the Feather River Canyon and forming, with the D & RGW, one of the finest scenic routes through the mountains.

The first train from the Atlantic to the Pacific was the 'Transcontinental Excursion' consisting of Pullman 'Hotel Cars', sponsored by the Boston Board of Trade in May 1870. It took eight days from Boston to San Francisco.

The Chile end of the summit tunnel at La Cumbre on the Transandine Railway

A daily newspaper was published on the journey.

The first regular through sleeping-car service between the Atlantic and Pacific coasts of the USA did not begin until as late as 31 March 1946. Before that a change had to be made at Chicago or St Louis.

The first South African transcontinental railway linked Cape Town and Durban at Heidelberg in the Transvaal on 10 October 1895.

Another African transcontinental route was completed in 1928. It runs from Benguela, Angola, via the Congo and Rhodesia to Beira in Portuguese East Africa.

The first Trans-Australian Railway from Port Augusta to Kalgoorlie, 1693 km (1052 miles) standard gauge, was opened on 22 October 1917. Across the Nullarbor Plain it traverses the world's longest straight stretch, 478 km (297 miles) long. At Kalgoorlie it connected with the Western Australian 1·067 m (3 ft 6 in) gauge line from Perth. With the conversion of the Kalgoorlie–Perth section and of the section from Port Pirie to Broken Hill from 1·067 m to standard gauge, completed on 29 November 1969, a through route entirely on standard gauge was opened up from Perth to Sydney, 3960 km (2461 miles). The section from Perth to Northern is dual-gauged. The 'Indian Pacific Express' was inaugurated on 1 March 1970 by the opening of the new standard-gauge line between Sydney, New South Wales, and Perth, Western Australia.

The Transandine Railway between Los Andes, Chile, and Mendoza, Argentina, was opened on 5 April 1910. It is metre gauge with Abt triple-rack sections, and climbs to an altitude of 3191 m (10 466 ft) at the 3·167 km (3463 yd) long La Cumbre Tunnel.

At Mendoza it connects with the 1·676 m (5 ft 6 in) gauge line from Buenos Aires. The total distance is 1448 km (900 miles).

The Northern Transandine Railway from Antofagasta, Chile, to Salta, a distance of 904 km (562 miles) is metre gauge and was completed in 1948. It reaches a height of 4475 m (14 682 ft) at Chorrillos; 4000 m (13 120 ft) at Muñano and over 3050 m (10 000 ft) at four other summits. At Salta it connects with the metre-gauge main line from Buenos Aires.

TRANSALPINE RAILWAYS

The first transalpine railways were those over the Semmering, opened on 15 May 1854, and the Brenner Pass, opened on 24 August 1867. This is the only main line which crosses the Alps without a major tunnel, and its altitude of 1370 m (4496 ft) makes it one of the highest main lines in Europe.

The only metre-gauge transalpine route was opened on 1 July 1903 and forms part of the Rhaetian Railway in Switzerland. Between Chur and St Moritz the railway passes through the Albula Tunnel, 5·865 km (3 miles 134 yd) long, at an altitude of 1823 m (5981 ft). It is the highest of the principal Alpine tunnels.

From St Moritz to Tirano in Italy the Bernina Railway, opened throughout on 5 July 1910, crosses the Alps in the open at an altitude of 2257 m (7403 ft). **It is the highest through railway in Europe.**

The first railway across the main range of the Alps was opened over the Mont Cenis Pass on 15 June 1868. It operated with the centre-rail friction-drive system invented in 1863–9 by John Barraclough Fell (1815–1902). It worked until 18 September 1871 when the Fréjus or Mount Cenis Tunnel was opened. This, **the first of the major Alpine tunnels**, was begun on 31 August 1857 and took 14 years to complete. It is 13·657 km (8 miles 555 yd) long and links the Italian and French railway systems, but is operated by the Italian State Railways.

The St Gotthard Railway and Tunnel were opened to goods traffic on 1 January 1882 and to passenger trains on 1 June 1882. The tunnel, 14·998 km (9 miles 662 yd), with double track, was begun on 13 September 1872. The engineer Louis Favre died of a heart

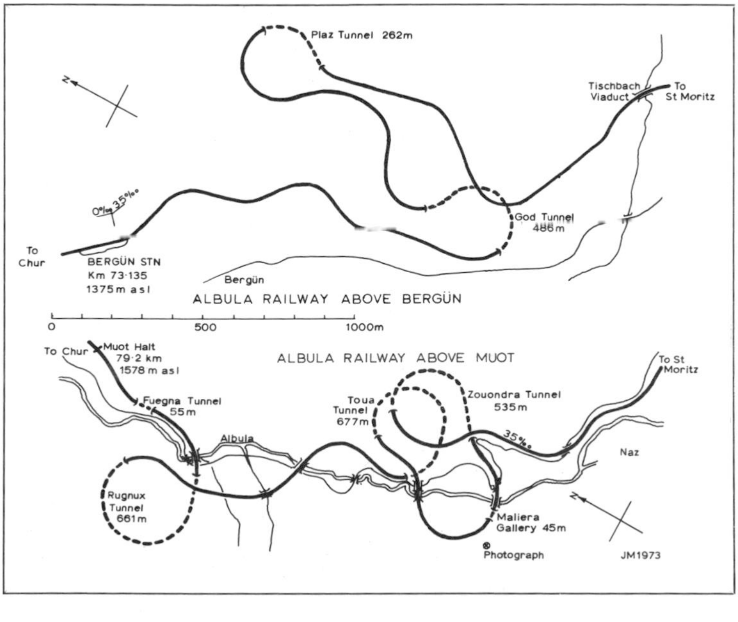

Map of Rhaetian Railway Spirals

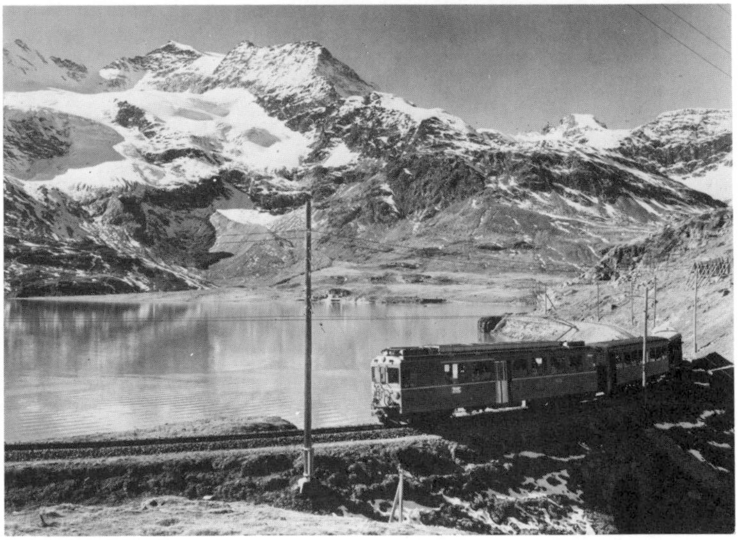

Train from St Moritz to Alp Grüm passing Lago Bianco at the summit of the Bernina Railway, the highest through railway in Europe (Swiss National Tourist Office)

attack inside the tunnel on 18 July 1879. The two bores met on 28 February 1880.

In this tunnel, in 1879, diamonds were successfully used for the first time in rock drills.

The principal railway through the Alps from east to west is the Arlberg Railway in Austria. It was completed with the opening of the Arlberg Tunnel for double track, 10·250 km (6 miles 650 yd) long, on 20 September 1884. It traverses a greater distance through magnificent mountain scenery than any other railway in Europe.

The Simplon Railway between Switzerland and Italy was completed with the opening of the first single-line Simplon Tunnel 19·803 km (12 miles 537 yd) long, on 1 June 1906. The second tunnel was opened on 16 October 1922 and is 19·823 km (12 miles 559 yd) long

The second railway between Austria and Italy was opened by the Austrian Federal Railways on 7 July 1909 after the completion of the Tauern Tunnel, 8·551 km (5 miles 551 yd) long, near Bad Gastein. (See also 'Railway Bridges', p. 55.)

The value of the Simplon route was greatly increased by the opening of the single-track Berne–Lötschberg–Simplon Railway on 15 July 1913. It included the double-track Lötschberg Tunnel under the Bernese Oberland Mountains, 14·612 km (9 miles 140 yd) long. The tunnel deviates from a straight line

Austrian Federal Railways train entering the western end of the Arlberg Tunnel, behind Co–Co electric locomotive No. 1110–12, on 11 August 1975

The Swiss end of the Simplon Tunnel in July 1966 as a two-car Trans Europe Express enters on the left and a train emerges on the right behind Bo–Bo locomotive No. 11473

to avoid a section where, on 24 July 1908, an inrush of water and rock caused the loss of 25 lives.

THE LIMITS

The most northerly railway in the world was a 2·414 km (1½ miles) long 889 mm (2 ft 11 in) gauge line at King's Bay, Spitsbergen, on latitude 79°N only 1207 km (750 miles) from the North Pole. It connected coal-mines with the harbour, and was used in summer only. It was built in 1917 and had five German 0–4–0 tank engines. The line was closed in 1929 but was reopened from 1945 to 1949.

The most northerly 'main-line' railway in the world is at Pechenga in Murmansk Oblast, north-west Russia, 330 km (205 miles) north of the Arctic Circle, latitude 69°33′N. The most northerly point reached is by an extension of 32 km (20 miles) to a wharf at Litsnayamari, but this carries no passenger service.

At Narvik in Norway the Lapland iron-ore railway, opened in July 1903, is about 209 km (130 miles) north of the Arctic Circle.

In Russia work is now in progress on a 400 km (250 mile) railway to the tip of the Yamal Peninsula, from Vorkuta to Kharasavei, 73°N, on the coast of the Karu Sea which will make it **the world's most northerly railway**. It will serve towns and settlements in the Yamal Peninsula. Gas from rich deposits in the area will be piped parallel to the railway. The route will involve a ferry across the Baydaratskaya Gulf, 60 km (37 miles) wide for which special ice-breaking train ferries will be used. The main problem is permafrost, but Soviet Railways now have considerable experience with this. Heavy bridging and tunnelling will be required through the Urals. Regular traffic is expected to begin in 1980.

The most northerly railroad in North America is at Fairbanks, Alaska, northern terminus of the standard-gauge Alaska Railroad, 756 km (470 miles) long from Seward, opened in June 1923. Fairbanks is just south of latitude 65°N, about 209 km (130 miles) south of the Arctic Circle. **The Alaska Railroad is also the most westerly line in North America**, at Anchorage, on longitude 150°W. It is also the only State-owned railway in the USA.

Farthest north and west was reached about 1910 by the now-closed Seward Peninsula Railroad at Nome, 165°24′W. Its northern end was at Lane's Landing, north of 65°N.

The farthest west reached by rail in Europe is now at Tralee in County Kerry, Ireland, 9°42′W, to which the 1·600 m (5 ft 3 in) gauge Great Southern & Western Railway was opened in 1859. In 1887 a branch was opened from Tralee to Fenit, 9°51′W, but this became disused about 1972.

Previously the honour was shared by Valentia Harbour, Ireland, 10°15′W, terminus of the 1·600 m (5 ft 3 in) gauge branch of the Great Southern & Western Railway from Killorglin opened on 12 September 1893, and by Dingle, terminus of the 914 mm (3 ft) gauge Tralee & Dingle Railway, opened on 31 March 1891, both in County Kerry. These are now abandoned.

The farthest west on the European mainland is at Cascais, 9°25′W, terminus of a 1·665 m (5 ft 6 in) gauge branch about 29 km (18 miles) west of Lisbon in Portugal.

The most westerly railway in Africa is at Dakar, on the metre-gauge Senegal Railways, latitude 17°24′W. The line from Dakar via Thiés to Saint-Louis was opened in 1885. The extension from Thiés to Kayes (Mali) was begun in 1907 but not completed until 1924.

The most southerly railway in the world is the Ramal Ferro Industrias Rio Turbio, an isolated 750 mm (2 ft 5½ in) gauge Argentine Coal Board line from Puerto Gallegos, about latitude 51°5′S, to the Rio Turbio coal-mines at the southern foot of the Andes in Argentina, close to the frontier with Chile. It runs due west from the South Atlantic coast for about 261 km (162 miles) and is used mainly to transport coal for shipment by sea from Puerto Gallegos. It was opened in 1958. The coal is carried in block trains of up to 1700 tons hauled by Japanese-built 2–10–2 tender engines, the largest and most powerful locomotives ever built for this gauge. Winds in this region frequently reach 100 mph (161 km/h).

At the Atlantic port of Deseado in Argentina, latitude 47°45′S, is the terminus of the 1·676 m (5 ft 6 in) gauge railway from Colonia Las Heras.

From 1910 to 1948 a 610 mm (2 ft) gauge

Preserved locomotive and coach at Ushuaia, Argentina, from the 610 mm (2 ft) gauge railway which operated from 1910 to 1948 to timber works and which employed convicts. The locomotive is a 0–6–0 well tank built by Orenstein & Koppel, Berlin. Photographed on 20 March 1974 (A. Eaton)

railway operated at Ushuaia in southern Argentina at 54°40′S, 68°05′W. One of the locomotives has been preserved (see photograph).

Farthest south by rail in Europe is Algeciras near Gibraltar, Spain, southern terminus of the 1·676 m (5 ft 6 in) gauge branch from Bobadilla.

The most southerly point reached by rail in Asia is Bentjulak on the island of Java on the 1·067 m (3 ft 6 in) gauge Indonesian State Railways, at latitude 8°0′S.

The farthest east in North America is operated by the Canadian National Railways. The 1·067 m (3 ft 6 in) gauge railway to St John's, Newfoundland, longitude 52°54′W, was opened in stages from 1884 until 1897 when trains began running through to Port-aux-Basques, 880 km (547 miles). The formal opening was on 29 June 1898.

The farthest east by rail in Asia is the 1·067 m (3 ft 6 in) gauge line at Nemuro on the island of Hokkaido, Japan, longitude 145°34′E.

The farthest west in Asia is in western Anatolia, Turkey, just north of Izmir on the line to Manisa, 27°E, completed 1866.

The limits of British Rail are:

North, at Thurso on the former Highland Railway, opened on 28 July 1874.
South, at Penzance, Great Western (West Cornwall) Railway, opened on 11 March 1852. Until 1964 it was at Helston on the GWR, opened on 9 May 1887.
East, at Lowestoft Central on the former Great Eastern Railway, opened on 3 May 1847.
West, the West Highland Railway between Arisaig and Morar, opened on 1 April 1901, longitude 5°53′W.

This is almost equalled by the Highland Railway branch from Dingwall to Kyle of Lochalsh, opened on 2 November 1897, longitude 5°43′W near Kyle, and by Penzance, longitude 5°33′W.

Farthest south on British Railways: Penzance station, Cornwall

RAILWAY BRIDGES*

One of the world's oldest bridges still carrying a railway is that built in 1810 as an aqueduct to carry the Paisley & Johnstone Canal over the River Cart near Paisley, Scotland. It was converted to a railway in 1885, becoming part of the Glasgow & South Western system.

The first iron railway bridge in the world carried the Stockton & Darlington Railway over the River Gaunless at West Auckland. It was built in 1825 and was replaced in 1901. It has been re-erected at the National Railway Museum, York.

The first skew-arch masonry railway bridge in Britain, also on the Stockton & Darlington

*See also 'Some North American Bridge Records'.

The world's first iron railway bridge, carrying a branch of the Stockton & Darlington Railway over the River Gaunless at St Helen Auckland, County Durham, built in 1825 and replaced in 1901. It has been re-erected at the National Railway Museum, York. The spans are 3·759 m (12 ft 4 in)

Railway, carried the Haggerleases Branch over the River Gaunless. It was built in 1829 and still stands.

The first railway suspension bridge was built in 1830 to carry the Middlesbrough extension of the Stockton & Darlington Railway over the Tees. Its lack of rigidity caused its early replacement. Originally Timothy Hackworth had designed a plate-girder bridge, but it was an untried design and the directors made the unwise choice of the suspension bridge. The type has rarely been used since for railways, except for light rapid-transit systems.

The only transporter bridge to carry railway vehicles was built in 1916 to connect the soap and chemical works of Joseph Crosfield & Son Ltd on both sides of the River Mersey at Warrington, Lancashire. It has a span of 57 m (187 ft) at a height of 23 m (75 ft). Although it has been out of regular use since 1964, it is maintained in working order.

RAILWAY BRIDGES OVER 61 METRES (200 FT) HIGH

The world's highest railway bridge spans the Mala Rijeka Gorge near Kolasin at a height of 198 m (650 ft) on the Belgrade–Bar line in Yugoslavia. It consists of five steel spans on concrete piers. The railway was opened on 1 June 1976 after nearly 25 years of work. It includes 254 tunnels totalling 114 km (71 miles). The summit at Kolasin is at 1032 m (3386 ft).

The Pfaffenberg-Zwenberg Bridge on an improved alignment on the south ramp of the Tauern Railway in Austria (opened on 25 July 1909) is a great concrete arch with a span of 200 m (660 ft), **the world's longest**, and height of 120 m (394 ft). It was opened on 30 July 1971, and it eliminated two tunnels and a smaller bridge and considerable sharp curvature.

Further improvements on the south ramp of the same railway include the Falkenstein Bridge, 396 m (1299 ft) long and 75 m (246 ft)

(Continued on p. 65)

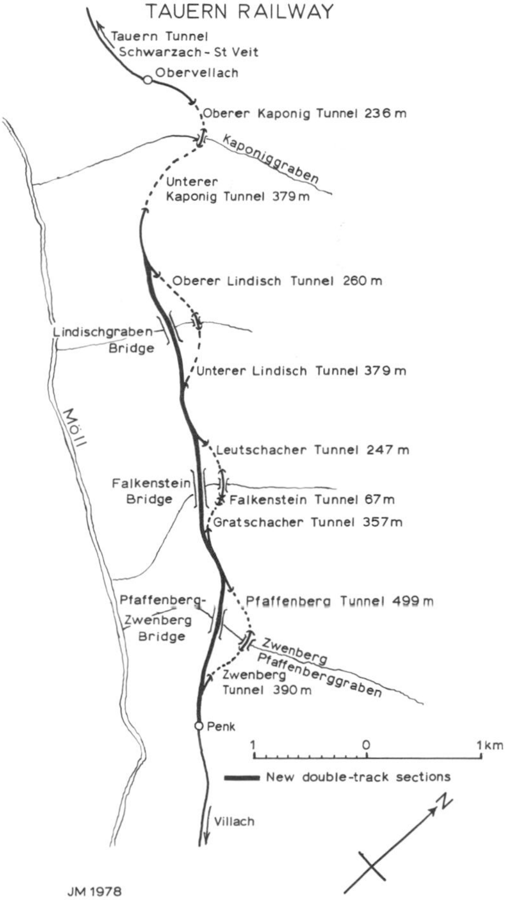

Map of the improvements on the south ramp of the Tauern Railway in Austria, between Obervellach and Penk, one of the most exciting pieces of railway engineering in Europe in recent years

RAILWAY BRIDGES OVER 61 M (200 FT) HIGH

Bridge	Railway	Position	Height m	Height ft	Date opened	Details
Mala Rijeka Viaduct	Yugoslav Railways (JZ)	Kolasin on Belgrade–Bar line	198	650	1 June 1976	Steel spans on concrete piers
Vresk	Iranian State	220 km (137 miles) from Bandar Shah on Caspian Sea, Trans Iranian line	152	500	1938	Masonry arch 55 m (181 ft) span
Fades Viaduct	French National	Clermont-Ferrand–Montluçon line	132·5	435	1909	Steel spans on masonry piers
Khotur	Iranian State	Khotur River near Khoi	131	430	1973	Steel arch spans 223 m (732 ft)—9 spans. Total length 443 m (1455 ft)
Victoria Falls	Rhodesia Railways	Livingstone	128	420	1904	Steel arch span 152 m (500 ft). Total length 198 m (650 ft)
Pfaffenberg-Zwenberg	Austrian Federal	Mallnitz–Spittal	120	394	30 July 1971	World's longest span concrete arch railway bridge, 200 m (660 ft) span. Double track. Replaced steel bridge on old line 68 m (223 ft) high; main span 56 m (184 ft).
Viaur	French National	Tanus, Rodez–Albi	116	381	1902	Steel cantilever span 220 m (722 ft)
Garabit Viaduct	French National	Neussargues–Mallnitz	112	367	1884	Steel arch 165 m (541 ft) span. Formerly 122 m (400 ft) high
Müngstner	German Federal	Müngsten, over River Wupper	107	350	1897	Double track. Main steel arch span 160 m 525 ft
Rio Grande	Costa Rica	Near San José	105	346		
Vance Creek	Simpson Timber Co	Shelton, west of Tacoma, Washington, USA	105	346	1928	Steel arch span 128·8 m (422 ft 6 in)
Tramo Sobre	Former Buenos Aires Great Southern, Argentina	Rio Negro	104	344		
Viaduct No. 2	Turkish State	Between Konakler and Günaykoy on Izmir–Afyonkarahisar line, 199·3 km from Izmir	103	338	1900	Lattice girders below rail-level—6 spans of 30 m (98 ft). Total length 195 m (640 ft)
Faux-Mau-Ti	Chinese Peoples Republic	Yunnan section	102	335	1910	Main span 55 m (180 ft 6 in) over Nam Ti River

Vresk Bridge on the Trans Iranian Railway, 152 m (500 ft) above the bottom of the gorge

Garabit Viaduct, now 112 m (367 ft) high. Until the water level was raised by a dam it was 122 m (400 ft) high

Müngstner Bridge, the highest in Germany, built in 1897, and carrying a double-track railway 107 m (350 ft) above the River Wupper with a span of 160 m (525 ft)

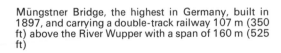

RAILWAY BRIDGES OVER 61 M (200 FT) HIGH

Bridge	Railway	Position	Height m	Height ft	Date opened	Details
Rio Chinipas	Chihuahua–Pacific Mexico	On Ojinago–Topolobampo line	101	330		Steel trusses on concrete piers. Total length 310 m (1019 ft)
Corte	Corsica	Corte	100	328	1894	Masonry arch
Lindischgraben	Austrian Federal	Tauern Railway Obervellach–Penk	100	328	3 Nov 1977	Concrete arch span 154 m (505 ft). Total length 283 m (928 ft)
Ten Tze	Chinese Peoples Republic	Yunnan section	*c* 100	*c* 328	1910	
Sitter	Bodensee–Toggenburg, Switzerland	Near St Gallen	99	324	3 Oct 1910	Steel span 120 m (394 ft) on stone piers
Malleco	Chilean State	Collipulli, on Santiago–Puerto Montt line	97·5	320	26 Oct 1890	7 steel spans on steel towers. Total length 347 m (1138 ft). Over Rio Malleco River
Gokteik	Union of Burma Railways	Mandalay–Lashio	97·5	320	1900	Steel trestle over River Nam Pan Hse which flows through a natural tunnel 251 m (825 ft) below the track
Pecos	Southern Pacific, USA	352 km (219 miles) west of San Antonio, Texas	97·5	320	21 Dec 1944	Continuous steel cantilever 424 m (1390 ft) long. Central span 114·15 m (374 ft 6 in) long, over Pecos River. Replaced an earlier steel structure built in 1892
Crooked River Canyon	Oregon Trunk Railroad, USA	Madras–Bend, Oregon	97·5	320	1911	Steel arch span 103·63 m (340 ft)
Mahoka Viaduct	New Zealand	34 km (21 miles) south of Waiora on Napier–Gisborne line, North Island	97	318	June 1937	Steel trestle 277 m (908 ft) long
Lethbridge Viaduct	Canadian Pacific	Oldman (formerly Belly) River, Alberta	95·7	314	1909	34 spans on steel towers 1624 m (5327 ft) long
Deep Creek	British Columbia Railway, Canada	Lillooet–Quesnel	95	312	Aug 1921	Lattice steel spans on steel towers
Stoney Creek	Canadian Pacific	East of Connaught Tunnel	93·6	307	1894	Replaced wooden trestle built 1886
Kinzua Viaduct	Erie Lackawanna Railway, USA	Bradford, Pennsylvania	92	301	Sept 1900	Steel trestle 626 m (2053 ft) long with 41 spans of 18·28 m (60 ft). Replaces iron trestle built 1882

RAILWAY BRIDGES OVER 61 M (200 FT) HIGH

Bridge	Railway	Position	Height m	ft	Date opened	Details
Solis	Rhaetian Railway, Switzerland	Thusis–Filisur	89	292	21 Oct 1902	Masonry arch 42 m (138 ft) span over Albula River
Wiesen	Rhaetian Railway, Switzerland	Davos–Filisur	88	289	1 July 1909	Masonry arch 55 m (180 ft) span over Landwasser River
Trisanna	Austrian Federal Arlberg line	St Anton–Landeck	87·4	287	20 Sept 1884	Main steel span 120 m (393 ft 8 in) on masonry piers
Drau	Austrian Federal	Bleiburg–Wolfsberg	87	285	1963	5 steel spans on concrete piers. Total length 428 m (1404 ft)
Ulla Viaduct	Spanish National	Sierra de la Culebra line	86	282	1959	Masonry: 219 m (718 ft) long
Here Dere	Turkish State	Near Radjoun	85·3	280		Steel truss bridge
Lawyers Creek Trestle	Burlington Northern, USA (former Northern Pacific)	Craigmont, Idaho	84	276		Steel trestle 407 m (1335 ft) long
Esla	Spanish National Sierra de la Culebra line	Zamora–Pueblo de Sanabria, near Andavias	84	276	1940	Total length 481 m (1578 ft). Main concrete arch span 197 m (645 ft)
Paderno d'Adda	Italian State	Over Adda River at Paderno d'Adda	80·7	265	1 July 1889	Iron arch by Gustav Eiffel. Span 150 m (492 ft). Total length 226 m (873 ft)
Nirihuao River	Argentine	20 km (12 miles) east of San Carlos de Bariloche, Rio Negro	80·4	264	1934	Steel arch span 70 m 229 ft 8 in). Carries 1·676 m (5 ft 6 in) gauge San Antonio–Bariloche line.

Bodensee–Toggenburg Railway train to St Gallen crossing the bridge over the Sitter at a height of 99 m (324 ft). The bridge, opened on 3 October 1910, has a main steel span of 120 m (394 ft)

Right Trisanna Bridge, on the Austrian Federal Railways Arlberg line. With a clear span of 120 m (393 ft) it carries the rails 87·4 m (287 ft) above the Trisanna River. The photograph, taken on 10 August 1975, shows the present span built in 1964–5 to replace the earlier iron bow-string truss built in 1884 which was stengthened by the addition of two steel bow-string girders underneath in 1922–3 (Andrew Marshall)

RAILWAY BRIDGES OVER 61 M (200 FT) HIGH

Bridge	Railway	Position	Height m	Height ft	Date opened	Details
Vivario	Corsica	4 km ($2\frac{1}{2}$ miles) north of Vivario	80	262	1894	Steel truss on stone piers 140 m (459 ft) long
Gisclard suspension bridge	French National	Mont Louis–La Cabanasse	80	262	18 July 1910	Carries metre-gauge Cerdagne line over River Têt. Length 234 m (768 ft); main span 151·5 m (497 ft)
Niagara Canyon	Canadian Pacific	22·5 km (14 miles) north of Victoria, Vancouver Island on Nanaimo line	79	260	*c* 1912	Steel cantilever 161 m (529 ft) long. Replaced wooden trestle. Used from 1884 to 1910 to carry main CPR line across Fraser River south of Lytton, BC.
Meienreuss (middle bridge)	Swiss Federal	St Gotthard line, above Wassen	79	260		Concrete arch faced in stone. Replaces steel bridge of 1882
Makatote	New Zealand	11 km (7 miles) south of National Park, North Island	78·6	258	10 July 1908	Steel trestle 262 m (860 ft) long
Bietschtal	Lötschberg, Switzerland	Brig–Goppenstein	78	255	15 July 1913	Steel span 95 m (312 ft)
Waikare	New Zealand	Just north of Putorino, North Island	78	255	Aug 1937	Steel trestle 1868 m (613 ft) long

Budd rail diesel car crossing the Niagara Canyon Bridge on the Canadian Pacific Victoria–Nanaimo line on Vancouver Island. This cantilever span, constructed in 1884, formerly carried the CPR main line across the Fraser River below Cisco. When it was replaced by the present bridge in 1910 it was re-erected here to replace a timber trestle. It is 161 m (529 ft) long and carries the line over the canyon at a height of 79 m (260 ft), 22·6 km (14 miles) north of Victoria (Canadian Pacific Limited)

The Bietschtal Bridge on the Lötschberg Railway in Switzerland, leaping across the gorge at a height of 78 m (255 ft), between two tunnels, with a span of 95 m (312 ft). The railway was opened on 15 July 1913

RAILWAY BRIDGES OVER 61 M (200 FT) HIGH

Bridge	Railway	Position	Height m	Height ft	Date opened	Details
Carrion	Peru Central	84·48 km (52 miles) from Callao	77	253	1937	Steel truss on steel towers. Length 219 m (720 ft). Replaced the 1891 bridge which replaced the Verrugas Bridge of 1870
Isorno	Centovalli, Ticino, Switzerland	Intragna	77	253	27 Nov 1923	Steel arch 90 m (295 ft) span over Isorno River
Van Staaden's Gorge	South African	Port Elizabeth–Avontour line	76	250	1905	Steel trestle 195·7 m (642 ft) long. Carries 610 mm (2 ft) gauge line
Hurricane Gulch	Alaska Railroad	Near Anchorage	76	250	June 1923	Two-hinged steel arch. Total length 280 m (918 ft)
Ingiustria	Centovalli, Ticino, Switzerland	Corcapolo–Verdasio	76	249	27 Nov 1923	Masonry viaduct; 3 arches 25 m (82 ft) span
Falkenstein	Austrian Federal Tauern line	Mallnitz–Spittal	75	246	13 July 1974	Two concrete arches of 120 m (394 ft) and 150 m (492 ft) span
Grandfrey Viaduct	Swiss Federal	Fribourg	74·7	245	2 July 1860	Over Saane River
Puente de las Vacas	International Railways of Central America 914 mm (3 ft) gauge	Near Guatemala	74·7	245		Steel trestle
Vecchio	Corsica	Vecchio	74	243	1894	Masonry arch
Tunkhannock Creek Viaduct	Erie Lackawanna, USA	Nicholson, Pa	73·15	240	7 Nov 1915	Double-track, reinforced concrete viaduct 724 m (2375 ft) long with 12 arches of 63·4 m (208 ft) and an approach arch of 30·48 m (100 ft) at each end
Göltzchtal Viaduct	German State (DR)	Reichenbach–Plauen, Vogtland, East Germany	73·15	240	1851	Arched viaduct in 4 tiers with brick piers and granite arches, 570 m (1870 ft) long
Brallos	Hellenic Railways Organisation Ltd	Over Kifissos River on Athens–Thessaloniki line 8 km south of Brallos Tunnel	73·2	240	6 Sept 1908	Steel trestle
Tardes Viaduct	French National	Montluçon–Eygurande	73	240	1883	Built by Gustav Eiffel
Niagara Gorge	Conrail, USA Formerly Michigan Central	Niagara Falls, NY/Ontario	73	240	16 Feb 1925	Braced spandrel steel arch, span 195 m (640 ft). Replaced 1883 cantilever bridge

RAILWAY BRIDGES OVER 61 M (200 FT) HIGH

Bridge	Railway	Position	Height m	Height ft	Date opened	Details
Trout Creek	Canadian Pacific	11·7 km (7·3 miles) west of Penticton, BC	72·5	238	1915	188 m (618 ft) long. 2 plate girder spans of 13·7 m (45 ft) and 1 of 79·2 m (260 ft) and 1 76·2 m (250 ft) lattice deck truss and 2 timber spans
Makohine Viaduct	New Zealand	11 km (7 miles) south of Mangaweka, North Island	72·5	238	1902	Steel trestle 228·6 m (750 ft) long
Staircase Viaduct	New Zealand	West of Springfield, South Island	71·6	235	1914	Steel trestle 146·3 m (480 ft) long

Carrion Bridge, the highest in the Peru Central Railway, built in 1937 to replace the 1891 bridge which had been built after the original bridge of 1870 had been swept away in a flood. The first bridge here was named Verrugas after the disease which killed many of the workers on the bridge. The present bridge is named after Dr Daniel Carrion who lost his life in a study of the disease. The bridge is 219 m (720 ft) long and carries the rails 77 m (253 ft) above the gorge

The steel trestle bridge carrying the 610 mm (2 ft) gauge Port Elizabeth–Avontour line over Van Staaden's Gorge in South Africa at a height of 76 m (250 ft). It was built in 1905

Göltzchtal Viaduct between Reichenbach and Planen in Vogtland, East Germany, now scheduled as a national monument. It was built in 1846–51, of brick and granite. With a length of 570 m (1870 ft), in four tiers with a total height of 73·15 m (240 ft), it is one of the largest structures of its kind in the world

RAILWAY BRIDGES OVER 61 M (200 FT) HIGH

Bridge	Railway	Position	Height m	Height ft	Date opened	Details
Waikoau Viaduct	New Zealand	45 km (28 miles) north of Napier, North Island	71·6	235	Aug 1937	Steel trestle 160 m (525 ft) long
Gennessee River Bridge	Erie Lackwanna, USA		71·3	234		Steel trestle
Cottonwood River Viaduct	British Columbia Railway, Canada	Quesnel–Prince George	71·3	234	1952	Steel trestle
Altier Viaduct	French National	Alès–La Bastide	70	230	16 Mar 1870	Masonry viaduct 246 m (807 ft) long
Maliko Gulch Trestle	Kahului Railway, Hawaii	Maui Island	70	230		
Felizon Gorge	Dolomites Rly	North of Cortina d'Ampezzo	70	230	15 June 1921	Lattice girder bridge 27·2 m (90 ft) long
Castellaneta	Italian State	Bari–Taranto	70	229	1928	Masonry viaduct; arches 25·5 m (83 ft 7 in) span. Replaced iron viaduct opened 15 September 1868
Gidur Viaduct	Turkish State	Between Hacikiri and Bucak on Ulukisla–Yenice section, 69·7 km (43 miles) from Ulukisla	69	226	1918	Steel spans on masonry piers. Total length 215 m (705 ft)
Niagara Gorge	Canadian National Railways	Niagara Falls, NY/Ontario	68·9	226	1897	Steel arch bridge 237·7 m (780 ft) long, span 167·6 m (550 ft). Replaced suspension bridge of 1855. Carries road beneath railway.
Jocketa Viaduct	German State (DR)	Near Plauen, Vogtland	68·3	224	1851	Granite arches, 279 m (915 ft) long
Cisco	Canadian National	11 km (7 miles) south of Lytton	68	222	4 Oct 1915	Steel arch 129·5 m (425 ft) span over Fraser River
Devils Canyon	Atchison, Topeka & Santa Fe, USA	41·8 km (26 miles) west of Winslow, Arizona	68	222	1944	Replaces 1900 trestle
Arbutus Canyon	Canadian Pacific	24 km (15 miles) north of Victoria, Vancouver Island	67	220		141 m (462 ft) long. 6 deck plate girder spans on steel towers. Replaced timber trestle
Dead Horse Gulch	White Pass & Yukon	Between Glacier and White Pass, Alaska	66	215	Feb 1899	Cantilever span 914 mm (3 ft) gauge line
Montangas bridge	French National	Bellegarde–Chezéry	66	215		Masonry arch 81·38 m (276 ft) span. Metre-gauge line
Maungatu-ranga Viaduct	New Zealand	24 km (15 miles) south of Waiora, North Island	65·5	215	June 1937	Steel trestle 243·8 m (800 ft) long

RAILWAY BRIDGES OVER 61 M (200 FT) HIGH

Bridge	Railway	Position	Height m	Height ft	Date opened	Details
Matahoura Viaduct	New Zealand	5·6 km (3½ miles) south of Putorina, North Island	65·5	215	Aug 1937	Steel trestle 141 m (463 ft) long
Landwasser Viaduct	Rhaetian. Albula line Switzerland	Filisur	65	213	2 Oct 1902	Masonry viaduct 6 arches of 20 m (65 ft 7 in) span
Angerschlucht	Austrian Federal Tauern line	Hofgastein	65	213	7 July 1909	Steel arch 110 m (361 ft) span
Torres Querido	Spanish National	Cuenca–Utiel	65	213		Masonry viaduct, 23 arches over Narboneta River
Fontpédrouse (Séjourné) Viaduct	French National Cerdagne line	La Bastide–Alès	65	213	18 July 1910	Masonry viaduct 236·7 m (777 ft) long. Centre arch in 2 tiers. Named after the engineer, Paul Séjourné (1851–1939)
Ruinacci	Centovalli, Switzerland	Camedo	65	213	27 Nov 1923	Steel arch 65·92 m (216 ft) span
Pembina River Viaduct	Canadian National	West of Winnipeg, Manitoba	65	213	1909	Steel trestle
Poughkeepsie	Conrail (former New York, New Haven & Hartford)	120 km (75 miles) north of New York City	64·5	212	1889	Cantilever bridge over Hudson River, 2063 m (6768 ft) long including 2 cantilever spans of 167 m (548 ft), 2 spans of 160 m (525 ft) and 2 anchor spans of 61 m (201 ft)
Weissenbach Viaduct	Bodensee–Toggenburg, Switzerland	St Gallen–Herisau	64	210	3 Oct 1910	Masonry viaduct 282 m (925 ft) long
Polvorilla	Argentine, North-Western Region, North Transandine	8 km (5 miles) west of Antonio de Los Cobres, Salta	64	210	1941	Steel trestle 225 m (738 ft) long on 6 piers on curve of 200 m (10 chains) radius. Carries metre-gauge line at altitude of 4267 m (14 000 ft)
Grueize Viaduct	French National 'Ligne des Causses'	Near Marvejols	63·4	208	3 May 1884	Masonry viaduct 218·78 m (717 ft) long
Black Lick Viaduct	Virginian, USA	Over Black Lick Creek near Princeton, W Va	63	207		227 m (910 ft) long
Bralo Viaduct	Hellenic State	On Livadia–Lianokladi section	63	207	6 Sept 1908	Steel trestle 320 m (1050 ft) long. 4 spans: 3×106 m (347 ft) and 120 m (394 ft)

RAILWAY BRIDGES OVER 61 M (200 FT) HIGH

Bridge	Railway	Position	Height m	Height ft	Date opened	Details
Margologio Viaduct	Centovalli, Italy	Verigo–Marone	62	203	27 Nov 1923	Masonry viaduct 3×29 m (95 ft)
Langwies	Rhaetian Rly Chur–Arosa section, Switzerland	Langwies	62	203	12 Dec 1914	Concrete arch 96 m (315 ft) span
Morlaix Viaduct	French National	Morlaix, Paris–Brest line, Brittany	61·2	201	1861	Masonry viaduct in 2 tiers 292 m (958 ft) long
Eglisau	Swiss Federal	Eglisau	61	200	1897	Steel lattice span of 90 m (295 ft) over Rhine. Masonry arch approaches. Total length 457 m (1500 ft)
Douro (Pont de Pia Maria)	Portuguese	Porto	61	200	1877	Steel arch, similar to Garabit Viaduct, France, also by Gustav Eiffel. Total length 354·5 m (1163 ft) Main span 160 m (525 ft)
Cowlitz River	Cowlitz, Chehalis & Cascade Rly, Washington, USA	Cowlitz River	61	200		Timber trestle
Gouritz River	South African	Worcester–Mosel line near Albertinia	61	200	1931	Steel cantilever

This list is intended to be comprehensive, but I am conscious of several bridges whose height could not be established. The height of a bridge above ground or water is the dimension which concerns the design or maintenance engineer the least, and consequently it is not always mentioned in details of the bridge. Also, heights are variable. Sometimes they are measured from a stream-bed, or from water-level which, under the Garabit Viaduct in France, for example, can be raised by a dam, so reducing the height of the bridge above water. Variations occur again at the upper end where measurements are sometimes given to the underside of the bridge, or to rail-level, or to the top of a parapet. In this list I have tried to establish the height of the rails above ground or water.

(Continued from p. 55)

high with one span of 120 m (394 ft) and one of 150 m (492 ft). This was begun on the day the Pfaffenberg–Zwenberg Bridge was opened, and came into use on 13 July 1974, shortening the route by 167 m (549 ft).

On the same day, 13 July 1974, work began on yet another great bridge, the Lindischgraben Bridge, with a span of 154·4 m (505 ft), 100 m (328 ft) high, opened on 3 November 1977. These new works reduce curvature from a minimum of 250 m (820 ft) radius to 450 m (1476 ft) radius and enable speeds to be raised from 60 km/h to 90 km/h (37 to 56 mph). Work will now begin on improvements to the north ramp.

The highest bridge in South America was the Loa River Viaduct on the Antofagasta & Bolivia Railway near Chuquicamata in Chile, 102 m (336 ft) high and 244 m (800 ft) long, at an elevation of 3048 m (10 000 ft) above sea-level. The railway was completed from Antofagasta, Chile, to Uyuni, Bolivia, in 1889 and to Oruro in 1893. It was built to a gauge of 762 mm (2 ft 6 in), but in 1926–8 the gauge was changed to metre and the Loa Viaduct was bypassed by a 12 km (7½ mile) deviation on easier grades.

The Gokteik Viaduct, Burma, carries the metre-gauge Lashio line 251 m (825 ft) above

Load test on the newly completed Lindischgraben bridge on the Tauern Line of Austrian Federal Railways. The arch has a span of 154·4 m (505 ft) and is 100 m (328 ft) high. Its opening on 3 November 1977 marked the completion of improvements on the south ramp between Spittal and the Tauern Tunnel, involving construction also of the Pfaffenberg–Zwenberg and Falkenstein bridges, a total of four great concrete arches, to eliminate sections of severe curvature. The gradient can be seen in the photograph at the centre of the arch (Austrian Federal Railways)

the River Nam Pan Hse. The tallest of the 18 steel towers stands on the natural tunnel over the river and is 97·54 m (320 ft) high. The viaduct was built in 1900 by the Pennsylvania Steel Company of the USA; it is 688·65 m (2260 ft) long, consisting of sixteen spans of 12·192 m (40 ft), seven spans of 18·288 m (60 ft) and ten spans of 36·58 m (120 ft).

The highest viaduct in India is the Ehegaon Viaduct on the line up the Thull Ghat, built in 1865. It is 58 m (190 ft) high and consists of three main girder spans of 42·7 m (140 ft), and two masonry arches of 12 m (39 ft 9 in) at each end. The total length is 229 m (750 ft). The girders were renewed in 1897.

The highest masonry railway bridge in Europe is near Corte in Corsica carrying the metre-gauge Corsica Railway over a gorge at a height of 100 m (328 ft).

On the metre-gauge Rhaetian Railway in Switzerland the Solis Bridge over the Albula River, built in 1902, is 89 m (292 ft) high with an arch of 42 m (138 ft). The Wiesen Bridge, built in 1908–9, crosses the Landwasser River at a height of 88 m (289 ft) with a span of 55 m (180 ft).

The highest railway bridge in Great Britain was the iron Crumlin Viaduct in Wales, built by T W Kennard for the Newport, Abergavenny & Hereford Railway and opened in June 1857. It was 60 m (197 ft) high with a total length of 505 m (1658 ft). It was demolished in 1965. The highest is now the Ballochmyle Viaduct (see below).

The highest railway bridge in England was the Belah Viaduct in Westmorland on the South Durham & Lancashire Union line of the former Stockton & Darlington Railway. It was built by Thomas Bouch in 1859 and was 317 m (1040 ft) long and 60 m (196 ft) high. It was closed in 1962 and dismantled in 1963.

The world's longest span concrete arch railway bridge is the Pfaffenberg–Zwenberg Bridge in Austria (see p. 55). The second longest is the Esla Viaduct in Spain on the single-line 1·676 m (5 ft 6 in) gauge Sierra de la Culebra Railway between Zamora and Pueblo de Sanabria near Andavias. It is 481 m (1578 ft) long, with a main arch over the Rio Esla of 197 m (645 ft) span, and about 84 m (275 ft) high. It was opened in 1940. The height varies with the level of the water in the reservoir.

Next in order are: Plougastel Bridge at Brest, France, opened in 1929, with a span of 186·54 m (612 ft); Stockholm, Sweden, opened in 1935, with a span of 181 m (593 ft). These carry both rail and road. The bridge over the Aare at Berne, Switzerland, with a span of 151 m (495 ft) was built in 1937–41 to replace the former lattice-girder steel spans, and carries four tracks into Berne Station.

Previously the record was held by the

Belah Viaduct on the former Stockton & Darlington Railway between Kirkby Stephen and Barnard Castle, opened in 1861 and closed in 1962. The design was prepared under the direction of Thomas Bouch. It was the highest in England, 60 m (196 ft)

Langwies Bridge on the metre-gauge Chur–Arosa section of the Rhaetian Railway in Switzerland, built in 1912–13. This has a span of 96 m (315 ft) and a height of 62 m (203 ft).

The longest-span masonry arch railway bridge is the Salcano Bridge carrying the railway from Trieste to Jesenice across the Isonzo Gorge at Salcano, about 16 km (10 miles) north of Gorizia (Görz), with a span of 85 m (279 ft) and a total length of 226 m (741 ft). It was built by the Austrian State Railway and opened on 19 July 1906. It was demolished during the First World War and was temporarily replaced by a Wagner military bridge. The territory was ceded to Italy in 1919 and in 1927–8 the bridge was rebuilt to the original design by Italian State Railways. In 1947 it was again transferred and it now belongs to Yugoslav Railways.

The metre-gauge Bellegarde–Chézery Railway in the Ain Department of France was carried over the gorge of the Valserine at a height of 66 m (217 ft) by a masonry bridge with a clear span of 81·38 m (267 ft). It was built by Alfred Picard (1844–1913), engineer.

The largest masonry arch railway bridge in Britain is the central span of the Ballochmyle Viaduct over the River Ayr on the Glasgow & South Western main line from Glasgow to Carlisle in Scotland. It was begun in March 1846 and finished in March 1848. The arch has a semi-circular span of 55 m (181 ft), 304·8 mm (1 ft) longer than the Wiesen Bridge in Switzerland. It carries the line 51·5 m (169 ft) above the river-bed. **It is now the highest railway bridge in Great Britain.**

THE WORLD'S LONGEST RAILWAY BRIDGES

The earliest of the long railway bridges was the Victoria Bridge across the St Lawrence River at Montreal. The original bridge, begun in 1854 and opened on 17 December 1859, was a single-line tubular structure designed by Robert Stephenson. It was 3·134 km (1 mile 1668 yd) long and carried the Grand Trunk Railway, later part of the Canadian National Railways. It had a central span of 107 m (350 ft) and 24 other spans of 73·76 to 75·28 m (242 to 247 ft).

The smoke nuisance and increasing traffic led to its reconstruction under engineer Joseph Hobson as an open girder bridge carrying double track and two roadways on the original piers. When reopened on 13 December 1898 it was named the 'Victoria Jubilee Bridge'.

The longest railway bridge in Europe is the Tay Bridge in Scotland. It is 3·552 km (2 miles 364 yd) long and it carries the Edinburgh–Aberdeen line across the Tay Estuary at Dundee. The original single-line bridge

The first Tay Bridge from the south in 1879

designed by Thomas Bouch was opened on 1 June 1878.

Cast-iron columns were badly designed and made, and construction was poorly supervised. On 28 December 1879 the centre spans were blown down in a gale while a train was crossing. Of the 78 passengers and crew there were no survivors.

The present double-track bridge, designed by W H Barlow and built by William Arrol, was opened on 20 June 1887. The deck trusses of the original bridge were reused as the centre girders of the present deck spans.

The Storstrøm Bridge, Denmark, opened on 26 September 1937, connects the islands of Zealand and Falster. It carries a single-line railway, a road and a footpath, and has a total length over water of 3200 m (10 500 ft). It consists of steel spans on concrete piers: from Zealand 21 plate-girder spans beneath the deck, alternately 57·8 m (189 ft 6 in) and 62·2 m (204 ft) span, 3 bow-string truss spans of 103·9 m (340 ft), 137·8 m (450 ft) and 103·9 m giving a clearance of 25·5 m (83 ft 8 in) above mean sea-level, and 26 more plate-girder spans. The bridge took four years to build.

The Tay Bridge from the south in July 1961. The stumps of the piers of the first bridge can be seen to the right of the bridge, exposed by the low tide. Wormit station in the foreground was closed on 5 May 1969

Crossing the Hardinge Bridge over the Ganges in 1944

The Hardinge Bridge over the Ganges in Bangladesh north of Calcutta was opened on 4 March 1915. It has 15 steel spans of 106·68 m (350 ft) and a length of 1·798 km (1 mile 207 yd) between abutments. The main piers are carried down to a depth of 48·77 m (160 ft) below the lowest water-level and were the deepest foundations of their kind in the world. It consumed more than 1 100 353 m^3 (38 860 000 ft^3) of masonry and 1 700 000 rivets. The engineer was R R Gales.

It carried the main line northwards from Calcutta to Siliguri at the foot of the Himalayas. It was damaged in the 1971 conflict and was temporarily repaired in 1972–4.

Britain's longest viaduct is the original London & Greenwich Railway, the first railway in London. It is 6 km (3·75 miles) long and consists of 878 brick arches. It was designed by Lieutenant-Colonel G T Landmann (later engineer of the Preston & Wyre Railway) and was opened in December 1836, first to an intermediate station at Deptford, on 14 December.

The longest masonry viaduct across a valley in Britain is the Harringworth Viaduct in Rutland on the former Midland Railway. It is 1166 m (3825 ft) long with 82 brick arches of 12·192 m (40 ft) span and a maximum height of 18·29 m (60 ft). It was opened in 1880. It consumed about 15 000 000 bricks. The resident engineer was Crawford Barlow.

One of the highest masonry viaducts in Britain is the Dee Viaduct at Cefn, Wales, on the Shrewsbury–Chester line. It is 45 m (148 ft) high and is 466 m (1530 ft) long, with 19 arches of 18·3 m (60 ft) span. It was designed by Henry Robertson (1816–88), engineer of the

Harringworth Viaduct on the former Midland Railway; Britain's longest viaduct across a valley, in June 1954

Shrewsbury & Chester Railway, and was built in 1848 by Thomas Brassey.

It is closely rivalled by the Templand Viaduct of 14 arches, carrying the former Glasgow & South Western Railway 44 m (145 ft) above the Lugar Water north of Old Cumnock.

The greatest number of viaducts per mile on a British railway is in Cornwall. In the 120 km (75 miles) between Saltash and Penzance there are 34 viaducts.

The Settle & Carlisle line of the former Midland Railway has 19 viaducts and 14 tunnels in 116 km (72½ miles).

The world's first large embankment, or fill was built in 1726 as part of the Tanfield Wagonway in County Durham, England. It is 30 m (100 ft) high and 91 m (300 ft) wide at the base. It carried trains until 1964. (See 'Tanfield Arch'.)

To connect the islands of Honshu and Shikoku as part of the Shinkansen system the Japanese National Railways are constructing a line from Naruto to Kobe which will include two large suspension bridges. The Oh-Naruto Bridge, begun in July 1976, by the Honshu Shikoku Bridge Authority which was established in July 1970, will have a centre span of 876 m (2874 ft), making it the 16th longest in the world. The Akashi Kaikvo Bridge, with a centre span of 1780 m (5840 ft) will be the world's longest.

Another railway, between Sakaide and Kajima, will include the South Bisanseto Bridge with a suspension span of 1100 m (3609 ft), the 6th longest, the North Bisanseto Bridge with a span of 990 m (3248 ft), the 12th longest, and the Shimotsuiseto Bridge with a span of 920 m (3018 ft), the 14th longest.

The earliest and largest 'elastic arch' railway bridge in Britain is at West Wylam on the former North Wylam Branch of the North Eastern Railway, Northumberland. It was designed by William George Laws on the principle of Leather's bridge over the Aire at Leeds, and has a span of 74·67 m (245 ft). It was built by the Scotswood, Newburn & Wylam Railway and was opened in October 1876, becoming part of the North Eastern system in 1883. It was the 'father' of the arch bridges at Newcastle upon Tyne, Sydney, the Hell Gate in New York, and others. The railway was closed on 11 March 1968, but the bridge remains, and is used as a footbridge.

The first cable-stayed railway bridge in Europe, Lyne Bridge, carrying the Virginia Water–Chertsey line of the Southern Region of British Rail over the new dual four-lane M25 motorway, was completed at the end of 1978. It consists of two skew spans of 55 m (180 ft) formed of continuous concrete beams, at an angle of 28° to the motorway. The towers stand 26 m (85 ft) above the tracks. The cable stays are primarily intended as external prestressing cables. It was formally opened by Sir Peter Parker, Chairman of British Railways, on 7 February 1979. The first trains crossed on 12 February.

The Solway Viaduct was designed by James Brunlees (qv) and was begun in March 1865 and completed in July 1868. It was part of the Solway Junction Railway between Dumfriesshire in Scotland and Cumberland in England, opened on 1 September 1869 for freight and on 8 July 1870 for passengers. Until the Tay Bridge was built it was the longest railway bridge in Europe, 1765 m (5790 ft) long. The rails were 10·363 m (34 ft) above the bed of the Solway. In January 1881 45 piers were demolished by ice-floes causing 37 spans to

One of the most unusual bridge designs in Britain, carrying the Manchester–Bury Line over the M62 motorway. It was designed by W F Beatty, chief engineer of London Midland Region of British Rail, and built in 1967–9 by Leonard Fairclough Ltd. It consists of a 161·5 m (530 ft) long beam built up of trapesoidal box sections carrying the tracks on prestressed concrete cantilever shelves, 19·8 m (65 ft) above the motorway. It absorbed 96 km (60 miles) of pre-stressing rods and stands, and 7500 tons of concrete in addition to 5000 tons of concrete in the foundations. It is one of the longest pre-stressed concrete beams in Europe, and it is built to withstand mining subsidence expected to amount to 3·35 m (11 ft) in the next 30 years

The Forth Bridge, from the south in July 1961. The road bridge, of which one tower can be seen under the south cantilever, was then under construction

fall and leaving others suspended. One ice-floe was 25 m (81 ft) square and 2 m (6 ft) thick. The bridge was reopened on 1 May 1884. The last train crossed on 21 August 1921 and the viaduct was dismantled in 1934–5 after a period during which Scottish drinkers used it as a footpath to English pubs on Sundays.

The largest steel arch span in the world is the Sydney Harbour Bridge in New South Wales, Australia, with a main span of 503 m (1650 ft). It was opened on 19 March 1932 and carries two railway tracks, six road lanes, footway and cycle track each of 3 m (10 ft), at a height of 51·82 m (170 ft). Its total length is 1149 m (3770 ft). Originally it had four rail tracks, two of which were used by trams until the late 1950s.

The greatest of all railway bridges, and the oldest railway cantilever bridge is the Forth Bridge in Scotland, opened on 4 March 1890. It was designed by John Fowler and Benjamin Baker and built by William Arrol. The three cantilever towers are 110 m (361 ft) high and the double-track railway is carried 47·55 m (156 ft) above high water. The two main spans are 521 m (1710 ft) and the total length of the bridge is 2528 m (8298 ft).

Work began in November 1882. The main columns, 3·658 m (12 ft) diameter, stand on piers 18·3 m (60 ft) diameter and rise to a height of 104 m (343 ft), leaning inwards from 36·5 m (120 ft) apart at the base to 10 m (33 ft) at the top, 110 m (361 ft) above high water. The piers of the shore towers are spaced 47 m (155 ft) apart and the Inchgarvie piers 82·3 m (270 ft).

The bridge consumed over 54 000 tons of steel, the Inchgarvie piers supporting 18 700 tons and the other piers 16 130 tons each. All this was held together by 6 500 000 rivets, themselves representing over 4000 tons. The piers consumed 21 000 m³ (740 000 ft³) of granite masonry, 35 400 m³ (46 300 yd³) of rubble masonry, 49 000 m³ (64 300 yd³) of

Some idea of the vast size of the Forth Bridge is gained from this photograph from the top of the north cantilever tower. A freight train is passing 61 m (200 ft) below, itself 46 m (150 ft) above the water. The main upright tubes are 3·35 m (11 ft) diameter

concrete and 21 000 tons of cement. Of the 4500 workers employed on the bridge 57 were killed in accidents. Work was completed, at a cost of £3 000 000, at the end of 1889 and the first train crossed on 22 January 1890. Since then it has needed constant painting by up to 29 men taking about 3 years to apply *c* 45 000 litres or 56 tons of paint to the 59 ha or 145 acres of steelwork. On completion of this it was time to start again. Since 1976 four painters have used two small diesel-powered paint-sprayers which can spray paint at up to 8·3 litres a minute and pump up to a height of 61 m (200 ft), each powering two spray-guns. The paint used is a British Rail formulation with red oxide.

SOME NORTH AMERICAN BRIDGES

The oldest railroad bridge in the USA still in use is at Mount Clare, Baltimore, across Gwynn's Falls. It is a stone arch of 24·384 m (80 ft) span with a clearance of 13·411 m (44 ft) above the water. It carries the double-track Baltimore & Ohio Railroad and was opened in December 1829.

The oldest stone viaduct in the USA is the Thomas Viaduct of eight arches carrying the Washington Branch of the Baltimore & Ohio Railroad across the Patapsco River in Maryland, completed on 4 July 1835. It was built in local granite by McCartney, contractor, who erected a monument at one end bearing his own name. The viaduct has eight elliptical arches about 17·7 m (58 ft) span and is 188 m (617 ft) long and 18·288 m (60 ft) high. The engineer was Benjamin Henry Latrobe (1806–78).

The first iron tubular bridge in the USA was built in 1847 at Bolton, Maryland, on the Baltimore & Ohio Railroad.

The first iron truss bridge, also built in 1847, was near Pittsfield, Massachusetts, on the Boston & Albany Railroad.

The first all-steel bridge was opened in 1879 at Glasgow, Missouri, on the Chicago & Alton Railroad. It was 823 m (2700 ft) long.

The world's first successful railway suspension bridge was built across the Whirlpool Rapids below Niagara Falls by John A. Roebling (1806–69) who developed the modern wire-cable suspension bridge. It measured 250 m (821 ft 4 in) between the towers and carried a single-line railway on the upper deck 68·9 m (226 ft) above the water, and a road beneath. It was opened on 18 March 1855, and it connected the Great Western Railway of Canada with the railways of the USA. It was replaced by a steel arch bridge, constructed round the suspended span, in 1897. (See the 'World's Highest Bridges'.)

The world's largest railway suspension bridge is the Benjamin Franklin Bridge over the Delaware River between Philadelphia and Camden. It was designed by Ralph Modjeski (1861–1940) in 1921 and was his last and greatest work. (See also 'Crooked River Bridge' and 'Metropolis Bridge'.) When opened on 4 July 1926 it was the longest single

The world's first successful railway suspension bridge, across the Niagara Gorge, used from 1855 until replaced by a steel arch bridge in 1897

The steel arch which replaced the suspension bridge over the Niagara Gorge in 1897

A train of logs of the Simpson Timber Company crossing the Vance Creek Bridge in Washington, USA, the highest railroad bridge in North America, 105·8 m (347 ft) above the floor of Vance Creek (Simpson Timber Company)

span in the world, with an over-all length of 2·527 km (8291 ft) between the portals and with a central span of 533·44 m (1750 ft) 42·67 m (140 ft) above the river. It cost $37 078 894. (See Japanese railway suspension bridges, p. 70.) A railway was opened over the bridge on 7 June 1936, operated by the Philadelphia Rapid Transit Company. The trains were under-used and last ran across the bridge on 28 December 1968. A new company, the Port Authority Transit Corporation of Pennsylvania and New Jersey (PATCO) has built a fine modern rapid transit line over the bridge. It opened between Philadelphia and Camden on 15 February 1969. Trains run at 120 km/h (75 mph).

A railway which went out to sea was the 206 km (128 mile) long Key West Extension, Florida. It was built by Henry Morrison Flagler (1830–1913), was begun in 1905, partly wrecked in a 201 km/h (125 mph) hurricane in 1909, and was opened to Key West on 22 January 1912. Between the mainland and Key West there were 27·8 km ($17\frac{1}{4}$ miles) of bridges and 32 km (20 miles) of embankment through shallow water. The remainder was on the 'keys'. The longest bridge was the 11 km (7 mile) long steel girder Little Duck Viaduct. The railway was closed after being damaged by a hurricane on 2 September 1935 and has been replaced by a road. The rail journey took $3\frac{3}{4}$ hours.

The highest railroad bridge in North America is the Vance Creek Bridge at Shelton, west of Tacoma in Washington State, USA. It is owned and maintained by the Simpson

Burlington Northern diesel-electric locomotive on a train of 'gallery cars' at Aurora, terminus of the Chicago suburban service, in August 1977

London (Paddington)–Bristol High Speed Train leaving Box Tunnel, in March 1978 (see p. 178) (Andrew Marshall)

Santa Fe 'Super C' freight at Coal City, Illinois, headed by one of the locomotives decorated to commemorate the bicentenary of Independence on 4 July 1976 (Paul Meyer)

Two Union Pacific 'Centennial' class diesel-electric locomotives, 6912 and 6941, with locomotives 8059 and 8074 at Salt Lake City, Utah, on a long freight for Los Angeles. The 'Centennials' are the world's largest and most powerful diesel-electric units. The first appeared in 1969, and the class is named, and numbered, to commemorate the centenary of the completion of the first American transcontinental railway, in 1869

Midland Railway 4–2–2 No. 673 in steam at the Midland Railway centre at Butterley near ipley, Derbyshire, on 27 August 1978. One of these locomotives reached a record speed of 44·8 km/h (90 mph) in 1897

The first Pecos High Bridge, which remained the highest railroad bridge in North America from 1892 when it was completed until the Vance Creek Bridge was built in 1928 (Southern Pacific Transportation)

The second Pecos High Bridge, completed in 1944, which replaced the 1892 bridge, the highest mainline railroad bridge in North America, carrying the Southern Pacific at a height of 97·54 m (320 ft) above the river. The superstructure contains 2650 tons of steel and the tallest pier is 78·5 m (257 ft 4½ in) high (Southern Pacific Transportation)

Timber Company, and it was built in 1928 by the American Bridge Company. It is of steel construction with a main arch span of 128·8 m (422 ft 6 in) carrying the rails 105·8 m (347 ft) above the floor of Vance Creek. The total length of the bridge is 252 m (827 ft 4 in).

The highest railroad bridge on a main line in North America is the Pecos Bridge carrying the Southern Pacific Railroad over the Pecos River a few miles above its confluence with the Rio Grande, 352 km (219 miles) west of San Antonio, Texas. The original high bridge, which took 103 days to build, was completed in March 1892. It replaced the earlier line, opened on 5 January 1883, which ran down into the Rio Grande Gorge and across the Pecos by a low-level bridge in 1882.

The present bridge, opened on 21 December 1944, is a continuous cantilever steel

Crooked River Canyon Bridge

structure, 413·784 m (1390 ft) long with seven spans, the longest being 114·15 m (374 ft 6 in). It carries a single line, 97·54 m (320 ft) above the river.

The Oregon Trunk Railroad crosses the Crooked River Canyon at a height of 97·54 m (320 ft) by a single steel arch span of 103·63 m (340 ft). It was designed by Ralph Modjeski (1861–1940), engineer of the Huey P. Long, San Francisco Bay, and other bridges, and was erected in 1911.

The Pit River Bridge on the Southern Pacific in Shasta County, California, about 22·5 km (14 miles) north of Redding was, when opened on 24 May 1942, one of the highest railway bridges in the world. It was built by the US Federal Government as part of the California Central Valley Water Project. Bids for construction of the bridge were received on 5 October 1939.

It is a riveted steel through Warren truss bridge carrying a double-track railroad, and a road above the top chords. The total length of the road deck is 1093 m (3588 ft) and of the rail deck 839·4 m (2754 ft). The longest of the 13 spans is 187·5 m (615 ft). The greatest height was just east of pier 3, under span 5, where the rails were 132 m (433 ft) above the bed of the old Pit River. Pier 3 is 108·8 m (357 ft) high and contains about 26 750 m^3 (35 000 yd^3) or 70 000 tons of concrete.

On completion of the Shasta Dam the water in the reservoir rose to 9·2 m (31 ft) below the bridge. The bridge is owned by the US Government Bureau of Reclamation.

The Kinzua Viaduct, south of Bradford, Pennsylvania, is 626 m (2053 ft) long and carried the Erie Railroad across a valley at a height of 92 m (301 ft), making it the third highest railroad bridge in the USA. The original iron trestle viaduct was begun on 10 May 1882 and was completed in four months at a cost of $167 000. In 1900, from May to September, the viaduct was rebuilt in steel. It has 41 spans of 18·288 m (60 ft). It is now out of use, but under a preservation order and with no funds for maintenance it is rusting away.

The world's largest reinforced-concrete viaduct carries the double-track line of the Delaware, Lackawanna & Western Railroad across Tunkhannock Creek at Nicholson, Pennsylvania. It is 724 m (2375 ft) long with 12 arches of 63·4 m (208 ft) span and an approach arch of 30·48 m (100 ft) at each end, and is 73·15 m (240 ft) high.

Deep Creek Bridge on the British Columbia Railway, 533 km (331 miles) north of Vancouver, is 95 m (312 ft) high. The line was opened in August 1921.

The highest railway bridge in Canada is the Lethbridge Viaduct carrying the Canadian Pacific Railway over the Oldman (formerly Belly) River in Alberta at a height of 95·7 m (314 ft). It was completed in 1909 and is 1623·63 m (5327 ft) long with 34 spans on steel towers. It consumed 12 000 tons of steel and is dead straight.

The highest bridge on the Canadian National system carries the main transcontinental line over the Pembina River west of Edmonton, Alberta, at a height of 64·924 m (213 ft). It is a steel trestle structure 274·32 m (900 ft) long.

The world's largest cantilever span is the Quebec Bridge over the St Lawrence River,

Lethbridge Viaduct, Canadian Pacific Railway

Prototype Advanced Passenger Train trailer unit 370001 at Carnforth in July 1978 during trials, showing the driving end and nose module (see p. 179)

One of the new Amtrak General Electric P30 diesel units with a train of Amcoaches at Kankakee, Illinois (see p. 190) (Paul Meyer)

The *Inca* and *Ollanta* at Guaqui, Bolivia, on Lake Titicaca, at a height of 3819 m (12 500 ft) above sea-level (see p. 196)

York Station, built on the North Eastern Railway and opened on 25 June 1877. The main roof span measures 24·69 m (81 ft) and the adjoining spans on each side 16·76 m (55 ft) across (see p. 226) The train is headed by a Class 40 diesel-electric locomotive. Photographed on 23 August 1977 (Andrew Marshall)

A train at the upper terminus of the Gornergrat Railway, Switzerland, 3088·7 m (10 133·5 ft), the world's first electric rack railway and the highest open-air railway in Europe. Beyond is the Matterhorn (see p. 208)

Quebec Bridge (Canadian National Railways)

The eastbound *Canadian* transcontinental train of the Canadian Pacific Railway crossing the Stoney Creek Bridge. The 16-car train includes two vista-dome cars (Canadian Pacific Limited)

Canada, opened on 3 December 1917 by the Canadian National Railways. It had cost $ Can 22 500 000 (then £4 623 000). The total length of 987 m (3238 ft) includes a main span of 548·6 m (1800 ft) and shore spans of 171·45 m (562 ft 6 in). The central suspended span of 205·74 m (675 ft) is the second one to be built. The first collapsed, causing the loss of ten lives while being hoisted into position on 11 September 1916 and now lies at the bottom of the river.

The first attempt by the Phoenix Bridge Company of Pennsylvania to erect a bridge here ended in disaster on 29 August 1907 when the south cantilever collapsed, killing 75 of the 86 men working on it.

The Stoney Creek Bridge on the Canadian Pacific Railway 6·5 km (4 miles) east of the Connaught Tunnel was originally built in 1886 as a timber Howe-truss deck-type bridge of two spans of 61 m (200 ft) and one of 30 m (100 ft) supported on timber towers. At the time it was the highest wooden bridge in the world.

In 1893–94 it was replaced by a steel arch span of 102·4 m (336 ft) designed by H E Vautelet and erected by the Hamilton Bridge Company of Ontario without interruption to traffic. It was unique in being probably the only parallel double-chorded arch with its main hinge-pins in its lower chord, unlike the Garabit Viaduct in France (p. 57) in which the chords converge at the springings.

In 1929 the bridge was reinforced by an additional arch on each side, additional supports for the railway, and new deck girders. From track-level on the centre-line of the bridge to the bottom of the gorge the height is 93·574 m (307 ft). (See map on p. 104.)

On Vancouver Island, British Columbia, the Malahat Logging Company's railway was

(Continued on p. 84)

Bear Creek Trestle on Vancouver Island, demolished in the 1950s. With a height of 77·5 m (254 ft) it was one of the highest wooden bridges in the world

THE WORLD'S LONGEST RAILWAY BRIDGES

Bridge	Length m	Length ft	Date opened	Details
Huey P. Long New Orleans, USA	7082	23 235	16 Dec 1935	Owned by the New Orleans Public Belt RR and used by the Southern Pacific, Missouri Pacific and Texas & Pacific RRs. Crosses Mississippi by 8 river cantilever spans totalling 1074 m (3524 ft). Main channel span 241 m (790 ft).
London–Greenwich	*c* 6000	*c* 19 000	14 Dec 1836	Viaduct of 878 brick arches. World's longest brick viaduct.
Hell Gate, New York	5862	19 233	1917	Steel arch span of 298 m (977 ft 6 in) and long approaches including a 4-span bridge nearly 366 m (1200 ft) long across Little Hell Gate, and two 53·54 m (175 ft) spans over Bronx Kill. Carries 4 tracks of former Pennsylvania RR, now Conrail, 43 m (140 ft) above water.
Savannah River, S. Carolina, USA	3962	13 000	1909	Plate girder and truss spans on concrete piers, and 1 swing span. Carries single line of Seaboard Coast Line RR at Hardeeville. Clearance above water 3·6 m (12 ft).
Lower Zambezi, Mozambique	3678	12 064	1934	33 main spans of 793 m (262 ft 5 in), 7 of 50·3 m (165 ft), 6 approach spans 22·2 m (66 ft 5 in) at east end and a steel trestle viaduct at west end. Carries 1·067 m (3 ft 6 in) gauge railway from Marromeu to Tete.
Venice Viaduct, Italy	3600	11 811	1846	222 arches across Lake of Venice. Road alongside.
Tay, Scotland	3552	11 653	20 June 1887	Main steel spans total 3130 m (10 269 ft). Carries double-track Edinburgh–Dundee line. Replaces former single-line bridge opened 1 June 1878 and which was blown down on 28 December 1879.
Storstrøm, Denmark	3212	10 537	26 Sept 1937	Carries a railway, 5·5 m (18 ft) road, and cycle path.
Victoria, Montreal	3135	10 284	17 Dec 1859	Built by Robert Stephenson as a single-line tubular bridge with central span of 100·5 m (330 ft) and 24 spans of 73·76–75·28 m (242–247 ft). Rebuilt as a double-track steel-truss bridge and reopened as Victoria Jubilee Bridge on 13 Dec 1898. Carries Canadian National Railway over St Lawrence River.
Upper Sone, India	3064	10 052	27 Feb 1900	Carries Calcutta–Delhi main line over River Sone near Sasaram.
Ohio River, USA	3011	9877	1929	177 spans; height 28 m (92 ft). Carries Conrail (formerly New York Central) between Louisville, Ky, and Jeffersonville, Ia. Replaced 1895 bridge.
Hwang Ho, China	3009	9873	Nov 1905	102 spans. Carries Peking–Hankow Railway across Hwang Ho (Yellow) River.
Godavari, India	2772	9096	6 Aug 1900	Carries Calcutta–Madras line over Godavari River.
Forth, Scotland	2529	8298	4 Mar 1890	Steel cantilever structure. Two main spans 521 m (1710 ft). Carries double-track Edinburgh–Dundee line 47·55 m (150 ft) above high water.
Benjamin Franklin, Philadelphia, USA	2527	8291	4 July 1926	Suspension bridge. Central span 533·44 m (1750 ft), 42·67 m (140 ft) above the Delaware River. Carries rapid transit trains between Philadelphia and Camden.

THE WORLD'S LONGEST RAILWAY BRIDGES

Bridge	Length m	ft	Date opened	Details
St Charles, Missouri, USA	2400	7876	1936	Steel cantilever structure on concrete and masonry piers, carrying the single-line Wabash RR 16·7 m (55 ft) above the Missouri River. Main bridge 500·4 m (1645 ft); max span 183 m (600 ft).
Cairo, Illinois, USA	2396	7864	1899	Carries Illinois Central Gulf RR over Ohio River. Height 31·1 m (102 ft). Steel truss spans on masonry piers.
Amur, Khabarovsk, USSR	2300	7546	1916	On Trans-Siberian Railway. 22 spans. Longest in Russia.
Newark Bay, New Jersey, USA	2259	7411	1926	Steel deck-plate-girder spans on concrete piers, and two vertical lift spans of 65·8 m (216 ft) and 40·8 m (134 ft), rising to give a clearance of 41·4 m (135 ft). Carries Jersey Central RR between Bayonne and Elizabeth.
Pont de Cubzac, France	2198	7211	1886	Between Chartres and Bordeaux. Iron girder spans; max height 20·5 m (67 ft).
Mahanadi, India	2106	6909	11 Mar 1900	Carries South Eastern Railway over Mahanadi River at Cuttack.
Salado, Santa Fé, Argentina	2044	6705	1892	Carries 1·676 m (5 ft 6 in) gauge single track of Argentine Central Region over River Salado. Longest in Argentina.
Izat, Allahabad, India	1945	6381	1 Jan 1905	40 spans of 45·72 m (150 ft). Carries the North Eastern Railway across the Ganges.
Havre de Grace, Maryland, USA	1877	6108	Jan 1910	Replaced 1886 bridge. Carries Baltimore & Ohio RR across the Susquehanna River. 40 steel spans.
Hardinge, Bangladesh	1798	5900	4 Mar 1915	15 spans of 106·68 m (350 ft) and 6 land spans of 22·9 m (75 ft). Clearance at high water 12·2 m (40 ft). Carries former Bengal & Assam Railway over the Ganges near Sara.
Santiago del Estero, Argentina	1788	5868	1891	Carries 1·676 m (5 ft 6 in) gauge single-track branch of Argentine Central Region over River Dulce.
Rakaia, South Island, New Zealand	1744	5720	1939	Replaces trestle bridge built in 1870s. 143 steel-plate spans of 12·2 m (40 ft) on concrete piers. Clearance above water 2·74 m (9 ft).
Martinez–Benicia, California, USA	1708	5603	1930	Steel spans on concrete piers. Central lift span 100 m (328 ft) giving max clearance of 41·1 m (135 ft). Carries Southern Pacific across arm of San Francisco Bay.
Great Bridge, Wuhan, China	1700	5576	1957	Double-track railway; road above.
Lethbridge Viaduct	1623	5327	1909	Carries Canadian Pacific Railway over Oldman River, Alberta, at a height of 95·7 m (314 ft). Highest and longest in Canada.
Ohio River, Louisville, Kentucky, USA	1604	5263	1918	Carries double track of Conrail (former Pennsylvania RR). Steel truss spans, max 192 m (630 ft).
A H Smith Memorial Bridge, Castleton, NY, USA	1602	5255	1924	52 steel girder spans on steel towers and 2 steel through-truss spans of 183 m (600 ft) and 124 m (408 ft) on concrete piers. Clearance 44·1 m (145 ft). Carries Conrail (former New York Central) across Hudson River.
Nanking–Pukow, China	1600	5249	1 Oct 1969	Carries double-track railway with road above across Yangtze River. 9 main truss spans of 160 m (525 ft).

THE WORLD'S LONGEST RAILWAY BRIDGES

Bridge	Length m	Length ft	Date opened	Details
Lake Pend d'Oreille, near Sanspoint, Idaho, USA	1453	4767	1902	78 deck-plate-girder spans of 15·2 m (50 ft) and 4 through-plate-girder spans of 23 m (75 ft) and 2 of 30·5 m (100 ft) and 1 pin-connected draw span of 60·9 m (200 ft). Clearance 9·8 m (32 ft). Carries Burlington Northern (former Northern Pacific) RR.
Batraki, USSR	1432·5	4700		Carries Syzran–Kuibishev line over Volga River by 13 main spans.
Moerdyk, Netherlands	1400	4592	1880	14 spans of 100 m (328 ft). Carries Antwerp–Rotterdam Railway across the Hollandsch Diep.
Ohio River, Pittsburgh, Pennsylvania, USA	1388	4555	1933	Carries 2 tracks of Conrail (former Pennsylvania RR). Steel truss spans, max 157 m (515 ft).
Fuji River, Japan	1373	4505	1 Oct 1964	On Shinkansen system. Steel through-truss spans.
Sacramento River Viaduct, California, USA	1325	4346		71 steel spans on steel towers and 3 deck-truss spans. Carries Southern Pacific RR.
Memphis, Tennessee, USA	1235	4909	1917	Steel cantilever structure on concrete and masonry piers. Max span 241 m (791 ft). Carries double-track Chicago, Rock Island & Pacific RR and 2 carriageways across Mississippi. Clearance 35·6 m (117 ft).
Yellow River Bridge, China	1225	4020	1911	Single track. 9 steel truss and 3 cantilever spans on piers. Clearance 19·1 m (62 ft 8 in).
Ava, Burma	1203	3948	1934	9 spans of 109·73 m (360 ft); 1 of 79·25 m (260 ft) and 6 of 18·29 m (60 ft). Carries metre-gauge line of Burma Railways across the Irrawaddy River from Ava (east bank) to Sagaing.
Rotterdam Viaduct, Netherlands	1180	3870		Carries Rotterdam–Dordrecht line through Rotterdam by 59 steel spans of 14–16 m (46–52 ft) and 6 approach spans, on masonry and steel piers. Tracks are 7 m (23 ft) above ground-level.
Sheyenne River Viaduct, Valley City, N Dakota, USA	1177·4	3863	1908	3 deck-plate-girder spans of 30·8 m (101 ft), 27 of 23 m (75 ft), 1 of 18·3 m (60 ft), 30 of 13·7 m (45 ft), all on steel towers, and timber trestle 45·7 m (150 ft). Max height above ground 49·4 m (162 ft). Carries single line of Burlington Northern (former NP) RR.
Weldon, N Carolina, USA	1165	3822	1910	Steel truss and plate-girder spans on concrete piers. Longest span 46 m (152 ft). Clearance above water 26 m (85 ft). Carries single line of Seaboard Coast Line RR.
Susquehanna River Bridge, Rockville, Pennsylvania	1161	3808	1902	48 masonry arch spans of 21·3 m (70 ft). Carries 4 tracks of Conrail (former Pennsylvania RR).
Sydney Harbour, New South Wales, Australia	1149	3770	19 Mar 1932	Main steel arch span 503 m (1650 ft); headway 51·82 m (170 ft); south approach 1 span 72·5 m (238 ft), 4 of 53·19 m (174 ft 6 in); north approach 5 spans of 50·9 m (167 ft). Carries double-track railway, road, tramway and footways.
Tsien-Tang-Kiang Bridge, China	1073	3420	1937	Steel truss spans on piers. Carries single-track Chekiang–Kiangsi Railway and road.

THE WORLD'S LONGEST RAILWAY BRIDGES

Bridge	Length m	ft	Date opened	Details
Upington, South Africa	1071	3514		Crosses Orange River with steel spans of 9·14 m (30 ft), 24·38 m (80 ft) and 30·48 m (100 ft).
Harrisburg Viaduct, Pennsylvania, USA	1069	3507		46 arches. Carries Reading Co Line across Susquehanna River. Max low-water clearance 22·7 m (74 ft 6 in).
Fort Madison, Iowa, USA	1020	3347	1927	Steel deck-girders and through-truss spans on concrete and masonry piers, and draw-span of 160 m (525 ft). Carries double track of Santa Fé RR and road across Mississippi. Replaced single-track bridge of 1887.
St Louis Bay, USA	1015	3330	1908	2 draw spans of 146 m (479 ft) and 129·5 m (425 ft); 1 pin-truss span 48·7 m (160 ft). Remainder pile and timber trestle. Carries Burlington Northern (former NP) RR between Superior, Wisconsin, and Duluth, Minnesota.
Kiso River, Japan	1001	3284	1 Oct 1964	On Shinkansen system.
Quebec, Canada	987	3238	3 Dec 1917	Steel cantilever bridge. Main span 548·6 m (1800 ft) including suspended span of 205·7 m (675 ft); shore spans 168·25 m (562 ft 6 in). Carries track of Canadian National Railways over the St Lawrence.

(Continued from p. 80)

carried across Bear Creek by a wooden trestle at a height of 77·5 m (254 ft), 274 m (900 ft) long. It was demolished in the 1950s. It claimed to be one of the largest wooden bridges in the world.

America's longest drawbridge span of 160 m (525 ft) forms part of the Atchison, Topeka & Santa Fe Railroad bridge over the Mississippi at Fort Madison Iowa, Illinois, opened in 1927.

The longest swing spans on American railroads are the Willamette River Bridge at Portland, Oregon, of 159 m (521 ft), completed in 1908; and the East Omaha Bridge over the Missouri of 158 m (519 ft) completed in 1903.

The longest railroad vertical-lift bridge span carries the Baltimore & Ohio Railroad connection to the Staten Island Rapid Transit across Arthur Hill, New York. It was opened on 25 August 1959 and replaces the earlier swing bridge. The centre span of 170 m (558 ft) is suspended from two 65·53 m (215 ft) steel towers. It can be raised to its maximum height of 41·14 m (135 ft) or lowered to its closed position 9·5 m (31 ft) above the water in 2 minutes.

The second longest carries the New Haven

THE LARGEST RAILROAD CANTILEVER BRIDGES IN THE USA

Bridge	Location	Main span m	ft	Year
Baton Rouge	Mississippi	258	848	1940
Cornwall	St Lawrence	257	843	1899*
Vicksburg	Mississippi	251	825	1930
Huey P. Long	New Orleans	241	790	1935
Memphis (Harahan)	Mississippi	241	790	1916
Memphis	Mississippi	241	790	1892

* Removed when the St Lawrence Seaway was established in 1954.

& Hartford Railroad across the Cape Cod Canal, Massachusetts. It was built in 1933–5. The 165·8 m (544 ft) span can be raised from 2·13 m (7 ft) to 41·14 m (135 ft) in 2½ minutes.

The world's longest stone arch railway bridge over a river carries the former Pennsylvania Railroad over the Susquehanna at Rockville, Pennsylvania. It was built in 1902 to replace the iron truss bridge of 1877 and is 1122 m (3680 ft) long.

The longest simple-truss span on USA railroads is the 219·5 m (720 ft) of the Chicago, Burlington & Quincy (now Burlington Northern) Railroad's Metropolis Bridge over the Ohio River, opened in 1917. The truss is 33·5 m (110 ft) deep. It was designed by Ralph Modjeski (see 'Crooked River Bridge', and 'Benjamin Franklin Bridge').

The longest continuous-truss railroad-bridge span in the USA is the 236·2 m (775 ft) of the Sciotville Bridge, also over the Ohio River, opened in 1918.

The world's longest railway water crossing is on the Southern Pacific Railroad, USA, across the Great Salt Lake, just west of Ogden, Utah. The original Central Pacific line climbed over Promontory at a maximum height of 1496 m (4907 ft). It was on this section that the record track-laying length was laid (see p. 96) and the last spike was driven (p. 47).

The Lucin Cut-off was opened on 8 March 1904. It crossed the lake on a 32 km (20 mile) long trestle which required 38 256 piles and other timber from 10·36 km² (4 miles²) of forests in Louisiana, Texas, Oregon and California. Gradually the trestle was filled in to form an embankment until latterly 19·082 km (62 605 ft), or just under 19·2 km (12 miles), remained. As most of it was single-track, and it was several times attacked by fire, it was the most vulnerable part of the Southern Pacific system. In May 1960 198 m (650 ft) were burnt out.

In 1955 work began on a broad embankment 20·4 km (12·68 miles) long to replace the trestle. A total of 34 673 000 m³ (45 480 000 yd³) of rock, sand and gravel were consumed, mostly from quarries on Promontory Point. A maximum of 1 835 000 m³ (2 400 000 yd³) was placed in one month. For

An aerial view from the east through a telephoto lens, of the new 20·4 km (12·68 mile) fill across the Great Salt Lake, Utah, during construction in 1958. The original timber trestle, completed in 1904, was formerly 32 km (20 miles) long but was gradually filled in until at the end only about 19 km (12 miles) remained. The Southern Pacific trains began running over the new embankment on 27 July 1959 (Southern Pacific Transportation)

the base of the fill 11 738 139 m³ (15 352 000 yd³) was dredged from the lake to a maximum depth of 26 m (85 ft) below the water surface, to a width of 183 m (600 ft). The top of the fill, 4 m (13 ft) above water, is 16 m (53 ft) wide.

The new line was opened on 27 July 1959. Together with the crossing of the Bear River by the Bagley Fill, the total length of embankment in the water is 44·39 km (27·58 miles).

The total number of bridges on railroads in the USA in 1937 was 191 779 totalling 6212 km (3860 miles), in a total length of 378 197 km (235 000 miles).

TUNNELS

The world's first railway tunnel was an underground line at Newcastle upon Tyne, England, built in 1770.

Chapel Milton Tunnel on the Peak Forest Tramway in Derbyshire, England, was opened

The two bores of Marc Brunel's Thames Tunnel as seen from Wapping Station on the East London Railway. The tunnels were begun in 1825, opened for pedestrians in 1843 and for the railway in 1869. Electric trains began running through the tunnel on 31 March 1913. Today the shaft in the foreground is occupied by a lift from a large platform just above the tracks, brought into use on 4 October 1915 (London Transport Executive)

on 1 May 1800. This was a plateway with L-section rails. At Ashby de la Zouch in Leicestershire, England, a tunnel 282 m (308 yd) long was built for the Ticknall Tramway (which also used L-section rails) in 1800–5. It was enlarged by the Midland Railway for the Ashby-Melbourne Branch opened on 1 January 1874. Passenger trains ran until 22 September 1930. Hay Hill (or Haie Hill) Tunnel on the Forest of Dean Tramroad in Gloucestershire, England, was opened in September 1809 and was 973 m (1064 yd) long. In 1854 it was enlarged by Brunel to accommodate the 2·134 m (7 ft) gauge Forest of Dean Branch from the South Wales Railway to Cinderford. It was converted to standard gauge in 1872 and was closed on 1 August 1967. Talyllyn Tunnel on the Hay Railway in Breconshire, Wales, was opened on 7 May 1816 and was 616 m (674 yd) long. In 1860 it became part of the Brecon & Merthyr Railway and was enlarged in 1862. It was closed on 2 May 1964.

The first railway tunnel to be used for passenger traffic was Tyler Hill Tunnel on the Canterbury & Whitstable Railway opened on 4 May 1830. It was 766 m (838 yd) long. Passenger traffic ended on 1 January 1931 and the line closed completely on 1 December 1952.

The second was Glenfield Tunnel on the Leicester & Swannington Railway opened on 17 July 1832. It was 1642 m (1796 yd) long. Passenger trains ran until 24 September 1928 and the tunnel was closed completely on 4 April 1966.

The first underwater public railway tunnel was the Thames Tunnel on the East London Railway. The two parallel bores were built by Marc Brunel, begun in 1825 and opened on 25 March 1843 for pedestrian traffic. They were incorporated in the East London Railway under the supervision of the engineer Sir John Hawkshaw and opened on 7 December 1869. The railway now forms part of the London Transport system.

Britain's longest railway tunnel is the Severn Tunnel built by the Great Western Railway to shorten the route between London and South Wales. It was opened on 1 September 1886 after 14 years' work. It is 7·011 km (4 miles 628 yd) long, but of this length only about 2 km ($1\frac{1}{4}$ miles) are actually under water even at high tide. The engineer was Sir John Hawkshaw.

Turkey is to build a tunnel between Istanbul and Haydarpasa to connect the European and Asian systems of Turkish State Railways. This was announced on 20 September 1977.

The longest underwater tunnel in the USA is the Bay Area Rapid Transit (BART) Trans Bay

(Continued on p. 90)

THE WORLD'S LONGEST RAILWAY TUNNELS

Tunnel	m	miles	yd	Date	Railway	Position
Siekan*	53 850	33	809		Japanese National	Honshu–Hokkaido
Daisimizu*	22 280	13	1483		Japanese National	Jōmō–Kogen–Echigo
Simplon No 2	19 823	12	559	16 Oct 1922	Swiss Federal	Brig–Iselle
Simplon No 1	19 803	12	537	1 June 1906	Swiss Federal	Brig–Iselle
Shin Kanmon	18 713	11	1105	10 Mar 1975	Japanese National	Honshu–Kyushu
Apennine	18 519	11	892	12 Apr 1934	Italian State	Florence–Bologna
Rokko	16 250	10	171	15 Mar 1972	Japanese National	Osaka–Shinkobe
Gotthard	14 998	9	562	1 Jan 1882 (a)	Swiss Federal	Göschenen–Airolo
Nakayama*	14 650	9	180		Japanese National	Takasaki–Jōmō–Kogen
Lötschberg	14 612	9	140	15 July 1913	Bern–Lötschberg–Simplon	Goppenstein–Kandersteg
Haruna*	14 350	8	1612		Japanese National	Takasaki–Jōmō–Kogen
Hokuriku	13 870	8	1089	10 June 1962	Japanese National	Maibara–Fukui
Mont Cenis (Fréjus)	13 657	8	855	17 Sept 1871	Italian State	Turin–Modane
Shin Shimizu	13 500	8	684	Aug 1961	Japanese National	Takasaki–Niigata
Aki	13 030	8	170	10 Mar 1975	Japanese National	Mihara–Hiroshima
Cascade	12 542	7	1397	12 Jan 1929	Burlington Northern USA	Spokane–Seattle Washington
Flathead	12 479	7	1327	7 Nov 1970	Burlington Northern	Libby–Whitefish, Montana
Kitakyushu	11 747	7	528	10 Mar 1975	Japanese National	Kokura–Hakata
Kubiki	11 353	7	96	May 1969	Japanese National	Nou–Nadachi
Zao*	11 210	6	1698		Japanese National	Fukushima–Shin–Shiroishi
Lieråsen	10 700	6	1142	3 June 1973	Norwegian State	Oslo–Drammen
Santa Lucia	10 262	6	662	22 May 1977	Italian State	Naples–Salerno
Arlberg	10 250	6	650	20 Sept 1884	Austrian Federal	Bludenz–St Anton
Moffat	9997	6	373	27 Feb 1928	Denver & Rio Grande Western USA	Denver–Glenwood Springs
Ichinoseki*	9730	6	79		Japanese National	Ichinoseki–Kitakami
Shimizu	9702	6	50	1 Sept 1931	Japanese National	Doai–Tsuchitaru
Kvineshei	9064	5	1112	17 Dec 1943 (b)	Norwegian State	Kristiansand–Stavanger
Bingo	8900	5	933	10 Mar 1975	Japanese National	Fukuyama–Mihara
Kaimai	8850	5	878	12 Sept 1978	New Zealand Govt	Waharoa–Apata North Island
Rimutaka	8798	5	821	3 Nov 1955	New Zealand Govt	Upper Hutt–Featherston, North Island
Uonuma*	8650	5	658		Japanese National	Urasa–Nagaoka
Ricken	8603	5	608	1 Oct 1910	Swiss Federal	Wattwil–Uznach
Grenchenberg	8578	5	581	1 Oct 1915	Swiss Federal (c)	Moutier–Grenchen
Otira	8563	5	564	4 Aug 1923	New Zealand Govt	Christchurch–Brunner, South Island
Tauern	8551	5	551	7 July 1909	Austrian Federal	Bad Gastein–Spittal
Fukuoka	8488	5	482	10 Mar 1975	Japanese National	Kokura–Hakata
Haegebostad	8474	5	467	17 Dec 1943 (b)	Norwegian State	Kristiansand–Stavanger
Ronco	8291	5	277	4 Apr 1889	Italian State	Genoa–Milan

THE WORLD'S LONGEST RAILWAY TUNNELS

Tunnel	m	miles	yd	Date	Railway	Position
Hauenstein (new)	8134	5	95	8 Jan 1916	Swiss Federal	Tecknau–Olten
Tenda	8099	5	60	30 Oct 1914	Italian State	Turin–Nice
Fukushima*	8090	5	46		Japanese National	Koriyama–Fukushima
Connaught	8083	5	39	6 Dec 1916	Canadian Pacific	Field–Revelstoke
Karawanken	7976	4	1683	1 Oct 1906	Austrian Federal	Rosenbach (Austria)–Jesenice (Yugoslavia)
Borgallo	7972	4	1679	1 Aug 1894	Italian State	Parma–La Spezia
New Tanna	7958	4	1663	1 Oct 1964	Japanese National	Tokyo–Shizuoka
Somport	7874	4	1572	18 July 1928	French National	Oloran (France)–Jaca (Spain)
Tanna	7804	4	1493	1 Dec 1934	Japanese National	Tokyo–Shizuoka
Ulrikken	7662	4	1338	1 Aug 1964	Norwegian State	Bergen–Oslo
Hoosac	7562	4	1230	9 Feb 1975	Boston & Maine USA	North Adams, Mass (Boston–Albany)
Monte Orso	7562	4	1230	28 Oct 1927	Italian State	Rome–Naples
Lupacino	7514	4	1178	24 Sept 1958	Italian State	Aulla–Lucca
Castiglione	7390	4	1040	24 Feb 1977	Italian State	Rome–Florence
Vivola	7355	4	1004	28 Oct 1927	Italian State	Rome–Naples
Monte Adone	7132	4	760	22 Apr 1934	Italian State	Florence–Bologna
Jungfrau	7123	4	750	1 Aug 1912	Jungfrau, Switzerland	Above Lauterbrunnen
Borgallo	7077	4	699	12 July 1894	Italian State	Fidenza–La Spezia
Toyohara*	7030	4	647		Japanese National	Nasu–Shine–Shirakawa
Severn	7011	4	628	1 Sept 1886	British Rail	Swindon–Newport
Sainte Marie aux Mines (Lusse)	6870	4	474	9 Aug 1937	French National	Saint-Die–Selestat
Shin-Kinmeiji*	6822	4	419		Japanese National	Shin-Iwakuni–Tokuyama
Itsukaichi*	6640	4	220		Japanese National	Hiroshima–Shin-Iwakuni
Ohirayama	6585	4	160	10 Mar 1975	Japanese National	Tokuyama–Ogori
San Giacomo	6514	4	83	12 May 1977	Italian State	Savona
Marianopoli	6475	4	42	1 Aug 1885	Italian State	Valledolmo–Enna, Sicily
Tsukiyono*	6460	4	25		Japanese National	Jōmō-Kogen–Echigo-Yuzawa
Turchino	6446	4	10	18 June 1894	Italian State	Genoa–Asti
Wochein (Podbrdo)	6339	3	1652	9 July 1906	Yugoslav State	Jesenice–Nova Gorica
Zlatibor	6202	3	1503	1 June 1976	Yugoslav State	Belgrade–Bar
Sozina	6170	3	1466	1 June 1976	Yugoslav State	Belgrade–Bar
Mont d'Or	6097	3	1388	16 May 1915	French National	Vallorbe (Switzerland)
Urasa*	6020	3	1302		Japanese National	Urasa–Nagaoka
Col de Braus	5949	3	1226	30 Oct 1928	French National	Turin–Nice
Albula	5865	3	1134	1 July 1903	Rhaetian, Switzerland	Filisur–Samaden
Gyland	5717	3	972	17 Dec 1943 (b)	Norwegian State	Kristiansand–Stavanger
Sant'Oreste	5710	3	962	6 Dec 1976	Italian State	Rome–Florence
Totley	5697	3	950	6 Nov 1893 (d)	British Rail	Sheffield–Chinley
Metropolitana	5666	3	910	28 Sept 1925	Italian State	Naples

THE WORLD'S LONGEST RAILWAY TUNNELS

Tunnel	m	miles	yd	Date	Railway	Position
Shin Karikachi	5647	3	896	Oct 1966	Japanese National	Ochiai–Shin Karikachi
Peloritana	5446	3	676	20 June 1889	Italian State	Palermo–Messina, Sicily
Puymorens	5414	3	641	21 July 1929	French National	Foix (France)–Puigcerda (Spain)
Monte Massico	5378	3	601	28 Oct 1927	Italian State	Rome–Naples
Senzan	5361	3	583	10 Nov 1937	Japanese National	Shikoku
Gravehalsen	5312	3	529	10 June 1908	Norwegian State	Bergen–Oslo
Fukasaka	5173	3	379	1 Oct 1957	Japanese National	Omi-Shintsu–Shinhikida
Biassa	5146	3	348	14 Nov 1933	Italian State	Genoa–La Spezia
S Elia-Ianculla	5142	3	343	5 Dec 1960	Italian State	Reggio Calabria–Brindisi
S Cataldo	5141	3	342	30 July 1894	Italian State	Agropoli–Supri (Naples–Reggio Calabria)
Mount Royal	5073	3	268	21 Oct 1918	Canadian National	Montreal
Ohara	5063	3	256	11 Nov 1955	Japanese National	Ohara–Katsuura
Otowayama	5045	3	327	1 Oct 1964	Japanese National	Tokyo–Osaka
Amanus	4905	3	83	1918	Turkish State	Adana–Aleppo
Woodhead New (e)	4888	3	66	14 June 1954 (f)	British Rail	Sheffield–Manchester
Standedge (g)	4888	3	66	5 Aug 1894	British Rail	Stalybridge–Huddersfield

(a) For goods traffic; passengers from 1 June 1882.
(b) Wartime opening under German Occupation. Full traffic began 1 March 1944.
(c) Grenchenberg Tunnel owned by the Bern–Lötschberg–Simplon Railway but worked by Swiss Federal Railways.
(d) For goods traffic; passengers from 1 June 1894.
(e) Superseded two single-line tunnels 4848 m (3 miles 22 yd) long, opened 23 December 1845 and 2 February 1852.
(f) Formally opened 3 June 1954.
(g) Two adjacent single-line bores opened 1 August 1849 and 12 February 1871 are now abandoned.
* Under construction (1977).

In Russia the Lena River–Tyndin section of the Baikal–Amur line, opened in 1977, includes a tunnel about 15 km (9 miles) long, but precise information is not yet available.

On the Paola–Cosenza line a base tunnel 14 944 m (9 miles 502 yd) was started about 1969 and is still only half finished.

In Italy the following tunnels were under construction at the time of writing in 1978:

Tunnel	m	miles	yd	Projected opening date	Position
San Donato	10 954	6	1419	1980	Rome–Florence *direttissima*
Orte	9371	5	1447	1979	Rome–Florence *direttissima*
Cravere	5573	3	813	1981	Busseleno–Salbettrand (part of track doubling between Turin and Modane)
Tanze	5433	3	660	1979	Busseleno–Salbettrand (part of track doubling between Turin and Modane)

The east end of the Severn Tunnel, from the train

(Continued from p. 86)

Tube carrying rapid transit trains beneath the bay between San Francisco and Oakland. It is 5·79 km (3·6 miles) long, the underwater section being the longest in the world. It was opened on 14 September 1974.

The 1837 m (2009 yd) long single-track St Clair Tunnel, linking Canada and the USA under the St Clair River between Sarnia and Port Huron was opened on 27 October 1891 for freight and on 7 December for passengers. It cost $2 700 000. In 1908 it was electrified with single-phase ac 3300 V, 25 Hz. It was operated by the St Clair Tunnel Company, a subsidiary of the Grand Trunk Railroad of Canada which gained access to Chicago by a series of links which became the Grand Trunk Western. The GT and its subsidiaries including 2598 km (1614 miles) in the USA came into the possession of the Canadian Government on 21 May 1920. It became part of the Canadian National system in 1959. When the use of diesel locomotives became universal the electrification through the tunnel was dismantled.

The Grand Trunk's main competitor, the then Michigan Central, also built a tunnel under the St Clair River between Detroit and Windsor in 1906–10. This consists of two single-track tubes 2553 m (2792 yd) long of which 813 m (889 yd) are beneath the water. This section was built by dredging a trench and sinking the pairs of steel tubes into it. It was originally electrically operated, but as in the St Clair Tunnel the electrification was abandoned with the advent of diesel-traction.

The Channel Tunnel between England and France first came into prominence in 1874 when the South Eastern Railway (England) obtained Parliamentary powers to sink experimental shafts and in 1881 to acquire lands between Dover and Folkestone. The Submarine Continental Railway Company Limited, incorporated on 12 December 1881, took over the SER works and drove a pilot tunnel about 1920 m (2100 yd) out under the sea. The chief engineer was Sir John Hawkshaw. Work was suspended in 1883, largely for military reasons. In 1875 a Channel Tunnel Company and a French Submarine Railway Company obtained powers to carry out works and the latter drove a 2·414 km ($1\frac{1}{2}$ mile) gallery under the sea from Sangatte. In 1886 the English company was absorbed by the Submarine Continental Company and in 1887 the name became the 'Channel Tunnel Company'. The original SER interests are now held by the British Railways Board.

In July 1957 the Channel Tunnel Study Group was formed to carry out extensive economic, traffic and revenue, and engineering studies. In March 1960 it submitted its report recommending a twin railway tunnel, and on 6 February 1964 the British and French Governments decided to go ahead with the project. Survey work was completed in October 1965. In 1966 it was proposed that private capital should be raised for the tunnel, being repaid through a royalty arrangement on all goods and traffic using the tunnel. It was emphasised that the tunnel would not be built at the tax-payer's expense. The estimated cost in 1973 was £468 000 000 of which the British and French Channel Tunnel Companies would each contribute half. Because of inflation the final cost in 1980 was expected to be between £820 000 000 and £850 000 000. Traffic forecasts prove the tunnel to be a sound economic investment. Trains would operate at a $2\frac{1}{2}$ minute headway and would make possible the carriage of 4500 cars per hour in each direction, the capacity of a dual three-lane motorway, in addition to through express passenger and freight trains. On the car-trains passengers would ride in their own cars; no advance booking would be necessary, and tolls would be up to 20 per cent less than sea-ferry charges. Trains would operate on a 24 hour, 365 days a year basis, taking 35 minutes between tunnel terminals near Folkestone and near Calais.

The electric trains, with 6000 hp locomotives operating on the 25 kV 50 Hz system would connect the main lines of Britain and France, and would travel between London and Paris in 3 hours 40 minutes.

The Dover Strait is about 34 km (21 miles) wide with a maximum depth of water of about 61 m (200 ft). The tunnel would pass through the Lower Chalk strata at a depth of about 49 m (160 ft) below the sea-bed, with gradients of 1 in 100.

The tunnel would be about 51·5 km (32 miles) long and consist of two single-line track bores 6·858 m (22 ft 6 in) diameter inside and fully lined. A pilot tunnel bored ahead of the main tunnel would act as a probe to detect any water ingress. On completion the pilot tunnel 4·419 m (14 ft 6 in) diameter, would be joined to the main tunnels every 250 m (273 yd) to provide an access and service tunnel.

The tunnel was expected to come into service in 1980. To connect it with London a new railway was to be built. It was proposed to site the new passenger terminal at White City where there would be good connections with the Midlands, the North and the West, and with the rest of London by the Underground Railways. Of its 129 km (80 miles), 14·5 km (9 miles) would be in tunnel and the remainder would be alongside existing railways. In November 1974 this high-speed rail link was abandoned because of expense. In January 1975 the British Government decided to abandon the entire Channel Tunnel project.

The political decision to divide responsibility between the British and French Governments, financing companies, project managers and railways prevented co-ordinated planning and was a major influence in the British Government's decision. The Cairncross Report (*The Channel Tunnel and alternative cross-Channel Services*, HMSO, 1975) stated: 'We have been conscious as our work proceeded that everything seemed to be happening in the wrong order.'

After its abandonment there was an enormous increase in cross-Channel juggernaut traffic obstructing British roads. Following a vote in the European Parliament on 4 July 1977 in favour of a viability study, there is still a hope that it will be built. 'In the face of all adverse circumstances the tunnel remains the cheapest and most efficient method of handling cross-Channel traffic.' (See above.)

The only alternative worth considering is a bridge. Experience with oil-rigs has made this appear more feasible, but shipping collisions remain a hazard.

The physical problems of the Channel Tunnel are minor compared with those of the Seikan Tunnel in Japan (see below), already more than half finished. The difficulties with the Channel Tunnel project are entirely man-made; political and economic. The technical expertise, the materials, machinery and skilled labour are all readily available.

The Channel Tunnel Project. The day of breakthrough in a 287 m (312 yd) long tunnel being driven through Shakespeare Cliff, Dover, as part of the Channel Tunnel project. The tunnel will connect a site adjoining the Old Folkestone Road, about 65 m (214 ft) above sea-level, to the site of the Old Dover Colliery on a plateau at the foot of the cliff, and will provide a road access to the lower site for men and contractors' plant and equipment. A second tunnel (centre, foreground) about 480 m (523 yd) long, is being driven under the cliff from the lower site to give contractors access to the point at which work would start on the Channel Tunnel itself. This tunnel is adjacent to the existing Folkestone–Dover railway tunnel (left). Phase II of the project, begun in November 1973, provided on the British side for the construction of approximately 2 km (1·3 miles) of service tunnel under the sea from the Kent coast, and the proving of tunnelling machines (The British Channel Tunnel Company Limited)

The latest information at the time of writing is the result of discussions in September 1978 between the British Railways Board and French Railways. Consideration is to be given to a single-line bore as a first step, using a 'tidal flow' system of operation which could handle an estimated 8 000 000 passengers and 8 000 000 tons of freight a year. Doubling could follow later.

The Seikan undersea railway tunnel between Honshu and Hokkaido in Japan, 53·85 km (33·4 miles) long with 23·3 km (14·4 miles) undersea, will have a maximum depth below sea-level of 240 m (786 ft). Work began in

A Northern Line tube train entering the world's longest railway tunnel at Morden. The train, travelling via Bank, will emerge at East Finchley after an underground journey of 27·8 km (17 miles 528 yd)

Shin Kanmon Tunnel, 18 713 m (11 miles 1105 yd) long, on the Japanese Shinkansen line between Honshu and Kyushu, opened on 10 March 1975, showing the paved concrete track (PACT) (Japanese National Railways)

1964 on shafts and pilot tunnels and is not expected to be completed before 1982. The tunnel will pass 100 m (330 ft) below the seabed in badly faulted granite containing water-filled seams of broken rock, compared with the clay-chalk of 'cheese-like consistency' with no faults expected in the Channel Tunnel. Approach gradients are 1 in 83·3 (1·2 per cent). Work has been delayed by serious flooding; one flood in January 1974 halted work for a year.

It is now 3 years behind schedule, and the estimated construction cost had risen to 355 400 000 000 Yen (*c* £794 000 000) by January 1978. About 4000 men are employed working in three 8-hour shifts. By December 1977 20 had been killed in the work, mostly crushed by the electric trains carrying spoil.

The world's longest continuous railway tunnel is on the London Underground railway system from East Finchley to Morden via Bank, 27·842 km (17 miles 528 yd). There are, however, 25 stations and 3 junctions in the tunnel. The tunnel is 3·7 m (12 ft) diameter and the station tunnels are 6·8 m (22 ft 2½ in). It was completed in 1939. A journey through it takes about 55 minutes, including stops.

The longest ordinary railway tunnel is the 19·823 km (12 miles 559 yd) Simplon Tunnel between Switzerland and Italy. (See 'Trans-alpine railways'.)

The world's longest underwater tunnel and also **the longest double-track railway tunnel** is the Shin Kanmon Tunnel in Japan, between Honshu and Kyushu, 18·713 km (11 miles 1105 yd), opened on 10 March 1975. The next longest double-track tunnel is the Apennine Tunnel in Italy on the *direttissima* line from Florence to Bologna. It was opened on 22 April 1934 and is 18·519 km (11 miles 892 yd) long.

The longest tunnel in Scotland is Greenock, on the former Caledonian Railway from Glasgow to Gourock, 1920 m (1 mile 340 yd), opened on 1 June 1889.

The longest tunnel in Wales is Ffestiniog, 3407 m (2 miles 206 yd), on the Llandudno Junction to Blaenau Ffestiniog Branch of the former London & North Western Railway, opened on 22 July 1879.

The highest tunnel in Britain was at Torpantau on the Brecon & Merthyr Railway in Wales, 609 m (666 yd) long. The west portal was 400 m (1313 ft) above sea-level. It was opened on 1 May 1863 and closed on 2 May 1964.

Today the highest is Shot Lock Hill Tunnel on the Settle & Carlisle section of the former Midland Railway, at an altitude of about 349 m (1153 ft). It was built in 1871–3 and is 97 m (106 yd) long. Freight traffic began on 2 August 1875 and passenger traffic on 1 May 1876.

The deepest tunnel in England is Cowburn between Chinley and Edale in Derbyshire, 267 m (875 ft) below the surface at its deepest

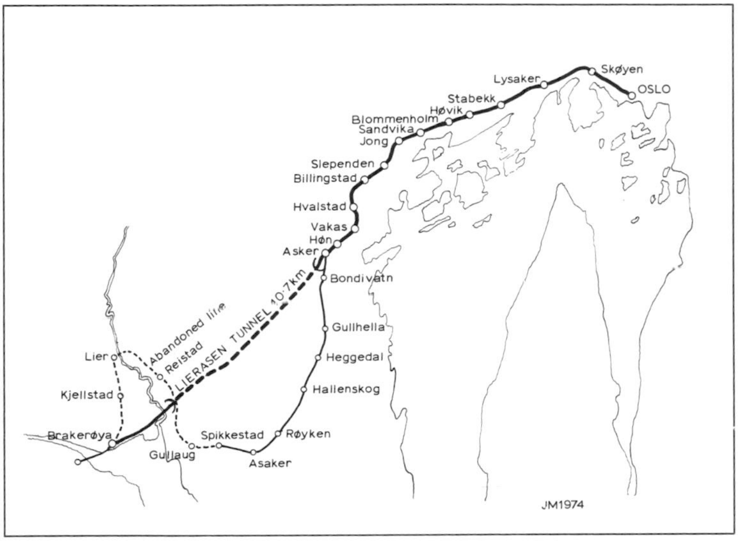

Map showing the position of the new Lieråsen Tunnel, Norway

point. It is 3384 m (2 miles 182 yd) long. It was built by the Midland Railway and opened on 6 November 1893.

The total number of tunnels in Great Britain was 1049 in 1938. By then several lines had been abandoned and the total could have been about 1060. This includes 'long bridges' classed as tunnels.

Europe's longest tunnel north of the Alps is Lieråsen between Asker and Brakerøya on the Oslo–Drammen line in Norway, begun in 1963 and opened on 3 June 1973. It is 10·7 km (6 miles 1142 yd) long, shortens the rail journey between Asker and Drammen by 12·5 km (7·767 miles) and permits speeds up to 120 km/h (74½ mph).

The longest tunnel on French Railways is the Somport Tunnel, actually between France and Spain. It is 7874 m (4 miles 1572 yd) long, and was opened on 18 July 1928. It carries a single line, and is operated by the French National Railways (SNCF).

The longest tunnel entirely in France is the Lusse (Vosges) Tunnel, 6870 m (4 miles 474 yd), opened on 9 August 1937.

Tunnels on Japanese National Railways total 1779 km (1105 miles).

The longest railway tunnel in Russia is the Suran Tunnel, nearly 4 km (2½ miles) long, on the Poti Baku line in the Caucasus.

One of Europe's shortest railway tunnels, Kleine Krausel Tunnel, 13·83 m long, on the Semmering Railway, Austria

A new 8 km (5 mile) tunnel is being built through the Pambak Range on a new railway to link Yeveran, capital of Armenia, with Akstafa, a junction in Azerbaijan.

The Baikal–Amur line, expected to be opened in 1982, includes a tunnel *c* 15 km (9 miles) long.

The longest railway tunnel in North America is the Henderson Tunnel (qv). The longest 'through' railway tunnel is the Cascade on the Burlington Northern (qv).

The longest tunnel in the Southern Hemisphere is on a 30 km (18·6 mile) long industrial mining line between Toquepala and Cuajone in Peru, officially opened on 6 December 1975.

Rimutaka Tunnel in the North Island, New Zealand, 8798 m (5 miles 821 yd), completed in 1955 to cut out the climb over the Rimutaka Range which included the 5 km (3 mile) Rimutaka Incline with Fell centre rail (New Zealand Railways)

A 1285 hp 'Ea' class Bo–Bo electric locomotive leaving the Otira portal of the 8563 m (5 mile 564 yd) Otira Tunnel on the Canterbury–West Coast line in the South Island, New Zealand, photographed in 1968 (New Zealand Railways)

It is 14·7 km (9·134 miles) long. Tunnels on the line total 27 km (16·78 miles), leaving only 3 km (1·86 miles) in the open.

The longest tunnel in New Zealand is an 8·85 km (5½ mile) tunnel through the Kaimai Range forming part of a new 24 km (15 mile) cut-off line between Apata and Waharoa in the North Island, opened on 12 September 1978. The tunnel is straight, on a gradient of 1 in 333 (0·3 per cent) rising from west to east. Paved concrete track (PACT, qv) is used throughout for the single line.

Also in the North Island is the single-track Rimutaka Tunnel on the railway from Wellington to Masterton. It was opened on 3 November 1955 and is 8798 m (5 miles 821 yd) long. It replaced the line over the Rimutaka Ranges involving the famous Fell incline of 5 km (3 miles) at 1 in 14–16 (see p. 209).

The Otira Tunnel in the South Island, New Zealand, between Christchurch and Greymouth, is 8563 m (5 miles 564 yd) long and was opened on 4 August 1923. It has a gradient of 1 in 33 (3 per cent), rising from Otira to Arthur Pass, and at the time of building it was the longest tunnel in the British Empire and fifth longest in the world. It is electrically worked, at 1500 V dc.

New Zealand Railways have over 180 tunnels totalling about 85 km (53 miles).

The longest tunnel in Argentina carries a 1·676 m (5 ft 6 in) gauge freight-only single line of the D F Sarmiento National Railway (formerly Buenos Aires Western Railway) under the city of Buenos Aires. It is 4·8 km (about 3 miles) long and was opened on 14 February 1916. The line leaves the surface tracks 1·207 km (¾ mile) west of Once de Septiembre Station and from the tunnel entrance descends at 1 in 67 to reach an average depth of 15 m (49 ft) below street-level, and emerges in the Port Zone. It is electrified with the standard 800 V dc third rail through the tunnel and with overhead conductors in the Port Zone.

The longest tunnel in Chile is Las Raices on the 1·676 m (5 ft 6 in) gauge branch from Pua to Lonquimay, about 625 km (388 miles) south of Santiago. It is 4545 m (2 miles 1450 yd) long.

The longest railway tunnel in South Africa is the twin-bore Hilton Road Tunnel between Boughton and Cedara on the Natal main line. They are 4948 m (3 miles 131 yd) long. Next are the Hidcote Tunnels, 3295 m (2 miles 84 yd). Both are on the South African Railways system. No others are over 1609 m (1 mile) long.

The only tunnel on the Rhodesia Railways is at Wankie. It is 254 m (278 yd) long, and was opened on 20 January 1957.

The first railway tunnel in Australia was the double-track Elphinstone Tunnel on the 1·600 m (5 ft 3 in) gauge Victorian Government Railways Bendigo line north-west of Melbourne, opened in 1862. It is 382 m (418 yd) long and lies on a gradient of 1 in 60 (1·66 per cent) and a curve of 120·7 m (60 chains) radius, and is still in use.

The longest railway tunnel in Australia is the Woy Woy Tunnel on the New South Wales Public Transport Commission's North Coast line between Sydney and Newcastle. It is double-track, 1789 m (1 mile 197 yd) long, and was opened in July 1886.

The longest would have been the Cox's Gap Tunnel, 1931 m (1 mile 352 yd), on the proposed Sandy Hollow to Maryvale Branch in New South Wales, sanctioned in 1911 but never completed. This tunnel and four others were finished, however, and are now used for road traffic.

The only spiral tunnels in Australia are one on the Brisbane to Sydney main line at Cougal just south of the Queensland–New South Wales border, opened in 1932; and one at Bethungra on the Sydney–Melbourne main line, in southern New South Wales, opened in 1946.

The most notorious tunnel in Australia was the Otford Tunnel on the NSW Railway's Illawarra line south of Sydney, opened in 1886. It was 1550 m (1695 yd) long on a gradient of 1 in 40 (2·5 per cent) against loaded trains. Engine crews suffered so much from smoke inhalation and scalding that, after a forced ventilation system was installed with little success, a deviation was built and opened in October 1920 and the tunnel was abandoned.

The railway with the greatest number of tunnels is the Sierra de la Culebra Railway, Spain. Between Puebla de Sanabria and Carballino, 173 km (107½ miles), there are 182 tunnels amounting to 78 km (48½ miles), the longest being the 5949 m (3 miles 1226 yd) Padornelo Tunnel, opened in 1957–9.

The Bergen–Oslo line in Norway has 178 tunnels in 491 km (305¾ miles) amounting to 36·2 km (22½ miles). It was opened on 1 December 1909.

The east portal of Galera Tunnel under the Continental Divide in the Andes, from Galera Station. It is the highest tunnel in the world, its peak being 4781 m 15 688 ft) above sea-level. It is 1176 m (1287 yd) long on a gradient of 4 per cent or 1 in 25. The mountain above is named Mount Meiggs after the engineer Henry Meiggs (see p. 41) (Brian Fawcett)

In Japan, the San-yo Shinkansen standard-gauge line from Okayama to Hakata, 398 km (247 miles), opened on 10 March 1975, includes 111 tunnels totalling 222 km (140 miles) and representing 56 per cent of the whole route. They include the Aki Tunnel, 13 030 m (8 miles 169 yd); Shin Kanmon, 18 713 m (11 miles 1105 yd); Kita-Kyushu 11 747 m (7 miles 528 yd) and Bingo, 8 900 m (5 miles 933 yd).

The highest tunnel in the world is the Galera Tunnel on the Central Railway of Peru, opened on 14 November 1893. It is 1176 m (1287 yd) long at an altitude of 4781 m (15 688 ft). (See map on p. 42.)

Compressed-air rock drills were first used in tunnel construction in the Hoosac Tunnel in the USA (see p. 103) in 1855. In Great Britain they were first used in the Clifton Tunnel on the Clifton Extension Railway, Bristol, in 1874.

SOME USA FACTS AND FEATS

(See also 'Some North American Bridges'.)

The railway spike with a hooked head, for holding flat-bottomed rails to sleepers, or ties, was designed in 1830 by Robert L. Stevens, first president of the Camden & Amboy Railroad (now part of Courail) in New Jersey. The first patent for a machine for making spikes was issued to Henry Burden of Troy, New York, in 1840. Stevens also designed the T-section iron rail and a 'fish-plate' for joining rail ends in 1830 (see p. 32). Flat-bottomed iron rails, rolled in England, became standard on the Camden & Amboy Railroad in 1832. They were 76·2 mm (3 in) wide across the base, 50·8 mm (2 in) across the top, 88·9 mm ($3\frac{1}{2}$ in) high, with a 12·7 mm ($\frac{1}{2}$ in) thick web.

Bessemer steel rails were first rolled in the USA at North Chicago Rolling Mills on 25 May 1865. By the end of the century they had almost completely replaced iron rails.

The record for laying the greatest length of track in one day was achieved during the construction of the Central Pacific Railroad in Utah on 28 April 1869 when 16·110 km (10 miles 56 ft) of a single track were laid. Charles Crocker (1822–88), in charge of construction, prepared the materials and briefed his men for several days beforehand. On the day over 4000 men, many of them Chinese, with hundreds of horses and wagons, were employed. The track advanced at 1·609 km (almost a mile) an hour, 800 men laying rails at the rate of about 73·15 m (140 ft) in 1 min 15 s, about as fast as a leisurely walk. Ahead of them were men preparing ties and spikes and behind them were the ballasters. The section included many curves on the western slope of Promontory Mountain where rails had to be bent. When work ended at 7 pm 25 800 ties, 3520 rails 9·144 m (30 ft) long, 24 948 kg (55 000 lb) of spikes, 14 080 bolts and great quantities of other material had been used. Each rail-handler had lifted 125 tons of iron during the day, in addition to his heavy tongs. To crown the achievement one Jim Campbell drove a locomotive back over the new line at 64 km/h (40 mph).

The whole of this section was abandoned in 1942 and the rails were removed. The original rails, of course, had been replaced long ago. (See 'The world's longest water crossing'.)

Laying part of the 16 km (10 mile) section of the Central Pacific Railroad, Utah, on 28 April 1869 to establish the record for the greatest length of track laid in one day (Southern Pacific Transportation)

During construction of the Canadian Pacific Railway in autumn 1883, 183 m (600 ft) of track were laid in 4 min 45 s, certainly a record in Canada.

Gauges. In 1871 there were 19 different gauges in use in the USA, ranging from 914 mm (3 ft) to 1·829 m (6 ft). Subsequently many 0·610 m (2 ft) gauge lines were built.

Between 1867 and 1871 it was possible to travel from New York to St Louis on 1·829 m (6 ft) gauge tracks via the present Erie route to Dayton, Ohio, and the present Baltimore & Ohio through Cincinnati to St Louis. In 1868 the Missouri Pacific Railroad was converted from 1·676 m (5 ft 6 in) to standard, and in 1871 the Ohio & Mississippi (now the Baltimore & Ohio) Railroad from 1·829 m (6 ft) to standard. These influenced other conversions, and so by 1887 nearly every important railroad in the USA was operating on standard gauge, the most outstanding exception being the Denver & Rio Grande Western Railroad which in 1888 operated a maximum of 2692 km (1673 miles) of 914 mm (3 ft) gauge.

The world's biggest gauge conversion was carried out on the Louisville & Nashville Railroad which was built to a gauge of 1·524 m (5 ft). On 30 May 1886 about 8000 men converted over 3220 km (2000 miles) of track to a gauge of 1·447 m (4 ft 9 in). Standard gauge was adopted gradually 10 years later. One section foreman and his gang converted 17·703 km (11 miles) in 4½ h. One shop changed 19 locomotives, 18 passenger cars, 11 cabooses, 1710 revenue freight cars and several other works vehicles between dawn and dusk on 30 May. The total cost of the conversion was $195 095.69, minus $29 605 raised by the sale of redundant third rails.

Altogether 21 000 km (13 000 miles) of route in the Southern States were converted at about the same time.

In 1920 USA railroads employed over 2 000 000 persons. In 1960 793 071 employees earned $4 956 902 360; in 1975 487 789 people earned $7 474 750 000. However, since 1916 the USA has abandoned nearly 80 500 km (50 000 miles) of railroad. This is almost 2·5 times the maximum railway mileage in Great Britain, in 1930.

Year	US railroad mileages km	miles	Great Britain km	miles
1830	37	23	c 190	c 120
1840	4535	2818	2388	1484
1850	14 517	9021	9790	6084
1860	49 286	30 626	14 594	9069
1870	85 167	52 922	21 826	13 563
1880	150 094	93 267	25 035	15 557
1890	263 289	163 605	27 799	17 274
1900	311 183	193 366	30 037	18 665
1910	386 735	240 313	32 152	19 979
1916	408 762 (maximum)	254 000		
1920	406 935	252 865	32 710	20 326
1930	401 711	249 619	32 902 (maximum)	20 445
1940	376 869	234 182	32 551	20 227
1950	361 015	224 331	31 848	19 790
1960	350 104	217 551	30 208	18 771
1970	336 345	209 001	18 988	11 799
1972	336 340	208 998	18 986	11 798
1975	c 322 000	c 200 000	18 017	11 258

The State with the highest railroad mileage is Texas, with 21 413 km (13 306 miles) in 1975. Its first railroad, from Harrisburg to Alleyton, was opened in 1860. Next is Illinois with 17 014 km (10 572 miles), the earliest being Jacksonville to Meredosia opened in 1838.

The smallest mileages are in District of Columbia with 42 km (30 miles) and in Rhode Island with 224 km (139 miles).

The following States had railroads open before 1835:

Alabama; Tuscumbia–Decatur, 1834
Connecticut; Northwich–Killingly, 1832
Delaware;* Newcastle–Frenchtown, 1831
Florida; Tallahassee–Port Leon, 1834
Louisiana; New Orleans–Lake Pontchartrain, 1831
Maryland; Baltimore–Ellicott's Mills, 1830
Michigan; Detroit–St Joseph, 1832
New Jersey;* Camden–South Amboy, 1834
New York; Albany–Schenectady, 1831
Pennsylvania;* Leiperville–Ridley Creek, 1809
South Carolina; Charleston–Hamburg, 1833
Virginia; Weldon, N.C.–Petersburg, Virginia, 1833
West Virginia; Baltimore–Harpers Ferry, 1834

The largest railroad abandonment in the USA was the 871 km (541 miles) New York, Ontario & Western on 29 March 1957. Next were the Missouri & Arkansas, 539 km (335 miles) in 1948; and the Colorado Midland (see below), from Colorado Springs to Glenwood Springs, 356 km (221·3 miles) in 1919.

The longest continuous curve in the USA is probably the Pontchartrain curve between Ruddock and Tunity in Louisiana on the Illinois Central Railroad, skirting the western shore of Lake Pontchartrain. It is 15·192 km (9·45 miles) long with only slight changes of radius.

The Southern Railway, shortly before entering New Orleans, skirts the same lake on a curve nearly 14·5 km (9 miles) long.

The longest uniform curve is on the Texas & Pacific Railroad between Alexandria and Chencyville, also in Louisiana. It has a radius of 10·5 km (6·5 miles) throughout its 9·173 km (5·7 miles).

SUMMITS IN COLORADO

The highest adhesion-worked summit in North America was on Mount McClellan, 4159 m (13 644 ft), reached by the Argentine Central (later Argentine & Gray's Peak) Railway,

*The three earliest States in the Federation, admitted 1787.

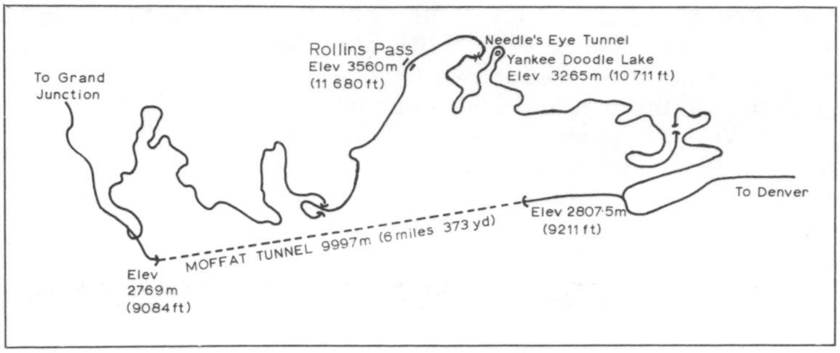

Map of the Denver & Salt Lake Railroad over the Rollins Pass

from Silver Plume, Colorado, a 914 mm (3 ft) gauge line built by Edward Wilcox in 1906. The 6 per cent, or 1 in 16·67, grades and switchbacks were worked by Shay geared engines (qv) which could pull two or three Colorado & Southern cars to the summit. Petrol cars were introduced in 1914. The 9·6 km (6 mile) long railway closed in 1917. (See also **'The highest railway in North America'**.)

A Shay geared locomotive and train at the summit of Mount McClellan, 4159 m (13 644 ft), on the Argentine Central Railroad, Colorado, which operated from 1906 to 1917. The lower terminus was at Silver Plume (see Georgetown Loop Railroad, p. 244)

The highest adhesion-worked standard-gauge line was the Denver & Salt Lake Railroad or 'Moffat Road' over Rollins or Corona Pass, at an altitude of 3560 m (11 680 ft). Opened in 1904 it was used until the Moffat Tunnel was completed in 1928. It is now a road.

The record was then held by the branch of the Denver & Rio Grande Western from Leadville up to Ibex, Colorado, at an altitude of 3509 m (11 512 ft). This was closed in 1944.

The Colorado Midland was a standard-gauge railway from Colorado Springs to Leadville and Grand Junction, completed in 1890. West of Leadville it climbed to a 659 m (720 yd) long tunnel under Hagerman Pass at a height of 3515 m (11 530 ft). In 1891 this was replaced by the Busk–Ivanhoe Tunnel, 2864 m (1 mile 1372 yd) long at a height of 3337 m (10 984 ft), considerably shortening the route and reducing the climb and curvature. The entire railway was abandoned in 1919 (see above).

The highest summit on a through line in North America is the 3121 m (10 239 ft) at Tennessee

Needle's Eye Tunnel on the approach to Rollins Pass on the former Denver & Salt Lake Railroad, now a 'dirt road' passable for light motor traffic

Photograph of an old Colorado Midland Railway poster showing the line climbing to Hagerman Tunnel above Leadville, Colorado, in 1890, before the construction of the Busk–Ivanhoe Tunnel which left the original route at the lowest bend, in the centre of the picture

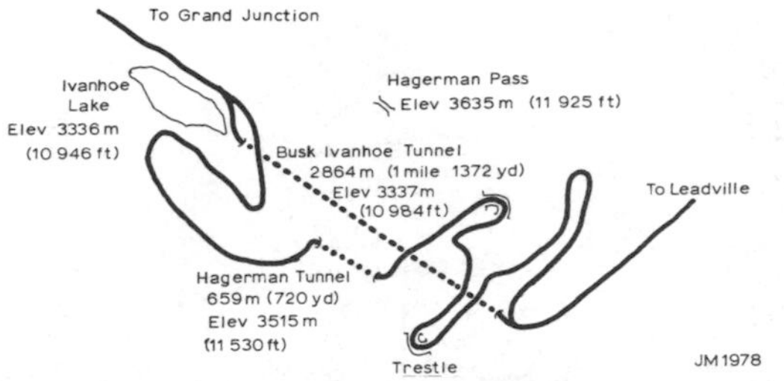

Map of the Colorado Midland Railway under Hagerman Pass, Colorado

Pass Tunnel on the standard-gauge Denver & Rio Grande Western Railroad north of Leadville. Before the 785 m (859 yd) long tunnel was opened in 1890 the earlier 914 mm (3 ft) gauge line crossed the pass at 3177 m (10 424 ft). In November 1945 a new concrete-lined tunnel, 777 m (850 yd) long, was opened and the original timber-lined tunnel was abandoned.

The Denver, South Park & Pacific Railroad, a 914 mm (3 ft) gauge line completed from Denver to Gunnison in 1882, crossed the Continental Divide in Alpine Tunnel 539·5 m (590 yd) long at an elevation of 3512 m (11 523 ft). From Como a branch, completed in 1882, reached Breckenridge over the Boreas Pass at 3503 m (11 493 ft) and in 1884 over Fremont Pass at 3450 m (11 318 ft) to Leadville. On 12 January 1899 the DSP & P. became part of the Colorado & Southern Railroad.

The line through Alpine Tunnel was closed in 1910; the remainder of the system closed in 1937. The section from Leadville to Fremont Pass was rebuilt to standard gauge and

South end of the Tennessee Pass Tunnel on the Denver & Rio Grande Western Railroad, Colorado. The new tunnel on the left was opened in November 1945 to replace the old timber-lined tunnel on the right, now filled in

The remains of the western end of Alpine Tunnel on the Denver South Park & Pacific Railroad, at a height of 3512 m (11 523 ft)

Burlington Northern Bo–Bo diesel No. 828 with a box car at the upper end of the spur to the Climax Molybdenum Company's Mill at a height of 3472 m (11 390 ft), now the highest adhesion-worked line in North America

reopened in 1943. It is operated by the Burlington Northern, successor to the Colorado & Southern since 1970. At the Fremont Pass this branch reaches a height of 3450 m (11 318 ft). A spur from here to a mill of the Climax Molybdenum Company on the pass reaches a record height of 3472 m (11 390 ft). **This is now the highest adhesion-worked railway summit in North America.**

The Silverton Northern (1906–41), 914 mm (3 ft) gauge, reached a height of 3408 m (11 180 ft) at Animas Forks.

The remaining summits over 3050 m (10 000 ft) were on 914 mm (3 ft) gauge lines:

Marshall Pass, 3306 m (10 846 ft), on the Denver & Rio Grande main line to Gunnison, opened 1881, closed 1955.

Lizard Head, 3124 m (10 248 ft) on the Rio Grande Southern Railroad, opened in 1891 and closed in December 1951.

Colorado & Southern Leadville line, 3111 m (10 207 ft), opened in 1884.

Monarch, Denver & Rio Grande Western 3093 m (10 148 ft), opened in 1883. This is now standard gauge.

Cumbres Pass, 3053 m (10 015 ft), on the Denver & Rio Grande Western from Antonito to Durango, opened in 1880. Today it is operated as a tourist line by the Cumbres & Toltec Scenic Railroad. (See p. 244.)

TUNNELS IN THE USA

On its 408 762 km (254 000 miles) of railroad in 1916 the USA had 1539 tunnels with a total length of 515 km (320 miles). This total number was only 50 per cent more than the total on 32 902 km (20 445 miles) in Great Britain in 1930.

The first American railroad tunnel was the Staple Bend Tunnel, Pennsylvania (qv).

The longest railway tunnel in North America is the Henderson Tunnel in Colorado. It is really a long mine adit, built by the Climax Molybdenum Company (a section of Amax Inc) to tap an immense body of molybdenum ore buried deep inside Red Mountain on the Continental Divide. The ore was discovered in 1975 just after the death of Robert Henderson who pioneered the exploration and after whom the mine is named. Shafts were sunk in

The portal of the Henderson Tunnel showing a train of molybdenum ore emerging behind one of the ASEA Bo–Bo locomotives (Climax Molybdenum Company)

the Clear Creek Valley near Empire 64 km (60 miles) west of Denver for access to the ore body. The main shaft, 8·534 m (28 ft) diameter and 945 m (3100 ft) deep, is the largest shaft in North America.

For extraction of the ore a tunnel was bored about 15·4 km (9·6 miles) long on a rising gradient of 3 per cent (1 in 33), emerging in the Williams Fork Valley on the west side of the Continental Divide. The exact length of the tunnel is difficult to establish because it has only one open end; the other end is inside the mine. A 7·7 km (4·8 mile) open stretch leads to the only suitable site which could be found within a radius of 40·2 km (25 miles) of the mine where there was enough flat area for the extensive processing and storage facilities without spoiling the environment.

Driving of the tunnel began at the west portal on 10 January 1971, and the tunnel was holed through on 15 July 1975 with a vertical error of 127 mm (5 in) and horizontal of only 25 mm (1 in). Surveying calculations had to

Diesel train emerging from the east end of the Cascade Tunnel, Washington. The buildings house the ventilating plant used to blow fumes out of the tunnel. For this purpose the portal is closed by a sliding door which opens automatically as a train approaches. From its opening in 1929 until the change to diesel traction the section through the tunnel was operated by electric locomotives. This tunnel replaced the first Cascade Tunnel of 1900 (Burlington Northern Inc)

allow for the curvature of the earth. The finished tunnel is 4·6 m (15 ft 2 in) high and 5 m (16 ft 6 in) wide, and contains a double-track 1·067 m (3 ft 6 in) gauge railway. In the centre is a ventilation shaft 3·35 m (11 ft) diameter and 483 m (1585 ft) deep to exhaust hot air from the tunnel. Its site was so remote that helicopters had to be used to transport men and materials. The altitude of the east end of the tunnel, 945 m (3100 ft) underground, is 2286 m (7500 ft) and of the west portal 2766 m (9075 ft) above sea-level.

Operation of the railway, which came into use in August 1976, is completely automatic. Six unmanned trains operate at a constant speed of 40 km/h (25 mph) between the mine and the processing mill. Each train, with four locomotives, one at each end and two in the middle, carries 660 tons of ore in 30 cars and makes 45 trips in 24 h. The locomotives were built by ASEA (Allmanna Svenska Elektriska Aktiebolaget) of Stockholm, and were designed to withstand a temperature range of −45·6 °C (−50 °F) to 29·4 °C (85 °F). Within the mine loading area the locomotives use a 600 V dc overhead system and from there to the processing mill a 1400 V dc overhead system fed by six transformer rectifiers from a 13·8 kW supply.

At a rate of extraction of 30 000 tons of ore per day it is expected that the known ore body will take 30 years to mine.

The longest through tunnel in the USA is the Cascade Tunnel on the Great Northern (now Burlington Northern) main line from Spokane to Seattle in Chelan and King Counties in Washington State. It is 12 542 m (7 miles 1387 yd) long. It was opened on 12 January 1929 and replaced an earlier line which climbed to a summit tunnel 4229 m (2·63 miles) long. While this was being built trains crossed the summit by a spectacular series of zigzags in a line 19·712 km (12¼ miles) long opened in 1892 and used until the tunnel was finished in 1900 (see map and illustration).

The second longest tunnel in the USA and seventh longest in the world, is the Flathead Tunnel in north-west Montana, also on the Great Northern. It was made necessary by the Federal Government's Libby Dam project which flooded much of the former main line beneath Lake Koocanusa. It is on a new 96 km (59½ mile) diversion and passes under the Elk Mountain from Wolf Creek to Fortina Creek.

Guided by laser beam the workers holed through on 21 June 1968 after 630 days drilling from both ends. The tunnel is 12 479 m (36 970 ft) or 10 ft under 7 miles, including a 'cut and cover' section 509 m (1670 ft) long at the western end, and is 5·486 m (18 ft) wide and 7·162 m (23 ft 6 in) high above rail-level.

The tunnel was officially opened on 7 November 1970 when the photograph was taken, the special train running from Libby to Stryker via the new line and returning via the old route.

The north portal is closed by a door after the passage of a train and two 2000 hp fans, 2616 mm (103 in) diameter with a capacity of 8963 m³ (307 000 ft³) per min clear the fumes from the tunnel in 17 min and provide cooling air for the engines as they pull up the grade towards the east.

The third longest tunnel is the Moffat Tunnel, 9997 m (6 miles 373 yd), under James Peak,

A passenger train climbing the series of zigzags which carried the Great Northern Railway over the Cascade Range while the first Cascade Tunnel was being built, from 1892 to 1900. This temporary line was itself a remarkable piece of railway engineering (Burlington Northern Inc)

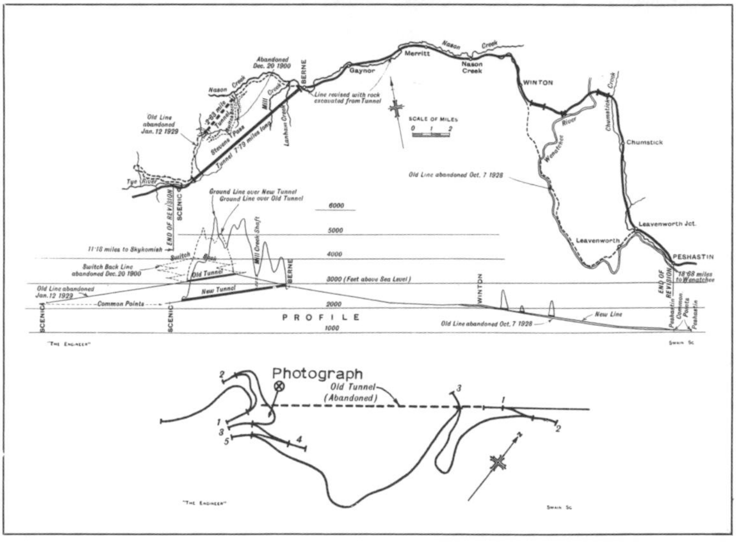

Plans and sections showing the positions of the first and second Cascade Tunnels, the old and new lines and the course of the temporary zigzags, and also the position from which the above photograph was taken (*The Engineer*)

Colorado, on the Denver & Salt Lake Railroad, the 'Moffat Road'.

In 1921 the people of Denver and near-by counties voted and passed a bond issue of \$15 470 000 to construct the Moffat Tunnel, thus creating the 'Moffat Tunnel District'. Work began in 1921 and the tunnel was holed through on 12 February 1927. It was opened on 27 February 1928, at an altitude of 2822 m (9257 ft), replacing the original line over the Rollins, or Corona, Pass at an altitude of 3554 m (11 660 ft). With the Dotsero Cut-off it shortened the route from Denver to Salt Lake City by 278 km (173 miles). The original pioneer bore carries water from the western slope of the Rockies to Denver where it is part of the main supply.

On 11 April 1947 the D. & SLRR merged with the Denver & Rio Grande Western Railroad which rents the tunnel from the Moffat Tunnel District. The bonds will mature in 1982.

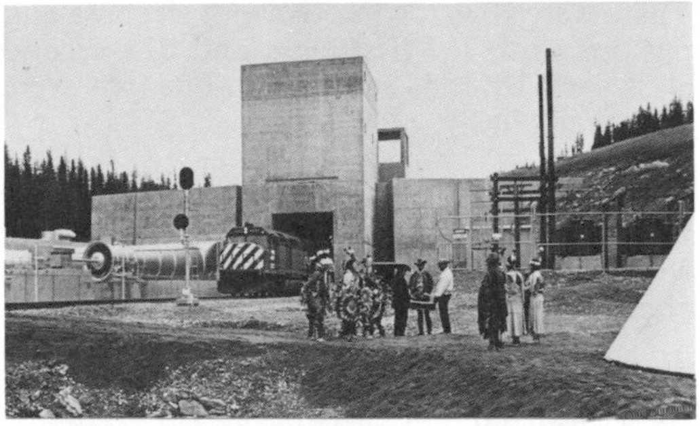

Red Indians at the dedication ceremony at the opening of Flathead Tunnel, Montana, on 7 November 1970. The photograph shows the eastern portal (Burlington Northern Inc)

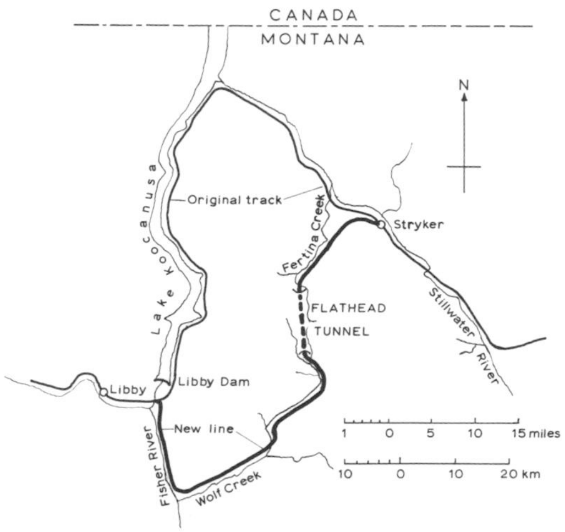

Map showing the position of Flathead Tunnel

The most difficult tunnel in America was the Hoosac Tunnel on the Boston & Maine Railroad in Massachusetts, on the main line from Boston to Albany. It was begun in 1851 and took 14 years to complete, at a cost of $20 000 000. The engineer was Herman Haupt (1817–1905). It was opened on 9 February 1875 and is 7562 m (4 miles 1230 yd) long. In 1911 it was electrified at a cost of $541 000. The electrification was abandoned on 24 August 1946 when the entire operation went over to diesels.

The shortest tunnel in the USA is Bee Rock Tunnel near Appalachia, Virginia, on the Louisville & Nashville line from Corbin, Kentucky, to Norton, Virginia, opened in 1891. It is 9 m (10 yd) long.

A natural tunnel was used on the Bristol–Appalachia section of the Southern Railway system at Glenita about 72 km (45 miles) west of Bristol, Tennessee. In the course of surveying the line along the Stock Creek Valley in 1880 the party reached a natural amphitheatre with a rock wall 61 m (200 ft) high and an arched tunnel entrance 27 m (90 ft) high and 36·5 m (120 ft) wide into which the stream flowed. It was eroded by waters east of Purchase Ridge forcing through the mountain wall into Clinch Basin. The tunnel was found to be 240 m (788 ft) long and averaged 30 m (100 ft) high and 40 m (130 ft) wide. After blasting through about 5 m (16 ft) of rock the engineers were able to construct the railway formation beside the stream.

The eastern portal of Moffat Tunnel showing the door closed to enable air to be blown through the tunnel

SOME CANADIAN FACTS AND FEATS

At the time of the union of the Canadian Provinces on 1 July 1867 Canada had 15 railways totalling 4015 km (2495 miles), employing 9391 persons. There were 485 locomotives, 310 first class and 374 second class cars which carried a total of 2 920 000 passengers in the year, and 4214 freight cars which carried 2 260 000 tons.

Prince Edward Island entered the Confederation in 1873 while its railway system was under construction. The 338 km (210 miles) of line were taken over by the Federal Government and opened for traffic in April 1875.

In 1882 the Grand Trunk and the Great Western railways, which had 1455 km (904 miles) of route, were amalgamated, together with another 761 km (473 miles) of line in Western Ontario.

Twenty years after Confederation, in 1887, Canadian railway route length was 18 815 km (11 691 miles), of which the Canadian Pacific system owned 6717 km (4174 miles) and the Grand Trunk system 4181 km (2598 miles). There were 1633 locomotives, 74 sleeping and parlour cars, 762 first class and 514 second class cars. By 1888 some main-line cars were electrically lit.

The first steel rails in Canada were used about 1871. In 1876 it was reported that there were 3659 km (2273¾ miles) of steel rails in Canada, about 45 per cent of the main routes.

The first railway in Newfoundland, from St John's to Hall Bay, was begun on 9 August 1881, against much local opposition and violence. The 870 km (547 miles) of 1·067 (3 ft 6 in) gauge line, from St John's to Port aux Basque, were completed in 1896. The first passenger trains ran on 29 June 1898.

The first iron railway bridge in Nova Scotia was built in 1877 at Elmsdale to replace the timber bridge. It was decided at this time to replace all Canadian wooden bridges by iron.

By the end of the 19th century Canadian railway route length had grown to 28 133 km (17 481 miles) of which the Canadian Pacific

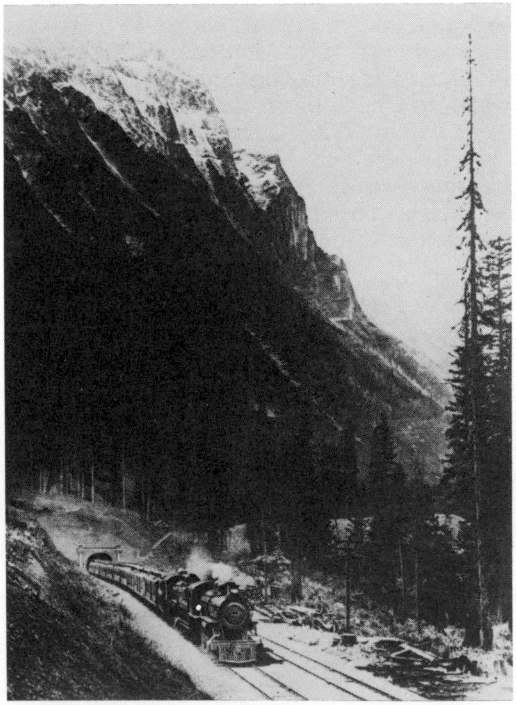

Steam train emerging from the east end of Connaught Tunnel. Today the track through the tunnel is singled to enable 'piggy-back' trains to operate

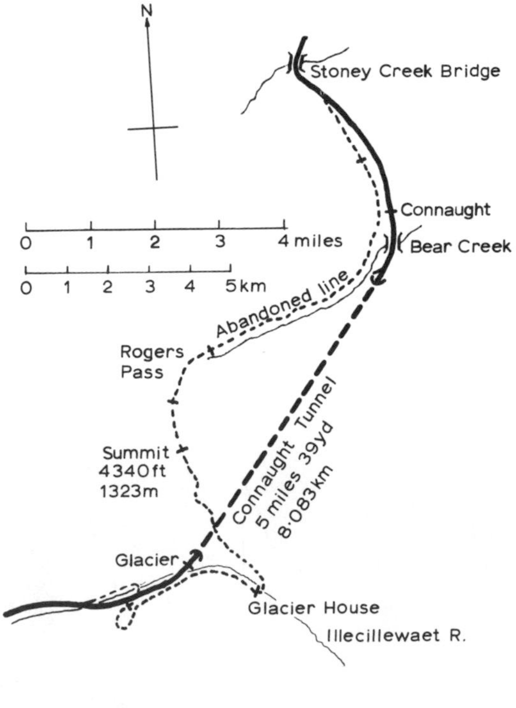

Map showing the Connaught Tunnel and the original line over Rogers Pass

Railway had 11 061 km (6873 miles), the Grand Trunk Railway 5050 km (3138 miles), and the Intercolonial Railway 2432 km (1511 miles).

One of the loneliest railways in Canada, the Temiskaming & Northern Ontario Railway, was completed to Moosonee on an estuary of James Bay in 1931.

The Canadian Northern and the Grand Trunk Pacific Railways were completed in 1915 by which year Canada had three transcontinental routes. The Canadian Northern ran from Quebec to Vancouver and the GTPR, including the National Transcontinental Railway, extended from St John, New Brunswick, to Prince Rupert in British Columbia.

The Canadian route length was now 57 264 km (35 582 miles), more than double that in 1900. In addition the Canadian Pacific Railway and the Grand Trunk Railway owned extensive mileage in the USA.

The Canadian National Railways was formed in 1917. For an outline of its history see p. 48.

Newfoundland entered the Confederation in 1949 when its 1135 km (705 miles) of 1·067 m (3 ft 6 in) gauge lines were absorbed by the Canadian National Railways. Of this, 880 km (547 miles) are on the main 'Overland Route' from St John's to Port aux Basques. In 1948 the Newfoundland lines carried 274 497 passengers and 856 560 tons of freight.

Today Canadian railways own 3311 locomotives of which 3292 are diesel and 19 electric; 2444 passenger cars and 188 770 freight cars. Each year they operate 153 000 000 000 revenue ton-km (95 000 000 000 ton-miles) of freight service and 4 900 000 000 passenger-km (3 000 000 000 passenger-miles).

Carry Brothers Tunnel in the Lower Kicking Horse Canyon on the Canadian Pacific Railway. The first tunnel of 1884 was abandoned in 1887 following collapse and the line was taken round the hill on sharp curves. This second tunnel, 213 m (700 ft) long and concrete lined, was opened in 1906. After further trouble, in the 1950s the ground was removed from above the tunnel but the concrete shell was left as a shelter from snow drifts

The Canadian eastbound transcontinental train in 1970 near the Great Divide at the summit of the Canadian Pacific Railway, 1435 m (5332 ft), the highest railway summit in Canada (Canadian Pacific Ltd)

The longest tunnel in Canada is the 8083 m (5 mile 39 yd) Connaught Tunnel in the Selkirks on the Canadian Pacific Railway. The headings met, below the 2890 m (9483 ft) peak of Mount Macdonald, on 19 December 1915. The double-track bore, opened on 6 December 1916, replaced the difficult route over the Rogers Pass which reached an altitude of 1323 m (4340 ft) and was threatened every winter with snow blockage despite 6·5 km (4 miles) of snow-sheds. It shortened the route by 7·24 km (4½ miles), lowered the summit by 165 m (540 ft) and eliminated curves amounting to seven complete circles.

Track was singled in 1959 to give greater clearances for 'piggyback' trains. At its deepest point the crown of the tunnel lies beneath a mile of rock.

The second longest tunnel is the 5073 m (3 mile 288 yd) Mount Royal Tunnel at Montreal on the Canadian National Railways. It was built by the Canadian Northern Railway at a cost of $3 000 000 and was opened on 21 October 1918. There are no other tunnels in Canada over 5 km (3 miles) long.

The highest railway summit in Canada is at the Great Divide on the Canadian Pacific Railway, 1435 m (5332 ft), where it crosses the Alberta-British Columbia boundary.

Canadian railway route length totals 72 089 km (44 794 miles). Of this Canadian National Railways owns 38 962 km (24 210 miles) in addition to 1146 km (712 miles) of 1·067 m (3 ft 6 in) gauge line in Newfoundland.

Canadian Pacific announced its new corporate identification programme on 17 June 1968, from which date its various interests became known as CP Rail, CP Air, CP Ships, CP Transport (road vehicles), CP Express, CP Hotels and CP Telecommunications. On 5 July 1971 supplementary Letters Patent were issued to the company changing its corporate name from 'Canadian Pacific Railway Company' to 'Canadian Pacific Limited' in English and to 'Canadian Pacifique Limitée' in French. In 1973 CP Rail operated 26 696 km (16 286 miles) in addition to 8000 km (4724 miles) in the USA, with 1181 diesel locomotives, 53 diesel railcars, 403 passenger cars and 72 501 freight cars.

CP Air operates 22 jet planes over 80 500 km (50 000 miles) of unduplicated route linking five continents. CP Hotels has five city and resort hotels across Canada.

Section 3
MOTIVE POWER

LOCOMOTIVE TYPES

Steam locomotives are generally referred to by the system of wheel arrangements invented in 1900 by Frederic M. Whyte (1865–1941), an official of the New York Central Railroad. It can easily be worked out from the examples below. All locomotives are imagined facing to the left.

2–2–2

2–4–0

4–4–2 ('Atlantic')

0–4–0

0–6–0

4–6–2 ('Pacific')

2–8–0

2–10–4

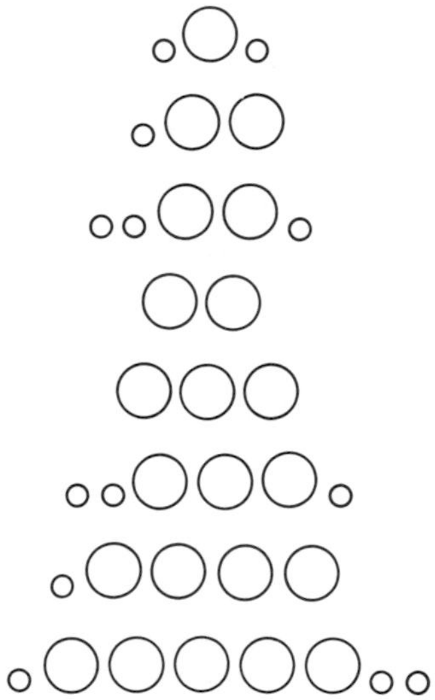

The European continental countries use an axle system, thus a 4–6–2 is a 2C1. Germany and Switzerland denote the number of driving-axles as a fraction of the total number of axles: for example, a 4–6–2 is a 3/6, a 2–8–0 a 4/5.

Electric and diesel locomotives are referred to by a letter indicating the number of driving axles: A is one, B two, C three and D four.

A locomotive on two four-wheeled bogies with a motor to each axle is a Bo Bo. The small 'o' indicates that the axles are not coupled. If the wheels were coupled it would be a BB. A locomotive on two six-wheeled bogies with all axles driven but not coupled is a Co Co; if the axles are coupled it is a CC; if the centre axle is not driven it is an A1A A1A. If the trucks are articulated by a connection taking buffing and drag stresses a plus sign is used; for example the locomotives of the Furka–Oberalp and Brig–Visp–Zermatt railways in Switzerland are Bo + Bo.

LOCOMOTIVE PROGRESS

The first railway locomotive was built in 1803 by Richard Trevithick at Coalbrookdale Ironworks in Shropshire for the 914 mm (3 ft)

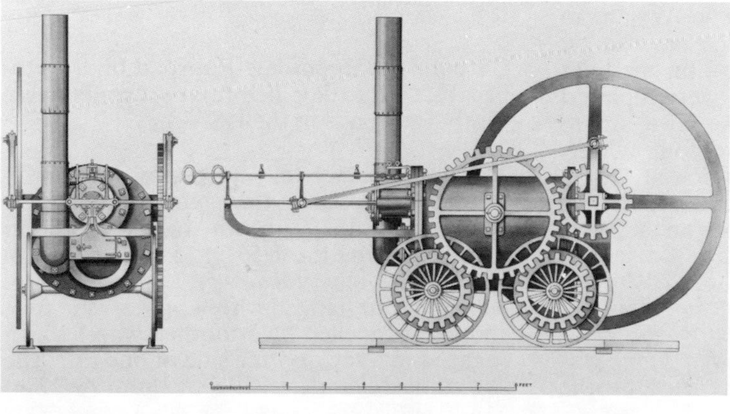

Drawing by the Science Museum, London, of Trevithick's Coalbrookdale Locomotive of 1803, the world's first steam locomotive, probably intended for the tramway at Coalbrookdale Ironworks, Shropshire. No evidence has been discovered, however, to prove that it actually ran gauge plateway there. It is shown in the drawing on p. 107, and a model of it can be seen at the National Railway Museum at York. It had a single horizontal cylinder mounted inside the boiler and it ran on flat-tyred wheels with no flanges.

Trevithick's second locomotive was built while he was employed as engineer at the Penydarren Ironworks near Merthyr Tydfil in South Wales. On 22 February 1804 it pulled 10 tons of iron, 70 men and five extra wagons for 15 km ($9\frac{1}{2}$ miles) at nearly 8 km/h (5 mph). This was the first locomotive to have a return-flue boiler, steam blast in the chimney, and all four wheels driving, by gearing. Drawings of this can be seen at the Science Museum, London.

The locomotive was introduced to Northumberland, England, by Christopher Blackett, proprietor of Wylam Colliery. He ordered an engine on Trevithick's principle through his engineer John Steel and it was built at Gateshead, County Durham, by John Whinfield. However, when it was tried in 1805 it was too heavy at over 5 tons and was rejected. **It was the first locomotive to have flanged wheels.**

The short 'D'-pattern slide-valve was introduced by Matthew Murray at Leeds, England, in 1806.

The first locomotive built entirely at Wylam, Northumberland, was built in 1813 by Timothy Hackworth and Jonathan Forster assisted by William Hedley. It ran on four flanged wheels and had a 1·219 m (4 ft) diameter boiler 3·048 m (10 ft) long. The two vertical cylinders at the rear drove the wheels through levers and connecting-rods to a centre jack-shaft geared to the two axles. It was known as the *Grasshopper*.

The next two engines built at Wylam in 1814–15 were of the same type but ran on eight wheels to spread the load on the light track until the cast-iron rails were replaced by wrought iron in 1830. Two more 'Grasshopper'-type engines on four wheels were built by Foster and Rastrick at Stourbridge, Worcestershire, as late as 1828. One, named *Agenoria*, was put to work on the Shutt End Railway from Lord Dudley's Colliery at Kingswinford to the Staffordshire & Worcestershire Canal. It is now in the National Railway Museum, York.

The other, named *Stourbridge Lion*, was sent to the USA where it was tried on the Carbondale–Honesdale Railroad on 8 October 1829, the day before the opening (see 'Early Railroads in the USA'.)

The last of the 'Grasshoppers', *Agenoria* built at Stourbridge, Worcestershire, by Foster and Rastrick in 1828 and now preserved at the National Railway Museum, York. The system of links forming the parallel motion to maintain the piston rod in the axis of the cylinder can be understood from this photograph and the two previous illustrations. From this date crossheads became universal and the parallel motion was dispensed with

The first commercially successful locomotive was most probably that built by Matthew Murray in 1812 to an order by John Blenkinsop for the 1·53 m (5 ft $\frac{3}{4}$ in) gauge Middleton Colliery Railway, Leeds, England. It ran on four flanged wheels which were free, and was propelled by a toothed wheel which engaged in a rack on the side of one rail. The two vertical cylinders, 229 × 559 mm (9 × 22 in) drove cranks set at right angles and geared to the rack wheel. It weighed about 5 tons. (For further details see p. 11.)

The spring-loaded safety valve was introduced in 1812 by James Fenton at Leeds, England.

The locomotive bogie was patented by William Chapman in 1813.

A locomotive propelled by two legs working at the rear and pushing it along was patented on 22 May 1813 by William Brunton (1777–1851). An example was built at Butterley, Derbyshire, for Newbottle Colliery near Newcastle. In 1815 it was fitted with a new boiler which exploded on 31 July 1815 killing five, fatally injuring nine and maiming 43 others.

George Stephenson's first locomotive, named *Blücher*, was completed at Killingworth near Newcastle upon Tyne on 25 July 1814. It had a boiler 863 mm (2ft 10in) diameter and 2·438 m (8 ft) long, in which the two 203 × 610 mm (8 × 24 in) cylinders were mounted vertically along the centre. They drove the wheels through counter-shafts geared to the two driving-axles.

In February 1815 Stephenson with Ralph Dodds, viewer at Killingworth Colliery, patented an engine in which the wheels were driven directly and coupled by either rods or chains.

The first engine under this patent was built in 1815. Its wheels were coupled by rods working on cranked axles. **This was the first use of cranked axles in a locomotive**, but they were abandoned as not strong enough and for a time wheels were connected by endless chains.

The loose-eccentric valve gear was introduced by George Stephenson in 1816 with the assistance of Nicholas Wood, and was used on the 'Rocket'- and 'Planet'-type engines until 1835.

Carmichael's valve gear with a single fixed eccentric was introduced in 1818. The end of the eccentric rod was fixed to two V-shaped 'gabs' in the form of an X which could be raised to engage the forward valve-pin or lowered to engage the backward pin. These pins were at opposite ends of a centrally pivoted lever.

The first locomotive to have its wheels coupled by rods was *Locomotion*, No. 1 of the Stockton & Darlington Railway, built by George Stephenson in 1825. The two vertical cylinders 241 × 610 mm ($9\frac{1}{2}$ × 24 in) were in line along the centre of the single-flue boiler and each drove one of the axles through rods and crank-pins on the wheels. Because these cranks were set at right angles one end of each coupling-rod had to be attached to a return crank.

The first four-cylinder locomotive was built by Robert Wilson of Newcastle upon Tyne, England, and was sold to the Stockton & Darlington Railway at the end of 1825. The vertical cylinders were in pairs on each side of the engine and drove the rear wheels.

The multi-jet blast-pipe was introduced in 1826 by Sir Goldsworthy Gurney (1793–1875). The fusible plug (a soft metal plug in the firebox crown which melts if uncovered by water and allows steam to damp down the fire) and expansion valve gear (allowing steam to be used expansively) were also introduced by him in the same year.

The first six-coupled locomotive was Hackworth's *Royal George* built at Shildon, County Durham, in 1827. It was also the first engine in which the cylinders drove directly on to the wheels without intermediate gearing or levers. The piston-rods, however, were guided by Watt-type parallel motion, not a cross-head. Cylinders were 279 × 508 mm (11 × 20 in) and exhausted into a single blast-pipe. It weighed 8·4 tons.

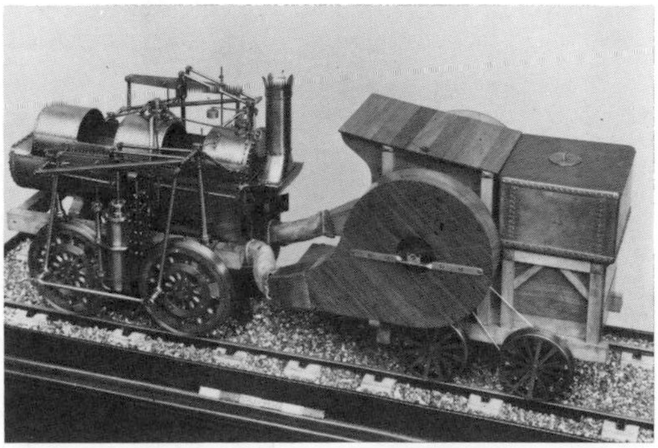

Model of Marc Seguin's locomotive in the Science Museum, London. In addition to being the first French steam locomotive, built in 1829, it was the first to have a multi-tubular boiler (The Science Museum, London)

The multi-tubular boiler was patented in 1827 by Marc Séguin and it was used on the first French steam locomotive, built by him and first tested on 7 November 1829 on the Saint-Etienne–Lyon Railway, opened in 1830. A forced draught was provided by two rotary fans on the tender, driven by the wheels. The engine weighed nearly 6 tons in working order and could haul 30 tons on a gradient of 1 in 167 at 7·25 km/h ($4\frac{1}{2}$ mph). A model of this engine can be seen in the Science Museum, London.

The first locomotive in which the wheels were driven directly from the piston-rod working in a crosshead was Stephenson's 0–4–0 for the Bolton & Leigh Railway where it was named *Lancashire Witch* in 1828. The 229 × 610 mm (9 × 24 in) cylinders mounted on the rear of the boiler drove the front coupled wheels which were 1·292 m (4 ft) diameter. This engine also incorporated expansion valve gear in a primitive form. It was the first locomotive to be entirely suspended on leaf springs.

Stephenson's *Rocket* of 1829 incorporated the same arrangement of cylinders which, however, were only 203 × 419 mm (8 × $16\frac{1}{2}$ in). It was the first engine to combine a multi-tubular boiler and a blast-pipe. Driving-wheels were 1·435 m (4 ft $8\frac{1}{2}$ in) diameter and the weight of the engine was only $4\frac{1}{4}$ tons. It won the £500 prize at the Rainhill Trials. The design was mainly by Robert Stephenson.

The first inside-cylinder engine (or 'inside connected') engine, driving on to a crank-shaft, was *Novelty* built by Braithwaite to a design by Ericsson. It was also the first well-tank engine. The 152 × 305 mm (6 × 12 in) vertical cylinders drove the front axle through bell-cranks. It was entered in the Rainhill Trials in 1829, but failed.

The first locomotive powered by a horse walking on a moving platform was designed by T S Brandreth. In the Rainhill Trials *Cycloped* achieved a speed of 24 km/h (15 mph).

In the USA a similar locomotive was designed by D C Detmold for the South Carolina Canal & Railroad in 1830. It was named *Flying Dutchman* and won a $300

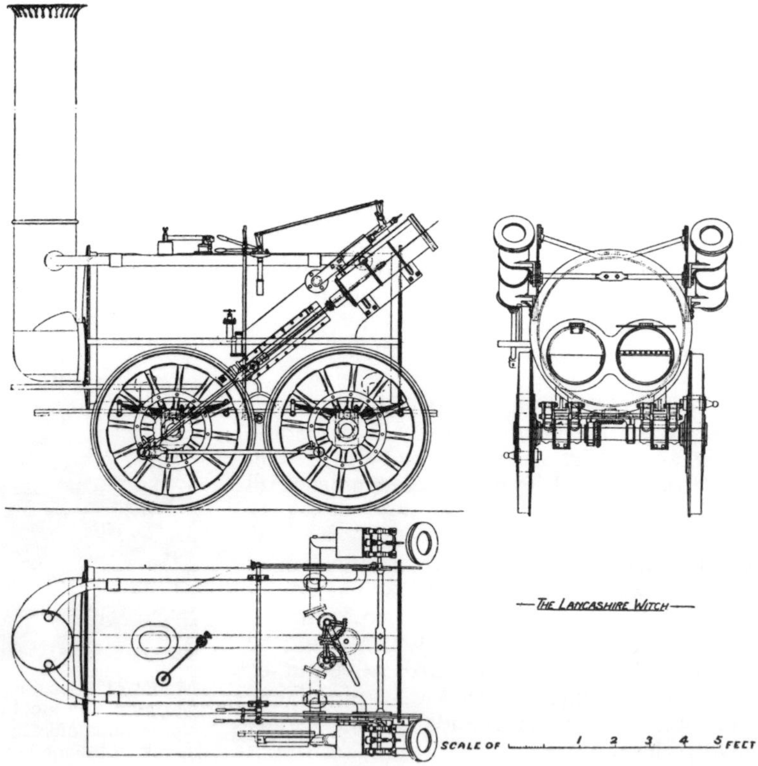

Stephenson's *Lancashire Witch* built in 1828 for the Bolton & Leigh Railway in Lancashire (*The Engineer*)

prize. On an experimental trip it pulled twelve passengers at 19 km/h (12 mph).

The bar-frame and haycock firebox first appeared in the 0–4–0 *Liverpool* built by Edward Bury, largely to the design of James Kennedy (1797–1886), and tried on the Liverpool & Manchester Railway in June 1830, two months before the line opened. It had 304 × 457 mm (12 × 18 in) cylinders driving on to a cranked axle. It was a highly advanced engine at the time. The inside cylinders became standard British practice and the bar-frame standard American practice. The multi-tubular boiler and smokebox were replacements soon after construction.

It was sold to the Petersburg Railroad, USA, in 1833 (see p. 116).

The first engine to be built with a smokebox was the Stephensons' *Phoenix* built in 1830 for the Liverpool & Manchester Railway. The *Rocket* was soon afterwards rebuilt with this feature which became universal.

Stephenson's 2–2–0 engine *Planet* built in 1830 for the Liverpool & Manchester Railway had inside cylinders enclosed within the smokebox. **It was the first engine to be built with outside sandwich frames and outside bearings**, a feature of British practice which survived in Stephenson's designs for many years. (The 'sandwich' frame consisted of a slab of oak or ash between two iron plates.)

Hackworth's first inside-cylinder 0–4–0 was built at Shildon in 1830 for the Stockton & Darlington Railway and was named *Globe*. The 229 × 406 mm (9 × 16 in) cylinders were mounted beneath the driving-platform at the rear.

The first locomotive in which the outside cylinders were attached to the frame instead of to the boiler was the *Union* built by Rothwell, Hick & Rothwell of Bolton, Lancashire, in 1831 for the Bolton & Leigh Railway. It was a 2–2–0 with a vertical boiler, 229 × 457 (9 × 18 in) cylinders and 1524 mm (5 ft) driving-wheels.

The first locomotive of Stephenson's 'Planet'-type inside-cylinder 0–4–0 to be delivered to America was originally named *Stevens* in honour of John Stevens (see 'Early Railroads in the USA'), but was renamed *John Bull*. It went into service on the Camden & Amboy Railroad on 12 November 1831. Because of a

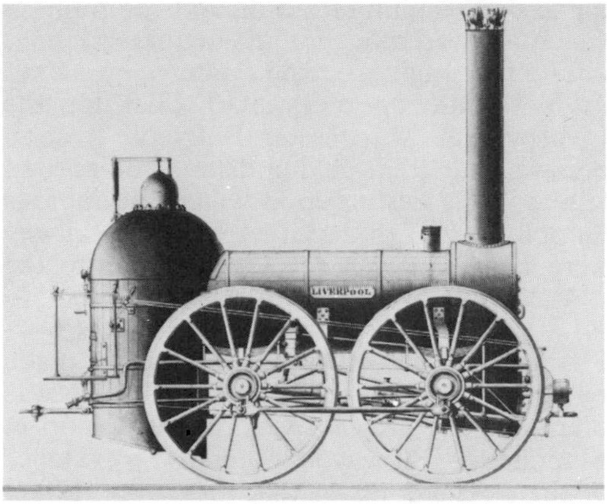

Edward Bury's inside-cylinder 0–4–0 *Liverpool* built at Liverpool in 1830 for the Liverpool & Manchester Railway. In 1833 it was sold to the Petersburg Railroad, USA, and it was probably this locomotive which established the bar-frame construction which became universal in North American locomotive practice (The Science Museum, London)

tendency to leave the rails a two-wheeled truck and pilot was fitted in front. This was **the first locomotive pilot, or 'cowcatcher'**. It ran until 1865 and is now preserved in the Smithsonian Institution, Washington, DC. In 1893 it travelled to the Chicago World's Fair under its own steam.

The classic British 'single-wheeler' was established by Robert Stephenson in a patent on 7 September 1833. It was a development of the 'Planet' type with a pair of wheels behind the firebox, becoming a 2–2–2, the success of

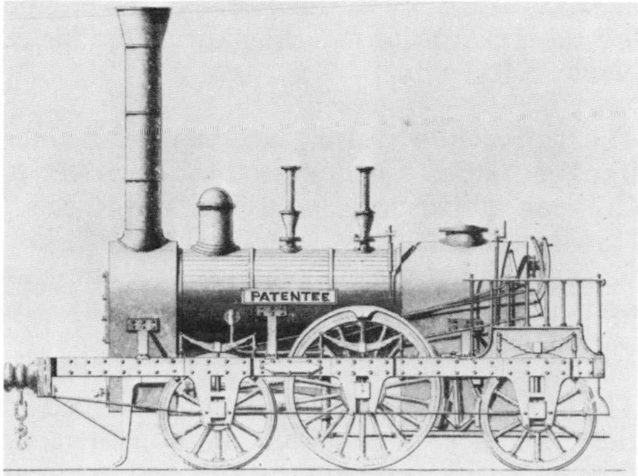

Stephenson's 2–2–2 *Patentee*, the first of the 'classic' British single-wheelers, built by Robert Stephenson & Company in 1833 for the Liverpool & Manchester Railway (The Science Museum, London)

the design resulting from the outside framing which allowed space for an adequate firebox.

The first engine, named *Patentee*, was built at Newcastle upon Tyne in 1833 for the Liverpool & Manchester Railway. It soon became widely adopted in Britain and abroad and was the design upon which the famous Gooch 'Singles' of the Great Western Railway were based. It was developed also into the 0–4–2 and 0–6–0 goods engines.

First experiments with piston-valves were made by Robert Stephenson in 1832. A design was prepared for a locomotive for the Liverpool & Manchester Railway, but there is no evidence of their behaviour, or that they were in fact used.

The 'petticoat' blast-pipe was also introduced by Robert Stephenson in 1832, by flaring the base of the chimney and extending it down into the smokebox to achieve a better smokebox vacuum.

A steam-trumpet was introduced on the Leicester & Swannington Railway following an accident at a road crossing on 4 May 1833.

The steam-brake was introduced by Robert Stephenson in 1833, and was incorporated in his 'Patentee'-type 2–2–2.

The first inside-cylinder 0–6–0, a development of the Stephenson 'patent' type, was built by Robert Stephenson in 1833.

The bogie was first used on a British locomotive in 1833 on J. & C. Carmichael's 0–2–4 engine for the 1·372 m (4 ft 6 in) gauge Dundee & Newtyle Railway.

The 'gab motion' (valve gear) operated by four fixed eccentrics was first used by Forrester & Company, Liverpool, in 1834–6, and R. & W. Hawthorn of Newcastle upon Tyne in 1835. Robert Stephenson & Company used the gear first on the 'patent'-type 0–4–2 *Harvey Combe* built in 1835.

The cylindrical smokebox was introduced in the USA in 1834 and was common there by the mid 1850s. It became established in Great Britain about 1900, but the old 'D' type was still being made by the London, Midland & Scottish and the Southern railways in the 1930s.

The balanced slide-valve was first patented by Hiram Strait of East Nassau, New York, on 25 June 1834. Its purpose was to eliminate the direct pressure of the steam on the top of the valve. It was first used on a railway engine by John Gray on the Liverpool & Manchester Railway in 1838. George W. Richardson patented an improved balanced slide-valve in the USA on 31 January 1872.

John Gray's expansion valve gear was first used in 1839 on the North Midland Railway. It was a complicated gear known as the 'Horse Leg' motion. Its purpose was to cut off the steam at varying positions of the piston stroke to allow the remaining work to be done by the expansion of the steam.

The variable blast-pipe was introduced by Peter Rothwell of Bolton, Lancashire in 1839. It was in the form of a hollow cone which could be raised or lowered inside the blast-pipe orifice from a lever on the footplate. It was used on Sharp's heavy goods engines of 1848–9.

The locomotive superheater was introduced by R. & W. Hawthorn of Newcastle upon Tyne in 1839.

Long-travel valves, giving greater cylinder efficiency, were first used on the Hull & Selby Railway by John Gray in 1840. They had about 152 mm (6 in) travel.

They first became established in the USA. It was about 1900 before they were regularly used in England, on the Great Western Railway by G J Churchward and in 1909 by George Hughes (1865–1945) on the Lancashire & Yorkshire Railway, but it was nearly 30 more years before they were universally adopted in Britain.

Hall's brick arch in the firebox for smokeless combustion of coal was first tried in 1841. Previously engines had burned coke or, as in North America, wood. It did not come into general use for several years but is stated to have been used on the Scottish North Eastern Railway by Thomas Yarrow from about 1857.

The Stephenson 'Long-boiler' locomotive was introduced in 1841, with the *North Star* for the 1·524 m (5 ft) gauge Northern & Eastern Railway. To obtain a large heating surface with a longer boiler, without increasing the wheelbase, the firebox was placed behind the rear axle. Mainly 4–2–0s, 2–4–0s and 0–6–0s were built to this design, but they were unsteady at speed.

The first British application of sanding gear, to sprinkle sand on the rails to help the driving-wheels to grip, was applied by Robert Stephenson in 1841.

The Stephenson (or Howe) Link Motion—valve gear with two fixed eccentrics—was first used on locomotives for the North Midland Railway by Robert Stephenson in 1843.

The 'stationary-link' motion was first used by Daniel Gooch on the Great Western Railway and by his brother John Viret Gooch (1812–1900) on the London & South Western Railway in 1843.

Walschaert's valve gear was invented by Egide Walschaert in 1844. Its first use in Great Britain was on a Fairlie 0–6–6–0 built by the Yorkshire Engine Company, Sheffield, in 1876, and used on the East & West Junction Railway until converted by the makers to a 2–6–6–2 in 1881 for sale to the Nitrate Railways, Peru. In 1878 it was used on a 0–4–4 tank built by the Fairlie Engine Company, London, for the Swindon, Marlborough & Andover Railway. For its first use in the USA in 1874, see p. 119.

The pneumatic brake was invented by James Nasmyth (1808–90) in 1844.

The dial pressure gauge, replacing the mercurial gauge, was first proposed in Germany by Schinz in 1845. It was perfected in 1849 by Eugène Bourdon (1808–84) of Paris.

The balancing of locomotive driving-wheels was first applied on the London & Birmingham Railway in 1845 as a result of experiments with models carried out in Birmingham by George Heaton of Shadwell Street Mills. His models are preserved in the Museum of Science and Industry, Birmingham.

The first three-cylinder locomotive was built by Robert Stephenson for the Newcastle & Berwick Railway in 1846.

The compounding of locomotive cylinders (in which the steam is used twice, first at boiler pressure and then in partly expanded form at a lower pressure) was invented by John Nicholson, and in 1850 was first tried on the Eastern Counties Railway (see 'Von Borries', 'De Glehn', 'Du Bousquet', and 'W M Smith'.

The double-beat regulator valve was introduced by John Ramsbottom on the London & North Western Railway in 1850. His famous **duplex safety-valve** was introduced in 1856 together with the **screw reverser**, instead of the hand lever, and the **displacement lubricator**. It is possible that the screw reverser was used on the Aberdeen Railway a few years earlier.

The first all-steel tyres for locomotive wheels were produced by Alfred Krupp (1812–87) of Essen, Germany, in 1851 and examples were displayed at the Great Exhibition in London in that year. The first manufacturer in the USA was James Millholland (1812–75) of the Philadelphia & Reading Railroad in the early 1850s. In Great Britain they were introduced by Naylor and Vickers on the London & North Western Railway in 1859.

Steel tyres lasted for 322 000 to 483 000 km (200 000 to 300 000 miles), compared with 96 500 km (60 000 miles) for iron tyres.

The drop-gate, to facilitate fire-cleaning, was introduced by Edward Bury in 1852.

A smokebox superheater for steam locomotives was used in 1852 by J E McConnell (1815–83) at Wolverton on the London & North Western Railway.

Feedwater-heaters were first tried in 1854 by Joseph Hamilton Beattie on the London & South Western Railway and were first applied in 1855. His double firebox and combustion-chamber to enable engines to burn coal without producing smoke were introduced in 1859.

The straight-link motion, invented by Alexander Allan (1809–91), was first used on locomotives of the Scottish Central Railway in 1854.

The firehole deflector plate to assist combustion was first applied by G K Douglas on the Birkenhead, Lancashire & Cheshire Junction Railway early in 1858.

The combination of brick arch and firehole deflector plate was devised by Charles Markham (1823–88) while assistant locomotive superintendent on the Midland Railway under Matthew Kirtley (1813–74) at Derby. It was first used in 1859 on a Midland engine. It enabled coal to be burnt without the complication of the Beattie firebox.

The steam injector (for forcing water into a locomotive boiler against pressure) was invented by Henri Giffard (qv), the French balloonist, and was first used on locomotives by Sharp Stewart & Company, Manchester, England, in 1859. By 1860 nearly 30 injectors were in use on British locomotives. It was introduced in the USA by William Sellers (1824–1905) in 1860. In the first year he supplied 2800.

A steel locomotive firebox was first tried by Alexander Allan on the Scottish Central Railway in 1860. Steel fireboxes became general in American practice, but European engineers tended to continue with the copper firebox.

Steel boilers in place of wrought iron were first used by George Tosh on the Maryport & Carlisle Railway in 1862.

Steam tenders were introduced on the Great Northern Railway, England, in 1863 by Archibald Sturrock (1816–1909), the locomotive superintendent. Fifty were built, to increase the power of his 0–6–0 goods engines. Various troubles, including heavy maintenance costs, and complaints from men who were 'driving two engines and only getting paid for one' led to their withdrawal.

Some were rebuilt into small locomotives in 1870–3 by Isaac Watt Boulton (1823–99) at his famous 'siding' at Ashton-under-Lyne near Manchester.

While Sturrock was the first to use steam tenders extensively, they were first applied by the Verpilleux brothers, of Rive-de-Gier, France, who patented the invention on 26 September 1842.

The radial axlebox was invented by William Bridges Adams (qv) and was first used on some 2–4–2 tanks for the St Helens Railway in Lancashire, built by Cross & Company of St Helens in 1863.

The counter-pressure brake in which the engine is reversed so that the cylinders act as compressors thereby absorbing power and avoiding wear on tyres and brake-blocks, especially on long inclines, was first used with water-injection by F. Holt on the South Staffordshire Railway in 1856. The Le Châtelier system using hot water was introduced on the London & North Western Railway in 1868.

The water-tube firebox was introduced by Johann Brotan (1843–1923) in Austria about 1870. His semi-water-tube boiler was first used in 1902 and over 1000 were built in the following 25 years.

The compressed-air brake was first used by the Caledonian Railway, Scotland, by Steel and McInnes in 1871.

The non-automatic vacuum brake was introduced by J Y Smith on the North Eastern Railway, England, in 1874.

The hydraulic brake was introduced by Francis William Webb (1835–1906) on the London & North Western Railway.

Gresham's automatic vacuum brake was invented by James Gresham (1836–1914) and was first used in 1878. By this system the brakes are automatically applied on both portions of the train if it breaks in two. Gresham began his work on brakes while with Sharp Stewart & Company, Manchester, where, in 1864, he began improving the Giffard injector by providing means for adjusting the combining cone in relation to the steam cone.

The 'pop' safety-valve was patented in Britain by T. Adams in 1873 and was first used in 1874. A second patent in 1875 covered an annular pop chamber. In the USA, however, pop safety-valves were used from about 1867 (see p. 119).

On the Lancashire & Yorkshire Railway, England, a pop safety-valve was introduced by Henry Albert Hoy (1855–1910) about 1900.

The Ross pop safety-valve was patented in 1902 and 1904 by fitter R L Ross of Coleraine Shed on the Belfast & Northern Counties Railway. It was first used on a locomotive by

Bowman Malcolm (1854–1933), then locomotive superintendent of the B. & NC, on his 2–4–0 No. 57 in 1908. The first new engine to be fitted was the B. & NC 914 mm (3 ft) gauge compound 2–4–2 tank No. 112, also in 1908. It did not achieve extensive use in Great Britain until the 1920s.

The advantage of the 'pop' safety-valve was the small pressure difference, only about 0·07–0·14 kg/cm² (1–2 lb/in²) between opening and closing compared with 0·35 kg/cm² (5 lb/in²) or more in the Ramsbottom type.

Speed-indicators for locomotives were first used by John Ramsbottom on the London & North Western Railway in 1861. A superior pattern was devised by William Stroudley (1833–89), locomotive engineer of the London, Brighton & South Coast Railway, in 1874.

Steam reversing gear was first used by James Stirling (1800–76) on the Glasgow & South Western Railway in 1874.

The Davies & Metcalfe exhaust-steam injector, making use of exhaust steam for forcing water into the boiler, was introduced in 1876.

Steel plate frames instead of wrought iron were first used by F W Webb on the London & North Western Railway in 1886. The plate frame was peculiar to British and European locomotive practice. American practice used the built-up bar-frame, first used by Edward Bury at Liverpool.

Steam sanding gear, devised by Gresham and Holt (Francis Holt, 1825–93, works manager, Midland Railway, Derby), was introduced on the Midland Railway in 1886. By forcing sand beneath the driving-wheels it brought about a revival of the 'single-wheeler' locomotive in Britain where it was built until about 1900 and lasted until the mid-1920s.

The British four-cylinder simple engine was introduced by James Manson (1846–1935) on the Glasgow & South Western Railway in 1897, with the 4–4–0 No. 11.

The smoke-tube superheater was introduced in Germany by Wilhelm Schmidt in 1897. It was first used in Britain in May 1906 on the Great Western Railway two-cylinder 4–6–0 No. 2901 *Lady Superior* and on the Lancashire & Yorkshire Railway in two 0–6–0s.

A smokebox-type superheater was used by J A F Aspinall (1851–1937), chief mechanical engineer of the Lancashire & Yorkshire Railway, on his 4–4–2 No. 737 in 1899. **This was the first British superheated locomotive.**

The Lentz poppet-valve gear was first applied in Germany by Hugo Lentz in 1905. It used the type of valves familiar in internal-combustion engines. In Britain it was applied by H N Gresley (qv) to several types of London & North Eastern Railway locomotives.

The Caprotti poppet-valve gear was first fitted to an Italian locomotive in 1920.

The first British engine to be fitted with a booster was the Great Northern Railway 4–4–2 No. 1419 in 1923, later No. 4419 on the London & North Eastern Railway. The booster, common in America, was tried only on the LNER in Britain. It consisted of an auxiliary engine on the trailing truck which could be engaged and put into or out of operation as required.

The LNER tried boosters also on two 2–8–2 freight engines, two North Eastern Railway 'Atlantics' and a Great Central Railway 0–8–4 tank. The boosters were removed after a few years' trials.

The Giesl ejector for steam locomotives was developed over a long period by the Austrian

The Giesl Ejector was much used in its country of origin. Here is an example of its application to a 762 mm (2 ft 6 in) gauge 0–8–0 tank on the Steyrtalbahn at Garsten in Austria in 1975

engineer Dr Giesl Gieslingen, and was finished in 1951. Multiple exhaust jets along the centre-line of the smokebox exhaust into a chimney of oblong section with a length many times its width. It provides an equal draught through the boiler tubes for less back-pressure in the cylinders compared with the conventional blast-pipe.

It was widely applied in Austria and Czechoslovakia and was tried in Australia (NSW Government Railways 'C36' Class 4–6–0 No. 3616), India and East Africa. On British Railways it was tried on only two engines: standard 2–10–0 No. 92250, and a rebuilt Southern 'Pacific'. The National Coal Board, however, used it quite extensively and it was claimed to be 'worth several more wagons'.

NORTH AMERICAN LOCOMOTIVES

The reason that North American steam-locomotive development was generally anything up to 20 years in advance of British was probably that workers in the USA were better paid. As long as British railways could obtain good coal for a few shillings a ton, or could employ experienced fitters at about £1 a week in well-equipped works, it was of little consequence if the typical British inside valves and motion did take days instead of hours to dismantle and assemble, or if engines were inefficient.

All the biggest advances in steam locomotive development such as superheaters, coned boilers, cylindrical smokeboxes, large bearings, outside valves and motion, long-travel valves, side-window cabs, were well established in the USA many years before they became standard practice in Britain. Inside-cylinder engines were abandoned in the USA in the 1850s and inside valve gear soon after 1905. British Railways were still building them at Swindon in the 1950s.

The first locomotive 'pilot' (or 'cowcatcher') was fitted, together with a pair of leading wheels, to the *John Bull* on the Camden & Amboy Railroad (see p. 111). The engine, originally a 'Planet'-type 0–4–0, was built by Robert Stephenson & Company, Newcastle upon Tyne, in 1831. The pilot was fitted by Isaac Dripps, master mechanic on the C. & A.

The first locomotive headlight consisted of a fire of pine knots on a flat car pushed in front of the locomotive on the South Carolina Railroad in 1831. During the 1840s and 1850s candles and whale oil were burned in reflector lamps. Gas and kerosene lamps were introduced in 1859. Electric headlamps first appeared in 1881. The 'figure 8' oscillating headlight was introduced in 1936, and the sealed-beam headlight in 1946.

The first American 'national type' engine was the 4–2–0, originated by John B. Jervis (1795–1885) with the *Experiment* built at West Point Foundry, New York, in 1832 for the Mohawk & Hudson Railroad. It was **the first bogie locomotive in the world**. In its day it was also the fastest in the world, covering 22·5 km (14 miles) in 13 minutes. It was claimed that it reached 128·75 km/h (80 mph) over a 1·609 km (1 mile) stretch. The type was taken up by the Norris Brothers who redesigned it with the firebox behind the driving-axle to give more adhesive weight. Between 1835 and 1842 the 4–2–0 type formed nearly two-thirds of the total locomotives in the USA.

The iron bar frame for locomotives was introduced in the USA in 1833 by the 0–4–0 *Liverpool*, built by Edward Bury of Liverpool in 1830 and, after several rebuildings and changes of ownership, sold to the Petersburg Railroad in 1833. (See illustration p. 111.) Other Bury locomotives were exported to the USA in the 1830s.

The first recorded American-built iron-frame locomotive was the *Comet*, completed at West Point Foundry, New York, in January 1835 for the Tuscumbia, Courtland & Decatur Railroad, but this was a bolted framing with pedestals for the journals. George E. Sellers claimed to have built the first iron frame, but his first engine was completed in September 1835. Previous American locomotives had wood frames. The Bury-type bar frame was specified for several 4–2–0s built by Stephenson and Tayleur, Newton le Willows, Lancashire, in 1835.

The earliest use of American-built bar frames cannot be established. They are shown on a drawing of the 4–4–0 *Gowan and Marx* built in 1839 by Eastwick & Harrison (Philadelphia 1839–42) but it is not certain if they were actually used on this engine. This firm certainly built them in 1842 for the *Mercury* for the Boston & Worcester Railroad. The bar frame probably became

Norris 4–2–0 *Lafayette* of 1837 (The Science Museum, London)

The first American 4–4–0, designed by Henry R Campbell in 1836 while he was chief engineer of the Philadelphia, Germantown & Norristown Railroad, and completed in 1837. Two years later it was superseded by the 'classic' American 4–4–0, illustrated on pp. 26 and 238 (The Science Museum, London)

popular in American practice because it could be forged by a blacksmith.

Bells were first fitted on American locomotives in 1835 when the State of Massachusetts passed a law requiring this warning device.

The first locomotive to be exported from the USA was *Columbus* built by Ross Winans (1796–1877) of Baltimore for the Leipzig & Dresden Railway in 1837.

The archetypal American 4–4–0 was first patented on 5 February 1836 by Henry R. Campbell (*c* 1810–*c* 1870), chief engineer of the Philadelphia, Germantown & Norristown Railroad.

The first American 4–4–0 was completed in Philadelphia on 8 May 1837. The 'classic' American 4–4–0 with 'three-point suspension' first appeared in 1839. It was a direct development of the Norris 4–2–0.

About 1870 83–85 per cent of locomotives in the USA were this type of 4–4–0. Between 1840 and 1890 about 20 000 were built.

The first steam locomotive in Canada was the *Dorchester* built by Robert Stephenson & Company, Newcastle upon Tyne, England, in 1836 and delivered to the Champlain & St Lawrence Railway (opened between St John and Laprairie, Quebec, on 21 July 1836) where it worked until it blew up in 1867 and was scrapped.

The first American locomotive whistles known to have been fitted were on two locomotives built at Lowell, Massachusetts, in 1836, appropriately under the supervision of the engineer George Washington Whistler. The *Hicksville* entered service at Jamaica, on the Long Island Railroad, and was reported to make 'a shrill, wild, unearthly sound, like drawing a saw flat across a bar of iron'. The *Susquehanna* was tried at Wilmington, Delaware, at 56–64 km/h (35–40 mph), and was said 'to give awful notice of its approach to any point'.

A whistle was also fitted to the first Rogers engine, 4–2–0 *Sandusky*, built in 1837 for the Paterson & Hudson River Railroad (qv). It was the first locomotive in the State of Ohio. During its first trip on 6 October 1837 from Paterson NY, to New Brunswick, NJ, the whistle was used so much that the engine ran short of steam.

Sandboxes were first fitted to American locomotives in 1836 following a plague of grasshoppers in Pennsylvania. On 1 August it was decided to use them on the Tuscumbia, Courtland & Decatur Railroad. The sand was sprinkled on to the rails and it prevented the engines slipping on the squashed insects.

The steam brake was first used on a locomotive in the USA in 1848 by George S. Griggs (1805–70), master mechanic of the Boston & Providence Railroad. But many years elapsed before it was widely used.

The first variable cut-off valve gear in the USA was produced by Eltham Rogers of the Cuyahoga Steam Furnace Company of Cleveland, Ohio, in 1849 and was first used on the *Cleveland* engine for the Cleveland, Columbus & Cincinnati Railroad in March 1850.

In Canada, as in the USA, wood was the standard locomotive fuel for many years. Apart from the three locomotives of the short coal line in Nova Scotia in 1839 (see p. 19) the first experiments with coal were made about 1858–60; but it was into the 1870s before coal became generally used.

At first engines covered about 58 km (36 miles) on a cord of wood, but by 1859 this had risen to 80 km (50 miles). A 'cord' of wood was a stack 2·438 × 1·219 × 1·219 m (8 × 4 × 4 ft).

The Bissell truck, a short bogie with the pivot behind the rear axle and using inclined planes to support and to centre the front of the locomotive, was patented by Levi Bissell (1800–73) of Newark, NJ, on 4 August 1857. It was patented in Britain in May that year but was not used on a British locomotive until 1860. It rapidly replaced the centrally pivoted short truck. Bissell patented a two-wheeled pony truck in 1858. The most familiar application of the Bissell truck was on the 4–4–0 tanks built for the Metropolitan and District railways, London, by Beyer Peacock & Company, Manchester.

Bissell also patented an 'air spring' for locomotive suspension on 11 October 1841.

The early adoption in the USA of large numbers of driving-wheels was to obtain the necessary adhesion without excessive axle loading for the light track then in use.

The first 0–8–0 type was built for the Baltimore & Ohio Railroad in 1841 by Ross Winans of Baltimore. He later developed the 'Mud-Digger' type.

Baldwin's first 0–8–0 type appeared in 1846 when 17 were built for the Philadelphia & Reading Railroad. The two leading axles were mounted in a flexible truck.

The world's first 4–6–0, 'ten-wheeler', was *Chesapeake*. It was ordered in October 1846 by the Philadelphia & Reading Railroad and was delivered in March 1847 by Norris Brothers. Almost at the same time another, *New Hampshire*, was completed by Holmes Hinkley (1793–1866) for the Boston & Maine Railroad.

The first 2–6–0 was *Pawnee*, built in 1850 by James Millholland (1812–75) for the Philadelphia & Reading Railroad. This was a rigid machine. The proper 'Mogul'-type 2–6–0 followed the invention of the two-wheeled Bissell truck in 1858. The first 'Moguls' were built in 1860 by Baldwin of Philadelphia for the Louisville & Nashville Railroad.

The first engine in North America to have a boiler made entirely of steel was the inside-cylinder 0–6–0 *Scotia* built at the Hamilton Works of the 1·676 m (5 ft 6 in) gauge Great Western Railway of Canada in 1860. The steel was imported from England and cost 16 cents a pound. The total weight of the boiler was 4652 kg (10 356 lb) without the copper tubes.

The first 12-coupled engine was a 'camel'-type 0–12–0 tank named *Pennsylvania* designed by James Millholland and built at the Philadelphia & Reading Railroad's shops in 1863. It was used for banking coal trains over the summit between the Schuylkill and Delaware rivers. In 1870 it was rebuilt into a 0–10–0 tender engine.

The first regular 2–8–0, named *Consolidation*, in honour of the merging of the Lehigh & Mahanoy and Lehigh Valley railroads, was designed by Alexander Mitchell (1832–1908) in 1865. It gave its name to the type. It was

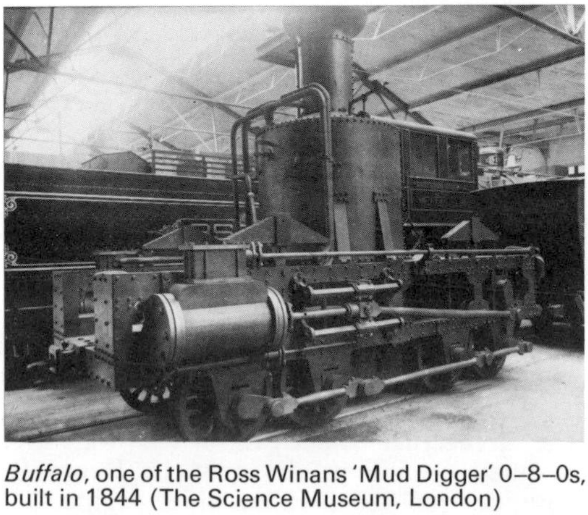

Buffalo, one of the Ross Winans 'Mud Digger' 0–8–0s, built in 1844 (The Science Museum, London)

The first 2–8–0, designed by Alexander Mitchell and built in 1866 by the Baldwin Locomotive Works for the Lehigh & Mahony Railroad. Its name *Consolidation* honoured the merger of the Lehigh & Mahony and the Lehigh Valley railroads.

built at Baldwin Locomotive Works, Philadelphia, in 1866 for the Lehigh & Mahanoy Railroad. It soon became the most numerous type in the USA.

In 1867 Mitchell introduced the 2–10–0 type for the Lehigh Valley Railroad.

The first 'pop' safety-valve was patented on 25 September 1866 by George W. Richardson of the Troy & Boston Railroad. (For its introduction and use in Great Britain see p. 114.)

Walschaert's valve gear was first used in the USA on a Mason-Fairlie double-bogie tank engine built in 1874 by William Mason (1808–83) for the Boston, Clinton & Fitchburg Railroad.

The wide Wootten firebox was invented in 1877 by John E. Wootten (1822–98) when general manager of the Philadelphia & Reading Railroad. It was designed to burn waste anthracite, or 'culm', which, because of its slow-burning qualities, required a larger area to give off the same heat as bituminous coal. It was first applied on the P. & R. 4–6–0 No. 411 in 1880. The grate area was 7·06 m^2 (76 ft^2). The cab was mounted midway along the boiler, ahead of the firebox, so that the engines became known as 'Camelbacks' or 'Mother Hubbards'. The firemen stood on a separate platform at the rear.

The first 'Pacific' or 4–6–2 type engine was built in 1886 at the Vulcan Iron Works, Wilkes Barr, Pennsylvania, to a design by George S. Strong for the Lehigh Valley Railroad. The class name 'Pacific' did not come into use until many years later.

The first 'Atlantic' or 4–4–2 type engine appeared in 1888, also built at the Vulcan Iron Works to a Strong design for the Lehigh Valley Railroad. The class name 'Atlantic' for the 4–4–2 type was suggested in 1894 by J K Kenly, general manager of the Atlantic Coast Railroad, for a group of 4–4–2s built by Baldwin.

The last, largest and fastest 'Atlantics' were the four oil-fired, streamlined engines built by the American Locomotive Company (ALCO) in 1935–7 to work the *Hiawatha* between Chicago and the 'Twin Cities' (Minneapolis and St Paul) on the Chicago, Milwaukee, St Paul & Pacific Railroad. They were the first steam locomotives in the world designed

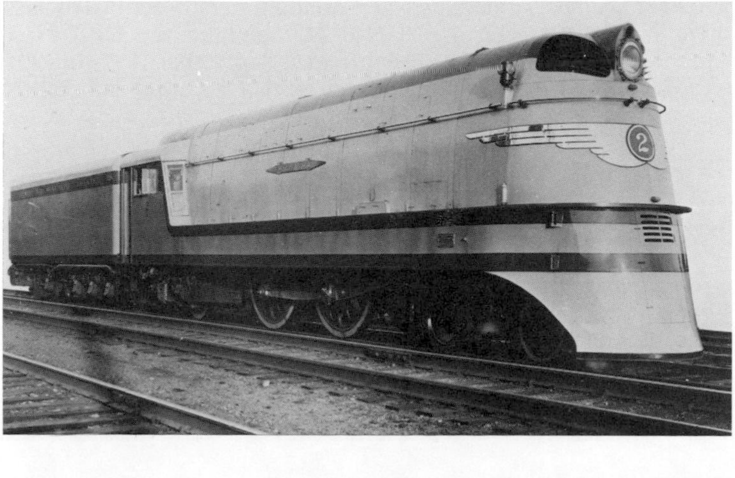

One of the four streamlined 'Atlantics', built by ALCO in 1935, for the *Hiawatha* between Chicago and the 'Twin Cities' on the Milwaukee Road. These were the first steam locomotives designed to run at speeds of over 161 km/h (100 mph) (The Milwaukee Road)

specifically to run at 161 km/h (100 mph) on every trip. They recorded speeds of over 193 km/h (120 mph).

The first 2–8–2 engines were built in 1897 by the Baldwin Locomotive Works for the 1·067 m (3 ft 6 in) gauge Japanese Railways. From these derived the class name 'Mikado'. It was introduced in the USA (where examples became affectionately known as 'Mikes') in 1903 on the Bismarck, Washburn & Great Falls Railway.

The Vanderbilt firebox was introduced by Cornelius Vanderbilt (1873–1942) in 1899 on 4–6–0 No. 947 of the New York Central & Hudson River Railroad, the railroad his great-grandfather Cornelius had established. The patent was for a boiler with a tapered barrel and a circular corrugated firebox resembling that introduced by Lentz in Germany in 1888. Although it had no stays, it gave trouble with leaks and breakages, and its limited grate area caused its early abandonment. Similar fireboxes were tried on the London & North Western and Lancashire & Yorkshire railways in England.

Vanderbilt also designed a tender with a cylindrical tank, which became popular on the Canadian National Railways from 1905 to 1930 and was widely used in the USA.

Wooden lagging for boilers, to prevent loss of heat, went out of use in the USA soon after 1900. Asbestos was first tried in 1873 on the Fitchburg Railroad, but it was not until about 1900 that, with magnesium lagging, it became widely adopted.

The first 2–6–2 or 'Prairie'-type tender engine was built by Baldwin Locomotive Works in 1900. It was No. 687 on the Chicago, Burlington & Quincy Railroad. Many were built for passenger and freight work on the Mid West lines and so gained the class name 'Prairie'.

The last examples in the USA were built in 1910, but the type became popular on some eastern European lines, and in Great Britain with Gresley's famous 'V2' Class introduced on the London & North Eastern Railway in 1936. The first of these, No. 4771 *Green Arrow*, is preserved at the National Railway Museum, York.

The 2–10–2 Santa Fe' type was introduced by the Atchison, Topeka & Santa Fe Railroad in 1903. These big Baldwin tandem compound machines were designed for helping heavy freight over the Raton Pass. The trailing-wheels assisted in running back down the grade.

The mechanical stoker of the Crawford plunger underfeed type was introduced on Pennsylvania Railroad 2–8–2s in 1905. From about 1915 it was gradually discarded in favour of the steam-jet overfeed system of the Street scatter type introduced about 1910, using a continuous chain belt. The Duplex stoker with screw conveyors was introduced in 1918 and replaced the Street type by 1920.

The Interstate Commerce Commission (qv) ruled that from 1 July 1938 the mechanical stoker should be used on all coal-burning passenger engines with over 72 570 kg (160 000 lb), and on freight engines with over 79 378 kg (175 000 lb), on the driving-wheels. As a general rule, grates of over 4·6 m² (50 ft²) merited mechanical stokers.

The first superheated locomotive in North America was Canadian Pacific Railway Class SR 4–6–0 No. 548, built in the CPR New Shops at Montreal in September 1891. In 1901 it was equipped with a Schmidt smokebox

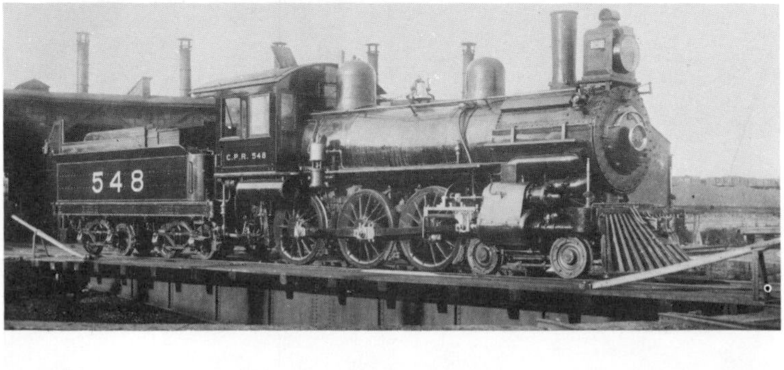

Canadian Pacific Railway 'SR' class 4–6–0 No. 548 as fitted in 1901 with a Schmidt smokebox superheater, said to be the first superheater application in the Western Hemisphere (Canadian Pacific Corporate Archives Collection)

superheater. It ran with this until 1911 when a CPR Vaughan & Horsey superheater was fitted. The engine was renumbered 392, Class D3c, in 1907; 7292 Class D4m in 1913; 292 Class D3c in 1922, and was scrapped in May 1929.

The Jacobs-Shupert firebox was introduced in 1908–9 on the Atchison, Topeka & Santa Fe Railroad. It dispensed with stay bolts and gave greater safety, but its numerous joints resulted in leaks and its use was not continued.

Boosters were first used in the USA on two-wheeled trailing trucks in 1915 and on four-wheeled trucks after 1925.

Baker valve gear, similar to Walschaert's but using a differently shaped link, was introduced in the USA in 1912–13.

The cast-steel one-piece engine frame, or bed, was first produced by General Steel Castings Corporation, USA, in 1925. At first the cylinders were separate. Later they were cast integrally with the frame and smokebox saddle, and this became universal from 1930. The whole was a triumph of the foundryman's craft and made possible the Lima 'Super Power' engines.

The four-wheeled trailing truck to carry increasingly heavy firebox loads was introduced in 1925 and with one-piece cast-steel frames in 1927. The six-wheeled truck first appeared in 1938.

The 2–8–4 'Berkshire' type originated in the USA in 1925, built by Lima Locomotive Works, Ohio, for the Illinois Central Railroad. It was the first of the Lima 'Super Power' engines.

The 2–10–4 type also originated in 1925 when Lima built some for the Texas & Pacific Railway. These gave the name 'Texas' to the type. The best-known examples were the magnificent 'Selkirks' of the Canadian Pacific Railway (see p. 126).

The popular American 4–8–4 type was introduced in 1927 on the Northern Pacific Railroad. The type represented the maximum power which could be obtained with eight coupled wheels. The type was widely adopted in the USA and Canada.

The first locomotive to be equipped with roller bearings throughout was a 4–8–4 built by ALCO in 1930 for the Timken Roller Bearing Company which numbered it 1111. Its rolling resistance was so small that on level track the 350 ton engine could be kept in motion by three girls. After demonstrations all over the country it was sold to the Northern Pacific Railroad, which numbered it 2626, in 1933.

A 'tender booster' or steam tender was fitted to the 2–10–4 'Texas'-type engines built by Baldwin for the Chicago Great Western Railroad in 1931. It added a further 8165 kg (18 000 lb) tractive effort making a total of 46 539 kg (102 600 lb). (See 'Steam Tenders'.)

The first all-welded boiler was fitted to a Delaware & Hudson Railroad 2–8–0 in 1934, and was given several years of trials before being passed as satisfactory by the Interstate Commerce Commission.

The most powerful non-articulated passenger steam locomotive was the Pennsylvania 6–4–4–6 'duplex' No. 6100 built at the Altoona shops in 1939. It ran for only 10 years. The 'duplexi' were not a success.

BRITISH AND EUROPEAN LOCOMOTIVE PROGRESS

The first British 4–4–0 was rebuilt from a Norris 4–2–0 of the Birmingham & Gloucester Railway between 1846 and 1850.

Daniel Gooch built ten 2·134 m (7 ft) gauge 4–4–0s for the Great Western Railway in 1855, but with a rigid wheelbase.

The first British bogie 4–4–0s to be built new were two by Robert Stephenson & Company for the Stockton & Darlington Railway in 1860 to a design by William Bouch (1813–76; brother of Sir Thomas). Next were the London, Chatham & Dover and Great North of Scotland railways. All these engines had outside cylinders.

The typical British inside-cylinder inside-frame 4–4–0 was introduced by Thomas Wheatley on the North British Railway in June 1871. The first of these, No. 224, went down with the first Tay Bridge in 1879. It was recovered and ran until 1919.

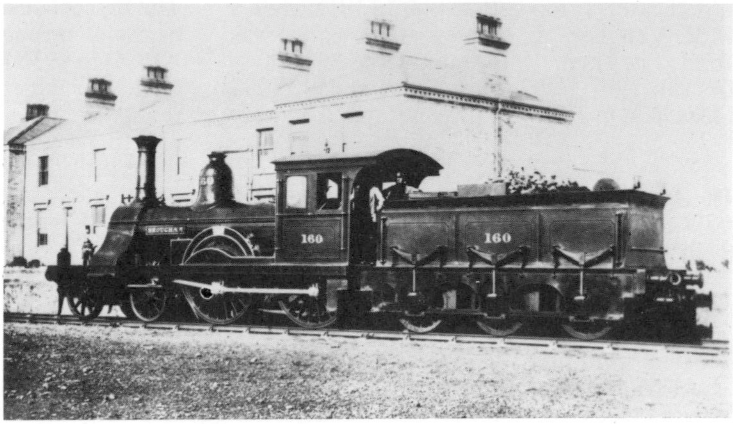

Stockton & Darlington Railway 4–4–0 No. 160 *Brougham* built by Robert Stephenson & Company in 1860 to designs by William Bouch, the first 4–4–0 bogie engine in Britain and the first with large American type cab (The Science Museum, London)

Great Western Railway 2–8–0 No. 2818 built at Swindon Works in December 1905, photographed near Sapperton Tunnel, Gloucestershire, in 1955. This was the first class of 2–8–0 in Britain. 2818 is preserved at the National Railway Museum, York, and 2857 on the Severn Valley Railway

The first 4–6–0 to run on a British railway, Highland Railway 'Jones Goods' No. 103, photographed at Stranraer in 1963. It is now preserved in the Glasgow Transport Museum

The first 2–6–0 or 'Mogul' to be built and to run in Britain appeared on the Great Eastern Railway in 1878. Fifteen were built by Neilson & Company of Glasgow to the design of William Adams (1823–1904).

The first eight-coupled main-line tender engines to run in Britain were two outside-cylinder 0–8–0s built in 1886 by Sharp Stewart in Manchester, originally for the Swedish & Norwegian Railway which, however, was unable to pay for them. In October 1889 they were acquired by the Barry Railway in South Wales where, in 1897, they were joined by two more of the same original order.

The first British inside-cylinder 0–8–0 was built in October 1892 at Crewe on the London & North Western Railway to a design by F W

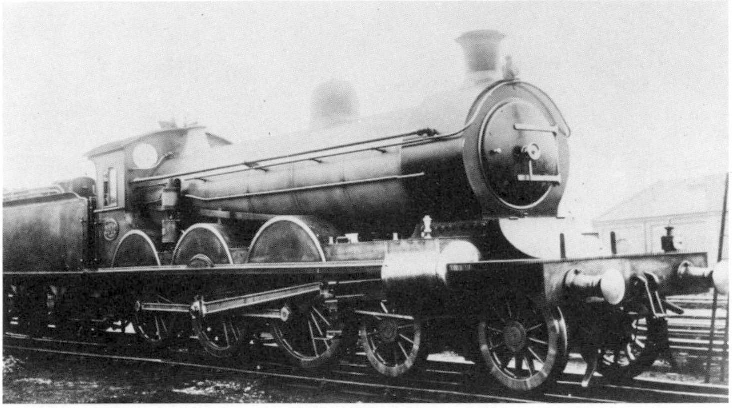

North Eastern Railway 4–6–0 No. 2002, one of the first two British 4–6–0 passenger engines, built at Gateshead in 1899 (The Science Museum, London)

Webb. It was Webb's only eight-coupled simple engine.

The 2–8–0 type was introduced in Britain by G J Churchward on the Great Western Railway in 1903, nearly 40 years after the type had become well established in the USA.

The first engine in service in Britain with a Belpaire firebox was the 0–6–2 tank No. 7 designed by Thomas Parker and built by the Manchester, Sheffield & Lincolnshire Railway at its Gorton Works in September 1891. It was renumbered 515 on 24 October 1893; became No. 5515, Class 'N5', on the London & North Eastern Railway in 1923; was renumbered 9250 in 1947 and was withdrawn in 1956 as British Railways No. 69250.

The first 4–6–0 to run on a British railway was Highland Railway No. 103 introduced in 1894 by David Jones (1834–1906). It ran until 1934 and, after a short spell working special trains in the early 1960s, it was placed in the Glasgow Transport Museum.

The first 4–6–0 passenger engine in Britain was the North Eastern Railway 'S' Class introduced in 1899 by Wilson Worsdell.

Britain's first 'Atlantic'-type locomotive was designed by H A Ivatt and was built at Doncaster in 1898 by the Great Northern Railway. The first, No. 990, was later named *Henry Oakley* after the GNR general manager. (See illustration.)

It was closely followed by the inside-cylinder 4–4–2 of the Lancashire & Yorkshire Railway designed by J A F Aspinall (1851–1937) and completed at Horwich Works in February 1899. This was remarkable for its

The first British 'Atlantic' heading a train out of Keighley, Yorkshire, on the Keighley & Worth Valley Railway, 8 October 1977. The engine was on loan from the National Railway Museum, York. The rear engine is British Railways standard Class 4 4–6–0 No. 75078

Britain's first 'Pacific', Great Western Railway No. 111 *The Great Bear*, designed by Churchward and built at Swindon in 1908 (British Railways)

2·210 m (7 ft 3 in) coupled wheels and high-pitched boiler.

Ivatt's large-boilered 'Atlantic' with wide firebox first appeared in 1900. Its appearance startled everyone at the time, but its performance was sadly inferior until it was rebuilt with superheater and piston-valves.

The first British 'Pacific' locomotive was built at Swindon in 1908 to a design by G J Churchward on the Great Western Railway. No. 111 *The Great Bear* was a large-boilered version of his successful four-cylinder 'Star' Class 4–6–0. Its weight restricted it to Brunel's London–Bristol railway, and the design was not repeated. It was withdrawn in 1923.

The first British 'Pacifics' to be produced as a class were designed by H N Gresley and built by the Great Northern Railway at Doncaster. No. 1470 appeared in April 1922 and was later named *Great Northern*. The most famous, No. 1472, appeared in January 1923 and was the first engine to be completed by the newly formed London & North Eastern Railway. It was renumbered 4472 and named *Flying Scotsman*.

The first ten-coupled engine in Britain was a three-cylinder 0–10–0 tank designed by James Holden (qv) and built at Stratford Works, London, on the Great Eastern Railway in 1902. Its purpose was to demonstrate that a steam train could accelerate to 48 km/h (30 mph) in 30 s, so defeating a proposal for a competing electric railway. It was the first three-cylinder engine in Britain since 1846 (see p. 113). Having fulfilled its purpose, it was rebuilt into a 0–8–0 in 1906.

Britain's other ten-coupled designs were the Midland Railway Lickey Banker 0–10–0 of 1919, the Ministry of Supply 2–10–0s of 1943 and the British Railways standard 2–10–0s of 1954.

The first 12-coupled tender engine in Europe was the 2–12–0 designed by Karl Gölsdorf for the Austrian State Railways. It was built in 1911 for the long 1 in 40 or 2·5 per cent grades on the Arlberg route.

The only other European 12-coupled engines were: 3 0–12–0 rack and adhesion tanks for the Austrian State Railways in 1911–12; 44 2–12–0s for the Württemburg State Railway in 1917–24; 10 0–12–0 tanks in

The most famous of the Gresley 'Pacifics', No. 4472 *Flying Scotsman*, fitted with headlight, bell and pilot (or 'cowcatcher'), photographed on 8 August 1972 when it was all but abandoned on Fisherman's Wharf, San Francisco. It was rescued by Mr W H McAlpine and returned to England in January and February 1973 and after a thorough overhaul it was made available again for steam-hauled trains in Britain. When not so used it is exhibited in the National Railway Museum, York

1922 and 20 2–12–4 tanks (12 two-cylinder in 1931 and 8 three-cylinder in 1942) for the Bulgarian State Railway; 2 2–12–2 rack and adhesion tanks for the German Reichsbahn (Austrian section) in 1941; a 2–12–0 six-cylinder compound for the French State Railways in 1947, and a metre-gauge 0–12–0 tank for the Zervanshja Mines, Yugoslavia, in 1947.

Britain's first eight-coupled passenger engine was the London & North Eastern Railway 2–8–2 No. 2001 *Cock o' the North* designed by H N Gresley and built at Doncaster in 1934. It was built with Lentz rotary-cam poppet valve gear and was later rebuilt with Walschaert's valve gear and a streamlined front. With five other 2–8–2s it worked between Edinburgh and Aberdeen. Their tractive effort of 19 714 kg (43 462 lb) was the highest of any British express locomotives. They had 1880 mm (6 ft 2 in) coupled wheels.

In 1943–4 all six were rebuilt into 4–6–2s by Edward Thompson, Gresley's successor.

The only other eight-coupled engines to be regularly used on passenger trains in Britain were the Great Western Railway '4700' Class 2–8–0s with 1727 mm (5 ft 8 in) wheels.

The first locomotive designed and built by the New Zealand Railways was a 2–6–2 tank, No. W192, in 1889.

RUSSIAN STEAM LOCOMOTIVES

The world's tallest locomotives are in Russia where the loading gauge permits engines 5·182 m (17 ft) high, 1·219 m (4 ft) higher than in Britain. They can also be up to 3·5 m (11 ft 6 in) wide.

The first Russian steam locomotive was probably a 2–2–0. It was built in 1833 at Nizhni-Tagil in the Urals by M. Cherepanov and it was run on a 0·8 km (½ mile) long 1·676 m (5 ft 6 in) gauge track.

The first locomotive in service in Russia was built by Timothy Hackworth at Shildon, County Durham, England, for the 1·829 m (6 ft) gauge 22·5 km (14 mile) long line from St Petersburg to Tsarskoe Selo in 1836. The engine cost £1885 including tender which was fitted with brakes. It was accompanied to Russia by T. Hackworth's eldest son John, then not quite 17 years old, and a group of men from Shildon. At Tsarskoe Selo John Hackworth was introduced to Tsar Nicholas. The engine was then given the blessing of the Greek Church before opening the railway, in November 1836.

In 1837 Hawthorns' of Newcastle upon Tyne built a 2–2–0 for the same railway.

The largest steam locomotives built in Russia were the two 'P38' simple expansion 2–8–8–4s built at Kolomna Works in 1954–5. They each weighed 214·9 tons and were 38·252 m (125 ft 6 in) long. They were the last main-line steam-locomotive type built in Russia.

The only 14-coupled steam locomotive was a 4–14–4 built in Russia in 1934. Its use was severely restricted by its rigidity and it saw little service before it simply 'disappeared'.

One of three 0–12–0 rack and adhesion tanks built in 1911–12 for the Eisenerz Railway between Leoben and Eisenerz in Austria, No. 197.303, photographed at Präbichl in 1975

Union Pacific Railroad 4–8–8–4 'Big Boy' No. 4019, one of the class of the world's largest steam locomotives, dating from 1941, hauling a freight train in Echo Canyon, Utah (Union Pacific Railroad)

THE POWER OF STEAM LOCOMOTIVES

Steam locomotive power can be represented in two ways. One is by **Tractive Effort** obtained by the formula $(D^2 \times S \times P)/W$ where D is cylinder diameter in inches, S is piston stroke in inches, P is steam pressure in lb/in² (usually 85 per cent of boiler pressure) and W is driving-wheel diameter in inches. Tractive effort is simply the force exerted at the rim of the driving-wheel. The use the engine can make of it depends entirely on its ability to grip the rails, or its adhesive weight, and the capacity of the boiler to supply the steam.

Horsepower includes a time factor (1 hp = 33 000 ft lb/min = 746 Joules/s or 746 Watts; in France 4500 kg m/min = 736 Watts). In a steam-engine this depends on the rate at which fuel can be burnt and water evaporated in the boiler, as well as cylinder efficiency.

With a steam locomotive there are so many variables that a horsepower rating is only approximate and is seldom used.

THE LARGEST AND MOST POWERFUL STEAM LOCOMOTIVES

(See also 'Articulated Steam Locomotives', and 'Garratt Locomotives'.)

The world's largest steam locomotives were the 4–8–8–4 'Big Boys' built by the American Locomotive Company in 1941–4 for the Union Pacific Railroad. Their over-all length was 39·852 m (130 ft 9¼ in), they stood 4·941 m (16 ft 2½ in) high and were 3·353 m (11 ft) wide. With tenders they weighed 508 020 kg (1 120 000 lb) and exerted a tractive effort of 61 405 kg (135 375 lb). On test they developed an indicated horsepower of 7000. The grate area was 13·96 m² (150·3 ft²); heating surface was 534·6 m² (5755 ft²) plus 189·8 m² (2043 ft²) of superheater. Working pressure was 21·1 kg/cm² (300 lb/in²). The four cylinders were 603 × 813 mm (23¾ × 32 in) and coupled wheels 1727 mm (68 in).

Twenty-five were built, for hauling heavy freights on the Sherman Hill section. They could run at speeds up to 129 km/h (80 mph). Seven have been preserved.

The largest locomotives in Canada were the 2–10–4 'Selkirks' of the Canadian Pacific Railway. The 'T1a' Class Nos. 5900–19 were built by the Montreal Locomotive Works in 1929; the 'T1b' Class, Nos. 5920–9 followed in 1938 and the 'T1c' Class Nos. 5930–5 in 1940. They had 1600 mm (5 ft 3 in) coupled wheels, a working pressure of 20 kg/cm² (285 lb/in²) and cylinders 635 × 813 mm (25 × 32 in). They worked passenger and freight trains through the mountain section of the CPR. No. 5934 is preserved at Calgary and No. 5935 at the Canadian Railway Museum near Montreal. **This was the last steam locomotive built for the CPR.**

The largest locomotives in South America were the 216 ton 1·676 m (5 ft 6 in) gauge 4–8–2s supplied by ALCO to the Chilean State Railways in 1940.

The largest metre-gauge engines in South America were the 181 ton 4–8–2 + 2–8–4 Garratts built by Beyer Peacock & Company,

Canadian Pacific Railway 'Selkirk' 2–10–4 No. 5921 of Class T1b, built in 1938, one of the largest steam locomotives in Canada (Canadian Pacific Railway)

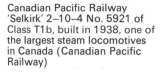

Virginian Railroad 2–10–10–2 Mallet No. 802, built in 1918. The ten engines of this class had the biggest boilers and biggest cylinders ever used on steam locomotives. The low-pressure cylinders in front were 1·219 m (4 ft) diameter and the engines stood 4·877 m (16 ft 7½ in) high. The last one ran until 1958

Manchester, in 1950 for the Antofagasta & Bolivia Railway.

The largest non-articulated locomotives in Australia were the ten '500' Class 4–8–4s Nos. 500–9 built in 1926 by Armstrong Whitworth & Company, Newcastle upon Tyne, for the 1·600 m (5 ft 3 in) gauge South Australian Government Railways. They were 25·653 m (84 ft 2 in) long with tenders and weighed 222·3 tons. They had 1·600 m (5 ft 3 in) driving-wheels. No. 504, withdrawn on 9 July 1962 with a mileage of 855 029 (1 375 993 km), was placed in the Mile End Railway Museum near Adelaide, maintained by the Australian Railway Historical Society, on 23 July 1965.

The world's most powerful steam locomotive on a tractive effort basis was a triplex articulated 2–8–8–8–4 Mallet compound tank engine built by Baldwin, Philadelphia, in 1916 for the Virginian Railroad—No. 700. It had a tractive effort of 75 428 kg (166 300 lb) working compound and 90 516 kg (199 560 lb) working simple, that is with high-pressure steam to all six cylinders. These were all 864 × 813 mm (34 × 32 in), coupled wheels were 1422 mm (4 ft 8 in), grate area 10·052 m² (108·2 ft²), total heating surface 754 m² (8120 ft²), total weight 377 tons.

The engine was under-boilered and quickly ran short of steam, and in 1921, following delivery of the ALCO 2–10–10–2s mentioned below, the engine was divided, the rear portion being rebuilt into a 2–8–2 tender engine and the front portion into a 2–8–8–0 Mallet, No. 610. This was later rebuilt into a 2–8–8–2 and was withdrawn in the early 1950s. It was the only Mallet to have existed in three-wheel arrangements.

The biggest boilers and biggest cylinders ever used on a locomotive were on the ten 2–10–10–2 Mallets built by ALCO in 1918 for the Virginian Railroad, Nos. 800–9. The boilers had a maximum diameter of 3·009 m (9 ft 10½ in). The grate was 2·743 × 3·658 m (9 ft × 12 ft). Evaporative heating surface was 799 m² (8600 ft²) plus 197 m² (2120 ft²) of superheater. The low-pressure cylinders were 1219 mm (48 in) diameter × 813 mm (32 in) stroke. The engines stood 4·877 m (16 ft 7½ in) high. Until the railway was electrified in 1926 they banked mile-long coal trains weighing 10 000 tons to over 15 000 tons up to 17·7 km (11 miles) of 2·1 per cent grade at Clark's Gap. They were withdrawn from 1948 to 1958.

Three-cylinder propulsion was introduced in the USA by ALCO in 1922 when New York Central 4–8–2 freight engine No. 2568 was so converted. The Holcroft/Gresley-type combination gear was used for the inside valve. Its success led to the development of the three-cylinder system by ALCO in a series of designs for switching, freight and passenger work, culminating in the giant Union Pacific 4–12–2 described below. Altogether 250 three-cylinder engines had been built when manufacture ended in 1930.

The largest three-cylinder engines ever built were the Union Pacific 4–12–2s. The first, No. 9000, was completed at Schenectady, New York, in April 1926. A total of 88 were built, the last, No. 9087 in 1930. They were also the

Union Pacific Railroad 4–12–2 No. 9000, the first of the class of 88 built in 1926–30. Besides being the largest three-cylinder engines they were the only 4–12–2s and the only 12-coupled engines to exceed 97 km/h (60 mph) in normal service. No. 9000 has been preserved in California (Union Pacific Railroad)

The largest French express passenger engine, three-cylinder compound 4–8–4 No. 242–A–1, rebuilt by Chapelon in 1942–6 from a 4–8–2. The engine incorporated so many advanced design features as to justify its description as the greatest steam locomotive ever built. Progress with electrification and dieselisation prevented the construction of further examples and this magnificent machine was tragically broken up in 1960 (French Railways Limited)

only 4–12–2s, and the only 12-coupled engines to exceed 97 km/h (60 mph) in normal service. Apart from the experimental Russian 4–14–4, they had the longest rigid wheelbase in the world, and they were the first non-articulated locomotives to exceed 30·5 m (100 ft) in length over drawbars. They were the first three-cylinder engines to have cast-steel cylinders.

In 1956 No. 9000 was presented by the UP to the Southern California Chapter of the Railway and Locomotive Historical Society (see p. 214) for preservation.

The largest French express passenger engine was the 242A1 three-cylinder compound 4–8–4 rebuilt by André Chapelon (1892–1978) in 1942–6 from a 4–8–2 three-cylinder simple No. 241.101. In many ways it was the finest steam locomotive ever built. It could maintain a continuous drawbar horsepower of 4000 at 70–100 km/h (44–62 mph), and 3800 hp at 120 km/h (74 mph). The triple Kylchap exhaust gave a high steaming rate at all speeds. The high-pressure cylinder had Trick valves with double admission, and the low-pressure cylinders had Willoteaux valves with double admission and double exhaust. Its coal and water consumption were remarkably low, only about two-thirds of that of a British Stanier Pacific for the same output. Coupled wheels were 1·95 m (6 ft 4¾ in) diameter and the engine weighed 148 tons. One of the greatest tragedies for locomotive history was that this engine was scrapped in 1960.

The largest tank engines to run on any British railway were the ten 4–6–4 'Baltics' built by the London, Midland & Scottish Railway at the former Lancashire & Yorkshire Railway Works at Horwich to the design of George Hughes (1865–1945), then the chief mechanical engineer. Thirty were to have been built, but insufficient suitable work led to the last 20 being turned out as 4–6–0 tender engines. They had four cylinders 419 × 660 mm (16½ × 26 in) and 1905 mm (6 ft 3 in) coupled wheels.

The last of the 4–6–4 tanks was withdrawn in 1941, largely because they were a non-standard class.

The largest locomotives in Ireland were the Great Southern Railway three-cylinder 4–6–0s of which three were built at Inchicore, Dublin, in 1939–40 to a design prepared under E C Bredin, chief mechanical engineer. They were built for the Dublin–Cork expresses.

The largest locomotive type in Ireland, Great Southern Railways three-cylinder 4–6–0 No. 800 *Maeve* at Cork in August 1948

Bristol & Exeter Railway 4–2–2 tank engine No. 46 built by Peter Rothwell at Bolton, Lancashire, in 1853. The 2·743 m (9 ft) diameter driving wheels were the largest in regular use in Britain at any time. In 1854 No. 41 of this type achieved a speed of 131·6 km/h (81·8 mph) which remained a world record until 1890 (British Railways)

The first, No. 800 *Maeve* (see illustration) is preserved at the Belfast Transport Museum.

The largest driving-wheels used on any engine in Britain were 3·048 m (10 ft) diameter on the freak Great Western 2–2–2 built by Mather, Dixon & Company of Liverpool to a specification by I K Brunel and delivered on 12 December 1838. It 'worked' until June 1840.

The largest driving-wheels in regular use in Britain were 2·743 m (9 ft) on the eight magnificent 4–2–4 tank engines built for the 2·134 m (7 ft) gauge Bristol & Exeter Railway by Rothwell & Company of Bolton, Lancashire, to a design by James Pearson in 1854. One of these, No. 41, achieved a record speed of 131·6 km/h (81·8 mph) on Wellington Bank, Somerset, in June 1854, which remained the highest authenticated rail speed until 1890. They were replaced by new B. & E. engines of the same wheel arrangement in 1868–73.

The largest coupled wheels ever used in Britain were 2·318 m (7 ft 7¼ in) diameter on Wilson Worsdell's 'Q1' Class 4–4–0s Nos. 1869 and 1870 on the North Eastern Railway. Two were built in 1896 for taking part in the railway races to the north (see p. 172).

ARTICULATED STEAM LOCOMOTIVES

The articulated locomotive with one or two swivelling power bogies was developed to provide great power on lines with severe curvature, or to spread the weight of a large locomotive over many axles to enable it to work on light track. The principal types have been the Fairlie, Meyer, Mallet and Garratt.

The world's first articulated locomotive was a 2–2–2–2 built at West Point Foundry, New York, in 1832 for the South Carolina Railroad, USA. It had a central firebox and four boilers, two at each end. It was designed by Horatio Allen and formed the basis of the Fairlie type. Each engine had one central cylinder.

The next stage towards the Fairlie design was the 0–4–4–0 built by John Cockerill et Cie of Seraing, Belgium, for trials on the Semmering line in Austria, in 1851.

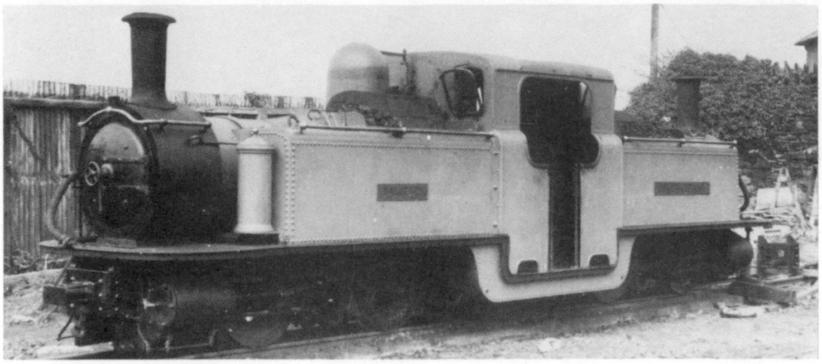

Festiniog Railway 0–4–4–0 Fairlie engine No. 3 *Taliesin* photographed in April 1957, shortly after restoration, at the Boston Lodge Works near Porthmadog where it was built in 1884. It was originally No. 11 *Livingston Thompson*: it was renamed Taliesin in 1931 following withdrawal of the early 0–4–4 'Single Fairlie' of that name. In April 1961, by permission of the Duke of Edinburgh the engine was renamed *Earl of Merioneth*

Robert F. Fairlie (1831–85) patented his double-bogie articulated locomotive design on 12 May 1864 in England and on 23 November 1864 in France. First to be built was 0–4–4–0 *Progress* in 1865. by Cross & Co, St Helens, Lancashire, for the Neath & Brecon Railway, Wales. It had a double boiler with a common firebox in the centre, and two power bogies. Most Fairlies were 0–4–4–0 and 0–6–6–0, the largest being some 0–6–6–0s built for Mexico in 1911. Fairlie also designed a single-boiler type with one power bogie, and many of these were built. In the USA this design was taken up by William Mason (1808–83), becoming known as the 'Mason-Fairlie' type. From 1871 to 1889 148 were built for gauges from standard down to 914 mm (3 ft). In 1890 the type was built by the Taunton Locomotive Manufacturing Co, Massachusetts, and later by the Manchester Locomotive Works, New Hampshire, and finally by the Schenectady Works of ALCO where the last were built in 1914 for the 914 mm (3 ft) gauge Boston, Revere Beach & Lynn Railroad which used this type exclusively until it was electrified in the 1930s.

Two double-boiler Fairlies survive today, on the 600 mm (1 ft 11½ in) gauge Festiniog Railway in Wales for which the first, *Little Wonder*, was built in 1870.

Jean Jacques Meyer (1804–77) and his son Adolphe (1840–91) of Mulhouse, France, patented the Meyer articulated locomotive on 15 March 1861 (French Patent No. 48993). It had the cylinders at the inner ends of the power bogies. The first type, 0–4–4–0, was built by Fives of Lille in 1868. The design restricted the ashpan, but the **Kitson-Meyer** type, developed at Leeds, England, overcame this by lengthening the frame and placing the firebox between the power bogies, each of which had the cylinders at the rear end.

The Kitson-Meyer was introduced in 1903 when three 0–6–6–0s were built, the first being No. 800 for the 1·067 m (3 ft 6 in) gauge Cape Government Railway, South Africa (Kitson No. 4179).

A later development, introduced in 1908, had the cylinders at the outer ends of the bogies. Some of these show the influence of the Garratt design but differ from this in having a single rigid frame mounted on the power bogies. The Garratt design gained in avoiding this duplication of framing.

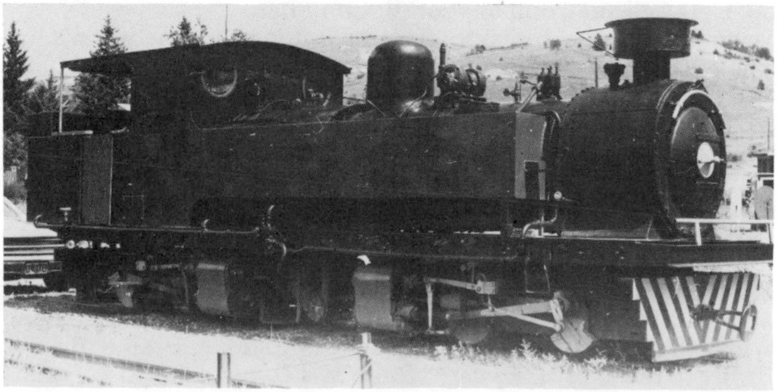

A Meyer 610 mm (2 ft) gauge 0–4–4–0 tank at Cripple Creek, Colorado

Erie Railroad 2–8–8–8–2 Mallet No. 5014 *Matt H. Shay*, first of three built in 1914–18 for banking freight trains up the 1 in 67 Susquehanna Incline in Pennsylvania. When built it was the world's largest locomotive. It pulled 250 freight cars weighing altogether 15 300 tons and stretching for 2574 m (1·6 miles) at a speed of 21·7 km/h (13·5 mph). They were withdrawn in 1929

One of the last active simple-expansion 'Mallets', a Baldwin 2–6–6–2 built in 1941 for the metre-gauge Teresa Cristina Railway in Brazil, photographed at Tubarao in October 1974

The first articulated locomotives in Africa were the 1·067 m (3 ft 6 in) gauge Kitson-Meyer 0–6–6–0s built by Kitson for Rhodesia in 1903. At the time they were the largest and most powerful engines in southern Africa.

Anatole Mallet (1837–1919), patented the type of articulated locomotive named after him in 1884 as a four-cylinder compound with the low-pressure cylinders on the pivoted front engine frame. The first Mallet was a 600 mm (1 ft 11½ in) gauge 0–4–4–0 tank built in 1887 by Ateliers Métallurgiques at Tubize, Belgium. Its advantage was that it provided high power while adapted to running on light track. In 1890 it was introduced on European main lines. In 1903 it was introduced in North America where it developed to its greatest extent. The Virginian Railroad 2–10–10–2 of 1918 had low-pressure cylinders 1219 mm (48 in) diameter, the largest ever used on a locomotive. (See p. 127 and photograph.) A triplex type with a third unit under the tender was also produced. These had two high-pressure and four low-pressure cylinders all of equal size. Three 2–8–8–8–2s were built for the Erie Railroad in 1914 and one 2–8–8–8–4 for the Virginian Railroad in 1916.

Mallet opposed the introduction of simple-expansion types, but with the use of superheaters this was a logical development. Mallets grew into the world's biggest engines, examples being the Chesapeake & Ohio Railroad 2–6–6–2s, the Northern Pacific Railroad 2–8–8–4s and the Union Pacific 4–8–8–4 'Big Boys', all over 500 tons.

The largest Mallet tanks (except the Virginian Railroad 2–8–8–8–4, p. 127) were the 0–8–8–0s built by Maffei in Germany for the Bavarian State Railways in 1913–14 and 1922–3. The first batch weighed 123 147 kg (271 500 lb) or 121 tons.

The first Mallet in North America was a 0–6–6–0 built by ALCO in 1903 for the Baltimore & Ohio Railroad. It was followed by five 2–6–6–2s built by Baldwin in 1906 for the Great Northern Railway.

The first of the Southern Pacific 'cab-in-front' Mallets was built in 1910. They were designed to enable the crews to escape the exhaust fumes in the numerous tunnels and snow-sheds in the Sierra Nevada, USA, in which the line climbs nearly 2133 m (7000 ft) from Sacramento to the summit in 161 km (100 miles) and 610 m (2000 ft) from Reno in 80 km (50 miles). The engines ran 'backwards' with the tender coupled beyond the smoke box. Oil fuel was delivered to the firebox under pressure.

The greatest of all Mallets, the Union Pacific 4–8–8–4 'Big Boys' first built by ALCO in 1941, were not strictly Mallets because they were not compounds. The engines are described on p. 126.

The first Beyer Garratt locomotive, 610 mm (2 ft) gauge compound 0–4–0+0–4–0 built by Beyer Peacock, Manchester (No. 5292), in 1909 for the North East Dundas Tramway, Tasmania. It is now restored at the National Railway Museum, York (North Western Museum of Science and Industry, Manchester)

The largest Russian locomotives, the 'P38' 2–8–8–4s of 1954–5, were likewise not true Mallets. They weighed 214·9 tons without tenders.

The last active simple-expansion Mallets are the 2–6–6–2s built by Baldwin in 1941–9 for the metre-gauge Teresa Cristina Railway in Brazil, Nos. 200–5. Some were still at work in October 1974 when the photograph was taken.

The world's most powerful steam locomotives on a potential horsepower basis were the 2–8–8–4 simple-expansion 'Mallets' of the Northern Pacific Railroad, USA. The first, built by ALCO in 1928, was the first locomotive to weigh over 453 600 kg (1 000 000 lb) with tender. Eleven more were built by Baldwin in 1930. They had a grate area of 16·9 m² (182 ft²), **the largest ever carried by any locomotive**, a heating surface of 712·3 m² (7666 ft²) plus 299 m² (3219 ft²) of superheater and a boiler pressure of 17·6 kg/cm² (250 lb/in²). This gave them the highest potential horsepower of any steam locomotive. The large grate, however, was designed to burn anthracite, so the steaming rate was lower than could have been achieved with bituminous coal. So the maximum potential power of these engines was never fully exploited. They had a tractive effort of 66 193 kg (145 930 lb) with a booster adding 6078 kg (13 400 lb). The ALCO engine was the first Mallet to have a booster.

The heaviest train ever hauled by a single locomotive was probably one of 15 300 tons made up of 250 freight cars stretching for 2·6 km (1·6 miles) at 21 km/h (13·5 mph), by the world's then largest locomotive, Erie Railroad 2–8–8–8–2 No. 5014 *Matt H. Shay*, the first of three built in 1914–18 for banking freight trains up the 1 in 67 Susquehanna Incline in Pennsylvania. The engines were withdrawn in 1929.

One of the most interesting articulated locomotive designs was produced by Gaston Du Bousquet (qv). It was a revival of the Wiener-Neustadt 0–4–4–0 tank locomotive built for the Semmering Contest, Austria, in 1851. The Du Bousquet was a four-cylinder compound 0–6–2+2–6–0 with cylinders at the inner ends of the power bogies. The first examples were built in 1905–11 for the French Nord and Est systems and the Peking–Hankow Railway, China, and in 1911 some further engines were built for the 1·672 m (5 ft 6 in) gauge Andalusian Railway, Spain.

GARRATT LOCOMOTIVES

Herbert William Garratt (1864–1913) invented the type of articulated engine named after him which was developed by the firm of Beyer Peacock & Company, Manchester, England. About 2000 were built altogether.

The first Garratts were two tiny 0–4–0+0–4–0s built in 1909 for the 610 mm (2 ft) gauge North East Dundas Tramway, Tasmania. They were untypical in that they were compounds and had the cylinders at the inner ends of the engine units. They ran until 1930. In 1947 No. K1 was shipped back to England and after being stored at Beyer Peacock's, Manchester, it was tried on the Festiniog Railway in Wales where, however, it was much too large. It is now restored for exhibition at the National Railway Museum, York.

The first conventional Garratt with four simple-expansion cylinders at the outer ends

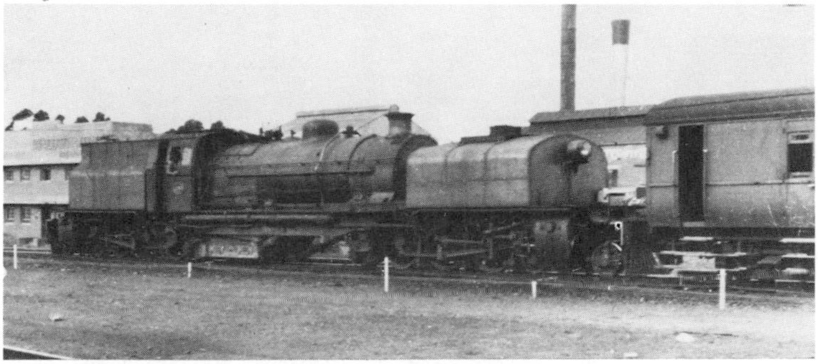

One of the Garratts built in Germany under licence from Beyer Peacock & Company for the South African Railways in 1927–8, 'GF' class 4–6–2+2–6–4, No. 2393, built by Hanomag, Hanover, in 1927, working a passenger train near Durban on 21 April 1943

of the engines was built in 1911 for the 610 mm (2 ft) gauge Darjeeling Himalayan Railway (see p. 212).

The Tasmanian Government Railway 'M' Class Garratt was a 1·067 m (3 ft 6 in) gauge 4–4–2+2–4–4 and was unique in having eight cylinders and for running at speeds up to 88·5 km/h (55 mph). The coupled wheels were 1·524 m (5 ft) diameter. Two were built in 1912.

The most powerful locomotives in South Africa are the South African Railways 'GL' Class Garratts—1·676 m (3 ft 6 in) gauge 4–8–2+2–8–4s—first built in 1929 by Beyer Peacock & Company. They weigh 211·1 tons and have a tractive effort of 35 675 kg (78 650 lb).

The world's first express passenger Garratts were built for the São Paulo Railway, as 2–6–2+2–6–2s, in 1927. In 1931–2 they were rebuilt as 4–6–2+2–6–4s. They regularly ran trains at 96·5 km/h (60 mph).

The largest and most powerful locomotive in Great Britain was the 2–8–0+0–8–2 Garratt built by Beyer Peacock in 1925 for the London & North Eastern Railway for banking coal trains from Wath up to Penistone in Yorkshire. It was numbered 2395 and classed 'U1'. Its two engine units were standard with H N Gresley's three cylinder 2–8–0s.

Britain's last Garratt was a 0–4–0+0–4–0 built in 1937 for the Baddesley Colliery near Atherstone, Warwickshire, where it worked until 1965. It had a 1·524 m (5 ft) diameter boiler and weighed 61·5 tons. It is now preserved at Bressingham, Norfolk. (See p. 233.)

The largest locomotives in New Zealand were the three 4–6–2+2–6–4 Garratts built in 1920. They weighed 145·8 tons. These were the only six-cylinder Garratts exported from England and were the first locomotives in New Zealand to have mechanical stokers, exhaust steam injectors, steam reversing gear and grease lubrication to coupled axleboxes.

They were too powerful, however, for the couplings then in use, and loops were too short for the trains they could pull. After transfer from the North to the South Island in 1936, the engine units were built into six 'Pacific'-type tender engines. But their design was faulty and in 1955–6 they became the first New Zealand main-line engines to be replaced by diesels.

The last Garratt to operate in Britain, the 0–4–0+0–4–0 *William Francis* at Baddesley Colliery near Atherstone, Warwickshire, in April 1964

New South Wales Government Railway 'AD60' Class Garratt. These standard-gauge engines, built in 1952, were the largest, heaviest and most powerful steam locomotives in Australia (North Western Museum of Science & Industry, Manchester)

The largest Garratt locomotive ever built, the single 'Ya-01' built by Beyer Peacock & Company for the Russian Railways in 1932 (North Western Museum of Science & Industry, Manchester)

The largest, heaviest and most powerful steam locomotives in Australia were the 'AD60' Class 4–8–4+4–8–4 Garratts on the standard-gauge New South Wales Government Railways. They were the first Garratts to have cast-steel engine-bed frames incorporating cylinders (see p. 121). They were introduced in 1952 and weighed 264·75 tons in working order. No. 6042, built by Beyer Peacock in 1952, was the last completed Garratt to be delivered to Australia and was the last steam locomotive in regular service in New South Wales, being withdrawn on 2 March 1973.

The largest Garratt locomotive ever built was completed by Beyer Peacock in 1932 for the USSR railways where it was classed 'Ya-01'. It was a 4–8–2+2–8–4 standing 5·182 m (17 ft) high, with bar-frames and a boiler 2·286 m (7 ft 6 in) diameter. It weighed 262·5 tons and had a tractive effort of 35 698 kg (78 700 lb).

The smallest Garratts ever built were the two 0–6–0+0–6–0s built in 1913 for the Arakan Flotilla Company of Burma, for 762 mm (2 ft 6 in) gauge, with a wheelbase of 7·320 m (24 ft 2 in). They weighed 23·55 tons.

GEARED STEAM LOCOMOTIVES

Geared locomotives were produced to three basic designs, principally to negotiate light temporary tracks over rough ground with steep gradients.

The 'Shay' geared locomotive was invented by Ephraim Shay (1839–1916) and was produced by the Lima Machine Works, Ohio, USA (from 1901 the Lima Locomotive & Machine Company). The first appeared in 1880. It had a two- or three-cylinder vertical engine on one side and the bogies were driven by a system of shafts, universal couplings and spur gears. On level track it could reach a speed of 30·578 km/h (19 mph) and on gradients of 6 to 14 per cent (1 in 16·7 to 1 in 7) it could move loads at 12 to 6·5 km/h (7·5 to 4 mph).

The Climax locomotive was built by the Climax Manufacturing Company of Corry, Pennsylvania. It had two sloping cylinders, one on each side, connected by gearing and longitudinal shafts to the two bogies. The company operated from 1884 to 1930.

Another type had a two-cylinder high-speed vertical steam-engine driving the bogies through a two-speed gear-box. A similar design was produced by the Baldwin Locomotive Works, Philadelphia.

The Heisler-type locomotive was first built by the Stearns Manufacturing Company, Erie, Pennsylvania, the first being completed on 20 August 1894 for service in Mexico. The Heisler Locomotive Works, Erie, began

Standard-gauge 'Shay' No. 3 of the Mayo Lumber Company at Cowichan Valley Museum near Victoria, Vancouver Island

production of this type in 1898. It had two cylinders arranged like a V beneath the boiler, driving a longitudinal shaft geared to the bogies. This was the neatest and soundest of the three designs, but the Shay was the most popular.

OIL FUEL FOR STEAM LOCOMOTIVES

Some of the earliest experiments with oil fuel were made in the 1870s by a British engineer Thomas Urquhart. Similar experiments began in France in 1869. The advantage of oil fuel over coal is principally the avoidance of ash, but its use depends largely on the price and availability of fuel. An oil-fired steam-engine is still an inefficient machine producing only half of the work done by a diesel engine using the same amount of oil.

In the USA early experiments with oil fuel were abandoned because of the cost and it was not taken up again until the 1890s.

The first regular use of oil fuel was on the Russian South Eastern Railway in 1883–4, using the Urquhart system.

In the USA an oil-burning locomotive made successful test runs from Altoona to Pittsburg, Pennsylvania, and back on 17–18 June 1887.

Oil fuel was first used in Britain by the Great Eastern Railway. In 1887 James Holden (qv), the locomotive superintendent, invented an arrangement for burning the waste product from the plant producing oil gas for carriage lighting. It was tried on the Johnson 0–4–4 tank No. 193 and was first regularly used on a 4–2–2 which was named *Petrolea*. About 60 engines were so fitted, but the apparatus was removed when the price of oil rose to an uneconomic level.

The first oil-burning locomotive in Canada was introduced about 1910, converted from a coal-burner for work in the Rocky Mountains. The first complete class of oil-burners was built by the Canadian Pacific Railway in 1917–19.

In 1947 many British locomotives on the Great Western, Southern and London & North Eastern railways, and on the Irish railways, were fitted up to burn oil fuel during the acute coal shortage in Britain. However, the increasing cost of oil led to its removal after very little use.

Strange fuels have been used for steam locomotives to keep railways running in difficult times. On a 600 mm (1 ft 11½ in) gauge branch of the Arica–La Paz Railway in Chile llama dung and dried moss were burned on two 0–4–0 tanks built by Orenstein & Koppel of Berlin. In South America, during a crop surplus, coffee beans were used as fuel.

In 1919, during a coal shortage, **dried fish** was used as locomotive fuel in Russian Turkestan. For this purpose the Soviet Government requisitioned 8000 tons from Aral Sea fishermen.

Electrically fired steam locomotives were tried on Swiss Federal Railways in 1943 when two 0–6–0 tanks were converted at Yverdon for shunting at St Gallen and Zollikofen, drawing power from the 15 000 V ac overhead wire. Current consumption was high for the power output compared with an electric locomotive, and the experiment was abandoned about 1948.

STEAM-TURBINE LOCOMOTIVES

The first steam-turbine locomotive was designed by Professor Belluzzo and was built in Milan, Italy, in 1908 by S A Officine Mechaniche. It was a 0–4–0 side-tank engine. The four turbines were single-wheel velocity compound type with the lower part of the blades for forward drive and the upper part for backward.

A steam-turbine-electric locomotive was designed by Sir Hugh Reid and W M Ramsey and was built in Glasgow in 1910 by the North British Locomotive Company of which Reid (1860–1935) was chairman and chief managing director. An impulse-type turbine with condenser was coupled to a variable voltage dynamo which supplied the four dc traction motors at 200–600 V.

A second Ramsey-type locomotive, a 0–6–6–2 type, was completed in 1922 and was tested by George Hughes at Horwich on the Lancashire & Yorkshire Railway, and on the North Eastern Railway. Turbines and electrical equipment were by Oerlikon, Switzerland. It was built by Armstrong Whitworth & Company, Newcastle upon Tyne.

The Zoelly turbine locomotive was converted from a Swiss Federal Railways 4–6–0 in 1921 by the Swiss Locomotive & Machine Works, Winterthur. It had a 1200 hp impulse turbine across the front of the machine, driving the wheels by gearing and a jack-shaft and side-rods. A surface condenser was positioned beneath the boiler. A similar engine built by Krupp of Essen, Germany, in 1922 ran on the German State Railways.

The Ljungstrom turbine condensing locomotive was first built in 1921 at the Ljungstrom Locomotive Works near Stockholm, Sweden. It was rebuilt in 1922 but was withdrawn in 1924.

The second, built at Trollhattan in 1924–5 to the metre gauge for the Argentine State Railway, was capable of travelling 805 km (500 miles) without rewatering.

The third, built by Beyer Peacock & Company at Manchester, England, in 1926 was given extensive trials on the Midland section of the London, Midland & Scottish Railway. It suffered in the numerous tunnels where soot entered the condenser and caused blockages. A fourth, and last, built in 1927, was similar in design and gave good service in Sweden for many years.

In 1932 some non-condensing Ljungstrom locomotives were built in Sweden and they worked iron-ore trains of 1831 tons on the Grängesberg–Oxelösund Railway from the Bergslag to the Baltic coast until displaced by electrification.

The Reid-Macleod turbine locomotive was built by the North British Locomotive Company of Glasgow in 1923–4. It was a 4–4–4–4 with high- and low-pressure turbines and an air-cooled condenser. It had an output of 1000 bhp.

The London, Midland & Scottish Railway turbine 'Pacific' No. 6202 was a non-condensing machine with one turbine for

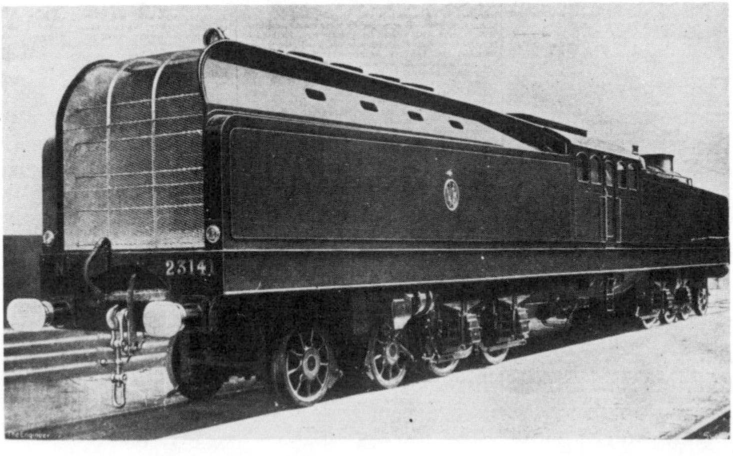

The Reid-Macleod turbine-condensing locomotive

forward running and a smaller one for reverse. It was built at Crewe in 1935 to the design of William Stanier (1876–1965) and ran successfully on the London–Liverpool expresses. In 1952 it was rebuilt into a conventional engine and named *Princess Anne*, but after only a few months' service it was involved in the collision at Harrow and Wealdstone Station on 8 October 1952 and was subsequently scrapped.

The Union Pacific Railroad, USA had a pair of steam-turbine-electric locomotives built by the General Electric Company in 1937–9. They were of the 2–Co–Co–2 type and could work either singly or together under the control of one man. They had a maximum speed of 201 km/h (125 mph). They each had high- and low-pressure turbines and condensers, and together had an output of 5000 hp. The semi-flash-type boiler worked at a pressure of 105·46 kg/cm² (1500 lb/in²).

The first direct-drive turbine locomotive in the USA was the Pennsylvania Railroad No. 6200, a 6–8–6-type non-condensing machine built by Baldwin in 1944 in co-operation with the Westinghouse Company. Like the LMS machine of 1935, described above, it had two turbines, one forward developing 6500 hp at 113 km/h (70 mph) and a reverse developing 1500 hp at 35·5 km/h (22 mph). This magnificent looking machine ran for only 5 years.

The Chesapeake & Ohio Railroad obtained three giant steam-turbine-electric locomotives built by Baldwin and Westinghouse in 1947–9. They were 47 m (154 ft) long 2–D+2–D–2 type with a starting tractive effort of 4445 kg (98 000 lb) and a continuous of 2177 kg (48 000 lb). They had a short existence because of the closure of the passenger service for which they were obtained, and also because of design faults.

The Norfolk & Western Railroad obtained a 4500 hp turbine-electric non-condensing locomotive in 1954, built by the Baldwin-Lima-Hamilton Corporation with the Westinghouse Company, and a boiler by Babcock & Wilcox. It measured 49 m (61 ft 1½ in) long and weighed 525 tons in working order. It could run up to 96·5 km/h (60 mph). It was numbered 2300. Although it showed marked economy in coal consumption, it was displaced in 1958 by diesels and was scrapped.

LARGE CLASSES OF STEAM LOCOMOTIVES

The largest class of locomotives to be built in Britain was the Ramsbottom 'DX' Class 0–6–0 of the London & North Western Railway, of which 943 were built between 1858 and 1874, including 86 for the Lancashire & Yorkshire Railway in 1871–4.

On the Great Western Railway a total of 863 0–6–0 pannier tanks of the '5700' Class were built between 1929 and 1950. The basic design dated back to the '645' Class of 1872 and the similar '1813', '1854' and '2721' Classes of which a total of 358 were built up to 1901. No. 5764 is still active on the Severn Valley Railway, Shropshire, and No. 5775 on the Keighley & Worth Valley Railway,

The impressive Pennsylvania Railroad 6–8–6 non-condensing turbine locomotive No. 6200, built in 1944 and withdrawn in 1949 (Altoona Area Public Library)

One of the numerous Ramsbottom DX class 0–6–0s, No. 417 of the Lancashire & Yorkshire Railway, one of 86 bought from the London & North Western in 1871. It ran until 1895

Yorkshire, both built at Swindon in 1929. No. 5786 (1929) is at Hereford (Worcester Locomotive Society); the Severn Valley Railway has also preserved No. 7714 (1930), while Nos. 7752 and 7760 (1930) are in working order at Birmingham Railway Museum at Tyseley. No. 7715 (1930) is at Quainton Road, Buckinghamshire; Nos. 3738 (1937) and 3650 (1939) are preserved at Didcot, Berkshire, by the Great Western Society, and Nos. 4612 (1942), 9629 (1945) and 9681 (1949) are also earmarked for preservation. So the '5700' class can also claim to be one of the most numerous classes of preserved locomotives. (See 'Largest class of diesel locomotives'.)

The railway with the greatest number of 0–6–0s in Britain was the Midland. In 1917 it had 1495, about 21 per cent of the total for the whole country. The '4F' 0–6–0s reached a total of 772. The next largest total of 0–6–0s was on the North Eastern Railway which had 777.

The largest class of modern locomotives in Britain was the London, Midland & Scottish Railway 'Class 5' 4–6–0 designed by William Stanier and first built in 1934. Including several variations in the design, the class eventually numbered 842 engines. A total of 13 has been preserved.

The first locomotive type to be adopted by the British Government for war service was the Great Central '8K' Class 2–8–0 designed by J G Robinson (1856–1943) and first built at Gorton, Manchester, in 1911. During the First World War many were built by the GCR and by other locomotive-builders making a grand total of 647 engines. After the war they were dispersed, most going to the London & North Eastern Railway (as successor to the GCR) where they were classed '04' and others to the Great Western Railway and to China, Australia and elsewhere. Many of them put in over 50 years' hard service. They were among the finest British freight engines.

The German 'Austerity' 2–10–0, introduced in 1941, numbered more than 8000 when the last was built in 1947.

The world's largest class of locomotives was the Russian 'E' Class 0–10–0 introduced in 1912 and at length numbering about 14 000 engines.

Between 1891 and 1923 9500 '0' Class 0–8–0s were built in Russia.

The largest class of steam locomotives to be built in the British Commonwealth was the Indian 1·676 m (5 ft 6 in) gauge 'WG' Class 2–8–2 first built in 1950 and eventually totalling 2450.

The largest classes in the USA were the USRA (United States Railroad Administration) 0–8–0s numbering 1375, and the 'light' 2–8–2s numbering 1266, built 1919–20.

The Canadian Pacific Railway 'D' Class 4–6–0s totalled over 1000, but there were ten different types and variations within these, built from 1902 to 1915. The 'D10' Class, built 1905–13, totalled 502.

Midland Railway 2–4–0 No. 158A, restored to MR livery and preserved at the Midland Railway Company's centre at Butterley near Ripley, Derbyshire. When withdrawn in July 1947 as London Midland & Scottish Railway No. 20002 it was 81 years old

VETERAN LOCOMOTIVES

One of the longest lived locomotives of British Railways was the former Lancashire & Yorkshire Railway 0–6–0 saddle tank, latterly No. 11305. It was built as a 0–6–0 tender locomotive in 1877 to an order of Barton Wright, locomotive superintendent, rebuilt to a saddle tank in 1891 and withdrawn in September 1964 aged 87.

A locomotive of the same class, No. 752 (Beyer Peacock 1881) is preserved on the Keighley & Worth Valley Railway in Yorkshire.

Another long-lived British locomotive was former Midland Railway 2–4–0 No. 158A, built at Derby in 1866 to a design of Matthew Kirtley and, after some rebuilding, withdrawn in July 1947 as LMS No. 20002, aged 81. It is now preserved in the National Collection and is on loan to the Midland Railway Company at Butterley, Derbyshire (see p. 233).

The oldest locomotive still active in Britain is *Prince*, No. 2 on the 600 mm (1 ft 11½ in) gauge Festiniog Railway in Wales. It was built by George England, London, in 1863 and was subsequently rebuilt in 1892, 1904, 1920, 1937 and 1955–6. (See also 'Narrow-Gauge Railways' and 'Railway Museums and Preservation'.)

The oldest steamable British locomotive is probably the 0–4–0 well tank *Shannon* built by George England & Company, London, in 1857 for the Sandy & Potton Railway, opened on 23 June 1857. In 1862 this became part of the Bedford & Cambridge Railway and this was absorbed by the London & North Western Railway in 1865. *Shannon* was used as a works shunter at Crewe until 1878 when it was sold for £365 8s 1d (£365 40½p) to the Wantage Tramway, Berkshire, where it became No. 5. It ran until the tramway closed in 1945 and in April 1946 was bought by the Great Western Railway for £100, renamed *Shannon*, and exhibited on Wantage Road Station. After the station closed, on 7 December 1964, the engine was acquired by the Great Western Society Limited at Didcot (see p. 232), and was so admirably restored that it became the oldest member of the Stockton & Darlington Railway 150th anniversary cavalcade on 31 August 1975, travelling under its own steam in the cavalcade.

The oldest active standard-gauge engine in Britain is the former London, Brighton & South Coast Railway 'Terrier' 0–6–0 tank No. 72 *Fenchurch* which entered service in September 1872, one of the first two of its type, designed by William Stroudley (1833–89). It is now at work on the Bluebell Railway in Sussex.

The fame and esteem which this class of 50 tiny engines inspired was out of all proportion to their size. No other locomotive type has gained such warm affection. Several others are preserved in England, and one can even be seen in the Canadian Railroad Historical Association's museum at Delson near Montreal. (See p. 236.) The design was even copied by the New South Wales Railways for working suburban trains in Sydney, Australia.

The longest-lived locomotive in Australia was a 1·067 m (3 ft 6 in) gauge 0–4–2 built in 1865 by Neilson & Company, Glasgow, for the Queensland Railways. In 1896 it was sold to Bingera Sugar Mill and in 1965 was lent to Queensland Railways for its centenary celebrations and was later donated to the QR. It last ran on 20 July 1967, on an Australian Railway Historical Society excursion and was then placed in the locomotive museum at Redbank, Queensland.

DYNAMOMETER CARS

Dynamometer cars for the testing of steam locomotives on the track were used in England by the Great Western, North Eastern and Lancashire and Yorkshire Railways. They were positioned between the locomotive and the train and were equipped to measure and record speed and drawbar pull in the form of graphs which could be used in conjunction with gradient profiles, fuel and water consumption, and indicator diagrams taken at the cylinders, to assess locomotive performance.

The North Eastern car was built at Darlington under Wilson Worsdell in 1906 and was based on the GWR car. It is now preserved at the National Railway Museum, York.

The LYR car was designed by George Hughes at Horwich, Lancashire, in 1911–12 and was based on the Belgian car designed by Jean Baptiste Flamme. It indicated speed and drawbar pull to give drawbar-horsepower-hours. It is being restored at the Midland Railway Centre, Butterley, Ripley, Derbyshire.

The latest dynamometer car is a standard vehicle designed for speeds up to 300 km/h (186 mph) by the Transport Systems Division of Messerschmitt-Bölkow-Blohm GmbH (MBB) in 1976. It is 26·4 m (86 ft 7 in) long, 4·05 m (13 ft 3 in) high, and it weighs 61·5 tons.

The first locomotive to be privately purchased from British Railways for preservation was Great Northern Railway 0–6–0 saddle tank No. 1247, purchased in 1959. It was built by Sharp Stewart & Company, Glasgow, in 1899 to a design prepared under H A Ivatt. It is at present at work on the North Yorkshire Moors Railway. (See also 'Railway Museums and Preservation'.)

LOCOMOTIVE BUILDING RECORDS

In February 1888 Francis William Webb (1835–1904), locomotive superintendent of the London & North Western Railway, had a 0–6–0 goods engine constructed in Crewe Works in 25½ hours.

The following June this record was reduced to 16¼ hours by the Pennsylvania Railroad at the Altoona Works, USA.

The all-time record was achieved by the Great Eastern Railway under James Holden at Stratford, London. On 10 December 1891 0–6–0 No. 930 was completely assembled and given one coat of paint in 9 h 57 min. It was steamed and tested on the line immediately afterwards. As London & North Eastern Railway 'J15' Class No. 7930 this engine ran until 1935.

THE LAST STEAM LOCOMOTIVES

The last main-line steam locomotives in Britain were the standard types designed under the supervision of R A Riddles, then Member of the Railway Executive for Mechanical and Electrical Engineering. They comprised three types of 4–6–2, Classes 6, 7 and 8; a 2–10–0 Class 9; two 4–6–0s, Classes 4 and 5; three 2–6–0s, Classes 2, 3 and 4; a 2–6–4 tank Class 4; and two 2–6–2 tanks, Classes 2 and 3. The first to appear was Class 7 4–6–2 No. 70000 *Britannia* (see colour photograph p. 39) in January 1951, and the 999th and last was the Class 9 2–10–0 No. 92220 *Evening Star* in March 1960.

As a whole, they represented the finest examples of steam-locomotive design on British Railways; but they were about 20 years too late, and they contained few features which were not standard practice in the USA in the 1920s and 1930s. By the 1950s the expense of design and development work on 12 new steam-locomotive types was an extravagance. Further construction of existing types even though, as with the standard engines, some of them may have given only a few years' service, could have kept the railways operating until more modern forms of traction had been developed.

The last steam locomotives in France were the American '141R' Class 2–8–2s, a fine rugged modern design by Baldwin imported after the Second World War to help in the rehabilitation of the French railways. They were equally at home on freight and passenger trains.

The last steam locomotives built in Russia were completed in 1956. They were the 'L' Class 2–10–0s, making a class totalling about 4700; the 'LV' Class 2–10–2s and the 'P36' Class 4–8–4s.

The last steam locomotive to be built for service in North America was the Norfolk & Western 'S1a' Class 0–8–0 switcher No. 224, outshopped from Roanoke Works in December 1953. It worked only until 1960 when steam finally disappeared from the N. & W.

The last steam locomotives built by Baldwin Locomotive Works, USA were 50 'WG' Class 2–8–2s for India, 1·676 m (5 ft 6 in) gauge, in 1955. Their price was about twice that tendered by European and Japanese builders. The last built for domestic use in the USA was a 2–8–0 for the US Army Transportation School at Fort Eustis, Virginia, in 1952.

The last steam locomotive on the Southern Pacific Railroad, USA made its last run, from San Francisco to Reno, in 1958.

The last steam locomotive to be built in Australia was 'B 18¼' Class 4–6–2 No. 1089 on the 1·067 m (3 ft 6 in) gauge Queensland Government Railways, completed on 13 March 1958 by Walker's Limited of Maryborough (Works No. 557). It was 18·354 m (60 ft 3 in) long and weighed 101·2 tons. It was withdrawn in 1969, one of the last to run, having covered only 398 470 km (247 450 miles), and it is preserved in the Queensland Railways Museum, Redbank, near Brisbane.

The last Australian State Government railway to make regular use of steam locomotives was Tasmania where one of the 'H' Class was used on the Hobart–Claremont–Hobart service in 1974 in an emergency following the Tasman Bridge accident.

Steam locomotives in Japan were withdrawn on 18 December 1975. The last steam-hauled passenger train ran on 14 December (see p. 186).

The last main-line steam locomotive to be built might be 'YG' Class metre-gauge 2–8–2 built by Indian Railways at the Chittaranjan Works and completed in February 1972.

The last express passenger engine built in Britain was the 'Class 8' three-cylinder Caprotti valve-gear 4–6–2 No. 71000 *Duke of Gloucester* completed at Crewe in 1954. It was the only one of its type. It was withdrawn in 1962 and after storage with a view towards preservation the valve gear was removed and was installed in the Science Museum, London. The remaining sections are now at Loughborough, Leicestershire, being restored by the Main Line Steam Trust.

At the end of 1973 a total of 26 300 useable steam locomotives remained in world stock. Of these 15 000 were in Asia, 5000 in Europe, and 3700 in Africa. India had over 8300, South Africa 2365, Japan and Federal Germany each over 1000. In Great Britain there were 181 in running order of which three belonged to British Rail, on the 600 mm (1 ft 11½ in) gauge Vale of Rheidol Railway.

(See also 'Last Steam Trains'.)

DIESEL RAIL TRACTION

The 'compression ignition' system was invented by Ackroyd Stuart (1864–1927) who developed the idea between 1886 and 1890.

Dr Rudolf Diesel (1858–1913) was born in Paris and became a professor at Munich. He invented his internal-combustion engine, in 1892, to use a fairly crude oil so as to be less costly to run than a petrol engine. It was first demonstrated in 1898. Dr Diesel who, apparently, refused to allow his engine to be used for war purposes, mysteriously disappeared from a steamer to Harwich during a journey to London in 1913.

Oil burned in a diesel engine produces 1·9 times as much work as the same amount burned in an oil-fired steam locomotive. A diesel locomotive will produce less atmospheric pollution than a steam locomotive for the same amount of work.

The major problem of high-power diesel rail-traction is the transmission from engine to wheels. Mechanical and hydraulic transmissions have been used, but electric transmission is now almost universal. It should be borne in mind that a diesel-electric is simply

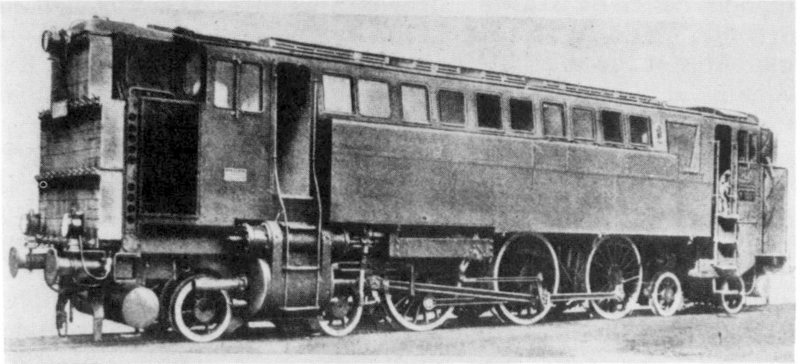
The German diesel/compressed-air locomotive, 1929

an electric locomotive carrying its own power-station on board. It produces only about a third, and at best less than half, as much power as a modern electric locomotive of equal weight, even though the latter includes a transformer and rectifier.

The first diesel locomotive was a direct-drive 1000 hp Diesel-Klose-Sulzer unit built in Germany in 1912–13, but it ran for only a few months, as an experiment.

The first diesel railway vehicle in revenue service was an Atlas-Deva 75 bhp diesel-electric railcar built in 1913 for the Mellersta & Södermanlands Railway, Sweden. It ran until 1939.

The first 'production' diesels were five 200 hp diesel-electric railcars built by Sulzer in Switzerland in 1914 for the Prussian & Saxon State Railways.

The first diesel-electric switchers (or 'shunters' in English) were three 200 hp units built in the USA by the General Electric Company in 1918.

The first 'commercially successful' diesel-electric locomotive in America was a 300 hp unit built by ALCO in 1923, with an Ingersoll-Rand engine and General Electric Company controls and transmission. It went into service on 20 October 1925, followed by four more. The first was sold to the Jersey Central Railroad, becoming No. 1000, and worked until 1957 when it was presented to the Baltimore & Ohio Transportation Museum (qv).

One of the most curious locomotives was the Kitson-Still steam-diesel locomotive built by Kitson & Company of Leeds, England, and tested on the London & North Eastern Railway in April 1927. It was a 2–6–2 tank engine with eight cylinders operating with internal combustion on one side of the piston and with steam on the other side. The internal-combustion engine helped in raising steam. It attempted to combine the power at slow speed of the steam-engine with the fuel economy of the internal-combustion engine. It gave good performance on freight trains between York and Hull, but was excessively noisy, and the design was not repeated.

The first experiment with diesel-traction on British railways was in 1924 when the London & North Eastern Railway tried an Austrian-built diesel locomotive for a short period.

The first main-line use of diesel-electric traction was on the Canadian National Railways in 1925 when eight railcars were put into service. They had eight-cylinder engines made by Beardmore of Scotland. One of these covered 4715 km (2930 miles) from Montreal to Vancouver in 67 hours.

The first main-line diesel-electric locomotives were the four 1200 bhp units built for the German State Railways in 1925 to a design by the Russian engineer Professor George V. Lomonossoff (1876–1952).

The Long Island Railroad was the first in the USA to run a diesel-electric locomotive in road service, in 1926.

The first 'road' or main-line diesel-electric locomotive in Canada was introduced by the Canadian National Railways in 1928. It was a twin unit of 2660 hp, Nos. 9000–1. It was scrapped early in 1949.

A curious form of transmission was tried in Germany on a 4–6–4 locomotive built in 1929 by Maschinenfabrik Augsburg Nürnberg AG. This was a diesel-compressed air machine. The 1200 bhp diesel engine drove an air compressor. The compressed air was taken through a heater through which the engine exhaust was passed, and the drive to the wheels was as on a steam locomotive with Walschaert's valve gear. The efficiency was stated to be higher than with electric transmission. The cylinders were 700 × 700 mm ($27\frac{1}{2} \times 27\frac{1}{2}$ in) and with a working pressure of 6·5–7 kg/cm² (92·3–99·4 lb/in²) the tractive effort was 12 000 kg (26 500 lb).

The first British diesel-electric train was adapted by the London, Midland & Scottish Railway in 1928 from an ex-Lancashire & Yorkshire Railway Manchester–Bury electric train, by fitting it with a 500 hp Beardmore engine and English Electric traction equipment. It ran for a time on the Preston–Blackpool service and was later reconverted to an electric train.

The first use of diesel-traction in Ireland was in 1929 when Kerr Stuart & Company of Stoke-on-Trent tried out a 0–6–0 diesel-mechanical locomotive on the Castlederg & Victoria Bridge Tramway in County Tyrone. It ran for about 6 months.

The first regular use of diesel-traction in the British Isles was on the 914 mm (3 ft) gauge County Donegal Railways in Ireland, in September 1931. The diesel railcar No. 7 was powered by a 74 hp Gardner engine. With a second, No. 8, built in November 1931, it was scrapped in 1939.

The first diesel locomotive in regular service in Britain was rebuilt from a Midland Railway 0–6–0 tank engine by the London, Midland & Scottish Railway in 1931. A Paxman engine was used with Haslem & Newton hydrostatic transmission.

The first British diesel railbus was produced by Hardy Motors Limited who converted an AEC 'Regal' road coach to run on rails in 1933, so beginning the long association of the Associated Equipment Company with railcars.

The first Great Western Railway diesel railcar was by Hardy Motors Limited in 1933, built by AEC with Park Royal coachwork. It was fully streamlined, was 19·379 m (63 ft 7 in) long and weighed 20 tons. It seated 70 third class passengers and had a top speed of 121 km/h (75 mph). After achieving considerable attention at the International Commercial Motor Exhibition in London it was sold to the GWR becoming their diesel car No. 1 and entering service in 1934.

The first high-speed diesel train, the streamlined *Flying Hamburger*, ran between Berlin and Hamburg and was introduced in the spring of 1932. It was scheduled to run at speeds of over 100 mph (161 km/h). On tests it reached over 198·5 km/h (124 mph).

The first diesel locomotives in main-line service in the USA were used on the Chicago, Burlington & Quincy and Union Pacific railroads in 1934. The first diesels on regular freight work went into service on the Santa Fe in 1940.

The 'Burlington Zephyr' of the Chicago, Burlington & Quincy Railroad entered service in 1934 as the world's first diesel-electric streamliner. On 26 May 1934 it travelled the 1633 km (1015 miles) from Denver to Chicago non-stop at an average speed of 125 km/h (77·6 mph). The train is preserved at the Museum of Science and Industry, Chicago, alongside a captured German submarine.

The first lightweight streamlined diesel passenger train went into operation between Lincoln, Nebraska, USA and Kansas City, Missouri, on 11 November 1934.

The first British streamlined diesel train was built by the London, Midland & Scottish Railway in 1938. It consisted of three articulated coaches powered by Leyland diesel engines and hydro-mechanical transmission. After successful service between Oxford and Cambridge, and Nottingham and London, it was stored throughout the war and afterwards was dismantled.

The greatest landmark in the progress of the diesel locomotive was the General Motors 'Electro Motive' No. 103, built in the USA in 1939. It was a four-unit freight machine rated at 5400 hp. In one year's trials it covered 133 572 km (83 000 miles) on 21 roads in 37

States in temperatures from −40 °C (−40 °F) to 43·3 °C (110 °F) at altitudes from sea-level to 3109 m (10 200 ft). Up the 40 km (25 miles) of 1 in 40 (2·5 per cent) on the Southern Pacific/Santa Fe climb to Tehachapi Pass from the west it hauled 1800 tons in one and a half hours, completely outclassing the biggest steam locomotives. From that moment the fate of the steam locomotive in America and round the world was sealed.

The first diesel-electric locomotive in road freight service in the USA was inaugurated by the Santa Fe Railroad on 4 February 1941.

The 'diesel revolution' in the USA took about 16 years. In 1945 there were 38 853 steam locomotives, 842 electric locomotives and 835 'other types'. In May 1952 the number of diesel locomotives, 19 082, became greater than the number of steam locomotives, 18 489. In 1961 there were 110 steam, 480 electric and 28 150 diesel units.

The first British main-line diesel-electric locomotives were built by the London, Midland & Scottish Railway in 1947—Nos. 10000/1. They were Co–Co types with English Electric Company 1600 hp engines and six nose-suspended traction motors, and weighed 128 tons each, a startling contrast to the 'Deltics' mentioned below, with a weight of 106 tons and horsepower of 3300, built only eight years later.

Rail Diesel Cars (known as 'RDCs') were introduced in North America by the Budd Company of Philadelphia, Pennsylvania, in 1949. They have two 300 hp General Motors diesel engines mounted under the floor, each driving one axle through a GM hydraulic torque converter and reverse gear. The single cars are 25·908 m (85 ft) long, weigh 51 620 kg (46·3 tons) (113 800 lb), seat 70 passengers and include a 5·182 m (17 ft) luggage compartment. For multiple-unit operation in trains, passenger-only trailer vehicles are also built with single engines.

By 1973 Budd had built about 500 RDCs. Most are in the USA and Canada. Others are at work in Australia, Saudi Arabia, Cuba and Brazil (Departamento Nacional de Estradas de Ferro—DNEF, and Rède Ferroviaria Federal Sa—RFFSA).

Diesel multiple-unit trains first appeared in Britain in 1954, and were first put to work between Leeds and Bradford via Stanningley on 14 June and between Carlisle and Silloth on 29 November.

Four-wheeled diesel railbuses of various designs were tried on lightly used lines in Britain for several years from 1958. Two are preserved for use on the Keighley & Worth Valley Railway, and another is on the North Yorkshire Moors Railway, Yorkshire, and two more are at Sheringham, Norfolk.

Multiple-unit diesel-electric trains on the Southern Region of British Railways were first used on the London to Hastings via Tunbridge Wells service on 6 May 1957. They are in six-car sets with a 500 bhp English Electric supercharged diesel engine and generator in each end car.

Hydraulic transmission was adopted by the Western Region of British Railways, prin-

The first British main-line diesel-hydraulic locomotive No. D600, built by the North British Locomotive Company in 1957–8 for the Western Region (British Rail)

cipally because of the greater power/weight ratio. The hydraulic transmission gear weighs considerably less than the generator and motors on a diesel-electric locomotive. For example, the Class '52' 'Westerns' introduced in 1961 had an output of 2700 hp and a maximum tractive force of 32 931 kg (72 600 lb), with a total weight of 109 tons. The Class '46' diesel-electrics, also 1961, had an output of 2500 hp, a maximum tractive force of 31 752 kg (72 000 lb), with a weight of 138 tons, a difference in weight equal to one coach.

The first British main-line diesel-hydraulic locomotive, No. D600, was built by the North British Locomotive Company, Glasgow, and was delivered to the Western Region of British Railways in March 1958. It was an A1A A1A type, weighed 117·4 tons, and had an output of 2000 hp and a top speed of 145 km/h (90 mph). It was the first of a class of five named, together with the following class of B-B locomotives, after warships, and carried the name *Active*. All five were withdrawn by the end of 1967.

Later in 1958 the first of the 71 B-B-type diesel-hydraulic locomotives of Classes '42' and '43' was completed at the Swindon Works, based on the successful German V200 Class, weighing only 78 tons and producing 2100 bhp. The WR version, however, built to the smaller British construction gauge, was not so successful and the entire class had been withdrawn by the end of 1972. Three have not been broken up.

The 58 1000 and 1100 hp B-B type of Class '22', weighing only 65 tons and built by the North British Locomotive Company, were introduced in 1959. They were among the less successful of the WR diesel-hydraulics and their working career was short. The last of the 1000 hp type was withdrawn in 1968, and of the 1100 hp type in 1971.

In 1961 the first of the 74 C-C 'Western' Class '52' locomotives was completed at Swindon. By the end of their career, in 1977, they had become one of the most popular and sought-after diesel classes on BR. Several have been preserved, including one at the National Railway Museum, York, and two on the Severn Valley Railway.

The 101 Beyer Peacock 'Hymek' B-B locomotives of Class '35', introduced in 1961, were more successful than the other B-Bs. With a weight of 74 tons they had an output of 1700 hp. The last of these was withdrawn in 1975. Three have been preserved, and three others were still in departmental use on BR in 1977.

The main difficulty with the WR diesel-hydraulics was the expense of maintenance. In traffic the 'Westerns' and 'Hymeks' were among the most efficient and economical of BR diesels.

Hydraulic transmission was also used on several classes of small 0–4–0 and 0–6–0 shunting locomotives, and some multiple-unit diesel passenger stock.

The first of the British Rail 'Deltic' diesels was introduced by the English Electric Company at their Vulcan Works, Lancashire, in 1955. It was then **the most powerful diesel-electric single-unit locomotive in the world**, rated at 3300 bhp with a weight of only 106 tons. After extensive trials on the London Midland Region an order was placed for 22 units for the East Coast main line between London and Edinburgh and delivery began in 1961. They are timed at speeds of 161 km/h (100 mph).

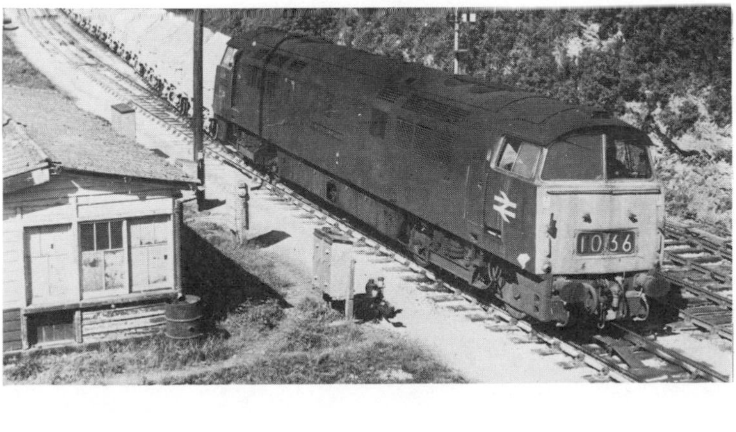

British Rail Western Region Class '52' diesel hydraulic C–C type No. 1036 *Western Emperor* on a china clay train at Par, Cornwall, in July 1976

Northern Rock, the newest locomotive on the 381 mm (15 in) gauge Ravenglass & Eskdale Railway in Cumbria, at Ravenglass on 28 June 1976 (see p. 211)

Welshpool & Llanfair Railway 762 mm (2 ft 6 in) gauge 0–8–0 tank No. 699.01. This locomotive was built as a 0–8–0 tender engine with short side tanks in 1944 by the Société Franco-Belge, Raismes, France, for the German military railways. On 6 January 1946 it was lent to the Salzkammergutlokalbahn, Austria, which bought it on 1 April 1950. In 1955 it was resold to the Styrian Provincial Railways, Austria, which rebuilt it in 1957 with full-length side tanks and bunker. In 1965 it was put into store until 1969 when it was bought by the W. & L. Behind it a coach from the Salzkammergutlokalbahn (see p. 240) (Simon Marshall)

A train on the 381 mm (15 in) gauge Romney, Hythe & Dymchurch Railway approaching New Romney from Hythe. The locomotive is 4–6–2 No. 8 *Hurricane* built by Davey Paxman in 1926 (see p. 211) (Simon Marshall)

A train for Devil's Bridge on the 600 mm (1 ft 11½ in) gauge Vale of Rheidol Railway, headed by 2–6–2 tank No. 9 *Prince of Wales*, ready to leave Aberystwyth Station in June 1975 (see p. 212)

The 'Hobby Train' at Mayrhofen on the 381 mm (2 ft 6 in) gauge Zillertalbahn, Austria, in July 1975, with 0–4–0 tank No. 6 built by Krauss (7182) in 1916

One of the 350 hp 0–6–0 diesel-electric shunters, Class 08 on British Rail, which were sold to the Netherlands Railways. This engine now works on the Appeldoorn–Dieren line north of Arnhem in conjunction with steam locomotives. Photographed at Loenen in August 1978

The original unit is now displayed in the Science Museum, London.

The first of the 'Deltics' to travel 2 000 000 miles (3 218 700 km) was No. 9010 *King's Own Scottish Borderer*, stationed at Edinburgh and working about 6437 km (4000 miles) a week, at speeds of 145–161 km/h (90–100 mph) between Edinburgh, London and Leeds. It is one of the class of 22 introduced in 1961, and it topped the 2 000 000 mark in the week commencing 15 January 1973. It is probably the first diesel-electric locomotive in the world to travel 2 000 000 miles in under 12 years.

By contrast the record-breaking 'A4' Class 'Pacific' *Mallard*, withdrawn for preservation in 1963, recorded only 2 294 943 km (1 426 000 miles) in its 25 years of service. The Great Western 'Star' Class 4–6–0 No. 4021 *King Edward* (renamed *British Monarch* in 1927) took 43 years to complete its 3 274 987 km (2 034 975 miles), and the 'Saint' Class 4–6–0 No. 2920 *Saint David* took 46 years for its 3 348 663 km (2 080 754 miles).

This illustrates the tremendous availability of diesel locomotives compared with steam.

The new numbering system for British Rail diesel and electric locomotives was introduced in 1968. Diesel classes run from 01 to 56, with blanks where classes have been withdrawn. Electric classes run from 70 to 87.

The largest class of British diesel locomotives is the 08 0–6–0 type of which 1193 were built to the same basic design. BR stock at the end of 1976 was 936. The design dates back to 1934.

The latest and most powerful diesel-electric freight locomotives on British Rail are the '56' Class Co–Co machines, first delivered in May 1976. With a change in 1974 to greater use of home-produced coal in Britain the railways were faced with an urgent need for more locomotives of adequate power for its haulage. The first 30 were erected in Romania and the second 30 at the Doncaster Works of British Rail Engineering Limited. A further 30 were ordered from BRE Ltd in 1976. The 16-cylinder engine develops 3250 hp at 900 rev/min. They weigh 128 tonnes and are designed for a service speed of 130 km/h (81 mph).

The world's most powerful single-unit diesel-electric locomotive is at present the Union Pacific Railroad 'Centennial' Do Do type, introduced in 1969, a hundred years after the completion of the first transcontinental railroad. At 29·261 m (96 ft) it is also the world's longest. It is rated at 6600 hp and weighs 229 000 kg (504 000 lb). The first was numbered 6900, and a total of 47 were ordered from the Electro-Motive Division of the General Motors Corporation. They have a maximum speed of 115 km/h (71 mph). See colour illustration on p. 75.

Canada's most powerful diesel-electric unit is the Canadian Pacific Rail No. 4744 built by Montreal Locomotive Works and delivered in 1971. It is a development of the 'Century' 636 design used in Australia. It is rated at 4000 hp.

The most powerful diesel-electric locomotives in Europe are the 20 3900 hp units, first built by Nydqvist & Holm and Frichs, Denmark, in 1972. They have General Motors (USA) 16–645–E3 engines, weigh 126 tonnes and have a maximum speed of 165 km/h (103 mph). More are at present on order for Spain.

The first diesel locomotive built in Australia was a 1·067 m (3 ft 6 in) gauge 'DL 1' Class 1C-type diesel-mechanical shunter weighing 17·5 tons, built by Queensland Government Railways at Ipswich Works, west of Brisbane, in 1939. It had a 153 hp Gardiner six-cylinder engine.

The first diesel-electric locomotive built in Australia was a 49 ton Bo Bo shunter, No. 350, completed in June 1949 for the 1·600 m (5 ft 3 in) gauge South Australian Railways at

British Rail Class '56' 3250 hp diesel electric freight locomotive No. 56002 undergoing trials with a train of 'Merry-go-Round' hoppers in July 1977. These 19·35 m (63 ft) long locomotives have special control systems to enable them to haul 'Merry-go-Round' trains at a constant speed of 1 km/h during loading and unloading (British Rail Board)

their Islington Works. Two were built, powered by English Electric 350 hp six-cylinder engines. They were still at work in 1975.

The first main-line diesel-electric locomotive in service in Australia was an A1A–A1A hood unit, No. 4001, introduced in November 1951 by the New South Wales Railways. It was built by Montreal Locomotive Works and was powered by an ALCO 1600 hp 12-cylinder engine. It was withdrawn in November 1971 and is now preserved in the New South Wales Rail Transport Museum. (See p. 234.)

The most powerful diesel-electric locomotives in Australia are the 'Century' 636 type introduced in June 1968 and owned by the Hammersley Iron Pty Limited on the north coast of Western Australia. They are 180 ton Co Co ALCO hood units of 3600 hp built under licence by Godwins of Sydney. Three units in multiple haul up to 240 cars each of 100 tons capacity and 120 tons gross weight, a total of 28 000 tons, at 64·374 km/h (40 mph).

The standard gauge Hammersley Railway carries a greater annual tonnage than any other single track in Australia. On a normal day six trains carry 90 000 tons of ore one way. It also uses the heaviest track in Australia, 67·5 kg/m (136 lb/yd).

The most powerful diesel-electric locomotives

Canadian Pacific 4000 hp Co–Co locomotive No. 4744, the most powerful diesel-electric unit in Canada and the most powerful single-engined diesel locomotive in the world (Canadian Pacific Limited)

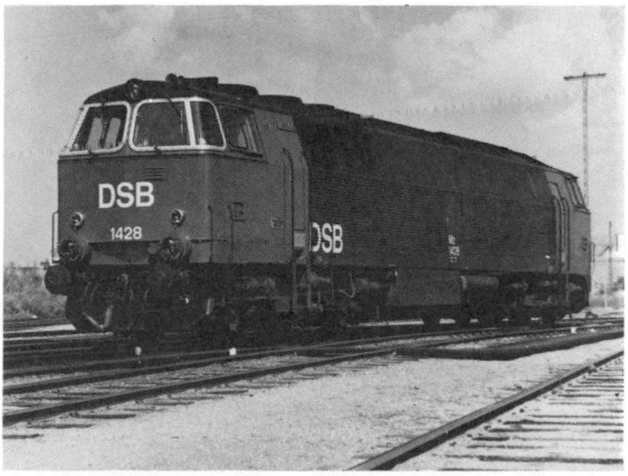

One of the Danish 3900 hp diesel-electric locomotives, the most powerful units in Europe, built in 1972. They have a top speed of 165 km/h (103 mph) (Danish State Railways)

The Railway Station (1862) by W P Frith, showing a scene at Paddington Station, London, in the days of the 7 ft gauge (see p. 224) (In the collection at the Royal Holloway College, University of London)

Istanbul Station, where East meets West. The portrait over the entrance is of Mustafa Kemal Ataturk (1880–1938), first president of the Turkish Republic and founder of modern Turkey

Various heraldic devices

on the 1·067 m (3 ft 6 in) gauge in Australia are the '11N' Class on the Western Australian Government Railways. The first was delivered in December 1976, built by Commonwealth Engineering.

The most powerful diesel-electric locomotives on an Australian Government railway are the Western Australian 'L' Class Co Co-type 3000 hp units built in 1968. They measure 19·354 m (63 ft 6 in) long, 2·946 m (9 ft 8 in) wide, and have a top speed of 134 km/h (83 mph). They are standard gauge. The Commonwealth Railways 'CL' class introduced in 1970 are of similar power.

Three-phase traction motors have been used in six pioneering 2500 hp Co Co diesel-electric locomotives which were ordered by Swiss Federal Railways in 1973 for operating the new Limmattal marshalling yard about 15 km (9 miles) east of Zürich. The first went into service on 2 November 1976. (For use of induction motors see p. 156.)

GAS-TURBINE LOCOMOTIVES

The gas-turbine was first applied to rail-traction in 1941 when a 2140 hp gas-turbine-electric locomotive was built for the Swiss Federal Railways by Brown Boveri & Company of Baden. It was 16·383 m (53 ft 9 in) long, 1Bo Bo1 type and weighed 92 tons.

The Great Western Railway in England ordered a Brown Boveri gas-turbine-electric locomotive with an output of 2500 hp which was delivered in February 1950. It was numbered 18000 by British Railways Western Region.

The first British-built gas-turbine-electric locomotive was a 3000 hp unit built by the Metropolitan-Vickers Electrical Company Limited for the Western Region of British Railways in January 1952 and numbered 18100. It was 20·320 m (66 ft 8 in) long and weighed 130 tons. It was withdrawn in January 1958 and was rebuilt into an electric locomotive for the 25 kV electrification for use in training drivers, and was numbered E1000 until withdrawn finally in 1968.

The first gas-turbine-electric locomotive to be built and operated in the USA began track tests on 15 November 1948 on the Union Pacific Railroad. The first unit entered regular pool service on 1 January 1952.

The largest gas-turbine-electric locomotives were the two-unit 8500 hp machines built by the General Electric Company at Schenectady, USA, for the Union Pacific Railroad. Forty-five were built, from 1957, following the success of the 25 UP 4500 hp gas-turbine-electrics built from 1952, which showed economies over diesels. The 1957 machines were 50·294 m (165 ft) long and weighed 408 tons.

Direct-drive gas-turbine locomotives were built by Renault in France in 1952 (1000 hp), and at Gotaverken in Sweden (1300 hp).

At the nationalisation of British railways on 1 January 1948 there were 20 024 steam locomotives. If, on average, including all passenger, freight and shunting work and standing idle, each evaporated 22 730 l (5000 gallons) of water in a day, then allowing for engines out of service British Railways were putting about 400 000 tons of water mixed

A1A–A1A gas-turbine-electric locomotive No. 18000 ordered by the Great Western Railway from Brown Boveri, Switzerland, in 1946 and delivered in 1950, photographed at Swindon in April 1960 after withdrawal from service

with waste products of combustion into the atmosphere every day. An express engine on a 644 km (400 mile) run would evaporate about 69 099 l (15 200 gallons), or nearly 70 tons of water, and burn about 8 tons of coal.

With considerably less fuel consumption and atmospheric pollution an equal amount of power is produced in an electric power-station which condenses most of its water and thereby runs at far higher efficiency, besides making more efficient use of fuel in boilers. At high voltages electricity can be transmitted over great distances with negligible power losses. High installation cost is the main obstacle to railway electrification and so it is justified at present only on lines with high traffic density. Future fuel shortages may alter this.

ELECTRIC-TRACTION

The first electric railway in the world was made by Thomas Davenport, a blacksmith in Vermont, USA, in 1835. It was a small railway powered by a miniature electric motor.

The first serious attempt at electric power on a railway was made by Robert Davidson in 1842 when he tried out a battery locomotive weighing 5 tons on the Edinburgh & Glasgow Railway where it ran at 6·5 km/h (4 mph).

The electric dynamo was perfected between 1860 and 1870 but its use as a motor came several years later.

The first practical electric railway was built by the German engineer Werner von Siemens (qv) for the Berlin Trades Exhibition—31 May to 30 September 1879. It was a 550 m (600 yd) long narrow-gauge line. The electric locomotive had a 3 hp motor, picking up current at 150 V from a centre third rail and returning it via the wheels and running rails. It could pull about 30 passengers on three cars at 6·5 km/h (4 mph).

The first public electric railway in the world was opened on 12 May 1881 at Lichterfelde near Berlin. It was 2·5 km (1½ mile) long. The car ran on a 100 V supply and carried 26 passengers at 48 km/h (30 mph).

The first public electric railway in Britain was Magnus Volk's Electric Railway at Brighton, first opened on 4 August 1883 with 610 mm (2 ft) gauge. It was rebuilt to 838 mm (2 ft 9 in) gauge and extended and reopened on 4 April 1884. It was taken over by Brighton Corporation on 1 April 1940. (See colour illustration, p. 34.)

The first electric railway to run on hydro-electric power was the 9·5 km (6 mile) long 914 mm (3 ft) gauge Portrush–Giant's Causeway Tramway, Ireland, formally opened on 28 September 1883. It was engineered by William Acheson Traill (1844–1933). Cars could run at 19 km/h (12 mph) on the level. At first an outside conductor rail was used, and the town section was worked by two steam-tram engines from W. Wilkinson & Company of Wigan. In 1899 the entire system was converted to overhead wire collection. It was closed in 1950.

The first electric underground railway in the world was the City & South London, opened on 18 December 1890. At first it used 14 four-wheeled electric locomotives built by Mather & Platt of Salford. By 1901 there were 52 locomotives. They ran until the line was reconstructed in 1924. One is preserved in the Science Museum, London.

The first electric locomotive in the USA for use on standard gauge was designed by L. Daft for the Mount Macgregor & Lake George Railroad in 1883.

The first electric train service in the USA began on the 11 km (7 mile) Nantasket Branch of the New York, New Haven & Hartford Railroad (now part of Conrail) on 28 June 1895.

Electric locomotives were introduced on the Baltimore & Ohio Railroad on 4 August 1895, on the Belt line from Henrietta Street, Baltimore (just south of Camden Station), to Waverley Tower—6 km (3¾ miles) through ten tunnels amounting to 48 per cent of the distance. Passenger traffic began on 1 May 1895, with coke-burning locomotives, and goods traffic began with the electrification. The first trials with electric-traction were on 27 June 1895, originally with an overhead slot pick-up, replaced in March 1902 by a third rail.

The world's first electric elevated city railway was the Liverpool Overhead Railway,

England. The first section opened on 6 March 1893. The line was closed, to avoid massive renewals, on 30 December 1956.

The Chicago Elevated Railway saw its first electric cars in 1895, after the system had been operated for a few years by the 'Forney'-type 0–4–4 tanks.

The Berlin Elevated Railway began as an electric line in 1902.

The world's first single-phase alternating current locomotive went into service in 1904 on the Seebach–Wettingen Railway, Switzerland. Originally it was built for a 50 Hz supply with direct current traction motors supplied by a motor generator, but in 1904 it was rebuilt for 15 000 V, 15 Hz, with ac motors. The railway was the pioneer of high-voltage single-phase systems. The locomotive remained in service on the Bodensee–Toggenburg Railway until 1958 when it was given a place of honour in the Swiss Transport Museum, Lucerne.

Railway electrification in North America, apart from suburban lines, has never been undertaken extensively because of the nature of the traffic. Electrification pays off only if the equipment is used intensively, such as on the London–Birmingham and Lancashire, or the St Gotthard route in Switzerland. In North America it is more economical to assemble the traffic into one enormous train, perhaps over a mile (1·6 km) long, which can be handled by a crew of three or four men. In Europe such trains are not possible; first, because the couplings are not strong enough, and second, the track layouts are not designed for trains of such length.

Electrification was undertaken in North America where there was the difficulty of ventilation in long tunnels such as Hoosac and Cascade, and of handling heavy trains on long climbs in the days of steam locomotives. The introduction of diesel power almost eliminated these troubles and consequently the electrical equipment could be dismantled and maintenance costs thereby reduced. The increasing cost of oil, however, may change this, and American engineers are watching with interest the development of the 50 kV system. (See p. 157.)

The longest electrified line in the USA was on the Chicago, Milwaukee, St Paul & Pacific (The Milwaukee Road). It had a total of 1056 km (656 miles) of electrified route out of a total route length of 17 125 km (10 641 miles).

In 1973 it was decided to abandon the electrification and to convert the entire line to diesel operation.

The Milwaukee is the only system in the USA operating over its own tracks all the way from Chicago to the Pacific Northwest. It was completed to Seattle in 1908.

The first British railway to be electrified at 1500 V dc with overhead catenary was the Shildon–Newport (now Tees-side) section of the North Eastern Railway. Electrically hauled coal trains with Bo Bo locomotives designed by Vincent Raven (1858–1934), the chief mechanical engineer, began running on 1 July 1915. It was proposed to adopt this system on the main line between York and Newcastle and a prototype 2–Co–2 express locomotive, No. 13, was built in 1922, but the Grouping into the London & North Eastern Railway and the severe shortage of money following the First World War prevented further progress.

With the decline of coal traffic, the Shildon–Newport section reverted to steam-haulage early in 1935. The locomotives were stored and subsequently scrapped. No. 13 survived the Second World War but was never used.

The 1500 V dc overhead system was recommended for adoption as a British Standard by the 1921 'Electrification Committee' Report and by the subsequent Pringle (1928) and Weir (1931) Reports.

The first British passenger railway to be electrified at 1500 V dc was the joint LNER and LMS line from Manchester to Altrincham where electric multiple-unit trains began running on 8 May 1931. On 3 May 1971 the line was changed to 25 kV ac.

The first mercury-arc rectifier to be installed on a British railway was at Hendon on the Morden–Edgware line of the London Underground in 1930. It marked one of the most important technical improvements in dc electric-traction and made unmanned substations possible. Previously permanently manned rotary converters had to be used.

The first British suburban railway electrification was inaugurated by the North Eastern

Railway between Newcastle (New Bridge Street) and Benton on 29 March 1904.

The Lancashire & Yorkshire Railway was a close runner-up when it introduced electric trains between Liverpool and Southport on 5 April 1904. In a desperate bid to beat the North Eastern Railway some trains were introduced before this, but the haste resulted in a partial breakdown and steam trains were not completely withdrawn until 13 May.

The first portion of the 'Southern Electric' was the South London line of the London, Brighton & South Coast Railway. Electric trains began on 1 December 1909 using ac at 6000 V with overhead collectors. It was later converted to 660 V dc third rail to conform to the other electrified lines south of London.

The first British main-line electrification was the Southern Railway London to Brighton and Worthing, brought into use on 1 January 1933. The system is 660 V dc third rail.

The use of electricity at very high voltages creates special dangers, necessitating precautionary notices even in the most unlikely places, such as this near Low Gill on the Lancaster–Carlisle section of British Rail

Electrification of the London (Liverpool Street)–Shenfield line, 32 km (20 miles), at 1500 V dc overhead came into operation on 26 September 1949. It was extended to Chelmsford, 15·289 km ($9\frac{1}{2}$ miles), on 11 June 1956 and to Southend (Victoria), 25 km ($15\frac{1}{2}$ miles), on 31 December 1956. It was converted to 25 kV ac in 1960.

Britain's first 'all-electric' main line (passenger and freight traffic) was the Manchester–Sheffield line of the former Great Central Railway. Through passenger services began on 14 September 1954 following the opening, on 3 June, of the new Woodhead Tunnel. The 'standard' 1500 V dc system was used. The passenger service was withdrawn from 5 January 1970.

On the Netherlands Railways 1646 km (1023 miles) are electrified at 1500 V dc out of a total route length of 2832 km (1758 miles). Steam-traction was withdrawn on 7 January 1958.

Following withdrawal of the Manchester–Sheffield passenger service in 1970 British Rail sold the seven Co–Co locomotives, Nos. 27000–6, to the Netherlands Railways in 1972.

The 25 kV single phase system at the industrial frequency of 50 Hz was pioneered in France in 1950.

The decision to adopt 25 000 V (25 kV) 50 Hz electrification as the future British standard was made on 6 March 1956.

The first British railway to operate on 25 kV was the 39·5 km ($24\frac{1}{2}$ mile) Colchester–Clacton–Walton line, on 16 March 1959.

The first British main line to operate on 25 kV was the Crewe–Manchester, on 12 September 1960. The Crewe–Liverpool line followed on 1 January 1962.

The first electric trains in Scotland (excluding the Glasgow District Subway) were the Glasgow suburban services—50 km (31 miles) of line at 25 kV. They began on 7 November 1960 but were withdrawn for alteration from 17 December 1960 to 1 October 1961.

The second stage—43·5 km (27 miles) of line south of the Clyde—was inaugurated on 27 May 1962.

The London–Manchester–Liverpool full service began on 18 April 1966. Some trains had run through from 22 November 1965. It was extended to the Birmingham area on 6 March 1967.

The extension of the electrification from London to Glasgow, covering the lines from Weaver Junction, Cheshire, to Motherwell in Lanarkshire, Scotland, was approved by the Minister of Transport in March 1970. It was opened throughout on 6 May 1974. The total cost was £75 000 000–£30 000 000 for electrification, £38 000 000 for resignalling and £7 000 000 for new electric locomotives.

The new '87' class electric locomotives, introduced in 1973 for the Scottish services, have an output of 5000 hp with a total weight of only 80 tons. They are **the most powerful locomotives on British Rail**. They have fully suspended traction motors and are designed to run at speeds of over 161 km/h (100 mph) and, unlike the other 25 kV locomotives, can be coupled and driven as multiple-units. Their output of 62½ hp/ton is twice that of the 'Deltics', the most powerful British diesel-electric units, but their adhesion at full power on adverse grades is at the mercy of the weather.

The first British Rail electric locomotive with thyrister control was No. 87 101, built at Crewe in 1975. The thyrister gives notchless control at constant tractive effort; tapchanger control produces variations in tractive effort in each notch.

At a ceremony at Piccadilly Station, Manchester, on 12 October 1977, No. 87 101 was named *Stephenson* by Mr A J Boston, President of the Stephenson Locomotive Society which provided the nameplates.

'The Great Northern Electrics' were introduced on the Moorgate (London)–Hertford/Welwyn Garden City service on 8 November 1976. They operate on 25 kV ac in the open and on 600 V dc on the underground section between Finsbury Park and Moorgate.

British Railways Southern Region mainline electrification to Southampton and Bournemouth was completed on 10 July 1967, enabling through trains to run from London, using third rail at 750 V dc. On the same day 145 km/h (90 mph) push-and-pull services were introduced, following successful tests at 161 km/h (100 mph). **The occasion marked the end of steam on BR Southern Region.**

Of the total British Rail network of 18 988 km (11 537 miles), 3570 km (2848 miles) are electrified with three systems: 600–750 V dc third rail (1770 km; 1100 miles), 1500 V dc (113 km; 70 miles) and 25 kV ac (1687 km; 1048 miles) overhead. This can be compared with the French Railways which, in a total of 35 180 km (21 860 miles), have electrified 9365 km (5819 miles), 4827 km (2999 miles) with 1500 V dc and 4299 km (2671 miles) with 25 kV ac.

The first silicon-rectifier locomotive in the USA, one of six, was delivered to an eastern railroad on 3 July 1962.

Induction motors for rail traction were first applied in 1965 on the *Hawk* diesel-electric locomotive by Brush Electrical Machines, Loughborough. At the time technology was insufficiently advanced and it was not a success. On the German Federal Railways the induction motor is being evaluated in three locomotives by Henschel/Brown Boveri. The

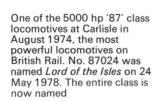

One of the 5000 hp '87' class locomotives at Carlisle in August 1974, the most powerful locomotives on British Rail. No. 87024 was named *Lord of the Isles* on 24 May 1978. The entire class is now named

advantage of the induction motor is that, having no commutator and brushes, maintenance is cheaper and it is less affected by dust and grit in industrial use.

The world's first 50 kV electric railway is the isolated 125·5 km (78 mile) standard-gauge line linking the Black Mesa Mines near Kayenta, Arizona, USA with the giant Navajo power-station which will have an output of 2250 MW, requiring 8 000 000 tons of coal a year. The high voltage requires only one feed point at one end of the line, so reducing installation and maintenance costs. The operation of the railway is entirely automatic. It was opened on 15 March 1974.

The six 6000 hp thyrister-controlled Co Co locomotives were built by the General Electric Company, USA. Two trains, each powered by three locomotives, make three round trips daily, carrying up to 10 000 tons of coal on each trip. The railway is regarded partly as a test-bed for future electrification in the USA.

North of Cape Town in South Africa a new 846 km (525 miles) 1·065 m (3 ft 6 in) gauge line from Sishen to Saldanha Bay has been electrified at 50 kV as a direct result of the oil shortage. It was built by the South African Iron & Steel Industrial Corporation (ISCOR). Tracklaying started on 11 November 1974 and was completed on 28 April 1976. The first trains ran on 7 May 1976. Ownership was transferred to South African Railways on 1 April 1977. Until electric operation began in mid 1978 trains were hauled by General Electric U26C diesel-electric locomotives in rakes of five. Trains of 204 wagons carrying 17 000 tons of ore, total weight 21 000 tons, are hauled at speeds up to 72 km/h (45 mph) by three GEC locomotives in multiple unit. Seventeen Co Co electric locomotives of 3780 kW (5069 hp) have been obtained, the world's most powerful locomotives on the 1·065 m gauge, weighing 168 tons each and measuring 20·12 m (66 ft) long over buffer beams. They have thyrister control, and four dynamic brake resistors capable of dissipating 4210 kW to hold the trains on the long down grades.

The locomotives were built in South Africa by Union Carriage & Wagon Company (Pty) Ltd with electrical equipment by GEC Traction, Manchester, England.

The world's most powerful electric locomotive was the Swiss Federal Railways experimental 1D2+2D1 No. 11852, built in 1939. It developed 11 100 hp at 75 km/h (46·6 mph).

The most powerful electric locomotives built as a class are the Swiss Federal Railways Re 6/6 Bo Bo Bo type. Four were built in 1972, two with articulated bodies, 11601–2, and two with rigid bodies, 11603–4, for trials on the St Gotthard line. Forty-five more with rigid bodies, 11605–49, were put into service in 1975–7. A supplementary order for 40 more was made in 1976 to be delivered at the rate of 12 per year, 1977–81, to make a total of 89 units. They have an output of 10 450 hp, a tractive effort of 88 600 lb (40 200 kg), weigh 120 tons, and have a maximum speed of 87 mph (140 km/h).

In 1979 Swiss Federal Railways will receive ten heavy shunting locomotives type Ee 6/6 II numbered 16811–20, all with triple-phase and group converters. These will replace the last of the Ce 6/8 II 'crocodiles' dating from 1920–2.

Two new types are being developed in Russia by CDK-Skoda, Class '55E', a Co Co type developing 8200 hp, and Class '66E', a (Bo Bo)+(Bo Bo) developing 10 900 hp for 200 km/h (125 mph) running.

Chopper circuits, now being used to control some electric locomotives, are solid-state switches capable of rapid closing and opening for controlling the voltage applied to dc traction motors. They consist of thyristers in conjunction with diodes, and capacitors to give continuous current flow. Chopper control results in a 20–25 per cent improvement in energy consumption and also facilitates regenerative braking.

The world's most powerful electric locomotives with chopper control, to be built as a production series, are the 7000 hp Co Co-type supplied by ACEC (Ateliers de Constructions Electriques de Charleroi Société Anonyme, part of the Westinghouse Electric Group) and La Brugeoise et Nivelles for the 3000 V dc Belgian National Railways (SNCB) and first delivered on 9 September 1975. They represented a great advance in the use of semiconductors for traction-power conversion.

Among the world's most advanced electric locomotives are the ten French four-system C C type built in 1965–6. They are designed to run on 25 kV 50 Hz single-phase ac and 1500 V dc (France); 3000 V dc (Belgium); or 15 kV

$16\frac{2}{3}$ Hz single-phase ac (Germany and Switzerland). They have an output of 4500 hp and a top speed of 240 km/h (150 mph). They are used on the Trans-Europe Express (TEE) services between Paris and Brussels, 314 km (195 miles) non-stop in 2 h 20 min.

In 1974 the Belgian National Railways (SNCB) obtained six four-system C C type locomotives of 5870 hp, 'Class 18'. With five three-system Bo Bos of 'Class 16' they provide a total of 19 Belgian electric locomotives for crossing frontiers. The four-system machines are equipped to run on the Belgian 3000 V dc, Netherlands 1500 V dc, French 25 kV ac 50 Hz and German 15 kV ac $16\frac{2}{3}$ Hz lines.

The longest electrified railway in the world is from Moscow to Irkutsk—5213 km (3240 miles)—on the Trans-Siberian Railway, Russia.

The first electric trains in Australia began running at Melbourne, Victoria, in 1919. The first electric locomotive was introduced there in 1923. The system is 1500 V dc.

The highest-capacity passenger trains in Australia are the double-deck electric suburban trains at Sydney, NSW, which carry 2500 passengers at speeds up to 96·5 km/h (60 mph). They were introduced on 12 January 1964.

In other countries outside Europe electrified railways began operating as follows:

Argentina: Buenos Aires district, 24 km (15 miles), 550 V dc OH 1909 (electric tramway vehicles)
General Bartolomé Mitre (former Central Argentine) Buenos Aires (Retiro)–Tigre (Central) 29 km (18 miles), 800 V dc third rail, 24 August 1916
Bolivia: Guaqui–La Paz Railway, La Paz-El Alto, 9·5 km (6 miles) 550 V dc OH 1908
Brazil: Corcovado Railway, Cosme Velho–Corcovado 3·2 km (2 miles) 750 V 3-phase ac OH 1910
Canada: CNR Montreal, 2700 V dc OH 1918
Chile: Bethlehem Chile Iron Mines–Tofo, Cruz Grande, 24 km (15 miles), 2400 V dc OH 1916

French quadri-current 4 5000 hp locomotive No. 40101 (French Railways Limited)

Valparaiso–Los Andes and Santiago, 232 km (144 miles), 3000 V dc OH 1924
Chilean Transandine, 75·5 km (47 miles), 3000 V dc OH 1927
Costa Rica: Pacific Railroad, 124 km (77 miles), 15 kV single-phase ac 20 Hz OH 1929
Cuba: Havana–Mantanzas, 145 km (90 miles), 1200 V dc OH 1920
India: Bombay–Poona, 1500 V dc OH 1925
Bombay-Virar, 1500 V dc OH 1928
Indonesia: Djakarta district, 8 km (5 miles), 1500 V dc OH 1925
Japan: Chuo line, 1500 V dc OH 1906
New Zealand: Otira–Arthur's Pass, 14·5 km (9 miles), 1500 V dc OH 1923
South Africa: Durban area, 3000 V dc OH 1926
Turkey: Sirkeci–Halkai 25 kV 50 Hz 1955
USA: Long Island Railroad, 700 V dc third rail 1905
Pennsylvania Railroad; 650 V dc third rail 1906 11 kV single-phase ac 25 Hz OH 1907
Reading Railroad, 11 kV single-phase ac 25 Hz OH 1906

The first electrified trunk railway in China, from Paochi in the Province of Szechwan, 676 km (420 miles), was opened on 1 July 1975. The first train was a Chengtu–Peking express hauled by a Chinese-built 5200 hp electric locomotive. The decision to electrify the line, at 25 kV 50 Hz, was made in 1958, and the first 100 km (62 miles) to Fenghsien was completed in 1961, using French equipment. The railway, built in 1953–7, has 304 tunnels and 981 bridges.

Section 4
TRAINS

PASSENGER CARRIAGES

The first railway passenger carriage was a mere 'garden shed on wheels' pulled by a horse on the Stockton & Darlington Railway in England in 1825.

The first scheduled passenger service on a railway began on the Stockton & Darlington Railway on 16 October 1826. The first coach, pulled by a horse, was named 'The Union'. It was simply an ordinary horse carriage mounted on railway wheels.

In the USA the first passenger car to make a regular scheduled run was another 'shed on wheels' pulled by a horse, on the Baltimore & Ohio Railroad in 1829.

On the Liverpool & Manchester Railway in 1830 passenger carriages were similar to horse road carriages mounted on a railway-wagon chassis on four wheels.

The last horse-drawn passenger service on a British railway was the 'Port Carlisle Dandy' operating on the branch of the North British Railway from Drumburgh to Port Carlisle in Cumberland (now Cumbria), opened on 28

Port Carlisle Dandy Car, built at St Margaret's, Edinburgh, in 1857, now in the National Railway Museum, York

August 1856. Dandy No. 1, illustrated, was built at the NBR works at St Margaret's, Edinburgh, and after brief service on the North Leith and North Berwick branches it replaced the first horse-drawn car on the Port Carlisle Branch in 1859. It accommodated 12 first and second class passengers inside and 15 third class passengers on the outside benches. It ran until the horse-drawn service ended on 4 April 1914. After being used for many years as a pavilion on a sports field it was rescued by the London & North Eastern Railway and restored for the Stockton & Darlington Centenary in 1925. After that it was displayed on Edinburgh's Waverley Station until 1939 when it was moved to Carlisle Station. It was beautifully restored again in 1975 for display in the National Railway Museum, York, where the photograph was taken.

Bogie carriages were introduced in the USA as early as 1831 by Ross Winans, engineer, on the Baltimore & Ohio Railroad and by 1835 they were being generally adopted. The reason was primarily the light track to which they adapted themselves more readily than a four-wheeled vehicle. A bogie carriage built about 1836 for the Camden & Amboy Railroad, and now preserved in the Smithsonian Institution, Washington, DC, is the **oldest eight-wheeled passenger car in existence.**

The first compartment coach was built by Nathaniel Worsdell (1809–86) for the Liverpool & Manchester Railway in 1834. It was named *Experiment* and consisted of three horse-carriage bodies on a four-wheeled truck. From this developed the standard compartment carriage used in Britain and throughout most of Europe.

The compartment carriage was never adopted in North America where passengers liked to move around and meet each other, and there the 'open' type of car was adopted. Through the influence of the Pullman Car Company this reached Europe in the 1870s

One of three replicas of early Liverpool & Manchester coaches, built by the London, Midland & Scottish Railway for the centenary in 1930, at the National Railway Museum, York. It is based on a design by Nathaniel Worsdell incorporating three horse-carriage bodies which was the origin of the British 'compartment' coach

and now, a century later, it is being adopted as the standard type in Britain where, however, many travellers still prefer the compartment carriage.

The first bogie carriages in Great Britain were built by the 600 mm (1 ft 11½ in) gauge Festiniog Railway, Wales, in 1870. They were designed by C E Spooner (see p. 210) and were 12·192 m (40 ft) long.

The first vestibule connections were provided in Connecticut, USA, in June 1853 when a passenger train was fitted with covered and enclosed passageways between the cars.

Gas lighting was introduced on North London Railway trains in 1863.

Oil-lamps were introduced on USA trains in 1850; gas-lighting came in 1860; Pintsch gas in 1883; electric light in 1885 and fluorescent light in 1938.

Steam-heating was introduced in the USA in 1881. In Britain hot-water cans continued in use until the end of the 19th century. Steam heating was introduced here only gradually after about 1890.

The Milwaukee Road (Chicago, Milwaukee, St Paul & Pacific Railroad) was the first railway in the USA to equip all its passenger cars with steam heating, in 1887.

Electric lighting was introduced on British trains in 1881. (See 'Pullman Trains'.)

The first trains in the USA to be fully equipped with electric lights ran between New York and Chicago, Boston and New York, New York and Florida and from Springfield to Northampton, Massachusetts, in 1887.

Corridor trains were introduced in Britain on the Great Western Railway on 7 March 1892. The connections between the coaches were at first locked and used only by the guards. Corridor trains next appeared on the northern lines out of London and then, in 1900, on the London & South Western Railway.

Vista-dome cars were invented and patented by T J McBride of Winnipeg, Canada, in 1891. The idea was simply a development of the roof-top cupola first fitted to freight-train cabooses on the Chicago & North Western Railroad in 1863 (see p. 169).

A vista-dome car was introduced on the Canadian Pacific Railway in 1902 and three more in 1906. They had a cupola at each end and a glazed centre portion with clerestory. They were withdrawn during the First World War.

The first cast-steel bogie-truck frame with integrally cast journal boxes was patented in the USA by William P Bettendorf in 1903. Its use became standard throughout the USA.

All-steel passenger cars were first placed in service in the USA on the Long Island Railroad in 1905. The LIRR was also the first to operate an all-steel-car passenger fleet, in 1927.

Articulated coaches were introduced in Britain by H N Gresley in 1907. He mounted the bodies of two old Great Northern six-wheelers on three bogies, thus improving the riding and reducing the weight and length. The idea was developed into the 'quad-arts', four-coach sets on five bogies, so familiar to a generation of long-suffering North London commuters.

Roller bearings were first used on rolling stock in 1926 on the Chicago, Milwaukee, St Paul & Pacific Railroad passenger stock because of the increased weight of the Chicago–Twin Cities (Minneapolis/St Paul) trains.

The Metropolitan Railway, England, experimented with roller bearings in 1924 and approved them for general use in 1929.

Air-conditioned cars first appeared in the USA as an experiment in 1927. They were first put into regular service in 1930. The world's first completely air-conditioned passenger train went into service on the Baltimore & Ohio Railroad between Washington and New York on 24 May 1931. In Canada air-conditioning came into regular use in 1935 when the sleeping car *Sturgeon Falls* was so equipped.

The first air-conditioned train in Australia was the lightweight diesel-mechanical railcar named *Silver City Comet*, introduced in 1937 between Parkes and Broken Hill, 676·5 km (421 miles), in New South Wales. Times were 9 h 45 min down and 9 h 35 min up.

British Rail's first air-conditioned coaches were introduced on 12 July 1971 when the Mark II coaches went into service between London (King's Cross) and Newcastle and in August between King's Cross and the West Riding of Yorkshire and Scotland, following trials with an experimental train introduced on 15 June 1964. The Mark IIE coaches were introduced on the London to Birmingham, Wolverhampton and Manchester services in 1972. They provide wider entrances and better luggage storage. By the end of 1972 450 were in service. The Mark III coaches designed for 200 km/h (125 mph) went into ordinary service in 1973. Their running is remarkably smooth and, for the passenger, silent. A regrettable feature of the Mark III design is that the 2nd class seating does not fit the window openings which are designed for the 1st class, and the passenger can find himself in a seat with no view out.

British Rail's Prototype 'High Speed Train' consists of seven Mark III air-conditioned passenger cars between two Bo–Bo power-cars, and is designed to run at 200 km/h (125 mph). It carries 96 first class and 276 second class passengers. Each power-car has one Paxman 12RP200L 'Valenta' 12-cylinder pressure-charged and intercooled diesel engine developing 2250 bhp driving a Brush Electrical three-phase 1430 kW alternator. This supplies the four 450 hp dc traction motors through the rectifier and control equipment. The two traction motors in each bogie are frame-mounted to reduce unsprung weight.

Features include double-glazed windows, air-conditioning, interior doors automatically operated by tread-mats, colourful upholstery, and public address system. Catering services include a trolley service to all seats, and a full range of meals cooked in modern micro-wave ovens.

On 12 June 1973 the train reached a world record speed for diesel-traction of 230 km/h (143 mph) between Thirsk and Tollerton while on test on the York–Darlington section. (For details of 'Inter City 125' service see p. 178.)

The APT-E, or Advanced Passenger Train (Experimental) is a four-car articulated set designed to operate at 250 km/h (155 mph) on standard track designed and signalled for 161 km/h (100 mph) trains. The four cars are carried on five two-axle bogies of which the two end ones have electric drive to both axles. The two power-cars each contain four Leyland 300 hp gas-turbine engines driving alternators, two providing the power for each driving-axle. A fifth gas-turbine engine drives an auxiliary alternator providing power at 415 V three-phase 50 Hz for auxiliary services including air-conditioning, heating, etc.

Features of the APT are body-tilting on curves and bogie-steering to reduce friction between flange and rail. Hydraulic braking systems enable the train to be stopped within the signalling distances designed for 161 km/h (100 mph) trains. (See also p. 179.)

On the conclusion of the stringent test programme the APT-E was delivered to the National Railway Museum at York where it is now displayed.

Vista-dome cars were introduced in the USA on 23 July 1945 between Chicago and Minneapolis on the Chicago, Burlington & Quincy Railroad (now part of Burlington Northern).

The **Canadian** transcontinental trains on Canadian Pacific Rail, running between Montreal/Toronto and Vancouver, consisting of new stainless-steel cars was inaugurated on 24 April 1955. It is the longest vista-dome train ride in the world, 4675 km (2904·8 miles) from Montreal to Vancouver. It required the purchase of 173 new cars from the Budd Company, Philadelphia. (See photograph of Stoney Creek Bridge, p. 80.)

The lightest passenger cars in the USA are the air-conditioned 'Pioneer III' cars introduced by the Budd Company in July 1956. They are 25·908 m (85 ft) long, seat 88 passengers and weigh 23·4 long tons or only 269·89 kg (595 lb) per passenger. In July 1958 the 'Pioneer III MU' (multiple-unit) cars were introduced on the Pennsylvania Railroad.

The 'Tightlock' automatic coupler for passenger cars was adopted as standard in the USA in 1946.

Gallery cars, with seats on two levels, were introduced by the Chicago, Burlington & Quincy Railroad on its Chicago suburban services in 1950. Each car accommodates 148 passengers, 96 on the main (lower) floor and 52 in the single seats in the galleries (see colour illustration).

The first 'double-decked' train in Britain, with seats on two levels, designed by O V Bulleid (1882–1970), went into service on the Southern Region of British Railways on 2 November 1949. Its higher capacity made longer station stops necessary and so its advantage was lost and it was withdrawn on 1 October 1971.

Canada's first gallery-car train, comprising nine air-conditioned cars built by Canadian Vickers Limited, went into operation on 27 April 1970 on the Montreal Lakeshore suburban service.

The first passenger train into Turkey left Vienna for Istanbul (then Constantinople) on 12 August 1888. On 1 June 1889 a through train was inaugurated between Paris and Constantinople taking 67 h 35 min. This became the famous '*Orient Express*'. It stopped running in August 1914. On 11 April 1919 the '*Simplon Orient Express*' began running from Calais to Istanbul via Paris, Milan, Vincovki, Belgrade and Nis, and also

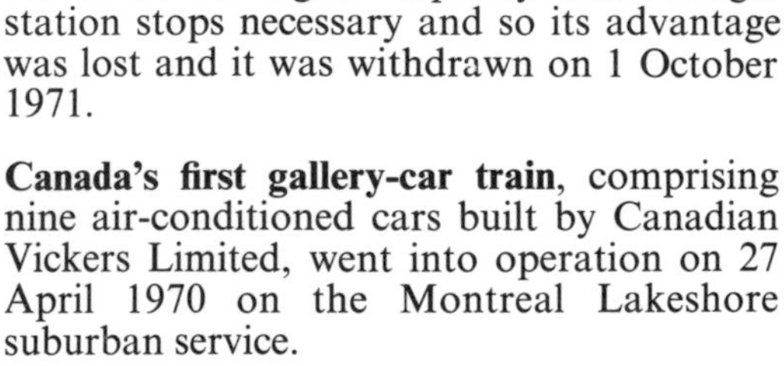

Now the only survivor of the through train service to Istanbul, the train to Frankfurt-am-Main about to leave Istanbul on 18 August 1976 behind Bo–Bo electric locomotive No. 4001 of the Turkish State Railways

Vincovki to Bucharest. The '*Direct Orient Express*' with coaches for Istanbul and Athens left the Gare de Lyon, Paris, for the last time at midnight on 19 May 1977. There are no longer through coaches between Paris and Istanbul and no sleeping cars east of Belgrade.

The Trans-Europ-Express (TEE) service was first proposed in 1954 by Den Hollender, then president of the Netherlands Railways. Services began on 2 June 1957, and they now cover nine countries: Austria, Belgium, France, Germany, Italy, Luxembourg, Netherlands, Spain and Switzerland, by 35 trains operating over 27 routes and serving 125 stations, and carrying 500 000 passengers a year in first-class accommodation with all seats reserved. The offices of TEE are at the headquarters of the Netherlands Railway at Utrecht. Trains are all painted red and cream.

Motive power and rolling stock is owned by the various administrations. The first trains were diesel multiple units. In 1961 Swiss Federal Railways introduced four five-coach multi-current electric trains. In 1972 only 7 out of 35 trains were diesels.

The 'Catalan-Talgo', introduced in Spain in 1969 for running between Geneva and Barcelona, has its bogies changed at Cerbère to run on the Spanish gauge of 1·676 m (5 ft 6 in) and the European standard gauge.

The most luxurious train in the world is the title claimed by 'The Blue Train' in South Africa. It was introduced on 4 September 1972 to replace the 33-year-old former 'Blue Train' on the Pretoria–Johannesburg–Cape Town service. It carries 108 passengers in 16 coaches and runs beautifully on air-cushioned bogies on 1·065 m (3 ft 6 in) gauge at speeds of 64·5–80·5 km/h (40–50 mph), and makes the journey in 26 h. Accommodation is entirely in private rooms, three of them with private bathrooms complete with baths; it is fully air-conditioned and sound-proofed, and ranks as a five-star hotel. Passengers normally dress for dinner.

'The Indian Pacific' in Australia, introduced in 1970, is probably the second most luxurious train in the world, crossing from Perth to Sydney in 65 h on standard gauge throughout. The streamlined, stainless-steel air-conditioned train provides sleeping accommodation for all passengers with showers and private toilets, a cocktail lounge, drawing-room and music-room with piano. Early morning and afternoon tea are wheeled round to all passengers.

New Zealand's 'Silver Star' introduced in 1972, runs overnight between Auckland and Wellington, covering the 743·5 km (462 miles) in 12 h 30 min, on 1·067 m (3 ft 6 in) gauge. It can claim to be the world's third most luxurious train. Mitsubishi of Japan built it in 1971. It includes the first dining car to run on NZR since 1915 and is the first all-sleeper with private toilets and showers in New Zealand.

The first modern trains with 'No Smoking' accommodation throughout began running on the Boston & Maine Railroad, USA, on 1 June 1970. They carry commuters only, 90 per cent of the journeys lasting under half an hour.

BRAKES

The energy stored in a train travelling at 100 km/h (61 mph) is sufficient to lift the entire train vertically through nearly 40 m (130 ft). The function of brakes is to absorb this energy as rapidly and as efficiently as possible. The two commonest methods are friction, and the regeneration of electrical power against a load which may consist of a resistance unit, or another train if on an electrified railway.

Braking may be assisted by a rising gradient, as at the approaches to stations on the London Underground system.

Early trains had no continuous brakes. The only brake power was on the engine tender and the guard's van. From a speed of 48 km/h (30 mph) a train might take 0·8 km (½ mile) to stop. Hence the great height of early signals, to be seen from a distance.

The earliest practical continuous brakes were mechanical systems such as those patented by George Newall of the East Lancashire Railway in 1852 and by Charles Fay (1812–1900), carriage and wagon superintendent of the Lancashire & Yorkshire Railway, in 1856.

George Westinghouse applied for an air-brake patent on 23 January 1869.

The Westinghouse continuous automatic air brake was introduced in 1872–3. 'Automatic' means that the brake applies itself on both halves of a train if it breaks apart.

The Gresham automatic vacuum brake was introduced in Britain in 1878, but it was about 1890 before all passenger trains were equipped.

Continuous automatic brakes became compulsory in Britain under the Regulation of Railways Act of 1889 (see 'Runaways'.)

Most of the world's railway systems use the air brake. Countries using the vacuum brake are mainly:

Europe–British Isles (except new British Rail stock); Austrian minor railways; Spain; Portugal
Australia–Western Australia; Tasmania
Africa–South Africa; Rhodesia; United Arab Republic
Asia–most railways in India and Pakistan; Malaysia; Thailand (Siam); Burma
South America–most railways except the Transandine; Antofagasta & Bolivia; high-altitude lines in the Andes; Central of Brazil.

PASSENGER CLASSES

Third class passengers were first carried in Britain in 1838, in open wagons without seats.

Gladstone's Railway Act of 1844 ruled that railways must carry third class passengers in closed carriages with seats at one (old) penny a mile on at least one train a day. 'Parliamentary' trains as they were known were often run at the most inconvenient times and at the slowest speeds.

The first British railway to carry third class passengers by all trains was the Midland Railway, on 1 April 1872. The Great Eastern Railway followed in the same year.

Second class was abolished on the Midland Railway and also on the joint services with the Glasgow & South Western Railway on 1 January 1875. They were the first.

Bogie carriages for first and third class were introduced in Britain by the Midland Railway in 1875.

The use of third class carriages by 'wearers of kid gloves and kid shoes' was strongly condemned by the chairman of the Lancashire & Yorkshire Railway, Thomas Barnes, in 1880, because of the danger of 'Americanising our institutions'!

Third class passengers were carried on all trains of the Great Western Railway from 1 October 1890.

First class was abolished on the Metropolitan and District railways, London, from 1 February 1940. From that date only one class operated on all London Transport services.

Third class was redesignated second class on British Railways on 3 June 1956 and by the Ulster Transport Authority (which had retained three classes) on 1 October 1956.

Greece and Turkey adopted two classes only from 1 January 1957, leaving only Spain and Portugal in Europe with three classes.

In Australia, on all systems, the second class was renamed 'economy' in 1971. Only the first class is now marked.

The last 'early-morning' (workmen's) tickets on British Railways were issued at the end of 1961.

'Ladies only' compartments were abolished on British Rail in 1977. Under the Sex Discrimination Act of 1976 they could be continued only if an equal number of 'Men only' compartments were introduced.

'Ladies only' compartments were introduced on the Great Western Railway in 1848. They allowed, for example, a woman wishing to feed a child at her breast a certain amount of privacy which, under the new law, is apparently no longer required.

On the Pakistan Western Railway a rule allowed a woman travelling alone at night in a first class compartment the company of 'a dog or servant but not both'.

SLEEPING AND DINING CARS

The world's first sleeping car was designed by Philip Berlin, manager of the Cumberland Valley Railroad, now part of Penn Central, USA. It operated between Harrisburg and Chambersburg in 1837. Sleeping arrangements were adapted from the seating.

Similar cars were also operated between Philadelphia and Baltimore in 1838, and on the Richmond & Fredericksburg Railroad (now Richmond, Fredericksburg & Potomac), Virginia, in 1839.

The first provision for sleeping on British trains was in 1838 when a makeshift bed was introduced. It consisted of two poles with strips of webbing between them which were laid across the compartment resting on the two seats.

The New York & Erie Railroad (now Erie & Lackawanna) operated experimental sleeping cars in 1843 and a regular sleeping-car service in 1856.

The Illinois Central introduced six stateroom sleeping cars, known as 'Gothic cars', in June 1856. Each was nearly 15·240 m (50 ft) long and nearly 3·048 m (10 ft) wide.

Night-seat coaches, with luxurious adjustable reclining seats, were put into service between Philadelphia and Baltimore in 1854.

The first sleeping-car patents were issued to T T Woodruff in the USA on 2 December 1856.

The world's first proper sleeping cars were designed by Samuel Sharp and built at Hamilton, Ontario, by the Great Western Railway of Canada in 1857. The design was adopted by the Wagner and Pullman companies. The first Pullman sleeping car appeared in 1859.

'Parlour cars' fiıst appeared in Canada in 1860 on the Grand Trunk, Great Western and Buffalo & Huron railways. They were fitted out with every possible luxury; the Grand Trunk even had a form of air-conditioning.

The first railway to serve meals on a train was the Baltimore & Ohio, USA. On 10 January 1853 it ran two special trains from Baltimore to Wheeling and back to mark the completion of the railway to that point. A caterer was engaged to provide food.

The world's first dining cars were operated by the Philadelphia, Wilmington & Baltimore (now part of Conrail) between Philadelphia and Baltimore in 1863. Two such cars, rebuilt from day coaches 15·240 m (50 ft) long, were fitted with an eating bar, steam-box and 'everything found in a first class restaurant'.

Canada's first dining cars, or 'hotel cars', appeared in regular service on the Great Western Railway in 1876.

A first class sleeping car was introduced in Britain by the North British Railway on the Glasgow–Edinburgh–London trains on 2 April 1873. It ran alternate nights each way, leaving Glasgow at 21.00 and arriving in London at 9.40 via the North Eastern and Great Northern railways. There was a supplementary charge of ten shillings (50p).

On 31 July 1873 the Great Northern Railway introduced a similar service so that it could operate every night.

The London & North Western and Caledonian railways introduced sleeping-car trains on the 'West Coast Route' between London and Scotland on 1 October 1873.

The Great Western Railway introduced sleeping-car trains in December 1877. In 1881 it built the forerunner of the modern sleeping car, with six double-berth compartments, three lavatories and an attendant's pantry. Passengers provided their own bedding. In 1890 the GWR introduced the first sleeping car equipped entirely with lateral berths in compartments.

The prototype British first class sleeping car was built by the North Eastern Railway in 1894. It had four compartments with single berths, two with double berths, a smoking compartment which could be adapted to sleep two, and an attendant's pantry with gas cooker.

Dining cars were introduced on the London–Leeds trains by the Great Northern Railway on 1 November 1879.

The 'Flying Scotsman' was provided with corridor stock throughout and with dining cars on 1 August 1900. The 20-min lunch stop at York was ended.

The first restaurant cars in Europe to use electricity for cooking were put into service on the metre-gauge Rhaetian Railway in Switzerland in 1929 by the Mitropa Company (Mitteleuropäische Schlafwagen und Speisewagen Aktiengesellschaft) of Berlin.

Third class sleeping cars were introduced in Britain by the London, Midland & Scottish, the London & North Eastern and the Great Western railways on 24 September 1928. For daytime use they had ordinary third class compartments which could be converted to four berths for sleeping. For bedding only a pillow and a rug were provided.

The first shower compartment in a British train was installed in a first class twin sleeping-car set by the London & North Eastern Railway in 1930.

A weekly through sleeping-car service between Togliattigrad in Russia and Turin in Italy was introduced on 1 June 1969. The 4000 km (2486 miles) are covered in 88 hours.

PULLMAN CARS AND TRAINS

George Mortimer Pullman (1831–97) converted two passenger coaches on the Chicago & Alton Railroad (now part of the Gulf, Mobile & Ohio Railroad) into sleeping cars at the railway company's shops at Bloomington, Illinois, in 1859. The first ran from Bloomington to Chicago on 1 September 1859. The first Pullman Car conductor was Jonathan L. Barnes. Pullman regarded these merely as experiments and in 1864 began building the first real Pullman sleeping car, named *Pioneer*, which went into service in 1865. Pullman sleeping cars were soon in common use throughout the USA.

Most sleeping-car services in the USA were operated by the Pullman Company until 1 January 1969. Since then they have been taken over by the individual railroads.

Pullman 'Hotel Cars' were introduced in 1867. They were sleeping cars equipped with kitchen and dining facilities. The first Pullman-built car providing only restaurant facilities, the *Delmonico*, was operated on the Chicago & Alton Railroad in 1868.

Pullman sleeping cars were introduced on Canadian railways in 1870. The Grand Trunk Railway cars were among the best appointed of their time. The convenience could be enjoyed for an extra payment of $1.

Pullman cars were introduced in Britain on 1 June 1874 on the Midland Railway between

London and Bradford. They were so popular that by the end of 1874 the MR had 36 in operation including 11 sleeping cars. In 1876 the services were extended to Edinburgh and Glasgow over the new Settle & Carlisle line and the Glasgow & South Western and North British railways.

The first 'restaurant car' in Britain was a Pullman named *Prince of Wales*, introduced on the Great Northern Railway between London (King's Cross) and Leeds on 1 November 1879.

The first all-Pullman train in Britain was on the London, Brighton & South Coast Railway in December 1881. It was also the first train in Britain to be electrically lit throughout. The London–Brighton 60-min Limited Pullmans (Sundays only) began on 2 October 1898.

The Pullman Company Limited was registered in England from 1882 to 1907. It was then purchased by Mr Davison Dalziel (1854–1928), an English newspaper proprietor, until 1915 when the Pullman Car Company Limited was formed under his chairmanship to acquire the interests.

Dalziel also controlled the International Sleeping Car Company from 1927 and negotiated purchase by this company of Thomas Cook & Son in 1928.

Pullman introduced the first vestibule train, in the USA, in 1887.

The Pullman Car Company introduced the first two all-steel trains in England in May 1928. They formed 'The Queen of Scots' on the London & North Eastern Railway and ran between London, Leeds, Harrogate and Edinburgh.

The all-Pullman 'Southern Belle' was introduced by the London, Brighton & South Coast Railway on 1 November 1908. At the same time Buckeye couplings and drawgear were introduced into Great Britain by the Pullman Company. 'The Southern Belle' was renamed 'The Brighton Belle' on 29 June 1934, having become an electric train on 1 January 1933. It made its last run on 30 April 1972.

The first air-conditioned Pullman car went into operation between Chicago and Los Angeles on 9 September 1929, following experiments begun in 1927.

The most famous all-Pullman train, the 'Golden Arrow' service between London and Paris, was introduced on 12 September 1926 with Pullman cars between Calais and Paris. From 15 May 1929 it became all-Pullman throughout the journey.

From September 1939 to 15 October 1946 the service was withdrawn. Second class Pullmans were introduced in October 1949, but these were replaced by ordinary coaches in May 1965. It made its last run on 30 September 1972. The 4000 ton cross-Channel steamer *Invicta* which carried 'Golden Arrow' passengers to their connection with the Calais–Paris 'Flèche d'Or' from 1946 was taken out of service at the same time.

The first diesel multiple-unit Pullman train was the six-car first-class-only 'Midland Pullman' inaugurated on 4 July 1960. It ran between London (St Pancras) and Manchester (Central). The 'Midland Pullman' was withdrawn in 1966 with the introduction, on 18 April, of the electrically hauled London to Manchester and Liverpool Pullman trains.

SLIP CARRIAGES

The earliest slip carriages were on the London & Blackwall Railway during cable operation from 1840 to 1849 when coaches were detached from the moving ropes at all intermediate stations between Minories and Blackwall.

The first coaches to be slipped from moving trains were on the London, Brighton & South Coast Railway in February 1858 when a portion for Eastbourne was slipped at Hayward's Heath from the 16.00 express from London Bridge to Brighton.

Three months later the South Eastern Railway slipped a portion for Canterbury off the 12.30 express from London Bridge to Ramsgate and Margate.

The first Great Western Railway slip carriages were introduced in December 1858 at Slough and Banbury.

In 1914 there were 200 slip-coach services, operated by most of the main-line companies in Great Britain and Ireland, of which the Great Western Railway operated 72. By 1918 the GWR total was down to 17.

The last slip working in Britain was at Bicester off the 17.10 Paddington–Wolverhampton train on 9 September 1960, at the end of the summer service.

SPECIAL TRAINS

The first excursion train was organised by the Nottingham Mechanics Institute, England, and was run to Leicester on 20 July 1840. The second, from Leicester to Nottingham on 24 August 1840, carried 2400 passengers.

In the 1860s the Lancashire & Yorkshire Railway carried excursion passengers in open cattle trucks. Only after numerous complaints in the Press were temporary roofs fitted.

Queen Victoria's first railway journey, from Slough near Windsor to London (Paddington) on the Great Western Railway, was on 13 June 1842.

The first royal railway carriage was built by the London & Birmingham Railway in 1842 for Queen Adelaide.

The first 'club trains' were run by the South Eastern and London, Chatham & Dover railways between London and Dover in 1889.

The first 'railway enthusiasts' rail tour in Britain was organised by the Railway Correspondence & Travel Society (see p. 214) on 11 September 1938 when the Great Northern Railway Stirling 2·438 m (8 ft) single-wheeler No. 1 took a train of old six-wheeled carriages from London (King's Cross) to Peterborough and back. The fare was five shillings (25p).

The first 'railway enthusiasts' rail tour in Australia was a rail-motor tour of the Moss Vale–Unanderra line south of Sydney run by the New South Wales Division of the Australian Railway Historical Society (qv) on 15 December 1946.

The greatest number of passengers carried in one locomotive-hauled train in Australia was on a special run by the New South Wales Rail Transport Museum, Sydney, on 10 December 1972. It was hauled by three '38' Class locomotives, 3801/13/20, and carried 900 passengers (700 more were turned away).

The longest passenger trains ever to run in Australia were of 42 carriages. One ran between Perth, Western Australia, and Port Pirie, South Australia on 27 December 1974. It was a combination of one 'Indian Pacific' and two 'Trans Australian' trains, because of delays caused by floods. Another ran over the same route on 11 February 1975, again because of serious delays. Both were operated by Commonwealth Railways.

MAIL TRAINS

Mail was first carried by train on the Liverpool & Manchester Railway on 11 November 1830.

The carriage of mails by rail in Britain was authorised by Act of Parliament in 1838.

The first travelling post office was an adapted horse-box operated by the Grand Junction Railway between Birmingham and Liverpool on 6 January 1838.

The first mail-sorting carriage to be specially constructed was designed by Nathaniel Worsdell and included the first apparatus for picking up and dropping mail-bags while in motion. It was built by the Grand Junction Railway at Liverpool in 1838.

Queen Adelaide's coach, 1842; the first royal coach, preserved in the National Railway Museum, York. It measures 6·64 m (21 ft 9 in) over buffers and stands 3 m (9 ft 10 in) high. The body is 5·03 m (16 ft 6 in) long and 1·68 m (5 ft 6 in) wide and has 10 seats. The vehicle has no brakes

The oldest named train in the world is 'The Irish Mail' running between London and Holyhead in Anglesey, North Wales, where it connects with the sailings to Dun Laoghaire. It began on 31 July 1848 and still runs, though the nameboards have been carried only since 1927. Until the completion of the Britannia Tubular Bridge over the Menai Strait on 18 March 1850 the train ran to Bangor and passengers made part of the journey by coach.

The first railway mail traffic in the USA was on the South Carolina Railroad (now part of the Southern Railway) in November 1831 and on the Baltimore & Ohio in January 1832. Soon after the B & O opened between Baltimore and Washington in 1835 a car was fitted up for carrying mail between the two cities.

From 1855 the Terre Haute & Richmond Railroad (now part of Conrail) west of Indianapolis operated Post Office cars in which mail was sorted and distributed on the journey.

A car equipped for handling overland mail for places west of St Joseph, Missouri, was introduced by the Hannibal & St Joseph Railroad (now part of Burlington Northern) on 28 July 1862.

Mail was first carried by rail in Canada on the Great Western Railway between Niagara and London in 1854, letters being sorted on the train under the supervision of P. Pardon, pioneer mail clerk of North America.

The first North American railway to use regular mail cars was the Grand Trunk Railway of Canada. In 1854 the baggage cars were replaced by specially fitted-up mail cars, at least ten years before such cars appeared elsewhere in North America.

The first permanent railway Post Office car in the USA for picking up, sorting and distributing mail on the journey was put into operation by the Chicago & North Western Railroad on 28 August 1864, between Chicago and Clinton, Iowa.

US railroads carry about 50 per cent of all domestic first class mail and about 80 per cent of all domestic bulk mail.

The first special postal train in the world was inaugurated by the Great Western Railway between London and Bristol on 1 February 1855. Passengers were carried from June 1869 when one first class carriage was attached.

The first mail train between London and Aberdeen was inaugurated by the London & North Western and Caledonian railways on 1 July 1885. It did not carry passengers.

Travelling sorting offices and exchange apparatus were discontinued in Britain from 22 September 1940 until 1 October 1945.

Apparatus for exchanging mail-bags on British Railways was last used on 4 October 1971, just north of Penrith.

FREIGHT SERVICES

Containers were first used in the USA on the Camden & Amboy Railroad in 1849. On the Pennsylvania Railroad they were first used in 1869.

The first recorded use of refrigerators on an American railroad was on 1 July 1851 when 8 tons of butter were carried from Ogdensburg, NY, to Boston, Mass., in a wooden box car stocked with ice and insulated with sawdust.

In 1857 box cars with ice compartments at each end were used for carrying fresh meat from Chicago eastwards over the Michigan Central Railroad (now Conrail).

The 'caboose' at the rear of an American freight train was originally known as a 'cabin car', 'conductor's van', 'brakeman's cab', 'accommodation car', 'train car' and 'way car'. The

Canadian Pacific 'Conductor's Van' photographed at Montreal about 1895 (Canadian Pacific Corporate Archives)

first recorded use of the term 'caboose' was in 1855 on the Buffalo, Corning & New York Railroad (now part of the Erie Lackawanna). The roof-top cupola appears to have been introduced in 1863 by T B Watson, a freight conductor of the Chicago & North Western Railway, Iowa. In parts of Canada, particularly on the Canadian Pacific, they are known simply as 'vans'.

The Railway Express Agency in the USA was established on 4 March 1839 by William F. Harnden (1812–45), formerly a passenger train conductor on the Boston & Worcester Railroad (now part of Conrail). Harnden contracted with the Boston & Providence (also now part of C) and a steamship company operating between Providence and New York for the carriage of his business.

The business grew rapidly and was extended to Philadelphia and elsewhere. The Railway Express Agency Company, established on 7 December 1928, was owned and operated by US railroads until 1960 when its name became 'REA Express'. It was purchased by a group of its executives in 1969. The handling of its business brings the railroads an annual income of over $40 000 000.

The first tank car specially built for transporting bulk oil in the USA went into service at Titusville, Pennsylvania, on 1 November 1865.

The first code of rules to govern the interchange of freight cars in the USA was adopted at a meeting of officials of six freight lines at Buffalo, NY, on 20 April 1866.

The Master Car Builders' Association was formed in the USA in 1867 to conduct tests and experiments towards the standardising of freight cars, brakes, couplers, etc. It subsequently became the Mechanical Division of the Association of American Railroads. (See p. 189.)

Containers were introduced in Britain and Europe during the early 1920s. These large boxes could be transferred bodily from train to truck or ship, so avoiding much loading and unloading.

First tests with automatic couplers in the USA were carried out by the Master Car Builders' Association beginning in 1869 and continuing for many years. Further tests from September 1885 led to the approval in 1887, by the MCBA, of an automatic coupler working in a vertical plane, invented by Major Eli Hamilton Janney (1831–1912) and patented on 21 April 1868. A second patent was issued on 29 April 1873 for the basic car-coupler design in general use today. Standard, interchangeable, automatic car couplers were introduced in 1887. The Janney automatic coupler was adopted as standard on Pennsylvania Railroad passenger cars in 1884. Link-and-pin couplers on passenger cars continued until about 1888. The fitting of automatic couplers and automatic air brakes became statutory in 1893. The 'Type F' interlocking coupler for freight cars was adopted as standard in 1953.

Automatic couplers were adopted on the Imperial Japanese Government Railway on 17 July 1925, after eight years of preparation. The conversion was completed in 24 hours.

The first 'Piggy-back' service in North America was introduced in September 1855 in Nova Scotia, with horse and buggy flat-car services for farmers. Farmers' truck-wagon trains were introduced on the Long Island Railroad, NY, in 1884.

'Piggy-backing' was reintroduced on USA railroads in the early 1950s. It is the transport of containers and motor-truck trailers on specially equipped flat-cars. Technically it is known as 'Trailer-on-Flatcar' (TOFC) or 'Container-on-Flatcar' (COFC). Its success resulted in an eightfold increase from 1955 to 1970 and in 1972 it handled a record number of 2 253 207 trailers.

Freight cars on USA railroads on 31 December 1975 totalled 1 723 605. This included 495 159 box cars; 363 186 hoppers; 186 773 gondolas (open wagons in England); 170 876 tank cars; 228 265 covered hoppers; 141 316 flat cars and 100 815 refrigerator cars. The average freight-car capacity is now 73·9 tons. New cars installed in 1975 had an average capacity of 89 tons.

The average length of an American freight train over a recent ten-year period was about 70 freight cars and a caboose. In 1929 the average was only 48 cars. Experimental trains have been run with as many as 500 cars. Freight cars vary in length from 7·620 to

38·104 m (25 to 125 ft) and average about 13·716 m (45 ft).

Plans for an Automatic Car Identification (ACI) systems in the USA to facilitate prompt location of freight cars were announced in October 1967. It began in 1970 in conjunction with Tele Rail Automated Information Network (TRAIN) with a central computer at the headquarters of the Association of American Railroads in Washington.

Freightliner services on British Railways were introduced between London and Glasgow on 15 November 1965; London and Manchester on 28 February 1966; London and Liverpool on 13 June 1966; Liverpool and Glasgow on 5 September 1966; Manchester and Glasgow on 12 September 1966; London and Aberdeen on 31 October 1966. By the end of 1966 about 27 000 loaded freightliner containers had been carried.

From 1 January 1969, under provisions in the Transport Act of 1968, Freightliner Services were taken over by Freightliners Limited of which 51 per cent is owned by the National Freight Corporation (see below) and 49 per cent by British Railways Board.

The National Freight Corporation was established under the Transport Act of 1968 to promote and to provide integrated freight services by road and rail in Great Britain and to ensure that goods go by rail where this is efficient and economic. Users of British motorways may well wonder if the Corporation is having any effect.

The British Railways service for carrying new cars between Dagenham, Essex, and Halewood near Liverpool using two-tier 'Cartic' (articulated car carriers) units began on 13 July 1966.

The first British 100-ton bogie tank wagon for Shell Oil Products was completed on 21 February 1967.

The Harwich–Zeebrugge container service between England and Belgium was introduced on 18 March 1968 using special cellular container ships and wide-span transporter cranes.

The first container shipped from Japan over the Trans-Siberian Railway arrived at Harwich, England, in May 1969 after a journey of 12 231 km (7 600 miles).

The longest and heaviest freight train on record was run on 15 November 1967 over the 253 km (157 miles) between Iaeger, West Virginia, and Portsmouth, Ohio. The 500 coal cars weighed 42 000 tons and stretched about 6·5 km (4 miles). The load was shifted by three 3600 hp diesels in front and three behind.

The heaviest single piece of freight ever carried by rail was a 32 m (106 ft) tall hydrocracker reactor weighing 549·2 tons, from Birmingham, Alabama, to Toledo, Ohio, USA, on 12 November 1965.

The heaviest load ever moved on rails was the 10 700 ton Church of the Virgin Mary built in 1548 in the village of Most, Czechoslovakia, in October and November 1975. In four weeks it was moved 730 m (798 yd) because it obstructed coal workings.

Some of the heaviest trains on the 1·067 m (3 ft 6 in) gauge are run on the Goonyella line of the Queensland Railways, Australia. Trains of 148 wagons carrying 8600 tons of coal are hauled by three locomotives linked by remote control to three more in the middle of the train. Each train is about 2 km (1¼ miles) long.

The heaviest load carried by British Railways was a 37·186 m (122 ft) long boiler drum weighing 275 tons from Immingham Dock to Killinghome, Lincolnshire, in September 1968.

The record run by a 'Super C' freight in the USA was made in January 1968 on the Atchison, Topeka & Santa Fe Railroad between Corwith and Hobart yards. The 3544 km (2202·1 miles) were covered in 34 h 35 min 40 s at an average speed of 102·355 km/h (63·6 mph).

A 'Super C' freight on the Santa Fe is booked over the 202·5 km (127·2 miles) between Winslow and Gallup in 105 min at an average speed of 117 km/h (72·7 mph). Another takes 175 min over the 330 km (205·2 miles) between Waynoka and Amarillo at an average speed of 113·2 km/h (70·3 mph).

Ton-miles on USA railroads reached a world record of 851 809 000 000 in 1973, but by the end of 1975 had fallen to 752 816 000 000.

Canada's first remote-controlled mid-train diesel locomotives in regular freight service, using the new 'Robot' radio-command system were first tested on the Canadian Pacific on 16 November 1967. The system is now in regular use in North America.

The longest freight train on record in Canada was a Canadian Pacific train of 250 loaded grain cars, powered by seven diesel-electric locomotives, about 4 km (2·5 miles) long. It ran on 22 October 1974 from west of Moose Jaw, Saskatchewan, to Thunder Bay, Ontario, where it had to be divided into three sections to be handled in the yards. It was part of experiments to increase trans-continental line capacity.

The heaviest trains in Australia are the ore trains in northern Western Australia, on the private railway of the Hammersley Iron Pty Ltd (see p. 149). Loads up to 250 wagons each carrying 100 tons of ore are hauled by three 3000 hp diesel-electric locomotives.

In January 1974 the Public Transport Commission of New South Wales introduced fast container trains, the first in an interstate network. They carry forty 6 m (20 ft) long containers, and run between Sydney and Brisbane in 17 h. (The Limited passenger trains take 15 h 20 min.) The new wagons have a maximum speed of 112 km/h (70 mph).

The Trans-Europ-Express Marchandises (TEEM) services were introduced in May 1961 to provide fast international goods services at speeds of 85–100 km/h (53–62 mph) on similar lines to the TEE passenger trains. They now operate 114 connections between 20 countries.

The largest marshalling yard in Europe is the German Federal Railways Maschen Yard near Hamburg. When new extensions are completed in May 1980 it will handle 11 000 wagons per day.

RAILCARS

The first railcar was a four-wheeled vehicle designed by James Samuel (1824–74), while resident engineer of the Eastern Counties Railway, England. It was built by W. Bridges Adams at Fairfield Works, Bow, London, and was named *Express*. It first ran on 23 October 1847. It had a vertical boiler. Although it could run at 75·5 km/h (47 mph) and burned only 0·9 kg of coke per km (3·02 lb/mile), it carried only four passengers and was hardly an economic proposition.

The first large railcar was again by J. Samuel and W B Adams, built in 1848 for the 2·134 m (7 ft) gauge Bristol & Exeter Railway. This vertical boilered car, named *Fairfield*, was put to work on the Tiverton Branch.

Their next, *Enfield*, built in 1849 for the Eastern Counties Railway, was the first with a horizontal boiler.

After a quarter of a century the railcar idea was again taken up and in 1873 Alexander McDonnell (1829–1904) of the Great Southern & Western Railway in Ireland produced a 0–4–4 tank with a staff saloon attached to the rear.

Other staff railcars were built by the Great Eastern Railway in 1874 to a design by William Adams (1823–1904); for the London, Brighton & South Coast Railway by William Stroudley in 1885 and the famous London & South Western Railway 'Cab', incorporating a single-driver engine, by Dugald Drummond (1840–1912) in 1899.

In Belgium the railcar was introduced in 1877 by M A Cabany of Malines. A total of 15 were built, some with six and some with eight wheels.

The next railcar phase came in 1903–11 when many railways were trying to economise on branch lines or on urban lines competing with street-cars. Most of these cars had a small 0–4–0 locomotive forming one bogie. About 25 companies in England, Scotland, Wales and Ireland produced about as many different designs. Among the best and longest lived were the Lancashire & Yorkshire Railway cars by George Hughes.

Geared steam railcars appeared in Britain in 1905 and later were developed by the Sentinel Wagon Works at Shrewsbury and by Cammell-Laird Limited in 1923. They had a vertical high-pressure water-tube boiler, and were in use all over the world. The biggest user of these cars in Britain was the London & North Eastern Railway.

The first British internal-combustion engined railcar was the 'Petrol-Electric Autocar' built by the North Eastern Railway in 1903. Two were built and they worked between Scarborough and Filey in August 1904 and in the winter between Billingham and Port Clarence. In 1908 they were put to work on the Selby-Cawood Branch.

Direct-drive gas (petrol)-engined vehicles were being tried at the same time in North America. In 1904 a Napier car fitted with flanged wheels was tested over 1609 km (1000 miles) of railway in the USA and Canada.

The 'gas-electric' car was introduced in the USA by the General Electric Company in 1906 when a combined passenger and baggage car was built for the Delaware & Hudson Railroad. It was 20·904 m (68 ft 7 in) long and weighed 43·8 tons.

Many railcars for light railways, particularly in Ireland, were adapted from old buses, the first being run on the 914 mm (3 ft) gauge County Donegal Railway in Ireland in 1928.

The 'daddy-long-legs' on the Brighton & Rottingdean Electric Tramroad, designed by Magnus Volk and built by the Gloucester Carriage & Wagon Company in 1896 (Brighton Public Libraries)

Pneumatic-tyred railcars were introduced in France by the Michelin Tyre Company in 1931. A similar car was tried on the London, Midland & Scottish and Southern railways in England in 1932. In 1935 the LMS tested the 'Coventry Pneumatic Railcar', a 16-wheeled vehicle by Armstrong Siddeley with Michelin tyres. Pneumatic-tyred cars, though much used in France, never went into public service in Britain.

(For developments in diesel railcars see 'Diesel Rail Traction', p. 141.)

The record for being the world's most extraordinary railcar must surely be held for all time by the Brighton & Rottingdean Seashore Electric Tramroad, Sussex, England. The line was 4·42 km (2·75 miles) long and was built by Magnus Volk on the seashore, with a total gauge of 5·486 m (18 ft). At high water the four rails were covered by about 4·572 m (15 ft) of water. The car stood on legs about 7 m (23 ft) high and had a cabin like a ship. It was the only railcar that carried a lifeboat and lifebelts as normal equipment. The railway opened on 28 November 1896 and ran until January 1901. The car was built by the Gloucester Railway Carriage & Wagon Co Ltd.

RAILWAY RACES

In the Great Locomotive Chase on the Nashville Chattanooga & St Louis Railroad on 12 April 1862, during the American Civil War, Captain James J. Andrews and his Yankee raiders seized the Confederate Rogers 4–4–0 *General* at Kennesaw about 40·2 km (25 miles) north of Atlanta, Georgia. They drove it 140 km (87 miles) to within 32 km (20 miles) of Chattanooga where it ran out of fuel and was caught by the Confederates in another 4–4–0, *Texas*. The chase was over light unballasted track at speeds of over 96·5 km/h (60 mph). For 80·5 km (50 miles) the *Texas* was running tender first.

Both engines are preserved; the *General* at Kennesaw Museum, Georgia, and the *Texas* at Grant Park, Atlanta.

In the race from London to Edinburgh in 1888 the West Coast companies (London & North Western and Caledonian) on 13 August covered the 643·25 km (399·7 miles) in 7 h 6 min at an average speed of 90·44 km/h (56·2 mph).

General in steam, passing over a trestle near Louisville, Kentucky, in 1970 (Louisville & Nashville Railroad)

On 31 August the East Coast companies (Great Northern, North Eastern and North British) set up a record over their 632·79 km (393·2 mile) route, taking 6 h 48 min at an average speed of 92·86 km/h (57·7 mph).

In the subsequent race from London to Aberdeen the West Coast companies set up a world speed record on 22 August 1895 by covering the 870·66 km (541 miles) in 512 min at an average speed of 101·87 km/h (63·3 mph) including three stops and the climbs over Shap and Beattock, but with only a 70 ton train.

The best East Coast time was 518 min for the 842·5 km (523·5 miles) on 21 August 1895, but they had reached Edinburgh in 6 h 18 min, averaging 100 km/h (62·3 mph) with three stops and with a 120 ton train, thereby beating their record of 1888.

When the Atlantic liners called at Plymouth there was great rivalry between the Great Western and the London & South Western railways in getting passengers and mail to London.

On 9 May 1904 the GWR 'Ocean Mail' ran the 205·673 km (127·8 miles) from Millbay Crossing, Plymouth, to Pylle Hill Junction, Bristol, in 123 min 19 s with the 4–4–0 locomotive *City of Truro*. Down Wellington Bank it reached a very high speed, but the reputed maximum of 164·631 km/h (102·3 mph) has since been seriously questioned and is no longer accepted. From the recorded data, however, there is now little doubt that a speed of about 161 km/h (100 mph) was reached.

The same train, behind 4–2–2 *Duke of Connaught*, covered the 191 km (188·7 miles) from Pylle Hill Junction to Paddington, London, in 99 min 46 s, with an average speed of 128·75 km/h (80 mph) over the 113·133 km (70·3 miles) from Shrivenham to Westbourne Park, a record for sustained high speed which stood in Britain until broken by the 'Cheltenham Flyer' in 1929.

The disastrous derailment at Salisbury at 13.57 on 1 July 1906 brought the racing to an end. The London & South Western Railway boat express was wrecked taking a sharp curve at excessive speed. Twenty-four passengers and four railwaymen were killed.

The world's longest non-stop run was established by the London & North Eastern Railway in the summer time-table of 1927 with the 431·788 km (268·3 miles) between London and Newcastle.

Not to be outdone the London, Midland & Scottish Railway immediately cut out the crew-changing stop at Carnforth in the run of the 10.00 train out of London (Euston), which had just been named 'The Royal Scot', and ran the 484·4 km (301 miles) non-stop to Carlisle (Kingmoor) shed where engines were changed.

On 1 May 1928 the LNER decided to run the 10.00 from London (King's Cross), the 'Flying Scotsman', non-stop between London

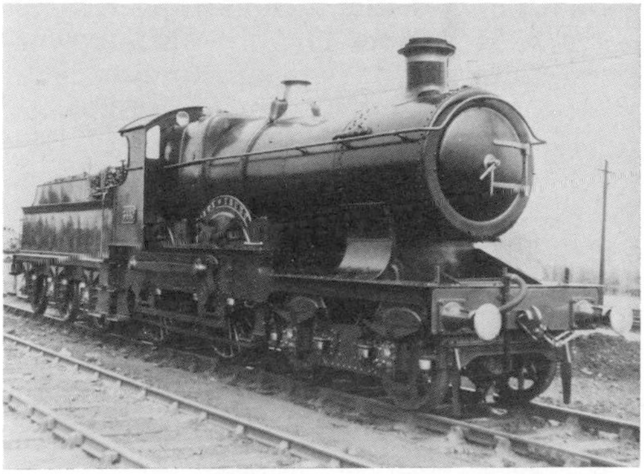

The record-breaking GWR 4–4–0 *City of Truro*. After withdrawal from service in March 1931 it was displayed in the York Railway Museum. In 1957 it was taken out, overhauled at Swindon, and put back into active service. For a time it was stationed at Didcot, where the photograph was taken in May 1957. It is now in the Great Western Railway Museum at Swindon

Stanier 'Pacific' No. 6201 *Princess Elizabeth* working a special train from Chester to Shrewsbury climbing Gresford Bank near Wrexham on 5 June 1976

and Edinburgh, 632·5 km (393 miles), thereby establishing another world record. For this purpose H N Gresley designed his famous corridor tender enabling the engine crew to be changed during the journey.

On the Friday before this, however, the LMS stole the glory by dividing the 'Royal Scot' and running the two halves non-stop between London and Edinburgh and Glasgow.

The Edinburgh portion of six coaches was taken by the 4–4–0 compound No. 1054 whose run of 643·251 km (399·7 miles) was certainly a British record for a 4–4–0, and probably a world record.

'Royal Scot'-type 4–6–0 No. 6113 *Cameronian* with the Glasgow portion achieved a world record with any locomotive by running the 646 km (401·4 miles) non-stop.

On 16 November 1936 the LMS crowned this achievement by running a special 230 ton train non-stop from London to Glasgow in 5 h 53 min 38 s at an average speed of 109·6 km/h (68·1 mph) behind the Stanier 'Pacific' No. 6201 *Princess Elizabeth*. The following day it returned with 260 tons in 5 h 44 min 15 s at an average speed of 112·65 km/h (70 mph).

The result of this exercise was the inauguration of the LMS 'Coronation Scot' streamlined train which ran between London and Glasgow in $6\frac{1}{2}$ h on 5 July 1937 stopping, however, at Carlisle for change of crew.

On the same day the LNER introduced the 'Coronation' between London and Edinburgh, streamlined from the front of the 'A4' Class 'Pacific' to the tail of the rear observation car. It called at York and Newcastle going north and at Newcastle going south. The journey time was 6 h.

The longest distance in Britain without an advertised stop is 909 km (565 miles) by the Night Motorail service from Kensington, Olympia, Greater London, to Inverness, Scotland, inaugurated in May 1973. It takes 13 h 20 min.

RAILWAY SPEED RECORDS

(See also 'Railway Races', p. 172.)

The train that arrived seven years late left Beaumont, Texas, on the Gulf & Interstate Railway, at 11.30 on 8 September 1900 for Port Bolivar, about 112·6 km (70 miles). At High Island, 53·1 km (33 miles) on, it was caught in a tremendous flood which washed away miles of track. The passengers and crew were saved, but the train remained isolated until after the impoverished railway company had been taken over by the Atchison, Topeka & Santa Fe Railroad which relaid the track. In September 1907 the train was overhauled and the engine steamed up and the journey, which should have taken 2 h 25 min, was completed. Some of the original passengers were there to greet the train on its arrival.

Several early rail speed records were claimed by the USA but most of these are unauthenticated and are not internationally accepted.

The earliest rail speed record worthy of mention was achieved by the Stephensons' *Rocket* at the Rainhill Trials on the Liverpool & Manchester Railway on 8 October 1829 when it ran at 46·8 km/h (29·1 mph).

On the opening day of the Liverpool & Manchester Railway, on 15 September 1830, the Stephenson 0–2–2 *Northumbrian* achieved 58 km/h (36 mph) while conveying the fatally injured William Huskisson from Parkside to Eccles. (See p. 180.)

A record speed of 91·3 km/h ($56\frac{3}{4}$ mph) was achieved down Madeley Bank in Staffordshire on the Grand Junction Railway by the 2–2–2 engine *Lucifer* on 13 November 1839.

The next three speed records were achieved on the Great Western Railway. In June 1845 the broad-gauge 2–2–2 *Ixion* reached 98·2 km/h (61 mph) between Didcot and London. On 1 June 1846 the 2–2–2 *Great Western* ran at 119·5 km/h ($74\frac{1}{2}$ mph) near Wootton Bassett,

Wiltshire, and in the same place on 11 May 1848 the 4–2–2 *Great Britain* reached 125·5 km/h (78 mph).

The Bristol & Exeter Railway 4–2–4 tank No. 41 achieved a record speed of 131·6 km/h (81·8 mph) down Wellington Bank in Somerset in June 1854. It was one of the class with 2·743 m (9 ft) diameter driving-wheels designed by James Pearson and built by Rothwell & Company of Bolton in 1853 (see p. 129).

The next speed record was achieved in France in 1889 when a Crampton 4–2–0 No. 604 reached a speed of 144 km/h (89½ mph) between Montereau and Sens on the Paris–Dijon line.

Britain re-established its claim to the world speed record in March 1897 when Midland Railway 2·362 m (7 ft 9 in) 4–2–2 No. 117 was timed by Charles Rous-Marten at 144·8 km/h (90 mph) between Melton Mowbray and Nottingham. The engine was then still new.

The record by *City of Truro* on 9 May 1904 is mentioned on p. 173.

On 15 June 1902 the New York Central & Hudson River Railroad inaugurated 'The Twentieth Century Limited' between New York and Chicago, covering the 1547 km (961 miles) in 20 h. On the same day the Pennsylvania Railroad introduced the 'Pennsylvania Special' between the same places, taking 20 h for the 1443·5 km (897 miles).

The NYC & HR route included a 24 km/h (15 mph) journey of 1·6 km (1 mile) through the main street of Syracuse which was replaced by a viaduct on 24 September 1936. The Pennsylvania Railroad route included 644 km (400 miles) through the Allegheny Mountains, round the famous Horseshoe Curve, and over a summit of 668·73 m (2194 ft).

'The Twentieth Century Limited' was accelerated to 18 h in 1908, but was later restored to 20 h until reduced to 18 again in April 1932. On 15 June 1938 the new streamlined trains reduced the time to 16 h. In 1929 the route had been shortened from 1547 to 1543 km (961 to 958·7 miles) by the Cleveland by-pass. Steam traction with the famous New York Central 'Hudson'-type 4–6–4s ended in March 1945. 'The Twentieth Century Limited' made its last run on 13 March 1967.

The earliest speed record with electric-traction was 162 km/h (101 mph) attained by a German double-bogie locomotive built by Siemens & Halske in 1901 and operating on 1500 V dc, but it severely damaged the track.

On 6 October 1903 a 12-wheeled electric railcar with motors by Siemens & Halske reached a speed of 203 km/h (126 mph) on the military railway between Marienfeld and Berlin. A similar car with AEG (Allgemeine Elektrizitäts-Gesellschaft, Berlin) equipment reached 210·2 km/h (130·5 mph) on 23 October 1903.

This record stood in Germany until 1974 when one of the prototype luxury four-car train sets of the German Federal Railways Class 'TE403' reached a speed of 215 km/h (133·6 mph) between Bielefeld and Hamm. These trains are designed for speeds of 200 km/h (124·3 mph) in public service and for experimental running up to 230 km/h (142·9 mph).

A new world speed record was established in Germany on 21 June 1931 when a petrol railcar driven by an airscrew maintained 230 km/h (143 mph) for 10 km (6·25 miles) between Karstädt and Dergenthin. The car was designed by Dr F. Kruckenburg.

'The world's fastest train' was the claim made by the Great Western Railway, England, on 6 June 1932 when the 'Cheltenham Spa Express' behind 'Castle' Class 4–6–0 No. 5006 *Tregenna Castle* ran the 124 km (77·3 miles) from Swindon to London (Paddington) in 56 min 47 s at an average speed of 131·3 km/h (81·6 mph). The maximum speed was 148·5 km/h (92·3 mph). The train became known as 'The Cheltenham Flyer', but the record was held only until 1935. For a brief period it was then held by the Canadian Pacific Toronto–Montreal service.

Germany established a record speed for steam-traction in May 1935 when the streamlined 4–6–4 No. 05.001 reached 200·4 km/h (124½ mph) on a test run between Berlin and Hamburg. The engine was built by the Borsig Locomotive Works, Berlin, in 1935. The second engine, No. 05.002, achieved 193 km/h (120 mph) with a 200 ton train in June 1935.

The fastest speed with a steam locomotive in Canada was on a test run when one of the five Canadian Pacific 'Jubilee' Class 4–4–4s No.

3000, reached 180 km/h (112½ mph) before making an emergency stop during brake tests at St Telesphore, Quebec, on 18 September 1936.

A record speed with diesel-electric traction was achieved in Germany on 23 June 1939 when 265·5 km/h (133·5 mph) was reached.

The diesel-electric 'Zephyr' of the Chicago, Burlington & Quincy Railroad, on 26 May 1934, ran the 1637 km (1017 miles) from Denver to Chicago at an average speed of 124·8 km/h (77·6 mph) throughout.

On 23 October 1936 it ran from Chicago to Denver in 12 h 12 min at an average speed of 147·4 km/h (91·6 mph); 1270 km (750 miles) were covered at 144·8 km/h (90 mph), 42·8 km (26·6 miles) at 169 km/h (105 mph) and a maximum speed of 186·7 km/h (116 mph) was reached.

The first American transcontinental speed record was made in June 1876 by the 'Jarrett and Palmer Special' when it ran the 5330 km (3312 miles) from Jersey City to San Francisco in 84 h 20 min, or about 3½ days.

Edward Henry Harriman (1848–1909), while president of the Union Pacific Railroad 1903 until his death, once covered the 5382 km (3344 miles) in a special train from Oakland, California, to New York in 71 h 27 min. This remained the transcontinental record until October 1934.

The Union Pacific Railroad achieved a record for diesel-traction with the first American streamlined diesel-electric express, the M10000. In October 1934 during tests it covered 96·5 km (60 miles) at 165·4 km/h (102·8 mph) and reached 193 km/h (120 mph). It crossed the continent from Los Angeles to New York—5245 km (3259 miles) in 56 h 56 min, at an average speed of 99·8 km/h (62 mph). In service it ran the 3657 km (2272 miles) between Chicago and Portland in 39¼ h. It was scrapped in 1942.

The Chicago, Milwaukee, St Paul & Pacific began experiments with high speeds in the early 1930s, and on 29 July 1934 'F6' Class 4–6–4 No. 6402, built in 1930, with a train of five roller-bearing steel cars, reached a speed of 166·5 km/h (103·5 mph) at Oakwood, Wisconsin, and averaged 149 km/h (92·62 mph) for 98·8 km (61·4 miles) between Edgebrook, Ill, and Oakwood, Wis. The average over the 137·9 km (85·7 miles) Chicago–Milwaukee run was 122·4 km/h (76·07 mph). This was the first authentic 161 km/h (100 mph) run in the USA.

The famous 'Hiawatha' service began on 29 May 1935, covering the 660 km (410 miles) Chicago–St Paul in 6 h 30 min. The Chicago-Milwaukee section was covered in 75 min at speeds of 161 km/h (100 mph). The locomotives were the four 'Atlantics', described on p. 119 which could run up to 193 km/h (120 mph).

The success of the 'Hiawatha' created heavier loadings which led to the introduction, in 1938, of the six 'F7' Class streamlined 4–6–4s. These shared the workings with the 'Atlantics', and from 21 January 1939 worked two additional Chicago–Twin Cities trains known as the 'Morning Hiawathas'. Later that year one of them averaged 193 km/h (120 mph) for 8 km (5 miles) and maintained over 161 km/h (100 mph) for 30·5 km (19 miles).

Today badly maintained track has forced Amtrak (National Railroad Passenger Cor-

Canadian Pacific 'Jubilee' Class 4–4–4 No. 3000. One of this type reached a speed of 180 km/h (112 mph), the fastest speed with a steam locomotive in Canada (Canadian Pacific Limited)

poration) to slow down the Chicago–Minneapolis service to over 10 h, about 3½ h longer than with steam in 1940.

In the course of a trial run from London to Leeds and back on 30 November 1934 the London & North Eastern Railway 'Pacific' No. 4472 *Flying Scotsman* with a load of 145 tons covered the 299 km (185·8 miles) outwards in 151 min 56 s. On the return, with 208 tons, it took 157 min 17 s. Down Stoke Bank between Grantham and Peterborough the dynamometer-car speed recorder gave a maximum of 161 km/h (100 mph) for 548·6 m (600 yd). However, this was disputed by the most experienced of all train-timers, Cecil J. Allen, who was on the train and who would accept nothing higher than 157·72 km/h (98 mph).

Bugatti railcars in France achieved some high speeds in 1935, one of them reaching 185·9 km/h (115·5 mph) near Le Mans.

A world speed record for steam was achieved by the London & North Eastern Railway on 5 March 1935 when the 'Pacific' No. 2750 *Papyrus* reached 173·8 km/h (108 mph) down Stoke Bank during a round trip of 863 km (536 miles) from London to Newcastle and back at an over-all average speed of 112·6 km/h (70 mph). The outcome of this test was a new four-hour service between London and Newcastle in October 1935.

The first of the Gresley 'A4' Class 'Pacifics', No. 2509 *Silver Link*, broke the record the same year, on 27 September 1935, when it twice reached 181 km/h (112½ mph) and averaged 173 km/h (107½ mph) for 40 km (25 miles), 161 km/h (100 mph) for 69 km (43 miles) and 147·7 km/h (91·8 mph) for 113 km (70 miles) continuously, with a 230 ton train.

An attempt to break this record was made by the London, Midland & Scottish Railway during a trial of the 'Coronation Scot' with 'Pacific' No. 6220 *Coronation*. Four reliable train-timers (Cecil J. Allen, D S M Barrie, S P W Corbett and O S Nock) independently recorded a speed of 181 km/h (112½ mph) at a point only 3·219 km (2 miles) south of Crewe Station. The LMS, eager to beat the LNER record, officially claimed a speed of 183·5 km/h (114 mph), but this is seriously doubted. It was followed by a hazardous entry into Crewe Station over crossovers, resulting in a heap of smashed crockery in the restaurant car.

The all-time record for stream-traction was achieved by the LNER on 3 July 1938 when the 'A4' Class No. 4468 *Mallard* with a seven-coach train weighing 240 tons reached 202·8 km/h (126 mph) on Stoke Bank between Grantham and Peterborough. Five miles (8 km) (mileposts 94–89) were covered at an average speed of 193·76 km/h (120·4 mph). The overrunning of the middle valve spindle (a fault of the Holcroft/Gresley combination gear) at a cut-off of over 40 per cent resulted in destruction of the bearing metal in the middle big end.

The driver, Joseph Duddington, retired in 1944 and died in 1953 aged 76. The fireman was Thomas Bray. *Mallard* is preserved in the National Railway Museum, York. (See photograph p. 231.)

New records were achieved in Italy by three-car electric units. On 27 July 1938 the 213·9 km (132·9 miles) from Rome to Naples were covered in 83 min at an average speed of 154·66 km/h (96·1 mph) and with a maximum of 201 km/h (125 mph).

On 20 July 1939 the 315 km (195·8 miles) from Florence to Milan were covered in 115·2 min at an average speed, start to stop, of 164 km/h (102 mph) with a maximum of 202·8 km/h (126 mph).

In Germany a record for a diesel train was made on 23 June 1939 with a speed of 214·85 km/h (133·5 mph).

The highest speed on sub-standard gauge was achieved on the 1·065 m (3 ft 6 in) gauge South African Railways on 11 November 1976 when a test coach hauled by a specially geared electric locomotive exceeded 200 km/h (124 mph). The purpose was to test the stability of the Scheffel cross-anchor bogie with its self-steering wheelsets widely used on the SAR.

The highest train speeds at the time of writing (1979) have been made in France. On 21 February 1953 Co Co electric locomotive No. 7121 with three coaches averaged 239·8 km/h (149 mph) for 4·8 km (3 miles) on the 1500 V dc line between Dijon and Beaune, reaching a maximum speed of 242·8 km/h (150·9 mph). The 4300 hp locomotive weighs 106 tons.

On 28 March 1955 No. 7107 of the same type reached 330·9 km/h (205·6 mph) with a three-coach train of 100 tons for 1·24 miles (2 km) between Facture and Morcenx on the Bordeaux–Hendaye line. The following day this speed was equalled by the 81 ton 4000 hp Bo Bo locomotive No. 9004, also 1500 V dc. The drivers were H. Braghet and J. Brocca.

A rail speed record of 378 km/h (235 mph) was achieved in France on 4 December 1967 between Gometz-le-Châtel and Limours by 'L'Aérotrain' powered by jet aero engines.

The world's highest speed for a flanged-wheel vehicle on rails of 410 km/h (254·76 mph) was achieved on 14 August 1974 by the Linear Induction Motor Test Vehicle of the United States Department of Transportation at its 9·97 km (6·2 mile) standard-gauge test track at Pueblo, Colorado.

A special Budd car fitted with two turbo-jet 'J-47' aircraft engines mounted on the forward end reached a speed of 296 km/h (183·85 mph) in July 1966 on the New York Central Railroad near Bryan, Ohio, between mileposts 350 and 345. The 8 km (5 miles) were covered in 1 min 39·75 s at an average speed of 291 km/h (181 mph). The record was achieved near milepost 347 over a length of 91·5 m (300 ft).

A maximum speed of 401 km/h (249 mph) was attained on 19 February 1976 by the Krauss-Maffei/MBB (Messerschmidt–Bölkow–Blohm) maglev research vehicle *Komet* on a 1300 m (1422 yd) track near Manching in south Germany. It was driven by six steam rockets, and reached a speed of 400 km/h (248½ mph) in 300 m.

The fastest train speed in the USA was 251 km/h (156 mph) recorded at Princeton Junction, NJ, on 24 May 1967 by a test train built as part of the Northeast Corridor Project.

The first regular scheduled service at over 161 km/h (100 mph) was introduced in Japan on 1 November 1965 on the then new standard-gauge Shinkansen line when trains began running between Tokyo and Osaka—(516 km, 321 miles)—in 3 h 10 min at an average speed of 163 km/h (103·3 mph) with a maximum of 210 km/h (130 mph), covering the 342 km (212·4 miles) between Tokyo and Nagoya in 120 min at an average speed of 171 km/h (106·2 mph). The trains, then 12 cars, weighing 720 tons, are now 16 cars weighing 950 tons.

The new service between Tokyo and Hakata, inaugurated on 10 March 1975, covers the 1069·1 km (664·3 miles) in 6 h 56 min at an average speed of 154·2 km/h (95·8 mph). On the 515·4 km (320·25 mile) Tokyo–Shin-Osaka section the average scheduled speed is 162·8 km/h (101 mph). (From *JNR Facts and Figures*, 1976 edition.)

The number of passengers carried on the Shinkansen system reached 1 000 000 000 on 25 May 1976. The record number of passengers carried in one day was 807 875 on 6 April 1975.

The highest speed with diesel-traction was recorded on 12 June 1973 when the prototype British 'High Speed Train' attained a speed of 232 km/h (143 mph) over 0·4 km (¼ mile) between Northallerton and Thirsk during a test on the Darlington–York section. The previous day the HST had covered 1·609 km (1 mile) at 226·9 km/h (141 mph) between Thirsk and Tollerton. The driver was Sidney Winford of York. On 6 June the same train, driven by Ernest Cockerham of Leeds, had broken the 35-year-old British rail-speed record by maintaining 215 km/h (131 mph) for 12·9 km (8 miles) between Northallerton and Thirsk.

British Rail's 'Inter City 125' High-Speed Trains gained a Design Council Award in 1978. The design work was mostly carried out at the BR Technical Centre at Derby.

The 'Inter-City 125' trains using the first 27 'production' HST (High Speed Train) sets went into operation between London (Paddington) and Bristol and South Wales on 4 October 1976. They were introduced on the East Coast main line on 8 May 1978, cutting the London–Edinburgh time from 5 h 27 min (by 'Deltic'-hauled express) to 4 h 52 min for the 632 km (392·7 miles) and London–York (302 km, 187·6 miles) from 2 h 31 min to 2 h 10 mins.

On the same day the London–Bristol and Cardiff times were cut by a further 3 min giving average speeds of 158·67 km/h (98·6 mph) between Paddington and Bristol Parkway.

The fastest run achieved by an HST set was by the *Jubilee Special* on 7 May 1977. Set No. 253019 covered the 189 km (117·65 miles) from Bristol to London (Paddington) in 68 min 20 s at an average speed of 166 km/h (103·3 mph), achieving a top speed of 206 km/h (128 mph) from Southall to Ealing. The return trip took 67 min 35 s, an average of 168 km/h (104·4 mph) with top speeds of 206 km/h (128 mph) from Maidenhead to Twyford and Steventon to Challow.

The British Rail gas-turbine-driven Experimental Advanced Passenger Train (APT-E) attained a speed of 244·6 km/h (152 mph) between Swindon and Reading on 10 August 1975.

Three 'prototype' pre-production Advanced Passenger Train sets classed '370' have been built at the Derby Works of British Rail Engineering Limited, each having five different types of passenger trailer coaches: 1, driving trailer with driving cab and seats for 52 second class passengers, and detachable nose module covering standard buffers and couplings; 2, intermediate trailer with 72 second class seats; 3, catering with kitchen and bar equipment for full meal and buffet facilities and with 28 second class seats; 4, intermediate with 47 first class seats; 5, van trailer with parcels section, guard's office and 25 first class seats. The trailers are articulated, two ends sharing one bogie, and the bodies are mainly aluminium. Driving and van trailers have single bogies at the 'outer' ends and share articulated bogies at the 'inner' ends. The 4000 hp 25 kV electric power cars, of steel construction, with two bogies, were originally intended to be positioned in the middle of the train, but it is now decided to incorporate a driving cab and nose module and to have it at one end, to give passengers free access to the entire train and to avoid duplication of catering facilities.

A 200 km/h (125 mph) train will have one power car and up to 11 trailers with over 500 seats; a 241 km/h (150 mph) train will have two power cars and up to 12 trailers with nearly 600 seats.

To stop a 241 km/h train within the present signalling system designed for 161 km/h (100 mph) trains special brakes are needed to absorb the enormous energy generated. For this purpose water-turbine brakes are used. To facilitate such high speeds on curves super-elevated for speeds up to 161 km/h a mechanism tilts the body inwards up to 9 degrees. On the power cars the pantograph is restrained centrally by a connection to the bogie.

Toilets are on the same principle as those in aircraft, with connections for pumping out and refilling with circulating water, and they flush on closure of the seat cover.

As tests proceed and production methods are evolved it is hoped to place orders for 60 or 70 eleven-vehicle trains at a cost of £2 000 000 each. Eventually they will operate on the main line out of London (Euston) giving journey times of London–Glasgow 4 h 5 min (present best time 5 h); London–Liverpool 2 h 1 min (2 h 31 min); London–Manchester 1 h 56 min (2 h 29 min); London–Birmingham 1 h 8 min (1 h 31 min). The first 200 km/h schedules are planned for October 1979. It is hoped to have 20 sets in service by 1982 and the complete fleet by 1985.

The fastest metre-gauge train in Europe is operated by the Rhaetian Railway in Switzerland. The 7·12 from St Moritz to Chur covers the 89·3 km (55½ miles) in 2 h, over a difficult mountain route with innumerable curves and long gradients of 1 in 28·6 (3½ per cent).

The highest recorded rail speed in New Zealand, 125·5 km/h (78 mph), was achieved on test by one of the 250 hp diesel railcars built by Vulcan Foundry Limited, Lancashire, England, in 1940. Only nine were delivered; one was lost at sea in a submarine attack. They have three-axle motor bogies and two-axle trailing bogies. Unofficial speeds over 145 km/h (over 90 mph) have been claimed.

The fastest steam locomotives in New Zealand were the 'Ja' Class 4–8–2s with a top speed of 120·8 km/h (75 mph).

The fastest speed achieved by a medium-gauged steam locomotive was 130 km/h (81 mph) on the 1·067 m (3 ft 6 in) gauge Japanese National Railways, by a C62 Class 4–6–4 of 1948 design. The JNR has the highest speed limit, of 120 km/h (75 mph) on the 1·067 m gauge.

A new Canadian speed record was made on 10 March 1976 during a test of a new LRC (Light Rapid Comfortable) train which achieved 207·6 km/h (129 mph) on the Canadian Pacific Railway Adirondack sub-division east of Montreal. It established another Canadian record by maintaining an average speed of 200 km/h (124½ mph) over a distance of 1 mile.

FASTEST SCHEDULED TRAINS IN THE USA AND CANADA

The Penn Central electric 'Metroliners' were introduced between New York and Washington on 15 January 1969, covering the 396 km (224·6 miles) with five stops in 2 h 59 min at an average speed of 121·2 km/h (75·3 mph). On 2 April 1969 a non-stop schedule of 2½ h was established at an average speed of 144·6 km/h (98·8 mph), but this was discontinued. In 1977 the times varied from 3 h to 3 h 4 min.

The 'North Coast Hiawatha' is Amtrak's name for the former Northern Pacific 'North Coast Limited'. This streamlined train runs three times weekly taking 50 h 29 min over the 3586 km (2228 miles) between Chicago and Seattle. In the reverse direction the time is 54 h 25 min. These times give average speeds of 71 km/h (44 mph) and 66 km/h (41 mph). The route crosses the Rockies at Momestake Pass and the Cascades at Stampede Tunnel, 2997 m (3278 yd) long.

The fastest scheduled services in Canada operate between Montreal and Toronto. The Canadian National 'Turbo' trains cover the 539 km (335 miles) in 4½ h with three stops, at an average speed of 120 km/h (74·4 mph); and the 'Rapido' trains take 4 h 55 min with the same three stops, at an average speed of 109·6 km/h (68·1 mph), in both directions. Between Guildwood, Ontario, and Dorval, Quebec, the 'Turbo' covers 500 km (310·9 miles) in 208 min at an average of 144·8 km/h (90 mph).

ACCIDENTS

Railway accidents and failures are classified under four headings:

1 Train accidents on or affecting passenger lines;
2 Movement accidents, to people injured by moving railway vehicles, excluding those in train accidents;
3 Non-movement accidents, to people on railway premises, not caused by movement of railway vehicles;
4 Failures of rolling stock, track and structures which could, but which may not, cause train accidents.

Under the Regulation of Railways Act, 1871, and the **Railway Employment (Prevention of Accidents) Act, 1900**, all train accidents on passenger railways in Britain and all accidents on railway premises resulting in injury or death must be reported to the Minister of Transport in accordance with the **Railways (Notice of Accidents) Order, 1965**. Under these Acts the Minister is empowered to order an inquiry into any of the reported accidents. The 1871 Act requires that all reports of accident inquiries are published.

The earliest known fatal railway accident on record occurred on Wednesday, 5 December 1821, when a carpenter, David Brook, was walking home from Leeds along the Middleton Railway in a blinding sleet storm. He failed to see or hear an approaching train of coal wagons drawn by one of the Blenkinsop/Murray engines (see pp. 10 and 108) and he was run over and fatally injured.

On the opening day of the Liverpool & Manchester Railway, on 15 September 1830, William Huskisson, Member of Parliament for Liverpool, was run over by the Stephensons' *Rocket* at Parkside near Newton le Willows. A thigh was fractured and he died later at Eccles near Manchester. He was taken there on the engine *Northumbrian*, driven by Joseph Locke who, on the journey, established a world speed record of 58 km/h (36 mph).

The first passenger-train accident in the USA occurred on 9 November 1833 on the Camden & Amboy Railroad between Spotswood and Hightown, New Jersey. One carriage overturned and 12 of its 24 passengers were seriously injured.

The first British railway accident to be investigated by an inspecting officer of the Board of Trade was at Howden on the Hull & Selby Railway on 7 August 1840 when a casting fell from a wagon and derailed a mixed passenger/goods train, causing six deaths.

The first large railway accident was in France on 8 May 1842. A 15-coach express from Versailles to Paris crashed when the axle of one of the two engines broke and several coaches piled on top of it. Locked compartment doors prevented people from escaping and 48 were burned to death. This ended the locking of train doors in France.

Canada's first major railway collision occurred on the Great Western Railway west of Chatham in 1854 when a train of ballast for the track collided with a passenger train, killing 47 people.

The worst railway accident in Canada was on the Grand Trunk Railway at Beloeil, Quebec, on 29 June 1864 when 99 people were killed. This stimulated safety-consciousness and led to the introduction of standard operating procedures on Canadian railways.

The first fatal railway accident in Australia was at Lidcombe, a suburb of Sydney, NSW, on 10 July 1858. A train took a curve too fast and was derailed, killing two and injuring 13.

Charles Dickens escaped with a shaking when he was involved in the derailment at Staplehurst, Kent, on the South Eastern Railway, on 9 June 1865, in which ten people were killed when the train ran on to a viaduct where repairs were being carried out. He never fully recovered and he died on 9 June 1870, exactly 5 years later.

The only major British railway disaster in which there were no survivors was on 28 December 1879 when the Tay Bridge collapsed in a gale while a train was crossing. All 73 passengers and crew of five were drowned. Some bodies were never recovered. (See 'Tay Bridge', p. 67.)

Britain's worst rail disaster occurred at Quintinshill near Gretna Green, in Scotland just north of Carlisle, on 22 May 1915. Signalling irregularities led to the overlooking of a train standing on the wrong line. A military special was accepted and it collided with the stationary train. The 195 m (213 yd) long train was telescoped to 61 m (67 yd). Fifty-three seconds later an express from the other direction ploughed into the wreckage. Fire added to the horror and destruction in which 227 lives were lost.

The world's worst railway disaster occurred at Saint-Michel-de-Maurienne in France on 12 December 1917. A packed troop train carrying 1025 soldiers in 19 Italian carriages weighing 526 tons behind a single locomotive, PLM 4–6–0 No. 2592, was ordered away from Modane at the north end of the Mont Cenis Tunnel at about 22.00. The maximum permitted load for this locomotive was 144 tons. Only the first three coaches had Westinghouse continuous brake and the rest had only hand brakes. Driver Louis Girard was unwilling to proceed but was unable to act against military commands. On the 10 miles of 1 in 33 (16 km of 3 per cent) falling grade the train ran out of control, brakes became red-hot and set fire to the coaches, the engine became derailed, breaking the coupling with the train, and finally the entire train was wrecked at 150 km/h (91 mph) on a curve at Saint-Michel-de-Maurienne. Of the 543 dead which could be accounted for in the wreckage 135 could not be identified. The driver miraculously survived and was freed of all blame.

The first serious accident to an electric train in Britain was at Hall Road on the Liverpool–Southport line of the Lancashire & Yorkshire Railway on 27 July 1905. A signalman's error led to a collision in which 21 people were killed.

England's worst railway disaster was at Harrow & Wealdstone Station on the London Midland Region on 8 October 1952. An express from Perth, running 80 min late, failed to stop at signals and ran at 90–95 km/h (56–59 mph) into the rear of a crowded local train in the platform. Almost immediately a double-headed express travelling northwards at the same speed crashed into the wreckage. The death toll was 112.

This accident would almost certainly have been prevented by automatic train control such as was in use on the Western Region (see p. 200) or the Advanced Warning System (AWS) now installed on most British main lines.

The worst accident on a London 'tube' railway occurred on Friday, 28 February 1975 when the 08.37 train from Drayton Park ran unbraked through Moorgate Station on the Highbury Branch and crashed into the end of a blind tunnel. The front 14 seats were compressed into a space of 61 cm (2 ft). A total of 43 died and 77 were seriously injured. The rescue operation was the most difficult ever undertaken on a British railway, in temperatures often exceeding 49 °C (120 °F). The last of the bodies was not recovered until late on Tuesday, 4 March.

The cause of the accident was the failure of Motorman Newson to stop the train. The reason for this could not be discovered. The station is now used by the new Great Northern Electric trains and is protected by a severe speed restriction and an automatic trip device.

The oddest collision on record occurred in February 1913 on the Memphis Branch of the Louisville & Nashville Railroad, USA, during a flood. A freight train collided in the dark with the shallow-draught packet-boat *Lochie S* which was sailing above the tracks at Cumberland, Texas. No one was injured, but the responsibility for damage was never properly settled.

A locomotive that disappeared was 0–6–0 No. 115 of the Furness Railway, England, built by Sharp Stewart & Company in 1881. On 22 October 1892 at about 8.16 it was shunting at Lindal, an area of extensive iron-ore mines, when the ground gave way beneath it and the engine began to sink in. The crew, Driver Postlethwaite and Fireman Robinson, jumped clear and by 14.15 the engine had disappeared completely. It fell to a depth of 61 m (200 ft), beyond recovery, and the hole was filled in.

One of Britain's most curious railway disasters was at Swinton near Manchester on 28 April 1953 when the roof of Clifton Hall (Black Harry) Tunnel collapsed under a filled-in shaft. A pair of semi-detached houses above collapsed into the crater, causing five deaths. The tunnel was on the Patricroft–Clifton Branch of the London & North Western Railway and was opened on 2 February 1850. The accident led to a review of all old tunnel records.

Grade crossing collisions cause the largest number of deaths on railroads in the USA amounting to about two-thirds of the total. There are about 180 000 unguarded grade, or level, crossings in the USA where about 1500 are killed and 3700 injured annually.

The worst level (grade) crossing accident in Britain was at Hixon, Staffordshire, on the Colwich–Stone section of the electrified main line from London to Manchester, on 6 January 1968. A transporter loaded with a 120 ton transformer was crossing at 3·2 km/h (2 mph) when the automatic barriers closed. A train arrived at 113 km/h (70 mph) before the crossing was cleared and struck the transformer, hurling it 6 m (20 ft). There were 11 deaths. The transporter was being escorted by the police who had failed to telephone the Colwich signalman for permission to cross with an exceptional load. The result was a change in the operation of all automatic half-barrier level crossings.

The hole at Lindal on the Furness Railway into which a locomotive disappeared on 22 October 1892. The engine still lies at a depth of 61 m (200 ft) (British Rail)

Hixon level crossing near Stone, 29 July 1969, showing the new warning notices following the accident on 6 January 1968. The picture also shows the lightness of the 25 kV catenary (T A Fletcher)

No passengers were killed on British railways in 1949, 1954, 1956, 1966 and 1976 in more than 15 000 000 000 journeys each year. In 1959,

WORST RAILWAY DISASTERS IN VARIOUS COUNTRIES

Country	Date	Place	No. Killed	Cause
France	12.12.1917	Modane	543	Runaway and derailment
Italy	2.3.1944	Balvano, nr Salerno	526	Stalled in Armi Tunnel
Spain	3.1.1944	Near Torre, Leon Province	500–800	Double collision and fire inside tunnel
Pakistan	29.9.1957	Montgomery	250	Collision
Argentina	1.2.1970	Near Buenos Aires	236	Collision
Scotland	22.5.1915	Near Gretna Green	227	Double collision
Poland	22.10.1949	Nowy Dwor	*c* 200	Derailment
Japan	29.1.1940	Osaka	200	Collision
Brazil	20.3.1946	Near Aracaju	185	Wreck
Jamaica	1.9.1957	Kendal	178	Derailed into ravine
New Zealand	24.12.1953	Near Waiouru	155	Bridge Collapse
Russia	13.7.1882	Near Tchery	*c* 150	Derailment
Nigeria	16.2.1970	Northern Nigeria	*c* 150*	
India	23.11.1956	Marudaiyar River	143	Derailment
Germany	22.12.1939	Near Magdeburg	132	Collision
England	8.10.1952	Harrow & Wealdstone	112	Double collision
Czechoslovakia	14.11.1960	Pardubice	110	Collision
USA	9.7.1918	Nashville, Tennessee	*c* 101	Head-on collision
Roumania	25.12.1938	Near Kishiney	*c* 100	Collision
Canada	28.6.1864	Beloeil, nr St Hilaire	99	Lack of control of train which ran through open drawbridge
Portugal	26.7.1964	Custoias, nr Oporto	94	Wreck
Indonesia	28.5.1959	Java	92	Derailed into ravine
Netherlands	8.1.1962	Woerden	91	Collision
South Africa	4.10.1965	Near Durban	81	Derailment
Northern Ireland	12.6.1889	Armagh	80	Runaway collision
Australia	17.1.1977	Granville nr Sydney	80	Collision with bridge
Burma	9.12.1965	Near Toungoo	76	Collision
Switzerland	14.6.1891	Münchenstein	71	Birs Bridge collapse
South Korea	31.1.1954	Near Seoul	56	
Philippines	2.9.1954	Negros Island	56	
Hungary	22.12.1968	Budapest	*c* 43	Collision
Yugoslavia	14.2.1971	Belgrade	34	Fire
Wales	20.8.1868	Abergele	33	Runaway collision

*A further 52 (survivors) were killed in a lorry on their way to hospital.

1963 and 1974 only one passenger was killed in each year.

On British railways in 1975 18 passengers were killed and 210 injured in train accidents; 65 were killed and 1872 injured in movement accidents; one was killed and 2409 injured in non-movement accidents, and trespassing and suicides resulted in 209 deaths and injured 105.

On the New South Wales Government Railways, Australia, during a period of 14 years there was not one fatal passenger accident on any part of the system. Unfortunately they now have had **the worst railway accident in Australia**. On 17 January 1977 a crowded commuter train from Blue Mountain to Sydney crashed into a bridge support at Granville near Sydney and a concrete span collapsed on to the train resulting in 80 killed and 81 injured.

USA statistics show that railway travel is the safest of all. In terms of fatalities per 100 000 000 passenger miles (161 000 000 km) the rate for the railroads is 0·1; for internal air services 0·3; for buses 0·24; and for cars and taxis 2·39.

In 1972 225 train accidents were caused on British Railways by vandals. In 1973 the number was 167. Thirteen per cent of all 'accidents' on BR are caused deliberately.

During 1973 an average of two bridges on BR were damaged every day by lorries carrying high loads. Many drivers never reported the damage and were not discovered.

RUNAWAYS

The first serious passenger-train runaway in Britain was on the Oxford, Worcester & Wolverhampton Railway at Round Oak near Wolverhampton on 23 August 1858 when part of a heavy passenger train broke away and ran back into the following passenger train. Fourteen lives were lost.

A similar accident occurred at Helmshore, Lancashire, on the Lancashire & Yorkshire Railway on 4 September 1860 when eleven died.

These led to experiments with continuous brakes, and the eventual adoption by law of automatic continuous brakes (see pp. 163, 199).

The most serious runaway in British railway history occurred on the Great Northern Railway of Ireland at Armagh on 12 June 1889 when the rear half of an overloaded excursion train, which had failed on a gradient and had been divided, ran back and collided with a following train, killing 80 passengers. The train had continuous but non-automatic brakes.

This accident led to the **Regulation of Railways Act** of 1889 (see p. 199) which gave power to the Board of Trade to order absolute block working on passenger lines (only one train in a section at one time), automatic continuous brakes on passenger trains, and the interlocking of points and signals.

The British unbraked freight train has been the cause of many runaways. The worst was at Abergele on the London & North Western Railway in North Wales on 20 August 1868 when some wagons being irregularly shunted on the main line ran away and collided with a passenger train, causing 33 deaths.

On 12 December 1870, at Stairfoot near Barnsley on the Manchester, Sheffield & Lincolnshire Railway, a similar runaway killed 15 passengers.

These accidents led to the installation of trap points to derail runaways on falling gradients.

Some runaways had amusing sequels, such as at Pinwherry, south of Girvan, on the old Glasgow & South Western Stranraer line. The story is still told of the string of wagons which broke loose on Pinmore Bank one night, ran back through Pinwherry and up Barrhill Bank, then back again, repeating this five or six times before coming to rest. A permanent-way inspector named Gallacher, who was spending the night at Pinwherry Station House, said next morning that it was the busiest country station he had ever tried to sleep at—there was a train every 10 minutes.

A record run of 100 miles (161 km) was made on the Chicago, Burlington & Quincy Railroad east of Denver on 26 March 1884 when a wind of tremendous force ripped off the roundhouse roof at Akron and set eight coal cars on the move. They ran on to the main line where the wind drove them along at speeds up to 64 km/h (40 mph). One downgrade stretch of 32 km (20 miles) was covered in 18 min. At Benkelman, 153 km (95 miles) from Akron, a freight engine gave chase and in a few miles was coupled to the cars and they were brought under control after covering 100 miles in under 3 h.

On the windswept Settle and Carlisle section of the former Midland Railway, England, a locomotive was once being turned at Garsdale when a freak wind caught it and kept it spinning round and round until the frantic crew managed to stop it by shovelling ballast into the turntable well. After this a stockade of old sleepers was erected round it.

BREAKDOWN, OR WRECKING, CRANES

'Accident cranes', known in North America as 'wrecking cranes' and more commonly as 'big hooks', and on the Canadian Pacific as 'auxilliary cranes', were originally hand-powered machines with a lifting capacity of 5–10 tons. As the weight of locomotives and rolling stock increased steam-power became necessary, but many British companies were unwilling to lay out capital on such equipment. The London & North Western, one of Britain's biggest railways and the largest joint stock corporation in the world, had no steam accident cranes until 1910.

The term 'breakdown crane' came into use in Great Britain during World War I.

The first steam accident cranes on a British railway were self-propelling machines of 5 tons capacity on four-wheeled trucks built for the Midland Railway by Appleby Brothers, London, in 1874–5.

Five years later the same firm built some of 10 tons capacity for the London & South Western Railway.

For many years the world's most powerful railway crane was one built for the Norfolk & Western Railroad, USA, by Industrial Works (later Industrial Brownhoist) of Bay City, Michigan, in 1912. It could lift a load of 134 tons (150 short tons) at a radius of 5·182 m (17 ft).

The most powerful British steam breakdown cranes are ten of 75 tons capacity built by Cowans Sheldon & Company Limited, Carlisle, and completed in 1962. Two more were built with diesel-power.

The world's most powerful railway breakdown crane has a lifting capacity of 226 800 kg (223·2 tons) (500 000 lb), at a radius of 5·33 m (17 ft 6 in). It was built by Cowans Sheldon & Company Limited, Carlisle, England, in 1960 for the Quebec Cartier Mining Company of Canada. It is powered by a Rolls-Royce 255 bhp supercharged oil engine through a hydraulic torque converter. It is carried on two three-axle trucks on standard gauge, and is designed to operate in temperatures down to −51 °C (60 °F below zero).

In 1961 Cowans Sheldon supplied the same Canadian Company with a wrecking crane of 136 080 kg (300 000 lb) or 134 tons capacity at 5·33 m (17 ft 6 in) radius. Both cranes can negotiate curves of 45·7 m (150 ft) radius.

Cranes of similar though not greater capacity have been built in the USA.

The world's most powerful breakdown crane, built by Cowans Sheldon, Carlisle, in 1960 for the Quebec Cartier Mining Company (Cowans Sheldon)

TRAIN FERRIES

The first wagon ferry was operated by the Monkland & Kirkintilloch Railway, Scotland, on the Forth & Clyde Canal in 1833. It was simply a barge fitted with rails and a turnplate.

The first railroad car ferry in the USA, the *Susquehanna*, went into operation on the Susquehanna River between Havre de Grace and Perryville, Maryland, in April 1836. In the winter of 1854 the river froze so solidly that rails were laid on the ice, and between 15 January and 24 February 1378 freight and other cars were hauled across.

The world's first 'train ferry' was designed by Thomas Grainger and was built in 1849 by Robert Napier & Sons on the Clyde. Named *Leviathan*, it ferried goods wagons across the Firth of Forth, Scotland, between Granton and Burntisland.

In 1858 a similar vessel, named *Carrier*, was put on the Tayport–Broughty Ferry crossing near Dundee.

Thomas Bouch is sometimes credited with the design of these; actually he designed only the loading mechanism.

The Harwich–Zeebrugge train ferry between England and Belgium began operating under Great Eastern Train Ferries Limited on 24 April 1924.

The Dover–Dunkirk train ferry was inaugurated on 14 October 1936. Through trains between London and Paris were operated by the Southern Railway of England, the Northern Railway of France, the Société Anonyme de Navigation Angleterre-Lorraine-Alsace, and the International Sleeping Car Company.

One of the most famous train ferries was the *Baikal* which operated across Lake Baikal in Siberia as a link in the Trans-Siberian Railway. It was launched on 29 July 1899 and

One of the Bosphorus train ferries, *Demiryolu II*, leaving Istanbul for Haydarpasa on the Asian side

entered service in April 1900, combining the duties of train ferry and ice-breaker. It remained in use as a ferry until the Circum–Baikal Railway round the south of the lake was completed in 1904, and it was destroyed in the civil war of 1918–20.

The largest fleet of train and automobile ferries is operated by Danish State Railways (Danske Statsbaner). There are six train ferries and three car ferries, and in addition train ferries operated jointly with the German Federal Railway, German State Railway and Swedish State Railways. The total distance covered is 208 km (129 miles). The speed with which the Danes handle the trains on to and off the ferries is almost unbelievable.

LAST STEAM TRAINS

The last steam-worked transcontinental trains on the Canadian Pacific Railway, after 67 years, ran in October 1954.

The last steam locomotive to pull a train on the CPR was 'A–1–e' Class 4–4–0 No. 29, built in 1887. It hauled a special from Montreal to St Lin and back on 6 November 1960.

The last regularly scheduled steam train in the USA ran on 27 March 1960 on the Grand Trunk Western system, operated by the Canadian National Railways.

Steam locomotives were finally withdrawn on the Canadian National Railways on 25 April 1960.

The last steam-worked branch line on British Railways was the Brockenhurst–Lymington Branch in Hampshire. It was opened on 12 July 1858 and was steam-worked until 30 March 1967. Electric trains began on 1 April.

Steam-traction was eliminated from British Railways on 8 August 1968, except for the summer-only service on the Vale of Rheidol narrow-gauge railway in Wales.

A commemorative 'Farewell to Steam' tour was operated by BR on 11 August 1968 from Liverpool to Carlisle and back. The fare was £15 15s (£15·75).

The last express worked by the famous French compound 'Pacifics' ran between Calais and Amiens on 26 May 1971.

The last regular steam passenger train in Australia ran from Newcastle to Singleton, NSW, in July 1971. It was hauled by 'C32' Class 4–6–0 No. 3246, built in 1893, which ran a total of 3 653 111 km (2 270 000 miles). No. 3242 of this type achieved **the record mileage for an Australian steam locomotive**, of 3 814 041 km (2 370 000 miles).

The last steam-powered goods train in Australia ran in NSW on 22 December 1972.

The last steam-hauled expresses in New Zealand ran between Christchurch and Dunedin in October 1971. However, two 'Ab' Class 'Pacifics' were returned to service for use on summer tourist trains between Lumsden and the Kingston railhead on the shore of Lake Wakatipu in Southland.

The last steam passenger train in Japan ran on 14 December 1976 from Muroran to Iwamizawa in Hokkaido, 140 km (87 miles), behind 'C57' Class 4–6–2 No. 135. At its final departure a Japanese National Railways band played 'Auld Lang Syne'.

The last scheduled steam-hauled train in West Germany ran on 22 May 1977.

The last passenger trains in Tasmania ran between Hobart and Wynyard on 28 July 1978.

Section 5
MISCELLANY

BRITISH AND IRISH RAILWAYS

Under the Railways Act of 19 August 1921, a total of 123 separate British railway companies were amalgamated into four groups; the London, Midland & Scottish, the London & North Eastern, the Great Western and the Southern. Certain inter-group joint companies continued to operate separately. The Grouping came into effect on 1 January 1923.

All Irish railways wholly in the 'Free State' (Eire), both 1·600 m (5 ft 3 in) and 914 mm (3 ft) gauge, were grouped into the Great Southern Railways on 1 January 1925.

The London Transport Executive was formed under the Transport (London) Act of 1969 which transferred the operation of the Underground Railways and the red buses from the former London Transport Board to the Executive, and financial and policy control to Greater London Council from 1 January 1970. The Executive owns 383 km (238 miles) of railway of which 378 km (235 miles) is electrified with third rail at 600 V dc, and operates over 248 km (154 miles) of route. The red buses run over 2799 km (1739 miles) of roads.

The background history goes back to the Act of 13 April 1933 when the London Passenger Transport Board was established to take over the Metropolitan Railway, the Metropolitan District Railway, the London Electric Railway, the Central London Railway, the City and South London Railway, all the street tramways (now abandoned) and nearly all bus and coach undertakings in its area. It became part of the British Transport Commission on 1 January 1948 and was renamed the London Transport Executive. On 1 January 1963 it was again renamed, becoming the London Transport Board when the British Transport Commission was dissolved under the 1962 Transport Act.

Under the Transport (London) Act 1969 control of LT finance and policy was transferred to Greater London Council from 1 January 1970 and operation of the red buses and underground railways passed to the new London Transport Executive. The green buses and coaches passed to London Country Bus Services Limited.

The Irish Transport Company (Coras Iompair Eireann), formed under the Eire Transport Act of 19 November 1944, began operation on 1 January 1945. Under it the Great Southern Railways and the Dublin United Transport Company Limited were merged.

From 1 October 1958 the portion of the Great Northern Railway in the Irish Republic was merged with CIE.

The proposal to nationalise British Railways was first announced by the Government on 19 November 1945. Canals and long-distance road haulage were included.

The Transport Act received the Royal Assent on 6 August 1947, nationalising British railways and canals from 1 January 1948.

At Nationalisation British Railways operated about 32 190 km (20 000 miles) of route with 20 024 steam, 55 diesel and diesel-electric and 16 electric locomotives. There were 6701 stations of which 4815 handled freight.

Under the guidance of Dr Richard Beeching BR went through a period of amputation mania during which the mileage dropped from 30 209 km (18 771 miles) in 1960 to 21 342 km (13 261 miles) in 1969. At the end of 1976 there were 18 012 km (11 258 miles) of route, three steam locomotives (610 mm, 2 ft gauge), 3338 diesel and diesel-electric locomotives and 351 electric locomotives. These totals do not include diesel, diesel-electric and electric multiple-unit sets. Rolling stock included 22 222 coaching vehicles and 187 000 freight vehicles. The number of stations had dropped to 2362 of which only 182 handled freight.

In 1975 BR train-km amounted to 328 000 000 (204 000 000 miles) with coaching stock and 75 600 000 (47 000 000 miles) with freight stock. The system was divided into regions: Scottish, North Eastern, London Midland, Eastern, Western and Southern. On 1 January 1967 the Eastern and North Eastern Regions were combined.

Although the statutory regional structure was abolished by the Transport Act of 1968, it has been continued from 1 January 1969 by the BRB as part of its management structure.

The Transport Act (Northern Ireland) 1948, incorporated the Ulster Transport Authority. The Northern Ireland Road Transport Board, the Belfast & County Down and the Northern Counties railways and other transport services were acquired by 1 April 1949.

On 1 April 1968 its assets were handed over to Northern Ireland Railways Company Limited, incorporated under the Transport Act (Northern Ireland) 1967.

The abbreviated title 'British Rail' and its new totem, two horizontal lines and two arrowheads, were adopted in the summer of 1964. The totem began to appear on rolling stock in February 1965.

The largest British railway scheme ever approved by Parliament in one Act was in the Great Northern Railway Act of 26 June 1846 authorising a railway from London to York via Peterborough, Grantham, Newark, Doncaster and Selby and a branch from north of Peterborough to Boston, Lincoln and Gainsborough to form a loop rejoining the main line near Bawtry, a total of 443 km (275 miles) with a capital of £5 600 000. However, only the sections from London to Doncaster, and Peterborough to Boston, 307 km (191 miles), were built under this Act. The main line ended at Askern Junction, about 6 km (4 miles) north of Doncaster, where it made an end-on junction with the Lancashire & Yorkshire Railway. The other sections were built under later Acts, some by different companies.

Eleven Acts of Parliament were obtained for the Uxbridge & Rickmansworth Railway. It was incorporated by Act of 1861, then abandoned after four more Acts, reincorporated in 1881 and abandoned again, after three more Acts, in 1888. In 1895 a third company was incorporated and in 1899 a further Act was obtained. Construction was never even started.

The last main line into London, the Great Central Railway (formerly the Manchester, Sheffield & Lincolnshire Railway) was opened to passengers on 15 March 1899. Coal traffic had begun on 25 July 1898 and general freight began on 11 April 1899. The railway was pioneered by Edward Watkin when he was chairman of the MS & L., the Metropolitan and the South Eastern railways and of the Channel Tunnel Company. He saw the London Extension as part of a main line linking Manchester, London and Paris. The Act of 28 March 1893 for the 'London Extension' of the MS & L. authorised **the greatest amount of capital in any British railway Act**, £6 200 000, equivalent in 1976 to £93 000 000. The name 'Great Central' was adopted on 1 August 1897.

The GCR became part of the London & North Eastern Railway on 1 January 1923.

The shortest independent standard-gauge railway in Great Britain was the Easingwold Railway from the East Coast main line at Alne, Yorkshire, 4 km ($2\frac{1}{2}$ miles) long. It was opened for goods on 1 July and for passenger traffic on 27 July 1891 and ran passenger trains until 29 November 1948. It was closed completely on 30 December 1957. It possessed only two engines, and only one at a time.

The longest name of an authorised British railway was the Sheffield, Rotherham, Barnsley, Wakefield, Huddersfield & Goole Railway Company, incorporated by Act of 7 August 1846. The section from Barnsley to Horbury Junction near Wakefield (14·5 km; 9 miles) was opened on 1 January 1850 and was vested in the Lancashire & Yorkshire Railway under an Act of 2 August 1858.

RAILWAYS, ROADS AND AIRWAYS

Information published by the **Railway Development Association** (Railway Development Society from 1 October 1978) in 1976 showed that while the railway deficit in Britain cost £21 per second, the capital and current cost of roads was £95 per second, tax allowances on company cars cost £32 per second, and government support for Leyland–Chrysler was estimated at £20 per second, a total of nearly £150 per second, all paid for by direct or indirect taxation.

Running down our railways puts more traffic on the roads where, in Britain in 1975, accidents cost a total of £816 000 000; 6366 persons were killed and 77 122 seriously injured. The average cost of a fatal accident was £41 400; a serious injury £2830; total costs of police, administration, medical and ambulance services alone were £79 000 000 (*Road Accidents in Great Britain 1975*, HMSO). Thus the total cost of fatal road accidents in 1975 was £263 532 400, or over £8 per second. Greater use of the railways could reduce both the rail deficit and the road cost, and an immeasurable amount of human distress.

A modern double-track railway can carry between three and four times as much traffic as a six-lane motorway while occupying only a third of the land space. One locomotive can easily haul a pay load of 1000 tons which would require a minimum of 40 lorries using more imported fuel, and highly paid drivers.

The Association of American Railroads (see below) has established that a railway can move an item of freight for a fifth of the fuel, a sixth of the accidents and a tenth of the land that road haulage requires for the same load, and can carry seven times as much freight per employee.

The true costs of air transport are not known because of deliberate concealment.

RAILROADS, OR RAILWAYS, IN NORTH AMERICA

Early railroads in the USA were given land grants, or loans, by the Federal Government under an Act passed by President Millard Fillmore on 20 September 1850. By 1871 the Government had granted 53 000 000 ha (131 000 000 acres) of land, then worth about $125 000 000, to over 80 railroads, for the construction of about 30 600 km (19 000 miles) of route. This amounts to less than a thirteenth of the total mileage built. Yet in exchange all American railroads were required to carry Government freight at half price and mail at a 20 per cent reduction. When Congress repealed this provision in 1945, from 1 October 1946, it was calculated that the railroads had saved the Government about $1 250 000 000, or ten times the value of the original land grants.

Some early railroads, however, were dishonest or ruthless. In the 1860s a group of railroad tycoons in North Carolina received $6 000 000 in bonds from the Federal Government for building 150 km (93 miles) of railroad worth under $1 000 000.

In 1867 Cornelius Vanderbilt, having gained control of two New York City lines, cut off rail access to Manhattan, thereby forcing the New York Central into his net, afterwards voting himself a personal bonus of $6 000 000 in stock. When his successor, his son William, was asked if he ran the NYC for the public benefit he replied 'The public be damned!' By the 1870s the Americans regarded their railroads as 'Public enemy No. 1'. Some of the legislation against which the railroads are fighting today originated in this period. They brought much of it upon themselves.

The Interstate Commerce Commission (ICC) was created by Act of Congress signed by President Grover Cleveland on 4 February 1887. It regulates rates, services and abandonments of services among railroads, motor carriers, pipelines, inland water-carriers and freight forwarders engaged in interstate commerce. While it regulates 100 per cent of railroad traffic, it regulates only 39 per cent of inter-city road haulage, 14·6 per cent of river and canal traffic, 4·4 per cent of coastal sea traffic and 1·1 per cent of Great Lakes traffic.

In the early 1900s the Interstate Commerce Commission encouraged road and water traffic to compete with the railroads (understandably in view of their over-exercised monopoly) by providing generous Federal assistance in the form of highways and waterways.

This pattern continues today. While the USA railroads pay 24 per cent of their profits in taxes, road operators pay 5 per cent, air lines 4 per cent, and water-carriers 0 per cent. In addition the competing carriers have received Federal assistance amounting to $246 000 000 000 in the period from 1955 to 1970.

The railroads of California, with 11 885 km (7385 miles), paid the highest taxes, $36 762 622, in 1973, followed by Illinois with 17 417 km (10 822 miles) which paid $35 592 897. Hawaii, which no longer has railroads, received $24 034 in railroad taxes.

Class I railroads pay over $900 000 000 in taxes per year, but receive meagre Federal assistance totally out of proportion to the contribution they make to the nation's economy.

Class 1 railroads are those with an operating revenue exceeding $5 000 000. All others are Class II railroads. Class I railroads operate about 95 per cent of the total mileage and employ about 92 per cent of the railroad workers. 'Line-haul' railroads are those operating between terminals. 'Switching' or 'Terminal' railroads operate between local yards or terminals.

There are about 544 operating railroads in the USA, of which 58 are Class I line-haul railroads and 486 are switching or terminal companies or Class II railroads. Amalgamations reduce these numbers, for example between 1916 and 1969 the number of line-haul railroads dropped from 1243 to under 375 of which only 74 are Class I railroads.

Standard Time was introduced in North America on 18 November 1883 when nearly 100 'local times' observed by the railroads were abolished. There are four time zones: Eastern, Central, Mountain, and Pacific, all one hour apart. Standard Time was sponsored and put into effect by the General Time Convention of Railway Managers, now part of the Association of American Railroads (see below), but it was not until 19 March 1918 that Congress passed the Standard Time Act, making this the official time.

The General Time Convention of Railway Managers, a predecessor of the Association of American Railroads, adopted the first standard code of train rules on 14 April 1887.

The Association of American Railroads, with headquarters in Washington, was formed on 12 October 1934 by amalgamation of the American Railway Association, The Association of Railway Executives, Railway Accounting Officers' Association, Railway Treasury Officers' Association, and the Bureau of Railway Economics. It acts as joint agency in research, operation, traffic, accounting and finance. Membership is open to all Class I railroads. In March 1971 there were 232 full-member companies including 116 line-haul railroads, 22 switching and terminal companies, and one leased line in the USA, five Canadian and five Mexican railroads.

The Department of Transportation, with headquarters in Washington, was established on 15 October 1966 by Public Law 89–670, and began operation on 1 April 1967. Eleven offices were transferred to it from other Federal agencies. It develops national transport at the lowest costs consistent with safety and efficiency, co-ordinates transport policies of the Federal Government, and administers the Uniform Time Act.

Railroads carry 70 per cent of the coal in the USA, 74 per cent of canned and frozen foods, 46 per cent of the meat and dairy products, 71 per cent of household appliances, 76 per cent of automobiles and parts, 86 per cent of pulp and paper, 78 per cent of timber, 63 per cent of chemicals and 68 per cent of primary metal products.

If the railroads in the USA were to shut down for one week the national income for the year would be reduced by nearly 6 per cent. An eight-week shut-down would reduce the gross national product for the year by 24 per cent and increase unemployment by 22 per cent.

USA railroads operate about 15 000 passenger-train cars. Of these about 8200 are passenger cars, and the others are dining cars, parlour cars, lounge cars, mail cars and baggage cars.

In 1975 USA railroads carried 268 861 000 passengers travelling 15 420 312 000 passenger km (9 582 000 000 passenger miles). This is less than 10 per cent of the total number of passengers on public or hire transport. This total itself is only about 10 per cent of the total passenger miles. The other 90 per cent travels by private car.

The National Railroad Passenger Corporation, known as 'Amtrak', was formed under the Rail Passenger Service Act of 31 October 1970. It took over the passenger services of 22 of the leading railroads of the USA. Operations began on 1 May 1971. The principal companies remaining outside were the Southern, Denver & Rio Grande Western, and the Rock Island & Pacific. Amtrak now operates about 200 trains daily over about 43 650 route km (27 125 route miles) connecting 440 cities in the USA, and into Canada, with about 2000 passenger cars including sleepers, diners, dome cars and chair cars, and about 400 locomotives. Its aim is 'To make the trains worth travelling again.'

Via Rail Canada was formed in January 1977 to operate all passenger train services in Canada. The first joint Canadian Pacific/Canadian National passenger timetable was issued, under the symbol VIA, in October 1976.

The Penn Central Company was formed on 1 February 1968 by the merging of the Pennsylvania and New York Central railroads. On 31 December 1968 the New York, New Haven & Hartford Railroad became part of the PC, which then owned 31 935 km (19 853 miles) and operated nearly 35 400 km (22 000 miles) of railroad of which 1170 km (727 miles) were electrified in 16 States, two Canadian Provinces and the District of Columbia. It carried nearly 3000 freight trains every 24 h with 4041 locomotives (174 electric and 3867 diesel-electric), 3109 passenger cars (including 766 multiple-unit electric cars) and 165 495 freight cars and other vehicles, and 2270 cabooses.

Conrail (Consolidated Rail Corporation) was formed on 1 April 1976. The new system is 27 353 km (16 996 miles) long and extends from the Mississippi River and Lake Michigan in the west, Canada on the north and the Ohio River on the south, to the Atlantic Coast. It serves major industrial areas such as St Louis, Chicago, Indianapolis, Columbus, Detroit, Toledo, Cleveland, Buffalo and Pittsburgh, connecting them with Boston, Providence, New York, Philadelphia, Baltimore and Washington in the North East and the Middle Atlantic States. It covers 16 States in the USA and two Canadian Provinces, and is divided into seven Regions and 28 Divisions. The Regions are: Atlantic, Central, Eastern, North East, Northern, Southern, Western. It includes the following systems: Central Railroad of New Jersey; Erie Lackawanna Railway Company; Lehigh Valley Railroad Company; Penn Central Transportation Company; Pittsburgh & Lake Erie Railroad Company; Reading Company; Pennsylvania–Reading Seashore Lines.

The Burlington Northern Railroad was formed on 2 March 1970 by the merging of the Chicago, Burlington & Quincy, the Great Northern, the Northern Pacific and the Spokane, Portland & Seattle railroads. It operates 37 230 km (23 603 miles) of route with 2136 diesel and diesel-electric units including railcars, 109 106 freight cars, 587 passenger cars, and extends from Chicago to Vancouver and Seattle.

One of the larger railroad systems in the USA with no recent amalgamations is the Southern Pacific Transportation Company, with headquarters at San Francisco, California. It operates 21 424 km (13 312 miles) of route (more than the entire British Rail network) serving 12 States by about 750 freight trains every day, representing more than 9 per cent of all the rail freight in the USA. Its trains cross the longest railroad bridge (Huey P. Long, New Orleans), and one of the highest (Pecos, Texas), and make the longest water crossing (Great Salt Lake, Utah) in the USA, and cross the deepest water on the Pit River Bridge (see pp. 76–85).

It owns nearly 88 000 freight cars and 2300 diesel locomotives. Its main line from Oakland, opposite San Francisco to Los Angeles and New Orleans, the 'Sunset Route', 4024 km (2513 miles), reaches an altitude of 1547 m (5074 ft) at Paisano, Texas, and a depth of 61 m (200 ft) below sea-level at Salton, California. From a height of 12·8 m (42 ft) at Sacramento its main line to Ogden climbs through the Sierra Nevada Mountains to a summit of 2147 m (7043 ft) in 100 miles with long grades of about 1 in 40 or 2·5 per cent. (See 'Articulated Steam Locomotives', p. 131.) Besides rail traffic it operates trucks over 26 000 miles of highway, and more than 2300 miles of pipe-line.

Other USA systems operating over 16 000 km (about 10 000 miles) are: Atchison, Topeka & Santa Fe 19 901 km (12 366 miles); Chesapeake & Ohio (Chessie System) 16 888 km (10 494 miles); Seaboard Coast Line Industries 16 371 km (10 172 miles); Chicago, Milwaukee, St Paul & Pacific 16 317 km (10 139 miles); Chicago & North Western 16 058 km (9978 miles).

The shortest and most exclusive railroad in the USA is a 183 m (600 ft) long subway connecting the Senate Office buildings with the Capitol at Washington, DC. It is used solely by Government officials. Trains shuttle to and fro 40 to 50 times an hour. New 32 km/h (20 mph) cars were installed in 1959, covering the journey from the old Senate Office Building in 41 s and from the new in 55 s. A new subway was completed in 1962.

LARGE NATIONALISED RAILWAYS

USSR Railways By 1913 the Russian railway network comprised 25 State and 13 private lines. The entire system was nationalised after the Revolution of 1917. The total route length on 1 January 1977 was 138 545 km (86 088 miles) of 1·520 m (4 ft 11$\frac{7}{8}$ in) gauge of which 39 716 km (24 678 miles) were electrified; 2809 km (1745 miles) of 600 mm (1 ft 11$\frac{1}{2}$ in) to metre-gauge lines; 761 km (473 miles) of 1·067 m (3 ft 6 in) gauge in South Sakhalin, formerly controlled by Japan, and 73 km (45 miles) of standard gauge. The Russian gauge was 1·524 m (5 ft) until 1 January 1972 when the standard was narrowed by 4 mm. In 1976 the USSR Railways carried 3545 000 000 passengers and 3 295 400 000 000 ton-kilometres of freight. They employ a staff of 2 031 200.

Canadian National Railways, operating 38 962 km (24 210 miles) of standard gauge and 1146 km (712 miles) of 1·067 m (3 ft 6 in) gauge, is dealt with on pp. 48 and 105. The now familiar CN monogram was adopted in 1960.

Chinese People's Republic railways The Chinese Government took over control of railways from 1908. The route length in 1977 was about 35 000 km (21 750 miles), mostly standard gauge.

South African Railways was formed in 1910 on the unification of the Cape, Orange River, Transvaal and Natal Colonies. The administration runs 21 726 km (13 499 miles) of 1·065 (3 ft 6 in) gauge lines of which 4492 km (2791 miles), or 21 per cent are electrified, and 706 km (439 miles) of 610 mm (2 ft) gauge.

The Indian Railway Board was constituted in its present form in 1951. Its owns 30 274 km (18 811 miles of 1·676 m (5 ft 6 in) gauge, 25 551 km (15 877 miles) of metre gauge, 3718 km (2310 miles of 762 mm (2 ft 6 in) gauge and 616 km (383 miles) of 610 mm (2 ft) gauge.

Japanese National Railways was formed under the Railway Nationalisation Law of 1906. In 1976 of a total route length of 21 272 km (13 218 miles) the standard-gauge Shinkansen accounted for 1177 km (731 miles). The remaining 20 095 km (12 486 miles) are 1·067 m (3 ft 6 in) gauge. The Shinkansen is electrified at 25 kV. Of the 1·067 m gauge lines 4603 km (2860 miles) are equipped with 1500 V dc electrification and 3210 km (1995 miles) with 20 kV ac. There are 5194 stations handling passenger traffic. The total length of bridges is 2174 km (1351 miles) and of tunnels 1179 km (733 miles). In 1976 the JNR carried 7 113 000 000 passengers, or 19 487 000 per day.

Argentine Railways were built largely with foreign capital. The railways were nationalised in 1948 and **Argentine State Railways** was established in 1956. The network is divided into four regional systems, as follows:

System	Gauge	km	miles
North West	750 mm (2 ft 5$\frac{1}{2}$ in)	77	48
	metre	13 451	8358
Central	1·676 m (5 ft 6 in)	10 902	6774
South West	1·676 m (5 ft 6 in)	12 656	7808
	750 mm (2 ft 5$\frac{1}{2}$ in)	403	250
North East	standard	3091	1920
	600 mm (1 ft 11$\frac{1}{2}$ in)	209	130
		40 789	25 288

Brazilian Federal Railways (Rede Ferroviaria Federal SA or RFFSA) was established on 30 September 1957. It is divided into four regions and operates a total of 24 546 km (15 252 miles) of route, mostly metre, but including 202 km (125 miles) of 762 mm (2 ft 6 in) gauge and 1673 km (1039 miles) of 1·6 m (5 ft 3 in) gauge.

National Railways of Mexico was formed by mergers and acquisitions beginning in 1908. It operates 14 151 km (8793 miles) of standard gauge of which 103 km (64 miles) are electrified, and 451 km (280 miles) of 914 mm (3 ft) gauge including 47 km (29 miles) of mixed gauge.

EUROPE

Belgian National Railways (Société Nationale des Chemins de fer Belges; SNCB) is the world's oldest nationalised system. The present administration, formed on 23 July 1926 took over the system operated by the Belgian State Railways. The system is one of the densest in the world for railway mileage per square mile of country. Route length at the end of 1974 was 4014 km (2494 miles) of which 1287 km (800 miles) were electrified at 3000 V dc, all standard gauge.

In addition **Belgian National Light Railways** operate 222 km (138 miles) of narrow-gauge and other light railways and 10 646 km (6615 miles) of bus route. The first line, Ostend–Nieuport Ville via Lombartsijde opened on 15 July 1885. In 1894 the company introduced the first electric traction in Belgium.

Czechoslovak State Railways was first established in 1919 and was re-established in May 1945. It operates 13 039 km (8102 miles) of standard gauge of which 2448 km (1521 miles) are electrified, 177 km (110 miles) of metre and 600 mm (1 ft 11½ in) gauge and 101 km (63 miles of the Russian 1·520 m (4 ft 11⅞ in) gauge, total 13 317 km (8275 miles).

French National Railways (Société National des Chemins de fer Français; SNCF) was formed on 31 August 1937. On 31 December 1975 it operated 34 703 km (21 563 miles) of standard gauge of which 9376 km (5826 miles) were electrified.

The German State Railway (Deutsche Reichsbahn) was established on 1 April 1920, but on 11 October 1924 by the Railway Act of 30 August, amended by the Act of 13 March 1930, the system was made independent of the Government. It was placed once more under State control on 30 January 1937. After the Second World War the name denoted only the system in East Germany. Today it operates 14 298 km (8884 miles) of standard gauge of which 1454 km (903 miles) are electrified at 15 000 V 16⅔ Hz; and 1012 km (629 miles) of narrow gauge.

The German Federal Railway (Deutsche Bundesbahn; DB) was formed by the State Railways Act of 13 December 1951 to operate the lines in Western Germany. On 31 December 1976 it consisted of 28 551 km (17 741 miles) of standard gauge of which 10 349 km (6431 miles) were electrified at 15 000 V 16⅔ Hz.

Italian State Railways (Ferrovie dello Stato; FS) was formed in 1905–7. It operates 16 077 km (9990 miles) of standard gauge of which 7941 km (4934 miles) are electrified at 3000 V dc.

The mountainous nature of the country has necessitated numerous bridges and tunnels. In 1951 there were 43 158 bridges and viaducts with over 10 m (32·8 ft) length of clearance. Of these 39 091 were of masonry and 4067 of steel, of which 77 masonry and 31 steel bridges and 36 viaducts had a clearance over 100 m (328 ft) long. There were 1849 tunnels totalling 911 km (566 miles), farther than from London to Inverness. The longest is the Apennine, 18 519 m (11 miles 892 yd); 21 others are over 5 km (3 miles) long. New lines are under construction with more large bridges and long tunnels. (See list of tunnels, p. 87.)

Spanish National Railways (Red Nacional de los Ferrocarriles Españoles; RENFE) was formed under the Law of 27 February 1943. It operates 13 380 km (8314 miles) of 1·676 m (5 ft 6 in) gauge, of which 3645 km (2265 miles) are electrified at 1650 and 3000 V dc.

The largest metre-gauge system in Europe is the Greek Pireus–Athens–Peloponnesus Railway (SPAP) with a route length of 800 km (497 miles). In September 1962 it was amalgamated with the Hellenic State Railways which now operates 960 km (597 miles) of metre-gauge lines and 1560 km (969 miles) of standard gauge.

The 24-hour time system was introduced on Italian Railways in 1898. Between then and 1912 it was adopted by Belgium, France, Portugal and Spain. Thomas Cook & Son first used it in the Cook's Continental Timetable in December 1919. It was adopted by British Railways in its timetables in summer 1964.

The first British Rail combined timetable operated from 6 May 1974 to 4 May 1975.

Cook's Continental Timetable was first issued in March 1873. From January 1977 it became the **Thomas Cook International Timetable** with the addition of a 64-page section of services outside Europe.

LOADING GAUGES

Britain pays a penalty for being first with railways by suffering a restricted loading gauge with universal dimensions of only 3860 mm (12 ft 8 in) high by 2692 mm (8 ft 10 in) wide. Some sections, however, such as the Great Northern, Great Central, Lancashire & Yorkshire and Great Western considerably exceed this. For most lines it is 3962 mm (13 ft) high by 2743 mm (9 ft) wide. The greatest is 4189 mm (13 ft 9 in) × 2946 mm (9 ft 8 in). On the Liverpool–Southport electric line the coaches were built 3·048 m (10 ft) wide.

The world's largest loading gauge for standard-gauge lines is in the USA, 4724 mm (15 ft 6 in) × 3277 mm (10 ft 9 in).

The Indian loading gauge for 1·676 m (5 ft 6 in) gauge lines is 4470 mm (14 ft 8 in) × 3200 mm (10 ft 6 in). In 1961 it was decided to increase it to 4725 mm (15 ft 6 in) × 4110 mm (13 ft 6 in).

The standard for European lines, as recommended by the Berne Conference, is 4279 mm (14 ft 0½ in) × 3150 mm (10 ft 4 in). **Australian standard-gauge** lines are about the same—4267 mm (14 ft) × 3200 mm (10 ft 6 in).

The world's biggest loading gauge is the Russian standard for the 1·520 m (4 ft 11⅞ in) gauge—5302 mm (17 ft 4¾ in) × 3413 mm (11 ft 2 in).

The South African loading gauge for its 1·065 m (3 ft 6 in) gauge lines is larger than the British standard—3962 mm (13 ft) × 3048 mm (10 ft).

The biggest loading gauge on metre-gauge lines is on the East African Railways—4115 mm (13 ft 6 in) × 3200 mm (10 ft 6 in), considerably larger than the British standard.

DIRECTION OF RUNNING ON DOUBLE LINES

The first railway to be planned and built as a double line was the Liverpool & Manchester Railway, opened on 15 September 1830. Left-hand running was adopted from the start.

Sections of the Stockton & Darlington Railway had been doubled previously, but in the form of extended passing loops. Doubling between Brusselton Incline and Darlington was not undertaken until 1831–2.

The following British railways adopted right-hand running from the beginning:

The Clarence Railway in County Durham of which the first portion opened in 1833. It became part of the Stockton & Hartlepool Railway on 1 January 1851 and of the West Hartlepool Harbour & Railway Company on 17 May 1853. The right-hand running continued until its absorption by the North Eastern Railway on 1 July 1865.

The London & Greenwich Railway, the first railway in London, opened in 1836–8. Right-hand running was adopted very early in the line's history and it continued until changed to left-hand running on 26 May 1901.

The Manchester & Bolton Railway, opened on 29 May 1838, changed from right- to left-hand running when it was joined at Clifton by the East Lancashire Railway which opened on 28 September 1846.

The Newcastle & Carlisle Railway, opened on 18 June 1838, changed from right- to left-hand running on 7 March 1864, after its absorption by the North Eastern Railway in 1862.

Right-hand running operates on the following railways:

Europe: Austria (some sections), Bulgaria, Czechoslovakia, Denmark, Finland, Germany, Hungary, the Netherlands, Norway, Poland, Spain (the former Madrid, Zaragoza & Alicante Railway only), Turkey, the USSR and Yugoslavia.
Asia: China (some sections) and the USSR.
North America: Canada and the USA (except the Chicago & North Western Railroad).

Other countries use left-hand running or have no double-line sections.

Using modern signalling methods, several railways in parts of Europe and in the USA are now equipped for either-direction running on both lines, with complete safety, so allowing one train to overtake another and so increasing line capacity.

LOCOMOTIVE DEPOTS

The oldest locomotive 'roundhouse' shed is the old No. 1 Shed of the former Midland Railway at Derby, England, built in 1839. It is now used as a crane repair shop.

The first mechanical locomotive coaling plants in Britian were installed at Crewe (North)

Shed in 1913 and at Hull (Dairycoats) shortly afterwards. Only one now remains, 'preserved' at Steamtown, Carnforth, Lancashire.

WATER-TROUGHS

The highest water-troughs in the world were at Garsdale on the Midland Railway Settle–Carlisle line, England, at 335 m (1100 ft) above sea-level, installed in 1907. Only 43·5 km (27 miles) away, on the London & North Western Railway at Hest Bank near Lancaster, the water-troughs were almost at sea-level.

The only water-troughs inside a tunnel were in the Diggle end of the three 4·888 km (3 mile 66 yd) bores of the Standedge Tunnels on the London & North Western Railway between Manchester and Huddersfield. The tunnels are the only level stretch on the whole route.

The total number of water-troughs in Britain was 141. Some, for example on the Lancashire & Yorkshire Railway, were steam heated in frosty weather.

Track-pans were used in the USA from 1870 to 1956. Britain and the USA were the only countries to make extensive use of water-troughs.

SNOW-PLOUGHS

The rotary snow-plough was invented by J W Elliott, a dentist of Toronto, Canada, who patented a 'compound revolving snow shovel' in 1869. The idea was not taken up, however.

The first rotary snow-plough was built by Leslie Brothers of Orangeville, Ontario, Canada, in 1883–4 and was tested by the Canadian Pacific Railway. Its success led to an improved design constructed in 1887 by the Danforth Cooke Company (which became part of the American Locomotive Company in 1901) and which was put into operation on the Union Pacific Railroad.

RAILWAY AIR SERVICES

The first air service operated by a British railway was by the Great Western Railway linking Cardiff, Torquay and Plymouth on 12 April 1933, in conjunction with Imperial Airways, using a three-engined Westland 'Wessex' plane.

Railway Air Services Limited was incorporated on 21 March 1934, in Great Britain. De Havilland 'Dragon'-type eight seater two-engined planes were used. In 1939 it became 'Great Western & Southern Air Lines'. It was suspended at the outbreak of war in September 1939 and was resumed afterwards by Imperial Airways, later British European Airways, now part of British Airways.

The railway with the most extensive air services is the Canadian Pacific (see p. 106).

DOCKS AND SHIPS

The earliest railway-owned docks and harbours were:

Carmarthenshire Dock, Llanelly, South Wales, opened in 1806 and owned by the Carmarthenshire Railway, authorised in 1802;
Lydney Dock, Gloucestershire, opened in 1813 by the Severn & Wye Railway Company;
Porthcawl Harbour, South Wales, opened about 1830 by the Duffryn, Llynvi & Porthcawl Railway.

Whitstable Harbour, Kent, opened in 1832 by the Canterbury & Whitstable Railway, was the first built and operated by a railway company using locomotive haulage and providing a passenger and freight service.

The first steamships to be owned by a British railway company appear to be three acquired in 1842 by the London & Blackwall Railway (opened 1841) for operating between Blackwall and Gravesend on the Thames. The ferry was later taken over by private owners.

The first British railway company to operate a sea-crossing service was the Chester & Holyhead Railway which, under the Act of 22 July 1848, operated ships from 1 August 1848 between Holyhead and Kingstown. The service was taken over by the London & North Western Railway from 18 March 1859. Also in 1848 the Hartlepool Dock & Railway

Company purchased three steamships to trade between West Hartlepool, Hamburg, Rotterdam and Cronstadt.

The first three Canadian Pacific ships, *Empress of India, Empress of Japan* and *Empress of China*, built at Barrow-in-Furness, England, in 1889–90, began operation in spring 1891. The CPR then advertised tours 'Around the World in 80 days', for $610! The name 'Canadian Pacific Steamships Limited' was adopted on 8 September 1921, and on 17 June 1968 it became 'CP Ships' (see p. 106).

The Lancashire & Yorkshire Railway operated more ships than any other British railway. Twenty-nine (including some owned jointly with the London & North Western Railway) were handed over to the London, Midland & Scottish Railway at the Grouping on 1 January 1923.

British Rail are the world's largest dock-owners with docks, harbours and wharves in 76 places, with a total quay length of 156 668 m (501 402 ft), or about 95 miles. At the end of 1972 BR used 13 518 m (44 350 ft) of quays in its own harbours.

British Rail 'Seaspeed' Hovercraft service between Southampton and Cowes, Isle of Wight, began operation on 5 July 1966, and a further service between Portsmouth and Ryde began on 26 March 1968. The first international car-carrying service went into operation between Dover and Boulogne on 1 August 1968. At the end of 1972 BR operated 4 Hovercraft and 49 ships.

PS *Wingfield Castle* (W. Gray & Company, West Hartlepool, 1934) at Hull on the crossing from New Holland. One of the last paddle-steamers operated by British Rail. It was withdrawn in March 1974

The last paddle-steamers operated by British Rail were engaged on the New Holland Pier-Hull ferry across the Humber. *Wingfield Castle*, withdrawn on 15 March 1974 (see illustration) was built by W. Gray & Company of West Hartlepool in 1934, and was 61 m (200 ft) long. It had coal-fired boilers and a triple-expansion three-cylinder engine. *Tattershall Castle* (Gray 1934) was withdrawn in June 1973. *Lincoln Castle* is similar, built by A. & J. Inglis of Glasgow in 1940. These coal-fired steamers had a draught of only 1·372 m (4 ft 6 in) to clear sandbanks at low tide. The service is expected to end when the Humber Bridge is opened.

The world's highest railway-owned ships are operated by the Southern Railway of Peru, now part of the National Railways of Peru, on Lake Titicaca in the Andes at a height of 3810 m (12 500 ft). The first ship, *Yavari* of 170 tons, was built in 1861 and was carried up from the coastal port of Mollendo in sections on the backs of mules and Indians to Puno on the lake. With the original steam-engine replaced by a diesel it is still in use.

Another ship, the 650 ton *Inca*—69 m (228 ft) long and 15·2 m (50 ft) beam—was built at Hull, England, in 1905, sailed out round Cape Horn to Mollendo, was dismantled and transported up the Southern Railway (completed to Puno in 1876) and reassembled on the lake (see colour illustration on p. 78). The flagship of the Titicaca fleet is the *Ollanta* of 850 tons, built in 1929. There are five ships at work on an itinerary of 2173 km (1350 miles). The longest voyage, Puno to Guaqui, takes 12 h for the 193 km (120 miles). Lake Titicaca is the highest navigable water in the world.

BRITISH RAIL WORKSHOPS

British Rail Engineering Limited, formed in January 1970 to enable BR workshops to compete with private engineering firms by tendering for outside work, is a wholly owned subsidiary of the British Rail Board. It manages the 13 main railway works and carries out all types of railway engineering for BR and for other companies. Export work is handled jointly by BRE and Metro-Cammel Limited. The works are at Ashford, Kent; Crewe, Cheshire; Derby; Doncaster; Eastleigh, Hampshire; Glasgow; Horwich, Lancashire; Shildon, County Durham; Swindon,

Wiltshire; Temple Mills, London; Wolverton, Buckinghamshire; and York.

RAILWAY ROAD SERVICES

The first railway-operated buses in Britain began on Monday, 17 August 1903, when the Great Western Railway inaugurated a service between Helston and the Lizard in Cornwall with Milnes Daimler buses that had originally been used in connection with the Lynton & Barnstaple narrow-gauge railway, where they were owned and operated by the railway chairman, Sir George Newnes.

Another service began on 31 October between Penzance and Marazion; meanwhile the North Eastern Railway introduced buses on 7 September 1903.

The London & South Western Railway began operating buses on 1 June 1904.

The first railway buses in Scotland were operated by the Great North of Scotland Railway between Ballater and Braemar on 2 May 1904. By 1911 the company operated six services.

By 1928 the Great Western Railway operated 330 buses on 154 routes. In the early 1930s, however, along with other railway companies, the road interests were sold to other bus companies operating in the area and a great opportunity for developing a unified transport system was lost.

ROAD-RAIL VEHICLES

A road-rail bus was placed in service by the London, Midland & Scottish Railway in 1931. Designed by J. Shearman of the LMS, it was a Karrier chassis with a Craven body and could be quickly adapted for rail or road use. It was used between Blisworth and Stratford-upon-Avon, being used on the road in Stratford. It could run at 113 km/h (70 mph) on rails and at 96·5 km/h (60 mph) on roads. It was scrapped after only a few years.

A road-rail truck was used by the London & North Eastern Railway on the West Highland section in Scotland for several years from 1934. It was a Karrier 2 ton truck on which the road wheels could be raised or lowered as on the bus just described. It was used in track maintenance.

In Austria villages remote from the railway are served by road trailers which carry railway wagons. These can be off-loaded onto a private 'siding' for loading and unloading. This was photographed at Fehring, near the border with Hungary, in August 1975

Daimler-Benz 'Unimog' road-rail truck. The guide-wheels in front and behind are raised and lowered hydraulically and the road tyres provide good rail adhesion

The most modern application of the road-rail principle is the German Daimler-Benz 'Unimog 406' shown in the illustration. This runs on the rails on its rubber-tyred wheels, guided by small rail wheels which can be raised or lowered by hydraulic jacks in front and behind. With a 2 ton ballast weight on the platform making a total weight of only 6·5 tons the 'Unimog' can pull a load of 300 tons on a gradient up to 1 in 200 or 150 tons up 1 in 100. It has high adhesion, even on wet rails. No special ramps are needed for transfer between rail and ground. When required only for rail running the guide wheels can be removed and the road wheels changed for Michelin pneumatic-tyred rail wheels with steel flanges. The operation takes 40 min and reduces the weight to 5 tons.

The first use of a 'steam navvy' or excavator on railway construction in England was on the West Lancashire Railway from Southport to

Preston. One was purchased from Ruston, Proctor & Company of Lincoln for £1150 on 12 June 1877.

The first extensive use of these machines was on the construction of the Hull & Barnsley Railway in 1881–3 and on the Great Central main line to London in 1894–7.

TRAMS/STREETCARS/TROLLEYS

These form a subject to themselves and only brief mention can be made here. For detailed information the reader should contact: **The Light Railway Transport League**, 64 Grove Avenue, London W7 3ES, and the **Tramway Museum Society** which runs the Crich Tramway Museum, Derbyshire (qv). For details of trolley museums in the USA see the *Steam Passenger Service Directory*, published by Empire State Railway Museum, New York.

The following books are useful:

Wilson, Frank E., *The British Tram* 1961; Bett, W H, and Gillham, J C, *Great British Tramway Networks* fourth edition 1962; Buckley, R J, *History of Tramways* 1975. There are also numerous books on tramways of various towns.

The first electric street tramway in Britain was at Blackpool, opened in October 1884. It ran about 3 km (2 miles) along the Promenade, using a conduit system. It was converted to the overhead trolley system in 1898–9. Blackpool's Car No. 1, built in 1884, is preserved at the Crich Tramway Museum. Today Blackpool operates the only remaining public tram service in Britain. Fine modern cars operate on a standard-gauge line 13 km (8 miles) between Blackpool and Fleetwood.

Single-deck Blackpool tram at Fleetwood, May 1962

The first electric trams in London were operated by the Metropolitan Tramways and Omnibus Company Limited between Finsbury Park and Tottenham and Wood Green from July 1904. The last London trams ran in July 1952.

The world's oldest section of tramway still in operation is in Geneva, between Place Neuve and Rondeau de Caronge, 2 km (1·24 miles), opened on 19 June 1862 as a standard-gauge horse tramway. Steam-traction was introduced later and it was electrified on 1 May 1896. It was converted to metre gauge in 1901 and is now part of Geneva's Route 12.

The tramway system with the greatest route length is in Leningrad where over 500 km (300 miles) are in operation. Extensions are still being opened.

The oldest continuously operating street railway in the world is the St Charles Street Car Line in New Orleans, Louisiana, USA. It was incorporated on 9 February 1833 as the New Orleans & Carrollton Rail Road Company and was opened on 26 September 1835. Electric car services began on 1 February 1893.

SIGNALLING

The first use of the electric telegraph on a railway was on the Great Western Railway in England, in 1839.

It was introduced in the USA by the Baltimore & Ohio Railroad on 24 May 1844. The first use of the telegraph for train dispatching in the USA was at Turner (now Harriman), New York, on 22 September 1851.

The block system with Cooke and Wheatstone's electric telegraph was first used at Clay Cross Tunnel on the North Midland Railway near Chesterfield in Derbyshire in 1841. In the USA it was introduced by Ashbel Welch in 1865.

The first record of a semaphore signal appears to be of one erected in 1841 by Charles Hatton Gregory (1817–98) on the London & Croydon Railway. From that time its use spread throughout the railways of Britain. Gregory was also responsible for the construction of a central lever frame with rudimentary interlocking at Bricklayers' Arms Junction, South London, in 1843.

The first railway to use the block system from opening was the Norwich & Yarmouth Railway, opened on 1 May 1844.

Staff working on single lines, to prevent two trains being on a section at once, was introduced on the London & North Western Railway in 1853.

Interlocking of points and signals was developed in France by Vignier who first installed it on the former Western Railway in 1855.

Interlocking was patented in England in 1856 by John Saxby and it was first installed in that year at Bricklayers' Arms. He installed the first interlocking frame, of the type that was to become universal, on the London, Brighton & South Coast Railway near Haywards Heath.

A somersault signal on the former Great Northern Railway near Nottingham in 1959

The first fully interlocked signalling system in Britain was installed at Kentish Town Junction on the Midland Railway by Austin Chambers in 1859.

Automatic block signals were introduced in the USA in 1866.

Track circuiting, in which the trains complete an electrical circuit via the rails, was first used in connection with signalling in USA by William Robinson in 1870.

Somersault signals, pivoted in the centre, were adopted by the Great Northern Railway, England, in 1876 following the double collision at Abbott's Ripton on 21 January 1876 caused by a signal being put out of order by frozen snow. They were also used on the Barry, Brecon & Merthyr and Rhymney railways in Wales and on the Belfast & Northern Counties Railway in Ireland.

The first use of telephone communication on USA railroads followed tests on 21 May 1877 at Altoona, Pennsylvania.

The tablet instrument for electric token operation of single lines was invented in 1878 by Edward Tyer (1830–1912), following the Norwich Thorpe accident on 10 September 1874 in which 25 were killed in a single-line head-on collision on the Great Eastern Railway.

The Regulation of Railways Act, enforcing the block system, interlocking of signals and points, and the provision of continuous automatic brakes on passenger trains on British railways, came into operation on 30 August 1889.

The first automatic track-circuit-controlled signalling system on a British main line was installed on the London & South Western Railway between Andover and Grateley, Hampshire, and was brought into use on 20 April 1902. This was a 'normally clear' system. Another system, using 'normally danger' was first used on the North Eastern Railway in 1904 on the main line between Alne and Thirsk Junction.

The first practical application of electro-pneumatic operation of points and signals in Britain was at Bishopsgate, London, on the

Great Eastern Railway early in 1899. The first complete electro-pneumatic installation was on the Lancashire & Yorkshire Railway at Bolton in 1904.

Audible cab signalling was introduced by the Great Western Railway, England, on the double-track Henley Branch on 1 January 1906 and on the single-line Fairford Branch on 1 December when the ordinary distant signals were removed.

The Great Western Railway audible cab signalling was first installed on a main line in 1908, on the four-track section between Slough and Reading, Berkshire, and was extended to London (Paddington) in 1912. About this time the automatic brake application was added, becoming known then as the 'Automatic Train Control' (ATC). Between 1931 and 1937 4587 km (2850 miles) of route were equipped.

The last GWR ATC equipment was removed from the Birmingham–Stratford-on-Avon line early in 1979 after replacement by BR AWS equipment (mentioned below).

The Hudd Intermittent Inductive ATC Apparatus was installed at 112 distant signal locations on the London–Southend line in 1938. On the London & North Eastern Railway Edinburgh–Glasgow line the system came into use on 13 August 1939.

Electric colour-light signals of the two-aspect type were first used in Britain on the Liverpool Overhead Railway in 1920. Their first use on a main line was in 1923 when three-aspect colour-light signals were installed by the London & North Eastern Railway between London (Marylebone) and Neasden. Four-aspect signals were introduced in 1926 by the Southern Railway between Holborn and Elephant & Castle, London.

Electric interlocking, instead of mechanical, was installed by the Southern Railway at North Kent East Junction in 1929.

The Panel type of power interlocking, now extensively used, was first installed by the London & North Eastern Railway at Thirsk on the main line between York and Darlington in 1933.

Centralised Traffic Control (CTC) was introduced in the USA on a 64 km (40 mile) route at Berwick, Ohio, on 25 July 1927. It has since been installed on over 64 300 km (40 000 miles) of track.

Train to land radio telephones were first used on the Canadian National Railways in 1930.

Radio channels for exclusive railway use were allocated by the Federal Communications Commission, USA, on 17 May 1945 and the first construction permit was granted on 27 February 1946.

The first train to land telephones in the USA were installed in 1947 on the Baltimore & Ohio *Royal Blue*, New York Central *Twentieth Century Limited* and the Pennsylvania *Congressional, Potomac* and *Legislator*.

In Europe telephones are installed on many trains used by business executives in France and Germany.

The first passenger train in Great Britain to use train radio was inaugurated on the 381 mm (15 in) gauge Ravenglass & Eskdale Railway on 28 May 1977 when a special train was run to mark the event. Previously train radio had been used in Great Britain only on private industrial lines. The R. & E. equipment is similar to that used on the Zillertalbahn in Austria.

Two-way radio communication between drivers and central control was extended throughout the London Transport Bakerloo line in 1977.

The first push-button route-selecting signalling control system in Britain was brought into operation by London Transport at Ealing Broadway on 29 November 1952. London Transport's last electro-pneumatic semaphore signal was removed from service on 21 November 1953.

The largest and busiest signalling centres in Great Britain are at Motherwell, London Bridge and Trent.

Motherwell Signalling Centre near Glasgow was completed in 1973. It replaced 67 mechanical signal-boxes and one power box (Newton) and now controls 200 km (124 miles) of route with 555 signals and 329 point machines, the largest control area in Britain.

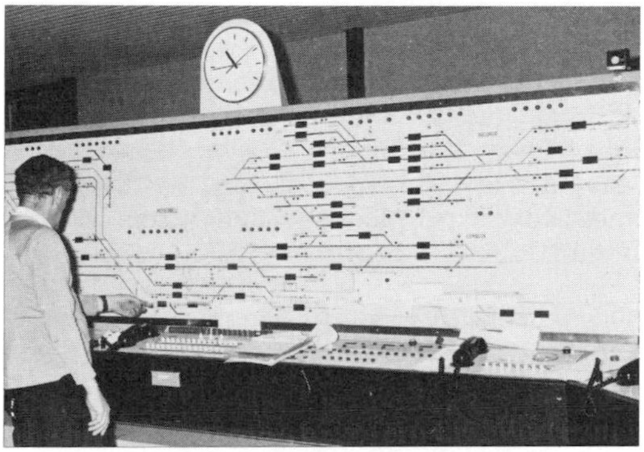

The control panel in Motherwell Signalling Centre near Glasgow which controls 200 km (124 miles) of route (British Rail)

This includes 137 km (85 miles) of the main London–Glasgow line extending from Kirkpatrick, 19 km (12 miles) north of Carlisle to Cambuslang, 8 km (5 miles) south of Glasgow. An average of 500 trains pass through Motherwell station every 24 h.

London Bridge Signalling Centre, although controlling only 75·6 km (47 miles) of route, handles over four times the volume of traffic handled by Motherwell.

Trent Signalling Centre between Nottingham and Derby controlling 119 km (74 miles) of route, 336 km (209 miles) of track, with 613 signalled routes, handles the most traffic of any in Great Britain. At any time there are at least 40 trains displayed on the console. About 250 passenger and 300 through freight trains pass through daily in addition to freight workings north of Toton and trips workings to many collieries.

The largest signal-box in England will be at Clapham Junction, south of London, when it is completed in 1983. It will control 430 km (267 miles) of track on the approaches to Holborn Viaduct, Blackfriars and Victoria stations from as far out as Epsom, Croydon, Sevenoaks and Longfield. It will replace 36 manual boxes at a cost of £35 000 000 with two signal panels, each 22 m (72 ft) long. Its area includes 70 stations.

British Rail's Advanced Warning System (AWS) for use with non-electric traction was approved by the Minister of Transport on 30 November 1956.

The first automatic level-crossing barriers on British Railways were installed at Spath Level Crossing near Uttoxeter, Staffordshire, on the now-abandoned Churnet Valley line, and came into use on 6 February 1961.

STATIONS

The world's oldest railway station is the Mount Clare Station in Baltimore, Maryland, USA, opened on 24 May 1830 by the Baltimore & Ohio Railroad. The first trains were drawn by horses. See p. 17.

The World's oldest station building is at Cuautla, Mexico. It was built in 1657 and was used as a convent until 1812. It became part of the railway station about 1860.

The oldest station built for a 'modern' steam-powered railway is at Liverpool Road, Manchester, England; the original terminus of the Liverpool & Manchester Railway, opened on 15 September 1830. Its passenger services ended, however, when Manchester (Victoria) was connected to the L. & M. on 5 May 1844 and it was used as a goods station until it was finally closed on 30 September 1975. It was subsequently sold to Greater Manchester Council, for £1. It is hoped to restore it for the 150th anniversary of the Liverpool & Manchester Railway in 1980.

Persons interested in the project should communicate with the **Liverpool Road Station Society (Manchester)**; Secretary, 2 Fairbourne Drive, Wilmslow, Cheshire, SK9 6JF.

Mount Clare Station, Baltimore, on the Baltimore & Ohio Railroad, completed on 24 May 1830. This is the oldest surviving railway station in the world (Baltimore & Ohio Railroad Company)

Liverpool Road Station, Manchester; the original buildings used from the opening of the line on 15 September 1830 until 5 May 1844, still standing, but only just! The need for restoration is urgent, if this valuable historic site is to be preserved for future generations

Doveholes Station, now the highest in England at about 335 m (1100 ft), between Whaley Bridge and Buxton in Derbyshire

The world's highest railway station is at Condor, Bolivia, on the metre-gauge line from Rio Mulato to Potosí, at an altitude of 4787 m (15 705 ft). The railway was completed in 1908.

The highest station on standard gauge is Galera on the Peru Central, 4777 m (15 673 ft). It was opened on 14 November 1893.

The highest station on British Rail is Corrour on the West Highland line from Glasgow to Fort William, 153 km ($94\frac{3}{4}$ miles) from Glasgow. It is 411 m (1347 ft) above sea-level. The line was opened on 7 August 1894.

Until closure on 3 May 1965 the highest station was Dalnaspidal on the former Highland Railway main line from Perth to Inverness, 82 km (51 miles) from Perth, 433 m (1420 ft) above sea-level. (See also p. 46.)

The highest station in England is Doveholes, Derbyshire, between Buxton and Whaley Bridge.

The World's largest station is the Grand Central Terminal, New York. It has 44 platforms, all below ground, on two levels, with 41 tracks on the upper and 26 on the lower level, and covers 19·4 ha (48 acres). It was built in 1903–13. It is used by 550 trains and 180 000 people daily. On 3 July 1947 it handled 252 288 people.

The world's busiest station is probably at Moscow where, in 1972, 2 740 000 passengers were handled daily.

Other large stations are:

Pennsylvania Terminal, New York	32 platforms
Union Station, Washington	32 platforms
Saint-Lazare, Paris	27 platforms

Clapham Junction, besides being the largest station in Britain, in area, is also the busiest junction, with an average of 2391 trains passing through every 24 h.

The world's busiest rail interchange is at Châtelot, Paris. In the peak hour 144 trains pass through the junctions at each end.

Carlisle Station was used by more railway companies than any other British station. Until the Grouping on 1 January 1923 it was used by the North British, North Eastern, Midland, London & North Western, Maryport & Carlisle, Glasgow & South Western, and Caledonian railways. Carlisle Station was administered by the Carlisle Citadel Station Joint Committee, established under an Act of 22 July 1861.

The largest span station roof ever built was the 91·44 m (300 ft) span of the second Broad Street Station, Philadelphia, USA, built in 1892 by the Philadelphia & Reading Railroad. The engineer was William Henry Brown, 1836–1910.

The Pennsylvania Railroad Station at Jersey City, built in 1888, had a roof span of 76·810 m (252 ft).

The largest station roof in Great Britain is at London (St Pancras), built by the Midland Railway, with a span of 73·15 m (240 ft) and 30·48 m (100 ft) high above rail-level. It was designed by William Henry Barlow, and the station was opened on 1 October 1868.

The large central roof span of 70·283 m (236 ft) at Milan Central Station

The largest station roof in South America at Retiro Station, Buenos Aires, Argentina, on the 1·676 m (5 ft 6 in) gauge General Mitre System. A four-car diesel multiple unit train is leaving

Milan Central Station, designed by Ulisse Stacchini and completed in 1930, has a central roof span of 70·283 m (236 ft). The main building is one of the most grandiose in existence.

The largest station roof in South America is at the Retiro terminal at Buenos Aires. It is 250 m (820 ft) long with two spans totalling 100 m (328 ft) wide and each 25 m (82 ft) high. It was built in the late 1920s by the former Central Argentine Railway.

Smoking was not permitted at stations on the London, Brighton & South Coast Railway. This rule continued until 1923, when the company became part of the Southern Railway.

At Dartmouth, Devon, is a station which has never had any trains. It was opened on 16 August 1864 and is connected by a ferry with Kingswear Station across the Dart Estuary. Since 30 October 1972 the section from Paignton to Kingswear has been owned by the Dart Valley Railway and operated by the Torbay Steam Railway.

A similar arrangement existed at Hull Corporation Pier where the Great Central Railway had a booking office connected by the Humber Ferry (see 'Last paddle-steamers of BR', p. 196) with New Holland Pier Station.

At Chester Station trains to London via the former London & North Western Railway and Great Western Railway routes left in opposite directions.

Similar situations could be seen at Plymouth (North Road), Exeter (St David's), Nottingham (Midland), and Trent now demolished, between Nottingham and Derby. Also at Trent, trains to and from London could call at the same platform going in the same direction.

The first station escalator was installed at Seaforth Sands Station on the Liverpool Overhead Railway in 1901.

LARGEST BRITISH STATIONS

	Platforms	Total length m	ft	Area hectares	acres
Clapham Junction	17	3409	11 185	11·229	27¾
Waterloo, London	23*	4679	15 352	9·813	24½
Victoria, London	17	5611	18 412	8·8	21¾
Crewe	16	3473	11 394	9·307	23
Waverley, Edinburgh	19	4360	14 305	7·28	18
London Bridge	21	4157	13 574		
Liverpool Street, London	18	3478	11 410	6·475	16
Paddington, London	16	4580	15 025	5·968	14¾

*Including two Waterloo & City Railway platforms below ground.

LONGEST RAILWAY STATION PLATFORMS

	m	ft
Chicago, Illinois (State Street Centre subway)	1066	3500
Khargpur, Bihar, India (formerly Bengal–Nagpur Railway)	833	2733
Perth, Western Australia (standard gauge)	762	2500
Sonepur, India (formerly Bengal & North Western Railway)	736	2415
Bulawayo, Rhodesia	702	2302
New Lucknow, India (formerly East India Railway)	685	2250
Bezwada, India (formerly Madras & Southern Mahratta Railway)	640	2100
Jhansi, India (formerly Great Indian Peninsula Railway)	617	2025
Colchester, England	603·8	1981
Kotri, India (formerly North Western Railway)	578	1896
Mandalay, Burma	545	1788
Bournemouth, England	533	1748
Perth, Scotland	522	1714
York, England	516, 480	1692 and 1575
Edinburgh (Waverley), Scotland	486	1596
Trichinopoly, India (formerly South India Railway)	471	1546
Ranaghat, India (formerly Eastern Bengal Railway)	464	1522
Crewe, England	460	1509
London (Victoria), England	457	1500
Dakor, India (formerly Bombay, Baroda & Central India Railway)	448	1470
Newcastle upon Tyne, England	423	1389
Cambridge, England	382	1254

UNDERGROUND RAILWAYS

The first underground passenger railway in the world was the Metropolitan Railway, London. It was opened, with mixed 2·134 m (7 ft) and standard gauge, from Bishop's Road to Farringdon Street on 10 January 1863 and extended to Moorgate on 23 December 1865. The broad-gauge outer rails were removed on 1 March 1869. Trains were lit by gas.

With the Metropolitan District Railway, the first section of which was opened from Kensington to Westminster on 24 December 1868, the Metropolitan formed a circular route known as the 'Inner Circle' which was completed on 6 October 1884, together with the opening of the connection with the East London Railway through Marc Brunel's Thames Tunnel. It was electrified from 12 September 1905 and the last steam trains ran on 23 September.

The world's first 'tube' railway was the Tower Subway beneath the River Thames in London. It was opened, using cable-traction, on 2 August 1870, though it had worked experimentally since April. From 24 December 1870 it closed as a railway and was used as a footway until March 1896. It then carried a water main, now abandoned.

The shortest underground railway is probably the Istanbul Metropolitan, 650 m (711 yd) long. It has a 'gauge' of 1·51 m (4 ft 11½ in) with cable haulage on a steep gradient. It was opened on 17 January 1875 and was operated by a steam-engine until electrification and modernisation from 26 November 1971. It now has a concrete track and two pneumatic-tyred cars.

The Mersey Railway between Liverpool and Birkenhead was opened on 1 February 1886. It includes 1 in 27 (3·7 per cent) gradients under the River Mersey, and at its lowest point it is 39·2 m (128·6 ft) below Ordnance Datum. At first it was worked by steam locomotives, one of which, Beyer Peacock 0–6–4 tank No. 5 *Cecil Raikes* (1885), is preserved at Southport awaiting restoration. The photograph opposite shows it at work at Shipley Colliery near Nottingham on 20 April 1940. On 3 May 1903 the Mersey Railway became the first steam underground railway to be electrified. It now forms part of the *Merseyrail System* (see p. 206).

The first electric underground railway in the world was the City & South London, opened on 18 December 1890 (see 'Electric Railways', p. 153).

London Transport's oldest tube coach, known as the 'padded cell' because of its high upholstered seat backs, ran on the City & South London Railway from Stockwell to the

Mersey Railway 0–6–4 tank No. 5 *Cecil Raikes* (Beyer Peacock No. 2605, 1885) photographed on 20 April 1940 when it was working at Shipley Colliery, Derbyshire. It is now on loan from Liverpool Museum to Steamport at Southport, Lancashire, where it is to be restored

City in 1890. Passengers were warned not to travel on the roof. For 35 years it was on display at the old Queen Street Railway Museum at York. It now forms part of the London Transport collection to be housed at Covent Garden, London.

The Glasgow District Subway was opened on 14 December 1896. It was 1·219 m (4 ft) gauge, cable operated, and consisted of two parallel tunnels, for either direction, forming a loop round the city centre, twice crossing beneath the River Clyde. It was electrified at 600 V dc in 1935, the 'inner circle' coming into operation on 28 March and the 'outer circle' on 5 December. It was the first electric passenger railway in Scotland. It is now being modernised.

The first section of the Paris Underground (the Métro) from Port de Vincennes to Porte Maillot was opened on 10 July 1900.

The first driverless underground railway was built in 1910 by the Post Office in Munich. It was a 360 mm (14·17 in) gauge double-track line and ran from the Post Office in Hofenstrasse to the Starnberger railway station, about 800 m (½ mile). The tunnel was 2·34 m (7 ft 8 in) wide and 1·2 m (4 ft) high. Trains used a 160 V overhead system and ran at 12–14 km/h (7–8 mph). It had to be re-routed before construction of the Munich Olympic Underground line which was opened on 8 May 1972.

The first driverless underground railway in Britain was the Post Office Subway in London. It was begun in 1914 and fully opened in December 1927. It is 610 mm (2 ft) gauge and 10·5 km (6½ miles) long, from Paddington Station to the Eastern District Post Office. The main double-track tunnels are 2·743 m (9 ft) diameter. It carries about 30 000 mail-bags a day.

London Transport Executive railways have a total route length of 405·5 km (252 miles) of which 383 km (238 miles) are administered by LT, the remainder by British Rail. A total of 159 km (99 miles) are underground of which 124 km (77 miles) are in small-diameter deep-level tube tunnels and 35 km (22 miles) are in sub-surface, mostly 'cut and cover', tunnels. The greatest depth below the surface is 67·3 m (221 ft) below Hampstead Heath, 579 m (1900 ft) north of Hampstead Station on the Northern Line. There are 279 stations of which 250 are managed by LT. Ventilation is provided by 93 fans handling nearly 2400 m^3 (84 756 ft^3) of air per second, excluding the Victoria Line which has 16 fans handling 531 m^3 (18 752 ft^3) per second. At 31 stations on the older system and at all stations on the Victoria Line draught relief shafts are provided, to cope with the air moved by the trains. London Transport owns 3118 motor cars, 1401 trailer cars and 330 other rail vehicles. Electric supply is by third rail at 600 V dc. In 1975 the system handled 636 750 000 passengers.

Of 1 250 000 journeys to work in Central London, London Transport carries 34 per cent by Underground and 14 per cent by bus.

The Post Office Subway, London, showing wagons being loaded

British Rail carries 460 000, or nearly 40 per cent, and two-thirds of this on the Southern Region. Thus the private cars which choke London's streets represent less than 12 per cent of the people travelling.

The maximum number of passengers passing over one track in 1 h on the London Underground system is as high as 28 000 on the Central Line.

The most frequent service is on the southbound Bakerloo Line between Baker Street and Waterloo at the morning peak; 33 trains in 1 h, 18 in one peak ½ h.

The Victoria Line was completed throughout from Walthamstow Central to Brixton on 23 July 1971.

The latest extension, of the Piccadilly Line to Heathrow Central for the Airport, was opened by Her Majesty Queen Elizabeth II on 16 December 1977.

The Jubilee Line (formerly known as the Fleet Line) is at present under construction.

The first London Transport train with automatic driving equipment entered experimental service on the District Line on 8 April 1963. Full-scale trials on the 6·5 km (4 mile) Woodford–Hainault shuttle service on the Central Line began on 5 April 1964. The entire service on the Victoria Line is operated by automatic trains.

The deepest lift shaft on the London Underground is at Hampstead Station, 55 m (181 ft) deep. The lift operates at a maximum speed of 243·8 m (800 ft) a minute. Hampstead is the deepest station on LT, 58·5 m (192 ft) below ground.

The first escalators on the London Underground were at Earl's Court between the District and Piccadilly line platforms, brought into operation on 4 October 1911. The last lifts, or elevators, on the London Underground were installed at Broad Street, Central London Railway, in 1913.

The longest escalator on the London Underground is that serving the Piccadilly Line at Leicester Square Station. The shaft is 49·3 m (161 ft 6 in) long with a vertical rise of 24·6 m (80 ft 9 in).

The newest British Underground railway system is the **Merseyrail** Loop and Link, designed to ease traffic congestion in Liverpool and Birkenhead. The central portion consists of the original Mersey Railway (p. 204). This has been extended under Liverpool to form the Loop and another line, the Link, connects the former Lancashire & Yorkshire lines to Southport, Ormskirk and Kirkby with the Loop and with the former Cheshire Lines Railway to Garston. (See map.) Under Birkenhead a new burrowing junction greatly increases the traffic capacity of the junction between the Rock Ferry and West Kirby/New Brighton lines. Parliamentary powers for the

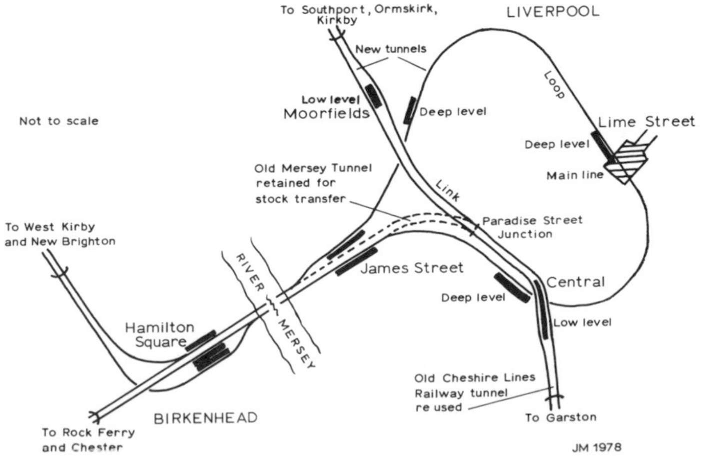

Map of the Merseyrail Link and Loop lines

Southport train leaving the tunnel near Moorfields on the Merseyrail Link line. The old Exchange Station, abandoned, can be seen above

Loop and burrowing junction were obtained in 1968 and after grants for construction had been arranged work began on the Loop in March 1972. Powers for the Link line were obtained in 1971 and construction began in spring 1973. On 2 May 1977 the Link line was opened from the north to Moorfields and Central and electric trains were extended up the Wigan line as far as Kirkby. The Link line was completed on 3 January 1978 when trains began running through to Garston. On 9 May 1977 the Loop was opened, with James Street and Central stations only, and the burrowing junction. Lime Street was opened on 30 October 1977 leaving Moorfields to be opened later. Trains use the 600 V dc third rail system as on the former LYR, Mersey and Wirral lines.

The world's longest station escalator is on the Leningrad Underground with a vertical rise of 59·5 m (195 ft). On the Moscow Underground is one with a rise of 50 m (164 ft)

Underground Railways were first opened in other towns as follows: Boston, USA 1898; New York, 1900; Berlin, 1902; Philadelphia, 1908; Hamburg, 1912; Buenos Aires, 1914; Madrid, 1919; Barcelona, 1924; Sydney, 1926; Tokyo, 1927; Moscow, 1933; Osaka, 1933; Chicago, 1943; Stockholm, 1950; Toronto, 1954; Rome, 1954; Leningrad, 1955; Cleveland, Ohio, 1956; Nagoya, 1957; Lisbon, 1959; Haifa, 1959; Kiev, 1960; Milan, 1964; Montreal, 1966; Rotterdam, 1968; Munich, 1971, San Francisco 1972.

Pneumatic-tyred trains were introduced on the Paris Métro on 8 November 1956.

RAPID TRANSIT RAILWAYS

Rapid Transit Railways are being planned, built or opened in numerous cities where it is realised that they are a better investment than ever more roads and bigger car-parks which simply create more traffic.

To attract the car-owner, particularly where railways are regarded as outmoded, trains must be fast and comfortable. **Free parking of cars and bicycles**, as provided on the San Francisco system, is a step in the right direction. Niggling parking fees which barely cover attendants' wages merely antagonise the motorist and repel traffic.

In Britain Liverpool, Newcastle and Glasgow are developing rapid transit railways; Manchester has rejected one.

MOUNTAIN AND RACK RAILWAYS

The first railway with a central rack was the Jefferson Incline on the north bank of the Ohio River near Madison, Indiana, built in 1847. The eight-coupled engines had a separate vertical-cylindered engine for driving the rack mechanism.

The first mountain rack railway was opened on 3 July 1869. It was built by Sylvester Marsh (1803–84) to carry passengers to the 1918 m (6293 ft) summit of Mount Washington in

Locomotive No. 9 *Waumbek* at the base depot of the Mount Washington Cog Railway in 1970

New Hampshire, USA. The railway is standard gauge, 4·8 km (3 miles) long, and has a maximum gradient of 1 in 3·1 (32·26 per cent). A wrought-iron ladder-type rack was used.

Nicholas Riggenbach (1817–99) designed a similar rack, patented in 1863, and first used on the 7·25 m (4½ mile) standard-gauge line from Vitznau to the summit of the Rigi, Switzerland, opened on 23 May 1871. The last 3·2 km (2 miles) were opened on 27 June 1873 to a summit level of 1750 m (5741 ft). It was electrified on 3 October 1937.

The Riggenbach rack is used also on the metre-gauge Brünig and Bernese Oberland railways in Switzerland.

Roman Abt (1850–1933) invented his rack system in 1882. It was first used in 1885 on a railway at Blankenburg in the Harz Mountains.

Three-quarters of the world's rack railways use the Abt system in which two or sometimes three flat steel bars having teeth in their upper edge are fixed side by side so that the gap in one comes opposite the tooth of the next or, in the triple rack, a third of the space of one tooth.

The steepest rack railway in the world is the Mount Pilatus Railway in Switzerland, with a gradient of 1 in 2 (50 per cent). A special rack was devised by Edward Locher (1840–1910). It has horizontal teeth on each side which prevent any possibility of slipping or derailment. The railway was opened on 4 June 1889 with steam and was electrified on 15 May 1937.

For this railway a gauge of 800 mm (2 ft 7½ in) was chosen. Roman Abt adopted this as his standard and it was used for eleven mountain railways in Switzerland, and others elsewhere.

The Snowdon Mountain Railway in Wales, 800 mm (2 ft 7½ in) gauge, uses the Abt double rack and Swiss-built steam locomotives. It was opened on 6 April 1896. In its 7·25 km (4½ miles) it climbs from Llanberis to the summit at 1064 m (3493 ft) on gradients of 1 in 5·5 (18 per cent). (See colour illustration on p. 35.)

The Abt system is used on 'main lines' on the Furka–Oberalp and Brig–Visp–Zermatt railways in Switzerland.

Car No. 15 at the 4300 m (14 109 ft) summit on the standard-gauge Manitou & Pike's Peak Railway in Colorado, the highest railway summit in North America

The world's first electric mountain rack railway was the Gornergrat Railway at Zermatt, Switzerland, opened on 20 August 1898. It is metre gauge, 9·35 km (5·8 miles) long, with Abt rack and operates on three-phase ac at 725 V. With a summit at 3088 m (10 134 ft) it is the second highest railway in Europe and the highest in the open. (See colour illustration.)

The highest railway in North America is the Manitou & Pike's Peak Railway in Colorado. This standard-gauge line is 14·3 km (8·9 miles) long with an average gradient of 1 in 6 (16·66 per cent). The lower terminus is at 2298 m (7538 ft) and the summit is 4300 m (14 109 ft). On Windy Point Hill it climbs for 3·219 km (2 miles) at 1 in 4 (25 per cent). It was opened on 1 June 1891 with steam-power, using Vauclain compound Abt system rack locomotives. These worked until 1958 when a petrol-driven railcar was introduced. In 1959 a diesel-electric locomotive was tried and was followed in 1961 by two diesel-electric single-unit railcars built by the Swiss Locomotive & Machine Works, Winterthur. Another two came in 1968. The newest cars are two diesel-hydraulic twin-unit sets built by SLM and delivered in 1976. One of the steam locomotives is preserved at Manitou and another at the Colorado Railroad Museum at Golden near Denver.

The highest railway in Europe is the metre-gauge Jungfrau Railway in Switzerland, opened on 1 August 1912. At Jungfraujoch it is 3454 m (11 332 ft). The upper section is entirely in a tunnel 7·123 km (4 miles 750 yd) long. The Strub rack was used until 1955 when it was replaced by the Lamalle system.

Switzerland's only steam mountain railway is now the Brienzer Rothorn Railway, 800 mm (2 ft 7½ in) gauge with Abt rack. It was opened on 17 June 1892. The summit is at 2349 m (7707 ft).

John Barraclough Fell (1815–1902) invented the centre-rail friction-drive system named after him in 1863–9. It was devised for the railway over the Mont Cenis Pass, opened in 1868 and used until the Mont Cenis Tunnel was completed in 1871.

A similar system had previously been invented by C E Vignoles and John Ericsson and jointly patented on 7 September 1830.

The most famous Fell centre-rail railway was the Rimutaka Incline in New Zealand on the line from Wellington to Masterton, opened on 12 October 1878. Gradients were 1 in 14–16 (7–6 per cent) for 4·8 km (3 miles). It was closed when the Rimutaka Tunnel was opened in 1955 (see p. 94).

The Fell centre-rail is used on the 1·067 m (3 ft 6 in) gauge Snaefell Mountain Railway in the Isle of Man, but for braking purposes only. The electric cars climb to the top, 620 m (2034 ft), by adhesion. It was opened on 21 August 1895.

The first and only railway to the top of a volcano was built on Vesuvius in Italy. The funicular railway, with gradients as steep as 1 in 1·9, was opened in 1880 to the summit station at 1213 m (4012 ft) just below the crater.

The composer Luigi Denza (1846–1922) wrote a popular song 'Funiculi-Funicular' to celebrate the occasion. Richard Strauss thought this was a Neapolitan folk-song and incorporated it in the Finale of his symphonic fantasy *Aus Italien* (1886).

The railway was destroyed in the eruption on 20 March 1944. It has been replaced by a bus between Pugliano and Lower Station and a chair lift from there to the crater.

MONO RAILWAYS OR MONORAILS

The first recorded mono railway was patented by Henry Palmer in 1821 for transporting foodstuffs at the Royal Military Yard, Deptford, London. It consisted of boards supported on posts straddled by the cars which were pulled by horses.

The first passenger-carrying monorail was built in 1876 by General Roy Stone in Fairmont Park, Philadelphia, as part of the city centenary exhibition.

The first commercial monorail was also American, built in 1880 to connect Brooklyn and Coney Island, New York. It ran for a few months but failed for lack of revenue.

Three types of monorail have achieved success. The type invented by Charles Lartigue in 1883 was used for the Listowel & Ballybunion Railway in County Kerry, Ireland. This 14·5 km (9 mile) line was opened on 1 March 1888. The twin-boilered locomotives and cars straddled the rail which was supported on trestles, as shown in the photograph. The most comical pieces of the equipment were the mobile steps which were marshalled into the train to enable passengers to cross the line. Loads had to be balanced. Once when a piano had to be transported it was balanced by a cow. The cow had to be returned by balancing it with two calves which were then sent back one on each side. The railway was closed in October 1924.

Lartigue-type monorails were also built in North Africa, central France, Russia, Guatemala and Peru.

The Tokyo–Haneda Monorail in Japan is a modern version of the Lartigue system. It was opened in October 1964 to connect Tokyo with the international airport at Haneda. Trains cover the 13 km (8 miles) in 15 min.

A similar monorail was opened in Seattle, USA, in 1962 in connection with the World's Fair. It is about 1·6 km (1 mile) long.

The second type of monorail, still in operation, is the 13 km (8 mile) long Wuppertalbahn from Elberfeld to Barmen in Germany. This is the Langen suspended type, much of it straddling the Wupper River. The first section was opened on 1 March 1901. By 1960 it had carried 1 000 000 000 passengers. It was this system which inspired the Swiss engineer Feldmann to build the first mountain aerial ropeway, up the Wetterhorn, opened in July 1908 and closed in 1914. It is electrically operated, and stock now consists of 28 articulated carriages.

The Ewing monorail system, which used an 'outrigger' wheel for balancing, was used by

One of the twin-boilered locomotives—complete with headlamp—on the Listowel & Ballybunion Railway in Ireland (National Library of Ireland)

The Langen suspended railway, Wuppertal, Germany

C W Bowles when State Engineer for the Patiala Government in India. He laid down a system totalling about 96 ·km (60 miles), known as the **Patiala State Monorail Trainway**. The single rail was laid along the edge of a road and the balancing wheels ran on the road. About 95 per cent of the load was carried on the rail and 5 per cent on the sprung road wheel. The rail wheels had double flanges.

In March 1909 four 0–3–0 steam locomotives were built for this monorail by Orenstein & Koppel, Berlin. One of these engines has been restored and it operates at the Indian Railway Museum, New Delhi. (See p. 236.)

NARROW-GAUGE RAILWAYS (less than 1 m gauge)

The current fascination with narrow-gauge railways is largely because, while other railways have progressed continuously, narrow-gauge railways stopped progressing about 1900–10 and so represent steam railways of that period or earlier. Many people find in them a relief from the rush of modern travel, *provided the journeys are not too long*.

Many such lines were built to open up backward areas and their ultimate closure in the face of road competition can be seen more as a measure of their success than of their failure.

GAUGES

914 mm (3 ft) Formerly extensively used in Colorado, USA, and in Ireland, and the Isle of Man. Still in use in Central America, Colombia, Peru, Mexico, Newfoundland, Canada (on the Canadian section of the White Pass & Yukon Railway) and Alaska

891 mm (2 ft 11 in) Some lines in Sweden

800 mm (2 ft $7\frac{1}{2}$ in) Mountain and rack railways

762 mm (2 ft 6 in) Austria, Yugoslavia, Czechoslovakia, India, Sri Lanka (Ceylon), Wales (Welshpool & Llanfair Railway), and on the former Leek & Manifold Valley Railway in England

750 mm (2 ft $5\frac{1}{2}$ in) Argentina, Brazil

610 mm (2 ft) and 600 mm (1 ft $11\frac{1}{2}$ in) Sierra Leone and secondary lines in Wales, South Africa, India, Pakistan, southern Chile, north-west Argentina. Also the Lynton & Barnstaple and Ashover Light railways in England, both abandoned.

The first narrow-gauge steam locomotives were five 0–4–0 saddle tanks designed by John Ramsbottom for the 457 mm (18 in) gauge internal railway at the London & North Western Railway Works at Crewe, and built there in 1862–70. One of these, *Pet* of 1865, is preserved at the Narrow Gauge Railway Museum at Towyn, Wales (qv).

The world's first public narrow-gauge railway was the 600 mm (1 ft $11\frac{1}{2}$ in) gauge Festiniog Railway in Wales, engineered by James Spooner (1789–1856) and opened for slate traffic on 20 April 1836. Trains ran by gravity from Blaenau Ffestiniog to Portmadoc and empties were pulled back by horses which rode down on the trains. Steam locomotives were introduced, for the first time on a narrow-gauge railway, in 1863 by Charles Easton Spooner (qv), son of James. Passenger traffic officially began on 6 January 1865, but passengers had been carried unofficially for years before that. Traffic declined during the Second World War and the railway was closed in 1946. In 1954 the Festiniog Railway Society Limited was formed and passenger services were resumed on 23 July 1955. (See p. 239.)

James Spooner was also engineer to the 686 mm (2 ft 3 in) gauge Tal-y-llyn and Corris railways in Wales.

The first narrow-gauge railroad in the USA was the 914 mm (3 ft) gauge Denver & Rio Grande Railway from Denver to Colorado Springs, opened on 26 October 1871. The locomotive *Montezuma* which was used was the first narrow-gauge passenger engine built or operated in the USA.

After attaining a maximum of about 4800 km (3000 miles) the 3 ft gauge in Colorado was finally abandoned in the late 1960s except for the 72 km (45 mile) long Durango–Silverton Branch and the Alamosa–Durango line between Antonito and Chama, 105 km (65 miles), over the Cumbres Pass, 3053 m (10 015 ft), both now preserved as tourist attractions. At present the Cumbres & Toltec Scenic Railroad (CATS) is the **longest preserved railway in the world**, and the highest, and to many the most scenic. (See p. 244.)

Typical of the Colorado 3 ft lines was the Uintah Railroad which, in 21 km (13 miles), had 233 curves from 434 m (1425 ft) to 22 m (72 ft) radius, including 27 sharper than 34·7 m (114 ft) radius. It had 8 km (5 miles) at a record 7·5 per cent or 1 in 13·3 and crossed into Utah at 2572 m (8437 ft) at Baxter Pass. It was abandoned in 1938.

In contrast, the Denver & Rio Grande Western between Villa Grove and Alamosa, Colorado, in the heart of the Rockies, was dead straight for 85 km (52·82 miles), falling from 2408 m (7900 ft) to 2301 m (7550 ft) at Alamosa.

The 3 ft gauge is still used on the White Pass & Yukon Railway, 178·5 km (111 miles) long, of which 32 km (20 miles) are in Alaska and the rest in Canada. It was **the first railway in Alaska**, opened in stages from 21 July 1898 and completely from Skagway to Whitehorse on 8 June 1900.

The first 610 mm (2 ft) gauge line in the USA was the Bedford & Billerica Railroad which opened on 28 November 1877. There were 14 systems operating 2 ft gauge in the USA ten of which were in Maine. The last to close was the Monson Railroad in December 1944.

Two feet gauge steam may still be enjoyed in the USA on the 8·85 km ($5\frac{1}{2}$ mile) Edaville Railroad at South Carver, Massachusetts; Silver Dollar City, Missouri; Cripple Creek, Colorado and a few short lines elsewhere.

The total mileage of narrow-gauge railroad in the USA in 1890 was about 10 000 (16 000 km), operated by about 500 independent companies.

Ireland's first 914 mm (3 ft) gauge line opened in 1875. Over 800 km (500 miles) were built. The last, the West Clare, closed on 1 February 1961.

The Ravenglass & Eskdale Railway in England's Lake District, was opened as a 914 mm (3 ft) gauge line on 24 May 1875, carrying passengers from November 1876, for 12 km ($7\frac{1}{2}$ miles) into the Cumbrian Fells. It was rebuilt into a 381 mm (15 in) gauge line in 1915–17. Today it is operated by a preservation company formed on 30 March 1961 (see colour illustration on p. 146).

The world's smallest public railway is the 381 mm (15 in) gauge Romney, Hythe & Dymchurch Railway in Kent, England. It was authorised in 1925 under the Light Railways Act of 1896 and was opened on 16 July 1927. It is 21 km (13·8 miles) long and from Hythe to New Romney, 13·5 km (8·3 miles), is double-track. It is the only double-track 381 mm (15 in) gauge railway in the world on which passenger trains pass each other many times daily at speeds of 32–40 km/h (20–25 mph). The railway possesses ten steam locomotives designed by Henry Greenly and built in 1925–31 (see colour illustration on p. 146).

The first narrow-gauge railway to carry standard-gauge wagons on transporter trucks was the 762 mm (2 ft 6 in) gauge 16·8 km ($8\frac{1}{4}$ mile) long Leek & Manifold Valley Light Railway in Staffordshire, England. It opened on 27 June 1904 and closed on 10 March 1934. The transporters were designed by the engineer, Everard Richard Calthrop (1857–1927), for the Barsi Light Railway, India, of which he was also engineer, but they

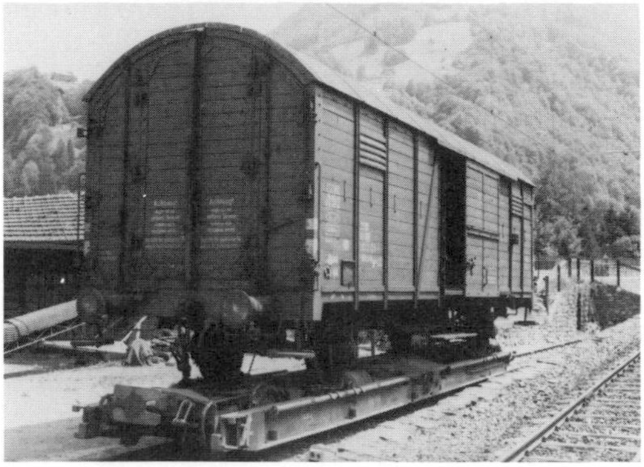

Metre-gauge transporter wagon carrying a standard-gauge van at Schiers on the Landquart–Davos line on the Rhaetian Railway in Switzerland

Train passing through Ghoom, 2557 m (7407 ft) above sea-level, at the summit of the 610 mm (2 ft) gauge Darjeeling Himalayan Railway, India, in May 1944

were first used on the Manifold Valley line. They are now widely used in several countries, on different gauges.

British Rail's only steam railway is the 610 mm (2 ft) gauge Vale of Rheidol Railway, Wales, opened on 22 December 1902 from Aberystwyth to Devil's Bridge (see colour illustration on p. 147). It is 19 km (12 miles) long.

The Zillertalbahn from Jenbach to Mayrhofen in Austria, 34 km (21 miles) long, 762 mm (2 ft 6 in) gauge, was opened on 2 January 1900. Today it is one of the most popular narrow-gauge railways in Europe. Its oldest locomotive is the 0–6–2 tank No. 2 *Zillertal* built at Linz in 1900.

A popular feature is the 'Hobby Train' which may be driven by amateurs, under supervision, at the upper end of the line.

One of the world's most spectacular narrow-gauge railways is the 610 mm (2 ft) gauge Darjeeling Himalayan Railway in India. It was opened from Siliguri, then the northern terminus of the Eastern Bengal Railway from Calcutta, to Darjeeling in the Himalayan foothills, in July 1881. From Sukna, 162 m (533 ft) above sea-level, and about 563 km (350 miles) from the sea, 11 km (7 miles) beyond Siliguri, the railway climbs for 64 km (40 miles) mostly at 1 in 25 (4 per cent) to a height of 2557 m (7407 ft) at Ghoom from where it drops to 2076 m (6812 ft) at Darjeeling. The total length is 82 km (51 miles). The line includes five spiral loops and three reversing zigzags to gain height. One of the loops includes the sharpest curve on the line, only 18 m (59½ ft) radius.

A branch of 45 km (28 miles) along the magnificent Teesta River Valley to a station below Kalimpong was opened in 1915. This is now closed.

Throughout most of its existence the railway has been worked by 0–4–0 saddle tanks of a type first built in 1888 by Sharp Stewart in Glasgow. For a time a 0–4–0+0–4–0 Garratt was used, built by Beyer Peacock, Manchester, in 1910. It was their second design (see p. 132) and the first normal simple-expansion Garratt with the cylinders at the outer ends.

The greatest narrow-gauge engineering in India is found on the 762 mm (2 ft 6 in) gauge Kalka–Simla Railway in the north-west Himalayan foothills. It was built in 1899–1903 to give access to Simla where the Indian Government made its summer headquarters. From a height of 653 m (2143 ft) at Kalka where it connects with the 1·676 m (5 ft 6 in) gauge line from Delhi, it climbs by gradients of 1 in 33 to a height of 2075 m (6808 ft) at Simla in 95 km (59 miles). There are 103 tunnels, the longest being Barogh, 1144 m (1251 yd). The track is of 'main-line' standard with 29·76 kg/m (60 lb/yd) rails.

The principal steam locomotives were the 'K' Class 2–6–2 tanks first built in 1908 by the North British Locomotive Company, Glasgow.

Section 6
RAILWAYS IN HUMAN AFFAIRS AND THE ARTS

RAILWAY WORKERS

The railroads of the USA employed 1 660 850 persons in 1929 earning an average rate of $1743 per annum. In 1975 the number had fallen to 487 789 earning an average of $15 324. Railroads of Illinois employed the highest number, 48 010, followed by Pennsylvania with 41 020, New York with 27 850 and Texas with 27 180.

The first railroad in the USA to institute a formal pension plan for all ranks of employees was the Pennsylvania, on 1 January 1900. It applied to all employees from the age of 70 which from that date became the compulsory retiring age.

The Federal Railroad Retirement Act (USA) came into effect for all railroads on 1 July 1937, replacing voluntary retirement and disability benefits on about 80 major railroads.

In 1972 British Rail employed 196 635 persons, an average of about 17 per mile of route, compared with about 2·5 in the USA. This comparison, however, does not take into account the density of population and traffic.

The first woman railroad employee in the USA was Susan Morningstar who was hired to help to clean the Baltimore & Ohio terminus at Baltimore, Maryland, in February 1855.

The first 'train hostess', Miss Kathryn Sullivan, began her work in 1935 on 'The Rebel', one of the first American streamlined trains, on the 1209 km (751 miles) run between St Louis and New Orleans on the Gulf, Mobile & Ohio Railroad.

The youngest locomotive engineer ever appointed was probably Richard Peacock (1820–99). He was appointed locomotive superintendent of the Leeds & Selby Railway in 1838 at the age of 18. In 1841 he became locomotive superintendent of the Manchester, Sheffield & Lincolnshire Railway and founded its works at Gorton, Manchester.

In 1854, when aged 34, he joined Charles Beyer (1813–76) to found the famous locomotive works of Beyer Peacock, also at Gorton.

Daniel Gooch was just 21 when he was appointed first locomotive superintendent of the Great Western Railway, under I K Brunel in 1837. He founded the famous works at Swindon in 1841–3.

Bowman Malcolm (1854–1933) was appointed locomotive engineer at the age of 21 on the Belfast & Northern Counties Railway in 1876. He remained in that position until his retirement 46 years later in 1922 at the age of 68. He had served the railway for 52 years. He died on 3 January 1933 aged 79.

Robert Stephenson was only 19 years 8 months old when he was appointed manager of Robert Stephenson & Company, Newcastle upon Tyne, in 1923, one of the world's first locomotive-manufacturers.

RAILWAY SOCIETIES AND ENTHUSIASTS

The oldest British society for railway enthusiasts is the Railway Club, London (112 High Holborn, London WC1 V6JS), founded in 1899. Its *Journal* was first issued in 1902, but is no longer published. A bulletin is published twice yearly.

The Stephenson Locomotive Society with members throughout Britain and all over the world (34 Durley Avenue, Pinner, Middlesex

HA5 1JQ) was formed in 1909. It maintains a lively monthly *Journal*, catering for the serious enthusiast with an interest in technical matters and in railways generally, first published in 1924.

The Newcomen Society for the study of the history of engineering and technology was founded on 4 June 1920 and incorporated on 3 May 1961. The *Transactions* contain many articles of great interest to railway historians. (The Science Museum, London SW7 2DD.)

The Railway Correspondence & Travel Society, like the Stephenson Locomotive Society with a widely dispersed membership, was founded in Cheltenham in 1928. Its monthly journal, *The Railway Observer*, first published on 1 May 1928 as the *Railway News*, first appeared in March 1929. It keeps members up to date with locomotive stock changes and allocations. (95 Chestnut Avenue, Forest Gate, London E7 0JF.)

The Railway & Canal Historical Society was founded on 4 September 1954. Besides an interesting journal members enjoy lectures in various centres and a comprehensive programme of outdoor visits to railways and canals. (435 Upper Richmond Road, London SW15.)

All the above societies organise programmes of lectures, the Railway Club in London and the others in centres throughout Britain. Other activities include rail tours and visits.

The Transport Trust, of Great Britain, is a charitable organisation concerned chiefly with the safeguarding of all forms of transport relics, documents, books, photographs, films and other historical material, and with co-ordinating the preservation of all forms of historic transport objects throughout the nation. It was constituted in 1965 and registered as a charity in 1967. Membership is open to all. (18 Ramillies Place, London W1V 2BA.)

The Irish Railway Record Society was founded on 24 October 1946. (24 Avondale Lawn, Blackrock, Co Dublin.) The *Journal* is published twice yearly.

The Railway & Locomotive Historical Society of the USA was founded in 1921 and incorporated in 1926. (Baker Library, Harvard Business School, Boston (63), Mass.)

The National Railway Historical Society, USA, was founded in 1935 and incorporated in 1937 to further the preservation of historical railway material. It publishes *The Bulletin* bi-monthly. (Suite 312–14, Empire Building, 13th and Walnut Streets, Philadelphia, Pa. 19107.)

The Canadian Railroad Historical Association was founded on 15 March 1932 at the Château de Ramezay Museum, Montreal. The *Bulletin* was first published in 1938, but ceased in 1941. In August 1941 the Association obtained a Charter. The *News Report*, now *Canadian Rail* has been published monthly since October 1947. The Association operates an extensive railroad museum at Delson near Montreal. (Box 22, Station B, Montreal 110, Quebec.)

The Upper Canada Railway Society was founded in 1941 and incorporated in 1952. It serves enthusiasts of both steam and electric railways. (PO Box 122, Terminal A, Toronto.)

The Australian Railway Historical Society was founded in 1933 as the Australian Railway Circle. It then became the Australasian Railway and Locomotive Historical Society. The name was changed to its present form in November 1951, and the Society now has divisions in all the States. It publishes the *Bulletin* monthly. (Hon Secretary: 24 Flora Street, Stepney, South Australia 5069.)

The New Zealand Railway & Locomotive Society was founded in 1944. It publishes the **New Zealand Railway Observer** monthly (PO Box 5134, Wellington C1).

The Association Française des amis des Chemins de Fer was founded in 1929. It publishes a monthly journal *Chemins de Fer*. (Gare de l'Est, Paris 10).

The Swedish Railway Club (Svenska Järnvägsklubben) was founded in March 1958. Its main interests are in railway history. (Box 124, 10121 Stockholm 7, Sweden.)

The Norwegian Railway Club (Norsk Jernbaneklubb) was founded in 1969 to foster interest in railway history, modern railways and railway modelling. It co-operates closely with Norwegian State Railways (NSB), the Railway Museum at Hamar (see p. 230), and the Museum of Science and Industry, Oslo. It operates trains on a 26 km (16 mile) freight line between Vikersund and Kroderen. (Postboks 1492, Vika, Oslo 1.)

The Railway and Tramway Society (Schienenverkehr Verband) of Austria includes the **Vienna Railway Enthusiasts Society**. It was founded on 7 May 1947. (Box 20, A-1016, Vienna.)

The German Railway Enthusiasts Society (Bundesverband deutscher Eisenbahn-Freunde EV) was founded on 29 June 1958. (3 Hannover 1, Viethof 3, Postfach 1163.)

The Railway Enthusiasts Society (Eisenbahn Kurier GmbH) was founded on 1 January 1965. (D-7800 Freibourg, PO Box 5560.)

The German Railway History Society (Deutsche Gesellschaft für Eisenbahngeschichte EV) was founded on 22 April 1967. (D-7500 Karlsruhe, Postfach 2063.)

The above addresses were correct at the time of writing. They are mostly of honorary secretaries, and it is well to check addresses in the current *Directory of Railway Officials and Year Book* or recent railway periodicals.

King Boris III of Bulgaria (1894–1943) had a keen interest in all things mechanical and frequently drove Bulgarian locomotives. On 5 November 1937 at the invitation of the London, Midland & Scottish Railway he drove 'Pacific' No. 6220 *Coronation*, reaching a speed of 142 km/h (88 mph). Afterwards Lord Stamp, then chairman of the LMS, presented him with a model of the locomotive.

One of the world's most distinguished railway enthusiasts was King Frederick IX of Denmark. He was born on 11 March 1899 and succeeded to the throne on 20 April 1947. He had an encyclopaedic knowledge of Danish railways and was a competent engine-driver. He died on 14 January 1972 and, in accordance with his wish, his funeral train on 24 January made the 32 km (20 mile) journey from Copenhagen to the ancient capital of Roskilde behind two 'E' Class 'Pacifics', Nos. 978 and 994.

RAILWAY PUBLICATIONS

The first British periodical devoted to railways was *The Railway Magazine* which first appeared in London in May 1835 and ran weekly until December 1840 when it became *Herapath's Railway Magazine* (later *Journal*) until December 1903 when it merged with *The Railway Times*.

The longest running railway periodical is *The Railway Magazine* (London) first published in July 1897 and monthly ever since except from May 1942 to December 1949 when it was issued every other month.

Until March 1974 the record for the longest run was held by *The Railway Times*, first published in London on 29 October 1837 and issued weekly until 28 March 1914, 76 years 7 months.

The oldest American railroad periodical was the *American Railroad Journal*, first published on 2 January 1832. From 1887 to 1892 it became *The Railroad and Engineering Journal*, then *The American Engineer and Railroad Journal* until 1911. Subsequent changes were: January 1912–May 1913 *The Railway Mechanical Monthly*, June 1913–December 1915 merged with *Railway Age Gazette* (1909); 1916–49 *Railway Mechanical Engineer*; 1950–2 *Railway Mechanical and Electrical Engineer*; from 1953 *Railway Locomotives and Cars*.

The oldest American magazine for enthusiasts is the *Railroad Magazine*, founded in 1906 and published monthly in New York.

The popular American monthly magazine *Trains* was first published in 1940 in Milwaukee, Wisconsin.

RAILWAYS IN LITERATURE

The earliest English poem about railways by an important writer is 'Steamboats, Viaducts and Railways' by William Wordsworth (1770–1850), No. 42 of his *Itinerary Poems* (1833). Three of his poems are anti-railway: 'On the projected Kendal and Windermere Railway', and 'Proud were ye, Mountains', Nos. 45 and 46 of his *Miscellaneous Sonnets* (1844); and 'At Furness Abbey', No. 48 (1845).

Robert Louis Stevenson (1850–94) wrote two railway poems, 'From a Railway Carriage' from *A Child's Garden of Verses*, and 'The Iron Steed'. In conjunction with his stepson, **Lloyd Osbourne**, he wrote a novel *The Wrong Box* in which a railway accident and a joker changing the labels on packages in a guard's van result in some exquisite situations.

Thomas Hardy (1840–1928) left us two railway poems: 'Midnight on the Great Western' and 'Faintheart in a Railway Train', as also did **Siegfried Sassoon** (1886–1967), 'A Local Train of Thought', a homely picture of a branch-line train, and 'Morning Express', a vivid account of a train's arrival and departure.

This poem, and 'From a Railway Carriage' by R L Stevenson, was set to music by Arthur Butterworth as part of his *Trains in the Distance*, performed at the NRM, York, on 13 June 1976 (see p. 229).

Other railway poems were written by **Edmund Blunden** (1896–1974) and **Rupert Brooke** (1867–1915). The most prolific writer of railway poems and essays is **John Betjeman** (b 1906).

Wystan Hugh Auden (b 1907) wrote a poem *Night mail* for a British Railways documentary film of that name.

Hans Christian Andersen (1805–75), the Danish fairy-tale author, wrote a remarkable piece in *Le Figaro* describing trains and train journeys. This was in 1840, seven years before the first railway was opened in Denmark, and was one of the earliest pieces of railway writing by a fiction author.

Railway fiction is mainly in the form of the short story. In 1845 **'Tilbury Tramp'** (C J Lever) (1806–72) published *Tales of the Trains*, five short stories based on train journeys.

William Makepeace Thackeray (1811–63) has left us *Jeames on the Gauge Question*, a short story of a journey from London to Cheltenham with changes of carriage at Swindon and Gloucester and the confusion arising from the transfer of 93 packages and a baby.

Arthur Quiller Couch (1863–1944) produced several works containing references to railways: *Delectable Duchy* (1893) in his native Cornwall, *The Destruction of Didcot* (1908) and *Pipes in Arcady* on a Cornish branch line, reprinted in *Sixteen On* edited by Charles Irving (1957).

One of the 'Reginald' stories, *The Mouse* (1930) by **H H Munro** (Saki) (1870–1916), takes place in a railway carriage. D H Lawrence (1885–1930) wrote a short story called *Tickets please*, based on a journey on the Nottingham–Ripley street tramway, and L A G Strong (1896–1958) wrote two, *Departure* (1929) at a country station, and *The Gates* (1931) about a crossing keeper.

Railways and crime have often been linked in author's minds. Although railway journeys are frequently mentioned in the 'Sherlock Holmes' stories of **Arthur Conan Doyle** (1859–1930), in only one, *The Adventures of the Bruce Partington Plans* (1924), do railways feature. In this the Metropolitan Railway, forms an important part of the story. 'The Lost Special' from his *Round the Fire Stories* (1908) describes the events leading to the total disappearance of a train.

Three of the 'Dr Thorndike' stories by **R. Austin Freeman** (1862–1943) have railway settings, or railway incidents form an essential part of the plot: *The Moabite Cipher*, *The Blue Sequin* and *The Case of Arthur Brodski* (1928).

The Mysterious Death on the Underground Railway by **Baroness Orczy** (1865–1947) is another example of a crime story where the railway setting is an important ingredient. F W Crofts (1879–1957) wrote several crime stories with railway settings: *Crime on the Footplate*, *Death of a Train*, *Death on the Way*, *The Level Crossing*, *The Mystery of the Sleeping Car Express* and *Sir John Magill's Last Journey*.

Three of the well-known crime books by Dame Agatha Christie (1890–1976) have railway settings: *Mystery of the Blue Train* (1928); *Murder on the Orient Express* (1934) and *4.50 from Paddington* (1957). *Murder on the Orient Express* has recently been filmed by EMI Films, using French National Railways '230G' Class 4–6–0 No. 353 and four coaches restored by the Wagon Lits Company to conform to the 1930s period.

Novels with railway settings tend to be written mainly by authors with particular interest in railways. However, in his novel of the 'Hungry Forties', *Sybil* (1845), **Benjamin Disraeli**

(1804–81) makes considerable references to railways.

Charles Dickens (1812–70) was fascinated by railways and they figure prominently in many of his works. In *Dombèy and Son* (1848) Chapters 6 and 15 contain accounts of the London & Birmingham Railway; *Our Mutual Friend* (1864–5) refers to the London & Greenwich and the Great Western railways and Paddington Station, not entirely accurately, and in a postscript Dickens describes his experiences in the Staplehurst accident in 1865 (see 'Accidents', p. 181). *The Uncommercial Traveller* refers to railways in Kent. *The Mystery of Edwin Drood* (unfinished at his death in 1870) makes reference to the South Eastern Railway. Of his other works, his story *A Flight* is based on a journey from London Bridge to Folkestone. Four of the 'Mugby Junction' stories (1866) are by Dickens: *Barbox Brothers*, *Barbox Brothers & Co.*; *Main Line: the Boy at Mugby*; and *No. 1 Branch Line: the Signalman*. These stories came to be written as a result of an enforced stop at Rugby Junction on the London & North Western Railway, following a fire in the coach in which Dickens was travelling. Finally, *Lazy Tour of Two Idle Apprentices* contains references to the LNWR in the Chester district.

Besides his terrible experience in the Staplehurst disaster, Dickens had other railway adventures. During a journey to Holyhead, *en route* for Ireland, his train was snowed up near Bangor for four hours, with no train heating. On one of his American journeys, between Rochester and Albany, he was caught in one of the worst floods on record when nearly 482 km (300 miles) of line were inundated. After he had spent an enforced night at Utica the railway company got him to Albany through floods and floating blocks of ice, taking ten hours for a journey normally taking three.

The great American writer of Western thrillers, Zane Grey (1872–1939) gave a vivid picture of the construction of the Union Pacific Railroad in *The UP Trail* (1918) describing the experiences of a young engineer and a girl.

An even better story on the same subject is *The Mountain Divide* (1912) by **Frank Hamilton Spearman** (1859–1937). Another UP book is *Building the Pacific Railway* (1919) by **Edwin L. Sabin**.

Probably the most successful railroad novel written in the USA is *The Big Ivy* (1955) by **James McCague**.

Edith Nesbit (Bland) (1858–1924) produced one of the best loved of all railway stories, *The Railway Children* (1906) in which three children prevent a train from running into a landslip. A successful film version was made on the Keighley & Worth Valley Railway in Yorkshire. In *Hatter's Castle* (1931) by **A J Cronin** (b 1896) the villain, Denis, perishes in the Tay Bridge disaster. This made a dramatic sequence in the film version, in which the deceived heroine had left the train at a signal stop.

Bhowani Junction (1954) by **John Masters** (b 1914) is a vivid portrayal of the Indian railway scene and of the Anglo-Indian community during the Second World War. Some readers, however, may find the sensuous aspect somewhat overdrawn. This has also been made into a film.

Hamilton Ellis (b 1909), the well-known railway writer and artist, has produced two novels about railways: *The Grey Men* (1939), a mystery story on the West Highland Railway, and *Dandy Hart* (1947) set in southern England in the period 1830–60. In *The Engineer Corporal* (1940) he gives a vivid account of 'The Great Locomotive Chase' during the American Civil War. This story is also told in 'The Railway Raid in Georgia' from *A Book of Escapes and Hurried Journeys* (1925) by John Buchan (1875–1940).

L T C Rolt (1910–74), best known for his biographies of Telford, the Stephensons and Brunel, wrote a novel *Winterstoke* (1954) set in an imaginary Midlands town in the nineteenth century during the financing and construction of rival railway projects.

The first, and probably only, novel to be dedicated to a railway was *Blue Eyes and Grey* (1928) by Baroness Orczy. It was dedicated 'To the President, Directors and all connected with that marvellous organisation the Canadian Pacific Railway'. The romance was based on the author's CPR journey in 1925.

It is in the form of the essay that railway literature achieves its greatest profusion. Many, written as articles for periodicals, of an amusing, light-hearted or ephemeral nature, can hardly be classed as 'literature', but there are some by **Paul Jennings** (b 1918), **Hamilton Ellis** and others which can be read repeatedly

140 JAHRE ÖSTERREICHISCHE EISENBAHNEN
ELEKTRISCHE LOKOMOTIVE REIHE 1044
S 3
REPUBLIK ÖSTERREICH
140 JAHRE ÖSTERREICHISCHE EISENBAHNEN
»AUSTRIA« ERSTE DAMPFLOKOMOTIVE IN ÖSTERREICH
S 1.50
REPUBLIK ÖSTERREICH
140 JAHRE ÖSTERREICHISCHE EISENBAHNEN
SCHNELLZUGSLOKOMOTIVE REIHE 214
S 2.50
REPUBLIK ÖSTERREICH
Stephenson's Locomotion
7p
1825 Stockton and Darlington Railway
Waverley Class
8p
1876 North British Railway Drummond
Caerphilly Castle
10p
1923 Great Western Railway Castle Class
High-Speed Train
12p
1975 British Rail Inter-City Service HST
125th ANNIVERSARY of the RAILWAY
THE PROJECTOR - 1845
JAMAICA 3c
125th ANNIVERSARY of the RAILWAY
ENGINE 54 - 1944
JAMAICA 15c
125th ANNIVERSARY of the RAILWAY
ENGINE 102 - 1967
JAMAICA 50c
JERSEY 2½p
"NORTH WESTERN"
Centenary - Inauguration of Jersey Eastern Railway
G DRUMMOND
COURVOISIER S.A.
JERSEY
"CALVADOS"
Centenary - Inauguration of Jersey Eastern Railway
G DRUMMOND
COURVOISIER S.A.
JERSEY
"CARTERET"
7½p
Centenary - Inauguration of Jersey Eastern Railway
G DRUMMOND
COURVOISIER S.A.
JERSEY
GOREY
"CAESAREA"
9p
ST HELIER
Centenary - Inauguration of Jersey Eastern Railway
G DRUMMOND
COURVOISIER S.A.

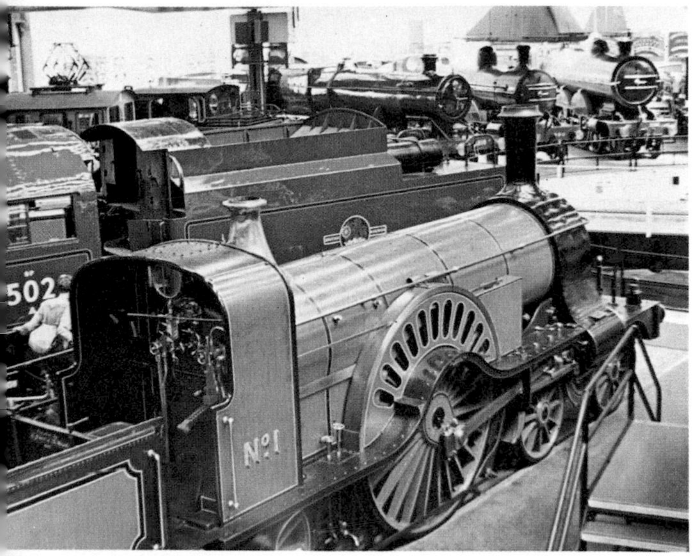

Locomotives in the National Railway Museum, York, on 6 July 1976. In the foreground is the Stirling 4–2–2 No. 1 of the Great Northern Railway. Exhibits are constantly being changed (see p. 231)

Metropolitan Railway 'A' class 4–4–0 tank No. 23 (Beyer Peacock No. 710, 1866) at the London Transport Museum at Syon Park in July 1978. The museum was closed shortly afterwards for removal to Covent Garden, London

with enjoyment. Among well-known writers who have given the railway consideration in essays are **Robert Lynd** (1879–1949) who wrote three: *In the Train*, *Railway Stations I have loved*, and *Trains*; **A A Milne** (1882–1956) who gave us *A Train of Thought* (1921); and **J B Priestley** (b. 1894), *Man Underground* (1932) in which he philosophises on travelling beneath London.

An example of factual literature on railways is *Across the Plains* (1892) by Robert Louis Stevenson. **Pierre Berton** of Canada (b 1920) has written two volumes on the building of the Canadian Pacific Railway which contain fine historical writing and deserve consideration as literature: *The National Dream, The Great Railway, 1871–1881* (1970) and *The Last Spike, The Great Railway 1881–1885* (1971).

The railway does not figure prominently in drama. John Galsworthy (1867–1933) wrote a one-act comedy in three scenes, *The Little Man* (1915) set on railway platforms and in a railway carriage compartment. Perhaps the best-known play is *The Ghost Train* (1925) by Arnold Ridley (b 1896) which has been made into a film on several occasions. In *Brief Encounter* by **Noël Coward** (1899–1973) part of the action is set in a railway station. The most completely 'railway' play is probably *The Knotty*, first produced by the Victoria Theatre, Stoke-on-Trent, in 1966, a musical documentary outlining the history of the North Staffordshire Railway. Extracts are now available on a gramophone recording.

RAILWAYS IN THE CINEMA*

The first cinema show by the French brothers Louis and Auguste Lumière, on 28 December 1895, included a scene entitled 'Arrival of a train at La Ciotat Station'. Members of the audience leapt from their seats as the train came towards them 'out of the screen'.

The first railway film was a single scene called 'Black Diamond Express' on 13·106 m (43 ft) of film produced in the USA by Thomas Edison (1847–1931) on a device known as the 'Kinetescope', in 1896. It showed Locomotive No. 665 of the Lehigh Valley Railroad passing on a train to Buffalo.

*This section is not intended to be a catalogue, or 'screenography'.

The first British film taken from the front of an engine was made in 1896 between Exeter Central and St David's stations, down the incline and through the tunnel. It was followed in 1897 by a similar film 'Railway Ride over the Tay Bridge'.

The first railway film to tell a dramatic story was 'The Great Train Robbery', produced in the USA by Edwin S. Porter (1870–1941), a collaborator with Edison, on the Delaware, Lackawanna & Western Railroad in 1903. It was one of the most important landmarks in the first 15 years of the cinema industry.

Train wrecks made exciting film scenes. In 1897, 1898 and 1908 some excellent shots were made using models. In 1914 Vitagraph of the USA produced *The Wreck*, the first film of a train wreck using actual old locomotives and stock on a specially rented track. Its success led to a spate of films and even public events of deliberately contrived crashes.

The Great Locomotive Chase (see p. 172) provided a perfect story for an exciting film. It was first filmed in 1911 in *Railroad Raiders of '62*. A 90-min film by Buster Keaton in 1927 used replicas of the locomotives *General* and *Texas*.

One of the last of the silent railway films, *The Wrecker*, a British production by Gainsborough Studios in 1929, was based on a stage play by Arnold Ridley and Bernard Merivale. It was filmed principally on the Southern Railway, partly on the Basingstoke & Alton Light Railway, which still had passenger trains until 12 September 1932.

One of the most popular stories for a film was *The Ghost Train* based on the play by Arnold Ridley. It was first produced by C. Bolvary as a silent film in 1927, running for 108 min. A second version, produced by Walter Forde with sound in 1931, ran for 72 min. In 1937 a third version was produced with sound for BBC Television, transmitted on 20 December. Gainsborough produced a fourth version, running for 84 min, in 1941, and a further television presentation was made by the BBC on 20 December 1948.

The first British sound film on a railway subject was *The Flying Scotsman* produced by British International Pictures in 1930. Three reels had been shot as a silent film then, after half an hour, it suddenly became 'talkie'. For the film the London & North Eastern Railway 'Pacific' No. 4472 *Flying Scotsman* was used for 6 weeks followed by running rights on ten successive Sundays between London (King's Cross) and Edinburgh.

The three best loved of British railway films are probably *Oh! Mr Porter* (Gainsborough 1937), filmed on the Basingstoke & Alton Light Railway in Hampshire (closed to all traffic on 30 May 1936); *The Titfield Thunderbolt* (Ealing Studios 1952), inspired by the preservation of the Tal-y-llyn Railway in Wales, filmed in colour on the Limpley Stoke–Camerton Branch of the Great Western Railway in Somerset; and *The Railway Children* based on the story by Edith Nesbit (1858–1924) and filmed in 1969, also in colour, on the Keighley & Worth Valley Railway in Yorkshire. All three films provide entertainment of a high order and an abundance of universal human interest, but *The Titfield Thunderbolt* is marred by two impossible scenes, one a battle between a locomotive and a steam-roller and the other in which a Great Western 0–4–2 tank locomotive is driven along roads. Both, however, are highly amusing.

RAILWAYS AND ART

The earliest railway pictures of any value are those produced as series of prints made during the construction or soon after the opening of some of England's earliest main lines. Chief among these are:

The Liverpool & Manchester Railway, a series of coloured aquatints by **Thomas Talbot Bury** (1811–77), published by Ackermann & Company in 1830. Rudolf Ackermann lived from 1764 to 1834.

The Newcastle & Carlisle Railway, a series of drawings by **James Wilson Carmichael**, a marine artist (1800–68), published in Newcastle in 1837 and reprinted in 1970.

The London & Birmingham Railway and **The Great Western Railway**, two series of hand-coloured lithographs by **John Cooke Bourne** (1814–96), produced in 1837–9. The GWR pictures were reprinted in 1969 and the L. & B. in 1970. Bourne's view of Camden Shed, shown here, illustrates the use of stub points.

The Manchester & Leeds Railway, a series of lithographs by **Arthur Fitzwilliam Tait** (1819–1905), published in both black and white and colour in 1845 and reprinted in 1972. Tait was primarily a landscape and animal painter. He emigrated to the USA in 1850.

J C Bourne's lithograph of Camden locomotive depot; one of the series illustrating the London & Birmingham Railway, which he produced in 1837–9, showing stub points. The locomotive is 2–2–0 No. 32 build by Mather, Dixon & Co. in 1836

Festiniog Railway 597 mm (1 ft $11\frac{1}{2}$ in) gauge train at Porthmadog Station on 11 October 1975. The locomotive is tank-tender 0–4–2 *Linda* (Hunslet No. 590, 1893), built as a 0–4–0 and formerly one of the engines working the Penrhyn Railway (see p. 239)

Tal-y-llyn Railway 686 mm (2 ft 3 in) gauge 0–4–2 tank No. 1 *Dolgoch* (Fletcher Jennings No. 42, 1865) at Towyn on 4 July 1976 (see p. 239)

Stanier 2–8–0, No. 8233 on a train of restored Great Western coaches at Bewdley on the Severn Valley Railway, on 12 April 1977 (see p. 242) (Simon Marshall)

K1 class 2–6–0 climbing the steep incline into Goathland Station on the North Yorkshire Moors Railway, in August 1977 (see p. 242) (Simon Marshall)

ssarro's painting known as *Penge Station, Upper Norwood*, actually Lordship Lane Station on the Crystal Palace High Level anch of the London, Chatham & Dover railway (see p. 224) (Courtauld Institute Galleries, London)

All these pictures, besides being works of art in themselves, possessed the additional advantage of technical accuracy and are valuable historical documents.

The first great artist to be inspired by the railway was Joseph Mallord William Turner (1775–1851) whose famous painting *Rain, Steam and Speed, the Great Western Railway* (1844) shows a 'Firefly' Class locomotive on a train crossing Brunel's Maidenhead Bridge towards Reading. It is in oil on canvas 908 mm × 1219 mm (35¾ in × 48 in). (National Gallery, London.)

David Cox (1783–1859), an English landscape-painter and one of the greatest English water-colourists, was inspired by Turner's painting to paint his *Wind, Rain and Sunshine* (1845) which recaptures some of the atmospheric effects but is really a landscape with a small train in the background. He also painted *The Night Train* about 1857, another landscape with a small train motif. (Both Birmingham City Art Gallery.)

Adolf Friedrich Erdmann von Menzel (1815–1905), a German historical and genre painter and illustrator, produced *Die Berlin–Potsdamer Bahn* in 1847. The curve of the railway is an important element in the composition, and a train is shown. (Berlin Nationalgalerie.)

Gustave Doré (1832–83) in his sketches of London published in 1872 (reprinted 1971) included two showing railways. *Ludgate Hill* shows a street scene which makes modern traffic appear insignificant. Over the bridge above a train of the London, Chatham & Dover Railway is entering the Ludgate Hill Station. In *Over London by Rail* we look through an arch of a railway viaduct along a row of cramped, overcrowded tenements to another viaduct over which a train is passing.

In 1871 the French landscape painter **Camille Pissarro** (1830–1903), on a visit to London with Claude Monet (see below), by way of escaping from the Franco-Prussian War, produced the painting which has been known as *Penge Station, Upper Norwood* (Courtauld Institute Galleries, University of London). The picture shows an early signal and a train approaching through a cutting in a bright, spring-like setting.

Actually the station was Lordship Lane on the branch of the London, Chatham & Dover Railway from Peckham Rye to Crystal Palace High Level, opened on 1 August 1865, quite close to Penge, and looking towards Nunhead. It was closed on 20 September 1954 and is now a housing estate.

The Dutch landscape-painter **Paul J C Gabriel** (1828–1903) of Amsterdam painted his **Train in Landscape** about 1887. (Kröller-Müller Museum, Otterloo near Arnhem.) It shows a train approaching beside a canal in a typically flat Dutch landscape.

Claude Monet (1840–1926), French landscape artist and one of the greatest of the Impressionists, was greatly inspired by Turner's work during his London visit in 1871. His earliest known railway picture is *Train dans la Champagne*, probably before 1870 (Louvre, Paris). In 1875 he painted his *Le Train dans la Neige* (Marmottan Museum, Paris) and *Railway Bridge at Argenteuil* with a train passing over (Philadelphia Museum of Art). His best-known railway paintings are his series of ten of the Gare Saint-Lazare, Paris, in 1877. At the time he was still an unknown and impecunious artist. He put on his best clothes and introduced himself to the station superintendent as 'Claude Monet, the painter'. The superintendent, knowing nothing of art, believed he was a world-famous artist and had trains stopped and arranged specially for his benefit, and when Monet had finished he was graciously bowed out by uniformed officials. Today the series is scattered. One is in New York, one in Harvard University, and one in the Marmottan Museum, Paris.

Perhaps the best loved of all railway pictures is *The Railway Station* (1862) **by William Powell Frith** (1819–1909) showing a bustling scene at Paddington Station, London, with one of Gooch's broad-gauge engines, *Great Britain* of 1847, on the left, and on the right the arrest of a criminal. Above all are the leaping arches of Brunel's great station roof. (See colour illustration on p. 150.) The original canvas, 2·565 m × 1·168 m (8 ft 5 in × 3 ft 10 in), hangs in the Art Gallery of Royal Holloway College, Egham, Surrey. It was commissioned by L V Flatow, an art-dealer in Haymarket, London, and Frith was paid £4500 plus £750 for waiving his right to exhibit it at the Royal Academy and for allowing it to be exhibited at Flatow's Gallery where 21 150 people paid to see it in 7 weeks. It was exhibited at the International Exhibition, Paris, in 1878, and at the British Empire Exhibition, Wembley, London, in 1924.

The railway carriage compartment was a popular setting for some Mid-Victorian paintings. **Abraham Solomon** (1824–62) produced a pair of paintings in 1854 entitled *First Class—The Meeting* and *Second Class—The Parting*. In the first a girl is fascinated by a young officer while her father talks animatedly between them. (In the original version the father was asleep in the corner, but this did not accord with Victorian decorum!) The second shows the sad parting of a mother and her son who is emigrating.

Honoré Daumier (1808–79) produced a vivid impression of travelling conditions in the mid-19th century in *The Third Class Carriage* about 1862 (Metropolitan Museum, New York).

August Leopold Egg (1816–63) left us *The Travelling Companions* (1862), now in Birmingham City Art Gallery, showing two extravagantly attired women, one asleep and the other reading, in a first class compartment, totally oblivious of the beautiful coastal scenery near Menton on the French Riviera.

To Brighton and back for 3s 6d by **Charles Rossiter** (1827–97) is a colourful painting of a group of mid-19th century excursionists, in a third class carriage with wooden seats and roof but no windows and with the rain driving in from the left (Birmingham Museum and Art Gallery).

Most of the increasing number of railway artists today are ardent railway enthusiasts. **Hamilton Ellis** is mentioned in 'Railways and Literature' on p. 219. His numerous paintings are distinguished for their technical accuracy. The paintings of **Terence Cuneo** (b 1907) are remarkable for their animated life and energy. An outstanding example is his reconstruction of the opening of the Stockton & Darlington Railway.

Nathaniel Currier (1813–88) and James Ives (1824–95) formed a partnership in the USA in 1857 and for over 50 years mass produced about three lithographs every week, hand-coloured by one girl per colour. They depicted accurately every aspect of American life, and a great many were pictures of railways.

The earliest known photograph of a locomotive is a Calotype of the Crampton 4–2–0 No. 134 *Folkstone* [*sic*] built by Robert Stephenson & Company for the South Eastern Railway in 1851. It was exhibited at the Great Exhibition of 1851 in the Crystal Palace in Hyde Park, London, where the photograph was taken. The Calotype process was patented in 1841 by William Henry Fox Talbot (1800–77).

RAILWAY ARCHITECTURE

In Victorian England the railway was almost alone in maintaining a high standard of architectural design. The most outstanding examples of fine design were the great viaducts and tunnel entrances, displaying a simplicity of form unique at the time. Some of the leading architects applied their skills to

The earliest known photograph of a locomotive, showing South Eastern Railway Crampton 4–2–0 No. 134 *Folkstone* at the Great Exhibition in the Crystal Palace, London, in 1851. The elliptical plate on the original clearly reads: 'Stephenson & Co. Engineers Newcastle—Crampton Patentee—South Eastern Railway—London to Paris via Folkstone [*sic*] & Boulogne & Dover & Calais' (Victoria & Albert Museum, London)

railway stations, but for these they often chose exotic and extravagant styles.

Famous examples were:

London, Euston Station, the Doric Arch and Great Hall designed by Philip Charles Hardwick (see p. 22).
Newcastle upon Tyne Station built in 1846–55 in the Classical style, by John Dobson (1787–1865).
London King's Cross Station, 1851–2, in a style of the utmost dignity and simplicity by Lewis Cubitt (1799–1883).
Huddersfield Station designed by J P Pritchett & Son has a magnificent central edifice flanked by Corinthian Colonnades. It was built in 1847–8.
London St Pancras Station, 1866–75, is one of the greatest pieces of Victorian Gothic, by Sir Gilbert Scott (1811–78). To pass through this building and to emerge beneath Barlow's tremendous arched roof is a startling experience.
York Station on the former North Eastern Railway is one of the finest examples in England, constructed in 1871–7 with three great arched roofs laid out in a long curve. The architects were Thomas Prosser, Benjamin Burley and William Peachy. (See colour photographs, pp. 39 and 79.)

Outstanding examples in Europe and America are:

Paris, Gare du Nord, 1861–5, by Jacques Ignace Hittorf (1793–1867), and **Gare de l'Est**, 1847–52, by François Duquesney (1800–49).
Boston, Massachusetts, Kneeland Street Station by Gridley J F Bryant (1816–97) was the most completely equipped station in America when it was completed in 1847.
Philadelphia, Broad Street Station on the Reading Railroad, designed by F H Kimball (1849–1919) and built in 1891–3, has a distinguished building displaying Renaissance features, and the greatest of all arched roofs, of 91·44 m (300 ft) span, by Wilson Brothers & Company, Engineers.
Helsinki Station, designed in 1905 by the Finnish architect Eliel Saarinen (1873–1950) was not completed until 1914. It is one of the finest in Europe.
Stuttgart Station, the work of the German architect Paul Bonats (1877–1951), is a leading example of modern station architecture. It was built in 1928.

Central Station, Newcastle upon Tyne

St Pancras Station, London

Some of the finest examples of modern station design are to be found on the London Underground system, mostly built in the 1920s and 1930s, by Adams, Holden and Pearson, largely inspired by Frank Pick (1878–1941).

The station at Thornaby, Teesside, Yorkshire, exhibited a notice asking passengers: 'Have you observed the varied carvings on the string cornices of the station buildings?' The notice has gone, but the carvings remain and are worth examining.

Detail of string cornice and chamfered stone, brick and woodwork on Thornaby Station, Teesside. The string cornice goes round all the buildings in fantastic variety. Were it inside one of our English cathedrals it would attract wide recognition (Simon Marshall)

RAILWAYS AND STAMPS

The first postage stamps with a railway subject were three issued in New Brunswick, Canada, in 1860. They were of 1 cent value, coloured brown-purple, purple and dull claret, and showed an inside-cylinder 4–4–0 with spark-arresting chimney.

The United States depicted the opening of its first transcontinental line in 1869 with a blue 3 cent stamp showing a Norris-type 4–4–0 with inclined cylinders and spark-arresting chimney. In 1944 the 75th anniversary of the transcontinental railway was marked by the issue of another blue 3 cent stamp showing the famous last spike ceremony.

The Pan American Exhibition at Buffalo in 1901 was marked by the issue of special stamps, one, a red 2 cent, showing the 'Empire State Express' headed by New York Central & Hudson River Railroad 4–4–0 No. 999.

Peru issued three stamps in 1871 showing arms and an early 2–2–2 locomotive. By 1962 Peru had issued 34 different stamps carrying railway subjects.

Belgium was the first country to issue rail parcel stamps, when the railway-operated parcel service began in 1879. The first issues, 1879–82, carried a winged wheel emblem. Issues from 1882–94 showed an early locomotive in the background. By 1964 a total of 387 different stamps had been issued.

The United States issued a set of parcel-post stamps in 1912–13. One of these, a rose-carmine 5 cent, showed a mail train headed by a 2–6–2 'Prairie' locomotive.

The Central American States, Mexico and West Indies have issued many stamps carrying railway subjects. **Guatemala** introduced railway tax stamps in 1886. **Nicaragua** produced ten stamps in 1890 bearing arms and a train, and by 1937 had issued a total of 113 stamps carrying railway subjects. **Salvador** issued 16 stamps in 1891 showing a train and a mountain. **Mexico** made ten issues in 1895–8 illustrating an early mail train. **Honduras** followed in 1898 with eight issues showing an early steam train.

The first Asian country to issue stamps of railway subjects was North Borneo, in 1912, with two showing an early train.

China issued its first stamp with a railway subject in 1913. By 1966 a total of 156 had been issued.

Russia produced a stamp showing a train in 1922, and by 1966 had issued a total of 111.

A century of friendship between the USA and Canada, 1848–1948, was celebrated by the issue of a USA blue 3 cent stamp showing the Niagara gorge suspension bridge of 1848 as strengthened by Roebling to carry trains in 1855. (See 'Some American Bridge Records'.)

Belgium was the first country to issue railway centenary stamps, in 1935, with a set of over 20 railway parcel stamps from 1 Fr to 100 Fr, of 15 different colours, showing the first locomotive built in Belgium, State Railways 2–2–2 No. 6 *Le Belge*, built by John Cockerill at Seraing to a Stephenson design. They marked the centenary of the opening of the Brussels–Malines line on 5 May 1835. In 1949–52 there appeared a set of 18 railway parcel stamps featuring famous Belgian locomotives, the first again showing *Le Belge*. An extra 300 Fr stamp (purple) issued in 1952 showed an electric train of 1951.

Germany celebrated the opening of the Nuremberg–Fürth line on 7 December 1835 by the issue of a set of stamps in 1935 showing the Robert Stephenson 2–2–2 *Der Adler* (The Eagle).

French stamps issued on 31 May 1937 to celebrate the 13th International Railway Congress in Paris. Swedish stamps issued on 27 August 1975, showing 0–6–0 tank *Fryckstad* of 1855; 0–6–0 tank *Gotland* of 1878, and Beattie 2–4–0 *Prinz August*, built by Beyer Peacock, Manchester, 1856.

Switzerland's first locomotive *Limmat* appeared on a 5 cent stamp in 1947 to celebrate the centenary of the opening of the Zürich–Baden line on 9 August 1847. In addition there were three other stamps showing railway scenes and four showing Swiss stations.

Other countries which marked their railway centenaries on stamps included: Austria, 1937; Italy, 1939; Hungary, 1946; Denmark, 1947; Yugoslavia, 1949; Chile, 1951; India, 1953; Australia, Brazil, Norway, 1954; Sweden, 1956; Argentina, Egypt, 1957.

The USA missed its railway centenary, but made up by celebrating the 125th anniversary of the Baltimore & Ohio Railroad Charter of 1827 with a blue 3 cent stamp in 1952, showing a horse passenger-carriage, an inaccurate replica of the first steam locomotive, *Tom Thumb*, and a diesel-electric locomotive.

Similarly Australia's 125th anniversary in 1962 and Jamaica's in 1970 were celebrated by stamp issues.

Japan issued the first two stamps, both 20 yen, in a series of ten showing steam trains, on 26 November 1974.

Great Britain issued its first railway stamps on 13 August 1975 to commemorate the 150th anniversary of the opening, on 27 September 1825, of the Stockton & Darlington Railway. The stamps, designed by Brian Craker, showed Stephenson's *Locomotion* of 1825 (7p); North British Railway 4–4–0 *Abbotsford* of 1876 (8p); Great Western Railway 'Castle' Class 4–6–0 *Caerphilly Castle* of 1923 (10p); and the British Rail High Speed Train of 1975 (12p). The subjects were cleverly chosen to satisfy the English, Scottish and Welsh.

The Isle of Man and Jersey both issued their own railway centenary stamps in 1973, of $2\frac{1}{2}$p, $7\frac{1}{2}$p and 9p values. They carried pictures of locomotives.

The Railway Philatelic Group makes a special study of Railway Stamps. Honorary Secretary: Peter Johnson, 20 Rockley Road, Leicester LE4 0GJ.

The carriage of letters by rail was legalised in Britain by agreement with the Postmaster-General in 1891. The additional rate was 2d (two old pence). On 15 January 1920 it was

Cover of a letter posted on the South Eastern Railway in February 1881 showing the railway postage stamp in addition to the two Post Office Half-penny stamps. This was 10 years before the carriage of letters by railway was legalised in Britain

increased to 3d when the Post Office letter rate was 1½d. It was again increased to 4d on 1 September 1920 when postage became 2d. (The Post Office rate was later reduced, again to 1½d.) The stamps were green and identical except for the name of the railway company. The last stamps were issued in 1920.

RAILWAYS AND MUSIC

One of the earliest composers to be influenced by the railway was the Dane, Hans Christian Lumbye (1810–74), whose *Københavns Jernbane Damp-Galop* or *Jernbane Galop* (Railway Galop) is an exhilarating orchestral item.

Hector Berlioz (1803–69) composed his *Chant des chemins de fer* (Railway Song) for tenor, chorus and orchestra in 1846. It was a setting of a poem by the French journalist, novelist and critic Jules Gabriel Janin (1804–74), commissioned to celebrate the opening of the Chemins de fer du Nord and first performed at Lille on 14 June 1846. In Britain the first performance of the full score was given by the Royal Philharmonic Orchestra and John Aldis Choir at a concert in the Royal Albert Hall, London, to celebrate the 150th anniversary of the Stockton & Darlington Railway, in September 1975. It was performed again, by the Huddersfield Philharmonic Orchestra, College of Ripon and York St John Choir and Saddleworth Musical Society, at a promenade concert of railway music conducted by Arthur Butterworth (see below) in the National Railway Museum, York, on 13 June 1976 as part of the York Festival.

Johann Strauss junior (1825–99) wrote a fast polka *Vergnügungszug* (Excursion Train), opus 281, in 1864.

His brother Eduard Strauss (1835–1916) composed an entertaining polka, *Bahn Frei*, opus 45, a musical train ride complete with guard's whistle and engine hooter, and followed it by *Mit Dampf* (With Steam), opus 70.

The Czech composer Antonin Dvořák (1841–1904) was a keen railway enthusiast and made daily visits to the Franz Josefs Station in Prague where he was friendly with many engine crews. On one occasion he was too busy to go, so he asked his future son-in-law, Josef Suk, to go and note the number of the engine on a particular train. The young man returned with the number of the tender by mistake, and Dvořák remarked to his daughter 'So this is the sort of man you intend to marry!'

The Swiss composer Arthur Honegger (1892–1955) was fascinated by the steam locomotive and in 1924 wrote his famous symphonic movement for orchestra *Pacific 231*. The figures 231 refer to the French axle notation. In the Whyte system a 'Pacific' is a 4–6–2.

The Brazilian composer Hector Villa-Lobos (1887–1959) gave us a delightful musical picture of a Brazilian narrow-gauge train in 'The Little Train of the Caipira' which forms the final toccata section of his second *Bachianas Brasilieras* (Brazilian Bach pieces), composed in 1930.

Vivian Ellis (b 1904) wrote a short orchestral piece (about 4 min) entitled 'Coronation Scot' about 1937–8. Actually it was inspired by the rhythms of trains on the Great Western Railway in Somerset. The title was given by the publisher, because the *Coronation Scot* of the London, Midland & Scottish Railway was much in the news at the time. It was published in a piano arrangement in a cover carrying a crude picture of the London & North Eastern Railway *Coronation* train.

The British composer **Arthur Butterworth (b 1923)** composed *Trains in the Distance* to a commission for the Saddleworth Festival, Yorkshire, in 1971. It is scored for orator, tape recording, chorus and orchestra, and is a setting of poems about trains by Gilbert Thomas, Charles Armstrong Fox, Thomas Wolfe, Siegfried Sassoon, Robert Louis Stevenson, Vivian de Sola Pinto, Alfred Noyes, Lawrence Durrell and Horatio Browne. It formed the first part of the concert in the National Railway Museum on 13 June 1976 (see above).

The British composer and conductor **Eugene Goossens (1893–1962)** was a knowledgeable railway enthusiast, as was **Constant Lambert** (1905–51). There have been many other organists, conductors, composers and performers with a keen interest in railways.

Section 7
RAILWAY MUSEUMS AND PRESERVATION

The earliest museum devoted wholly to transport grew out of an industrial exhibition at Nuremberg in 1882 in the form of a collection recording the development of the Bavarian railways. It was opened to the public in 1899.

The first true railway museum to be opened to the public was established at Hamar in Norway, about 128 km (80 miles) north of Oslo, in 1897. It is administered by Norwegian State Railways supported by the Norwegian Railway Club. It displays standard- and narrow-gauge locomotives and rolling stock and a varied collection of railway equipment.

The first British museum to display railway equipment was the 'South Kensington Museum of Science and the Pure and Applied Arts', London. It was an outcome of the Great Exhibition of 1851, following a proposal by Prince Albert, and was established in 1857. The first railway locomotive to be acquired, in 1862, was the Stephensons' *Rocket*, followed in 1864 by *Sans Pareil* by Timothy Hackworth (qv) which was presented by John Hick of Bolton. In 1874 the scientific, engineering and art collections were united as the South Kensington Museum until, in 1899, the name became the Victoria and Albert Museum. In 1909 the scientific and engineering collection was rehoused in a separate building as the **Science Museum**. It houses a fine collection of railway material. Locomotives include *Puffing Billy*, the first Great Western 'Castle' Class 4–6–0 and the pioneer 'Deltic' diesel-electric. There is also one of the finest collections of scale models of locomotives and rolling stock to be found anywhere. Other exhibits include track, signalling, and bridge models. Admission is free and the museum is open 10.00–18.00 on weekdays and 14.30–18.00 on Sundays.

The first steps towards a British railway museum were taken in the 1890s when a council was formed to consider the idea. It included Archibald Sturrock (1816–1909), former locomotive superintendent of the Great Northern Railway; W M Acworth, the railway historian; and Alfred Rosling Bennett (1850–1928), author of *The Chronicles of Boulton's Siding*. The president was Charles Rous-Marten (1844–1908), the well-known recorder of locomotive performance. The scheme was actively discouraged by the railway companies and was dropped. Bennett tried to revive it but Rous-Marten, probably trying to maintain his favour with the railway companies, discouraged it and it made no progress.

On the North Eastern Railway, however, progress was being made. As so frequently happens in matters of this kind, everything depended on the enthusiasm and determination of one man, John Bradford Harper (1853–1935), whose entire working life was spent on the NER. One of the constituents of the NER was the Stockton & Darlington Railway which was absorbed in 1863. To celebrate the 50th anniversary of the opening of the S. & D., in September 1875, the NER organised a jubilee celebration in Darlington. Harper had in mind this rich historical heritage when, in 1890, he became station master at York. He immediately began to collect railway items of historical interest which he stored at York. On 31 December 1922 Harper retired from the position of assistant general superintendent and on the following day the NER became part of the London & North Eastern Railway which thereby inherited the historical relics.

Soon steps were being taken to celebrate the centenary of the S. & D. in 1925. Following this great event the LNER housed various old locomotives in the machine shop of the former

The world's fastest steam locomotive, London & North Eastern Railway *Mallard*, as exhibited in the Museum of British Transport at Clapham, London in 1970

GWR 0–6–0 No. 2516, designed by William Dean and built in 1897, at the Great Western Railway Museum, Swindon

York & North Midland Railway at York. Into it went **Britain's first privately preserved locomotive**, the 0–4–2 No. 214 *Gladstone*, designed by William Stroudley for the London, Brighton & South Coast Railway and built at Brighton in 1882, and purchased by the Stephenson Locomotive Society in 1927.

In 1928 the collection was opened to the public as **the first British railway museum**. New items were constantly moved in and by 1 January 1948 when, with nationalisation of the railways, the museum was taken over by the British Transport Commission, it was becoming overcrowded. Admission charges were introduced in 1957.

At this time work was in progress on two other railway museums. In London the **Museum of British Transport** was established in a former London transport garage at Clapham under the guidance of John Scholes. As its name implied, this was a museum of all forms of transport, and besides railway equipment it contained marine exhibits, horse carriages, buses, trams, fire-engines, in fascinating variety, collected together on a 'shoestring' budget and well displayed. It was fully opened in 1963.

At Swindon, the home of the Locomotive Department of the Great Western Railway, a museum was opened in Faringdon Road on 23 June 1962. **The Great Western Railway Museum** is housed in a building of historical interest in itself. It began as a hostel for GWR employees; in 1869 it became a Wesleyan chapel where the locomotive superintendent Joseph Armstrong (1816–77) was a local preacher. It contains a full-size replica of the 2·134 m (7 ft) gauge *North Star*; the 4–4–0 *City of Truro*; the only remaining 'Star' Class 4–6–0; a Dean 0–6–0 and a pannier tank, as well as numerous GWR items. It is maintained by Swindon Borough Council and is open on weekdays 10.00–17.00 and Sundays 14.00–17.00.

After 4 years of uncertainty, in which BR expressed growing concern at the losses sustained on the railway museums, the Transport Act of 1968 provided for the closure of the museums at Clapham and York and for the opening of a new railway museum at York, with responsibility transferred to the Department of Education and Science, as a branch of the Science Museum.

Clapham Museum was closed on 23 April 1973, despite the fact that there was more than enough material at York and in the National Collection scattered around the country to fill the new museum at York without removing anything from Clapham except for exchange. In its 4½ years it was visited by nearly 1 750 000 people. Following its closure its creator, John Scholes, declined; and he died on 1 July 1977 at the age of 63.

The National Railway Museum, Leeman Road, York YO2 4XJ, is housed in part of the former North Eastern Railway locomotive depot, suitably rebuilt. It was opened by the Duke of Edinburgh on 27 September 1975, the 150th anniversary of the opening of the Stockton & Darlington Railway. The main exhibits stand on tracks radiating from two turntables. This permits any item to be removed without difficulty, facilitating exchange of items with other museums or the removal of a locomotive for running under its own steam. Permanent exhibits include the Great Northern Railway 4–2–2 No. 1 by Patrick Stirling (1820–95), with its 2·438 m (8 ft) driving-wheels; and a sectioned Southern Railway 4–6–2 by Oliver Bulleid.

Attendances at the NRM exceeded expectations: the millionth visitor arrived on 22 April 1976, the two millionth on 9 September, less than a year after opening, and the three millionth on 28 June 1977, an average of over 6000 on every day opened. The record was 50 804 on 19 April 1976. The museum includes a library for serious researchers, a bookshop and restaurant facilities.

The primary function of the NRM is education. Hence a large portion of its visitors consists of school parties, assisted by the absence of admission charges. In these respects it differs from the Clapham museum where the emphasis was more on display and contrast, leaving the interested visitor to learn what he could. It is open 10.00–18.00 weekdays and 14.30–18.00 on Sundays. Closed New Year's Day; Good Friday; May Day; Christmas Eve; Christmas Day; Boxing Day.

Darlington, North Road Station Museum. Following the opening of the National Railway Museum, on 27 September 1975, the Duke of Edinburgh travelled to Darlington, on the prototype High Speed Train, and there opened the North Road Station Museum. This occupies the former Stockton & Darlington Railway Station of 1842 on the Bishop Auckland branch. Locomotives on display, on loan from the NRM, all have close associations with Darlington: Stephenson's *Locomotion* of 1825; the Hackworth 0–6–0 *Derwent* of 1845, built by Kitching of Darlington; North Eastern Railway 'Tennant' Class 2–4–0 No. 1463 of 1885; and a Stockton & Darlington Railway coach. Other items on temporary loan may also be seen. The museum, run as a charitable trust, welcomes and needs support. It is open daily, 10.00–17.00 and on Sunday afternoons in summer, for a small admission charge.

Great Western Preservations Limited, Didcot Railway Centre, close to Didcot Station, Oxfordshire. Here is the largest collection of GWR locomotives and rolling stock to be seen anywhere. The museum is open 11.00–17.00 on Sundays from Easter to September, with steaming displays at holiday times. It is less than 30 km ($18\frac{1}{2}$ miles) from Swindon, and by careful timing both museums can be seen on one day.

The Narrow Gauge Railway Museum, Towyn, Gwynedd, Wales, must be included in a visit to the Tal-y-llyn Railway (see p. 239). It began with the donation by the Guinness Brewery at Dublin of one of their 0–4–0 locomotives in 1956. Other items accumulated and a new building was erected at Towyn Station. The museum was opened by John Scholes on 29 September 1959. Among the various locomotives is the 457 mm (18 in) gauge 0–4–0 saddle tank *Pet*, designed by John Ramsbottom and built in 1865 for the internal railway at the LNWR Works at Crewe. The engines built for this system from 1862 were **the earliest narrow-gauge locomotives**. The museum also contains many railway items associated with the Welsh slate industry. Open 09.00–17.00 at Easter, and daily from May to October.

The slate industry is also represented at the **Penrhyn Castle Museum**, owned by the National Trust, at Llandegai near Bangor, Gwynedd. Here also is a unique locomotive, the 0–4–0 *Fire Queen*, one of two built by A. Horlock of Northfleet Iron Works, Kent, in 1848, for the 1·219 m (4 ft) gauge Padarn Railway. This is probably **the oldest sub-standard-gauge locomotive in existence**. An extraordinary feature is that it has no frame, everything being attached to the boiler. The museum is open daily from 1 April to 31 October.

Birmingham Railway Museum, Warwick Road, Tyseley, Birmingham, was established in the former GWR Engine Shed at Tyseley and is operated by the **Standard Gauge Steam Trust**. It houses an LMS 'Jubilee' 4–6–0 and an interesting collection of GWR locomotives. Open Sunday afternoons.

Birmingham Museum of Science and Industry, Newhall Street. Open weekdays and Sunday afternoons; admission free. Among several steam locomotives on display is one of the few built in Birmingham, the 826 mm (2 ft $8\frac{1}{2}$ in) gauge *Secundus* (*c* 1874) from the Furzebrook Tramway in Dorset. By contrast there is also the Stanier LMS 'Pacific' No. 46235 *City of*

Birmingham (1939). The museum also contains numerous fascinating examples of steam-engines and machinery.

Bressingham Steam Museum, Norfolk, 4 km (2½ miles) west of Diss on the A1066 Diss–Thetford road, was established in 1963–4 by Alan Bloom as an addition to his nursery gardens. A magnificent collection of standard-gauge locomotives is displayed, including four from the National Collection. There are two 'Pacifics', and the last 'Garratt' to work in Britain (see p. 133). Visitors can ride on three narrow-gauge steam railways of 241 mm (9½ in), 260 mm (10¼ in) and 600 mm (1 ft 11½ in) gauges. There are also steam road vehicles, traction engines, steam-rollers, organs and a steam roundabout. Open Thursdays, Sundays and Bank Holidays, May to September.

The Midland Railway Trust, Butterley near Ripley, Derbyshire, is rapidly developing a project in conjunction with Derby Museum. Locomotives on display include three from the National Collection: Kirtley 2–4–0 No. 158A, originally built in 1866 (see 'Veteran Locomotives'); Johnson 4–2–2 No. 673 built in 1899; and LMS 0–6–0 Class '4F', 1924. The largest engine is LMS Pacific No. 6203 *Princess Margaret Rose* (1935). Ultimately the railway from Butterley to Pye Bridge will be restored as a typical stretch of the Midland Railway on which the stock will operate. This museum is only about 8 km (5 miles) from the Crich Tramway Museum described below. It is open at week-ends. (See colour photograph of the MR 4–2–2, p. 75.)

Crich Tramway Museum, Crich, near Ambergate, Derbyshire, houses the largest collection of electric trams (or streetcars) in Great Britain. The **Tramway Museum Society** was founded in 1955 and the museum was begun in 1959 in a large limestone quarry which was opened by George Stephenson in 1841. (See 'The first metre-gauge railway' p. 29.) A 1·2 km (¾ mile) line has been laid on which the trams operate a passenger service. The terminus recalls the Edwardian British tramway scene. Besides British trams there are examples from Czechoslovakia and Portugal and a steam-tram engine built by Beyer Peacock, Manchester, in 1885. Open Saturdays, Sundays and Bank Holidays April to October, 11.30–19.30; Tuesdays to Thursdays also in July and August.

Dinting Railway Centre near Glossop, Derbyshire, about 20 km (12 miles) from Manchester, was established in 1968 as a home for the privately preserved LMS 'Jubilee' Class 4–6–0 No. 5596 *Bahamas*. The large new shed now houses an impressive collection of locomotives including the Great Central 2–8–0 from the National Collection. The Centre is open most weekdays and at weekends for a small admission charge.

Liverpool Museum, William Brown Street, Liverpool L3 8EN, houses some interesting material concerning the Liverpool & Manchester Railway, including the 0–4–2 *Lion* built by Todd, Kitson & Laird, Leeds, in 1838; and facsimiles of two L. & M. coaches. There is also an 0–6–0 saddle tank built at Bristol in 1904 for the Mersey Docks & Harbour Board.

The museum houses a valuable collection of

Glasgow Corporation tram No. 22 of 1922, beautifully restored to its original condition and now operating at the Crich Tramway Museum, Derbyshire. The tower above the quarry face is the memorial to men of the Sherwood Foresters Regiment, who fell in the 1914–18 war locomotive drawings from Vulcan Foundry Limited, Newton le Willows, Lancashire, from 1833 to 1904. A catalogue is on sale and copies of drawings may be ordered. Open weekdays 10.00–17.00, Sundays 14.00–17.00; admission free.

Steamtown, Carnforth, close to Carnforth Station, Lancashire, and just off the M6 at Junction 35. It is served by Lancaster–Barrow trains. Carnforth Engine Shed was closed in 1968 when the final steam locomotives were withdrawn from British Railways, and a private company was formed to purchase the entire depot with extensive yards, turntable, coaling tower (the only preserved example in Britain), as a home for preserved locomotives. Besides a varied collection of British main-line and industrial locomotives, there is also a large three-cylinder 'Pacific' from Germany, a four-cylinder compound 'Pacific' from France, and a German tank engine. Locomotives are in steam most week-ends.

Stanier 'Jubilee' class 4–6–0 No. 5596 *Bahamas* (1935) being prepared for steaming at the Dinting Railway Centre near Glossop, Derbyshire

Locomotives on display at Steamtown, Carnforth on 12 August 1974. On the extreme left is the French compound 4–6–2

Glasgow Museum of Transport, 25 Albert Drive, Glasgow S1, was opened by the Queen Mother on 14 April 1964. It is owned and run by Glasgow Corporation. Railway exhibits include **the first 4–6–0 on a British railway**, the Highland Railway 'Jones Goods' No. 103 of 1894 (p. 122); the Caledonian Railway 4–2–2 No. 123 of 1886 which took part in the races from London to Aberdeen; 4–4–0s from the North British and Great North of Scotland railways; and a Glasgow & South Western Railway 0–6–0 tank. Other exhibits include trams and all kinds of road vehicles, and aeroplanes. Open 10.00–17.00 weekdays and 14.00–17.00 Sundays; admission free.

Belfast Transport Museum, Witham Street, Belfast 4, was opened on 15 June 1962. It houses a magnificent collection of locomotives from all over Ireland, of 1·600 m (5 ft 3 in) gauge and 0·914 m (3 ft) gauge, including 4–6–0 No. 800 *Maeve* (1939), one of the three largest locomotives in Ireland (see p. 128). There is also a representative collection of rolling stock. Open weekdays 10.00–18.00 (21.00 Wednesdays).

AUSTRALIA

New South Wales Museum of Applied Arts and Sciences at Ultimo, Sydney. This museum houses **the first locomotive to work in NSW**, which was presented in 1884, and a second/third class carriage of about 1855. Various other locomotives await exhibition when the transport section of the museum is completed.

New South Wales Rail Transport Museum, Enfield, near Sydney. The museum displays a collection of 48 locomotives, 21 carriages and ten wagons, and railway equipment, in two old locomotive roundhouses. Sixteen of the locomotives are in operating condition. The museum is open at week-ends.

Australian Railway Historical Society Museum, North Williamstown, Melbourne, Victoria, contains 18 steam locomotives, four carriages and three goods wagons, the oldest items dating from the 1870s. Open week-ends 14.00–17.00.

Queensland Government Railways Museum near Redbank, 27 km ($16\frac{3}{4}$ miles) west of

Brisbane on the Brisbane–Ipswich line. It houses 14 steam locomotives dating from 1866 to 1958, including a large 4–8–2+2–8–4 Garratt built by Beyer Peacock, Manchester, in 1950. The Queensland Government Railways also maintains several steam locomotives, including a Garratt, for use on enthusiast specials.

Australian Railway Historical Society Museum, Railway Terrace, Mile End, Adelaide, South Australia, contains a varied collection of 19 steam locomotives dating from 1886 to 1954, two railcars, one petrol and two diesel locomotives and items of rolling stock, on a total of five different gauges. It is open from 14.00 to 17.00 on the first and third Sunday each month, when a 457 mm (18 in) gauge railway is operated.

Australian Railway Historical Society Museum at Bassendean, Perth, Western Australia, displays 21 steam locomotives, one electric locomotive and 18 items of rolling stock.

AUSTRIA

Austrian Railway Museum, A-1140 Vienna XIV, Mariahilferstrasse 212. This splendid museum, established in 1885, can easily occupy the interested visitor for one or two days. It is open Tuesdays to Fridays 09.00–16.00 and week-ends 09.00–13.00. Inside are six steam locomotives ranging from 1841 to 1900, and an enormous collection of models of locomotives, rolling stock, bridges, and other railway items, as well as full-size pieces of equipment connected with signalling, electrification, and every aspect of railway working. Dated maps and pictures line the walls all round. Here one can study the whole history of Austrian railways. Outside is a collection of steam locomotives arranged in a circular display, perfect for photographing. The adjoining Science Museum should be visited also.

CANADA

National Museum of Science and Technology, 1867 St Laurent Boulevard, Ottawa, Ontario K1A OM8. At the entrance to the museum stands a big CNR 4–8–4, No. 6200. Inside are nine steam, one diesel and one electric locomotives and various items of rolling stock dating from the earliest days of Canadian railways. A steam locomotive is frequently operated on a stretch of line outside the museum. Admission is free.

Canadian National Railways 4–8–4 No. 6200 when in course of restoration outside the National Museum of Science & Technology, Ottawa, in June 1970. It was built by Montreal Locomotive works in 1942

London & North Eastern Railway 'A4' class 4–6–2 No. 60010 *Dominion of Canada* (1937) on display alongside Canadian Pacific 4–4–0 No. 144 of 1886 at the Canadian Railroad Historical Association Museum, Delson, near Montreal, in June 1970

Canadian Railroad Historical Association Museum, Delson, about 16 km (10 miles) from Montreal on the south side of the St Lawrence River. Here is a vast collection of Canadian steam locomotives and electric trolley cars, and two British engines; A4 Class 'Pacific' No. 60010 *Dominion of Canada*, and London, Brighton & South Coast Railway 'Terrier' 0–6–0 tank No. 54 *Waddon* of 1875; also a French 0–6–0 built in 1883. Greatest of all is the Canadian Pacific Railway 'Selkirk' 2–10–4 No. 5935, the last steam locomotive to be built for a Canadian main-line system, and one of the largest. Open daily June to August 10.00–17.00, and week-ends May, September and October.

Ontario Rail Association, Box 64, Brampton, Ontario, was formed to preserve, restore and operate old Canadian railway equipment. It is developing the Credit Valley Railway on 11 km (6·8 miles) of abandoned branch line between Georgetown and Cheltenham Park, Ontario, 50 km (31 miles) north-west of Toronto, where it operates steam trains on summer week-ends.

DENMARK

Railway Museum (Jernbanemuseet), Slvegade 40, DK-1349 Copenhagen K. Twenty-five steam and two diesel locomotives are displayed, with twelve carriages, a crane, an electric suburban train and a diesel express train, presenting a comprehensive survey of Danish railway traffic. There is also a reference library of 8500 volumes, 10 000 photographs and 1000 drawings. Open Wednesdays April–October, 12.00–16.00; admission free.

EGYPT

Egyptian Railways Museum, main Railway Station, Cairo. This museum was opened on 15 January 1933 in connection with the International Railways Conference held in Cairo in that year. The exhibits include the 2–2–4 steam railcar for Said Pasha, built by Robert Stephenson & Company and delivered in 1862; a sectioned 'Atlantic' by North British Locomotive Company; and a Robert Stephenson 0–6–0 of 1865. There are also signalling exhibits, permanent way, and a magnificent collection of models and photographs illustrating not only railways but a history of transport in Egypt over a period of nearly 5000 years. Open Tuesday to Sunday 8.30–14.00; admission 2 Piastres. Closed Monday and public holidays.

FRANCE

Railway Museum, Mulhouse-Nord, rue Josué Hofer. Thirteen steam locomotives and rolling stock are temporarily displayed in the former locomotive roundhouse until completion of a permanent museum building at Mulhouse-Dornach where a total of about 48 steam and ten electric locomotives and many examples of rolling stock will be displayed.

GERMANY

Nuremberg Transport Museum, Lessingstrasse 6, displays locomotives ranging from a 2–4–0 of 1853 and a Crampton 4–2–0 of 1863 to a 4–6–4 which recorded a speed of 200 km/h (124 mph) in 1936. There is also a collection of rolling stock and other railway equipment. The museum was established in 1882 and the present building was opened on 22 April 1925.

INDIA

Indian Rail Transport Museum, Chanakyapuri, New Delhi. The first positive steps towards the establishment of this museum were taken in 1970. Adviser, and one of the prime movers in the project, was Mr M G Satow. At its opening on 1 February 1977 there were 28 locomotives of various gauges and 15 items of rolling stock. At present the museum covers only 10 of the 26 acres available; when completed it may well be the largest railway museum in the world. Inside the museum building are galleries depicting the history of Indian railways since 1850, locomotive and rolling stock development, and civil engineering. Among the locomotives is an 'N' Class 4–8–0+0–8–4 Garratt (1929) from the 1·676 m (5 ft 6 in) gauge Bengal–Nagpur Railway; the 16 engines of this class were the largest in India. The oldest engine is the 5 ft 6 in gauge East Indian Railway 2–2–2 well tank No. 22 *Fairy Queen* (1855). The oddest engine is the 0–3–0 tank No. 4 (1908) from the Patiala State Monorail Trainway

The last steam locomotive to operate on Netherlands Railways, 4–6–0 No. 3737 built in 1911 by Netherlandsche Fabriek van Werktuigen en Spoorwegmateriel, Amsterdam (No. 272), at the Netherlands Railway Museum, Utrecht

One of the first two electric locomotives in Switzerland, No. 2 of the Burgdorf–Thun Railway, type E2E, built at Winterthur in 1899 with electrical equipment by Brown Boveri, Baden, and now one of the exhibits in the Lucerne Transport Museum. The BTB was opened on 21 July 1899 and originally operated on 3-phase alternating current 750 V, 40 Hz. Next to it is the Seebach–Wettingen locomotive of 1904 described on p. 154, the world's first single-phase alternating current locomotive

(see p. 210). Enthusiasts for narrow gauge will be pleased to see one of the 0–4–0 tanks from the 610 mm (2 ft) gauge Darjeeling Himalayan Railway, No. B777 (1889). The museum is closed on Mondays.

NETHERLANDS

Netherlands Railway Museum, Utrecht, was established in 1951 at the Maliebaan Station (in Joan van Oldenbarneveltlaan) which was opened in 1874 and disused from 1939. The eight steam locomotives displayed range from a replica of *Arend* of 1839, the first locomotive to run in the Netherlands (see photograph p. 24), to the last steam locomotive, the four-cylinder 4–6–0 No. 3737 built at Amsterdam in 1911. There are numerous models and small exhibits and a model railway. Open daily except Monday.

SWITZERLAND

Swiss Institute of Transport and Communications (Verkehrshaus der Schweiz) Lidostrasse 5, Lucerne. This museum, situated beside the St Gotthard Railway, was opened on 1 July 1959 and is now **the largest and most comprehensive of its kind in Europe**. Besides a vast collection of railway material including steam and electric locomotives of various gauges, mountain rack-railway equipment and rolling stock, there are road vehicles and even a complete paddle-steamer, the *Rigi* of 1848, the oldest Swiss lake steamer, used as a restaurant. Open daily.

USA

In a vast country where the level of interest in railways is matched only by that in Britain and in Australia, there are numerous preserved locomotives and steam-operated railways. Seven of the principal railway museums are described below. For a fuller list the reader should consult the *Railway Directory and Year Book* published annually and accessible at most reference libraries.

Colorado Railroad Museum, 17155 West 44th Avenue, Golden, is easily approached along 44th Avenue out of Denver. It was established in 1958 and now houses a collection of standard and 914 mm (3 ft) gauge locomotives and rolling stock, a large 'HO' scale model railway, and a great display of Colorado railway items. The largest exhibit is a 4–8–4 built in 1940 by the Chicago, Burlington & Quincy Railroad. It stands beside the oldest engine in Colorado, Denver & Rio Grande 3 ft gauge 2–8–0 No. 346 of 1881. There is also one of the Vauclain compound rack engines from the Manitou & Pike's Peak Railway (qv). Complete narrow-gauge trains are exhibited. A large shop supplies books, photographs and pictures. Open all year, 09.00 to sunset.

National Museum of History and Technology, Smithsonian Institution, Washington, DC, displays several locomotives and items of railway rolling stock and equipment, and provides research facilities and a library for the serious student of railroad history. Open 09.00–18.30 in summer and to 16.30 in winter; admission free.

Museum of Science and Industry, Jackson Park, Chicago (near 57th Street Suburban Station), contains items of great historical interest. Besides the 0–4–0 *Mississippi* of *c* 1836 from the Natchez & Hamburg Railroad there is a replica of John Stevens's pioneer locomotive of 1825 and another of the Stephensons' *Rocket*. Outside are the record-breaking New York Central 4–4–0 No. 999 of 1893, its original 2·184 m (7 ft 2 in) drivers replaced by 1·727 m (5 ft 8 in), a giant Santa Fe 4–8–4 of 1943 and the pioneer Burlington Zephyr, the first diesel-powered streamlined train in the USA. Admission is free.

Baltimore & Ohio Transportation Museum, Pratt and Poppleton Streets, Baltimore, Maryland. This museum, opened on 2 July 1953, centres on one of the most historic railroad sites in North America, in **the world's oldest station**, opened on 24 May 1830, through which **the first telegraph messages** were sent on 24 May 1844. (See p. 201.) The main exhibits are housed in the huge 22-sided passenger car roundhouse built in 1883–4 and include a replica of Peter Cooper's *Tom Thumb* of 1829 (see p. 17); two vertical-boilered 0–4–0s of 1832 and 1836; a Norris 4–2–0 of 1837; one of the world's first 0–8–0s, of 1848; a Mason 4–4–0 of 1856; a 4–6–0 of 1863; a 'camelback' 4–6–0 of 1873; a Jersey Central 'camelback' or 'Mother Hubbard' 'Atlantic' of 1901; a large three-truck Shay (see p. 134) from the Western Maryland Railway, one of the last and finest of this type to be built, in 1945; and the first streamlined diesel locomotive, built for the B. & O. in 1937. Examples of old passenger cars and freight vehicles are also displayed. The Museum Annexe, built in 1891, houses a fascinating collection of small exhibits. Open Wednesday to Sunday 10.00–16.00. Admission free.

The Baltimore Streetcar Museum at 1901 Falls Road, Baltimore, has a collection of horse and electric cars which operate on a 800 m (½-mile) line.

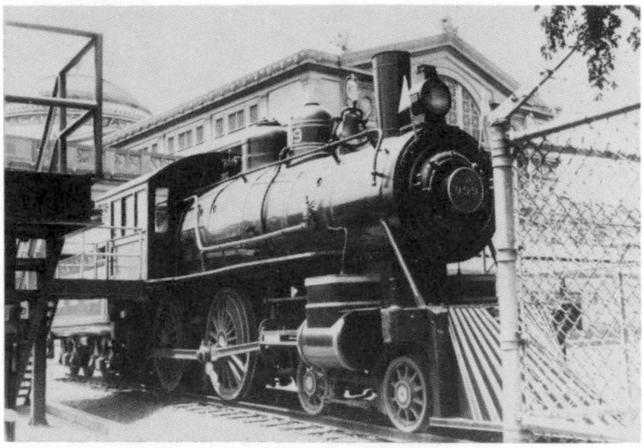

The record-breaking New York Central 4–4–0 No. 999 of 1893 standing outside the Museum of Science & Industry, Chicago, in 1970, having long ago lost its giant 2·184 m (7 ft 2 in) driving wheels

Former Ferrocarriles Mexicano 762 mm (2 ft 6 in) gauge 2–8–0 No. 12 (Baldwin, Philadelphia, 1912) at Edaville Museum, South Carver, Massachusetts

Edaville Railroad and Museum, South Carver, Massachusetts. Founded in 1946 by Ellis D. Atwood who named the railway after himself. It was later purchased by F. Nelson Blount, founder of Steamtown Museum. Besides displaying an interesting range of locomotives and rolling stock of gauges from 610 mm (2 ft) to standard, the 2 ft gauge Edaville Railroad operates passenger trains on an 8·85 km (5½ mile) circuit in the heart of the Cranberry country.

Steamtown USA Museum, 3 km (2 miles) north of Bellows Falls, Vermont. Here is the largest collection of steam locomotives to be found in the USA, and probably in the world; about 50 ranging from little 0–4–0 saddle tanks to the Union Pacific 4–8–8–4 'Big Boy' No. 4012 of 1941, an example of the world's largest steam locomotive type. Locomotives from England, Ireland and Belgium are also on display. It was established by F. Nelson

Canadian Pacific 4–6–2 No. 1246 (Montreal 1946) on a train on the Green Mountain Railroad at the Steamtown Railroad Museum at Bellows Falls, Vermont. The engine is named *F. Nelson Blount* after the founder of the Museum

Blount (1918–67). Adjoining the Museum is the Green Mountain Railroad on which passengers can travel 21 km (13 miles) out and then back in old-time passenger cars behind veteran steam locomotives. Open daily from 09.30.

This is a brief selection from a great number of museums. Addresses of others and of preservation societies can be found in the current *Railway Directory & Year Book*; and in the annual *Steam*, the official Year Book and Steam Guide of the Association of Railway Preservation Societies, published by Haraton Ltd, are addresses of all railway museums and preservation societies in the British Isles.

RAILWAY PRESERVATION SOCIETIES

(See also 'Narrow-Gauge Railways'.)

There are numerous railway preservation societies in Great Britain and abroad operating both working lines and preservation centres. Membership is open to all and provides opportunities for interesting work, whatever one's skills, and for making friends. The railways and societies are listed with addresses in *The Railway Directory and Year Book*, in most large libraries. Times of trains on operating British preserved railways are contained in the full British Rail timetable.

The first privately preserved railway was the 686 mm (2 ft 3 in) gauge Tal-y-llyn Railway from Towyn to Abergynolwyn in Wales, 11·7 km (7¼ miles) long. It was first opened for slate traffic in December 1865 and for passengers in October 1866. Following the death of the owner, Sir Henry Haydn Jones, in July 1950 a group of enthusiasts led by the late L T C Rolt took over the railway and its equipment and continued the passenger service. In the following years track was renewed, new locomotives and rolling stock were acquired and old ones rebuilt. A new 1·2 km (¾ mile) extension from Abergynolwyn to Nant Gwernol was opened in May 1976. Its success inspired the restoration of the Festiniog Railway and the railway preservation movement throughout the world. The full story of the rescue and restoration is told in Rolt's book *Railway Adventure*, 1953. Address: Wharf Station, Towyn, Gwynedd.

The Festiniog Railway, 597 mm (1 ft 11½ in) gauge (see 'The world's first public narrow-gauge railway') ended its passenger service in 1939 and slate traffic in 1946. It lay derelict until the early 1950s when a controlling interest was bought by Mr Alan Pegler. With the assistance of a voluntary preservation society trains began running again over the Cob at Porthmadog in 1955. Gradually the line was rebuilt until, in 1958, trains worked through to Tan-y-Bwlch, 12 km (7½ miles). After 10 years of consolidation a further 3·2 km (2 miles) were opened in 1968. Meanwhile, in 1955, the then British Electricity Authority began work on a pump-storage hydro-electric power-station involving compulsory purchase of part of the line near Tan-y-Grisiau. After **the longest series of court cases in British legal history** (involving two Lands Tribunals and a House of Lords Committee), in 1971 compensation was obtained enabling the company to construct a deviation round the power-station including a tunnel 645 m (705 yd) long through which the first official trains passed on 25 June 1977. Part of this deviation was opened on 8 July 1977 enabling trains to run to a temporary terminus at Llyn Ystradau and it was fully opened to Tan-y-Grisiau on 24 June 1978. It is hoped to have the railway completed to a new central station at Blaenau Ffestiniog by Easter 1980. The total length of run will be 21 km (13 miles). (See C E Spooner; Robert Fairlie.) Address: Harbour Station, Porthmadog.

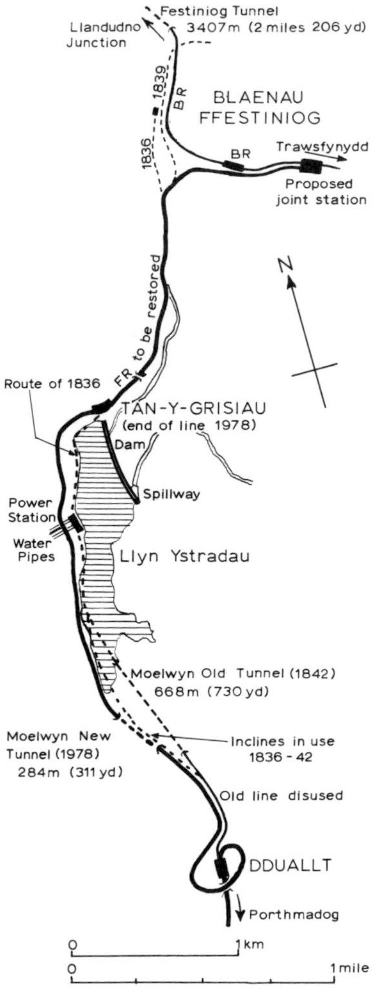

Map of the Festiniog Railway, Dduallt–Blaenau Ffestiniog. Plans are being prepared for a joint BR/FR station at Blaenau Ffestiniog on the site of the former GWR station near the town centre, to open in the early 1980s

The Welshpool & Llanfair Railway, Montgomeryshire, is a 762 mm (2 ft 6 in) gauge railway 13 km (8 miles) long, with severe gradients including a mile of 1 in 30 (3·3 per cent). It was opened on 4 April 1903. Passenger services ended on 7 February 1931 and freight on 31 October 1956. A preservation society was incorporated on 4 January 1960 and part of the railway was reopened from Llanfair Caerinion on 6 April 1963. Running was extended to Sylfaen on 15 July 1972. There are some interesting locomotives including the two original Beyer Peacock 0–6–0 tanks, a Bagnall, (Stafford) Meyer type 0–4–4–0 articulated tank engine of 1953, **the last narrow-gauge steam-engine to be built in Britain for ordinary commercial use there**; and a 0–8–0 tank, **the most powerful narrow-gauge steam locomotive in Wales**. It was built in 1944 as a 0–8–0 tender engine with short side tanks by the Société Franco-Belge, Raismes, France, for the German Military railways. On 6 January 1946 it was lent to the Salzkammergutlokalbahn, Austria, which bought it on 1 April 1950. In 1955 it was resold to the Styrian Provincial Railways, Austria, which rebuilt it in 1957 with full-length side tanks and bunker. In 1965 it was put into store until 1969 when it was bought by the W. & L. (See illustration on p. 146.) There is also a large 0–6–2 tank built in 1927 by Kerr Stuart, Stoke on Trent, for the Antiguan Sugar Company, and acquired by the W. & L. in 1971. Among the passenger stock are some four-wheelers from the Zillertalbahn, Austria (see p. 212), built in the early 1900s. Address: Llanfair Caerinion Station.

Isle of Man Railway. The first section of the 914 mm (3 ft) gauge Isle of Man Railway was opened from Douglas to Peel on 1 July 1873. The branch to Port Erin opened on 2 August 1874. The system was completed by the Manx Northern Railway from St Johns on the Peel line to Ramsey, opened on 23 September 1879 and the Foxdale Branch opened in June 1886. The system totalled 74 km (46 miles).

Following heavy losses the system was closed in 1965 but was reopened as a private venture in 1967. This, too, failed and it was decided to maintain the Douglas–Port Erin line of 25 km (15½ miles) assisted by the Isle of Man Steam Railway Supporters' Association. In 1975 this was reduced to the Castletown–Port Erin section and traffic, divorced from Douglas, dwindled. After difficult negotiations services were restored between Douglas and Port Erin on 15 May 1977 with financial support from Tynwald, the Manx Government. The railway is operated by Beyer Peacock 2–4–0 tanks, some over a century old. It provides one of the most delightful train journeys in the British Isles. Address: The Railway Station, Douglas.

The first British standard-gauge railway to be preserved was the Bluebell Railway between Sheffield Park and Horsted Keynes in Sussex, 8 km (5 miles). It is part of a route from East

Beyer Peacock 2–4–0 tank No. 14 *Thornhill* on a Douglas–Ramsey train at St Johns on the 914 mm (3 ft) gauge Isle of Man Railway in 1959. This section is now abandoned and trains operate only between Douglas and Port Erin

Restoring Southern Railway 'N' class 2–6–0 No. 1618 at Sheffield Park on the Bluebell Railway

Grinstead to Culver Junction north of Lewes built by the London, Brighton & South Coast Railway and opened on 1 August 1882. It was finally closed on 16 March 1958. **The Bluebell Railway Preservation Society** was formed in June 1959 and the piece of line was reopened on 7 August 1960. At Horsted Keynes it connected with the branch from Haywards Heath, but when this closed on 28 October 1963 it was severed from British Railways. The oldest locomotives are LBSCR 'Terrier' 0–6–0 tanks No. 72 *Fenchurch* (1872) and No. 55 *Stepney* (1875). There is also a Fletcher Jennings (Whitehaven) 0–4–0 tank of 1877. Another engine of great value is the Adams 4–4–2 tank No. 488 of 1885, built by the London & South Western Railway; and a Bulleid 'West Country' 'Pacific' built in 1946 and restored to Southern Railway livery as No. 21C23 *Blackmore Vale*. Trains operate at week-ends all year and on weekdays in summer. Address: Sheffield Park Station, near Uckfield, Sussex.

The longest British preserved railway is operated by the **North Yorkshire Moors Historical Railway Trust**, 29 km (18 miles) from Pickering to Grosmont through the great Newton Dale, an ancient glacial spillway. It is part of the former Whitby & Pickering Railway built by George Stephenson and opened in 1836. In 1847 it was absorbed by the York & North Midland Railway which, in the same year, extended it southwards to join the York–Scarborough line near Malton. In 1854 it became part of the North Eastern Railway. The original rope-worked incline below Goathland was replaced in 1865 by the present steeply graded line. Traffic was always heavy. However, under Dr Beeching it was decided in London that the line was losing money and so it was closed from 6 March 1965, despite vigorous local protests.

The first meeting of the preservation society was held on 3 June 1967 under threat of imminent track removal by BR. It was decided to aim to preserve the entire section from Grosmont, still served by trains between Whitby and Middlesbrough, to Pickering. A company known as the 'North Yorkshire Moors Railway Limited' was formed to negotiate with BR. South of Pickering the track was unfortunately removed, ostensibly to eliminate several level crossings. After a

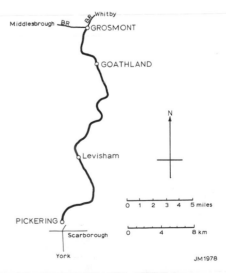

Map of the North Yorkshire Moors Railway

long hard struggle the society raised enough money to acquire part of the line. In March 1972 the preservation society and the limited company combined to form the North Yorkshire Moors Historical Railway Trust, with charitable status. Work went ahead and on 1 May 1973 the line from Grosmont to Pickering was officially reopened by HRH The Duchess of Kent, and with the granting of a Light Railway Order a public train service was reinstated.

The North Yorkshire Moors Railway can justifiably claim, with the Festiniog, the finest scenery traversed by any preserved railway in Britain.* An interesting collection of locomotives and rolling stock has been assembled, and no one who visits the line and travels on it will come away feeling unrewarded. Membership inquiries should be addressed to Pickering Station, North Yorkshire, YO18 7AJ. (See colour illustration on p. 223.)

The Keighley & Worth Valley Light Railway Ltd operates the 7 km (4½ mile) branch from the Midland Railway at Keighley, Yorkshire, up the valley past Haworth, the home of the Brontës, to Oxenhope. It was opened on 15 April 1857 and was operated by the Midland. Passenger services were withdrawn on 30 December 1961. In March 1962, three months before final closure of the line, a preservation society was formed. It was incorporated on 8 February 1966. After an immense amount of voluntary work two Light Railway Orders were obtained, in 1967 and 1968, and the line was reopened on 29 June 1968. Since then many thousands of passengers have been carried. With the Severn Valley Railway (qv) it has one of the two **largest collections of preserved steam locomotives in Britain**, among them being four from the former Lancashire & Yorkshire Railway including an 0–6–0 built in 1887. One of the most interesting engines, still awaiting restoration, is an 0–6–0 well tank built at St Helens, Lancashire, in 1874. Steam trains run every week-end and on Wednesdays in summer. This railway formed the setting for the filming of *The Railway Children*. (See p. 221.) Address: Haworth Station, Keighley, Yorkshire. In 1977 it carried nearly 150 000 passengers, a record for a private railway.

*In fact the scenery is the main 'selling point'. The North Yorkshire Moors National Park Authority encourage tourists to leave their cars at Grosmont or Pickering and to travel on the train.

The Severn Valley Railway Company was incorporated on 24 May 1967. It operates the second longest British preserved railway, 21 km (13 miles) between Bridgnorth in Shropshire and Bewdley in Worcestershire, and also a portion of the branch from there to Kidderminster. It was opened between Hartlebury north of Worcester and Shrewsbury on 1 February 1862 and became part of the Great Western Railway on 1 August 1863. On 1 June 1878 the GWR opened the branch from Kidderminster to Bewdley. Through traffic ended on 9 September 1963. The Severn Valley Railway Preservation Society was formed on 6 July 1965, just in time to prevent dismantling. A Light Railway Order was obtained in May 1970 and on 23 May trains began running again between Bridgnorth and Hampton Loade, 7 km (4½ miles). The service was extended to Bewdley on 18 May 1974 and to Foley Park on the Kidderminster Branch in September 1976. The SVR is distinguished by owning the finest bridge on any British preserved railway, the Victoria Bridge across the River Severn, a great cast-iron arch of 61 m (200 ft) span, designed by John Fowler and built by the Coalbrookdale Company in 1861. Steam trains are run every week-end, with a great variety of locomotives and stock. The SVR has **the largest collection of main-line locomotives** (as distinct from industrial types)

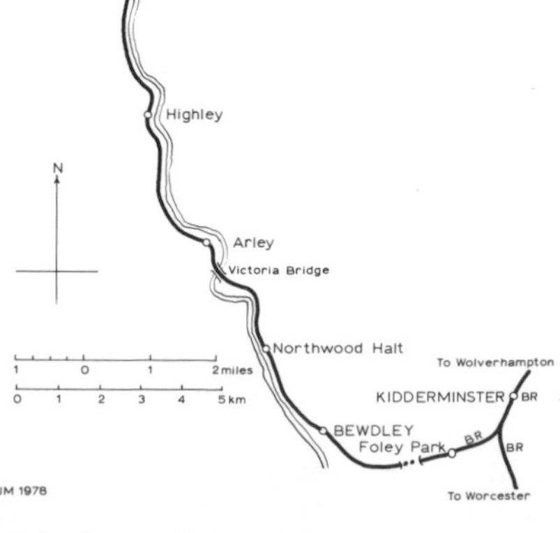

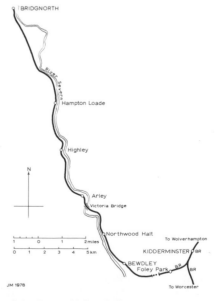

Map of the Severn Valley Railway

in Britain. Address: The Railway Station, Bewdley, Worcestershire.

The Dart Valley and Torbay Steam Railways in South Devon operate in close connection. The Dart Valley Railway Limited was incorporated in 1965 to operate part of the branch from Totnes to Ashburton. It was opened as a 2·134 m (7 ft) gauge line on 1 May 1872, standard gauged in May 1892, and absorbed by the GWR in 1897. Passenger services ended on 3 November 1958 and the line was finally closed on 10 September 1962. Under the new company the branch was reopened on 5 April 1969 between Totnes and Buckfastleigh, 11 km (6¾ miles). The section from Buckfastleigh to Ashburton was sacrificed to road works. Trains operate from April to October with a collection of GWR engines.

The neighbouring **Torbay Steam Railway** was opened in 1972 to continue passenger services on the 11 km (6¾ miles) section of line from Paignton to Kingswear. The 7 ft gauge branch was opened for passenger trains from Aller Junction near Newton Abbot through to Kingswear on 16 August 1864. It was changed to standard gauge in May 1892. Services beyond Paignton were discontinued by BR in October 1972. Locomotives include several former GWR types. Trains run daily from April to October, and give the passenger fine views of Torbay and the Dart Estuary on either side of the 450 m (492 yd) Greenway Tunnel. Address: Buckfastleigh Station, Buckfastleigh, Devon TQ11 0DZ.

AUSTRALIA

The Puffing Billy Preservation Society, in conjunction with Victorian Railways, operates a 13 km (8 miles) long 762 mm (2 ft 6 in) gauge railway between Belgrave and Emerald at week-ends and on public holidays, with four steam locomotives, 23 coaches and 16 wagons. There is also a narrow-gauge railway museum at Menzies Creek in conjunction with this railway. It contains various locomotives and rolling stock and is open on Sundays 10·00–17·00.

Victorian Railways also retain four steam locomotives and 16 coaches for operating special enthusiast trips on its 1·600 m (5 ft 3 in) gauge system. Address: 38 Wash Street, Melbourne, Victoria 3000.

FRANCE

Tourist and Mountain Railways. When the Vivarais Network of metre-gauge railways of 204 km (127 miles), built between 1886 and 1891, was closed in 1968 a group of local enthusiasts determined to save part of the system. In June 1969 the 33 km (21 miles) section from Tournon, about 64 km (40 miles) south of Lyon, to Lamastre was reopened with steam trains and diesel railcars. It is a magnificent scenic line with gradients of 1 in 30 (3·3 per cent). From 1 June to 15 September there are one steam and two railcar services each way daily. Steam locomotives include three 0–6–6–0 compound Mallet tanks built by the Swiss Locomotive & Machine Works, Winterthur.

There is also the St Hilaire du Touret Funicular Railway, a 1·5 km (⅞ mile) cable line on a gradient of 1 in 1·2 (83 per cent). Address: BP 37, 69 Lyon (2e).

SWITZERLAND

Blonay–Chamby Tourist Railway, a 3 km (1·86 mile) metre gauge preserved railway between Chamby, on the Bernese Oberland Railway above Montreux, and Blonay on the Vevey-sans electric line. An interesting collection of Swiss steam locomotives has been assembled including 0–4–4–0 and 0–6–6–0 Mallet tanks and Rhaetian and Furka Oberalp 2–6–0 tanks. Trains run at week-ends only. Address: Case Postale 187, CH-1001 Lausanne.

USA

Current information on preserved railways in the USA is contained in the *Steam Passenger Service Directory* published annually by Empire State Railway Museum Inc, PO Box 459, Wall Street Station, New York, NY 10005.

From a great number four of the most interesting for scenery and engineering have been selected, three of these in the Colorado Rockies.

California Western Railroad. This 64 km (40 miles) standard-gauge line from Willits, north of San Francisco, down through the redwood forest to the Pacific coast at Fort Bragg was opened on 19 December 1911. Its primary

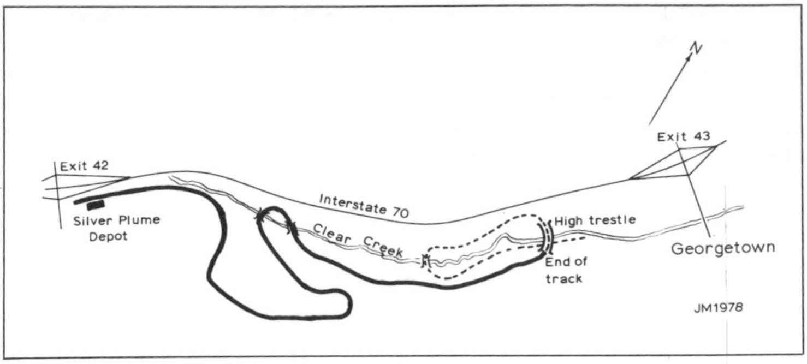

Map of the Georgetown Loop Railroad

purpose was haulage of logs. The line includes two tunnels, and climbs from 12 m (39 ft) above sea-level at South Fork to a summit of 530 m (1740 ft) above Willits in 46 km (29 miles). The top section of the climb consists of a series of 'hairpins' affording fine views. Though not a 'preserved' railway the CWR now provides the only steam-operated standard-gauge passenger service in Western USA. Trains are worked by a 2–8–2 (Baldwin 1926) and a 2–6–6–2 Mallet (Baldwin 1937), both with coupled wheels only 1·118 m (3 ft 8 in) diameter.

Cumbres & Toltec Scenic Railroad. The Denver & Rio Grande Railway completed its 914 mm (3 ft) gauge line over the 3053 m (10 015 ft) Cumbres Pass west of Antonito in 1880. It formed part of a through route from Denver to Durango and Silverton completed in 1882. Regular passenger services ended in 1951 and after freight finished in 1968 the line became derelict. In 1970 the most scenic section of 103 km (64 miles) between Antonito and Chama was purchased jointly by the States of Colorado and New Mexico and reopened on 27 June 1971, operating tourist trains with 2–8–2 steam locomotives. **It is the longest preserved railway in the world.**

Denver & Rio Grande Western Railroad: Durango–Silverton. Following withdrawal of through passenger services between Denver, Alamosa and Durango in 1951, the Silverton line with its magnificent scenery along the Animas Canyon became a major tourist attraction. This 74 km (46 mile) line was opened in July 1882. Today it carries more passengers than any other section of the D. & RGW, through some of the most spectacular scenery in the Rockies. As on the Cumbres line, trains are hauled by 2–8–2 steam locomotives. Advanced booking is necessary, at Durango Station, Colorado.

The Georgetown Loop Railroad. This is one of the most exciting railroad restoration projects in North America. In 1884 the Georgetown, Breckenridge & Leadville Railway (a subsidiary of the Union Pacific) reached Silver Plume from Georgetown by a 914 mm (3 ft) gauge line of 7·25 km (4½ miles) in which it climbed 194 m (638 ft) on a maximum grade of 1 in 28·5 (3·5 per cent), climbing over itself on a high trestle and looping through nearly three and a half circles. It soon became one of the major tourist attractions in Colorado, but by 1939 traffic had declined and it was closed and dismantled.

California Western Railway 2–8–2 No. 45 at the Pacific coast town of Fort Bragg on a train to Willits, in 1972

In the late 1950s the State Historical Society began restoration of the valley as an industrial museum and in 1973 began reconstruction of the railway. Steam trains are now running from Silver Plume a distance of 4 km (2½ miles) down to the upper abutment of the high trestle which will be rebuilt when funds are available. Track will then be restored through to Georgetown. Two powerful 2–8–0s (Baldwin 1921) are in use. Access is from exits 42 or 43 on Interstate 70. This is a fine scenic ride.

BIBLIOGRAPHY

The number of railway books from British and American publishers is so vast that a full bibliography for a book of this scope is impracticable. For books on British railway subjects the reader should consult *A Bibliography of British Railway History* compiled by George Ottley (Allen & Unwin 1965). Since then numerous books have appeared, not all of reliable authenticity, and discrimination is needed in their selection. A useful guide is *Railways, a readers' guide* by E T Bryant (Clive Bingley 1968) which also contains critical comments. So also does *Steam Locomotive Development* by Kevin P. Jones, published in 1969 by the Library Association. A classified bibliography used to be published annually in the *Railway Directory and Year Book*, but from the 1978 edition this is limited to books published since the last issue. Earlier issues should be available at most good libraries. For American books the reader may find it useful to consult the *Bibliography of railroad literature* published by The Association of American Railroads, Washington.

The principal publishers of railway books in Britain are Ian Allan, of Shepperton, Surrey; Allen & Unwin, of London; David & Charles, of Newton Abbot, Devon; Oakwood Press, of Blandford, Dorset; and it is worth approaching them for their current catalogues. The Railway Correspondence & Travel Society (see p. 214) publish some magnificent locomotive histories, chiefly of the Great Western and London & North Eastern railways and the Southern companies.

In North America many railway books are published by Bonanza Books, New York; Howell North, Berkeley, California; and Kalmbach Publishing Company, Milwaukee, Wisconsin. The Macmillan Company of New York is bringing out a series of comprehensive histories of the various large railroad companies of North America.

The following list is of books of general railway interest; it omits scholarly and deeply researched histories of single railway companies and the numerous albums of photographs, many of which are directed towards those to whom serious reading makes little appeal.

Some of the books are out of print, but should be available through the library service.

REFERENCE BOOKS

Biographical Dictionary of Railway Engineers, by John Marshall, David & Charles 1978

Bradshaw's Railway Manual and Shareholders' Guide and Directory 1869 David & Charles 1969

British Rail Atlas Ian Allan 1967

Fodor's Railways of the World Hodder & Stoughton (USA) 1977

Gradients of the British Main Line Railways Railway Publishing Company 1947

Janes World Railways (Annual) Low, Marston & Co

Railway Directory & Year Book (Annual) IPC Transport Press

Railway Enthusiast's Handbook (Annual) David & Charles

GENERAL RAILWAY HISTORY

A Regional History of the Railways of Great Britain (not yet complete) David & Charles: Vol 1 *The West Country* David St John Thomas 1966; Vol 2 *Southern England* H P White 1964; Vol 3 *Greater London* H P White 1963; Vol 4 *The North East* K. Hoole 1966; Vol 5 *The Eastern Counties* D I Gordon 1968; Vol 6 *Scotland, Lowlands and Borders* John Thomas 1971; Vol 7 *The West Midlands* Rex Christiansen 1973; Vol 8 *South and West Yorkshire* David Joy 1975; Vol 9 *The East Midlands* Robin Leleux 1976; Vol 10 *The North West* Geoffrey O. Holt 1978

Acworth, W M, *The Railways of England* (5th edition 1900) Ian Allan 1964

Bagwell, Philip, *The Railway Clearing House in the British Economy 1842–1922* Allen & Unwin 1968

Ellis, Hamilton, *British Railway History* Vol 1 1956; Vol 2 1959 Allen & Unwin

Ellis, Hamilton, *Railway Carriages in the British Isles from 1830 to 1914* Allen & Unwin 1965

Holbrook, Stewart H., *The Story of American Railroads* Crown (Bonanza Books) New York 1947

Jackman, W T, *Development of Transport in modern England* (2nd edition) Frank Cass & Co Ltd 1962

Jackson, A A, & Croome, D F, *Rails through the Clay* (a history of London's Underground railways) (2nd edition) Allen & Unwin 1964

Lee, Charles, *The Evolution of Railways* Railway Gazette 1937

Lewin, Henry Grote, *Early British Railways* Locomotive Publishing Company 1925

Lewin, Henry Grote, *The Railway Mania and its Aftermath 1845–52* (1936) David & Charles 1968

Lewis, M J T, *Early wooden Railways* Routledge & Kegan Paul 1970

Nock, O S, *Fifty Years of Railway Signalling* Institution of Railway Signal Engineers (Ian Allan) 1962

Pratt, Edwin A., *A History of inland transport and communication* (1912) David & Charles 1970

Priestley, Joseph, *Navigable Rivers, Canals and Railways* (1831) David & Charles 1969

Robbins, Michael, *The Railway Age* Routledge & Kegan Paul 1962

Simmons, Jack, *The Railways of Britain; an historical survey* Routledge & Kegan Paul 1961

Stover, John F., *American Railroads* University of Chicago Press 1961

Whishaw, Francis, *Railways of Great Britain & Ireland* (1842) David & Charles 1969

LOCOMOTIVE HISTORY

Ahrons, E L, *The British steam railway locomotive* (1927) Ian Allan 1961

Aston, R L, *The Diesel Locomotive* Thames & Hudson 1957

Brownlie, John S., *Railway steam cranes* John S. Brownlie 1973

Bruce, Alfred W., *The steam locomotive in America* W W Norton & Co, New York 1952

Cooper, B K, *Electric trains and locomotives* Leonard Hill Ltd 1953

Cox, E S, *World Steam in the twentieth century* Ian Allan 1969

Dover, A T, *Electric Traction* (4th edition) Pitman 1963

Haut, F J G, *The History of the electric locomotive* Allen & Unwin 1969

Jones, Kevin P., *Steam Locomotive Development 1923–62* (a bibliography) Library Association 1969

Lowe, James W., *British steam locomotive builders* Goose & Son 1975

Dendy Marshall, C F, *History of locomotive design down to the end of the year 1831* Locomotive Publishing Company 1953

Poultney, E C, *British express locomotive development 1896–1948* Allen & Unwin 1952

Ransome Wallis, P. (ed), *Concise Encyclopaedia of world railway locomotives* Hutchinson 1959

Ransome Wallis, P., *Preserved steam locomotives of Western Europe* Vol 1 1971; Vol 2 1971 Ian Allan

Reder, Gustav, *The world of steam locomotives* Blandford Press 1975

Sinclair, Angus, *Development of the Locomotive Engine* (1907) MIT Press, Cambridge, Mass, 1970

Tuplin, W A, *British steam since 1900* David & Charles 1969

Warren, J G H, *A century of locomotive building 1823–1923* (1923) David & Charles 1970

White, John H. Jr, *American locomotives, an engineering history 1830–80* John Hopkins Press, Baltimore, Md 1968

Wiener, Lionel, *Articulated locomotives* (1930) Kalmbach Publishing Company, Milwaukee, Wis 1970

Locomotive Cyclopaedia 7th edition (1925) 1973; 14th edition 1950–2 Simmons Boardman Publishing Company, New York

Index

M

N

O

P

Ebooks in Education: Realising the Vision

Edited by
Hazel Woodward

]u[

ubiquity press
London

Published by
Ubiquity Press Ltd.
Gordon House
29 Gordon Square
London WC1H 0PP
www.ubiquitypress.com

First published 2014

Cover Image by Daniel Sancho
(Flickr / teclasorg)

ISBN (Hardback): 978-1-909188-37-2
ISBN (EPub): 978-1-909188-38-9
ISBN (PDF): 978-1-909188-39-6
ISBN (Kindle): 978-1-909188-40-2

DOI: http://dx.doi.org/10.5334/bal

Suggested citation:
Woodward, H (ed.). 2014. *Ebooks in Education: Realising the Vision.* London: Ubiquity Press. DOI: http://dx.doi.org/10.5334/bal

To read the online open access version of this book, either visit http://dx.doi.org/10.5334/bal or scan this QR code with your mobile device:

Contents

Foreword

Madeleine Atkins
Higher Education Funding Council for England

In 1840, the essayist Thomas Carlyle wrote that "the true University of these days is a collection of books". On this evidence alone, it's safe to say that Carlyle may not recognise the universities of today. Decades of significant developments in pedagogy, research methods and journal publishing, enabled by expansion, globalisation, research assessment, and the impact and knowledge exchange agendas have transformed our understanding of what a university can be, for the better. The UK's universities are dynamic, innovative and inventive places, geared up to embrace and solve the challenges of the 21st century.

Were he alive today, Carlyle would however no doubt be comforted to see that books of all sorts – textbooks, monographs, edited collections, critical editions and exhibition catalogues – continue to be hugely important to authorship, scholarship and education in many disciplines. He might therefore be somewhat disconcerted to learn that many people feel that the book is falling out of favour in academic life, with electronic journal articles and electronic course materials becoming more prominent in all universities, and with one university in the USA even having opened a new library containing not one single physical book.

Whether the book is in jeopardy is debatable. But the great challenge to conventional print books is obvious: the twin developments of digital text and the internet have brought about major and rapid advances in all areas of our lives. All of us are now accustomed to writing and producing our own documents electronically, communicating electronically, storing and retrieving information

How to cite this book chapter:
Atkins, M. 2014. Foreword. In: Woodward, H. (ed.) *Ebooks in Education: Realising the Vision.* Pp. v-vi. London: Ubiquity Press. DOI: http://dx.doi.org/10.5334/bal.for

electronically, and, increasingly, accessing it anywhere on a wide range of devices. In this context, the humble print book can feel rather anachronous and students will rightly expect at least basic electronic access to their course books in the same way that they can access almost everything else they need: freely, immediately and online. As students' demands change, a transition to the print book's successor, the ebook, therefore seems both necessary and inevitable.

This publication by Jisc Collections describes very lucidly the current state of such a transition. Through some really eye-opening examples, we see how ebooks have been incorporated successfully into educational practice, improving the learning experience for students, particularly students with disabilities and distance learners. We see exciting partnerships with research institutes, the development and promotion of an ebook app, the creation of an open living book, and new collaborations with ebook publishers and vendors to provide access to e-textbooks to students. Such success stories reflect well on e-books more generally, showing us that they are reaching the level of maturity needed for widespread adoption. And the benefits here extend beyond the purely practical, as described neatly by the University of Leicester who recognise that ebooks can help them improve teaching, reduce costs and enhance the student educational experience.

If the encouraging stories told in this publication reveal anything, it is that ebooks are perhaps even more necessary and inevitable than previously thought. But in examining the situation further, we are acquainted with some of the significant challenges that ebooks have yet to overcome, most chiefly around functionality, curation and access. These challenges are not insignificant and should not be underestimated. One of the most pressing of these is the challenge of delivering open access to research publications, maximising their potential readership and impact on wider society. Open access has its own distinctive drivers and opportunities, as have been outlined here by Peter Suber, and are fully recognised by HEFCE in our own policy for open access in the next REF exercise. But open access for books has substantial cultural, technological and financial challenges, many of which are not well understood. I am also delighted that this publication will be followed up in 2015 by a much-anticipated report by Professor Geoffrey Crossick on the opportunities and challenges for monographs and open access, which will help to illuminate our understanding of this difficult area.

In the 21st century, universities must be at the forefront of embracing the opportunities brought about by new technologies as well as understanding and overcoming their limitations. For these reasons, I warmly welcome this new publication on ebooks in education, which sheds much-needed light on the significant opportunities for ebooks to transform and improve the learning experience for students. Throughout this publication the inventiveness and perspicacity shown by academics and librarians to deliver improvements to education by embracing the opportunities of ebooks are striking. It is clear that the future of ebooks in higher education is in safe hands.

Ebooks in higher education: a strategic priority?

Christine Fyfe
University of Leicester

University leaders and managers concern themselves with developments that align with institutions' strategic priorities, deliver competitive advantage, improve teaching and research performance, reduce costs and enhance value for money. Ebooks have the potential to engage with all these strategic priorities. Following the successful integration of ejournals into the academic workflow, ebooks promise much to universities aspiring to enhance students' educational experience, enrich research resources and streamline services. They have greater potential to transform the reader experience than ejournals and yet they have experienced a long and difficult birth, suffering from digital rights management, integration, discoverability and functionality challenges. It is taking much longer than expected to arrive at a position in which ebooks have a dominant and realiable part to play in students' learning and in universities' provision of texts to support both teaching and research. Indeed in the UK, while ebook provision and use via libraries is growing rapidly (for example, the University of Leicester Library acquired 1086 ebooks in 2008/9 rising to 406,576 in 2012/13) library spending on books is still dominated by spending on print. The 2011/12 Annual Library Statistics published by the Society of College, National and University Libraries (SCONUL 2013) report that

How to cite this book chapter:
Fyfe, C. 2014. Ebooks in higher education: a strategic priority? In: Woodward, H. (ed.) *Ebooks in Education: Realising the Vision.* Pp. 1–7. London: Ubiquity Press. DOI: http://dx.doi.org/10.5334/bal.a

across the 147 higher education institutions making returns total expenditure on printed books was £46.4 million and on ebooks £14.8 million.

Both the higher education sector and the publishing industry are undergoing a prolonged process of experimentation with service and provider models in a complex environment characterised by many variables and choices. As a consequence of this complexity, and of the fast pace of change, there has been insufficient time to pause and reflect on key topics such as user behaviour, the impact of the changing balance between electronic and printed books (either at individual user level, or at provider level), the rate of change towards e-only provision, and the future role of libraries.

Faced with this bewildering landscape, university leaders may easily fail to appreciate the transformative potential of ebooks to help to address a range of challenges encountered by institutions. In this chapter I attempt to explore some of the roles which ebooks may play in building successful educational institutions.

Key strategic drivers

Ebooks have the potential to engage with three key strategic priorities common to most universities: to enhance the student experience and academic outcomes within an increasingly competitive environment; to drive innovation in learning, teaching and research; and to help to use space and human resources more effectively and efficiently.

Enhancing the student experience is clearly a key strategic driver for all universities, sharpened by ever increasing global competition for well-qualified students. The abolition of student number controls in England from 2015/16 and the introduction of new private providers will drive further striving for competitive advantage between institutions. Students' (and their parents') expectations of value for money and investment in their education continue to rise within a context in which many will have a much wider choice of institution than in the past. A recent report by Moody's (2014) painted a picture of a stratified competitive environment for English higher education institutions in which responses depended on institutions' market position. Moody's described an environment in which most institutions will need to jostle for position, making strategic investments in order to attract students. League tables, which are highly influential in student choice of institution, constitute a further element of the competitive landscape. Competition clearly is not limited to student recruitment; universities also strive to improve the educational outcomes of their students in order to prepare them for employment and to reinforce institutional reputations.

Ebooks contribute to this scramble for competitive advantage by offering the exciting possibility of enhancing the student experience – what it is like to be a student – and producing better educated students. At a fundamental level, ebooks enhance educational benefit by improving access to titles that students are expected to read. Ensuring timely access to key books has been a fundamental, and largely intractable, challenge for universities and their libraries for many years, and lack of sufficient copies has regularly featured as the top complaint in student surveys over many years. Ebooks enable libraries to move away from inadequate and unpopular solutions to high demand for particular books, such as reliance on short-loan print collections. Making access to books more convenient, anytime, anywhere helps to meet student expectations and to assist students who are juggling the demands of study with complicated personal commitments. There remain significant challenges with institutional licensing or purchase of online textbooks in particular, but nevertheless ebooks are having a significant impact on improving student satisfaction with book provision.

There is evidence also that ebooks are not only becoming widely accepted, but also embedded in students' expectations of core provision. The University of Leicester Students' Union annual Student Voice Report for 2014 chose to ask two questions on learning resources. In answer to the question "How much of your reading is available online?" 65% of the 769 respondents indicated that most or all of their reading was available electronically. Most of this, at undergraduate level, would be books and book chapters. The second question asked "How useful would each of the following [resources] be to your learning?". Ebooks topped the list which included lecture capture, journal subscriptions, more physical books in the library and social learning space. Of the respondents, 60% deemed ebooks to be "very useful" to their learning, compared with 44% awarding physical books in the library the same judgment. It is telling that the student compilers of the survey highlighted these as the most important questions to ask, and that ebooks received strong support against other hot topics. The survey aligns with national usage statistics for ebook sections which record over 123 million requests in 2011/12 (SCONUL 2013), demonstrating that for students they have entered the mainstream.

Students increasingly resent the expectation that they should purchase books themselves, especially in the context of increased tuition fees. The National Union of Students and individual student unions have run successful campaigns to highlight what they see as hidden and unacceptable additional charges of undertaking a programme of study. Some universities, including my own, have supplied individual copies of core print books or ebooks for students which serve to enhance student satisfaction and perception of value for money. Further potential is offered by ebooks to personalise the provision of reading material to enhance the attractiveness of the offer to students.

Ebooks evidently enable universities to enhance substantially the range of titles available to students through the purchase of large packages of titles assembled by aggregators or by individual publishers. While there is inevitably some redundancy in large packages, the level of use of the popular titles and the penetration across the package will often justify the cost. As was evident when digital journal backsets became available, the opening up of back-list titles in electronic form boosts usage and helps to support the wider reading required for writing essays and dissertations in a much more convenient way than traditional print-based document supply. Academics at the University of Leicester confirm that they and their students read and cite more titles if the content is easily accessible.

The availability of patron- or demand-driven acquisition, in which a number of selected titles are made available to institutions, but the purchase of individual titles is triggered only when an agreed usage level has been reached, may seem to be a direct contrast with a strategy that relies on the purchase of large packages. In some institutions a more targeted approach to acquiring ebooks will be appropriate, but in others targeting can happily coexist with a range of other approaches. Both approaches are ways of maximising the chance that the reader will find and access what they want immediately, responding to an expectation of instant service. This contrasts with a considered collection building approach by libraries, highlighting a consumer focus that contributes to enhanced service and greater satisfaction.

Universities have long been involved in programmes that include professional placements, integrated work experiences or in other offerings that require students to study remotely. Students are now able to access key texts via mobile devices, and this has significantly enhanced the educational value of these activities. The educational power delivered by ebooks, of being able to access original texts from the patient's bedside, at the archaeological dig, or in the laboratory is enormous.

A further strategic benefit of ebooks is the part they can play in providing access to texts for students with disabilities. The ability to change font size, colour and contrast helps these students to have equivalent access to texts and a comparable experience to students without disabilities. In this way, ebooks support universities' widening participation agendas.

Driving innovation in teaching learning and research

The second strategic driver is innovation in teaching, learning and research. Ebooks can be embedded in online programmes or made available through virtual learning environments. The University of Leicester's MSc Security, Conflict and International Development by distance learning provides an instructive example of innovation. This programme, offered by the Department of Criminology, is aimed at those working, or intending to work, in international development. Students may be working in military environments, remote locations or as peace workers, far away from conventional study facilities. All students are provided with an iPad loaded with the course materials and relevant ebooks, and have access to a course app. Students are able to access material without an internet connection, which is often unavailable or unreliable in their employment environment. This is what the students say:

- I love the fact it is mobile, as I am constantly on the move. Travelling with books would be unrealistic.
- You can access all the materials without having to carry lots of books and means you can study any time any where.
- Firstly I am more motivated, as it is structured and organised. I am getting through more than I would if I was solely given a recommended reading list.
- My opinion of the course materials is very high: this is a fully immersive multimedia form of learning with core texts, videos and internet links etc presented in a clear flow. An extended bibliography gives you the option to explore the subject areas much wider.
- With the use of ebooks and the ability to download electronic academic documents from the library account, its almost paperless learning. For example, I will often be using a note taking app, ebook reader app and mindmapping app concurrently when studying while listening to music, also coming from the iPad. I only have to remember the charger!

It is striking how students respond positively not only to the accessibility of content, but also to the coherence and seamlessness offered by this approach to course design. Without ebooks, this distinctive programme would be considerably diminished, but the benefits of the approach are potentially applicable to all students. Only having to remember the charger neatly encapsulates the transformative potential of online delivery, of which an essential element is ebooks.

The rich potential offered by enhanced ebooks in terms of interactivity and multimedia is a further area for innovative design and delivery of content.

Ebooks have the power to enhance the approaches available to researchers who engage with text. The large scale digitisation of books, in addition to digitised copies of specialist collections, has made vast quantities of material discoverable and readily accessible, and has contributed to the growing importance of digital humanities. The ability to mine text (where permissible and practical) opens up new areas for enquiry and analysis, by identifying patterns across a corpus, or by highlighting features of texts that would not be discernible through traditional methods of reading.

Repurposing space

The 2011/12 SCONUL Annual Library Statistics (SCONUL 2013) record that its member libraries occupy a total of some 1.4 million square metres of space for traditional library activities, although it is not recorded what proportion of this space is occupied with the storage of printed books. This is an underestimate as not all libraries were able to provide the data. Commentators agree that print and ebooks will co-exist for a long time into the future, but it is evident that a continued move to ebooks will, over time, permit the reduction of prime space allocated to printed books, allowing significant quantities of space to be released for other purposes, including formal and social learning space. This move is already underway, promising to deliver significant financial and academic benefit to institutions. It will be possible in many institutions to reduce off-site book storage space, delivering further efficiencies.

A further consideration for university managers is the extent to which access to and use of ebooks will occur outside the library service (for example through texts being provided by academic departments) or outside the institution altogether. Large-scale book digitisation projects (such as Google Books and Project Gutenberg) are obvious examples where students and researchers access material independently from the institution. The growing interest in open access ebooks from commercial publishers (for example Brill Open Books, Palgrave Open), the emergence of specialist open access publishers, and the exploration of new models provide a further dimension to the ebook landscape. Interest in open access ebooks is further evidenced by a range of high level explorations, including the current HEFCE examination of open access monographs and long-form scholarly works, the OAPEN-UK research project and the Jisc work to investigate the need for and shape of a national monographs strategy.

Universities and libraries will also wish to develop as creators and publishers of ebooks, which may form an economically viable approach to reviving university presses and enable textbook production.

Closing comments

Students and researchers experience access to book content, either whole books or sections, via personal purchase of print or ebooks, library print collections, library individual ebooks (selected by library), library individual ebooks (selected by readers through demand-driven acquisition), open access ebooks and document supply (borrowing from other libraries). Ebooks are on the cusp of becoming mainstream in learning, teaching and research. They offer significant opportunities to enhance the richness and effectiveness of education across all these areas and to deliver advantages to institutions. If we are to realise the vision, we need more research into the complexities of delivery, production and access to provide leaders with the evidence they need to influence institutional strategies.

References

Moody's (2014) English Higher Education Reform: the strong get stronger while the rest jostle for position. *Sector Comment*, 17 April. https://moodys.com

SCONUL (2013) *Annual Library Statistics, 2011–12*. London: SCONUL.

Ebooks in further education

David Scott
Dundee and Angus College

The adoption of ebooks in further education (FE) colleges across the UK has been driven forward in large measure by the Jisc funded ebooks for FE project[1]. This initiative, which was established in 2009 and ended in August 2014, has provided all colleges in the UK with free access to a collection of approximately 3000 ebooks from a range of well-known publishers. In attempting to paint a picture of the landscape of ebooks across this very varied sector we have surveyed the views of librarians in 25 colleges which make heavy use of this collection, as well as taking note of recently published reports. The survey covered issues such as: ebooks strategies; access to ebooks; integration of ebooks with other institutional systems such as virtual learning environments (VLE) and library management systems (LMS); barriers to usage - cultural, technical; and the ebooks landscape in the next three years. It was sent to a range of colleges which reported high use of the ebooks collection by their students and staff, as defined by the monthly statistics provided by Jisc Collections. A high proportion of the institutions surveyed were in the top twenty of student users of the Jisc ebooks collection. Inevitably with such

[1] http://fe.jiscebooks.org/

How to cite this book chapter:
Scott, D. 2014. Ebooks in further education. In: Woodward, H. (ed.) *Ebooks in Education: Realising the Vision.* Pp. 9–14. London: Ubiquity Press. DOI: http://dx.doi.org/10.5334/bal.b

Technical issues are still a major source of frustration in accessing ebooks easily. This was reported in 2013 (Conyers and Dalton 2013, p.29), and in our survey most of the librarians complained about navigation issues for staff and students in using ebook platforms. There were strong views expressed about the need for standardisation across the range of suppliers' platforms. FE colleges subscribe to the Jisc ebooks collection as well as purchasing books from Dawsonera, Coutts and others. They all have different platforms which can be frustrating for the end user and can promote negative attitudes towards the use of ebooks to support their studies, particularly among those who are used to the ease of downloading and accessing books on to devices such as Kindles and iPads. The ease of use of these devices is often seen in contrast to the perceived difficulties of accessing ebooks. Equally, there were views expressed about the "clunky" look and feel of some of the platforms as well as the additional software and procedures related to digital rights management (DRM) often required to download ebooks.

Libraries are still facing difficulties in acquiring electronic versions of textbooks, particularly up-to-date versions. Textbooks are a vital element in the publishers' business model; they sell vast numbers directly to students as well as libraries. Jisc Collections are in a good position to work with publishers to ensure that more up-to-date and relevant books are available to the sector.

Innovations

Libraries have become increasingly adept at promoting their services to their users, and many employ a range of measures to ensure that ebooks are seen as an increasingly important part of the overall service. Apart from adding all the ebook titles to the library catalogue and also linking them in a variety of ways to specific courses developed by teaching staff on their institutional VLEs, they are also promoted in a number of creative and engaging ways. Colleges have developed a range of enhanced induction workshops, as well as working closely with curriculum staff on the development of study and research skill programmes which enable students to become aware of and adept at accessing and using ebooks. The advantages of ebooks are built into the teaching and learning process with lecturers demonstrating their use during lectures and classes, as well as devising activities and assessments which demonstrate their increased accessibility, flexibility and functionality. Some libraries have adopted the bookshop approach to signposting, using QR codes on shelves to provide further information and a direct link to the individual ebook. Complementary to this, some libraries are using DVD style boxes or cards to promote ebooks which they shelve or place adjacent to other relevant print-based textbooks. Posters, flyers and placing details of the ebook collection on the college website, student online portal and social media pages all play a part in their promotion.

Colleges have reported that their ebook collection has proved invaluable to their online and distance learning students. Not only has it enhanced the service to these learners but it has also enabled the library to reduce the administrative processes required to provide print-based texts by post. The benefits to this relatively small number of specific users could well be a key driver to support the information needs of many more full-time and part-time students at the increasing number of merged colleges across the country. A number of these merged colleges are geographically far apart, with practical difficulties for students in accessing resources at more than their local campus. For example, in 2012 there were 43 FE colleges in Scotland, but in April 2014 there were only 13, some of which have campuses more than 40 miles apart. Ebook collections will be even more important in ensuring that students have access to relevant resources when they need them.

Future prospects

All of the librarians we contacted thought that the demand for ebooks by students was likely to increase over the next three years. The increase in the number and range of smartphones has resulted in a consequent increased demand by students for mobile access to their timetables, course materials and as study support tools such as ebooks. It will become a focus for Jisc Collections and consortia such as the SHEDL and the Welsh Higher Education Libraries Forum (WHELF) to support the demand for up-to-date ebooks to ensure that student and staff demands are met. Further work is also required in trying to establish a set of standards in the processes involved in accessing, downloading and repurposing the content of ebooks. There are strong messages coming from the sector that the process for students is too cumbersome, with many confused and frustrated by the varying licence conditions.

Ebooks are now a significant element in the FE library service. I cannot overestimate how powerful a driver the Jisc Collections ebook initiative has been in providing a critical mass of materials freely available to students across the UK. There are now more ebooks on offer from publishers, and access to them has improved from the days of patchy arrangements focusing on fixed PCs with IP address authentication. Shibboleth access is now much more prevalent. There are creative partnerships in place in many colleges between library and lecturing staff which have promoted the practical uses and advantages of ebooks – increased accessibility, flexibility and functionality. Problems remain in the supply of ebooks, however; librarians find it hard at times to source good quality materials, and often the licences are complex and at times restrictive. There is work to be done by Jisc Collections on behalf of the FE sector nationally in securing a step-change in the supply of ebooks and the establishment of standards to ensure easy and effective access and usability.

References

Conyers, A. and Dalton, P. (2013) *Analysis of E-books in FE Project Data*. Birmingham: Birmingham City University.

Cox, J., Cox., L and Carden, M. (2010) *Migrating to E in UK further education*. London: Jisc Collections.

Ebooks and the distance learner

Claire Grace and Gill Needham
The Open University

What we can do for students now

Emily is in her second year studying psychology with the Open University (OU). She chose to study in this way while working full time as a classroom assistant in a primary school. Her best friend from school, Carole, is a year ahead, attending a campus university as a full-time student. Carole is also studying psychology, and the two friends meet up from time to time to share gossip, compare experience and sometimes help one another with their work. They meet for a coffee one Saturday. Carole is a little late. "I'm so sorry" she says "I've been queuing up in the library, trying to get hold of this book I need from short loan for the weekend – my essay's due in next week." "I get the feeling you weren't successful?" "No I wasn't, and I'm really stuck now – it's only published in print. I might just have to buy a copy – it's paperback, but it's £25 I would rather not spend." "Well, that's one problem I don't have" says Emily. "How does that work, exactly?" Carole asks "How do you get hold of library books?". "Well, the books we are expected to read are all there for us online – the only 'real' book I have for the course is the one set book I had to buy at the beginning".

Carole's question and Emily's subsequent explanation is the crux of the question we shall address in this chapter – "Why are ebooks important in

How to cite this book chapter:
Grace, C. and Needham, G. 2014. Ebooks and the distance learner. In: Woodward, H. (ed.) *Ebooks in Education: Realising the Vision*. Pp. 15–20. London: Ubiquity Press. DOI: http://dx.doi.org/10.5334/bal.c

distance education?". For OU students, all of whom study at a distance, their library service *is* the online library, and ebooks are increasingly important to their overall learning experience. It has always been a challenge to offer distance learning students a library experience which is at least equivalent to that of a conventional university. The OU library has been addressing this challenge for the last fifteen years with a significant amount of success.

In the early days the OU library was able to provide access to journal articles as they became available in digital form. But journal articles tend to be more relevant to students in the later stages of their degree, so there was little material available in digital form aimed at first- and second-year undergraduate students. The advent of ebooks, and in particular the growth in academic texts available in ebook form, has allowed us to deliver content online which is more relevant to students studying at levels one and two. Flexibility of access is of paramount importance. Like Emily, the majority of OU students are in full-time employment, and many are also juggling family commitments. Books have to be available to them anytime, anywhere and in the most appropriate formats.

During Emily's studies she will encounter and use ebooks in a number of different contexts. There are two distinct models of providing ebook material at the OU. Some "e-textbooks" will be embedded in the online course materials delivered via the Virtual Learning Environment (VLE) – Moodle, an open source platform that is used at the OU. These are currently procured by the University's production unit, known as Learning & Teaching Solutions (LTS), who will have arranged payment to clear the rights for either whole textbooks or individual chapters for use by students on this particular course. The university has now adopted a commercial textbook platform to provide easy access and integration with the VLE. Previous versions of Emily's psychology course included a course reader (a collection of rights-cleared journal articles and parts of books) in print. For the latest version of the course Emily is studying, the reader is online and is delivered via the University's structured content markup system that is used for all the core course materials. This means that the content can be delivered in any format and hence on to any desktop or device. "It's so flexible" says Emily "when I went on holiday I downloaded all the course materials and the readings onto my Kindle – I read them on the beach and by the pool, so I didn't get behind at all. I was even able to join in a tutorial while I was away."

The other model is provided by the OU library and is based on providing links to a selection of resources to support the course. These links are managed by the library to ensure that they are "persistent", i.e. they are robust and can cope with changes in supplier, and they are "pushed" into the VLE using RSS feeds. The OU library has recently developed a new back-end system, known as Liblink, that manages this process. When a new course module is developed, a librarian will work alongside the module team to identify and suggest relevant ebooks and other content to be used. Links are likely to be to chapters, rather than an entire book. So, for example, there may be an activity written around the chapter.

"Don't you ever have to go and look for books yourself?" asks Carole. "Yes of course – last year, when it was all a bit new to us, we would be given some keywords and told to go into the online library and search for books on a particular subject. This year, now we are at level two, we are expected to search the online library to find books and journals when we have an assignment to do. There are loads to choose from."

Students can search for ebooks via the library search interface, by title or keywords, or they might wish to browse specific collections like PsycBOOKS®. However, finding library ebooks is not a straightforward process and provides some challenges for students and libraries. The silos that libraries have been using to manage print and digital resources (library catalogues and knowledge bases) rely on metadata about the individual ebook titles being loaded into the appropriate systems. This can be time-consuming and some ebook collections only have metadata available for the collection rather than all the titles in it.

It is also difficult to provide a true browsing experience for our students that recreates the ability to scan the shelves in a physical library. We try to facilitate this by presenting "Selected resources for your study" lists on the website, and the fairly recent addition of book jacket images makes the experience more "real". The need for anytime, anywhere access has meant that our extensive collection of online reference books is highly valued by students (e.g. Oxford Reference Online, Credo Reference, CRC Netbases). Experience suggests that the online library can encourage a more interdisciplinary approach to learning. Emily, studying psychology, will have easy access to relevant books in medicine, management, education and other related disciplines. In a physical library she may perhaps have been less inclined to venture outside her subject area.

Like many other university libraries, the OU library is experimenting with different models for acquiring ebooks, and we suggest that the experience can have an added significance for us. In our first trial of the Patron or Demand Driven Acquisition (PDA/DDA) model, aimed at Emily and her fellow psychology students, we found that students were choosing a range of general, popular and self-help type books, which may well have been available in a conventional university library but would not have been included in our collections, because our content is generally selected in close liaison with module teams to relate strictly and directly to the curriculum.

The problems and their future solutions

While the first half of this chapter has hopefully demonstrated the value and importance of ebooks to our distance learners like Emily, and the efforts involved behind the scenes, we would not wish to give the impression that all is perfect. As part of our programme of eliciting student feedback, we were able to persuade Emily to join our ebooks focus group. Emily had a number of questions to ask us about her experience of ebooks as a component of her studies. These are the questions she posed:

1. Why do I seem to have to go to so many different places to get my ebooks?
2. Why do so many of the ebooks look completely different and have different rules about what I can do with them, how long I can read them for etc.?
3. Why can't I read them all on my Kindle?
4. Why can't it work like getting books from Amazon or music from iTunes?

We weren't able to provide Emily with satisfactory answers to all her questions. Instead we assured her that these questions would help us to improve services in the future, and to use our influence with publishers.

Let us try to explore the issues behind Emily's questions:

1. Why do I seem to have to go to so many different places to get my ebooks?

This is indeed frustrating and there are a number of layers to the answer. First: the e-textbooks which are procured by LTS and embedded into a module, as explained above, will be accessed on a totally different platform from the platforms that are used to access the ebooks provided by the OU library. Why should this be so? In some cases the e-textbook platform is provided by the same company as the library ebook platform and provides the same functionality – why can they not be combined? The answer is that, in the publisher's view, the different business models governing the sale of the content necessitate different rights management (DRM) to be applied to the two types of ebook and therefore access has to be via separate platforms. This view means that publishers often structure their business to separate the sale of ebooks to libraries from institutional procurement or sales to individual students. How can institutions and publishers improve this situation so that the needs of students are better met and they receive a more cohesive service?

Secondly: the OU library currently has no choice but to acquire ebooks from a range of publishers/suppliers all of which have different platforms which look and behave differently. Could we agree to buy them all from one supplier? This is unlikely while the market is so unstable, with publishers developing different platforms, licensing and access models, causing all offers to differ. Our responsibility is to find the best value and the best user experience in every case.

2. Why do so many of the ebooks look completely different and have different rules about what I can do with them, how long I can read them for etc.?

It would appear that publishers and suppliers are experimenting with various business and licensing models. These govern the need for different functionality to be delivered to the end user in different platforms. This makes perfect sense to the supplier but none whatsoever to the user. For Emily it would appear reasonable to expect every book to allow unlimited access and a reasonable amount of downloading and printing but this is far from the case, as the length of time allowed for access can vary significantly. As librarians we can and should continue to put pressure on our suppliers to take the issue of user experience far more seriously and deliver products which meet students' reasonable expectations. We need to be far more proactive in this area.

3. Why can't I read them all on my Kindle?

The Open University is now producing its course materials in standard EPUB format which can be rendered to any device. This is regarded as good practice in the digital world and is particularly important for distance learning students who need to access content wherever they are. As a library service we would appear to be failing our students if we are unable to deliver ebooks in the same way. It is hoped that the initial discussions carried out under Jisc's umbrella to establish publisher guidelines for mobile delivery will help to progress this issue. We are selling Emily and her fellow students short in failing to meet expectations in this regard.

4. Why can't it work like getting books from Amazon or downloading music from iTunes?

Indeed, these services should and do act as the benchmark for user experience in the digital world, perhaps more because of familiarity and content range than merely usability. Just as libraries have continued to fail to offer a search experience which meets the expectations of Google aficionados, we are unlikely to achieve this in our ability to provide flexible, seamless access to content. Sadly, the academic book industry has seemed to lack the vision and courage to come up with a truly game-changing business model. Can we help to move the process of experimentation forward by articulating a clear vision of what we would like to be offering to our students like Emily? Here are our suggestions for a future vision for ebooks, based on our experience of supporting distance learners.

- Ebooks in the future will provide far more sophisticated functionality than a print book or a single "popular" ebook on a handheld reader.

- Students will be able to search the content within the books, and access and use parts that are relevant to them, without barriers. This will include the ability to connect content within the ebook with content from other sources.
- Students will be able to access ebooks via a single interface or even a single platform. If there are different platforms, they will be able to move seamlessly between titles regardless of platform.
- Ebooks will meet the highest standards we set for accessibility (to meet the needs of our 12,000 students with disabilities) and they will work effectively on any mobile device.
- The platform(s) will provide a single sign-on authentication that allows students to download and use ebooks of all types wherever they are.
- Search will be integrated across e-textbooks, library ebooks and ebooks that the student has bought, so that the student can transfer between the different "types" of ebook through seamless search and discovery.
- Ebooks purchased by an individual student using their OU student identity would be discounted for them through prearranged deals with publishers. They would be able to annotate, comment on and share these books with their friends.

Although this chapter has focused on the experience of an OU student and the challenges faced by the library on her behalf, we believe that many of the same challenges will be increasingly relevant to the sector as a whole, as online learning moves from margin to mainstream. If librarians, publishers, suppliers and technologists work hard enough together, we may be able to realise the vision articulated above before Emily completes her studies and before all the future Caroles are affected to the same degree. We may have to wait a little longer for the iTunes moment – the true game changer.

Ebooks: the learning and teaching perspective

Suzanne Enright
University of Westminster

Ebooks are here to stay and have "come of age" as a fully accepted format for publishers, readers and libraries in the library and education sectors[1]. Ebooks (that is to say, electronic versions of academic books, textbooks, reference books, scholarly monographs, annuals and other "one-off" publications) are recognised as a strategic element for UK higher education (HE) library services, and their use as a tool to better serve the needs of our users remains a hot topic.

The key drivers pushing the University of Westminster to strengthen the digital aspects of our service (with the usual caveats about availability, price and appropriateness) are: strategic imperatives within the institution, changes to user behaviour and changes to the external environment, including the publishing model.

Context

Digital collections are a growing component of library services and the wider digital library development. The various drivers for the digital future

---

[1] Ebooks and Econtent 2014: Beyond Ebooks at University College London. https://www.ucl.ac.uk/dis/conferences/ebooks

---

How to cite this book chapter:
Enright, S. 2014. Ebooks: the learning and teaching perspective. In: Woodward, H. (ed.) *Ebooks in Education: Realising the Vision.* Pp. 21–33. London: Ubiquity Press. DOI: http://dx.doi.org/10.5334/bal.d

of the book (or monograph) as a component of today's academic publishing landscape, the benefits and barriers for universities – locally, nationally and internationally – have been articulated variously and often. There has been a plethora of research, surveys and conferences devoted to the wide ranging world of ebooks, and I do not intend to examine them here. However, I will highlight key aspects of today's environment that I think are of especial interest to library service designers and providers.

Three recent studies, all from the USA in 2013, contextualise today's environment around delivery of digital services: firstly, there is OCLC's report *Meeting the e-resources challenge* on the effective management, access and delivery of e-collections for HE libraries[2]. It presents case studies of experiences structured around key tasks in the e-resource management workflow, including: selection, acquisition, describing, discovery, access and renewal of licensed content within libraries' electronic collections.

Secondly, there is the *ECAR Study of Undergraduate Students and IT*[3] in which Educause collaborated with more than 250 USA HE institutions to collect responses from more than 112,000 undergraduate students about their technology experiences and expectations, and which explores the ways in which new, better, or more technology can impact students' relationship with information technology. It found the cost of textbooks was the most important value factor for students to use ebooks or e-textbooks, but a need for portability and availability outweighs that. As mentioned also in the context of my institution below, unfortunately the user experience is frustrating given complex platforms and incompatible devices.

Lastly, the *Ithaka S+R US Library Survey*[4] examines how the leaders of academic libraries are approaching systemic changes in their environment and the opportunities and constraints they face in leading their organisations. From a collections standpoint, it found that spend on ebooks hadn't really increased since 2010, and yet its Faculty Survey (2012) found more than half of faculty members assert that ebooks play an important role in research and teaching.

Local context at the University of Westminster

Our ebook collections

At time of writing (Spring 2014) the University of Westminster spends around 70% of our materials budget on electronic content (£330.3K in 2012/13). Our digital library collection includes nearly 87,000 ejournals, 330,000 ebooks and over 140 databases; these generate around 3 million electronic usages

[2] http://www.oclc.org/en-UK/publications/newsletters/enews/2013/36/02.html

[3] Educause Centre for Applied Research (ECAR) http://www.educause.edu/library/resources/ecar-study-undergraduate-students-and-information-technology-2013

[4] http://sr.ithaka.org/research-publications

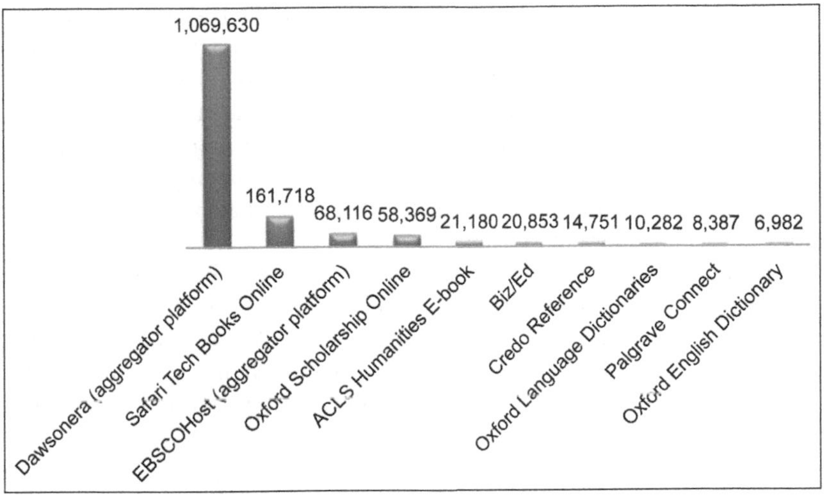

Figure 1: Top ten ebook resources — usage 2012–13.

annually. Access is these is split across about 1 million journal articles, 1.5 million ebook sections and 500,000 database searches, making this one of our key delivery areas. The ebooks we provide are, unsurprisingly, a mix of purchased, subscribed and open access (OA) including nearly twenty ebook collections. Notwithstanding the availability of the vast resource that is the Jisc Historic Books collection, the majority of our usage comes from single ebook purchases (course textbooks) which have been selected by the library, by our academics and through a Patron Driven Acquisition (PDA) pilot, and which are available through aggregator platforms such as Dawsonera, Safari Tech and EBSCOHost. The most popular collections support our faculties of Business, Science and Technology, Social Sciences & Humanities, and Law, as well as multidisciplinary reference (see **Figure 1**). Within the institution, strategies for ebook management rely on relationships with the academic community to support targeted and strategic collection development around high profile, high impact content such as one-off ebook, ebook collection and course text purchases; all purchases must be in support of strategies for learning and teaching, and research.

Ebook discovery and promotion

The integrated management and discovery of the digital collection is through the Ex Libris suite, with its Primo service badged for our users as *LibrarySearch*. During 2012/13 we logged over 650,700 physical visits to our libraries (we record visits to three out of four libraries) and made nearly 685,000 loans. This compares to about 6 million electronic visits (about 3m ejournal/ebook and database and about 3m LibrarySearch sessions). We ran a small pilot on PDA, and used what we found out to support evolving models and to drive up user satisfaction; this includes targeted ebook PDA rentals for "just in time" access to ebooks content to satisfy interlibrary loan requests (an increasingly common model in HE). It is feasible that more targeted use of PDA could benefit Westminster, but ongoing work would be needed to monitor use of patron selected titles, and provide management information comparing PDA titles against academic/library selected material to find a balance that works both for our users and for our budgets.

Meantime, we continue with advocacy to promote digital resources, and the benefits of our ebooks portfolio, ebook collections and new acquisitions to students and staff in order to optimise usage. We recognise the need to increase support for new students unfamiliar with the "user unfriendly" aggregator platforms, as most do not provide a satisfactory user experience;

Ebook learning and teaching strategy

In relation to the University's strategy for learning and teaching, Deans of Faculties and the Pro-Vice-Chancellor for Teaching and Learning are involved with the university's current Learning Futures initiative, including a strand on "transforming learning and teaching". This developmental work is based on the Community of Inquiry model (Garrison and Anderson 2011), which provides a coherent framework to underpin all the different strands of the Learning Futures programme. Of particular relevance to the library service are some of the key principles.

(a) A focus on the educational experience and higher-order skills, which puts the educational experience right at its heart. It places emphasis on critical thinking and reflection, but it also stresses the importance of the social dimension of learning. Work on Graduate Attributes, including digital and information literacy, will underpin this.
(b) A solid and realistic basis for integrating technology into higher education and promoting blended learning. The model recognises the potential of technology, but dismisses the use of technology for technology's sake. If technology is to be used, it must add value – it should provide a means through which learning is facilitated. This is true of the library's digital resources as well.
(c) Recognition of the enormous value of the face-to-face educational experience. Blended-learning approaches should not be viewed as replacing these experiences.
(d) A basis for the promotion of a blended-learning approach, which offers the potential to create a community of inquiry independent of time and location through the use of information and communication technologies. The power of blended learning is that it respects the advantages and preferences of face-to-face, whilst recognising the enormous

strengths of online learning. Realising the potential of e-learning does not imply that traditional education is obsolete, rather that e-learning's capabilities can actively enhance traditional educational ideals. The educational rationale for blended learning is the ability of a blended-learning design to engage participants in critical reflection and discourse by creating a flexible and sustainable community of inquiry. Blended-learning designs can extend time and tasks that sustain a community of inquiry beyond the limited frame of the traditional face-to-face classroom.

Aligning services to strategy

Our challenge is to align our services with the theoretical framework as it evolves. Meantime, I expect work to emerge within the Learning Futures initiative to explore user behaviour with students given the ongoing evolution in the use of digital resources, ebooks and changes to the supply model. Today, aggregators such as CourseSmart and VitalSource prefer conversations directly with academic colleagues to promote a 1 to 1 student textbook model, with associated class note sharing facilities, finding new ways to increase their market share by tailored cost negotiation based on full-time equivalent users/length of course, while bypassing the library as the traditional funder of such resources. This implies that libraries would not support a student-centric model which gives access to a set course book through the virtual learning environment (VLE), or direct via the publisher platform. Moreover, it implies that we do not want to engage with supporting access to resources after a student graduates as part of an institutional lifelong learning agenda. Such business models are challenging, as they expand the need to support content from more publishers on yet another dynamic platform. The library is usually better placed to manage the process including procurement, licensing and access management and to help users meet expectations of the experience whether through on- or off-campus access, and across a range of mobile devices.

Use of ebooks

A quick turnaround survey of taught course students via Blackboard around use of ebooks at the university in March 2014 showed that most respondents (60%) used ebooks weekly, or at least monthly, with most use being related to textbooks and reference works (90%) to help complete coursework assignments. Ease of use and access across multiple devices are considered essential, not just desirable. Anecdotally, ebook users utilise the content in short targeted bursts, and we know they use other resources including print books and content on other devices, at the same time. While it is difficult to compare the value of physical against virtual usage on such a small sample, these findings underline the digital shift and the importance of digital library activities to our users. Preliminary results from the 2014 LibQual survey at the university highlight again the message that students on taught courses need access to the "*main texts and readings I need for my work*" and make "*electronic resources accessible from home or office*" amongst their top requirements. While this is not a surprise, it underlines how we have to ensure we weave ebooks into our offering as a genuine way of improving the student experience, not as an add-on.

With regard to core texts in relation to learning and teaching, we are watching the current pilot for core text provision that the London Universities Purchasing Consortium (LUPC) is currently running with Queen Mary London. Phase 2 (from September 2014) will be opened up to a wider cohort of interested institutions and we are gauging faculty interest and funding. Some of our academics are also experimenting with WileyPlus fully integrated inside Blackboard for their modules.

IT challenges

Within our service we are exploiting access via the VLE (Blackboard), and have a project underway to bring in new reading-list software to further facilitate planning and budgeting. The reading-list software will offer new opportunities for the library to work with academic staff and students on managing lists, reducing out of date/out of print items previously listed, and positively acquiring alternative ebooks, subject to availability and pricing. For ease of deployment and to increase user engagement, it remains important to integrate access solutions into existing workflows and systems as much as possible. We use existing authentication systems to simplify access and to increase reliability and resilience (as an institution we use the Lightweight Directory Access Protocol (LDAP) internet standard) and we offer Shibboleth login where practical. There is new work under way in respect of institutional IT access and identity management, which we intend to help us exploit managed user groups' access more effectively. That said, for users, there are known, big problems to solve – the multiplicity of formats and platforms, the restrictions on use, the restrictions on using devices, formats and access routes they prefer, and the limited functionality and incompatibility with non-academic ebooks. Another aspect will be the "open" agenda – exploitation of Open Educational Resources (OER) as well as access to more OA ebooks as ways to manage cost and optimise impact.

I would add that Westminster has good support for visually impaired users, including sourcing of text files from publishers, and recent feedback has indicated that ebooks can be a viable offering. However, digital rights management (DRM) and the need to download specialist digital publishing software still present a barrier to usage, not least with a cost implication for users on- and off-campus. Not all visually disadvantaged users wish to use only the text-to-speech function, and more industry development in partnership with organisations such as Jisc TechDis will be required to provide a more viable solution. We look forward to the development of more user-friendly alternatives, including digital watermarking.

What the user wants

In terms of the user's learning experience, it is important to take a more user-based approach and to remember why s/he needs the content in the first place or what "job" they are doing (e.g. to get an assignment done). Often (in an ebook context) we focus on the function of delivery online or ebook formats. What has passed into the sector's folk memory is the presentation by Joshua Harding, a second year medical student at Warwick Medical School, at the 2013 UKSG Conference who (politely) took publishers and librarians to task for simply not moving fast enough to give him what he wants. What he said he wanted (and wasn't getting without paying for it personally) was everything integrated in his personal iPad based "ecosystem"; this included:

- Intuitive navigation
- Interactive features – movies, animations, music, podcasts, slideshows, images, 3D models
- Search function through the entire book
- Highlighting text, making notes and sharing them
- Purchasing per chapter
- Free content updates

"From my limited perspective, much of what is wrong with the system comes down to the fact that publishers and libraries have to plan well in advance and make changes slowly... Students on the other hand are able to change direction quickly and easily. The problem exists because the market has changed so radically in the past few years that students have been able to adopt the new technologies well before the industry and libraries were able to make changes to support these students."[5]

An "above campus" shared service

A second internal element is the requirement of greater efficiency and economy in the management of all professional and support services as the HE financial environment shifts and reshapes. Ebook management requires a

---

[5] http://www.slideshare.net/UKSG/0930-harding

heavy investment in staffing (time and skills sets) in every HE institution (HEI), as ebook procurement, metadata, licensing and accessibility are (and are increasingly) complex. As a member of the Society of College, National and University Libraries (SCONUL) Shared and Collaborative Services Strategy Group, I have been an active supporter of the development of KB+[6] as a centralised, shared, above-campus knowledge base of data useful to electronic resources management (ERM) at institutional level, recognising the potential for these activities to be integrated into a shared service "above campus" based on automated and integrated workflows to avoid single points of failure. As of May 2014, KB+ has data from over 170 institutions with some 550 registered users of the service.

Most recently, as part of the Jisc co-design programme, the KB+ project team, supported by the University of Huddersfield, undertook a consultation exercise to identify and assess the pain points relating to ebooks[7] and post-cancellation access[8] as reported by academic libraries and their users.

Drawn from over 500 delegate submissions across a range of HE libraries, a total of 47 pain points were identified by librarians and further validated through a voting process during the study. It grouped problems into four categories: ones that that seem intractable (too big/too complex/out of our control); ones we can solve locally ourselves; those requiring local resolution, but which would benefit from above-campus support; and those that can only be tackled through above-campus or community action (e.g. through a shared service). Each of the top 12 pain points (25%) received majority endorsement (over 66%) for "above campus" support as a solution. These "dirty dozen" are recognisable by any library service director:

- Improve e-book compatibility with mobile devices
- Compatibility with accessibility software
- Share knowledge on procurement issues
- Standardise and simplify licensing
- Adopt a community approach to negotiating with publishers
- Single ebook acquisition and discovery service including pricing and models
- Better usage statistics – Journal Usage Statistics Portal (JUSP) for ebooks
- Normalise ebook ISBNs
- Provide continuing and archival access
- Preservation of DRM-free content
- Finding out what ebooks are available
- Share techniques for local statistics collection

6 http://www.kbplus.ac.uk/kbplus/about
7 http://knowledgebaseplus.wordpress.com/ebooks-co-design-project/ebooks-full-report/
8 http://knowledgebaseplus.wordpress.com/pca-co-design-project/pca-full-report/

While this list will come as no surprise, it is disappointing that publishing models and services as they exist today cannot help us to solve them.

External drivers – a time of intense scrutiny

Today the digital future of the book in the HE environment is the focus of intense scrutiny; this is important for all aspects of HE services supporting learning, teaching and research. Four important initiatives – by funders, by Jisc and other sector bodies and library services – are currently taking place which are worthy of special mention here as their outcomes can help solve some of the wider, intractable issues:

(a) The Jisc pilot co-design project on a national monograph strategy: its report, expected be published in Spring 2014, forms the final output from the first phase of a project which ran from July 2013 until January 2014 in collaboration with SCONUL and Research Libraries UK (RLUK)[9]. Part of its work has been around identifying the need for an infrastructure that can give access to both digital and hard-copy monographs via a stable business model with appropriate collaborative approaches to licensing and digitisation, and which would offer innovative approaches to publishing and new formats.

(b) OAPEN (Open Access Publishing in European Networks)[10]: this primarily explores open access monograph business models in the humanities and social sciences, and the goal is to foster the creation of new content by developing future-orientated publishing solutions, including an open access library for peer reviewed books;

(c) The Higher Education Funding Council for England (HEFCE) expert reference group on Monographs and Open Access Publishing[11] has been set up to develop increased understanding about the challenges and opportunities for open-access monograph publishing.

(d) The Arts and Humanities Research Council (AHRC) and the British Library have launched a two-year research project on the academic book of the future in the context of OA publishing and continuing digital change.[12]

These developments are against the background of frustration with the publishing model, its unsustainable mixture of formats and platforms and changes in the behaviour and expectations of students and other users. As

[9] http://monographs.jiscinvolve.org/wp/

[10] http://oapen-uk.jiscebooks.org/oapen/

[11] http://www.hefce.ac.uk/whatwedo/rsrch/rinfrastruct/oa/monographs/

[12] http://www.ahrc.ac.uk/News-and-Events/News/Pages/The-Academic-Book-of-the-Future.aspx

a sector, we are also experiencing another shift with publishers withdrawing textbooks from unlimited concurrent users and imposing limits. For all HE library directors, the holy grail remains publishing models that are sustainable and affordable.

University publishing initiatives

Today some HEIs are considering moving to become e-textbook creators as well as OA publishers. In March 2014, Jisc Collections invited UK HE institutions to participate in a three-year national project to explore the viability of institutions becoming e-textbook publishers[13]. The project will assess the following question: *"Will the institution as e-textbook creator help students by providing a more affordable higher education, and promote a better, more sustainable information environment for libraries, students and faculty?"* The term "e-textbook" is defined by Jisc Collections as: "a coherent package of learning materials in electronic form that is fundamental to a course of study at an Further Education College (FEC) or HEI" and which should be reusable, accessible, interoperable, and durable. Moreover, as learning objects e-textbooks must be capable of supporting the different activities and interactions that teachers, or learning designers, might use or encourage; be capable of integration into a range of virtual/managed learning environments; support multiple uses through multiple devices in multiple environments (including offline where appropriate); be benchmarkable for functionality and range of learning materials against the products of accepted commercial market leaders; and be fully hospitable to FECs'/HEIs' requirements in terms of accessibility, such as supporting text-to-speech, magnification, choice of colours for backgrounds and texts, and adhere to recognised standards. An accompanying landscape report by David Ball sets out the current environment and issues in rich detail.

In Scotland, the Scottish Higher Education Digital Library (SHEDL) aims through collaboration and combined purchasing power to achieve a shared digital library with easier access to online content to support research and learning and teaching. Its HE libraries ebook purchase tender work has highlighted to the library community that the publishers they use are making available few (if any) of the textbooks that they want to be able to purchase collectively in their ebook packages; consequently they are all grappling individually with challenging and expensive data rights management when they wish to obtain textbook material. Given there is a common interest in addressing this, the libraries are discussing how they can cooperate to share the costs of e-textbook publishing, and then release the material by OA. SHEDL is to

---

13 http://www.jisc-collections.ac.uk/News/Institution-as-e-textbook-publisher-call-for-particiation/

explore this approach by commissioning a set of pilot e-textbooks to support undergraduate and postgraduate study in certain fields of suitable significant interest across the SHEDL partners (e.g. Scottish law, devolution and government, offshore renewable energy, science and policy, renewable energy in maritime high-latitude environments, and Gaelic language).

While OA methodologies are likely to provide a more cost-effective route to the provision of textbook information, the challenge of funding the research, authoring, publishing and maintenance costs remains. The SHEDL business model is being developed and they estimate the likely timetable for a full e-textbook production may take two years or even longer. The process will most likely invite competitive bids for the overall subject and individual chapter coverage, and they estimate that the costs of producing an e-textbook on a reasonably defined subject area may be in the region of £3000 to £5000, including an author royalty of £500 to £1000. It is anticipated they would seek to use of variants of models used by e.g. Knowledge Unlatched, Open Library of the Humanities, Jisc Collections and Ubiquity Press. Publishing models that are sustainable and affordable will be a paramount consideration.

At the time of writing, the University of Westminster is establishing the University of Westminster Press in partnership with Ubiquity Press for some of these same reasons. It will provide a university-branded dissemination channel for high-quality research, for the production of online articles and journals, digital and print-on-demand monographs, conference proceedings and other forms of peer-reviewed research output, increasing the profile and standing of Westminster's research, providing an income generation channel and supporting our research engagement and excellence missions. A Westminster thesis series is also under consideration. It is to be hoped that we can also move into the e-textbook publishing space over time. The press will provide us with an online publishing platform and service supported by international peer-review networks, and will demonstrate the university's commitment to the OA agenda and facilitate high quality publications (in particular from early career researchers).

This will contribute to the disruption of conventional commercial models of scholarly communication and advance the OA agenda, addressing issues prevalent in the current commercial model, by significantly reducing the costs of publishing and addressing problems such as loss of copyright. The Ubiquity Press is based on a collaborative model (Ubiquity Partners Network) involving a network of peer review, and a governance structure involving participation from members of the Ubiquity Partners Network. Our press will operate under the oversight of a board with editorial and governance responsibilities.

Standards of editorial practice will be benchmarked to those of established and reputed academic publishers. Peer review is facilitated through Ubiquity's partner network of expertise. In the initial three-year term, the aim is to publish three journals and five books. In the initial stages, it is anticipated that publications will be solely from Westminster, but further development is planned to enable publication of externally produced outputs. The publishing model is based primarily on a Gold OA approach, with article processing charges and book processing charges. The key difference from standard commercial models is that the charging system is designed to be affordable and sustainable, and charges will be significantly lower than those of commercial operators. The details of pricing are currently under consideration by the university. The inception of the university press is an important development for the university in the context of OA publishing, including the new REF OA requirements. We are seeking the active engagement of faculty research leaders and colleagues currently involved in academic publishing.

Closing comments

There are continuing and even increasing concerns about the processes involved in the management and delivery of ebooks, relating both to library functions and to the end-user experience. As the core texts model(s) and OA/OER resources mature, and student-as-consumer expectations grow, provision of core texts will not be an easy challenge. Varied and mixed economies are currently being experimented with, including text provision (print or electronic), text plus device provision, tokens towards text cost (used on Amazon, aggregator platform or on-site bookshop) and direct student purchase. The potential for change is still "around the corner", but the complexity of the issues and the seemingly intractable nature of the problems continue to exercise service directors, our staff and users.

It is likely that, with the spotlight now on the future of the monograph, the distinctiveness of an institutional ebook support offering will become a more important issue for institutions across HE. The drivers include content cost, current publishing models, active promotion of OA and even cohort size. It will interesting to see where the move to "blended content" takes us as libraries begin to exploit both our paid-for and open (OA/OER) content more systematically. That said, a large part of the innovation and "competition" is taking a very consumerist approach. Much of what service directors (and many scholarly publishers too) talk about is, naturally enough, from the supplier point of view (and this includes the library as supplier).

As service directors, we must always try to shift more towards a user perspective and constantly ask ourselves "is this going to change the user's learning experience?" What unites us all at a local level is the customer-centric drive to provide content to support both our current student cohort and lifelong learning. The big question is how and when we can all reimagine content so that the norm for ebooks is that they have become true "natively digital" in origin, with imaginative built-in interactivity features and multimedia elements, including video and 3D objects, to enhance the learning experience, rather than being a more or less faithful electronic version of a traditional print textbook with all the drawbacks inherent in that.

Reference

Garrison, D. R. and Anderson, T. (2011) *E-learning in the 21st century: a framework for research and practice* (2nd edition). London: Routledge/ Falmer.

elements, including video and 3D objects, to enhance the learning experience, rather than being a more or less faithful electronic version of a traditional printed book with all the drawbacks inherent in that.

Reference

Garrison, D. R. and Anderson, T. (2011) *E-learning in the 21st century: a framework for research and practice* (2nd edition). London: Routledge-Falmer.

Ebooks and accessibility

Alistair McNaught and Huw Alexander
Jisc TechDis and SAGE Publications

What do we mean by accessibility and what are the issues?

Accessibility is to ebooks what labelling is to the food industry. When you purchase a ready meal from a supermarket you expect to be able to check the ingredients straight away. Will it be suitable for my friend with the nut allergy? Is it suitable for vegetarians? By recognising that different people have different needs and preferences, the industry makes it easy for people to choose the things that suit them and many retailers make a point of signalling their "dietary accessibility" to boost sales. In a similar way, different readers have different needs and preferences, yet it can be very difficult for them to find out whether the book they are about to purchase or read will meet any of their reading needs or interoperate with their assistive technologies such as screenreaders or text to speech.

Happily, ebooks have the potential to meet a very wide range of accessibility needs. For example, with the right format and the right construction, ebooks can offer:

- Magnification with text reflow. Magnification alone is of limited benefit if it makes it harder to navigate the page. If, however, line lengths

How to cite this book chapter:
McNaught, A. and Alexander, H. 2014. Ebooks and accessibility. In: Woodward, H. (ed.) *Ebooks in Education: Realising the Vision.* Pp. 35–49. London: Ubiquity Press. DOI: http://dx.doi.org/10.5334/bal.e

can reflow when text is magnified so that the line still fits the width of the screen, reading speed is significantly improved.

- Colour/contrast changes. People with some visual impairments or dyslexics with scotopic sensitivity can find reading much easier if they can adapt text and background colours or contrasts. This also benefits people working in very dark or very light environments.
- Text-to-speech support. Text to speech is a mature technology that allows text on screen to be voiced by software. Good quality human sounding voices are commercially available in a wide range of languages.
- Alternative texts for images/tables. A text description of the main points of an image or table helps convey information to blind readers, but often helps sighted readers in their interpretation of the information.
- Compatibility with assistive technology devices. Screenreaders perform a text to speech role, but also allow audio-only access to the menus and other features of the delivery platform – provided the product has been produced to recommended accessibility standards.

Ebooks with these features are accessible to a very wide range of users, including non-traditional readers – for example people with print disabilities. The term print disability refers to any disability that hinders an individual's ability to access hard-copy printed text. It is more than visual difficulty, and includes those who have difficulty decoding printed text – for example dyslexic people. Equally, spinal injury or involuntary muscle spasms may hinder someone from physically holding a book. Ebooks can potentially transform access to content for these very varied users. However, the potential benefits are not always realised. It is not unusual for barriers to accessibility to be accidentally introduced at any stage of the supply chain. Typical barriers can include:

- File format choices influence accessibility – for example PDF documents that are a "photograph" of text cannot be read out, recoloured or reflowed to fit a larger font size. Flash-based "flipbooks" can be difficult or impossible to use if you need magnified reflowable text or access to text to speech,
- Lack of accessibility awareness in the production team – even if accessible formats are used, production decisions (like tagging headings for typographical appearance rather than semantic meaning) can strip away benefits for disabled users.
- The interface of the delivery platform (e.g. ebook library systems) may lack features like font and background colour change – even when the format of the ebooks supports it.
- Lack of information or communication of the accessibility features that exist – for example, many products have no accessibility guidance, despite print-disabled people being up to 10% of the readership.

- The hardware devices (e.g. ebook readers/tablets) on which the files are displayed may lack accessibility features – for example colour/contrast options.

Procurement checklist for library staff

One of the issues with accessibility is that it can seem to get bogged down with incomprehensible technicalities – if a sales representative says "it's Section 508 compliant" or "it was designed to WCAG specifications", it's difficult to argue even though neither of you has any clue what those statements mean in practice.

In 2012 Jisc TechDis was commissioned by a group of university libraries to research the provision of alternative formats[1]. The final report included good practice pointers in terms of procurement practices. Jisc TechDis is very focused on the user experience so the procurement advice from the report boils down to eight plain English questions – most of which can be demonstrated there and then with the product. These questions will not guarantee 100% accessibility for all assistive technology tools, but they will allow non-specialist decision makers to ask highly pertinent questions which will help weed out products with poor accessibility.

- What is the maximum font size and does text reflow when you enlarge the font?
- Can a user change background/foreground colours or contrasts?
- Are there keyboard-only equivalents for all mouse actions?
- Is text marked up so it can be navigated in a meaningful way (for example by heading level)?
- Can text be selected and read by text-to-speech tools?
- Are text descriptions available for graphics and images?
- Which assistive technology tools has the system been tested with?
- Where can I find guidance for all these features?

Risks and opportunities

Practice perpetuates culture and cultures perpetuate practices. The model described shows how a publisher or supplier with little awareness of accessibility gives end users little information on their accessibility features. Many print-impaired people have only a scant idea of how ebooks could meet their needs, and even library staff and disability officers are not necessarily aware of the wide benefits that accessible digital text provides. This ignorance can lead

---

[1] Jisc TechDis. Libraries and alternative formats research. Parts 1–5. http://www.jisc.techdis.ac.uk/techdis/multlinkres/details/main_site/laafr

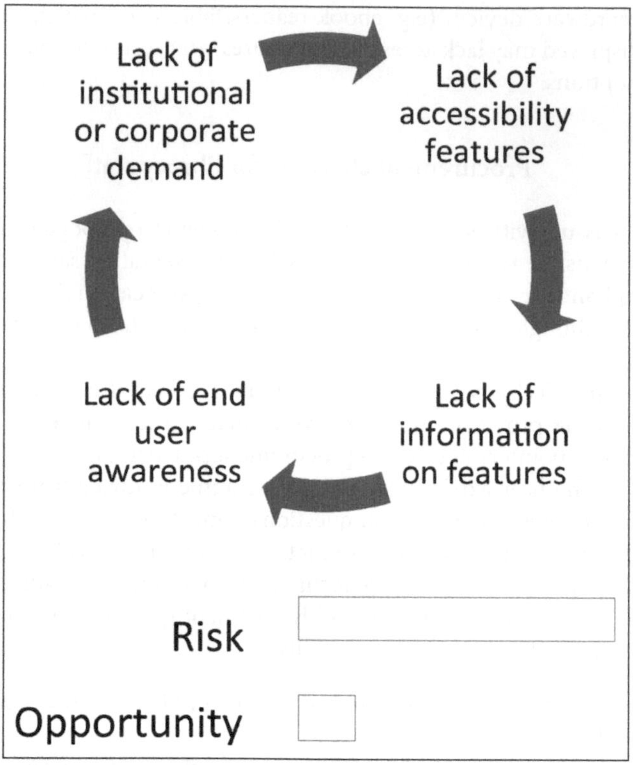

Figure 1: Flow diagram showing how lack of accessibility and accessibility information perpetuates end-user ignorance, reinforcing the status quo. This is a high-risk approach because customer awareness can change very rapidly, particularly if they come across a more accessible rival supplier.

to a dangerous complacency for less accessible publishers. Customer awareness can change in a single day by reading an article or attending a webinar or a conference. Research by Jisc TechDis[2] in 2012 showed that 10% of the 49 higher education institutions (HEIs) surveyed had accessibility as a "deciding factor" in their procurement policies. Colleges and universities can implement such policies faster than publisher workflows can adapt to keep in the market – giving accessible publishers a significant market advantage. **Figures 1** and **2** illustrate the difference between the "hope the issue will go away" approach and a more proactive "let's show the customer what we can provide" approach. The key point here is that accessible suppliers can sustain existing

[2] Libraries and alternative format research. Part 4: Are some organisational approaches more effective? pp. 3-5 http://www.jisctechdis.ac.uk/assets/Documents/laafr4.pdf

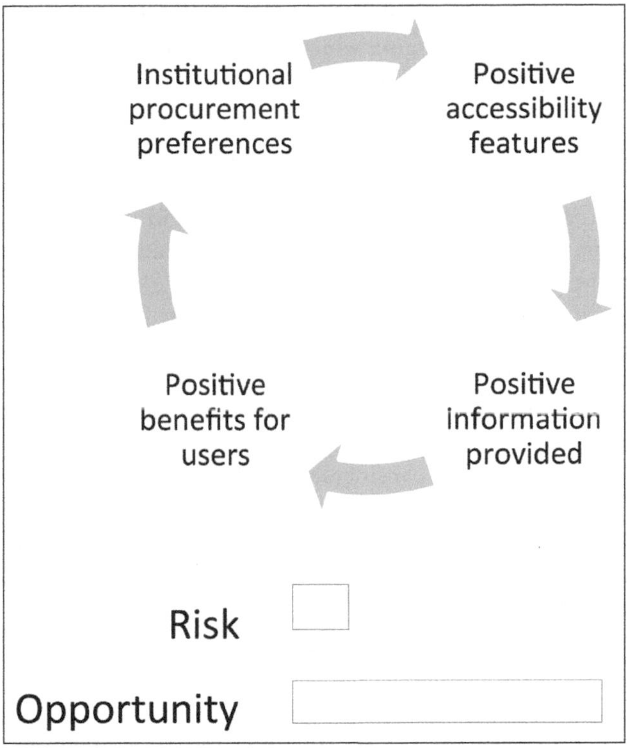

Figure 2: Flow diagram showing how proactive publishers perpetuate a demand for their accessible products.

markets and create new ones. As we see later in this chapter, proactive accessibility provides significant new opportunities.

How are accessible publishing practices evolving?

The transition to a digital publishing world has facilitated the provision of new, innovative products and content to our audiences. The natural corollary of this shift has been the opening up of content to people with visual impairments or print disabilities. Awareness of print disability within the education environment has risen sharply over the past decades, but it is only now that the tools have been made available to effectively meet the needs of this community. Previously the provision of content in an accessible form (Braille, spoken word) was a time-consuming and expensive process. The digital revolution is allowing for a wider range of content to be made available in a more timely and cost-effective fashion. The disadvantages experienced by the visually impaired or print-disabled student are being peeled away. In essence a level playing field is emerging which affords everyone equal access to the content that they require for their studies.

Changing mindsets

This new accessible environment is still nascent and there is much work to be done, but publishers are now much more embedded in the process. The redraft of the *Creative Skillset Nation Occupational Standards for Publishers*[3] resulted in 40 mentions of accessibility themes. The previous standards had zero. Content can be designed and created with accessibility at the forefront of publishers' minds. An "accessible" book now means a "better" book. This constitutes a tremendous shift in the mindset of publishers – one wrought by the need to design content with the delivery method as a central concern. Society itself has changed considerably in the last decade and the dependence on access to information in digital form at the point of demand, be it from a tablet or smartphone, has fundamentally altered the approach of publishers.

Changing opportunities

Digital has afforded a myriad of opportunities to publishers, both in the type of content that can be created and the ways in which in can be delivered. Fortunately, among the main beneficiaries of this sea-change are the visually impaired and print disabled communities.

HESA statistics[4] show that between 600–700 print impaired students could be expected in an average-sized university. If each learner only required two core texts a year that would still result in well over a thousand requests per institution. Current requests to publishers are well below that for most institutions[5] but they are rapidly increasing. They will increase even further. Changes in the disabled student allowance put more expectation on learning providers

[3] http://standards.creativeskillset.org/assets/0000/0572/Book_and_Journal_Publishing_2012_FINAL.pdf

[4] The range in values reflects the fact that whilst specific learning difficulties, visual and motor impairments are the main print impairments, other disabilities (like mental health) can create a need for alternative access. Within a single disability there can be a big variation on the impact on print impairment. Finally, the figures for average size university can be significantly skewed by the inclusion of the Open University. The figures quoted are regarded as a conservative estimate. https://www.hesa.ac.uk/dox/dataTables/studentsandqualifiers/download/Disab1213.xlsx

[5] http://www.jisctechdis.ac.uk/assets/Documents/laafrfull.pdf Median of annual alternative format requests to publishers = 5-15/year.... not the thousand plus that might be expected.

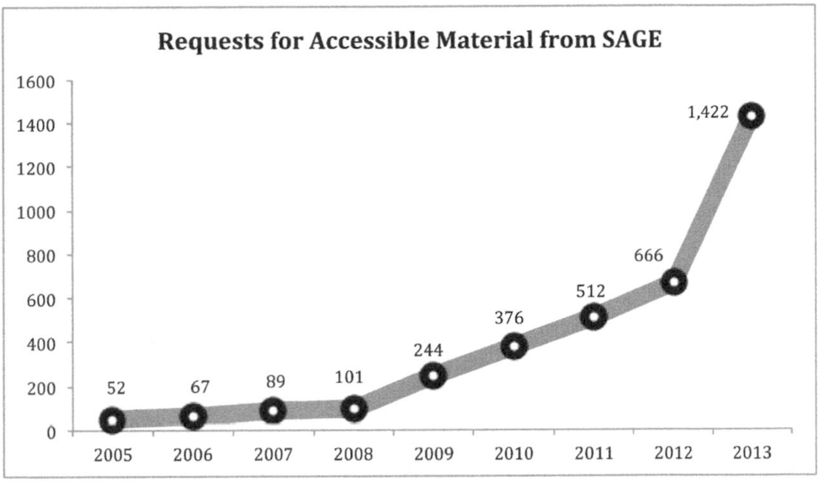

Figure 3: Graph illustrating a nearly 30-fold increase in accessibility requests over eight years with a gradually accelerating demand.

to take responsibility for sourcing accessible content in the first place. Annual requests for digital versions of textbooks by librarians and disability officers (by year) are shown in **Figure 3** for SAGE Publications.

As explored below, SAGE embraced the demand and made fundamental changes to effectively meet this challenge. But this has involved close collaboration with stakeholders, and has had far-reaching ramifications across the business. These kind of figures illustrate the drivers for change. Although the demand for physical copies of textbooks is unlikely to go away, publishers have a vested interest in ensuring that the processes that lead to either physical books or ebooks result in an accessible electronic version. The more accessible the mainstream products become, the fewer costs will be incurred in meeting specific learner needs.

Support and guidance for publishers

The Publishers Association, the Publish Licensing Society, EDItEUR, Jisc TechDis and the Royal National Institute of Blind People have provided the industry with invaluable advice on how to deliver content of the highest quality to our whole audience (see Further reading and resources). The *Accessible Publishing Best Practice Guidelines for Publishers*[6] is a truly indispensable guide

[6] Hilderley, S. (2011), *Accessible Publishing Best Practice Guidelines for Publishers*. http://www.accessiblebooksconsortium.org/inclusive_publishing/en/accessible_best_practice_guidelines_for_publishers.html

to the business of publishing not only accessible content but better books. The advice provided by the aforementioned groups is also supplemented by the conference circuit, where the provision of accessible content is a consistent discussion point. Attendance at events held at the London and Frankfurt Book Fairs, Association of Learned and Professional Publishers (ALPSP), University College London's Digital Forum, the Independent Publishers Guild (IPG) and the guidance provided by the Publishers Association Accessibility Action Group[7] will allow you to keep informed about the changes in the industry. The Trusted Intermediary Global Accessible Resources (TIGAR[8]) project currently being developed by the International Publishers Association will be a huge step forward in the provision of accessible content on a global scale. The opportunities are far-reaching and exciting, and publishers are endeavouring to make a difference, to disable barriers to access and enable learning environments. In the following case study we shall examine the reasons behind the decisions SAGE have taken to help foster this community and the benefits that have been reaped from these decisions.

SAGE and Accessibility: A Case Study

In 2008, SAGE saw firsthand the rise in interest amongst our customers for accessible content. Until this point the provision of files to the visually impaired and print disabled had been a fairly ad hoc process undertaken by the rights and permissions department. The rise in demand, however, was seen as an opportunity to build relationships with our customer base and champion the provision of content to the library community.

Engendering support within the business

The SAGE Vision Statement advocates that SAGE play "a creative role in society by disseminating teaching and research on a global scale, the cornerstones of which are good, long-term relationships, a focus on our markets, and an ability to combine quality and innovation." In redeveloping our approach to the provision of accessible content and support of students, we began by turning everything upside down. The central tenets of the business proposal presented to senior executives were those of speed and simplicity. The most consistent issue identified by librarians regarding content was the time it took publishers to provide the files. Solving this issue was intrinsic to implementing

[7] McNaught, A. (2014), *Overview of guidance for publishers*, compiled by A. McNaught to support the Publishers Association Accessibility Action Group presentation at the London Book Fair. http://tinyurl.com/LBFaccess

[8] TIGAR Service: http://www.accessiblebooksconsortium.org/tigar.en/

a successful makeover of our systems, and the answer was simple, if possibly controversial. The aim would be to respond to all enquiries within 15 minutes of receipt – a plan that would involve prioritising all requests for accessible content above every other project or request. SAGE provides all accessible content free of charge, and proposing that we prioritise a non-revenue stream above say Amazon had the potential for a difficult conversation with the upper echelons of the company.

This difficult conversation did not arise. The proposal was made that from a legal, ethical and commercial point of view implementing this proposal would serve to benefit SAGE both qualitatively and quantitatively. The goodwill generated by this approach would build stronger relationships with the library community, university faculty and students, and would support our commercial interests. The executives at SAGE immediately discerned the benefits and the ties that could be forged by reshaping our provision of accessible content in line with the SAGE Vision Statement. It was also, simply, the right thing to do.

Implementing a simple, customer-centric approach

The policy was swiftly adopted and the profile was raised across SAGE. The message was a simple one. All accessibility requests would be handled centrally through the sales department and everyone within the company knew this. It solved the speed issue in one motion, as any issue linked to accessibility could be passed to the appropriate person. The rise in the number of requests was thus met by a simplification in the processes for delivering the content files. Complicated licence agreements were pared down to simple usage rules, dedicated FTP sites were created, and the whole of our digital archive was redeveloped to focus on ease of discoverability of our own in-house content. In essence the process became a one-stop service whereby the librarian requested the content and we would deliver as soon as possible (the record being within two minutes of receipt). The workflow has been simplified in **Figure 4**.

The goal for SAGE was always to disseminate teaching, and the swiftness of our response would enable our visually impaired and print disabled customers by giving them the material at the same time as their peers. Again, the level playing field at work.

Influencing the bottom line

This decision was vindicated by the positive responses we received from our library partners, and ultimately we were honoured to receive the inaugural Jisc TechDis Publisher Lookup Award for Library Services in 2010. We are

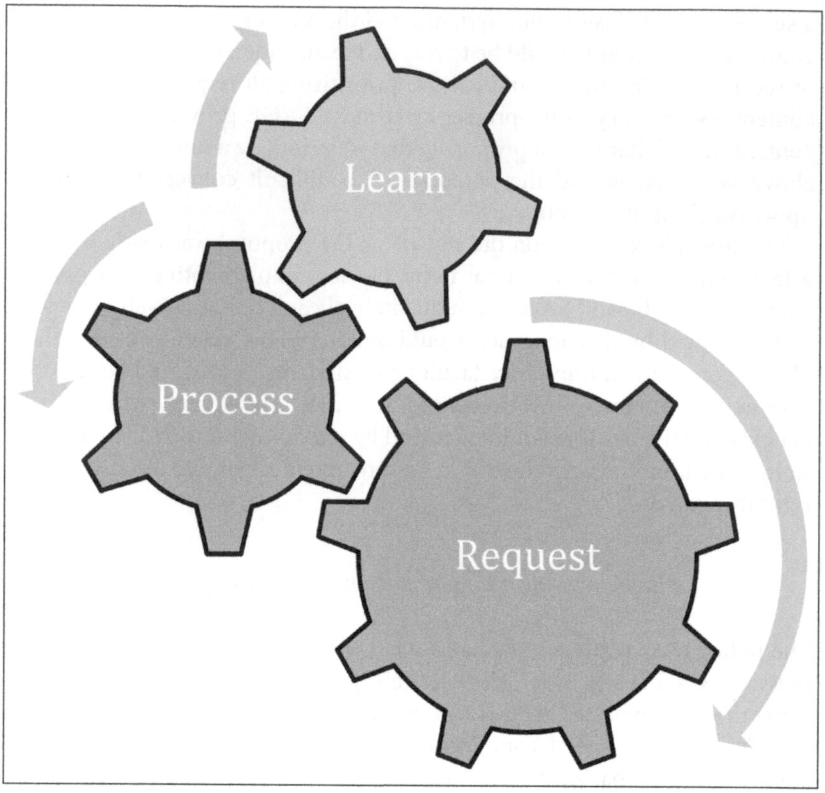

Figure 4: SAGE's workflow for the provision of accessible texts – the priority is to process the request then learn from process in order to improve the fulfilment of future requests.

happy to have developed close working relationships with over 500 academic libraries worldwide, a number that is growing every day.

The efforts made to promote accessibility within SAGE have also informed our publishing decision-making and the development of our own products and platforms. SAGE publishes in both the book and journal sectors, and the development of our digital platforms has been undertaken with a keen eye on the accessibility of the content. Accessible content is better content. It has not always been an easy process and it has been a steep learning curve at times, but the benefits have been manifold. An eye-opening comment from the recent ALPSP meeting by Rachel Thornton, Copyright Clearance Officer at Leeds Metropolitan University, was that librarians were requiring faculty to adopt only titles that had accessible content available. A fair request by librarians and one that SAGE is able to support through the systems we have put in place. No one should be left without access to content that their peers are readily able to consume.

The SAGE checklist for publishers

Based on SAGE's experience the following recommendations are aimed at publishers who are seeking to improve their dissemination of accessible content to the library community: the mnemonic should prove helpful... **A.C.C.E.S.S.I.B.L.E.**

Archive

Gather all your digital files into one central repository organised by year of publication and ISBN. Searching for content will be simplified and efficient. The dual benefit of this undertaking is that you will discover content that can be sold through conventional ebook channels.

Centralise

Assign responsibility to one person for accessibility issues within your company. So many of the issues surrounding the provision of content are explained by a lack of responsibility within the company, and requests falling through the cracks between departments. Define the role and the responsibilities and make sure that in-house staff know who to turn to when a request is received.

Communicate

As well as communicating internally make sure that your efforts are being advertised externally. Clearly state your policy on your website and make sure that your contact details are present on the Publisher Lookup website. Prepare a short FAQ document for customer-facing staff so that they know what to answer when faced with questions regarding accessibility. Giving field sales staff the opportunity to say "Yes, we can do that" will increase the chances of winning that adoption.

Explore

Keep yourself informed. Attend conferences and seminars on the issue of accessibility in publishing and wider society. The Accessibility Action Group set up by the Publishers Licensing Society is a hub of such information and news.

Simplify

Simplify everything from workflows to usage rules. The processes for supplying accessible content do not need to be complicated. Librarians and publishers are already inundated with work, so strip away the layers of bureaucracy and make the fulfilment of requests as simple as possible. Rules for the use of content do not need to be draconian – they need to be viable, straightforward and informative. If you cannot trust a disability librarian in this world, who can you trust?

Speed

From simplicity comes speed. Installing a bureaucracy-heavy approach to delivering content to the visually impaired or print disabled will only serve to take up your time and theirs. The aim should be to get the content and knowledge in their hands as swiftly as possible. Put yourself in their shoes. Imagine how hard university is at the best of times. Now imagine it without access to the books you need to study. Perfectly impossible. Make it possible.

Inform

Use the information gleaned from your accessible publishing programme to inform the decisions taken at the heart of your business. Develop your platforms in a manner consistent with your accessibility policies – make the best content possible for every audience. Identify trends in your accessibility requests that will inform your digital strategy – at SAGE if someone requests content that has yet to be digitised then it is processed as a priority and feeds into our commercial ebook channels. Use accessibility requests as a guide to demand.

Build

Build accessibility into your entire production workflow. Explore the opportunities afforded by EPUB2 and EPUB3 and a fully XML-first workflow. But don't ignore the humble PDF. A finely crafted PDF can be an example of great accessibility and a widely saleable asset in the library community.

Listen

Listen to your customers. They will all be saying the same thing, whether from within the accessibility community or outside. Everyone wants better access, better information, better platforms, better books. Do not let accessible issues be a secondary concern, make them central. The user experience is everything.

Enthuse

If you've done something good, produced something wonderful or made a terrible hash of it, share your experiences. We all make mistakes, it is how we learn from them that is important. Make appearances on the conference circuit to communicate what you have done, what worked and what didn't. Sharing ideas and policies is the only way to improve the services we each strive to offer.

Learning providers as catalysts for change – sourcing alternative formats and providing feedback

There are many different ways of obtaining text in digital format – and these were explored in some detail at the E-books and accessibility conference[9] coordinated by Jisc TechDis in 2013. A notable statistic from this was the annual cost of scanning textbooks[10] for print disabled learners – £50,000 to meet the needs of seven learners. Publishers able to provide accessible content either directly from their mainstream ebook offers or indirectly via an accessible PDF are an extremely attractive option compared to those that can't.

There are different ways in which accessible content can be obtained and Jisc TechDis have put together detailed guidance with a helpful flow diagram[11] that takes a number of different factors into account in order to help library and disability staff work out the quickest and most cost-effective way of meeting learners' needs.

The Publisher Lookup website[12] was created by Jisc TechDis and the Publishers Association in order to facilitate easy communication between library/disability staff and publishers. The Publisher Lookup website provides an opportunity for library and disability staff to leave feedback on publisher responsiveness – both to praise good practice and to highlight poor practice. Publishing is a complex business with multiple demands. The Right to Read Alliance has worked hard to make accessibility a positive marketing benefit. Jisc TechDis, a key member of the Right to Read Alliance, sponsored the Publisher Lookup awards to raise awareness of good practice in the industry. Providing positive feedback to publishers is essential in helping to justify changes to practice. The Publisher Lookup awards brought positive

---

9 E-books and accessibility ugly duckling or adolescent swan? (2013), Senate House, London, 13 Feb. http://www.jisctechdis.ac.uk/techdis/events/detail/2013/ebook13022013

10 McMahon, A. (2013), Presentation entitled: "Accessible books – who pays?" http://www.jisctechdis.ac.uk/assets/documents/events/130213ebooks_amcmahondundeeuni.ppt

11 http://www.jisctechdis.ac.uk/assets/Documents/guidetoaltformat.pdf

12 http://www.publisherlookup.org.uk

Figure 5: The Jisc TechDis Publisher Lookup Awards raised awareness of both good practice in the business process (Elsevier, Palgrave MacMillan and SAGE) and responsiveness to library requests (SAGE, Hodder Education and Wiley Blackwell).

publicity to five publishers including SAGE, who were successful in both awards (**Figure 5**).

Conclusion

Publishing has been able to make giant strides in recent years in the provision of accessible content. Help is now widely available to publishers unsure as to how to implement a successful accessibility programme. The emergence of organisations such as Load2Learn[13] in the UK and BookShare[14] and AccessText[15] in the USA provide platforms for the delivery of content, and removes the complexity from the process.

The numbers of students seeking accessible content will continue to grow in the years ahead. By engaging with the issue now, publishers will be able to shape the future by building relationships with the network of decision

13 Load2learn. Delivered by RNIB and Dyslexia Action. https://load2learn.org.uk

14 BookShare is the world's largest online library for individuals with print disabilities. https://www.bookshare.org

15 Accesstext Network. All post-secondary institutions in the USA are eligible to join the network at no cost. Members can request files and permissions from leading publishers with one simple form. http://accesstext.org

makers across higher education. Pressure also needs to be exerted on device makers and digital vendors so that content is open to all. It is then that we will see the true benefit of digital, and a convergence of demand and supply where anyone who wants to access information will be able to do so in the format that they desire. It is hopefully a day that is not too far away, and by working together we can accomplish it and just make books better. Inclusivity in every respect will be essential; we have the tools at our disposal and it is time to use them.

Further reading and resources

Copyright (Visually Impaired Persons) Act 2002. http://www.legislation.gov.uk/ukpga/2002/33/contents

Free online training resources on accessibility. http://www.visionip.org/inclusive_publishing/en/

Guidance on alternative text formats. http://www.jisctechdis.ac.uk/techdis/technologymatters/altformat

Jisc TechDis guidance for publishers. http://www.jisctechdis.ac.uk/techdis/keyinitiatives/publishers

Online accessibility self evaluation for library staff. http://www.jisctechdis.ac.uk/techdis/resources/oaseslibrary

Publishers Association's guidelines for provision of content to VIPs. http://www.publishersassociation.org.uk/index.php?option=com_docman&task=doc_download&gid=273&Itemid=

Research report on alternative format provision in HE. Sponsored by CLAUD group – Creating Libraries Accessible to Users with Disabilities. http://www.jisctechdis.ac.uk/techdis/multlinkres/detail/main_site/laafr

Academic ebooks and the mobile user experience

Mark Williams and Ben Showers
Jisc Collections and Jisc

How did you go bankrupt?

Two ways. Gradually, then suddenly.

Ernest Hemingway, The Sun Also Rises

These two trajectories – gradual, almost imperceptible change and then sudden, rapid transition – define much of the technological change that has confronted universities and colleges over the past few decades. While this progression is not unique to academia, it does seem particularly marked in the academic sector, from the initial caution shown to the web and the lack of institutional presence online to the experimentation with mobile learning, which remains experimental and largely peripheral. Serious change always seems such a long way off, until it changes everything.

In contrast to the development of the Kindle and iPad and the associated content platforms of Amazon and iBooks, the "revolution" in digital academic content seems to be indefinitely waiting in the wings. Much of the innovation in digital academic content has been in academic ejournals which have for a number of decades cemented themselves as the primary mode of delivery for

How to cite this book chapter:
Williams, M. and Showers, B. 2014. Academic ebooks and the mobile user experience. In: Woodward, H. (ed.) *Ebooks in Education: Realising the Vision.* Pp. 51–58. London: Ubiquity Press. DOI: http://dx.doi.org/10.5334/bal.f

scholarly articles. With increasing rapidity, however, students' and researchers' changing requirements and expectations mean that they expect an intuitive and mobile platform approach to the discovery of, and access to, ebooks and digital content. Academic users are no longer willing to make exceptions for scholarly content.

In this chapter we make an attempt to explore the changing requirements of students and researchers regarding access to scholarly digital content, and the challenges and implications for content and service providers in adapting to these changing expectations. Primarily, there is a focus on the consumption of ebooks and digital content by users, ensuring that institutions and publishers take a user-centric perspective in the ways digital content is delivered and used. It also provides an opportunity to explore the particular value of ebooks for the scholarly enterprise. They offer a way to enhance the experience of engaging with the texts themselves – access to the underlying data, interactive images, annotation functionality, and so on. There is also the potential for new models and approaches to inform the research process itself – being able to access the content in new ways, such as text and data mining, for example.

Fundamentally, this chapter is an attempt to move academic ebooks beyond the current paper (pdf) archetype and towards something which exploits the inherent potential of digital content. Ebooks deliver a user experience that exceeds the expectations of students, researchers and users.

The landscape

Plenty of reports on the web detail trends of mobile versus desktop usage and, although such reports may differ in terms of the timescales they predict, they mostly agree that mobile usage will exceed desktop very soon.[1] The fact that we no longer concern ourselves with statistics about smartphone sales versus feature phones shows how *de-facto* web consumption on a mobile device has become. The one distinction worth making is between the use of mobile tablets and the use of smartphones, although even this distinction loses relevance outside of conversations around content usability and authentication.

It is in this mobile ecosystem that academic ebooks have to exist. Even in the traditional desktop scenario, where publishers and institutions have tinkered with the ebook platforms and content to fit a reasonably consistent template, there is significant variability among the products, something that institutional librarians have had to take into account when developing their user guides.[2] Once the huge variety of mobile devices and operating systems is introduced into the equation, the consistency of the user experience can be severely compromised.

---

1 http://www.gartner.com/newsroom/id/2645115
2 http://adat.crl.edu/ebooks

It is user expectation that impacts the actual definition of what an ebook is. Users who are used to having a straightforward consistent experience when using an individual, commercially purchased ebook for their own leisure enjoyment are often confronted with a completely different experience with an academic ebook in a mobile context. So much so, one wonders whether the same definition of an ebook really applies to the two scenarios. Depending on the ebook provider, a user won't be able to read the book anytime, anywhere on their device, nor will they be able to lend the book, to underline passages, or to save the entire book. They may not even be able to open the book because of authentication issues, in which case the question needs to be asked: Do they even have in their virtual possession, a book?

It is this gap in user experience that causes consumption of an ebook on a mobile device to fall behind other experiences. Academic ebook provider platforms differ to such a degree that institutions are forced to develop bespoke instructions on their use, something which would be anathema to a large scale retailer of commercial ebooks – and something which certainly defies current web design best practice of intuitive interaction.

The equation is admittedly more complex than at first glance. An ebook is not simply a single file. Effectively it is the sum of a publisher platform. It is a file that holds content and supports discovery, a content file ideally developed to common standards such as EPUB[3]. In addition to this, there may be reader software such as Adobe Editions wrapped around the platform, and beyond this, there may also be variety of authentication procedures attached. All of these elements then have to operate on a variety of operating systems and devices. The sum of this complex relationship is greater than the challenge of any individual element.

Because of this complexity, the presentation of ebooks within an app in the mobile environment becomes very tempting. In an app, the developer has far greater control over the processes occurring, which should lend itself to a more bug-free and issue-free user experience. The tendency by publishers to focus on apps for mobile delivery can be attributed to both demand – after all, this is the way in which many users consume other content on their devices – and the fact that half the mobile tablet space is essentially app-driven by design, such as the iPad. So app deployment on smartphones can remove some of the usability issues discussed here – issues with the platform, such as discovery and download and with the content, and readability on a three-inch screen.

But app-driven ebooks pose significant authentication challenges. Many apps use device twinning, in which a user first authenticates to a platform in a traditional web environment, often using IP or federated access, and then requests a code that is then sent by email. They can then use this to authenticate their mobile device. It is a pragmatic solution, but one that in many ways

[3] http://idpf.org/epub/30

undermines the UK's current academic licensing models and authentication systems. By receiving a key code and twinning their account, the user is effectively authenticating the phone but not the user. If the phone is lost or stolen, or simply borrowed, access is often possible for periods of up to 90 days – there is no industry standard here. Only with the use of two-factor authentication or the use of activation lock software, making the user enable password protection on the phone, is this vulnerability mitigated. However, there is an ironic twist here. For the user to enable twinning and receive an initial authentication code to enable them to access their resource while mobile, they frequently need to be on campus in the first instance. They are required to be within the designated IP range, or to navigate a federated login on a very small screen, which is of course the very issue they are trying to avoid by enabling device twinning.

Device twinning is, however, still one of the more pragmatic solutions from the user's point of view. However, authentication can be far more complex. A user will often have to juggle logins for an app store, Adobe Digital Editions, a federated access account and a social ID just to access the same piece of content on a range of devices. There is often further difficulty arising from the policies of the user's own institution, if social web apps such as Facebook have been blocked. On a small-size mobile device screen, those additional obstacles can become unmanageable. The effects of a single bug or problem encountered by the user become multiplied as the number of processes necessary for a user to gain access to and read an ebook increases.

Fortunately, the additional tools that a user frequently has to download in order to read an ebook successfully, such as Adobe Editions, can at least be installed on a user's mobile device by the user themselves. But in a locked-down institutional desktop environment that may well be impossible. This again leads to users having a very different and inconsistent experience when accessing the same content on different platforms.

Consistency of experience is a must, with an expectation that users on a mobile device will require offline access, will be able to annotate on and offline, will be able to cut and paste according to the agreed licence, and have a flowing layout that is readable on and adapts to the full range of devices.

Providers of commercial mainstream content have learned the lessons that making content difficult to access can lead to users exploring alternative ways of getting that content. If an institutional user illegally streams a resource for which their institution already holds a licence, this tells us that it is not a question of affordability but one of usability. Platforms such as Adobe Digital Editions do offer ebook providers the ability to set up borrowing rather than purchase ebook offerings, but at a cost of ease of use. A poor first-time experience on an ebook platform for a user may well be their last as they explore other resources. This should be considered by publishers as they make choices as to what to protect through Digital Rights Management (DRM) and what not to protect.

Feedback from institutions also demonstrates that ebook performance on mobile devices is considerably "buggier" than in any other environment. Clearly, the range and limitations of the browsers, platforms and devices in question are larger than the typical desktop experience. This makes it harder to design and code for, and consequently requires more effort put into testing to allow for the range of devices to be used with the content. Simply emulating generic mobile experiences is not sufficient for this, and if it takes more resources to ensure an ebook product is properly tested and fit for mobile purpose, then that resourcing should be provided, rather than providing an experience that may just dishearten and drive users away. Additional associated costs should be worked into the ebook model.

Some studies have shown that many users prefer not to read ebooks on mobile devices, although the important question is – why?[4] If the discovery and delivery phase is so difficult, then this will surely cloud the user experience of the actual consumption of content. A reflexive answer that small screens are an issue for the user avoids confronting this, and flies in the face of the trend for larger mobile device screens. While we need to do more work on finding out what users want to use mobile devices for, we need to remove what barriers we can, and ensure that accessing ebooks on a mobile device is seen not just as added value, but as a core component of a licence and user experience of that resource.

Meeting user needs with academic ebooks

Removing the barriers for the enduser is essential if content and service providers are going to able to meet the expectations and requirements of our users. If we fail to remove this friction for the users, they will simply adopt the path of least resistance, finding easier, and possibly less trusted and secure, ways to find and access the content they need.

There have been over the past few years a number of efforts to begin collaboration and sharing of best practice and exemplars in the online and mobile delivery of ebooks and digital content. Some of these, like the Library Success Wiki[5] and the Mobile Technologies in Libraries blog[6] are collaborative, community attempts to impose some order on the disparate and fragmented mobile content environment in universities and colleges. Building on this work, Jisc, along with a group of academic librarians[7], hosted two workshops to see whether it was possible for the community (libraries, publishers,

4 http://blogs.lse.ac.uk/impactofsocialsciences/2013/06/11/what-do-academics-want-a-survey-of-behaviours-and-attitudes-in-uk-higher-education/

5 http://www.libsuccess.org/M-Libraries

6 http://mlibraries.jiscinvolve.org

7 http://mlibraries.jiscinvolve.org/wp/2013/07/25/jisc-collection-mobile-issues-workshop/

aggregators and systems vendors) to come together to clarify the ways they could meet user needs and overcome the shared challenges in achieving this. As a result of these workshops there has emerged what has been dubbed a "mobile manifesto" for improving mobile services to students and researchers.

A mobile manifesto for ebooks

To ensure that libraries and publishers can deliver the kinds of content and services that students and researchers expect, the manifesto aims to provide concrete activities that will fulfil the core requirements that emerged from the library and publisher workshops. These include a number of specific statements of intent, including:

1. Authoritative record of relevant mobile products

The proliferation of mobile resources and devices makes testing and assessment of resources an onerous task for any individual library or organisation. A crowd-sourced list, or record, has the advantages of spreading the workload and developing consensus on user experience. Libraries and publishers should develop this partnership and the process and ongoing end results need to be effectively surfaced for the community.

2. A mobile standard

While not quite a fully-fledged standard, this would be a checklist against which the functionality of a mobile resource can be measured. The work done by the Book Industry Study Group on the EPUB support grid[8] and the EPUB3 standard (which is designed for reflowable content) provides a model for how this might work. Librarians would be able to see instantly the kinds of functionality they could expect from a particular mobile resource and be able to advise users on what they can expect to be able to do with it.

3. Product roadmap/status updates

There is a clear need for a grading system for mobile products that express the status of the development. For example, grades may include whether a product is in trial or will have a continuous upgrade path. This could form part of the authoritative record of mobile products already discussed in section 1 above.

---

[8] https://www.bisg.org/epub-3-support-grid

4. Accessibility and compatibility

Any mobile development should enable content to be accessed easily and read on all mobile devices, using clear flowing text. This should meet not just WC3 accessibility standards[9] but also general ease of use requirements for all users accessing via mobile devices. Accessibility of content on mobile devices benefits everyone. Similarly, cross-platform compatibility is required to ensure that content and resources can be seamlessly accessed on different mobile devices. Users should be able to start reading an article on their desktop and pick up where they left off on their iPad as they travel home on the bus.

5. Access and authentication

Accessing content should be made as simple and intuitive for the user as possible. There are only a certain number of access scenarios, and all publishers should have the same common requirement of achieving secure authentication to their resources. This can be done through collaboration between libraries and publishers, and agreement and consolidation around agreed standards based on models previously discussed.

The manifesto is primarily a way to surface the shared challenges and concerns of the community in providing access to ebooks for its users and customers. It also provides a locus for discussion of these issues and a common source for exemplars and best practice to be shared and updated, both nationally and internationally.

Fundamentally, it is the beginning of the necessary collaboration between all the stakeholders involved in ebook creation and provision. They can begin working together to tackle the challenges that must be overcome to provide users with a positive mobile experience. It also marks the start in further work Jisc and the library partners would like to do to begin taking some concrete action in the mobile ebook space.

Conclusion

This chapter has highlighted some of the major challenges that currently confront institutions, libraries, publishers and other stakeholders in the scholarly content supply chain in providing mobile access to those resources. Taken together, these challenges form a systemic and "hard" problem; a problem which requires work on multiple fronts and in partnership and collaboration with others. It is not easy to overestimate the scale of the problem that is faced in delivering a mobile experience that students and researchers would expect when accessing and using scholarly ebooks.

[9] http://www.w3.org/standards/webdesign/accessibility

But progress is being made, and while there are a number of initiatives from the stakeholders involved, there is also a recognition that many of these problems cannot be solved without collaboration. And the need to solve these issues is a priority.

Overwhelmingly, the message is that we must begin to act. While change so far for academic content has been gradual, this will not be the norm. The pace of change is going to increase, user expectations will change in relation to these new developments, and the technology we are beginning to adapt to will disappear to be replaced with something else. If we cannot meet the needs of our users while the pressures on academic content remain relatively benign, then the inevitable suddenness of future change threatens to overwhelm our capacity to provide content and services at all.

Ebooks acquisition as a shared service

John Tuck
Royal Holloway University of London

The growing demand for ebooks has been evident in libraries for many years. Depending on your viewpoint, moderate or extreme, ebooks are deemed to play an important role in the development or the decline of libraries. A measured forecast is outlined in *Academic Libraries of the Future*, a report from a project sponsored by the British Library, Jisc, the Research Information Network (RIN) and the Society of College, National and University Libraries (SCONUL 2011, p.14):

"All the scenarios assume that at some point beyond 2020 libraries will have made significant progress towards completing the digitisation of paper-based records. Practically all scientific books, papers and other records post-1900 will have been digitised. Arts and humanities materials will have the majority of post-1950 books, papers and records digitised. Remaining paper materials required for teaching or research will normally be digitised on demand. Some special collections (e.g. extensive collections of frail manuscripts) are likely to be the exception. Libraries will develop and change to encompass the new practices and technologies."

On the other hand, in *Academic library autopsy report, 2050*, Sullivan (2011) considers e-books to have exerted a baleful influence:

"The academic library has died...Although the causes of death are myriad, the following autopsy report highlights a few of the key factors. 1. Book

How to cite this book chapter:
Tuck, J. 2014. Ebooks acquisition as a shared service. In: Woodward, H. (ed.) *Ebooks in Education: Realising the Vision.* Pp. 59–67. London: Ubiquity Press. DOI: http://dx.doi.org/10.5334/bal.g

collections became obsolete...Most of these collections originated in physical libraries, which signed their own death warrants with deals to digitize their books."

However, the specific feedback that provided the momentum for the idea of a shared ebook acquisition service came from more localised sources: the students and librarians within the M25 Consortium[1] and the Museum Librarians and Archivists Group (MLAG)[2] institutions and feedback from Royal Holloway students, in surveys such as the National Student Survey and i-graduate's Student Barometer. These included:

"The library has good books on critical theory that would have been helpful to read online especially as they were not in the library", "More ebooks would make it easier to access the material" and "More ebooks please!"

As for librarians, the growing importance of ebooks was demonstrated through their participation in an ebooks survey carried out in 2011 by the M25 Consortium, Jisc Collections and MLAG, a network of archivists and librarians working in museums and galleries throughout the UK. The survey elicited 55 replies from 50 institutions and covered ebook platforms and services used by member institutions, content formats, subjects and publishers of interest, ebook business models used and possible options for consortial purchase.

Based on an assumption that the two consortia or their nominated agents would consider negotiating and centrally administering the acquisition of ebooks collections on a collaborative basis, the institutions were asked about their views on the suitability of a number of options such as: individual title purchase, individual title subscription, package purchase, package subscription, patron driven acquisition, short-term rental and access on the basis of a limited number of simultaneous users. The survey highlighted some divergent views and issues needing clarification. For example, some respondents stated a preference for a strong, robust, national approach rather than the proposed regional, consortial approach, and others identified possible conflict with existing preferred ebook platforms. In some smaller specialist institutions, respondents raised the possibility of the specialism being a barrier to a consortial approach, while others held the view that the consortial approach would be an opportunity for specialist institutions to offer more ebooks and/or achieve better pricing on specialist titles. There were also questions on how an M25 Consortium and MLAG consortia agreement would fit with other purchasing consortia agreements. The Steering Groups of the M25 Consortium and MLAG considered the feedback from the survey, and

---

1 The M25 Consortium of Academic Libraries is a collaborative organisation geared to improving library and information services within London and south east England. It has 57 members including small colleges, large universities, national institutions, museums and societies (http://m25lib.ac.uk)

2 http://mlablog.org

noted that 26 of the respondents had indicated that a patron driven acquisition (PDA) approach seemed to be quite or very suitable.

This interest led to the setting up of a joint M25 and MLAG task force, not so much to deliver the service but to explore and respond to the questions raised by the survey. In timely fashion, the opportunity arose in March 2012 to submit a bid for funding under Jisc's Digital Infrastructure programme to address many of these questions and fulfil the specific aim of delivering reports, guidelines and navigation tools for consortia seeking to embark on collaborative purchasing of ebooks using PDA.

The successful bid was entitled E-BASS25 (E-Books Acquisition as a shared service in M25). The project was led by Royal Holloway University of London (RHUL) on behalf of the M25 Consortium. Specific named partners for E-BASS25 were Kingston University, the Science Museum on behalf of (MLAG), Jisc Collections and Sero Consulting Limited[3, 4].

What is meant by PDA?

Funding was awarded to the E-BASS25 project to identify experience and best practice from existing PDA examples and engage with stakeholders across the board in order to define their roles and expertise in this area.

A key starting point for the project was to provide a definition of PDA and investigate acquisition models that offered particular opportunities and benefits. PDA was defined as a "just in time" purchasing model which gives library users more control over which books are purchased and added to library collections. Although librarians still have a role in selecting the range of titles that are available to users, the library only pays for items that patrons use. Purchase, rental, usage, and evidence-based models were then defined and described as follows[5].

PDA purchase

This is a straightforward PDA model which uses the available funds to purchase ebooks based on demand from customers. A selection of available titles

---

3 All outputs of the E-BASS25 project can be found at: http://ebooksguidance.jiscinvolve.org

4 Thanks are expressed to all members of the E-BASS25 project team who delivered the goals of the project to schedule and who, between them, contributed most of the content of the above report: Dominic Tate, project manager (University of Edinburgh), Anna Grigson (LSE), Kim Coles (Royal Holloway University of London), Amy Warner (Royal Holloway University of London), Carolyn Alderson (Jisc Collections), Ben Taplin (Jisc Collections), Helen Woolfries (Kingston University), Anna Vernon (British Library), Rupert Williams (Library Services, University College London – Qatar), David Kay (Sero Consulting Ltd) and Owen Stephens.

5 These models are described in more details in a video *EBASS25 patron-driven acquisition (PDA) e-book purchasing models* (http://ebooksguidance.jiscinvolve.org/wp)

is agreed between the library/consortium and the supplier and MARC records are loaded in the library catalogues. Users have full access to the ebooks.

PDA rental

The library consortium spreads the available funding more widely, agreeing to rent access to content up to agreed limits, before purchases are triggered. A selection of available titles is agreed between the library/consortium and the supplier and MARC records are loaded in the library catalogues. Users have full access to the ebooks.

PDA usage

This model makes use of "micropayments" to count up the actual use of the ebooks in the collection, for example a charge per page viewed. The library sets up a PDA agreement with a supplier to make a range of ebooks available to users. Once the titles have been selected, the library makes the content visible and discoverable to users. Users have full access to the ebooks. Each significant use of a book triggers a charge to the library. If the total charges payable for the book reach a given level, then the book is deemed purchased and becomes a permanent part of the library's collection. If the library decides to end the PDA agreement, access to any books which have not been purchased is withdrawn, and the library removes records for these books from the catalogue.

Evidence-based selection (EBS)

The library sets up a PDA agreement with a publisher to make a range of ebooks available to users for a defined period. Typically, libraries select one or more of the publishers' collections to be made available for a year. The library pays a fee upfront, which is typically greater than the cost of subscribing to the collection, but less than the cost of purchasing the collection. This fee will eventually be used to purchase books, but no titles are selected at this stage. The library makes the content visible and discoverable to users and users have full access to the collection for an agreed period of time (typically a year). No further charges are made.

Identifying user needs

Led by Sero Consulting, two workshops, one at the beginning and one at the end of the project, focused on user needs. The first brought together 30 librarians from 19 institutions and the second more than 45 from over 30 institutions. The first workshop considered various acquisition models as well as the underlying drivers and motivations for each, from the perspective of libraries and suppliers. The participants were in strong support of an evidence-based PDA approach and a survey to explore further the drivers and motivations.

A survey was undertaken, predominantly of M25 Consortium members, and evoked 30 responses (more than 50% of M25 members) The responses indicated that PDA was viewed favourably by a significant majority and seen as a user-centred approach that should be applied to more aspects of the library collection (80% of respondents) and should not be dismissed as a temporary supplier-driven tactic (73%). The main motivations in offering user ebook choice were seen to be the availability of key titles (100%), encouraging user movement to e-access (80%) and supplementing the print collection (73%). The most significant blockages preventing ebooks from fulfilling their potential were identified as the business models offered by publishers (87%) and the availability of titles, especially e-textbooks (73%). Linked to this was the view that best value in ebook acquisition was potentially to be delivered by a range of models that contribute to collection development as well as satisfying immediate demand.

From the library perspective, library-driven purchase models, informed by usage statistics over a rental period, were valued highly (90%), as well as those involving the professional expertise of librarians and lecturers (73%). There was a challenge to the value of access based on models not leading to ownership (67%). As for views around the consortium approach to ebook acquisition, expectations were high for using scale to achieve the best price and making a bigger collection accessible (97% in both cases), more so than the reduction of the burden of procurement and administration (80%). The most significant concerns about working in a consortium to acquire ebooks were being driven by others' subject interests that are not relevant (80%), and domination by larger institutions (70%).

In many ways these responses were not unexpected. After all, the respondents were professional librarians grappling with the dual aim of serving the immediate needs of their users and managing longer term collection development in the context of shrinking budgets, while the costs of e-resources continue to rise disproportionately around them.

The views of publishers and aggregators

Through a work package managed by Jisc Collections, the four models were considered with a range of aggregators and publishers, addressing issues such as minimum thresholds of investment and commitment required from consortia entering into a PDA deal with suppliers. Questions were put to the suppliers by telephone interview and the unattributed responses were summarised by Ben Taplin and Carolyn Alderson in a report, *Publisher feedback on PDA models*[6].

The purpose of the interviews with seven publishers and two aggregators was to discover which models they thought were feasible or realistic as a consortium purchase and learn their thoughts on the practicalities of how these models would operate. The intention was then to use the information to construct guidelines for institutions considering embarking on a PDA consortium project.

Again unsurprisingly, the evidence-based selection (EBS) model proved popular with the publishers, as it would be relatively straightforward to implement, and would guarantee some upfront payment, helping sales forecasting and planning. Seven responses favoured this model. One publisher likened it to a "paid-for trial", and one suggested that the upfront payment would be an incentive to the institution to ensure the content was used. Others mentioned its greater flexibility and sustainability and one publisher suggested that the EBS model involves a higher level of trust and cooperation between both parties and is therefore "more interesting in the long term".

The other three models were generally seen as being complicated to manage for the publisher or aggregator, entailing a considerable amount of technical work with no guarantee of payment if content is not used. This complexity was seen to increase if micropayments from a large number of institutions were involved.

General reservations were expressed about the potential for each model to offer access to content for free, and the threat posed by ebooks to print sales was still considered as a concern to publishers, especially those in the textbook market. This threat was seen to be magnified by any consortial agreement in which single copies of books are shared across several institutions. This could mean that some publishers limit the titles they make available. However, despite these concerns and reservations, the consensus among the suppliers interviewed was a willingness to explore the practicalities of each model and be flexible in order to accommodate the requirements of a consortium.

Other purchasing consortia

Engagement also took place with the Southern Universities Purchasing Consortium (SUPC), and this led to guidance on identifying the most efficient procurement routes for setting up a consortium ebooks agreement through existing framework agreements such as the Joint Consortia Book Agreement (out to tender at the time of E-BASS25). This guidance is entitled *Procurement guidelines*[7]. It makes it clear that the agreement is flexible

[6] Available with all the other project outputs at http://ebooksguidance.jiscinvolve.org.

[7] http://ebooksguidance.jiscinvolve.org

and supports a range of business models including PDA. It provides a robust mechanism for institutions wishing to purchase ebooks, but draws attention to certain factors that might inhibit the evidence-based PDA approach and collaborative purchasing by a consortium such as the M25, for instance, lack of support for procurement directly from a publisher, and eligibility to use the agreement limited to English Higher Education (HE) sector regional purchasing consortia.

Developing systems guidelines

The technical issues to be addressed in implementing a PDA agreement, and how library systems can be exploited to maximise the staff time efficiency savings that PDA offers, were explored and guidelines were produced relating to each model[8]. The guidelines include: the use of MARC records in a library management system; the use of MARC records in a discovery service; the use of a knowledge base and link resolver; discovery in the native interface of the publisher/aggregator rather than locally; and discovery in "next generation" library service platforms.

Through an analysis of each option, the *Systems integration guidelines* draw attention to key points that need to be considered and assessed at institutional and consortium level before a decision is made to embark on collaborative acquisition. For institutions, the points for consideration include the need for clarity and understanding of the discovery method to be used, how frequently records will be updated, and the level of resource required for this. There is also a need for a methodology for the removal of candidate records, the maintenance of high quality records for purchased content, and an appropriate financial tracking procedure to be in place. At consortium level, points to consider were defined as how parity might be ensured across the institutions in terms of discovery procedures, how staffing and systems might be provided for centralised payment and how monitoring of usage would be centralised to coordinate closure at an appropriate payment limit.

Outcomes

Findings from the E-BASS25 workshops and the associated survey, together with the views expressed through the publisher interviews, pointed to a strong preference for the evidence-based model. This, in turn, led the project manager, Dominic Tate, to lay down the following challenge to the M25 Consortium (Tate 2013):

---

[8] These were entitled *Systems integration guidelines*, by Helen Woolfries of Kingston University. Accessible at http://ebooksguidance.jiscinvolve.org

"This brings us to the fourth model, PDA Evidence. Seemingly the most popular amongst librarians and publishers alike, this model allows patrons to access a whole range of content during the course of the agreement, with the guarantee that all the money will be spent on whole books at the end. Sounds ideal? Well, almost. Here's the rub. The library can choose which books they buy at the end of the agreement. This is great for library choice, but surely this is not actually PDA? There is an intervention between the patron and the purchase. Surely this adds an administrative burden that PDA was designed to eliminate? Perhaps this model could still achieve cost savings when scaled up to a large consortium? ... A consortium has strength to strike a deal with a publisher because its size maximises sales for the publisher and reduces their overheads of dealing with individual customers. Libraries similarly benefit through reduced overheads and similar costs so consortial purchasing is an obvious win-win. Through the size and diversity of its membership, M25 has the capability of putting together a sizeable consortium for the acquisition of ebooks and it seems obvious that the only way this could be achieved is by using the evidence-based model. Those wishing to participate would club their guaranteed spends together to achieve the highest possible discount. At the end of the term, those books every partner wants would be bought. The remaining fund could be divided up in line with the initial deposit, with each partner choosing their books. A number of publishers may also be interested in trialling this approach to see if success could be achieved in practice. Such an approach would be a departure from conventional purchasing practices and would require significant guidance from the consortium and there is always a chance it might not work, but, hey, perhaps M25 should give it a try? If we don't give it a try, we'll never know. Over to M25…"

This approach combines the features of library intervention with a guaranteed upfront payment for publishers. It cannot, therefore, be described as PDA in the purest sense. However, it does combine key elements of the PDA definition. Properly managed, it does give library users more control over which books are purchased and added to library collections and the library only pays for items that patrons use. It is in this spirit that the M25 Consortium is seeking to take up the project manager's challenge, and is undertaking discussions with Jisc Collections and publishers with a view to assessing the feasibility of a collaborative ebooks purchasing model based on the evidence-based approach and in line with the M25 Consortium strategy for 2013/14 to 2015/16[9].

In the meantime further important work on e-books has been undertaken under the Jisc Co-Design Programme. The *Ebooks co-design report* (Chowcat *et al.* 2014) set out to understand the "pain points" experienced by libraries in terms of management and user experience in dealing with ebooks in all their

[9] http://m25lib.ac.uk

guises and to identify actions that might be taken at local library, consortium or national levels and in the supply chain to address them.

It is the intention that the outcomes of the *Ebooks co-design report* and the E-BASS25 project can be used to guide and benefit the work of the M25 Consortium in order both to address some of the "pain points" and to deliver an improved and value-for-money service experience for the ebook user.

In other words, ebooks continue to develop in exciting, innovative and disruptive ways. They present challenges and opportunities to many stakeholders: librarians, users, publishers, aggregators, teachers, etc. This is why they are of such importance within the constantly shifting digital landscape.

As for the tipping point and the future of the printed book, perhaps clues can be found in a handwritten inscription recently found in the sixth printing of a Collector's Library edition of Virginia Woolf's *Mrs Dalloway*, first published in this edition by CRW Publishing in 2003, and purchased in an Oxfam bookshop in Reading in December 2013:

"To Kate,
In case your kindle breaks.
Happy birthday and
Happy sabbatical,
Lots of love…"

References

Chowcat, I., Kay, D. and Stephens, O., with Devenney, A. and Stone, G. (2014) Ebooks co-design report. http://knowledgebaseplus.wordpress.com/ebooks-co-design-project/ebooks-full-report

SCONUL (2011) Academic libraries of the future. http://www.sconul.ac.uk/page/academic-libraries-of-the-future

Sullivan, B.T. (2011) Academic library autopsy report, 2050. *The Chronicle of Higher Education*, 2nd January. http://chronicle.com.article/Academic-Library-Autopsy/125767

Tate, D. (2013) Reflections on the E-BASS25 project. http://ebass25.rhulo.ac.uk/2013/02/21/refections-on-the-e-bass25-project

Case Studies

Ebooks at the University of Portsmouth: a ten year success story

Anne Worden
University of Portsmouth

The University of Portsmouth Library has been making ebooks available since spring 2004, so we can now look back across ten years' provision. From an initial three suppliers and around 15,000 ebooks, Portsmouth staff and students can now access over 476,000 ebooks from 15 suppliers, and in certain subject areas ebooks are an essential part of the curriculum (the 15 suppliers are a mixture of aggregators such as ebrary and MyiLibrary, and individual suppliers such as Oxford University Press, Emerald and MIT Press, plus Jisc Historic Books). Not only do we have a significant number of ebooks, but national data shows that students and staff at Portsmouth access ebooks more than in most other UK universities (SCONUL Strategic Planning Data, 2012/13) with just over 4.7 million ebook section requests in the 2012/13 academic year. In addition to monitoring usage data closely, we have carried out surveys to track student reaction to ebooks in 2005, 2009, 2012 and 2014, with the latest survey gathering views from 1846 students. This case study will include selected results from our surveys.

Early success

Our initial offering of 15,000 ebooks, rather than just a few hundred, led to early success because it meant there was something for most subject areas.

How to cite this book chapter:
Worden, A. 2014. Ebooks at the University of Portsmouth: a ten year success story. In: Woodward, H. (ed.) *Ebooks in Education: Realising the Vision.* Pp. 71–77. London: Ubiquity Press. DOI: http://dx.doi.org/10.5334/bal.h

We also made sure that all our ebooks were in the catalogue to aid discovery; Nicholas *et al.* (2008) note that use of catalogued ebooks is double that of those not catalogued. A 2005 survey, together with Athens authentication data broken down across departments, showed us at this early stage that it was humanities and social sciences (HSS) students who were leading the way in the uptake of ebooks. This contrasts with the findings of Abdullah and Gibb (2006) at the University of Strathclyde, although Chelin *et al.* (2009) report HSS students at the University of the West of England coming second to law students in frequency of use of ebooks, and Levine-Clark is reported as finding that social sciences students use ebooks much more frequently than science and technology students (ProQuest 2014).

As there was proven student interest, we targeted HSS academics with hands-on ebook training at the end of academic year staff conference, and we arranged subject cluster training for groups who were less well represented at the conference. Academics could see at first hand the useful features available on ebooks and conversations sprang up across the room about how ebooks could be integrated into teaching. We believe these sessions were instrumental in leading to the continued high usage figures for ebooks at Portsmouth, because they convinced academics of the value of ebooks, and led to the adoption of ebooks as key weekly reading on various taught units. We continue to offer hands-on training on ebooks and other electronic sources before the start of each academic year for new lecturers and those who want a refresher. Gravett (2011) and Chelin *et al.* (2009) both stress the importance of promoting ebooks to academics to achieve success with them in a university setting.

In addition to this training for academics, we provided practice on ebooks as part of information literacy sessions for new undergraduates and postgraduates. As a result of this hands-on practice, students who might otherwise have been put off ebooks because of the technology involved saw how easy it was to search and find something relevant to their work. (Our 2009 survey showed that "Put off by technology" was the most common reason for not using ebooks; this reaction has mostly disappeared now, apart from with some mature students.) It is interesting to note from successive survey data that students in the Faculty of Technology – computing, maths and engineering – who do not have these hands-on introductions use ebooks (and ejournals) much less frequently, with their written comments indicating that some are not even aware of our ebook provision, e.g. "What are ebooks?" (first year mechanical engineering).

A further factor in our success with ebooks is the large number of distance learners registered at Portsmouth – around 1,000 in criminology and approximately 500 across the rest of the university. Extensive online support – including daily monitoring of student online discussion boards – is provided for these students in order to help them use ebooks. Naturally, the factors which make ebooks ideal for providing academic reading to distance learners, particularly 24/7 availability at any location across the world, also help students

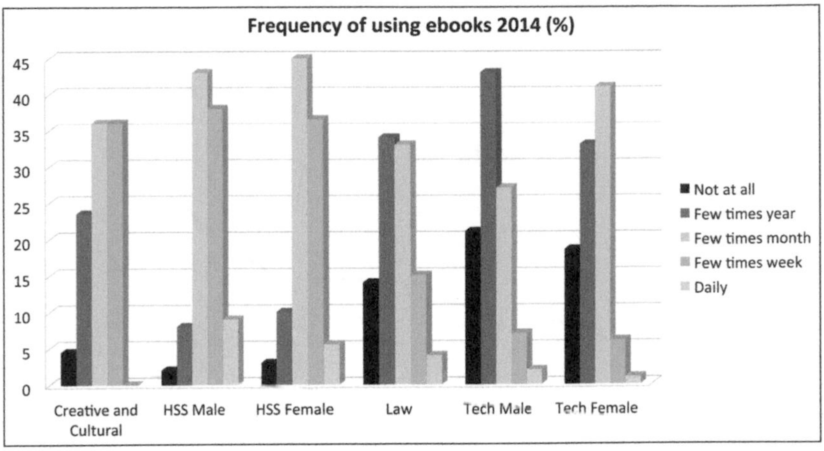

Figure 1: Frequency of using ebooks 2014 (%).

on campus who for one reason or another cannot get to the library. A second year campus-based criminology student provided this comprehensive comment in our 2014 survey of ebook usage (**Figure 1**):

"I use ebooks for different reasons; bad weather/severe winds or pouring rain; I'm running out of time and have to find the info I need quickly; the books I need are already borrowed by someone else; key words and terms/ definitions are easy to find and highlighted in yellow; ...or I feel lazy and want to stay in bed all day so I search for what I need online ☺; when I'm home and I can't take the books with me because I have luggage limits because I'm flying to get home for the holidays."

For several years our usage statistics showed that titles required by distance learners dominated the top 30, but this domination has dropped off over the last three academic years as campus-based students make even greater use of ebooks, perhaps because of the factors referred to in the next section.

Driving usage even higher

From 2004/05 to 2008/09 we saw a steady rise each year in use of our ebooks. However, in both academic years 2010/11 and 2011/12 we experienced steep increases. These steep rises coincided with deliberately buying ebooks to meet reservation requests (e.g. a book on the European revolutions of 1848 bought because of multiple reservations just before Christmas 2011 had 17,099 section requests in January 2012) and sustained work on increasing the number of online reading lists available to our students. Over the last three academic years we have been systematically checking reading lists to see whether ebooks are available, then linking them into the list if

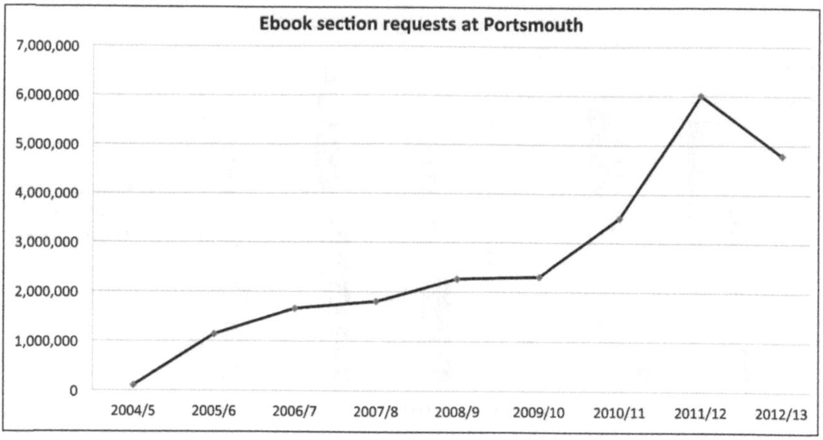

Figure 2: Ebook section requests at Portsmouth.

they are and attempting to buy them if not. Usage data for individual ebook titles in this same time period shows that the majority of books at the top of our usage tables are titles which we deliberately bought either for a reading list, or for a reservation: in 2012 for example, 92% of the ebooks in our top 50 via ebrary were ebooks which we had bought outright, with 76% being on reading lists. Our 2014 survey showed that 39% of HSS respondents and 36% of those in Creative and Cultural Industries (CCI) found ebooks via online reading lists whilst, just as reported by Bucknell (2012) and Chelin *et al.* (2009), the most common method of finding ebooks was by searching the library catalogue, at 76% of HSS and 79% of CCI respondents. In contrast, technology students most commonly use Google (46%), with the catalogue coming second at 39%.

Figure 2 charts the use of our ebooks over the last ten years. Although there was a drop in 2012/13, we believe this is accounted for by a combination of three factors: a smaller number of students in the final year than in the preceding two academic years; a change in the tally of ebook page views as a result of the move to the COUNTER 4 standard of recording ebook use; and a complete restructuring of the curriculum across the university which deliberately tried to reduce some of the assessment burden for students.

From ebooks being an "added extra", used to grab quick quotes or if the print copy was out on loan according to our 2009 survey, our 2014 results show that ebooks are now mainstream, a key part of student activity, certainly for students in HSS subjects (see **Figure 3**). Evidence from our 2014 survey leading to this conclusion includes: in 2009 40% of male HSS respondents and 42% of female HSS respondents claimed to use ebooks for every assignment, whilst in 2014 these figures have risen to 74% and 70% respectively, with figures for history being 87% of males and 89% of females. One male first-year history

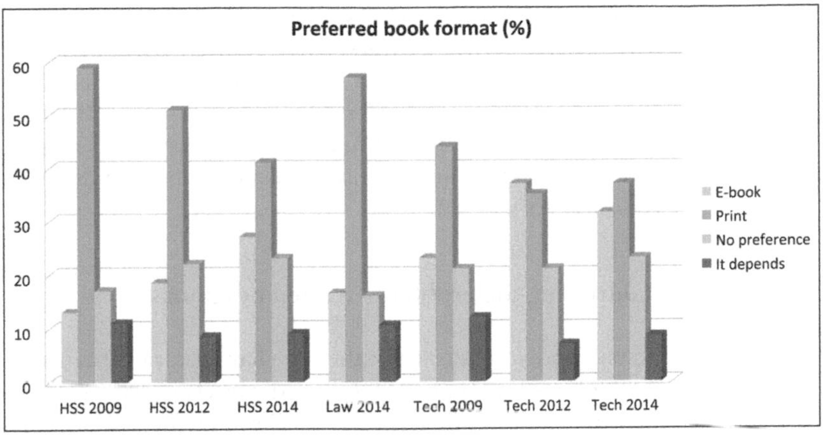

Figure 3: Preferred book format (%).

student stated "I can't get enough of 'em!"; over 80% of HSS and CCI respondents now say that ebooks are either very useful or quite useful for their course, with the figures reaching 93% of male history respondents and 98% of female history respondents (there were 122 replies from history). In 2009 58% of HSS respondents and 44% of those from technology said that, given a choice, they would prefer a print book, whereas in 2014 this had dropped to 40% for HSS and 37% for technology, with only law out of those subjects surveyed remaining above 50% preferring print. The biggest turnaround can be seen in history, where in 2012 56% of respondents expressed a preference for print books; in 2014 the figure had dropped to 38% for males and 24% for females, with only 10% of first year female history respondents saying they would prefer a print book. A factor which could explain this turnaround in history is that, in response to their subject area having the highest number of students in HSS complaining about not enough copies of books in the National Student Survey in 2011, we worked intensively with history lecturers to ensure that all history reading lists were available in our online reading list system. The online lists include links to as many ebooks as possible, plus scans of chapters from those not available as ebooks, and the lecturers ensured that the weekly seminar readings for core units were items available electronically. (History lecturers had been slower than others to adopt this practice in the past.)

Before concluding this section, we touch on our findings regarding the devices used to access ebooks. Contrary to expectation, PCs or laptops are still the dominant means of access, with 73% of technology students surveyed and 82% of HSS students stating they use those. HSS students aged 24–29, male technology students and those from CCI were most likely to use mobile phones at 17%, 13.5% and 13% respectively, compared to 7.5% for 18–23 year old HSS students and 4% for law students. HSS students aged over 30 were most likely to use an iPad, followed by HSS students aged 24 – 29 year-old and female technology students at 23%, 21% and 20.5% respectively, compared to 13% for 18 – 23 year-old HSS students and 11% for CCI. Use of other tablets was 5% or below for all groups except HSS students aged 24 – 29 at 10%, HSS students aged 30 and above at 8.5% and male technology students at 6.5%. These results indicate that mobile devices have, so far, played very little part in the success of ebooks at Portsmouth.

Addressing the problems created by ebooks

Despite the success of ebooks at Portsmouth, there have naturally been some problems too. Each of our surveys has highlighted concerns, many of which have been resolved by the time of the next survey. However, there always seem to be some people who simply do not like reading from a screen, although the number who mention this problem drops with each survey: "I don't really use them because I find them hard to read off the screen" (year two Illustration).

In 2009 students wanted a greater variety of ebooks and expressed frustration with the instability of the browser and login processes for ebooks, especially at home: "Whilst access is convenient, it is not that easy for off campus students – better options would be good!" (final year politics); "I have found that it crashes a lot" (final year history); "I find it a lot harder to access at home and it often takes ages to load up" (year two sociology). The browser issues were addressed by actions taken by our main ebook supplier, ebrary, who made changes which resolved the problems previously experienced. The issue of more ebooks was also partially resolved through ebrary adding thousands more ebooks to their Academic Complete subscription collection; faculty librarians also began buying more individual ebooks to complement our subscription holdings.

In 2012, students were still not satisfied with the number of ebooks available and wanted to download ebooks to any device they owned. The download problem was again solved via the actions of our ebook supplier, who introduced features enabling students to download the whole book for offline reading for a short period of time (typically two weeks); previously, our ebooks had only been accessible whilst the user was connected to the internet. Meanwhile, as publishers made more of their back-lists available as ebooks, faculty librarians were able to address the issue of quantity of ebooks by buying increasing numbers of titles from reading lists as ebooks. As mentioned earlier, we also tried to buy more ebooks matching reservation requests. Tackling reading lists and reservations finally seems to have resolved complaints over quantity, as this issue became insignificant in the 2014 survey.

In 2014 the big issue for students was the problem of not being able to access an ebook because someone else is already reading it, i.e. turnaways: "Don't understand the online book queuing system? Why do you need to wait for an online book?" (year one criminology); "When you have to wait in a queue for an ebook it is really irritating!" (year two criminology). From the beginning of 2014 we began addressing the problem of turnaways by generating a monthly report of top turnaways so that faculty librarians could purchase additional licences where possible. We hope that students will see the benefit of this in the next academic year. However, there remains concern over a small number of titles which prove impossible to upgrade.

Conclusion

Over the last ten years, ebooks have become firmly embedded at the University of Portsmouth, with lecturers and students being equally enthusiastic. Although initially the convenience of any time, any place access to a large variety of ebooks was a key attraction, over the last three years purchasing specific ebooks both for online reading lists and for reservation requests has led to even greater success. Since summer 2013 we have been experimenting with patron driven acquisition of ebooks, and it will be interesting to see what effect this has on our usage statistics.

References

Abdullah, N. and Gibb, F. 2006. A survey of e-book awareness and usage amongst students in an academic library [online]. In: *Proceedings of International Conference of Multidisciplinary Information Science and Technologies*, 25–8 October, Merida, Spain, http://strathprints.strath.ac.uk/2280/1/strathprints002280.pdf [Accessed 9 April 2014]

Chelin, J., Briddon, J., Williams, E., Redman, J., Sleat, A. and Ince, G. 2009. 'E-books are good if there are no copies left': a survey of e-book usage at UWE Library Services. *Library and Information Research*, 33(104), 45–65.

Bucknell, T. 2012. Electronic books in academic libraries: a case study in Liverpool, UK. In: M. Fieldhouse and A. Marshall, eds. *Collection development in the digital age*. London: Facet, 71–82.

Gravett, K. 2011. Providing guidance, training and support for readers using e-books. In: K. Price and V. Havergal, eds. *E-books in libraries: a practical guide*. London: Facet, 163–179.

Nicholas, D., Rowlands, I., Clark, D., Huntington, P., Jamali, H. and Olle, C. 2008. UK scholarly e-book usage: a landmark survey, *Aslib Proceedings*, 60(4), 311–34.

ProQuest, 2014. ebrary and EBL data study sheds light on ebook use [online] http://www.proquest.com/about/news/2014/ebrary-EBL-Data-Study-Sheds-Light-on-Ebook-Use.html [Accessed 7 April 2014]

Instant fulfilment: the successful use of patron driven acquisitions to satisfy interlibrary loans

Annette Moore
University of Sussex

As ebooks continue to rise in popularity, the implementation of Patron Driven Acquisitions[1] (PDA), with EBL as the vendor, has already proven a very successful model at the University of Sussex. It allows our users to decide on ebook titles that may become permanent additions to our collection. Using technology to make content more accessible, EBL offers a flexible access model, including free browsing (time-limited), non-linear lending (multiple concurrent accesses to content) and short-term circulation, with the fourth loan triggering an automatic purchase.

With the economic realities of an agreed budget, we make only a subset of the entire EBL catalogue available to our users, carefully chosen with a focus on key subject areas as well as the most recent publications. In order to extend the use of the enormous repertoire of titles offered by EBL, we decided to pilot the use of the entire catalogue of approximately 450,000 ebook titles available through the EBL administrative dashboard LibCentral, to satisfy interlibrary loan (ILL) book requests. We were already offering desktop delivery to our users for journal articles through the British Library, and our aim was to extend desktop delivery to books, fulfilling book requests with ebooks wherever possible. The

[1] Patron Driven Acquisitions, also referred to as Demand Driven Acquisitions

How to cite this book chapter:
Moore, A. 2014. Instant fulfilment: the successful use of patron driven acquisitions to satisfy interlibrary loans. In: Woodward, H. (ed.) *Ebooks in Education: Realising the Vision.* Pp. 79–90. London: Ubiquity Press. DOI: http://dx.doi.org/10.5334/bal.i

pilot service was launched in February 2013 and evaluated through the Spring and Summer terms, generally our busiest months for ILL requests.

Using quantitative statistics on availability, subject coverage, cost and usage, as well as qualitative feedback from users, in this paper I evaluate the success of the pilot with reference to Ranganathan's (1931) five laws of library science:

1. Books are for use
2. Every reader his or her book
3. Every book its reader
4. Save the time of the reader
5. The library is a growing organism

Although Ranganathan first conceived the five laws of library science at a time when the term open access (OA) referred to the newly found freedom for users to browse along the open book shelves, there is an interesting similarity here with what is happening now with OA publishing. Again it allows users greater access to research material, but now outside of the constraints of the library building itself. Although technology has changed the information landscape beyond all recognition, Ranganathan's clearly elucidated laws are arguably (McMenemy 2007) still relevant today, and serve to refocus our attention firmly back on our library users, to reflect on how best we can serve their needs in a climate of economic constraints, higher user expectations and continual change.

Implementing desktop delivery for ILL book requests

We launched the pilot service in February 2013 as part of a new desktop delivery service for ILL with a new form for placing requests online. The default option for a journal article request was "secure electronic delivery"[2] to the requestor's email address, although users could choose from other delivery methods if preferred. For book requests, users were first offered access to an ebook, where available, but we would continue with a request for the hard copy ILL from the British Library, if print was the preferred format or the title was not available as an ebook.

Following discussions with our collection development librarian, we agreed to use the same access model for satisfying ILL book requests as for our current PDA model, largely because our users were already familiar with this. When a user opens a title for the first time, there is a five minute browse period (ten minutes for owned titles)[3] that is not counted as a loan instance. A

[2] Secure electronic delivery is a service offered by the British Library for supplying journal articles as encrypted PDF files using the FileOpen digital rights management tool – http://www.bl.uk/reshelp/atyourdesk/docsupply/help/receiving/deliveryoptions/electronic/index.html

[3] Titles your library has purchased or autopurchased via the EBL system

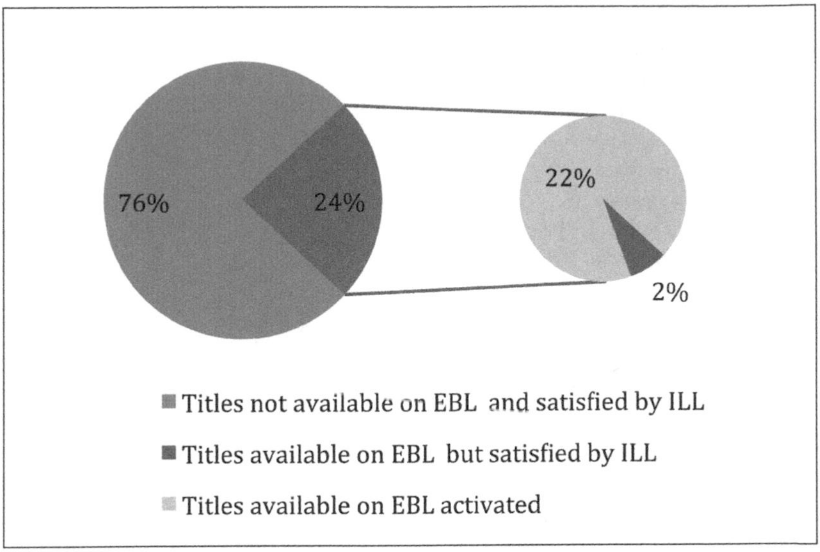

Figure 1: Percentage of ILL titles available on EBL.

loan is triggered by a user initiating a print, a copy or a download of the title or when the browse period expires. A loan period lasts for 24 hours and within this time an individual can read online, download the ebook, print and copy text, within certain limits, and access the ebook anytime within the 24 hour period. Additionally, we set a limit of £150 on the purchase price of an ebook and allocated £5,000 from the ILL budget for the pilot. Above £150, we would order through the ILL system unless no other lending locations were found.

Each day, all interlibrary book requests were checked against the full catalogue of EBL ebooks for a direct match, using the advanced search. We set up a list within LibCentral to track titles used to satisfy ILL requests and also set up a new fund code for ILL to track costs. Activating an ebook title is achieved simply by turning visibility on from the results page or from the item full record. The requestor was notified by email that the title was available as an ebook and a link to the ebook was sent along with further access information. Additionally, if an ebook was not their preferred option, the user was invited to get back to us and we would continue with a traditional ILL request and order a print copy from the British Library, in which case a £2 admin charge for obtaining an ILL would apply.

Once an ebook is activated in LibCentral, it becomes part of our Sussex EBL collection and is discoverable through Library Search (powered by ExLibris Primo)[4], although it does not appear on the library catalogue, Capita Prism,

[4] Primo is ExLibris' solution for discovery and delivery – http://www.exlibrisgroup.com/category/PrimoOverview – allowing users to search across the library catalogue as well as ebooks, ejournals and other online resources

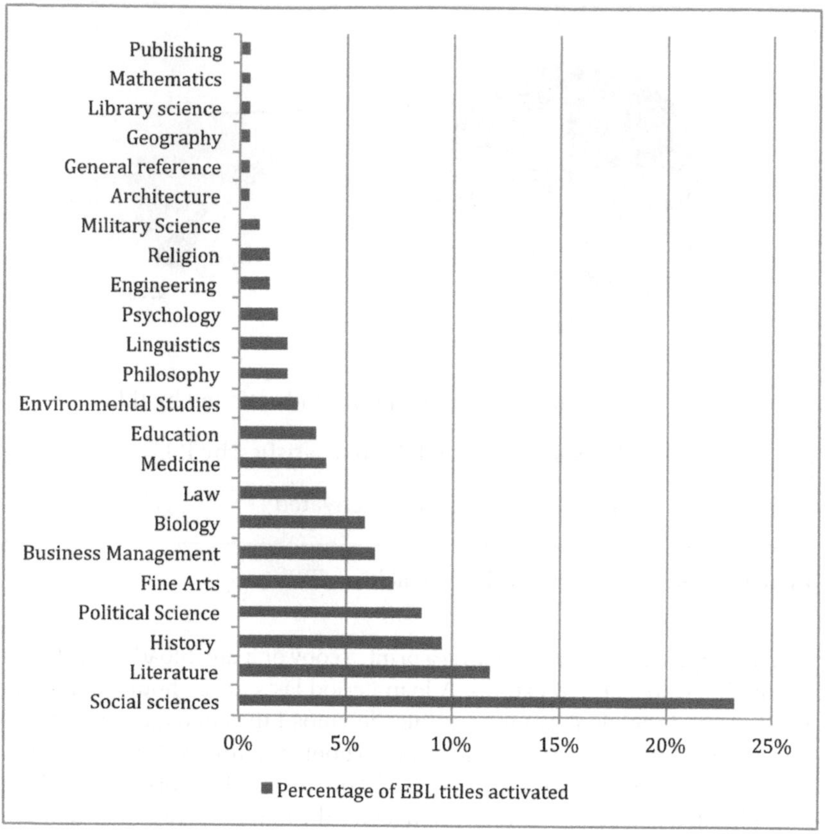

Figure 2: Subject categories.

unless the title becomes an automatic purchase on the fourth short loan. EBL provide a weekly list of purchased titles as well as the associated MARC records which are added to the library catalogue.

Summary of findings

Availability

Over the six month period of the pilot, we were surprised at the number of ILL book request titles that were available through the EBL full catalogue (**Figure 1**). Of the 996 interlibrary loan book requests fulfilled during this period, 238 (24%) of the titles were found to be available on EBL. Of these, 220 were activated and 18, although available, were not activated as the requestor's preference was for a print copy.

The reasons given by users for preferring a print copy to an ebook fell into several key categories:

	No. of Titles	% of titles	Cost (exc. VAT)	Average cost per title
EBL titles leading to automatic purchase (4th SL)	24	11%	£1,874	£78.08
EBL titles with between 1–3 SLs	130	59%	£2,000	£15.38
EBL titles browsed (less than 5 mins)	66	30%	£0	£0.00
Total	**220**		**£3,874**	£17.61

Table 1: Cost of EBL titles.

- Needing to read the whole book and not comfortable reading online for any length of time
- A problem accessing the ebook due to IT Services password not working [temporary problem with user's account]
- Technical restrictions on the number of pages that can be printed [this can vary from one publisher to another]
- Preference always for a print copy rather than an ebook

Overall the feedback from users has been very positive, with favourable comments on the speed of delivery offered by the new service in providing online access to the material requested. The traditional ILL takes five to ten days to arrive, depending on the lending location, compared to within 24 hours to provide access to the ebook. In addition to a small number of users with a preference for a print copy, there were an equal number of requestors that specified they would prefer an ebook, if available.

Subject coverage

The top five subject categories covered by ebooks used to satisfy ILL requests were: the social sciences (51 titles), literature (26), history (21), political science (19) and fine arts (16) (**Figure 2**). For comparison, the top five subject areas (based on the user's department) for the ILL requests were very similar English literature, art history, history, international relations and politics, and media and film. With around 450,000 titles made available for selection from key academic publishers, such as Taylor and Francis, Oxford University Press and Palgrave Macmillan, EBL offers a wide range of academic material that matches the needs of our users.

Costs

Of the 220 ebooks activated on EBL, only 24 titles became automatic purchases, triggered by the fourth short loan (**Table 1**). The majority of titles

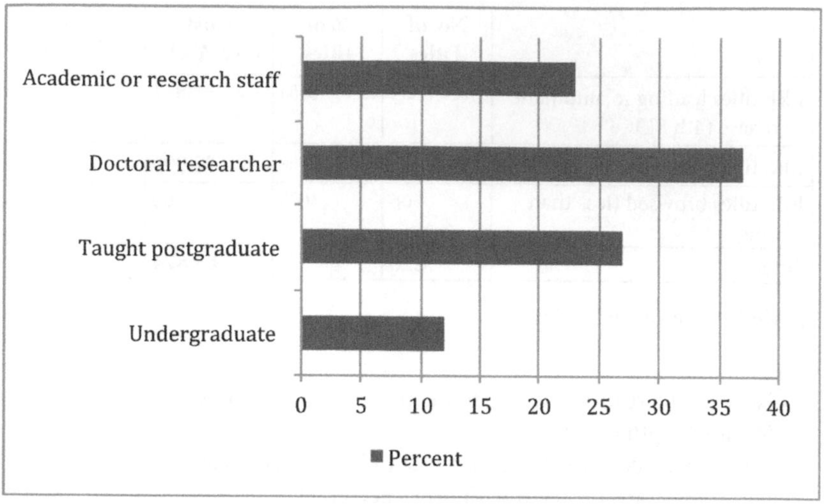

Figure 3: Borrower type.

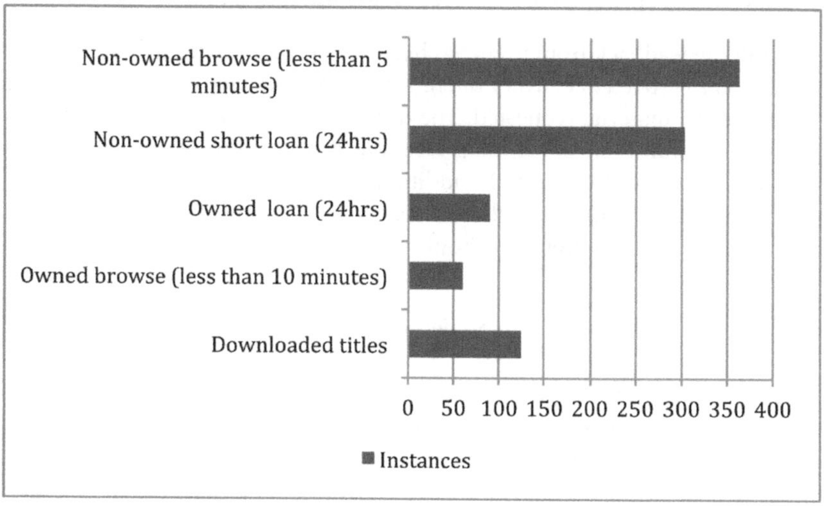

Figure 4: Usage type.

received only one short loan (30%), 14% received two short loans and 15% three short loans. The average cost per title varied considerably depending on whether the reader accessed the ebook for one or more 24-hour loan periods. The cost of a loan period is set by the publisher and can vary considerably; however a guide price for a 24 hour loan is 10–15% of the purchase price.

The most surprising result was the high percentage (30%) of ebooks that were only "browsed" by the reader and did not result in a short loan. The

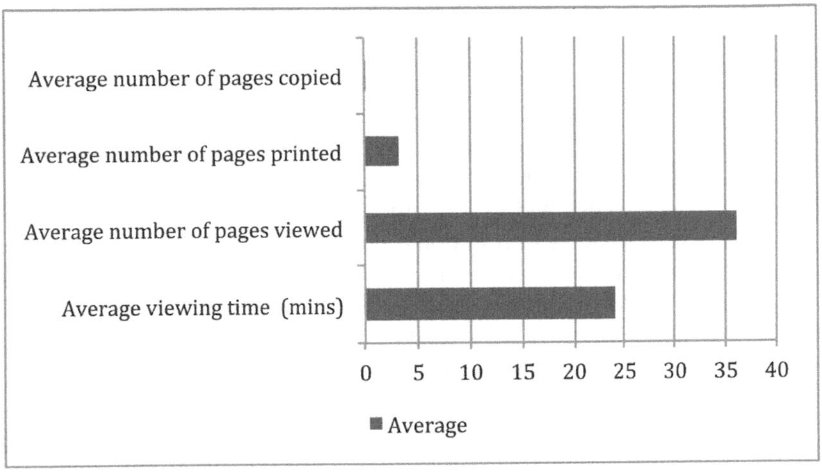

Figure 5: User activity.

browse feature of EBL allows the reader to view a non-owned ebook for up to five minutes without triggering a loan. With 66 titles viewed without a charge, this brought the average cost per title (loans and purchases) down to £17.61. Although this cost remains higher than the direct costs of a traditional interlibrary loan from the British Library, £11.60 (at the time of the pilot) plus return carriage costs, 24 titles became owned titles during the pilot and therefore remain part of our permanent collection. For comparison, if all 220 items had been obtained through the British Library, the full cost would have been £2,772, taking into account the £2 handling charge paid by the requestor on collecting an ILL.

User activity

The highest use of ebooks was by doctoral researchers (37%), closely followed by taught postgraduates (27%), academic and research staff (23%) and finally undergraduates (12%) (**Figure 3**). The combined figure for ILL requests received from postgraduates was 56%, academic and research staff 19% and undergraduates 25%. Comparing these figures indicates that the range of material offered by the EBL catalogue generally satisfies the readership level required by users of the ILL service.

Usage data within LibCentral revealed some interesting patterns (**Figure 4**). Downloading was very popular with over 50% of titles downloaded. During the pilot, we received very few queries from users regarding the technical issues of using EBL ebooks, indicating that users generally found the user interface easy to navigate and were able to download the ebook to a range of devices successfully.

Significant use of the free browsing period was an unexpected result. Our initial concerns at the start of the pilot were that a higher number of titles would result in automatic purchase, significantly raising the cost of the pilot above the allocated budget. In many instances, a browsed title subsequently results in a short loan at a later date; however, in other cases, previewing the contents of the book within the browse period was long enough for the user to decide they did not need to read any further. This pattern of user behaviour sometimes occurs with traditional ILL, where the item is collected from the library and returned almost immediately as the requestor realises that the book does not contain the level of information they were expecting.

Further analysis of use of individual titles revealed low levels of printing or copying of text from ebooks, suggesting that users' needs were met by reading online without the need to print out a paper copy of extracts from the work (**Figure 5**). However, this result may require further examination, as feedback from users indicated some issues regarding the limits of printing from an ebook. EBL uses digital rights management to prevent users printing or copying more than the number of pages allowed by the publisher. This amount varies according to the publisher, which is confusing to users and also acts as a barrier to using the material in different ways.

The average duration online of a short loan was 24 minutes and the average number of pages viewed was 36. This gave us some useful insights into the use of books requested through the ILL service and indicates that users are dipping into a book, with a focus on a particular section or sections, rather than reading cover to cover.

Evaluating the results

The results of the pilot were very encouraging, with plenty of positive feedback from users, costs comparable to traditional ILL, and the new service offering improved access to required reading anytime, anywhere. Revisiting Ranganathan's five laws of library science, we can measure the success of the pilot by examining how well the new service met the fundamental expectations of library users and contributed to the development of effective library services.

Books are for use

Ranganathan's first law of library science is about ensuring books are accessible and easily available for use, with consideration of the location of the library, the development of systems that accommodate the use of library materials, and shelves open stack for the user to browse. McMenemy draws our attention to the relevance of this law to the digital technologies of the 21st century, commenting:

> "Books are indeed for use, and if conversion from analogue to digital creates many more users for the one title, then I am sure Ranganathan would have welcomed such a process with open arms" (McMenemy 2007, p.98).

The PDA model of opening up access to a wider selection of scholarly material online has proven a great success with our users, expanding the boundaries of the library to access anytime, anywhere. Extending the use of the full catalogue of EBL PDA titles for satisfying ILL takes this one step further, providing desktop delivery of essential reading within 24 hours of request.

Every reader his or her book

Ranganathan (1931) devotes several chapters of his work to this second law emphasising the need for modern librarianship to serve the needs of *every* reader and to encompass a wide variety of interests and provide books in an accessible format. He is concerned with the equality of access to books and therefore access to education, with the role of the librarian being to remove any barriers to access and understand that individuals will have different needs.

> "On the other hand their [library staff] business is to know the reader, to know the books, and to actively help in the finding by every person of his or her book" (Ranganathan 1931, p.291)

The results of the pilot service has demonstrated that use of the EBL full catalogue of ebooks, with its wide subject coverage, has provided an excellent source for finding material required by our users. Additionally, the use of Primo, the discovery service behind Library Search, ensures that once activated ebooks continue to be easily discoverable by other library users.

In many cases, the ebook format is welcomed by the requestor; however, as the results on user activity show, some readers may prefer a print copy in certain circumstances and on these occasions we will use the traditional ILL service to obtain a print copy. Ebook loans satisfy the need of our distance learners very well in crossing the boundaries of space and time. But the barrier of technical protection measures prevents users from printing or copying more than a publisher has allowed under the licence which may restrict the reader from using the material in the desired way, something Ranganathan's second law warns against.

Every book its reader

The principle of the third law is the complementary reverse of the second law, "Every reader his or her book", stating that every book should be helped to find its reader. The interlibrary loan service is central to this law, where library staff are locating and connecting the book with the reader using a range of catalogues and online resources. Although satisfying interlibrary loan requests using ebooks makes this connection between the book and its reader, the results of the pilot indicate that it may not always have the desired result of satisfying the user's requirements as 30% of ebooks activated were only browsed rather than used extensively. Reflecting on this outcome, the flexible model provided by EBL allowing a five-minute browse period is a benefit to users if only to clarify their need for the information contained within the ebook. In terms of traditional ILL, the reader may only have seen the item as a citation in a list of references and may be requesting with the hope that it will be useful to their research. Any tool that allows the user to browse content before a cost is involved is clearly very useful.

Another benefit of the online access that ebooks provide within this context is the opportunity for full-text searching, which assists in the location of relevant information within the work.

Save the time of the reader

The fourth law is recognition of the measure of an excellent library service as its ability to meet the needs of library users efficiently. Ranganathan follows the path of a reader through the library, from returning books to leaving with new ones "critically examining each process that he has to go through, with an eye to the economy of time that can be effected at each stage" (Ranganathan 1931, p.337).

Saving the time of the reader is a central element of the new pilot service. Traditionally there is an expectation of waiting involved in obtaining an ILL from another library, as the speed of delivering a book is limited by the means of delivery, the parcel post or courier system. While journal articles are now routinely delivered by secure electronic delivery, the same improvement in efficiency has not been apparent with the delivery of books until now. Online requesting and desktop delivery of ebooks both serve to save our reader time, providing access to resources without the need to visit the library. Additionally, ebooks save the time of library staff as there are no further processes involved, such as making the book available for loan, renewing or processing the item for return to the lending library.

Leiter (2003, p.417) describes other ways of satisfying this law by "employing the best available technologies to provide quick access to materials". In terms of the pilot, the EBL ebook interface provides the reader with a user friendly, intuitive interface incorporating a range of tools for navigation and use of the resource online as well as downloading to a range of mobile devices.

The library is a growing organism

Ranganathan's fifth law uses the analogy of the library as a "growing organism", describing the ways in which a library must evolve and metamorphose, changing size, shape and format in an effort to remain healthy and stay relevant. This is nowhere more apparent than in the provision of PDA ebooks; new models of delivery, access and content provide a new environment for librarians to develop-added value services and for users to experience new ways of learning. As Wicht (2011) concludes in her article discussing the changing nature of resource sharing,

> "ILL departments in academic libraries are operating in a time of major change that presents new opportunities to expand and redefine services in ways that best serve evolving patron needs".

Conclusions

The results of the pilot service demonstrate that using ebooks to satisfying ILL requests complements our traditional ILL request service, offering a speedier delivery direct to the user's desktop, anytime, anywhere. Analysis of the results with reference to Ranganathan's five laws of library science highlights the benefits to our users, saving them time, recognising individual needs and helping them to find the essential books they need for their study and research.

In discussing the relationship between ebooks and ILL, Gee (2007) notes that:

> "... while some loathe ebooks, many others have become accustomed to using them, often even demanding e-articles for their research, and also are quickly adopting ebooks" (Gee 2007, p.24).

Gee also identifies the cost and efficiency benefits of satisfying requests through access to an ebook in satisfying patron needs. With the benefits of using ebooks for instant fulfilment clearly demonstrated during the pilot, this is a service that we were keen to continue offering and using ebook loans to satisfy ILL requests is now a key part of the service we offer our users.

Finally, revisiting their relevance in the 21st century, Ranganathan's five laws of library science continue to remain appropriate in the digital environment, providing a framework for reviewing service delivery and helping to ensure that every reader does have access to his or her book.

> "Five simple statements that say so much of what we are about and what we strive to achieve for society" (McMenemy, 2007, p.100).

References

Gee, W. (2007) The connundrum of e-books and interlibrary loan. *Against the Grain* [online], 19(2), 22–28. Available online at: http://docs.lib.purdue.edu/cgi/viewcontent.cgi?article=5047&context=atg [Accessed 4 February 2014]

Leiter, R. A. (2003) Reflections on Ranganathan's Five Laws of Library Science. *Law Library Journal* [online], 95(3) 411–418. Available online at: http://www.aallnet.org/main-menu/Publications/llj/LLJ-Archives/Vol-95/pub_llj_v95n03/2003-28.pdf [Accessed 4 February 2014]

McMenemy, D. (2007) Ranganathan's relevance in the 21st century. *Library Review* [online]. 56(2), 97–110. http://www.emeraldinsight.com/journals.htm?articleid=1599282 [Accessed 2 February 2014].

Ranganathan, S. R. (1931) *The Five Laws of Library Science* [online]. Madras: Madras Library Association. Available online at: http://babel.hathitrust.org/cgi/pt?id=uc1.$b99721 [Accessed 2 February 2014].

Wicht, H. (2011) The evolution of e-books and interlibrary loan in academic libraries. *Collaborative Librarianship* [online]. 3(4), 205–211. Available online at: http://www.collaborativelibrarianship.org/index.php/jocl/article/viewFile/163/116 [Accessed March 2014]

Creating open access books: a partnership between a university library and a research centre

Janet Aucock
University of St Andrews

This case study describes a partnership that has developed at the University of St Andrews between a particular research centre, the St Andrews Centre for French History and Culture[1] and the University Library. The product of this partnership since 2010 is a unique series of "midigraphs", which are shorter monographs and collaborative volumes of 25,000–50,000 words, published as the St Andrews Studies in French History and Culture. Six ebooks[2] have already been produced, and future publications are planned with a regular publication schedule. The library and the editor-in-chief of the ebook series have a close working relationship which enables this series to be made available as open access ebooks in the university repository, Research@StAndrews:FullText. The books are also published in paperback with a limited free print run (see **Figure 1**). Titles are rigorously peer-reviewed and, in keeping with the mission of the centre to "enhance public understanding of the Francophone world", the publications are free at the point of delivery and

[1] Centre website http://www.st-andrews.ac.uk/history/frenchcentre/publications.shtml
[2] http://research-repository.st-andrews.ac.uk/handle/10023/846/browse?type=title&submit_browse=Title

How to cite this book chapter:
Aucock, J. 2014. Creating open access books: a partnership between a university library and a research centre. In: Woodward, H. (ed.) *Ebooks in Education: Realising the Vision.* Pp. 91–103. London: Ubiquity Press. DOI: http://dx.doi.org/10.5334/bal.j

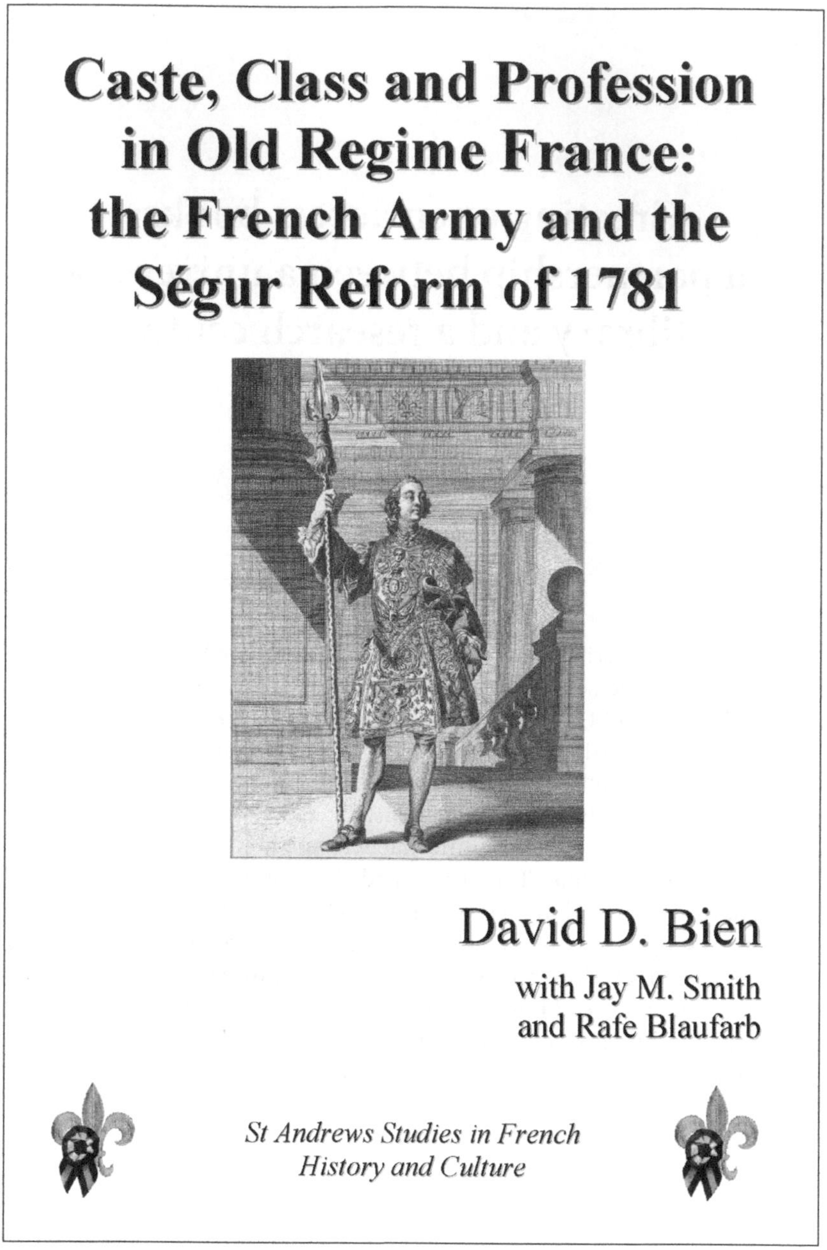

Caste, Class and Profession in Old Regime France: the French Army and the Ségur Reform of 1781

David D. Bien

with Jay M. Smith and Rafe Blaufarb

St Andrews Studies in French History and Culture

Figure 1: BIEN, D. D., SMITH, J. M., & BLAUFARB, R. (2010). *Caste, class and profession in old regime France the French: army and the Ségur reform* of 1781. Image from the title page reproduced by kind permission of the owner.

come with no charge for consultation, downloading, printing or circulation, either for private use or for educational purposes.

The development of this ebook series is of particular interest because of its short study format, its humanities disciplinary base, and its use of the repository for scholarly communication, discovery and archiving. However, this partnership was created organically and was never in fact a planned project. Rather, it was the result of the enthusiasm of the research centre for the development of a new platform and mechanism for communication of scholarly research, combined with the availability of open-access services within the university library. The collaboration began as a result of seeds sown in conversation between individual library staff and the research centre, and converged with the realisation that existing library services could be used to provide the institutional repository as a platform for open-access ebooks.

Each ebook in the series carries multiple acknowledgements on its title page verso to mark the collaboration of the St Andrews Centre for French History and Culture with its publishing partners, and it is satisfying to see that one of the partners listed is the University of St Andrews Library. This case study describes how that partnership came about and considers the perspective of the research centre, editor, library and authors, as well as exploring some aspects of the value, usage and visibility of the open-access ebooks. In conclusion, we look forward to the future of the series and its potential impact on publishing initiatives within the wider institution.

The research centre and editorial perspective

Dr Guy Rowlands, the editor-in-chief of the St Andrews Studies in French History and Culture, had the idea of developing a publication format shorter than a traditional research monograph back in 1998. He felt that this would fulfil a need in his discipline, but he was also determined that despite the shorter format the publications should be of exactly the same research quality as full-length research monographs. The idea took a further step forward when he got the inspiration for the name "midigraph" from his four-year-old son.[3] In 2005 he took up his appointment in St Andrews as the first Director of the Centre for French History and Culture. Part of his remit was to launch a publication for the centre. Between 2005 and 2009 he faced the challenges of starting a publication from scratch, getting authors on board, finding a publisher, planning for distribution and marketing. By 2007 the essential idea for the format and scope of the publication series was well developed and it was time to approach publishers with the idea for a print publication. He

[3] At the time his four-year-old son was in the middle of a childhood obsession with small and large vans. The cross between a long and short van was soon described as a "midivan". Thus the idea of a the midigraph was born!

approached two publishers. One, a large scale monograph publisher, could not see how the short monograph format would fit their existing publisher models and didn't buy into the concept. Another smaller publisher considered the idea, but required a substantial indemnity per publication of £2–3,000. This sort of financial investment broke the business model and was well in excess of the centre's annual budget. These setbacks in following traditional publishing routes were in fact the catalysts for a change in direction.

In the next couple of years the editor-in-chief and the newly formed editorial board became more aware of the ebook environment and much more familiar with digital delivery. They were naturally wary of "self-publication" but increasingly realised that digital delivery could be reputable and respected. Also, ebooks with rigorous peer review and quality layout could fulfil the needs of research communication and perhaps exceed the visibility the series might get if produced only in print and with a price tag. It was at this point that he made the connection with the university library. He realised that digital publication in-house, using institutional services and resources, could be a cost-effective and attractive solution.

A crucial element for success is quality peer review and editorial control. Much work has been done to develop and expand the editorial board across institutions and to bring particular experts on board on an ad hoc basis for individual titles. The editorial board has grown since the first ebook in 2010 and continues to expand.

All costs are funded from the research centre budget which is around £1,200—£3,000 per annum to cover all activities. Costing per issue comes in at the low to mid hundreds, and this allows for the production of two books per year. Costs include some technical work on layout, printing and postage. Editorial work is not costed but is absorbed into academic and research time. The library absorbs minimal staff costs to deposit the electronic books into Research@StAndrews:FullText and does value-added work such as metadata. The analysis of costs and use of existing centralised library services would suggest that this is very good value for money for the small budget available.

Marketing and publicity is targeted to coincide with the launch of each new book. Flyers are sent to all UK university libraries and selected overseas libraries. Alerts and announcements are posted online to major humanities networks such as H-France and H-Net[4] and are designed to reach the most relevant disciplinary audience of humanities researchers and French history and studies researchers. Posts are also made to other discussion forums and book-review sites, for example the Institute of Historical Research.[5] A limited

[4] http://h-net.msu.edu/cgi-bin/logbrowse.pl?trx=vx&list=H-Catholic&month=1002&week=a&msg=8glxfxcx2CgqTNKTUxhHGQ

[5] http://www.history.ac.uk/news/2012-08-31/new-book-centre-french-history-and-culture-university-st-andrews

print run, maximum 75 copies, is provided for authors and contributors, UK copyright library deposit and selected international libraries. The distribution of print is also another means of publicity.

As an institution St Andrews is very supportive of school initiatives and supports the development of research centres. The decision-making and budgetary control for this particular centre is devolved through the head of school for history, and the development of specialist centres in turn develops a group of disciplinary research experts and a fertile environment for the publication of research. This encourages sustainability.

The library and institutional perspective

The development of repository and open-access services in St Andrews has been well documented already (Aucock 2009, Proven and Aucock 2011). A research repository was introduced in pilot phase in 2002, and from 2006 the primary focus was a full service to support the deposit of electronic research theses. Since 2010, and the implementation of a Publication and Research Current Research Information Service, there has been increasing emphasis on open access to research publications authored by researchers within the institution. Activity has increased with the introduction of open-access mandates from funders. More recently, the Higher Education Funding Council for England (HEFCE) consultation and new policy statement in April 2014 has brought open access to centre stage in preparation for the post-2014 Research Excellence Framework.[6] Although monographs are excluded from the compliance requirements in this new policy, HEFCE has indicated a longer-term interest in understanding open-access monograph publishing by setting up an Expert Reference Group.[7] This project, in partnership with the Arts and Humanities Research Council and the Economic and Social Science Research Council, was due to report late in 2014.

There is a growing acknowledgement of open-access publishing developments from university research managers. The university has voiced a commitment to making research outputs available to a wider audience, as announced in its Open Access Policy[8], and states: "We encourage academic authors to consider open-access publication of monographs where possible."

The library open access and research publications team has worked hard to create a set of services and systems which can support open-access publication. A good example is the library journal hosting service using Open Journal Systems (OJS), which began in 2011 and to date hosts eight

[6] Policy for open access in the post-2014 Research Excellence Framework (HEFCE 2014/07) http://www.hefce.ac.uk/whatwedo/rsrch/rinfrastruct/oa/policy

[7] http://www.hefce.ac.uk/whatwedo/rsrch/rinfrastruct/oa/monographs

[8] http://www.st-andrews.ac.uk/library/services/researchsupport/openaccess/oapolicy

open-access journals.[9] The take-up of the journal hosting service has been primarily from humanities and social sciences disciplines, and has proved to be a useful exemplar of open-access publishing in precisely those disciplines where monographs are a primary vehicle of scholarly communication. This has sparked interest amongst researchers in these disciplines, and the services offer up the potential to become transferable to the monograph publishing environment.

Repository content has built up to a critical mass of quality full-text content, making it an attractive option for depositing and archiving full text in an institutional setting. Much work has centred on increasing awareness of open access and communicating the changing landscape of scholarly communication. It has concentrated on building relationships with academic schools, research groups and individual researchers, and engaging in dialogue with researchers to improve research support services. This in turn has created an environment which facilitates collaboration.

Rewards have come by steady progress in embedding our services within the research community of the university and being known to be open and receptive to new ideas and initiatives. So when the editor-in-chief had his first conversation with library staff he already expected that the library would play a supportive role and would engage with the publication process. The solution of using the institutional repository to host an ebook series has simplicity, but the library was able from the outset to offer robust and real services which give added value and essential infrastructure to support publishing initiatives.

The library provides a DSpace institutional repository as an established platform for hosting with underlying technical and development support from the Scottish Digital Library Consortium (SDLC). User support is provided by the open access and research publications team and deposit is mediated by the library on behalf of the ebook editorial team. The repository platform provides good discovery and visibility as well as centralised and secure archiving (multiple format versions of the ebooks in PDF and RTF are stored centrally). The repository also provides usage statistics for page views and downloads. Discovery and visibility are further enhanced by the creation of good quality metadata for each publication. Metadata is created using the Dublin Core schema and includes abstract, keywords, full headings for authors and editors, series headings and subject headings and classification using Library of Congress schema. Very similar detailed metadata is created in Machine Readable Cataloguing (MARC) format for the St Andrews library catalogue and both the Dublin Core records and the MARC records for the e-books are then made available for discovery and reuse in other databases and discovery systems. Metadata is harvested and made available in established services

[9] http://ojs.st-andrews.ac.uk

such as OAIster[10], WorldCat[11], COPAC[12] and other aggregator sites such as BASE[13] and CORE.[14]

The author perspective

The digital and open-access aspects of these books have not been perceived at all as inhibitors to their potential authors. Authors fully support the model and see this as an accepted way to publish. The shorter format may take some adjustment for authors used to publishing at article or full monograph length, but it can also fit well around collected essays and conference-length pieces and so can prove to be versatile and fulfil a need. A positive example of these publications being endorsed centred on a discussion about inclusion for a tenure portfolio for an academic author in the USA, where key benefits were visibility and access and the very real advantages of being read.

Authors have favourably compared their experience to the traditional print route, describing how their first monographs were expensive to purchase and royalties were small, even though print runs did sell out. Authors want to be read, so an open-access digital approach has high value. They also comment that a quality editorial board, high production values and rigorous peer review are also vital when migrating publication to a non-traditional format. There is now greater acceptance that online and high quality can go hand in hand. When academics publish in an ebook series such as this they are adding momentum to this acceptance process and endorsing it themselves. These ebooks can still be reviewed in specialist journals by peers and experts in just the same way as print books.

Immediate accessibility is seen as a distinct advantage. It can usefully be tied in with online publicity using blogs and author video interviews, and the reader can literally be anywhere in the world with suitable network access to follow the link instantly to read or download the digital copy. Readers don't have to wait for print copies to be ordered for their library at a cost. Academics, including the authors themselves, can easily recommend the material instantly for reading lists and assignments. The format is ready-made for online teaching, where it can be fully integrated as digital material in the course structure. Because the material is already in a good quality digital format, does not need to be scanned, and is already copyright cleared, then it can very quickly and conveniently be used for teaching without the extra burden of administrative overheads. The ebooks are open to the general public and to

---

10 http://oaister.worldcat.org
11 http://www.worldcat.org
12 http://copac.ac.uk
13 http://www.base-search.net
14 http://core.kmi.open.ac.uk/search

groups such as future students so they help to bridge the gap from scholarship to more general readership, as well as potentially influencing student recruitment and research collaboration.

Authors in the humanities understand and accept that traditional publishers and university presses still have a vital role, and that publishers who move to digital publication may still operate in a profit-making model. However, a specialised research centre can offer advantages over this model. A research centre is often much better placed to commission quality peer review than a traditional publisher. The elimination of any profit motive in publication can also give the editorial board and authors much more control and freedom in their publishing schedule and the choice of manuscripts.

Usage, reach and value

There are many and varied aspects to the usage, reach and value of these publications, some quantitative and some qualitative, and in both cases perhaps not always easy to measure and benchmark. What follows gives some indicators of the impact and visibility of these ebooks in the early stages of their open-access life.

Research@StAndrews:FullText[15] offers download and page view statistics on its content, based on data gathered by Google Analytics. Usage statistics on the ebook series are available for the collection as a whole and for individual ebooks, and can be aggregated over varying time periods. **Figure 2** shows downloads for all six titles in the series, and the current download total up to April 2014 is 1239 downloads, giving an average of over 200 downloads per title. **Figure 3** shows statistics for the latest book in the series, launched in September 2013, which already has figures of over 100 downloads in its relatively short existence. These statistics show healthy usage which compares favourably with the standard print runs and sales of traditional print monograph publications, quoted recently in the OAPEN-UK Project Plan, which notes that these have declined to "little more than 200 in the early years of this century".[16]

Analysis of the geographical origin of traffic to the set of publications indicates the UK, the USA and France as the top three sources. Drilling down to traffic from city level gives some interesting correlations with the subject matter of the books. Top city traffic comes from St Andrews and London, but in the next rank is Paris and then Blois. This would seem to indicate that there is potential direct interest to material related to the history of Blois coming directly from that location and facilitated by digital delivery of the content.

---

15 http://research-repository.st-andrews.ac.uk/gastatistics/collection?handle=10023%2F846&submit_simple=View+Statistics

16 http://oapen-uk.jiscebooks.org/overview/project-plan

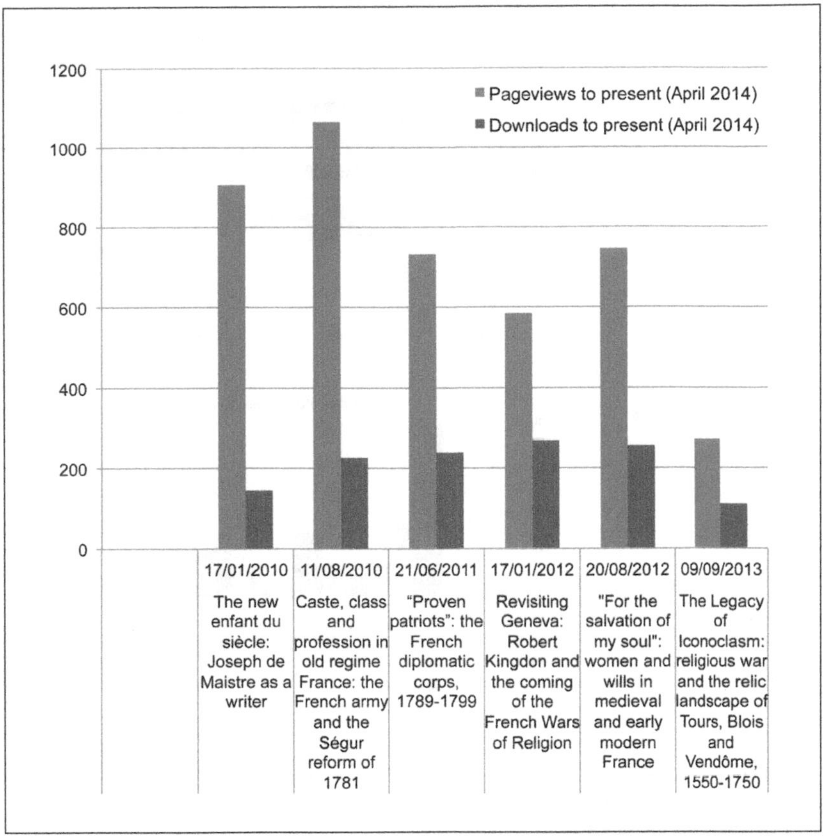

Figure 2: E-book series showing load date, title, page views and total downloads to April 2014.

Research@StAndrews:FullText as a whole received some 130,000 downloads from the site during the four years that these ebooks have been available, with monthly download figures now increasing to a steady average of 5,000 per month. Hits and page views on the site now average at more than 30,000 per month and the yearly increase of hits over the period shows a trend of steady upward growth. Just over 75% of these hits came from Google and Google Scholar, and the analytics for the geographical origin of traffic to the repository clearly show a global audience. The repository platform facilitates ease of digital discovery and delivery, especially because of its proven ability to provide good metadata content to search engines. An increasing amount of traffic is being driven to the site and this in turn has benefited the global visibility of specialist content such as the ebook series.

There are other facets to the reach and value of these publications. The series, and in particular its open-access ebook publication format, was

No. of Page views

Year/Month	Page views
2013/08	0
2013/09	92
2013/10	43
2013/11	24
2013/12	17
2014/01	29
2014/02	12
2014/03	30
2014/04	44
2014/05	28
2014/06	13
2014/07	12
2014/08	4
Total	*348*

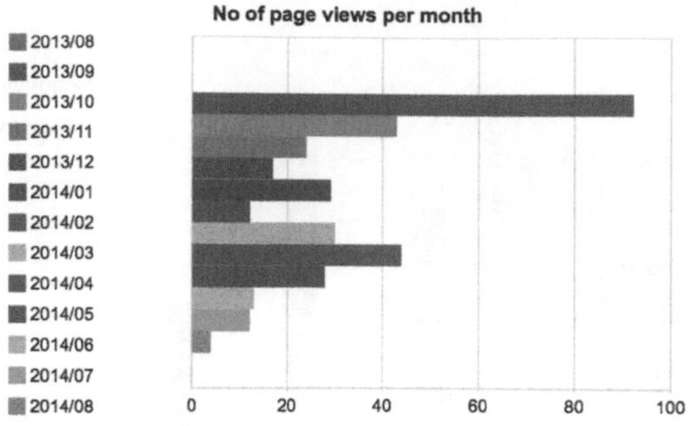

No. of Downloads

Year/Month	Downloads
2013/08	0
2013/09	40
2013/10	17
2013/11	8
2013/12	8
2014/01	15
2014/02	2
2014/03	10
2014/04	15
2014/05	11
2014/06	4
2014/07	4
2014/08	2
Total	*136*

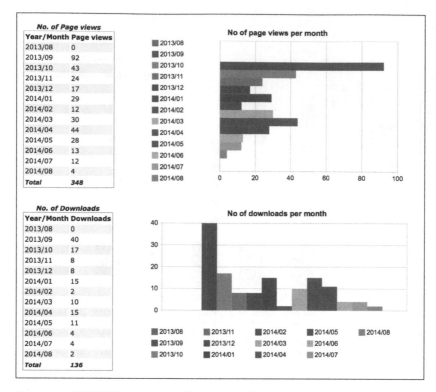

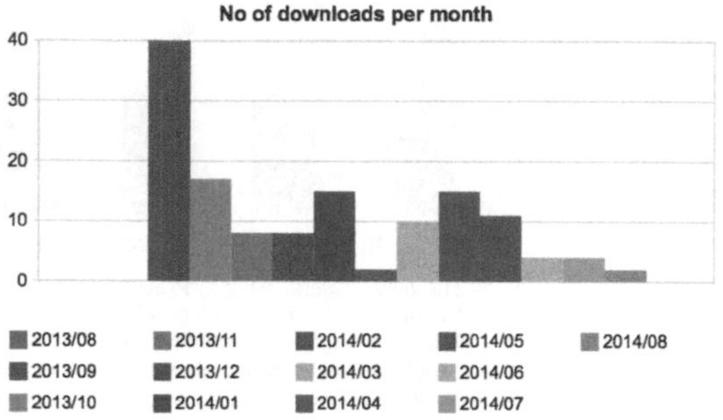

Figure 3: NELSON, E. (2013). *The legacy of iconoclasm: religious war and the relic landscape of Tours, Blois and Vendôme, 1550–1750.* http://hdl.handle.net/10023/4038 Page views and downloads since the book launch in September 2013.

specifically referenced and used as part of the evidence for research assessment in the School of History environment statement for the 2014 Research Excellence Framework (REF) assessment exercise. Environment statements count for 15% of the REF assessment and are assessed in terms of "vitality and sustainability".[17] This was in the context of the value of the St Andrews Centre for French History and Culture as an intellectual and social focus for staff and postgraduate students and as an exemplar of how the centre forges strong international links.

In the "author perspective" section, I gave strong indications of the value of this publication format for immediacy of access and teaching and for ease of reuse. Some examples of this are a publication being listed on a syllabus list at the University of California Santa Barbara for a course in Urban Space in Late

[17] http://www.ref.ac.uk/panels/assessmentcriteriaandleveldefinitions

Medieval and Early Modern Europe[18], and a subject guide at the University of Reading providing access to free internet resources for French studies, specifically referencing the ebook series.[19] The editor and centre have expressly stated that they want other libraries to make digital copies and provide links. The count of traffic coming in at city level from Exeter points to the links with the Centre for Early Modern Studies at the University of Exeter, where one of the publications' authors is based[20], and the inclusion of the records for the digital ebooks in the University of Exeter's library catalogue. The catalogue provides direct URL links and describes the books as being freely accessible at St Andrews, thus immediately promoting discovery and usage. At Cornell University one publication has been copied and included in their repository eCommons@Cornell monographs collection.[21] All these examples point to the development of a discipline-based open community of reuse around the ebooks.

There is clearly value to the research institute itself. It gains visibility and opportunities for collaboration by promoting its expertise and value through accessible quality publications. The value of the research institute is demonstrated and reinforced within the institution, and the academic institution in turn gets the same benefits.

At the level of personal and professional development, the editor of these publications develops an enhanced skill set as part of the process, such as aesthetic design, layout of publications and desktop publishing knowledge. In the longer term these may be skills that sit better with a centralised publication service, but in the short term they are highly beneficial skills to acquire and understand, and serve to better inform academic researchers about all aspects of the publication process, including business and costing models for open-access monographs.

From the library perspective what better way to demonstrate the effectiveness of open-access publication support services than by collaborating on a successful set of ebook publications? The library uses this series as an exemplar when giving support sessions to academic researchers and postgraduate students, and to raise open-access awareness. The existence of these ebooks can help to develop a dialogue, especially with other humanities researchers, and helps the library to understand the types of research support it needs to provide.

---

18 http://www.google.co.uk/url?sa=t&rct=j&q=&esrc=s&source=web&cd=24&ved=0CDoQFjADOBQ&url=http%3A%2F%2Fwww.history.ucsb.edu%2Fcourses%2Ftempdownload.php%3Fattach_id%3D6286&ei=nlROU-_VJ8vFPZqegaAB&usg=AFQjCNHdFPOp1zYSLYE5604fNH_bR_ya3Q&bvm=bv.64764171,d.ZWU&cad=rja

19 http://www.reading.ac.uk/library/finding-info/subjects/french/lib-french-Internet.aspx

20 http://humanities.exeter.ac.uk/history/research/centres/earlymodern

21 http://ecommons.library.cornell.edu/handle/1813/31546

The future

There are some practical aspects to the future development of these publications. The repository platform is functional, but there are plans to enhance it with a more professional look and feel, and to introduce extra publication formats to support more varied reading devices. Detailed licensing for the ebooks still needs to be finalised, and they can then be registered for the Directory of Open Access Books.

Within the university there is a growing buzz of interest and awareness of open-access and digital publication. Not yet a torrent, but rather a bubbling under of people talking and debating and watching the activities of their colleagues in this area and wondering if they should be considering similar initiatives. A series of ebooks may not of itself move the debate along, but as an exemplar of open access in practice, combined with many other drivers and influences, it can potentially change the scholarly communication culture in an institution or within a disciplinary area. The library has noticed a steady upturn in institutional requests to host new open-access journals on its hosting platform.

Another current debate in the university and an agenda item at library and academic strategic meetings is the question of setting up a University Press, which would include the publication of monographs and is very much in line with recent activities in other institutions such as University College London.[22] This might in particular offer opportunities for new researchers and young academics, for example to publish research theses selectively. The recently published "Policy for open access in the post-2014 Research Excellence Framework (HEFCE 2014/07)", also now hotly debated within the university, offers another potent driver for open-access monographs when it states that "Where a higher education institution can demonstrate that it has taken steps towards enabling open access for outputs outside the scope of this definition (currently journal articles and some conference proceedings), credit will be given in the research environment component of the post-2014 REF".

Meanwhile, the relative simplicity of the publication process for the St Andrews Studies in French History and Culture continues to promote sustainability and continuity. The next volume is in preparation and is a very topical publication on French civilians in World War One. It will be made available online and promoted following a well-established procedure. In addition it will almost certainly become part of collaboration with the library's own series of events commemorating 1914–1918 and another example of research centre and library partnership in action.

[22] http://www.ucl.ac.uk/library/ucl-press

Acknowledgement

I am indebted to the editor-in chief of the series Dr Guy Rowlands for his valuable contribution to this study and to Dr Eric W. Nelson, Professor in the History Department of Missouri University, for his extremely helpful insights into his experiences as an author of one of the books.

References

Aucock, J. (2009) Developing the Digital Research Repository at the University of St Andrews, *SCONUL Focus,* 46. http://hdl.handle.net/10023/4584

Proven, J. and Aucock, J. (2011) Increasing uptake at St Andrews: Strategies for developing the research repository, *ALISS Quarterly,* 6(3): pp. 6–9. http://hdl.handle.net/10023/1824

"Zap our App!"

Janet Morgan, Liz Chester, Jean Sullivan
and Elaine Edwards
Coleg Sir Gâr

"Zap our App!" shouts our poster. Our new library app gives mobile access to our catalogue, ebooks, e-mails, college files and even "ask a librarian".

Coleg Sir Gâr is a College of Further Education based in South West Wales offering a comprehensive range of academic and vocational programmes that includes 14–19, Further Education (FE), Work Based Learning, Adult and Community Learning and Higher Education (HE). Annually it enrols in excess of 10,000 learners. The college has five main campuses located at Llanelli, Carmarthen (Pibwrlwyd and Jobs Well), Ammanford and Gelli Aur, and primarily serves the unitary authority area of Carmarthenshire. The College has four libraries which cater for the needs of learners and lecturers across a wide range of curriculum areas, from entry level to higher education. Carmarthenshire is a rural area with 43.9% of the population being Welsh-speaking.

We are continually striving to increase awareness of our resources and improve our users' information literacy skills, so developing a library app seemed to be the perfect way to bring our resources closer to our audience.

How to cite this book chapter:
Morgan, J., Chester, L., Sullivan, J. and Edwards, E. 2014. "Zap our App!". In: Woodward, H. (ed.) *Ebooks in Education: Realising the Vision.* Pp. 105–112. London: Ubiquity Press. DOI: http://dx.doi.org/10.5334/bal.k

App development

During the summer of 2013 we carried out our initial investigations by looking at other FE academic library apps and we discovered that very few institutions had developed an app, let alone a specific library app. The main aim of an app was to take the library closer to our users, with the objective being to provide a broad range of information relating to the library, in particular quick and easy access to our ebooks and Jisc Collections resources.

At a library team brainstorming session, we established a structure for the app. As our library web-page had been redesigned in 2012 it could be used as a template for the information that would be made available, and we wanted it to support the college's Welsh-language policy, so all information on the app had to be bilingual.

The next step was to investigate app creator software; our requirements were that it should be compatible with both Apple and Android devices, free of initial outlay or follow-on fees, user-friendly, available to download freely via QR code, and be customer-focused software – making it easy for our users to get in touch via email or phone and most importantly enable easy downloading of ebooks from the library catalogue. We worked closely with several college departments to achieve our goal. We discussed the idea of a library app with the college's ILT co-ordinator, and Appshed[1] was suggested, as it had been recommended to the library by another college. We agreed that it was the most suitable free software available and was the way forward.

Two members of the library team then delivered a training session on how to start building it. Once the framework of the app was set up, we were left to our own devices to input all the information and links. We took only one afternoon to create it. Once it was developed, the college web graphic designer created the icons which identified the different pages, and our translators worked on the Welsh version. We spent a week testing the links to ensure that there were no glitches once the app went live (**Figure 1**).

The college's marketing department designed promotional "Zap our App" posters and bookmarks and, to keep costs to a minimum, they were printed in-house using the reprographics department. College senior management were consulted for final approval prior to the launch, and the marketing department wrote and distributed a press release, greatly adding to the sense of achievement!

The app development provided an opportunity to work closely with other departments within the college and these links can be further developed in future.

---

[1] http://appshed.com

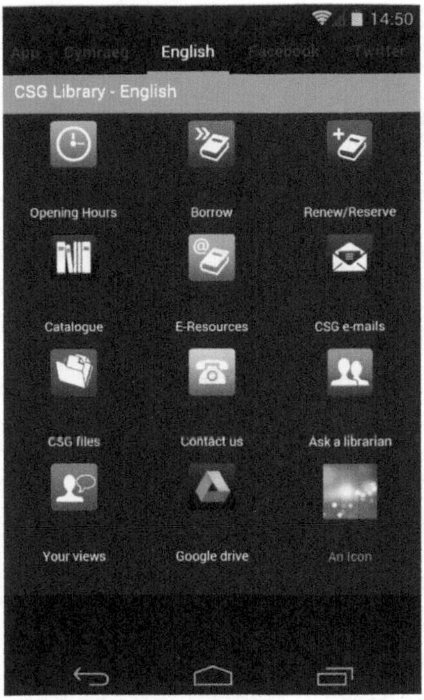

Figure 1: App layout.

Launch and promotion

We were ready to launch it at the beginning of the autumn term; all new and many returning learners were introduced to the app during their library induction. This has been an ongoing process for all new courses starting throughout the year. As our two ebooks suppliers, Dawsonera and ebrary, had produced instructions on how to download their books to mobile devices, we printed these and added them to our collection of library helpsheets. At inductions many of these were collected.

The library services manager was asked to give a presentation to the college's senior management team who gave very positive feedback. Other sessions were then delivered to various curriculum areas in order to increase awareness across the college.

The library holds an annual library open week in October, which gives learners who missed their inductions or were late starting college the opportunity of visiting the library to be informed of what resources are available and what services are provided.

To further promote the app and reach an even wider audience it was decided to run a library app roadshow to coincide with the library open week, thereby

Figure 2: Marketing poster.

taking the app to the users instead of waiting for users to come to us. A team of library staff and a member of the IT department visited each of our campuses and set up a stall displaying our posters (**Figure 2**) and bookmarks, including in the refectories, to make the most of the opportunity and engage with as many learners and academic staff as possible. We demonstrated the app in action and promoted the advantages of downloading it to mobile devices; learners and staff were encouraged to "Zap our App" using the QR code. All users were asked to create a shortcut to the app on their phone or tablet homescreen for the chance to be entered into a prize draw with the opportunity of winning one of four £20 Amazon vouchers (**Figure 3**).

It was a fun event for all involved and the response from all those who downloaded it was really positive, providing easy access to our catalogue, opening times and emails. It proved to be a great talking point and staff and learners were keen to give it a go! However, the downloading via a QR code proved to be a barrier as many people didn't have a pre-installed QR code reader on their mobile devices. Once this problem was identified the URL link for the app was added to all promotional material.

Figure 3: One of our competition winners.

Meanwhile, we were very busy delivering our autumn term digital literacy sessions, and our second-year PGCE learners in particular were thrilled to discover the app, downloading the ebooks on to their tablets and phones during the session. They were delighted to find how user-friendly the app was and to have digital access to library resources. All Library staff were also instructed on how to download the app, so that they could promote "Zap our App" in the library not only during the open week but throughout the year.

All four libraries produced eye-catching promotional displays using posters, flyers and bookmarks, and the roadshow was posted to the library web pages as well as the library, college and librarywales.org Facebook pages to further increase awareness (**Figure 4**). Notices encouraging participation were placed on the College Gateway message board seen by learners and staff. Generic and targeted emails were also sent to academic staff encouraging them to bring their tutor groups in to "Zap our App".

Figure 4: Our Facebook posting.

All this activity justified participation in the Wales Libraries Marketing Innovation Awards for which we received a highly commended in the FE category. Marketing the app has to be an on-going process. Most recently, at a college apprenticeship event, library staff could show the app to all attendees and several more of our academic staff downloaded it.

To continue to raise awareness, to extend the functionality of the app and to learn more about how it could support connection to ebooks on different devices, we are now experimenting with "on the spot" morning break sessions. Here, two of us offer help with downloading our app and with the unfamiliar navigation through to our ebooks. These encounters allow us to meet learners on their own ground and to show them that valuable library resources are accessible to them anywhere.

Supporting our users

We can observe how owners of smartphones and tablets use their devices. We have spoken to office staff, learner support workers, learners and tutors. Their phones are often so new to them that there is often uncertainty. We prevent potential mistakes, calm impatience and reassure. Users of phones touch links at speed and have very little patience if the desired outcome is not instant.

To help us with this flexible style of support, we purchased a library iPad on which to train and demonstrate. This has proved invaluable during our fortnightly drop-in sessions at our Jobs Well campus, which does not have a library on site. It has been, therefore, the perfect setting for promoting and demonstrating the advantages of the app. Our iPad was set up by the IT department so that wi-fi access to the internet is continuous (unlike personal phones and tablets which "drop out" when the device goes in to sleep mode). This has allowed us to demonstrate the app and all its features whilst using it to support users with all manner of library enquiries. However, the Safari default browser on the iPad was causing us download problems; being new to Apple computers, we asked our Apple Mac expert, who had a top tip: use Puffin!

We are a very rural college and at three of our four campuses there is not a reliable 3G connection; mobile access can be slower than a PC, and our wi-fi connection is not always reliable. Taking on this case study has pushed access to the top of our agenda. We know where there are problems and where some of the best hotspots are, such as a certain window ledge in our very rural Gelli Aur campus!

There are several processes to go through to download our ebooks, processes that create extra barriers to taking the first steps:

- Creating an Adobe account
- Signing in to Google Play or the iTunes store
- Downloading Bluefire or ebrary reader
- Signing in with Shibboleth

These requirements cannot all be set up for an individual during an "'on the spot" or "drop-in" session, so we encourage learners to have a go at starting a process that they can complete independently by following the help sheets or by contacting us in the library. Also, ebrary and Dawsonera use different ebook apps for downloads, and have different loan periods, interfaces and functions. We have to be careful to prioritise a book that will make a difference to the user so that confidence is built.

Such intensive testing has brought to light refinements we need to make:

- To bring closer together the labels and the icons on the app as it is a little confusing at the moment
- To move ebooks to the top of our "media type" list in the OPAC
- Possibly change the links to ebooks so that it is clear which provider the title sits with

We are also now more aware that learners have multiple misapprehensions, for instance, if they do not have an internet contract on their phone they may not know how to turn on the college free wi-fi access.

Conclusion

The software was free of charge and does not contain reporting functionality, so it has not been possible to track the number of users who have downloaded the app. In an attempt to capture data, the library will ask for a question about it in learner exit surveys.

We expect the app access to ebooks to drive ebook usage in the future. It provides an alternative way of accessing our services and resources that is already well-received and likely to grow. The app to ebook study has invigorated our testing of the app as well as of our own phones and tablets! It has extended library staff understanding of the barriers and challenges of mobile access, informing us for future refinements so that we can continue to improve our app to ebook functionality.

A living open book

Peter Suber
Harvard University

This is a case study of my short book, *Open Access* (Suber 2012a). The book is not "enhanced" in the way that a growing number of digital academic books are enhanced. It has no graphics, no multimedia, and no interactivity beyond links, and does not offer different layers or pathways for readers at different levels. From that point of the view the book is conventional and text-oriented. But it has two other enhancements worth highlighting. First, the full text is open access, which benefits authors and readers, and sometimes also publishers. Second, the book has a companion web site of open-access updates and supplements, which benefits all three groups.

Open access

MIT Press and I agreed from the start that the full text would eventually become open access. I wanted immediate open access, but understood why the press could not accommodate me. Our compromise was to make the book open-access under an open licence one year after publication. During year one, the book existed only in print and in non-open digital editions, such as a Kindle edition.

How to cite this book chapter:
Suber, P. 2014. A living open book. In: Woodward, H. (ed.) *Ebooks in Education: Realising the Vision.* Pp. 113–117. London: Ubiquity Press. DOI: http://dx.doi.org/10.5334/bal.l

I wanted the book to be open access for the same reasons that I want all research literature to be open access. In the book itself (Section 5.3), I discuss the reasons why open access is more difficult for books than articles, and nevertheless why it can be viable for authors and publishers. I won't digress here on the advantages of open access. The book should speak for itself on those. I'll merely say that my readers and I have realised the benefits for which I'd hoped. I'm grateful to MIT Press for its willingness to make this possible.

I'll focus here instead on the consequences for the press. A good number of anecdotes and studies suggest that open-access full-text editions can stimulate a net increase in the sales of print books. I collect the evidence in the book itself at pp. 109–110, especially notes 8–10 at pp. 200–202, and in the updates and supplements for pp. 109–110. The evidence is promising enough that dozens of academic presses now experiment with open-access editions that coexist with priced print editions.

The same anecdotes and studies suggest that the "net boost to sales" effect works for some books, or some kinds of books, and not for others. To see whether it worked for my book, MIT Press analysed its sales data before and after the first open-access editions appeared in mid-2013.

The open-access editions did not boost the net sales of my book. On the contrary, the month after the open-access editions appeared, print sales were one-third of what they were the month before, and were never as high again. However, two months out, print sales were higher than they were one month out. Instead of an immediate spike in sales followed by a slow decline, we saw an immediate drop followed by a mild bump.

The open-access editions caused a deeper drop in digital sales than in print sales. Not surprisingly, people who already prefer to read digital editions also prefer free digital editions. If the sales of print editions declined more slowly, part of the explanation lies in the appeal of print itself.

Ellen Faran, the director of MIT Press, and I have discussed why the "net boost to sales" phenomenon works for some books, including some academic books, but didn't work for my book. We both think the book's topic is a key variable. (This would be ironic only if increasing print sales were the purpose of open access rather than an occasional side effect.) The book's audience consists of people who care about open access. While some readers are undecided about open access, or critical of it, most support it and are eager to take advantage of it.

Ellen also wonders whether the book is perceived as a reference book more than a monograph. That would matter because the evidence suggests that the "net boost to sales" phenomenon works better for monographs than reference books. The thinking is that when readers have an open-access option, they're more likely to buy a book they want to read in full than a book they only want to consult for snippets. I admit that as I wrote the book, I thought of it more as a monograph than a reference book. But I've since seen evidence to support

Ellen's theory. Four months after she voiced it, *Choice* named the book an outstanding academic title for 2013 in the category of reference books.

Several universities (Cornell, Georgia Tech, Harvard, and the University of Florida) bought print copies of the book in bulk to give to new faculty members. Ellen believes that bulk purchases became harder to justify after the open-access editions appeared. We have no data on whether the open-access editions might have increased individual purchases of the print edition, while decreasing bulk purchases, with the net effect of decreasing print sales. If so, it's particularly regrettable because, as Ellen notes, giving out print editions has more impact than giving out links to an open-access edition.

Updates and supplements

While the book became open access one year after publication, I launched the book's web site on the very day of publication. I created it as soon as I could because I already had a growing collection of updates and supplements to post. These were of two kinds: evidence that I had before publication in mid-2012 but couldn't fit into a short book, and evidence that only appeared after I submitted my manuscript in mid-2011.

The book was supposed to be short. But because open access suffers from wide and deep misunderstandings, and because an overriding purpose of the book was to lay these misunderstandings to rest, I was especially concerned to document my claims in full. In the end, I exceeded my word count in order to include 41 pages containing 153 small-font notes. I'm grateful to MIT Press for letting me do so. Nevertheless, I still had to cut many relevant studies from the manuscript, and wanted to restore them as soon as possible through my online supplements. Moreover, the world of open access is fast-moving, and many new studies appeared during the year when the book was in production. This is one reason why some books are (nearly) obsolete on they day they are published. I didn't want that fate for my book. The online updates and supplements turned a short book into a long one. More importantly, they turned a frozen and dated book into a living book.

I could have kept the book alive in the traditional way by giving public talks and writing new articles. I did both, but I wanted all the updates and supplements to be easy to find and use. I wanted them all in one place, searchable, with links to their sources, and links back to the relevant passages of the book. If I wrote about new evidence in a new article, that article would reach one kind of reader. But at the same time, I wanted to write a paragraph-length summary of the new evidence, with a full citation and link, in the form of a footnote or endnote, for the book web site.

Another way to keep a book alive is to publish a second edition, or even a series of new editions over many years. I could ask MIT Press to consider this. But it might decline and it might be right to do so. Even if the new material was not voluminous, the sales might not justify new editions. More importantly, I might not want this solution myself. For example, I might want to write voluminous supplements. (It turns out that I do.) I also want to post my updates in real time, not just every few years. Above all, I want to write the updates that I want to write, without running them by an editor or publisher. The book itself went through the standard vetting process at MIT Press, but the updates and supplements are entirely under my control. This gives me a freedom that book authors seldom have. As a bonus, this control also means that I could decide the access terms on my own. Open access came to the main text one year late, but the web site was open access from the start.

Despite the fact that author supplements are not vetted by the publisher, the publisher can still point to them as an enhancement to the published book. MIT Press links to my book site from its own web page on the book, and added the site URL to the second printing of the print edition. Beyond letting me post updates and supplements, the book web site lets me link to reviews, translations, and other editions, including open-access editions. Before the open-access editions appeared, the supplements could only cite the main text by page number. But now that the whole book is open access, each supplement deep-links to the page it supplements. Moreover, readers can deep-link to each individual thread of supplements, and use them as public footnotes summarising the evidence for a claim they may want to assert themselves.

Recent developments

As I write this case study (late April 2014), the book web site has been viewed more than 89,000 times. It links to eight open-access editions, as well as the MIT Press page on the book. It links to 19 reviews with short excerpts. It points to ten translations in progress, and one already online. At least three of the translations are now under way because the translators saw my call for more translations on the web site itself.

Above all, the site contains 236 updates and supplements supporting 121 arguments and assertions from the book. The updates and supplements alone come to more than 38,000 words, or more than 80% of the word count of the original book. And of course the site grows in real time.

Here are three quick examples of the kind of updates and supplements I've been adding:

1. At p. 30 of the book I say, "[C]umulative price increases...forced the Harvard Library to undertake 'serious cancellation efforts' for budgetary reasons." In note 5 at p. 182, I cite two public statements from Harvard. By the time the book came out in mid-2012, I could cite seven public statements from Harvard to the same effect. I now excerpt, cite, and link to them all in my updates to p. 30.

2. At p. 40, I say, "Laid on top of this natural monopoly [created by the fact that different journals don't publish the same articles] are several layers of artificial monopoly." To keep the book short, I decided to give brief rather than detailed coverage to the evidence of monopoly in the journal publishing business. But in the updates to p. 40, I now point to eight articles and web resources for readers who want to go further.
3. At p. 152 I say, "At Congressional hearings in 2008 and 2010, legislators asked publishers directly whether green [open access] was triggering cancellations. In both cases publishers pointed to decreased downloads but not to increased cancellations." By the time the book came out, there had been a third Congressional hearing at which publishers were asked the same question with the same result. I described it and linked to it in my updates to p. 152. The same section of the site now includes additional new evidence that rising levels of green OA have not increased journal cancellations even if they have decreased publisher downloads.

Six months after the book came out, I wrote an article generalising the idea (Suber 2012b) of public footnotes growing in real time to keep the documentation current on important assertions in an article, book, or field. The result is a new container or structure for digital research. I called it an "evidence rack" because it allows any argument or assertion to become a hook on which to hang new evidence as it emerges. My book web site fulfils only part of the vision of an evidence rack, but I'm consciously letting it evolve in that direction.

For me, the book web site shows that a book can be a finished product of a certain length with an unfinished library of supplements of indefinite length. It lets me make additions in real time without delay or compromise. It lets me link to each growing thread of evidence, and because supplements are open access, it lets other scholars do the same. It also lets me expand the documentation and deepen the inquiry of the original book, thinking only about relevance, not length. If I had to keep my supplements short enough to fit into a new edition, then I'd have to omit most relevant new studies, which would recreate the problem that made supplements necessary in the first place. Finally, it lets me do justice, or try to do justice, to a rapidly growing field, together with its nuances and complexities, in a way that no single, short, dated book ever could.

References

Suber, Peter (2012a) *Open Access*, Cambridge, MA: MIT Press.

Suber, Peter (2012b) The idea of an open-access evidence rack, *SPARC Open Access Newsletter*, no. 166.

The Plymouth ebook project

Philip Gee
Plymouth University

"Puts everyone at an advantage right from the beginning of the course and not only the people who can afford books."

First year student, Plymouth University

Most of us will be familiar with the term "reading for a degree". All academics earnestly urge students to "read around" the topic of their lectures, and all are familiar with student essays showing little evidence of it. Should we be surprised? A lecturer may recommend reading Chapter 3, but to do so the student must have paid for a copy, or be able to borrow it from a library[1]. Even the best-funded library may be unable to meet demand for key texts near coursework deadlines or exams.

[1] There has always been another way for unscrupulous students to access books. Those with the skill and nerve could steal from a shop or library. But recently it has become possible to download pirated copies. The amount of skill and nerve required is much lower, and moral qualms may be easy to overcome for students used to getting music and movies that way. I think this will be a major challenge to academic publishers, and a compelling reason for them to encourage schemes such as ours.

How to cite this book chapter:
Gee, P. 2014. The Plymouth ebook project. In: Woodward, H. (ed.) *Ebooks in Education: Realising the Vision.* Pp. 119–124. London: Ubiquity Press. DOI: http://dx.doi.org/10.5334/bal.m

Library ebooks will ease the problem somewhat, but these typically have restrictions on the number of simultaneous users and limits on downloading for offline use. The experience of reading them with a slow internet connection can be frustrating, and they are hard to use on the smaller screens of tablets and mobile phones.

No cost to the students

In this chapter I describe the Plymouth ebook project, which provides a set of core textbooks to students at Plymouth University in ebook format, at no extra cost to the student. The project started with my own subject, psychology, and has since extended to cover a number of others.

As a lecturer in psychology, I have long since negotiated with publishers for discounts on textbooks I recommend. Students are more likely to read around the topics I cover if they have a personal copy. By 2010 I was programme leader for BSc Psychology. The Plymouth ebook project started in the autumn of that year, when a colleague suggested I should extend the range of books I negotiated on. Instead of just my own modules, why not all those we recommended to first years?

I set about compiling a list of core textbooks. What is a core textbook? Any lecturer will have encountered students who, having been given a reading list, says they can buy just one of the books. Which should it be? It is those we defined as core. It turned out that in the first year of the psychology degree there were 12 of them. My original plan had been simply to negotiate a price on behalf of our students, just as I had for print. However, my colleagues and I decided we should supply the books at no cost to the student. Even if we negotiated a fabulous bargain, if students had to pay some would choose not to. Giving them away means we can exploit the potential of the books in teaching and learning more effectively. We can teach knowing that every student has a copy of the core text. There were obvious benefits to inclusivity, too. Affordability would no longer be a barrier. Furthermore, with ebooks students can set the font size, background and text colours to suit their needs and preferences, and the text is accessible to assistive technology.

Negotiation with publishers

I explained my plan to the publishers. It soon became apparent that, where print copies were concerned, the discounts on offer were relatively small. I also became concerned about the practicality of delivering a bundle of 12 print books to each of 360 students. Ebooks seemed to offer a number of advantages. First, this relatively new format appeared to enable publishers to think more flexibly about price. There are longstanding agreements and commercial relationships to be taken account of in the supply of print, but digital material allows a more or less direct business relationship between publisher and university. The other attractions of a package of ebooks for publishers include savings in production and distribution, that their customer buys a copy for every student rather than their selling to only a proportion, and that ebooks are tied to an account and so cannot be sold second-hand. They also benefit from a more predictable customer, with the opportunity to develop multi-year agreements that provide a more stable business environment.

For academics, the main advantage is that they can teach in the knowledge that every student has access to the core reading, and that many have it to hand whenever they have their laptop, tablet or smartphone with them. Few students would carry heavy books around to all their classes, but they have these devices with them most of the time.

Collaboration with the library

I should explain at this point that it was I, as programme leader, who carried out negotiations with publishers, and the scheme was funded from departmental rather than central library funds. I conferred with and had help from library colleagues throughout, but the library budget for first year psychology texts was far too small to cover our ambitions, even if we had opted to spend all of it on these 12 titles. It was clear that if the school wanted to proceed, it would have to provide the funds.

Furthermore, our thinking was not that the books should replace library resources. Rather, we saw this as an opportunity to enhance them. The library had traditionally held around 30 copies of each new edition of core psychology texts. When we set up our ebook scheme, our library was able to redirect spending so we only took three. These catered to students who did not want to use an electronic text, and to those on other programmes who needed to consult a psychology text. Spending that had previously gone on the other 27 copies was redirected to books used by second- and final-year students. Holding more copies of texts that final-year students use, which tend to be more specialist and more expensive, and less likely to be needed for long periods, is a better use of library resources. In this way, supplying core texts to first years enabled us to better serve second- and final-year students.

The interface and software

When we first talked to publishers, they were keen that the books should be made available through their own platform. This would have meant students could only read books through an online browser, and using a different interface for each publisher. It also gives the user the impression that the books are a publisher's property that they have allowed limited access to. We made it clear we were only interested in books that students could have a sense of ownership over, that could be used offline, and that could be read on a mobile device. It should be a similar experience to buying a book for a Kindle.

That the student feels they own the text is important because we hope they will invest time and effort in making highlights and notes on their books, just as many do on personal copies of print books. That they should be downloadable for use offline is important because the internet is not always available; students may want to catch up on reading during a train journey, for example. That they could be read on a mobile device was important partly because reading from a tablet is more pleasant than a computer screen, and partly because they might find themselves unexpectedly with half an hour spare. If their books are on their phone, they can use that to fill the time productively. Indeed, we have had feedback from students who have read textbooks while queuing at a supermarket checkout.

We delivered our first batch of ebooks in September 2011. Students were sent an email containing instructions on how to set up an account with the suppliers of the software we were using, VitalSource Bookshelf, along with a redemption code for their books. We chose Bookshelf because at the time it was the only system that allowed download for offline use, and that would work on computers running Mac OS X or Windows, and on mobile devices running iOS or Android, as well as allowing access through a browser on any other device.

Survey of student views

After two weeks, I ran an anonymous web survey of our students. Feedback on the scheme was the most positive I had ever seen. A typical comment was: "Excellent scheme, very impressive use of new media technology. Can't honestly believe I'd be starting with every core book dropped into my lap, wonderful surprise."

Very few made negative comments, and those that did almost exclusively concerned extended reading from computer screens: "It can be difficult to sit and read through many chapters at once on a computer screen compared to sitting and reading a paper copy of the text. After a while it can cause strain to the eyes which can be uncomfortable and increases headaches." I believe that, as more students acquire tablets, much better devices for extended reading, this will become less of an issue.

I followed up this first survey with a more extensive one at the end of the autumn term, and again at the end of the academic year. These, and surveys in subsequent years, have given similar results; across more than 1,300 responses, a mean of 95% agree or strongly agree that the scheme is a good idea.

Text comments

One feature that students found especially valuable was that I could make text comments on my copy, and share these with them. I suspect I am not alone in not actually having read much of the main text recommended for my first year module. Each of my lectures ends with a suggestion to read Chapter *x* before next week, but I had never properly read Chapter *x* myself. That is not to say I had taken no care in choosing the recommended text. However, that care consisted of checking the table of contents and skim reading a few sections.

Given the opportunity to share notes with my students, I started to work my way through the text more thoroughly. As I went, I found sections to which I could add comments about examples given in lectures. I also found sections that I disagreed with, where I felt the authors were giving a biased view, that were not well explained, or where I could give a hyperlink to more recent research. Students who subscribed to my notes would see them appear in the relevant places on their own books. These notes had a valuable role in making clear that the textbook was a contestable document, not the last word on a subject. My notes proved popular, especially as some would indicate sections I wouldn't be asking questions on in the exam. The notes clearly helped draw students to the text.

Students also shared notes with each other in informal study groups. The relatively simple technology of note sharing has transformed reading from a solitary experience to a social one. It has helped foster a sense of membership of a wider scholarly community.

Conclusions

The ebook scheme was such a success that we offered to set up similar arrangements for colleagues in other schools. We launched ebook schemes in marine biology, environmental science, earth science, geography, and computer science in September 2012. In 2013, the scheme expanded even further to biology, biomedical sciences, maths and statistics, and accountancy. I now lead a project exploring the possibility of extending it across all undergraduate programmes at Plymouth, and am seeking funding to share our experiences with other universities.

If schemes such as ours are to become more widespread, they must be affordable. Surveys at Plymouth suggest that only about two-thirds of students buy any books at all in their first year. If you average those who do not with the ones who do buy books, the amount spent per student is about £62 (n = 700), and that is through retailers who typically take a 30% cut. If the academic publishing industry can be persuaded to supply books to schemes such as ours for the same revenue they currently get from sales to individual students, the approach will thrive. I am sure most universities would spend more than £62 per student to give first years a full set of core texts.

Widespread core ebooks schemes would benefit academic publishers, universities and, of course, students. They would protect publishers from declining sales, undermine the second hand-book market, and reduce the threat from piracy. Students and their universities would be the main beneficiaries, however. Students would save substantial amounts of money, have unprecedented access to core material, see increased spending on second- and final-year texts, and benefit from technological developments such as the interactive features Plymouth is helping publishers embed in future e-textbooks. And for academics, such schemes will restore the pleasure of teaching students who really are "reading for a degree".

E-textbooks at Coventry University: a pilot project

Sandy Forster
Coventry University

The government's decision to change the model of funding to institutions of higher education (HEIs) in 2012/13 had an impact on every UK university, and each institution had to formulate a strategy to deal with the changed situation. At Coventry University part of our response was to propose a variable fee structure for courses, based on the actual cost of their delivery. We then proceeded with a "no hidden extras" offering (referred to internally as the "promises" project), which was to provide further resources within the fees. This meant that each student entering the university within the 2012 fee band could expect to receive a pre-defined number of print credits each year of study, safety equipment, drawing materials, field trips and site visits, etc., depending on their course. Most students would also be provided with a number of essential core textbooks, as identified by their course tutors, for each year of their course.

In 2012/13 all students eligible to receive textbooks received them as print copies. We followed up the September 2012 distribution of print books with an online survey in February 2013, asking students if they would prefer ebooks to print. Fewer than 9% responded, and around 86% of those stated that they would prefer print. However, the reasons behind this are unclear. It

How to cite this book chapter:
Forster, S. 2014. E-textbooks at Coventry University: a pilot project. In: Woodward, H. (ed.) *Ebooks in Education: Realising the Vision.* Pp. 125–129. London: Ubiquity Press. DOI: http://dx.doi.org/10.5334/bal.n

is possible that many first-year students had little contact with ebooks other than ebook readers such as the Kindle prior to arriving at the university, and therefore were unable to appreciate the benefits of e-textbooks.

The library initiative

In the light of the small number of responses to the survey and the prospect of distributing a potential 40,000 printed texts to around 6,800 students studying on 240 courses, the library put forward a proposal in April 2013 to run a pilot project to provide e-texts as an alternative to the print across a limited number of courses. We hoped that this would become a viable replacement to the staff-intensive and therefore costly distribution of large numbers of print copies to an ever- increasing number of students. As the supplier of our print books, Ingram Coutts, were able to offer e-textbooks through their digital arm, VitalSource, this would also enable the pilot to run from Autumn 2013.

The potential benefits of distributing e-textbooks to students were numerous. They would be provided with a personal, downloadable copy of the e-textbook in PDF or XML format that they could store simultaneously on up to four separate devices for the duration of their course, no software downloads would be necessary, and the book could be searched, personalised with notes and annotations, and printed out subject to digital rights management (DRM) limitations. Students would be able to find and download their e-textbooks easily via a link in the university's virtual learning environment (VLE) CUOnline (Moodle).

The benefits to the university would also be substantial – a huge reduction in the logistical challenges and costs of ordering, distributing and ultimately returning uncollected items. As we would be delivering the e-textbooks online, this would also negate the need for us to distribute and/or allocate access codes. Other long-term benefits would include the ability to analyse the metrics that VitalSource provide, and a cost saving given the current tendency for e-textbooks to be (sometimes) cheaper than their print equivalent. However, even where the price differential is small, this is outweighed by the savings in distribution and administration costs over their print counterparts.

A small number of departments in the Business, Environment and Science, Engineering and Computing, and Health and Life Sciences faculties expressed an interest in being considered for the pilot, and the university's Promises Board finally agreed that the pilot would be run with the Computer Science Department, within the Engineering and Computing Faculty. Part of the reasoning behind this choice was that these students would also be receiving a tablet as part of their "promises package" and would, in theory, be more likely to engage with downloadable texts.

The pilot

A shortlist of eight book titles was quickly identified from the agreed course texts by early August 2013, to be supplied to Year 1 and 2 students across six courses with a total of 500 students being eligible. Within three weeks, the e-textbook title list was reduced to seven, as one of the books was still available only in print. By the end of September, VitalSource had provided the library with the links to the titles, and these were embedded in Moodle against the appropriate modules ready for the students to follow and redeem. At this point it was made clear that a further title was not available electronically, so we had to place another order for print copies instead. The pilot list of titles was now reduced to six.

Once we had completed the main distribution of print copies and returned uncollected items, it became clear that managing the e-textbooks would not be quite as easy as we had first thought. As the links to the e-textbooks would remain in Moodle throughout the academic year, they could be downloaded at any time, not just in the Autumn term. As there was some delay in obtaining the download statistics, it wasn't until February that the figures for the Autumn term became available to us. The summary information showed that 586 access codes had been redeemed, and this was disappointing since some courses were offering two e-texts and the total number of students was around 520.

More detailed reports were requested at the end of April, since the initial statistics didn't show the details of the courses the students who had downloaded the texts were studying on. Once this information had been provided and analysed, it revealed that our decision to put the links against the relevant module had not provided control at a granular enough level to prevent students on different courses also studying that module from downloading the texts. Other students who were not entitled to download the texts had also been able to do so. These included, for example, part-time students who were only given vouchers to cover half the value in "promises" received by full-time students, and those on pre-2012 fee bands who were not entitled to any "promises" at all. I also realised that other e-textbooks were included in the report which were not within the pilot set, as the Business School and Faculty of Health and Life Sciences had also purchased a number of e-textbooks.

Further analysis of the statistics

The conflict between module and course made analysis of the statistics much more difficult. It appeared that, of the 318 pilot e-textbooks claimed, 71 had been made by students who were not eligible to have them, some of whom were not even in the Faculty of Engineering and Computing. One particular textbook that was intended for 27 students on a course had been downloaded

17 students on another course in a different faculty (but still studying same module) and by only ten students on the course for which it was ıded.

e pattern of students claiming their ebooks is also worthy of note. There 249 e-texts redeemed in October, the first month of the term, with 180 se in the first week, followed by 21 in November, 20 in December, 11 in y and 5 in February. By shifting the analysis from course level to mod-el, I found that 53% of the 598 e-text "copies" on the relevant modules en redeemed. Usage also seemed encouraging – there had been a total 3 page views (1386 of which had been online from portable devices) une, with 29 highlights having been created within the e-texts. By way of contrast, the first-year students were all eligible to collect print textbooks which hadn't been available in e-text format, and out of the 208 students eligible for print books, only 37 collected them.

It is difficult to assess the apparent results of this pilot in relation to the e-text usage, particularly as there is nothing comparable to benchmark against within Coventry University. The figures supplied by VitalSource do, however, include some of our other e-textbooks on their platform and the one most used (by students in the Faculty of Health and Life Sciences) is showing 120 e-texts claimed over the same period with 4,589 page views – an average of 38 pages per student. The two other titles being reported on were bought for Stage 2 students in Business, and they are showing an average of 104 pages per student, so it would appear that the usage on these pilot titles is lower than for other texts bought by the University. That, however, could merely confirm that Engineering students are currently less likely to engage with books during their studies. We might dare to hope that they are more likely to use their e-textbooks than the traditional print.

Summary

Is it easy to make broad statements trying to establish why there has not been as good a take-up as we might have anticipated. It appears, however, that students in other departments are more likely to make use of e-textbooks – possibly because they are being encouraged to work both in the classroom and through lecturer-controlled areas on publishers' websites with close links to their textbooks, and are therefore more comfortable learning within this medium. We are also seeing a steady rise in the use of ebooks bought under the library access models across the institution as a whole. This is the first time that students in Engineering and Computing have been introduced to e-texts so that there is nothing to compare against; there is no way of measuring usage of the print textbooks that have been distributed, either to them or other students, so it is difficult to make informed conclusions about what the data means in real terms. The final analysis of the data also came at a stage where it was difficult to make contact with the students to have meaningful discussions and find out whether they had understood the personal nature of their e-texts as opposed to the ones made available through the library discovery system.

I am encouraged that just over half of the Engineering and Computing students accessed their e-textbooks when the generally accepted view is that these students don't usually engage with books or the library, and only 18% of the same students collected their free print textbooks. The usage statistics that we have been given do not yet give the full picture for the year, or whether these e-texts will be used again in the final year of the course. It is encouraging to note that the 2014/15 distribution includes new requests for e-texts from other departments, alongside those which have previously been requested as print books with associated e-access cards. The e-textbook continues to evolve, and I feel sure that Coventry University will continue to be engaged in and take an active role in this process.

Index